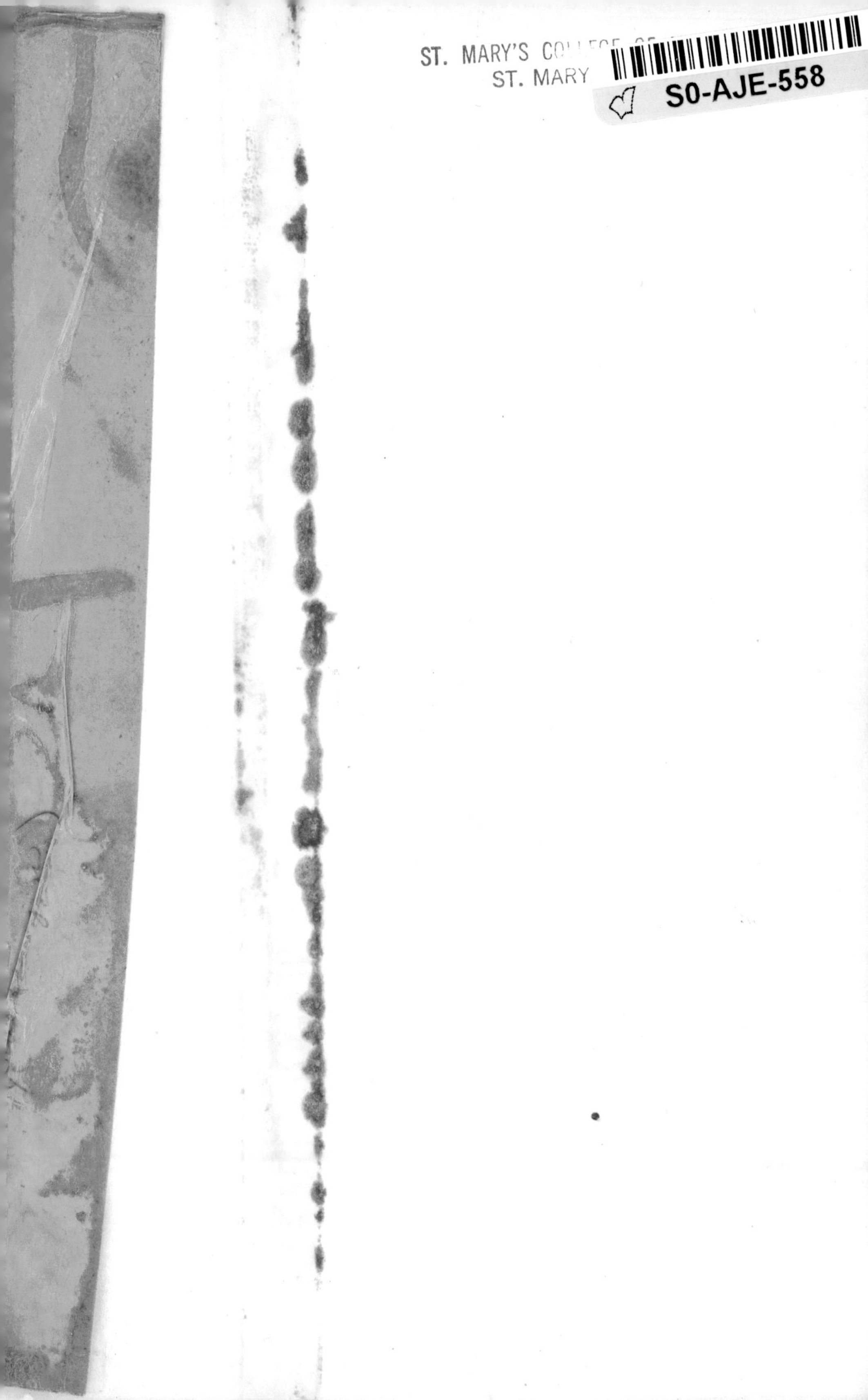

ST. MARY'S CO
ST. MARY
S0-AJE-558

mask for treason———

if among those drawn into the whirlpool set up by so sudden a subversion of the current of human affairs, there were any suffered an unjust doom, their innocence should be made clear beyond further question.

david miller dewitt
the assassination of Abraham Lincoln and its expiation

Vaughan Shelton——

mask for treason—

the Lincoln murder trial

stackpole books - harrisburg, pa.

copyright © 1965 by
vaughan shelton

first edition april, 1965

published in the u. s. a. by
the stackpole company
cameron and kelker streets
harrisburg, pennsylvania 17105

library of congress catalog card number: 65-13385

printed in the u. s. a. by telegraph press
harrisburg, pennsylvania

10

19850

respectfully dedicated to the late

Otto Eisenschiml———

without whose many questions on this subject no answers would have been possible

foreword

The assassination of Abraham Lincoln has been under continuous investigation for nearly a hundred years. Even before official inquiries were terminated, scholars and writers took up the task and have been at it ever since.

Considering the volume of mental effort that has been expended in trying to solve America's most famous mystery, the lack of positive results is something of a phenomenon. The basic history-book story of the crime is exactly the same as it was a century ago except in some very minor details. We have known almost as little about the *instigation* of the murder as those who were present in Ford's Theater when Booth pulled the trigger.

Any new investigation begins with a careful study of the work of others in the same field, both to profit from their findings and if possible to avoid their pitfalls. In this case a point of particular interest is why so many able investigators have drawn a blank—as evidenced by the lack of any alterations or corrections in the original version of what happened.

We didn't find—nor did we expect to find—any serious fault with the research procedure or reasoning of any responsible historian who has studied the assassination and published his theories. But we did find a common denominator that seemed significant. The unvarying practice has been to use the version of the "conspiracy" popularized at the Conspiracy Trial as an over-all target and then try to expose some weakness in that version which would open a clear avenue of inquiry leading to the core of the mystery.

Weaknesses by the dozen have been found. But probing them, rather than leading the investigator to the *instigators* of the assassination, merely turns up a new crop of riddles more baffling and controversial than those on the surface. We can suggest a reason for this frustrating situation.

There's very little controversy regarding the character of the Conspiracy Trial as a legal proceeding. It was probably the darkest page in the history of American jurisprudence. Even the apologists for Secretary of War Stanton, by whose order the military court was convened, admit that its purpose was to *convict* eight defendants whom the War Department had accused of having conspired with John Wilkes Booth. It isn't denied that the prosecutors violated every rule and tradition of impartial justice to obtain convictions and that the judges collaborated. Stanton's defenders offer his zeal for the punishment of Lincoln's murderers as his excuse.

The point is that, being "organized to convict," the Trial didn't undertake to search out the true facts of the assassination. Yet in spite of its unconcern for facts beyond those which seemed to confirm the guilt of the accused, the Conspiracy Trial produced a comprehensive *explanation* of the "conspiracy" which went into the history books forthwith—and has remained there.

We submit that any explanation of an event that is based upon partial information supplemented by conjecture is not history but legend. As such it could have no logical structure of action and reaction, cause and effect, motivation and opportunity, etc. that a rational investigator could explore to get to the root of the matter. The fact is that, being a legend, the version of the "conspiracy" advanced at the Conspiracy Trial *is impregnable to investigation.*

This is our first premise: that the legend doesn't provide a valid basis for study, and that any investigation of it is futile. Yet it's the only complete account of the assassination there is.

If the would-be investigator accepts this, he has only one alternative. He must collect all the available evidence on the assassination—that concealed and ignored at the Conspiracy Trial as well as that brought to light—and construct a new version of the conspiracy from the ground up.

Such a research procedure has many complications. When one is beginning from scratch, no evidence, testimony, records, or documents can be taken at face value. Every statement, written or spoken, must be weighed to determine whether its author was in a position to *know* the truth or not and whether it was his intention to reveal or to conceal what he knew. It is then necessary to check for agreement and disagreement among the various facts and witnesses.

Above all, the object is to reconstruct an authentic situation in which there is a logical relationship between motive and action, between cause and effect, and among the various parties to the event. Thus the acid test in any specific instance has to be *logic.* The conventions of historical research place great reliance upon *documents,* which when authenticated are assumed to be the most reliable form of evidence. But they must be used logically. The antiquity of a document is no guarantee that the writer knew what he was talking about or wanted to tell what he knew. If we can learn anything from what he wrote, it is because we understand him as a human type and have a reasonably clear idea of his connection with this historical episode.

The nature of this form of research also creates some complications in the presentation of the findings. In effect we begin with a mass of evidence but *no theory* as to what happened. To build a theory, we have to fit pieces of related evidence together as if they were parts of a giant jigsaw puzzle—completing as many small sections as possible, trying to get an idea of the over-all pattern or picture.

The principal characters in the assassination have to be identified and hypotheses established as to their probable actual roles in connection with the crime. In the course of this procedure a general pattern of a conspiracy begins to emerge.

Having rather firm hypotheses about each of the principal characters, we can begin testing to see whether these fit into the developing pattern of a conspiracy by the logical use of given data.

Thus the reader's conviction as to whether this new version of the conspiracy to murder Lincoln is valid or not will largely depend upon whether he feels that the available data is in fact logically put together and interpreted. To reach a conviction for or against this version, the reasoning process must be displayed for his examination.

Provision has been made for those who don't wish to expend the mental energy to follow the research through all its variations to final conclusions but do wish to know who did what and to whom. The first seven chapters convey the general foundation of the new version. The eighth through the fourteenth close with summaries which are adequate for the reader whose taste for details is not avid. By reading the summaries only, he can follow the thread of the research and proceed with the subsequent inductive chapters which concern the roles of the principal figures in Lincoln's assassination and the Conspiracy Trial.

Finally, we should point out an intellectual hazard that the advanced student of the assassination will encounter in a treatment researched and presented in this manner. Quite frequently, and from the very beginning, we depart radically from the "known facts" that are "established" by the traditional version of the "conspiracy." When these contradictions occur, there may be a temptation to stop and take issue with them—and perhaps lose the thread of the discussion. If it is kept in mind that the objective is to develop a substantially *new* version based upon accumulated evidence from all sources, these frequent departures from tradition will be much less distracting.

V. S.

acknowledgments

These paragraphs are addressed to exactly twenty-six people. It is doubtful that any of this group knew the final objectives of the undertaking or the unusual circumstances under which the research was conducted. Although its geographical range covered most of the eastern half of the United States, the only traveling done by the author from start to finish was between Virginia Beach and Washington, D. C.

All of the extensive research in other parts of the country was conducted by mail, with countless hours of searching being done by persons who had not (and still have not) met the author nor ever heard of him before. Their only reason for giving so generously of their time and effort was a mutual interest in the subject of this book. File folders bulge with their correspondence and the mass of data they gathered. An expression of thanks—even one laden with superlatives—couldn't adequately convey the author's gratitude for their exertions and support.

It is impossible to itemize the data contributed by each of these associates. It is also unnecessary, since each *knows* what he did, and would be misleading, since some spent long hours of searching in old records and volumes but were unable to find much material bearing on the case.

Although the help of these co-workers is acknowledged collectively in the following alphabetical list, an asterisk has been placed before the names of several persons whose contributions were so indispensable that the work could not have developed beyond the idea stage if any one of them had been withheld. It is the author's hope that each of these will have the personal satisfaction of knowing that he, individually, made this book possible.

Professor Rollin S. Armour, Stetson University, DeLand, Florida

Mrs. Amy Gillette Bassett, Cambridge, New York

Mr. W. J. Berry, Editor, Primitive Publications, Elon College, North Carolina

*Mrs. Thomas W. Botts, Columbia, Missouri

Mrs. Mary Givens Bryan, Director, Georgia Department of Archives and History, Atlanta, Georgia

Dr. Dorothy Dodd, State Librarian, Florida State Library, Tallahassee, Florida

Mr. Henry J. Dubester, Chief, General Reference Division, Library of Congress, Washington, D. C.

Mrs. Maude Engram, Orlando, Florida

Mr. Robert Fowler, Editor, *Civil War Times Illustrated*, Gettysburg, Pennsylvania

Dr. Woodford B. Hackley, Secretary, Virginia Baptist Historical Society, University of Richmond, Richmond, Virginia

Miss Ann K. Harlow, Chief, Readers Service Division, U. S. Military Academy Library, West Point, New York

*Mrs. Sarah Jackson, National Archives, Washington, D. C.

Mrs. K. M. Lattin, Santa Cruz, California

Mr. Herbert Law, Chief Clerk, County Court of Orange County, Orlando, Florida

Dr. Fred V. Lucas, Chairman, Department of Pathology, School of Medicine, University of Missouri

Judge John H. McCormick, County Judge of Hamilton County, Jasper, Florida

*Mr. Ray A. Neff, Avalon, New Jersey

*Mr. Elmer O. Parker, National Archives, Washington, D. C.

Mrs. W. O. Richey, Boyce, Louisiana

Mr. John A. Smith, Attorney-at-Law, Talbotton, Georgia

Mr. and Mrs. Francis Spickler, Westtown, Pennsylvania

*Mrs. Lucy S. Stewart, deceased

Mr. John E. Taylor, National Archives, Washington, D. C.

*Mrs. Ruth Thomas, Seattle, Washington

Mr. Rufus Webb, Gaithersburg, Maryland

*Mr. Howard P. Wright, Genealogist, Jacksonville Public Library, Jacksonville, Florida

contents

appendix 405

notes to chapters 457

index 471

list of documents

list of plates

1

the riddle of Louis Paine

At about 11:30 on the evening of April 17, 1865, a tall, robust young man named Louis Paine rapped at the front door of a Washington, D. C., boardinghouse on H Street. The establishment was located about four blocks from Ford's Theater, scene of the assassination of President Lincoln three nights earlier, on Good Friday, April 14.

The boardinghouse was a respectable three-story brick structure built flush with the sidewalk. It was operated by Mrs. Mary E. Surratt, a widow and the mother of three grown children. Her son John and daughter Anna lived with her. An older son was with the Confederate forces in Texas.

In answer to Paine's knock, the door was opened immediately by Captain Wermerskirch and Detective Morgan. These officers were members of a special detective detail that had arrived ten minutes earlier with orders from the War Department to arrest Mrs. Surratt and all the members of her household. Their instructions were also to search the house for evidence that any of the occupants had been involved in a suspected conspiracy to assassinate the President and other high officials of the government.

The search party was particularly interested in the whereabouts of Mrs. Surratt's son John. He was known to have been a Confederate mail courier between Richmond and Canada during the Civil War, which had ended or virtually ended eight days earlier with the surrender of General Lee at Appomattox. The War Department had known for several weeks that he was a close associate of John Wilkes Booth, the noted actor who had been identified as Abraham Lincoln's assassin. As of this night Booth was still at large, and a nationwide search for him was in progress. It was believed that young Surratt might know where the murderer could be found.

In addition, the authorities were looking for a man who had made a savage attack upon the invalid Secretary of State William Seward at almost the same time Lincoln was shot on the evening of April 14. Surratt was high on their list of suspects in connection with this crime.

Over the shoulders of the two officers the towering Paine could see activity in the gas-lighted hallway. Mrs. Surratt and three young ladies —seventeen-year-old Anna and two relatives who boarded there—were dressed for the street and being herded toward the door by other detectives.

"I guess I am mistaken," he murmured, and turned to leave.

It was too late. He had stepped across the threshold, and Morgan pushed the door shut.

"Who do you want to see?"

"Mrs. Surratt."

"You're right." Morgan's invitation was a command. "Walk in."

This was the *detectives'* explanation of how young Paine happened to be picked up during the raid on the Surratt house.

Three weeks and a few days later, on May 12, Louis Paine was one of eight civilians arraigned before a special military commission, a court martial appointed by Secretary of War Edwin McMasters Stanton. As a group, the seven men and one woman were charged with conspiring with John Wilkes Booth to assassinate President Lincoln, Vice-President Johnson, Lieutenant General U. S. Grant, and Secretary of State Seward.

The murder plot was alleged to have been hatched following the failure of a six-month-long conspiracy to kidnap the Chief Executive and carry him to Richmond as ransom for all the Confederate soldiers held in Northern prisons. This imaginative undertaking, under the leadership of Booth, was said to have been sponsored and directed by Jefferson Davis and certain leaders of the Rebel underground in Canada.

In addition to the sweeping general charges, Paine individually was accused of entering Seward's house on the night Lincoln was murdered and attempting to stab the Secretary of State to death. It was charged that he was thrown from his horse as he fled northeastward out of Washington and that he hid in the woods for three days, until hunger drove him to return to Mrs. Surratt's house that night, disguised as a laborer.

On June 30, at the close of a sensational six-week trial, all eight defendents were found guilty as charged. Three of them—Dr. Samuel Mudd, Samuel Arnold, and Michael O'Laughlin—were sentenced to life imprisonment. Ned Spangler, a very minor figure in the "conspiracy" described by the prosecution, was given a six-year term.

Shortly after one o'clock on the hot afternoon of July 7, 1865—only twenty-four hours after they had been informed of their sentences—Louis Paine, Mrs. Surratt, George Atzerodt, and David Herold were hanged together in the courtyard of the Washington arsenal.

the legend of the Booth conspiracy

The history of the controversial Conspiracy Trial of 1865 as most Americans know it is a textbook version pared down to a digestible nubbin. For history is a complex and highly speculative study at best, particularly with regard to the personal motivation of the actors, and has to be reduced to a fairly simple story which average students can understand and recite.

In this case the essentials are that a humanitarian president who had successfully steered his country through a bloody civil war was murdered by an insane actor to avenge the defeat of the Southern Confederacy. Twelve days later, after a countrywide search, the actor was traced to a farm near Port Royal, Virginia, and was shot to death by a Union cavalryman when he refused to surrender. The actor's gang of accomplices were rounded up and—after a trial of several weeks, in which they had every opportunity to defend themselves—were sentenced to various degrees of punishment, four of them being hanged.

This basic account, with some modifications, is the same one the engineers of the Conspiracy Trial set out to promulgate. In a way their success in planting such a version on the pages of American history was a triumph in propaganda. For even before the trial began, the first gusts of a storm of protest were shaking the legend.

From the time Edwin Stanton had taken office as Secretary of War in Lincoln's cabinet on January 20, 1862, he had increased the power of the War Department—which is to say, his personal power—to a frightening degree. Under the pretext of combating subversion, he had developed a Gestapo-like secret service headed by the notorious detective Lafayette C. Baker, who was responsible only to the War Secretary. He had assumed the power to make arbitrary arrests at his and Baker's sole discretion and to hold suspected individuals in prison for indefinite periods, incommunicado and without charges. Most importantly, he had instituted the practice of trying civilians before military tribunals which disregarded many of the accepted legal procedures and made rulings from which there was no appeal.

The Conspiracy Trial was just such a proceeding, but with a major difference. Whereas trials by military commission had previously been conducted in wartime in areas under military control, which gave them an atmosphere of both legality and necessity, the war was now over. The civil courts were functioning. The eight defendants at the Conspiracy Trial were all civilians and had a clear constitutional right to be tried individually in a civil court.

This legal aspect—the question of whether the military tribunal Stanton had appointed to try the "conspirators" had jurisdiction in the case—was under violent attack by some newspaper editors who were properly alarmed at the reluctance of the War Department to relinquish its dictatorial emergency powers with the coming of peace.

In spite of the campaign of vilification against the prisoners with which the War Department succeeded in convicting most of them in the public mind before the actual court proceedings began, the fact that one of them was a woman (and a woman had never before been sentenced to death in a national court) brought a strong emotional reaction from much of the press and a considerable segment of the public. When Colonel William E. Doster, who had acted as defense attorney for the prisoners Paine and Atzerodt, left the arsenal grounds on July 7 immediately after the executions, he noted that a large crowd of citizens was gathered before the gates shouting, "judicial murder."

From that time until the present, suspicions that the Conspiracy Trial resulted in a historic miscarriage of justice have been focused particularly upon the case of Mrs. Surratt. For years after the Trial a storm raged around her memory. The future political careers of several men who had a hand in her conviction and execution were blighted by the stigma of having hanged a woman, a woman who was widely believed to have been innocent. At least three men directly involved in the widow's execution—including the president of the military commission, General David Hunter—committed suicide, presumably from remorse.*

With the passage of time the sense of outrage at the widow's "judicial murder" extended itself to the other prisoners, at least as far as historians were concerned. Dr. Mudd's heroic exertions when yellow fever swept through his sunbaked prison on Dry Tortugas, killing prisoners and guards alike, gave him a mantle of nobility that covered any possible damage to his reputation suffered at the Trial. Atzerodt and Herold, two of the four who were hanged, and Booth's boyhood friends Arnold and O'Laughlin gradually became objects of considerable sympathy as harmless simpletons who had been led astray by the fanatical actor. Pathetic Ned Spangler, a scene-shifter at Ford's, was widely believed to have been an innocent bystander by observers at the Trial. When he and the other three were pardoned in 1869 at President Johnson's order, Dr. Mudd took tubercular Spangler home to his Maryland farm to die. O'Laughlin pined himself into the grave on Tortugas.

The only one of the eight defendants whose unmitigated guilt has never before, during, or since the Trial been questioned was the young man who tapped at Mrs. Surratt's door on the evening of Monday, April 17, 1865—Louis Paine.

---

* Preston King of New York and General James Henry Lane of Kansas prevented Anna Surratt from seeing President Johnson to appeal for clemency for her mother the day of the executions. King drowned himself in the Hudson River on November 13, 1865. Lane cut his throat on July 11, 1866.—*Records of the Columbia Historical Society*, XXVII, 143.

the riddle of louis paine

Of the eight prisoners, Louis Paine was the only one convicted on evidence that was not circumstantial, by the testimony of eyewitnesses to the specific crime of which he was accused. Even today, a century later, his image is unchanged from that given him by the prosecution at the Conspiracy Trial: A homicidal, half-witted brute without a flicker of remorse for the vicious crime he had attempted but bungled.

Paine, as the only prisoner the prosecution could connect with a particular act of violence, bore the brunt of their denunciation. In the absence of the dead Booth, he was the bull's-eye for a savage propaganda campaign to make all eight prisoners, together with Jefferson Davis and the prostrate Confederate government, objects of public loathing as the murderers of Abraham Lincoln.

The nine undistinguished military men whom Stanton had appointed as judges on the court martial were, if possible, more blinded by this artificially engendered prejudice than the general public. Throughout the whole proceeding, their partiality to the aims and wishes of the prosecution was scandalous from a legal standpoint. They were deaf to any appeal on Paine's behalf on any ground, and his being sentenced to hang was one of the foregone conclusions of the Trial from the first session, if not from an even earlier point.

But the persistence of the prejudice against this young man for a full century—generations after all his fellow defendants have received either exoneration or sympathetic understanding in the history books—is a phenomenon of mass thought-conditioning that has no parallel.

Even while the Trial was in progress, the possibility that the hate campaign being directed against the Booth "conspirators" was a screen for a less visible conspiracy in high places was being hinted in the press. With the passing months the accusations to this effect became louder, more widespread, and more explicit. In February of 1866 President Andrew Johnson, under violent attack by the Radical Republicans since he had reverted to Lincoln's conciliatory policies toward the conquered South, included a large class of Northern politicians and high government figures in this indictment shouted during a speech from the White House steps:[1]

> . . . Are those who want to destroy our institutions and change the character of the government not satisfied with the blood that has been shed? Are they not satisfied with one martyr? Does not the blood of Lincoln appease the vengeance and wrath of the opponents of this Government? . . . Have they not honor and courage enough to effect the removal of the presidential obstacle otherwise than through the hands of the assassin?

In spite of the fact that the legend of the Booth "conspiracy" presented to the nation at the Conspiracy Trial has remained the general basis for textbook versions of the episode for a hundred years, the suspicion of a plot within a plot has persisted among magazine and book writers on the subject. The high tide of this suspicion came in 1937, with the publication of the late Otto Eisenschiml's first report on his ten years' research on the assassination,[2] followed by its sequel in 1940.[3] Eisenschiml's two books amount to a catalogue of a large portion of the existing documentation on Lincoln's murder, the Conspiracy Trial, and the trial of John Surratt in 1867. The reader of these two extraordinary collections of historical material is left with a strong impression that Edwin Stanton and certain of his political and official associates must surely have had a hand in the intrigue to remove President Lincoln by assassination.

Dr. Eisenschiml—and perhaps it is evidence of his integrity as a historian—refused to reach absolute conclusions, allowing his readers to ponder upon the evidence presented and attempt to reach their own conclusions. So there the matter has rested since then. No subsequent account of the assassination and Trial has been or can be written without reference to Eisenschiml's monumental study; but commentators still display a wide divergence of opinion as to what, if anything, went on behind the scenes at the infamous Trial. Some still follow the line that Booth was the mastermind. Others have gone much farther than Eisenschiml was willing to go in the direction of pinning the guilt upon Edwin McMasters Stanton and his clique.

the legend of Louis Paine

In all the searching for the key to America's most famous mystery, though, no one to this writer's knowledge has looked for it in what might seem to be the most obvious place to find a weak spot in the War Department's case against the Booth "conspirators"—the case of Louis Paine.

Paine was the keystone in the structure of the interrelated guilt erected by the prosecution. Because of the universal prejudice against him, the evidence upon which he was convicted and hanged has never been analyzed closely. A study of it, from the viewpoint that the accusations against him may or may not have been well founded, leads the student step by step from one astonishing discovery to another—clear to the final conclusion that of the eight defendants at the Conspiracy Trial *he was the most innocent.*

This is a main thread in our study—the overwhelming evidence that Louis Paine didn't even know Booth, had nothing to do with the "conspiracy" for which he and the other defendants were tried, and had not attacked Secretary of State Seward.

From the foregoing statement it can be assumed both that the writer is convinced of Louis Paine's innocence and that he has sound evidence to support the belief. If that were the scope of the study—to show this young man not guilty of the crimes for which he was hanged—it would not be necessary to write a book on the subject. The evidence to that effect could be presented in a few hundred words.

But as mentioned before, the case against Paine was the keystone of the War Department's case against all eight defendants. When this keystone is removed through vindication, the entire aspect of the Conspiracy Trial changes. Exposure of the methods by which justice was corrupted to obtain Paine's conviction brings a chain reaction in the cases of the other seven prisoners, who were to a large degree convicted by precisely the same methods. And wherever the charges against them involve a relationship in the alleged "conspiracy" with young Paine, the validity of the charges becomes questionable.

So the case of Louis Paine is a sort of rear door to the Lincoln murder trial. Through it we can get behind the scenes and see a little of what was going on there while the legend of the Booth "conspiracy" was being presented to Americans of the time and those of the future on stage.

The grist of our investigation is in the actual proceedings of the Trial: the testimony of the witnesses for both prosecution and defense, the arguments of the attorneys, the judgment of the court. Fortunately for the sake of historical inquiry, these day-to-day proceedings were taken down by shorthand reporters and later published in book form. Several compilations are available for reference. In addition, the *original* records of the proceedings, preserved in the files of the War Department, are kept in the National Archives in Washington, D. C. They were consulted and compared with the published transcripts—which led to some very surprising discoveries.

Behind the outward aspect of the Trial as recorded in various forms, both published and unpublished, a considerable collection of original documents is preserved in the National Archives which shows us what was happening in the War Department during the tense period between the assassination and the beginning of the Trial about a month later. During this time officials of the Bureau of Military Justice were busy trying to form a picture of what had transpired to bring about the murder of the President and the attack upon Seward. Their interrogations of the prisoners, analyses of the information gathered, correspondence within the department and with officials elsewhere, etc. are all available in the original memoranda and letters, written in the longhand script of the men who helped to write the legend of John Wilkes Booth—and the legend of Louis Paine—a century ago.

Naturally we consulted the voluminous literature on the assassination and Trial, particularly the writings of persons who observed the events at first hand or took part in them. The later literature was referred to from time to time, although with the exception of Dr. Eisenschiml's study most of this is devoted to reviewing the Booth legend in an effort to make it add up logically. Since legends are only fantasy sparingly seasoned with fact, repeated analysis of them does not, unfortunately, bring us much closer to the truth.

Finally, our investigation called for considerable original research, notably in connection with antecedents of Louis Paine, the mystery man. At the time of his execution and since then, it has been the almost universal belief that his real name was Lewis Powell and that he was a former Confederate soldier from the state of Florida. There *was* such a man, and he played a leading part in the bloody events of Good Friday, April 14, 1865. But he vanished that same night and never reappeared under his own name, though he evidently lived for many years afterward.

Louis Paine was the *real name* of the young man who was tried, convicted, and hanged as a participant in the John Wilkes Booth "conspiracy."

2

confusion

In the spring and summer of 1865 the country was under the control of the military establishment. The power and national influence of the War Department under Edwin Stanton had grown to Frankenstein dimensions during four years of wartime emergency, and most informed citizens knew it. What they did not know was that this political monster was kept under control only by the firm but unobtrusive hand of Abraham Lincoln.

Even while Lincoln was dying in the Peterson house across Tenth Street from Ford's Theater, Stanton stepped forward to organize the nation's grief and focus it upon the project of finding and punishing the murderers. For three months the country was kept in a state of hysteria on this one theme, while the War Department performed its assumed role as Lincoln's avenger with a minimum of question or criticism as to its methods.

This favorable atmosphere of directed emotion allowed the Department's Bureau of Military Justice to stage a mockery of a trial and erect a legend to screen two ominous realities: First, that the assassination was one phase of a power grab within the federal government. Second, that the removal of Abraham Lincoln's restraining influence at a time when Congress was not in session had cleared the way for a military dictatorship headed by Secretary of War Stanton—and that plans were afoot to make it permanent.

We know now that the life of this dictatorship was brief, not because control of the country was voluntarily relinquished, but because the nation's spirit and institutions proved strong enough to resist and reject it.

The legend, however, persisted after its creators had been eliminated from the political scene. Even the nearly universal belief that the Conspiracy Trial was a miscarriage of justice hasn't enabled students to probe beyond its firmly rooted conceptions of how and why the murder of Lincoln occurred. As a whole the legend has a plausibility which resists any serious contradiction. Even the major damage done to it by Dr. Eisenschiml in the 1930's doesn't greatly impair our belief in it in the 1960's.

the bureau of military justice

The state of affairs inside the War Department during the three days immediately following the assassination was one of utter confusion. The War Department's prerogative of directing the search for Booth and his accomplices was not immediately made clear to the country's various law enforcement agencies, and many of these promptly launched private investigations of their own—scouring the cities and countryside of the middle Atlantic states and Maryland, tracing clues, arresting suspects, and keeping any information they found to themselves—in hopes of having the exclusive honor of bringing the President's murderers to justice.

Today we can get a very detailed view of the War Department's predicament for the first three days and the developing situation thereafter from the files of the Bureau of Military Justice, which are still preserved in the National Archives in Washington.* Thanks to the mere fact that the telephone had not yet been invented, communications between officials in the War Department were routinely conveyed in written form. The day-to-day progress from complete bewilderment to sudden enlightenment is thus well documented.

These same files reflect the state of hysteria which gripped the nation. Letters poured in from public officials and private citizens eager to contribute their opinions as to how the search should be conducted and, after April 20, eager to contend for the $100,000 reward offered by the War Department for the apprehension of John Wilkes Booth, John Surratt, and David Herold. While many of these letters came from cranks and professed clairvoyants and some of the writers merely wanted to cast suspicion on neighbors they didn't like, there was an element of horse sense in them. Several voiced the conclusion which now seems obvious—that Booth could not hope to make his escape through the aroused countryside and that, being a professional actor, he could be expected to assume a disguise and possibly even remain in Washington. Unfortunately for Booth, this element of horse sense was absent from the script he was enacting.

The Bureau officials who sifted this correspondence paid attention to some of the volunteered information and were greatly misled by it. Not knowing just whom or what they were looking for, they occasionally passed up clues that might have transformed the history of the pursuit and subsequent Trial. One farmer in northern Maryland described a stranger who had stolen his horse the Sunday after the assassination, but a hundred years passed before it was possible to see that the stranger had probably played a key part in the bloody events of April 14.

The Bureau's position was difficult. Stanton wanted the Trial to begin

*Army and Air Corps Branch, Lincoln Assassination Suspects File.

without a long delay in which public emotions would cool off. Judge Advocate General Joseph Holt and his assistants, Colonels Burnett and Bingham, were expected to build their case in a hurry. Holt was so unsure of his legal ammunition that he tried, unsuccessfully, to have the proceedings held in secret.

One reason for the uncertainty within the Bureau of Military Justice during the early period was that considerable information possessed by Stanton's efficient secret police system, headed by Lafayette C. Baker, was not communicated to the Bureau. It had to get along with whatever meager clues could be found and a not-too-enlightening collection of rumors that had been floating around the lower echelons of the War Department for several weeks.

the informant Weichmann

The principal source of these rumors was a gossipy young man named Louis J. Weichmann, a clerk in the Commissary of Prisoners. He was a former schoolmate of John Surratt's and had been a boarder and family friend of the Surratts since the widow had moved into the establishment the preceding November. He had told a Captain Gleason in his office that young Surratt, together with Booth and some other associates, was hatching a scheme to kidnap President Lincoln around the time of his second inauguration on March 4, 1865. His reason for wishing to cast suspicion upon a longtime friend was never made clear and remains a mystery to this day. In any case wartime Washington was one great rumor-mill, and no one in the War Department took Weichmann's revelations seriously until after the assassination had occurred.

At the Trial the informer said he had voluntarily surrendered himself the morning after the murder to Superintendent A. C. Richards of the Metropolitan Police and revealed what he knew about Booth and his "accomplices," George Atzerodt, "Payne," and John Surratt. He said he was sent to the office of General Augur, provost marshal general of the city.[1] If he was and if he divulged his information there, the War Department didn't act upon it. But Richards apparently thought it over and decided Weichmann might come in handy as an informant and as one able to identify Surratt. He made the young man his private property and sent him into southern Maryland on Saturday, to Baltimore on Sunday, and on Monday the seventeenth clear to Canada with two detectives who were to look for Surratt in Montreal.[2]

Just how valuable Weichmann proved to be to Superintendent Richards is hard to determine. The police chief had some information on Surratt even before the assassination, and only five hours after it occurred—at 3:00 A.M. Saturday morning—had sent some of his men to the boardinghouse and learned from the widow that her son had left for Canada eleven days earlier, on April 3. Anyway the purloined informer was kept beyond the reach of the Bureau of Military Justice until his return from Montreal on April 30 and may have had very little to do with the apprehension of any of the suspects, all of whom were in custody before that date.

On April 25 Stanton learned about the articulate Weichmann and learned that Richards had sent him to Canada on a "wild goose chase." He called the police chief to his office and proceeded to give him a tongue-lashing, until the indignant Richards retorted that the Canada excursion had been ordered by Stanton's chief of detectives, *Colonel Baker*. That cooled the acid little War Secretary off somewhat, but he still ordered Richards to leave immediately for Montreal and bring Weichmann back.[3] When the informer returned to the Capitol on April 30, he was promptly arrested by the War Department and, still under arrest, became its devastating star witness at the Trial, giving testimony which hanged Mrs. Surratt and giving much of that which sent Paine and Atzerodt to the gallows.

the arrests

On Sunday the sixteenth a party of plainclothes detectives arrived from New York City in charge of a certain Colonel H. S. Olcott, who was quickly installed in the Bureau of Military Justice with the title of Special Commissioner. The detectives were put up at the better hotels at the War Department's expense and during the rest of that day and the next were inconspicuous. On the evening of Monday, April 17, they suddenly went into action. Under the orders of Colonel Olcott, they swarmed into the Surratt boardinghouse and arrested all the occupants—as well as an odd fish named Louis Paine, who they said knocked at the door just as they were leaving. Within a week they had scooped up seven of the eight persons who would later be tried as Booth's accomplices, those arrested by other military and police agencies as well as by themselves. The male prisoners were isolated aboard two ironclad monitors anchored in the Navy Yard. Mrs. Surratt was held in Carroll Prison for a couple of days and then sent to a closely guarded cell in the Washington arsenal.

During this period of rapid developments, the officials of the Bureau were not sure just what was happening. The Capitol's jails had been filled with suspects of all descriptions, but Mrs. Surratt and the men confined on the *Montauk* and *Saugus* were clearly the only ones who mattered—or so they had been led to believe. Yet their interrogation of this hapless group of prisoners failed to reveal any concerted plot to murder the President. With the exception of Paine, and perhaps Dr. Mudd, all were known to have been acquainted with John Wilkes

Booth; and three of the men—Arnold, O'Laughlin, and Atzerodt—willingly admitted that they had been parties with the actor in a crackpot scheme to kidnap the President from a theater but that the scheme never got beyond the talking stage. Only Atzerodt, a grubby little carriage-painter from lower Maryland, would admit he had any notion that Booth's thoughts had finally turned to murder.

Even Colonel Olcott, who had been directly responsible for the arrest of most of the seven star prisoners, didn't know how they fitted into a conspiracy. His efforts to make the collected information from them add up were no more successful than those of Colonel John A. Foster, the regular War Department investigator who worked with him. Both men drew up various analyses of the "evidence" for Colonel Burnett, the Bureau's co-ordinator on the case, without arriving at a plot which would hang together, even though they frequently took the liberty of twisting the prisoners' statements to make the thing work out. The individual from whom Olcott was receiving his orders remained carefully unidentified in the official memoranda except for an occasional hint. Olcott was apparently not in a position to demand information on the suspects and their interrelationship from the man who had ordered him to arrest them.

The Bureau's frustration was communicated to Secretary Stanton, who—rather than screaming for Olcott's invisible puppeteer who was doling out intelligence by the spoonful, mostly in the form of depositions by the truculent plainclothesmen from New York—had the prisoners hooded to prevent them from talking to each other or their guards.

The vital question of course was the whereabouts of Booth, who could answer *all* the questions—who might even have more answers than Mr. Stanton had questions. On April 25, at almost the same time that a search party of detectives and soldiers was converging on the Garrett farm in Virginia, where Booth and Herold were secreted, the War Secretary ordered Colonel Foster to go back to the gunboats and interrogate the prisoners again "in hopes of getting a clue." [4]

On the evening of the following day the news arrived that Booth had been caught and killed—and that settled that. Herold joined the rest of the male "conspirators" on the monitors. With Booth dead, the Bureau would now have to rely upon its own ingenuity—and any handouts Olcott's boss felt like giving it—to construct a case against the prisoners. There were a lot of puzzles to work out before the Trial could begin, but Stanton and his associates, both visible and invisible, would solve them all one way or another.

the prisoner Paine

The greatest puzzle was the strange young man who had blundered into Mrs. Surratt's house at just the right moment—or the wrong moment, depending upon one's point of view. Louis Paine, at first willing to talk about himself freely, though he denied knowing anything about a conspiracy to assassinate the President, suddenly clamped his square jaw shut and refused to talk to anyone. The young giant with the smoldering dark-blue eyes was as impervious to threats and promises as a statue. He would sit or stand there with his wide mouth pressed into a narrow line and stare his interrogators out of countenance. No one could get a word out of him, and no one did until six weeks later, two weeks after the Trial had begun, when he just as suddenly decided to communicate with his baffled attorney, Colonel William E. Doster.

In this long meantime he was a thorn in the Bureau's side. Almost nothing was known about him. No one could be found who was *sure* he had ever seen Paine before. Some of the members of the Surratt household *thought* they recognized him, but they could not be positive. Yet the young colored boy who had opened the door to the man who tried to stab Seward to death the night Lincoln was shot had positively identified Louis Paine as that man. Thus any design for a grand conspiracy headed by Booth would have to include the silent giant.

As late as April 24, ten days after the assassination, a memo written in the Bureau of Military Justice listed the prisoners committed by Colonels Wells, Foster, and Olcott to that date. The list did not include Louis Paine, although he had been placed in the custody of Colonel H. H. Wells on April 19 and had been confined on the *Saugus* ever since. The Bureau was so uncertain whether it could find a place for Paine in Booth's "conspiracy" that on the twenty-fourth he wasn't even carried on the list of prisoners.[5]

A place was eventually found for Louis Paine of course, and it was an important one. But it wouldn't have been possible without the historic feat of treachery performed by the mystery man from whom Colonel Olcott took his orders.

3

Seward's assailant

mr. Stanton's telegrams

We are told that when Paine was arrested at Mrs. Surratt's house three nights after the assassination, he was taken to the headquarters of General Christopher Augur merely because the detectives considered him a "suspicious character."[1] William Bell, the Negro waiter who had answered the doorbell the night of the attack and let the intruder into the Seward house, was sent for; and as soon as he saw Paine, he made a positive identification of him.

This was the version of the "identification" sequence in the legend which was expounded by the prosecution at the Conspiracy Trial. It had certain elements of time, place, and characters which were correct, and it certainly reduced the incident to a simple and damning indictment of the prisoner. It succeeded in hiding one of the most insidious episodes in the search for the Booth "conspirators."

Sometime after 10:30 P.M. on the night of the assassination, as he was preparing to retire in the bedroom of his home on K Street, Secretary Stanton was brought the news that Seward had been stabbed at his mansion on Lafayette Square. Stanton immediately dressed himself again and, in company with the messenger, hastened to Seward's mansion.

Everything was confusion at Seward's. A large crowd of persons from the nearby embassies had gathered, and Stanton had to force his way through the crush to gain admittance. He went upstairs to the Secretary of State's bedroom (Seward had been injured in a carriage accident a few days earlier and was still a bed patient at the time of the attack), saw the grave condition of the victim in his blood-spattered bed, and talked with the doctors, family members, and servants. He then went to the next room and saw Seward's son Frederick, who had met the intruder at the top of the stairs and received a savage pistol whipping which had inflicted serious head wounds. After this, in company with Secretary of the Navy Gideon Welles, who had arrived a little earlier, he entered a carriage and went to Ford's Theater.[2] It was at Seward's house that Stanton heard the news that Lincoln had been shot.

By this time the dying President had been carried across Tenth Street to a back bedroom of the Peterson house. From the time of his arrival there before midnight until after seven o'clock the following morning Stanton attended the death watch, and at the same time received reports on the initial findings of the police investigators and dispatched four telegrams to General John A. Dix in New York which conveyed the first news of the tragedy for release to northern newspapers through Dix' headquarters.

The exact wording of these wires to New York is important to some subjects that will come up later, as well as to the immediate question of Paine's identification, so they are reproduced here in full:[3]

April 15, 1865–1:30 A.M.

Maj-General Dix,
New York:

Last evening, about 10:30 P.M., at Ford's Theater, the President, while sitting in his private box with Mrs. Lincoln, Miss Harris, and Major Rathbone, was shot by an assassin, who suddenly entered the box and approached behind the President. The assassin then leaped upon the stage, brandishing a large dagger or knife, and made his escape in the rear of the theater. The pistol-ball entered the back of the President's head, and penetrated nearly through the head. The wound is mortal. The President has been insensible ever since it was inflicted, and is now dying.

About the same hour an assassin (whether the same or another) entered Mr. Seward's home, and, under pretense of having a prescription, was shown to the Secretary's sick chamber. The Secretary was in bed, a nurse and Miss Seward with him. The assassin immediately rushed to the bed, inflicted two or three stabs on the throat and two on the face. It is hoped the wounds may not be mortal; my apprehension is that they will prove fatal. The noise alarmed Mr. Frederick Seward, who was in an adjoining room, and hastened to the door of his father's room, where he met the assassin, who inflicted upon him one or more dangerous wounds. The recovery of Frederick Seward is doubtful.

It is not probable that the President will live through the night. General Grant and wife were advertised to be at the theater this evening, but he started to Burlington at 6 o'clock this evening. At a cabinet meeting yesterday, at which General Grant was present, the subject of the state of the country and the prospects of speedy peace was discussed. The President was very cheerful and hopeful; spoke very kindly of General Lee and others of the Confederacy, and the establishment of government in Virginia. All the members of the Cabinet except Mr. Seward are now in attendance upon the President. I have seen Mr. Seward, but he and Frederick were both unconscious.

EDWIN M. STANTON
Secretary of War

seward's assailant—mr. stanton's telegrams

April 15, 1865—3 A.M.

Major-General Dix
(Care Horner, New York)

The President still breathes, but is quite insensible, as he has been ever since he was shot. He evidently did not see the person who shot him, but was looking on the stage as he was approached behind.

Mr. Seward has rallied, and it is hoped he may live. Frederick Seward's condition is very critical. *The attendant who was present was stabbed through the lungs, and is not expected to live.* The wounds of *Major Seward are not serious. Investigation strongly indicates J. Wilkes Booth as the assassin of the President. Whether it was the same or a different person that attempted to murder Mr. Seward remains in doubt.* Chief Justice Cartter is engaged in taking evidence. Every exertion has been made to prevent the escape of the murderer. His horse has been found on the road near Washington.

EDWIN M. STANTON
Secretary of War

The italics in this and the following telegrams are this author's. All the emphasized statements have direct or indirect bearing on the case of Louis Paine.

April 15, 1865—4:10 A.M.

Major-General Dix

The President continues insensible and is sinking. Secretary Seward remains without change. Frederick Seward's skull is fractured in two places, besides a severe cut upon the head. *The attendant is still alive but hopeless.* Major Seward's wounds are not dangerous.

It is now ascertained with reasonable certainty that two assassins were engaged in the horrible crime, Wilkes Booth being the one that shot the President, the other a companion of his whose name is not known, *but whose description is so clear that he can hardly escape.* It appears from a letter found in Booth's trunk that the murder was planned before the 4th of March, but fell through then because the accomplice backed out until "Richmond could be heard from."

Booth and his accomplice were at the livery stable at 6 this evening, and left there with their horses about 10 o'clock, or shortly before that hour. It would seem that they had for several days been seeking their chance, but for some unknown reason it was not carried into effect until last night. One of them has evidently made his way to Baltimore, the other has not yet been traced.

EDWIN M. STANTON
Secretary of War

April 15, 1865

Major-General Dix
New York

Abraham Lincoln died this morning at 22 minutes after 7 o'clock.

EDWIN M. STANTON
Secretary of War

In these four telegrams to General Dix, Stanton inadvertently gave us a number of important pieces of the historical jigsaw puzzle we are putting together. Some belong in sections which will be assembled in later chapters and will be passed by for the present. Before we begin fitting the rest into their proper places, there are a couple of aspects the significance of which should be mentioned briefly.

Stanton's reaction to the crimes

We are more likely to get a clear idea of Secretary Stanton's personal reaction to the shocking events of that night from these four wires than from any later statements or writings in which he referred to the subject. During the tense hours right after the assassination, harried by the going and coming of messengers, law officers, and dignitaries and obliged to issue orders of one kind or another having to do with the situation, he could hardly have had time to weigh his words with great care. The final wire suggested that he was not unaware of the certainty that his words would be recorded in history. But elsewhere he seemed to be writing hastily, expressing the thoughts which were foremost in his mind at the time.

These wires show a surprising difference in his attitudes to the murder of the Chief Executive and the wounding of the Secretary of State. In the first one he gives about equal attention to the two occurrences. In the second he takes three lines to say that the President is obviously dying, one and a half lines of which report that Lincoln did not see the person who shot him. Then he takes nearly six lines to say Seward will probably live and to give details of the affair at the Seward house.

In the third wire Stanton writes off the President in seven words and gets on with the subject which really seems to intrigue him, the attack upon Seward.

From our viewpoint in history it seems that the fatal shooting of such a noted individual as President Lincoln would be the more sensational happening of the evening, particularly since the Secretary of State was expected to survive—and even if he weren't, his death, though tragic, would not represent such a major political calamity for the nation.

Stanton's statements on Lincoln could suggest a certain lack of surprise. If he felt shock at the terrible thing which had happened, he controlled himself admirably. The reality of the situation—that Lincoln's imminent death would give *him* (Stanton) virtual control of the country (since he knew Johnson to be a political cipher at that time)—was not lost upon the Secretary of War.

The writer of the telegrams was giving a fair profile of his own early reactions. The murder of Lincoln apparently did not surprise him, but he was very much puzzled as to why anyone would want to kill Seward, who was not at the moment blocking anyone's pathway to power.

the letter in Booth's trunk

Reference in the third wire to the letter found in Booth's trunk at the National Hotel contains one of the implications against Stanton which are probably not well founded. The letter was one written to Booth on March 27 by his boyhood friend from Maryland, Samuel Arnold (see Appendix A, the "Sam" Letter). It was signed only "Sam," and although it referred in covert language to a project in which they had both been involved, it chided Booth for his resentment at Arnold's determination to withdraw from the business.

The "project" was Booth's harebrained idea to kidnap Lincoln from the presidential box in one of the theaters by lowering the trussed-up Executive to the stage and carrying him out to a waiting carriage, thence out of town and south to Richmond. On the face of it the idea was laughable, and Sam had hoped to be able to wash his hands of it without offending his old friend. In the letter he said nothing whatever about "before the 4th of March."

In his assumption that "Sam" was Booth's accomplice and probably the attacker of Seward, who had "evidently made his way to Baltimore," Stanton was simply adding two and two and getting five. An exhausted horse *had* been found northeast of the city in the direction of Baltimore, and it had probably been ridden by the man who attacked Seward. But that man was not Arnold. Mr. Stanton was far from the mark and rather indiscreet to flash his first impressions to the country's newspapers.

What he actually revealed was that he had heard the rumor circulated by the informer Weichmann that Booth had thought of trying to kidnap the President on Inauguration Day, March 4.

description of the suspect

So much for the sidelights. Now we return to the central consideration, the connection between Stanton's telegrams and Paine's identification. References to the attempt upon Mr. Seward's life in the first wire included the following two statements:

1. That there was uncertainty whether the man who shot President Lincoln was "the same [as] or another" than the one who attacked Mr. Seward.
2. That Stanton had visited the Seward house in person. Since we know

he did and had every opportunity to interrogate the witnesses there personally, this merely reaffirms it.

The second wire added these further particulars germane to our question:

1. That Stanton had received further reports from the Seward house since sending his first telegram.
2. That investigation had indicated that John Wilkes Booth was the assassin of the President.
3. That the doubt whether Lincoln and Seward were attacked by "the same or a different person" still remained. This was followed by a reference to "the murderer" in the singular.

The third wire reported additional important details:

1. That it was now believed "with reasonable certainty that two assassins were engaged in the horrible crime."
2. That John Wilkes Booth was believed to have shot Lincoln.
3. That the name of his accomplice (who attacked Seward) was not yet known, but that the authorities had a "description . . . so clear that he can hardly escape."

The collective intelligence of these several statements scattered through three telegrams amounted to this: *From Stanton's personal inquiries at the scene of the crime, plus information passed along to him in the course of the night, he was satisfied that the witnesses at Seward's house had seen the intruder clearly enough to be able to give an extremely good description of him—and that he was similar in appearance to John Wilkes Booth.*

It was asserted in telegrams one and two that Booth might have committed both crimes. Telegram number three reported that a "clear description" was available—and this could come *only* from the witnesses at the scene. These two circumstances added up to the foregoing conclusion.

Now Booth's outstanding physical and facial characteristics were (1) his underaverage height, about five feet seven inches,* and (2) his drooping black moustache.

Around three o'clock on the morning after the assassination, at about the same time Stanton was composing telegram number two, metropolitan police dispatched by Superintendent Richards conducted a raid on the Surratt boardinghouse. They were looking for John Wilkes Booth and *John Surratt* in connection with the attacks upon President Lincoln

*Booth may have been even shorter. For references to his lack of height, see Frances Wilson, *John Wilkes Booth* (Boston: Houghton Mifflin Co., 1929), pp. 10 and 15.

and Secretary Seward. Neither of them was found in the house of course, and the police went away without making arrests.

For the next three days John Surratt continued to be the prime suspect in the Seward affair. Most of the nation's daily newspapers reported that he was being sought in that connection. Some of the first newspaper reports on the arrest of a man who said his name was "Lewis Payne" indicated that the prisoner was thought to be John Surratt.

Surratt was a slender young man of twenty-three, about six feet tall. He had a hawk nose and brownish hair, and his distinguishing facial characteristic was a thin goatee.

Even though Booth and Surratt looked quite unalike in features and stature, and one wore a moustache and the other a goatee, it seems that they both conformed to the "clear description" of Seward's assailant which had been furnished by witnesses at the scene.

Almost exactly twenty-four hours after the attack upon Seward—at nine o'clock Saturday evening—Stanton's Assistant Secretary of War, C. A. Dana, telegraphed the following notice to police chiefs in the larger northern cities. The assumption that it was sent out by Stanton's order is quite reasonable: [4]

WASHINGTON, D. C., April 15, 1865

Chief of Police
Baltimore

The following is a description of G. A. Atzerodt, the assassin of Mr. Seward. He is twenty-six or twenty-eight years old, five feet eight inches high; light complexion, but browned from exposure; brown hair; long and rather curly mustache and goatee, dark from being dyed; wore dark pants, vest, and coat, and a long gray overcoat; was rather round-shouldered and stooping position; was in company with a man giving his name as S. Thomas, about thirty years of age; poorly clad in dark suit, low slouch hat; wore a mustache and heavy beard; was a rough and weather-beaten looking man.

C. A. DANA
Assistant Secretary of War

During the first few hours after the attack on Mr. Seward, the War Department decided that two types of men were acceptable as suspects: An undersized man who wore a drooping moustache and a tall, thin man who wore a goatee. Twenty-four hours after the crime, they telegraphed a "wanted" announcement to northern police chiefs which described a suspect who in height and facial adornment was an almost exact compromise between the two types which had been acceptable up to that time: A man of average height who wore *both* a moustache and a goatee!

Bizarre as this compromise seems, the War Department was getting down to cases at last—even *naming* the new suspect and giving an extremely accurate description of him. They didn't commit themselves altogether to Atzerodt, though, since John Surratt was still their favored suspect on Monday night, April 17, when Louis Paine was arrested.

This whole matter of the appearance of Seward's assailant raises a formidable doubt as to how well the witnesses at the scene had observed the knife-wielding intruder. When they took the witness stand at the Trial, those who described the stranger *at all* described a man as different from Booth, Surratt, *or* Atzerodt as it was possible for a man to be.

The text of Dana's notice to police chiefs contains internal evidence both as to where his information on Atzerodt came from and that this abortive announcement was merely a product of the War Department's helpless groping for information—and of their misinterpretation of what they found.

When Weichmann took the witness stand for the prosecution on May 18,[5] the sixth day of the Trial proceedings, he related how he had read the papers the morning after the assassination and had seen an article which said the intruder at Seward's had been wearing "a long gray coat." Recollecting that his acquaintance George Atzerodt had a long gray coat, he was overwhelmed by a sense of his patriotic duty and right after breakfast hastened over to Superintendent Richards' office, and then to General Augur's headquarters, to supply the authorities with a description of his acquaintance.

The identity of the man named "S. Thomas" also came out at the Trial. John Greenawalt, keeper of the Pennsylvania House, testified on May 17.[6] He said he was called to the desk at about 3:00 A.M. the morning after the assassination and found two men in the lobby who both wanted rooms. He told them he was short of space but they could share the same room if they wished. They wished, and both signed their names to the register: "George Atzerodt" and, the seedier of the two, "Sam Thomas." The hotelkeeper couldn't say whether the men had come in together or whether they were even acquainted. Thomas left around 5:00 A.M. to catch the early train; Atzerodt slipped out a little later without paying his bill.

Before any other tribunal except a military commission of the Civil War variety, the fact that Atzerodt registered under his own name at a hotel only a few blocks from the scene of either of the past night's crimes might have been construed as evidence that he had nothing much on his conscience. At the Conspiracy Trial this unconspirator-like behavior—as with all behavior which didn't fit in with the prosecution's preconceptions—was attributed to stupidity.

The conclusion we draw from the foregoing analysis is that the witnesses at Seward's house saw the intruder only vaguely and agreed only on the point that he wore a moustache, a goatee, or both.

4

Seward's assailant

colonel Baker's handbill

Lafayette Baker claimed to have masterminded the Conspiracy Trial. But his contempt for the truth was notorious, as was his reputation for taking credit for anything others did within his orbit which he considered an accomplishment. It's doubtful that any public servant in the history of the country was ever called a liar more often or more eloquently than Stanton's chief of detectives. He could hardly have earned this distinction without having been reasonably worthy of it.

In his ghostwritten autobiography, *The Secret Service in the Late War*, he states, "On my bureau devolved the task of procuring, compiling, and arranging this testimony. . . ."[1] He referred to the mass of forged, perjured, fabricated evidence by which the defendants were convicted. His chapters on the assassination recount his brilliant, heroic, and successful efforts to convict eight persons of "conspiracy" against the life of his beloved President. Being so largely devoted to the glorification of its author, the book hardly qualifies as a historical reference if taken literally. Yet it is remarkable how often Baker can be caught telling the truth, or revealing the truth (as in the foregoing quotation), when his statements are interpreted in terms of his *type*. He was an artist at deception. And this episode of American history was his masterpiece, which he dared not display. The temptation to boast of it became too great to resist, and he told it all—not in the printed word, but between the lines.

Many historians have sensed that a sinister force was in motion behind the scenes at the Conspiracy Trial, and they have usually associated it with Secretary of War Stanton, who was an offstage manipulator of unusual talent. But Stanton's type was one which tended to react to events rather than initiating them. By temperament and capacity he was an opportunist, and his personal political history documents it. In his connections with the backwash of the assassination, his obvious efforts to reap advantages from the murder placed him under persistent suspicion. Yet evidence that he was reaping where he himself had planted is largely lacking. He appears rather to have been reacting to stimuli supplied by his chief of detectives.

Baker's description of the assailant

In the preceding section we saw the fumbling performance of the War Secretary in a volcanic situation in which he was obliged to take action. In this section we shall see the prompt, decisive turn of events when the unseen hand of Lafayette Baker began to move.

According to Navy Secretary Gideon Welles' diary—a mother lode of intimate observations on the Washington scene in the 1860's—Colonel Baker had been out of favor with his boss for some time prior to the assassination, or so Stanton wanted it believed. Baker's memoirs inform us that he had been in New York investigating "frauds committed in the recruiting service . . . for some weeks previous to the assassination."[2] But he had been in the Capitol as recently as the day before the crime.[3] He was, however, at the Astor House in New York on Saturday, April 15, the day afterward.

Baker was in touch with General Dix's headquarters and got the news of the murder in the small hours of the morning—so early that the building in which his New York offices were located had been draped in black by a little after 6:00 A.M. at his direction. According to *his* account, he did nothing for the rest of the morning but sit around heartbroken and muse about his great personal loss in the death of Mr. Lincoln.[4] A more positive reaction might have been expected from the head of the national detective bureau—though there is some question whether that was still his function as of April 15. When he returned to the Capitol, he signed official communications with only the title "Agent of the War Department" after his name.

Sometime in the early afternoon, as Baker related it, a wire came from Secretary Stanton[5] which read:

> WASHINGTON, April 15, 1865
>
> COLONEL L. C. BAKER:
>
> Come here immediately and see if you can find the murderer of the President.
>
> EDWIN M. STANTON, *Secretary of War*

The detective's autobiographical version of his response to this order is told in two versions: First, quotations from an article written by New York *World* reporter George Alfred Townsend, based on an interview with Baker in his Washington headquarters.[6] Second, in a "brief official history" of the event by the author, via his ghost-writer.[7] Since both versions had the same source of information (Baker himself), neither can be taken as the literal truth. In both, confusion of days, dates, and events is most evident.

Baker's own account says he had difficulty with train connections but arrived in Washington Easter Sunday morning, April 16. After an emotional interview with the equally heartbroken Secretary of War, he spent the first day reviewing the chaotic search of the countryside by thousands of soldiers and all the police agencies—including metropolitan detective details *from as far away as Boston and New York*. The officials of none of the local agencies (particularly General Augur) would give him either co-operation or information; so he finally decided to pursue his own course, using the detective personnel which was subject to his own orders.

At this time, he relates, no co-ordinated pursuit had been organized, no photos or descriptions of the culprits had been circulated, and no rewards had been offered. Thus on Monday the seventeenth he composed the first public "wanted" notice on Booth and "Seward's assailant" in the form of a handbill. This was sent out by mail and wire, and was also distributed by his detectives in areas adjacent to Washington. The text of the handbill, according to Baker, was as follows:[8]

$30,000 Reward
Description
of
JOHN WILKES BOOTH

Who assassinated the President, on the evening of April 14, 1865. Height 5 feet 8 inches; weight 160 pounds; compact build; hair jet black, inclined to curl, medium length, parted behind; eyes black, and heavy eyebrows; wears a large seal ring on little finger; when talking inclines his head forward; looks down.

Description of the person who attempted to assassinate Hon. W. H. Seward, Secretary of State. Height 6 feet 1 inch; hair black, thick, full, and straight; no beard nor appearance of beard; cheeks red on the jaws; face moderately full; 22 or 23 years of age; eyes, color not known—large eyes not prominent; brows not heavy but dark; face not large but rather round; complexion healthy; nose straight and well formed, medium size; neck short and of medium length; hands soft and small; fingers tapering; shows no sign of hard labor; broad shoulders; taper waist; straight figure; strong looking man; manner not gentlemanly, but vulgar. Overcoat double-breasted; color mixed of pink and gray spots, small—was a sack overcoat, pockets inside and one on breast, with lapels or flaps; pants black common stuff; new heavy boots; voice small and thin, inclined to tenor.

The common council of Washington, D. C., have offered a reward of $20,000 for the arrest and conviction of these assassins, in addition to which I will pay $10,000.

L. C. Baker
Colonel, and Agent of the War Department

The description of Booth, the President's murderer, was so brief and superficial that we might wonder whether the writer of the handbill really wanted him caught.

But the description of "the person who attempted to assassinate Hon. W. H. Seward" could hardly have been more detailed and specific if Baker had been listing the features of someone he had known all his life.

This handbill's description of an unnamed man was *an almost perfect description of Louis Paine.*

Paine was arrested after 11:30 P.M. on Monday, April 17. Until that time and day, the War Department's official conception of the appearance of Seward's assailant—undoubtedly based upon interrogation of the witnesses to the crime—was of a man who looked like George Atzerodt, whose name and description had been telegraphed to metropolitan police chiefs in the North on Saturday night.

Thus, since the man supposedly described by the Seward witnesses and the suspect in Baker's handbill were so radically different in appearance, either the witnesses or Baker—one or the other—had to be wrong. If Baker was right, the witnesses had either not seen the intruder at all or had seen him under such unfavorable conditions that *they could not describe him accurately.* If the witnesses were right—well, let's look a little farther.

Baker's "official" report in his autobiography said he had arrived in the Capitol on the morning of April 16. But the Townsend article he quoted expressed it differently. Townsend wrote: "He returned on the third morning. . . ."

The *third morning* after the assassination was Monday, April 17. The detective's account of his frustrating first day back in Washington established beyond doubt that it had been entirely consumed with trying in vain to get information and co-operation from various police bureaus. Lafayette Baker's supreme unpopularity with the garrison officers and all police officials in the city, due to his cutthroat, self-glorifying methods, makes this non-co-operation extremely plausible. He himself said it was not until his *second* day in town that he wrote the handbill and had it printed and distributed.

Thus by his own timetable the handbill was not published until Tuesday the eighteenth. Was this revelation due to sloppy proofreading—or did Baker *intend* to insert the implication?

On May 2, Major H. W. Smith, one of the imported detectives who had raided the Surratt house, submitted an expense voucher to Colonel Olcott, under whose direct orders he was operating. It listed two items totaling thirty-two dollars: (1) The cost of a hack (to take Mrs. Surratt and the three young ladies to the police station) on April 17; (2) The expense of *handbill* distribution in the northern neck of Virginia.[9]

The order in which Smith listed these expenses is revealing. Apparently he did not feel it necessary to cover up a monstrous "irregularity" in a chit intended only for the attention of Colonel Olcott. Major Smith, as we shall see later in his testimony at the Trial, had participated in the arrest of Louis Paine on *Monday, April 17*—and distributed handbills in which Paine was described as Seward's assailant on *Tuesday, April 18*.

All of which adds up only one way: Lafayette Baker composed the handbill with its description of Louis Paine *after he had seen him in custody in General Augur's headquarters!*

The same evidence (Smith's distribution of Baker's handbill) identifies Colonel L. C. Baker as the mysterious individual under whose orders Colonel Olcott and the New York detectives were operating.

Later, at the Conspiracy Trial, two of the three persons who were alleged witnesses to the attack upon Secretary Seward would testify under oath that the gaslights at the house that night had been few and turned down quite low, leaving the hallways and Secretary Seward's room in semidarkness. The third witness did not describe the intruder at all.

In view of this, the very text of the handbill bears witness to Baker's treachery. The details he mentioned—straight and well-formed nose; soft, small hands with tapering fingers showing no signs of hard labor; a coat with mixed pink and gray spots, etc.—were features the witnesses did not and could not describe. They could not even say surely whether the intruder had been tall and beardless like Paine or medium-sized like Atzerodt, with a moustache and goatee.

The handbill description could have been written *only* after someone had observed its subject closely and at leisure under an excellent light, someone who had the authority to tell the prisoner to hold out his hands palms up.

the assailant's moustache

As we have seen, the man arrested at the Surratt house and charged with the attack upon Secretary Seward was of a physical and facial description radically different from the man the War Department had advertised for by name two days earlier. We can presume that the witnesses at Seward's who talked with Edwin Stanton only half an hour after the attack were not at that time involved in any scheme to corrupt justice, nor under any pressure to report the stranger as appearing otherwise than as they remembered him. So their initial impressions deserve consideration.

The clothing of the intruder was not a factor in this connection, since he could have changed it shortly after leaving the scene. His height would have been a feature on which they might well have disagreed or been mistaken—depending upon their own relative heights and the conditions under which they encountered him. The question of the reliability of their descriptions turns more on whether he wore facial hair in any style, as they seemed to think. There are good indications that he may have.

On the afternoon of Sunday, April 16, a bloodstained gray coat was found in the woods northeast of Washington[10] in the same general area where an exhausted one-eyed horse was picked up—which later proved to have once belonged to Booth. News of finding this coat seems to have gone out over the news wires the next day, before Paine's arrest. On Wednesday the nineteenth, the triweekly *Missouri Democrat* in St. Louis reported the finding of the coat and mentioned a further detail, which was never referred to throughout the Conspiracy Trial and which this writer has never noticed in *any* history of the affair.

This St. Louis paper said the pockets of the bloody coat contained "a false mustache, a pair of riding gloves, and a card bearing the name 'Mary J. Gardener 419.' "

Here was a perfectly acceptable explanation for the most glaring discrepancy between Baker's description of Seward's assailant and the one given earlier by the witnesses—a false moustache! Yet the prosecution never referred to it. Was it possible the War Department didn't know these objects were in the pockets of the coat which was found?

The War Department *did* know about them and had possession of them both before and after April 26. The following receipt is in the National Archives among the documents relating to the Trial:

Received from Col. H. S. Olcott
the package of clothes Taken from the
person of Lewis Payne on board the
Gunboat, also the over coat found
near Fort Bunker Hill, with ~~the~~
Contents of pockets.
Thos. T. Eckert.
Washington, D.C., Apr. 26th, 1865. Maj & A.D.C.

FIG. 1.—Major Eckert's Receipt for Paine's Clothing and "Contents of Pockets"

Major Eckert was head of the Office of the Military Telegraph and Assistant Secretary of War under Edwin Stanton—one of his closest, if not his closest, of confidants. There was *no one* more deeply involved with the capture, trial, and conviction of the Booth "conspirators" than he. He enters the picture at this point only because his signed receipt shows the War Department's knowledge of the contents of the coat pockets, including the false moustache.

As the War Department's prosecutors began the presentation of their case against Paine, it became clear that they had prepared themselves for the possibility that the defense might make an issue of the discrepancies between the original descriptions of the intruder given by the Seward house witnesses and the appearance of the prisoner in the dock—Louis Paine. On May 13, the very first day of testimony, Louis Weichmann, star witness for the state, was fed one of Judge Advocate Holt's characteristically leading questions with regard to the behavior of Paine during his alleged stay at the Surratt house sometime in the month of March:

"Did you observe any trace of disguise or preparations for disguises?"

Weichmann responded obediently with an incriminating bit of "evidence" which was never confirmed by any other witness. He referred to an occasion in March when, he said, "Payne" was boarding at Surratt's:

"One day I found a false moustache on the table in my room; I threw it into a little toilet box, and Payne searched for it and inquired for his moustache; I was sitting in the chair and did not say anything; I retained it ever since; it was found in my baggage. . . ."[11]

As it happened, the defense raised no questions regarding the early confusion as to whether the intruder had worn a moustache, so the prosecution's foresight to have a false one mentioned in the record had been unnecessary. The War Department's reason for injecting the false moustache in this contrived manner, rather than simply presenting the one found in the coat pocket as an exhibit, may be deduced from the nature of the other two items which were found in the pockets with it.

Louis Paine's hands were apparently quite small for a man of his size —so much so as to be a distinguishing characteristic. The riding gloves, to be used as evidence against him, would have to fit. If they did not, if they were noticeably too large, that fact might be used to argue that neither the gloves *nor* the coat were his.

The card reading "Mary J. Gardener 419" might have been even more risky to place in exhibit. For somewhere in the environs of Washington there was possibly a lady by that name. The prosecution, being completely in the dark as to Paine's personal history, due to his stubborn silence, could hardly risk publicizing the name. She might come forward herself, or the defense might find her and force her to appear, and she might be able to supply the prisoner on trial with a perfect alibi. Clearly, the claim of finding a false moustache by the pliable Weichmann involved much less risk.

did Lafayette Baker gamble?

From the foregoing it would seem as if Colonel Baker—quite apart from his treachery in going to such lengths to implicate Paine—was taking a fantastic chance by framing a man about whom he apparently knew very little. Though Paine refused to talk after the first few hours, he *might* have changed his mind and come up with an airtight alibi for his whereabouts at the time the crime was being committed at Seward's house, exposing Baker's perfidy in a public scandal. In his seamy wartime career, Baker had earned the reputation of a no-holds-barred scoundrel whose arsenal of crime-detection methods included forgery, blackmail, manufactured evidence, paid perjurers—every device of entrapment right down the list. But he was no fool. In fact he was a genius in his line. In this case he was probably not nearly so rash as he seemed to be.

Whoever it was who rang the Seward doorbell the night of April 14 and tried to stab Secretary Seward to death, it was not a solitary assassin acting on his own initiative. The stranger knew on which floor of the mansion and in which room to find his victim; yet he was not known to the Seward family or the servants. The attempted assassination almost *had* to involve someone else, who knew the layout of the Seward house. That is, the assailant was *sent* by someone—probably paid by someone—who could tell him the best time to arrive at the house and the floor and room where his victim could be found. He did not *search* the house for Mr. Seward; he went directly upstairs to the right bedroom.

Thus someone in official Washington, probably someone who had normal access to the Seward mansion on Lafayette Square, *knew* the real assassin. A later chapter will discuss the probable identity of this person. The man to whom suspicion points was a close acquaintance and collaborator with Baker at the time of Paine's arrest and throughout the Trial. It is more than likely that he was at General Augur's headquarters when the prisoner was brought in. It is *most* likely that he told Baker (if Baker didn't know it already) that Paine *resembled* the guilty man to a startling degree.

photographic evidence

Lafayette Baker's handbill was the first of a series of misrepresentations of Louis Paine, by which he was not only railroaded to the gallows but also portrayed to posterity in a character not remotely resembling his own. In addition, it was the leading end of a thread of treachery which we will be tracing through the whole course of the Conspiracy Trial.

Thus it is important that the writing and publication of this "wanted" notice on April 18—the day *after* Paine's arrest—be established to the reader's thorough satisfaction. To this end, we shall mention a circumstance which would ordinarily come up in a later chapter in the chronological sequence of events we are trying to follow.

Two coats were put in exhibit at the Trial by the War Department's prosecutors. One was a light-gray garment of flecked material with distinctive pocket flaps. The other was darker and somewhat larger—a single-breasted coat of the shade then called "Confederate gray." During a sharp exchange on May 19 between Colonel Doster and a witness—Major H. W. Smith,[19] one of Baker's detectives who had participated in Paine's arrest—it was established that the *first* coat, the lighter-gray one, was worn by Paine on the night he was arrested. The other was the one with blood stains on the sleeve which had been picked up near Fort Bunker Hill northeast of the city on Easter Sunday.

Fortunately, Paine was photographed wearing both coats: the one in which he was arrested, with no hat (see Plate 1-A); and the one found in the woods, with a hat which the intruder at Seward's was said to have lost in his scuffle with the witnesses at the scene (see Plate 1-B). When he knocked at Mrs. Surratt's door that night, the young man *had no hat.*

Now, comparing the text of Baker's handbill with the two photos, it is quite evident which outer costume is being described: The double-breasted design of the coat, pockets inside with lapels or flaps outside, lighter-color material, and no hat. Clearly Baker was describing Paine as he looked when the detectives brought him to General Augur's headquarters. If he had been describing the man who invaded Mr. Seward's home, he would have described the coat and hat the prisoner is wearing in Plate 1-B.

other parties to the frame-up

Apparently Baker was able to arrange to have documents placed in the War Department files which would, in the absence of the foregoing analysis, verify that the handbill had been published and distributed *prior* to Tuesday, April 18.

The National Archives contain three drafts of telegrams addressed to army officers in West Virginia and New York. Each reproduces the full text of the handbill as to "Seward's assailant." One is dated April 15, 1865, signed "by order of Captain Edward P. Hudson," and countersigned "Levi F. Burnett, Asst. A. Genl." The other two are dated April 15 and April 16 respectively and are signed by "Col. Fred. Townsend."

The dates alone show these telegram drafts to be faked documents; even Baker didn't claim to have written the handbill until the seventeenth. The name of Captain Hudson did not figure in the Trial, but Colonel E. D. Townsend was Assistant Adjutant General in the War Department; Colonel H. L. Burnett had the same title and was one of the three prosecutors at the Conspiracy Trial. First names are similar but incorrect, but the rank and title is accurate in each case. Since both officials customarily used the initials of their first two names when signing official documents, these messages would seem to be forgeries—or were written to *appear* to be forgeries. In any case, since Baker did not have personal access to the Judge Advocate's files, someone in that department helped him plant them there.

It appears that the text of the handbill which is reproduced in these telegrams was copied from Baker's *original* draft. For here, in the very middle of the description, we find additional details which do not appear in later versions: ". . . lips thin; upper lip protruded when he talked; chin pointed and prominent. . . ."

These are characteristics which might be noted by someone who saw Louis Paine in General Augur's headquarters; but they are features which would *not* be visible in a man who wore a moustache and goatee, or a *false moustache.* So Baker thought it discreet to omit them from his final draft.

5

mechanics of the trial

preparations

During the interim between the assassination on April 14 and the opening of the Conspiracy Trial on May 9, the staff of the Bureau of Military Justice under Judge Advocate General Holt earned its pay. A mountain of "evidence" relating to the crimes poured in from all quarters. Much of this, as previously noted, was worthless; but all of it had to be read and classified.

The variety and nature of these documents[1] were remarkable. The proportion of rumor and mere speculation, even in official communications from army and police investigators, was high. But there was a leavening of terse, business-like reports from officers who were involved in the pursuit and arrest of suspects and the search for evidence. Some of the depositions and transcripts of initial interrogation of prisoners and witnesses were informative in the extreme. Some were useful to the prosecutors in building their case. Others, ignored or suppressed by the Bureau of Military Justice, have played a vital part in our present study a century later.

From April 18 onward a class of "evidence" began to appear which revealed the invisible hand of Lafayette Baker. Depositions and letters by individuals who sometimes identified themselves as "detectives" but never mentioned Baker by name were received and noted by the three officials who were most active in the case-building task: Colonel John A. Foster, Assistant Judge Advocate; Colonel H. L. Burnett, Special Judge Advocate; and Colonel H. S. Olcott, with the title of Special Commissioner.

These depositions often made statements which were far different from those of other officers who had been involved in the same arrests. They sometimes disagreed with the depositions of other detectives who had interrogated the same prisoners—even disagreed with their own previous statements. But they had the effect of offering positive evidence of guilt and giving support to the theory that there really had been a "conspiracy." They were clearly welcomed by the Bureau's investigators in spite of their questionable character.

Foster, Burnett, and Olcott did most of the interrogation of the prime suspects, Mrs. Surratt and the seven men held on the monitors, who were to become the defendants at the Trial. In this task they were confronted with profound confusion. The stories of the suspects had a common denominator of sorts, in that some of them had been loosely associated with Booth in what appeared to have been a halfhearted notion to abduct the President and exchange him for thousands of Confederate prisoners.

Except for Mrs. Surratt, who denied everything, and Louis Paine, who would say nothing, the suspects were all communicative and gave consistent accounts of themselves whenever they were interrogated. But what they revealed didn't add up to any kind of co-ordinated plot. The only one who admitted having had an inkling of Booth's intention to kill the President was the frightened, scarcely understandable George Atzerodt, the carriage-painter from Port Tobacco.

In evaluating *all* the information obtained from these suspects, the investigators used a rule of thumb: In any instance where the statements of the suspects failed to agree with their gradually crystallizing theory of the "conspiracy," the suspects were lying. Thus they felt free to quote these prisoners, or those who testified *about* them, in any way which supported the War Department's contentions.

For example, Honora Fitzpatrick, a plain young lady who boarded at Mrs. Surratt's, was interrogated by Colonel Foster on April 28. She was asked to confirm the statement of a Negro maid in the household to the effect that three men had come to see Mrs. Surratt late one night around the time of the assassination; that they had said something about John Surratt's having been with Booth at the theater; that Miss Fitzpatrick had been present and had leaned over the supposedly sleeping maid to see if she were really asleep.

Honora denied any knowledge of the affair, and Foster was unable to trick her into changing her story. Since the girl was a friend of the widow's, Foster had some reason to be skeptical. But the point is that he described the night visit in his next summary as if its authenticity had been established—without reference to the fact that a named witness, who was not believed to have been a party to the alleged conspiracy, denied any knowledge of the occurrence.

The case of Louis Paine was the real puzzler. There was every indication that the young man was a total stranger in Washington, known to no one. The residents of the Surratt boardinghouse who were available prior to April 30 were unanimous in doubts that they knew him.

However there was a curious similarity in their stories, although they were interrogated separately without opportunity to agree among themselves as to what they would say about Paine. With one exception, he reminded each of them to some degree of a man named "Wood" who had called at the house several times to see John Surratt. But they did not agree that he *was* "Wood." Anna Surratt and Nora Fitzpatrick were sure he was *not*. Mrs. Surratt denied both that he looked like "Wood" and that she knew him at all.

In spite of this general uncertainty, the investigators recorded positively that Paine and "Wood" were the same person. On April 30 Louis Weichmann was arrested on his return from Baker's "wild goose chase" to Canada. He obligingly stated that Paine had stayed at the Surratt house for a couple of days "around the middle of March" and had said he was a Baptist preacher. Weichmann was happy to say he recognized him as "Wood," who had been at the house "about the last of February."

Even before Weichmann's return, though, the investigators had Paine pegged as "Wood" in disguise. Now they were able to refer to the latter as a "bogus preacher."

George Atzerodt made a "confession" to Colonel H. H. Wells which was duly recorded on April 25.[2] This officer had been put in charge of the prime suspects, and he contributed some reports of statements they made to him which are useful for comparison with other interrogations. According to this (and all his other statements), Atzerodt had learned of the murder plan only three or four hours before it was executed.

He was in a restaurant—so his statement goes—in the early evening of April 14, when Booth sent a message that he and "James Wood" wanted to see him at the Herndon House, where the latter was staying. When Atzerodt arrived there around 6:30 P.M., the actor said that he was going to murder the President and "Wood" had agreed to kill Seward. Booth wanted Atzerodt to join them. The little man said he refused to kill anyone; then they said they only wanted his help as guide on the escape route. So he agreed to that, in order to get out of the place, and then spent the whole evening wandering around the city getting drunk.

Foster's summary of the "confession," as he called it, recited the gist of it faithfully enough. But wherever the name "Wood" was mentioned he substituted the name "Payne," of whom Atzerodt had never heard.[3] The effectiveness of this deliberate transfer of identity from one man to another is seen in the fact that just before his execution the little German told a similar version to Mr. Butler, a Lutheran minister of Washington who was allowed to act as his spiritual counselor—but by that time Atzerodt too referred to "Wood" as "Payne."

In the same copy of Foster's summary as the one in which the switch of names was made, the investigator revealed his private doubt that Paine and "Wood" and Seward's assailant were all the same man. The italics in the following quotation from Foster are added here:

"At about 10 minutes past 10, Payne, *or a person precisely answering his description,* rode up to the house of Mr. Seward, fastened his horse at the post in front, dismounted, rang the doorbell. . . . "

Later on we shall be referring back to Foster's statement that the intruder rode up and tethered his own horse in front of the house. It contradicts a facet of the legend bearing on the case of David Herold.

The thorough cynicism of the War Department's case against Louis Paine is shown even more formidably by still other documents in the National Archives. Almost immediately after his arrest, the War Department had written communications from the provost marshal in Baltimore identifying three competent witnesses in that city who knew Paine as "Paine"—and could testify that he had been living at the boardinghouse there (and had not been away) during the entire period when "Wood" had been visiting the Surratt house.[4] Thus the investigators had substantial evidence nearly from the beginning that Louis Paine was *not* "James Wood." Yet they continued to identify these two as the same person throughout the Trial.

The question of whether Paine was *disguised* on the night of his arrest also came up during these pre-Trial investigations. *Everyone* concerned with the raid on Surratt's—arresting officers as well as prisoners—denied that the young man's appearance had suggested a disguise of any kind, although he was *said* to have entered carrying a pickax. But later the prosecution would charge and "establish" that he had returned to Mrs. Surratt's house three days after the assault on Seward *"disguised as a laborer."*

This trick of substituting a defendant's name for that of another person in an incriminating situation was used effectively by the prosecution against other defendants. A classic example of it occurred on May 16 during Holt's interrogation of Sergeant Silas Cobb, who had been guarding the Navy Yard Bridge over which Booth escaped on the night of the assassination.[5]

The soldier had testified that, having no reason to forbid him that he knew of, he had allowed Booth to cross into Maryland between 10:30 and 11:00 P.M. A second rider came up a few minutes later at a leisurely pace, identified himself as "Smith," said he was returning home after a night on the town, and was permitted to cross. A third horseman arrived a while later, but the guard didn't think he had sufficient reason for crossing so turned him back. This last man was a stableman named Fletcher, who according to his own testimony thought he had seen David Herold on the dark, crowded street riding a rented horse which was overdue. He said he went to the stable, saddled and mounted another horse, and gave chase. His assumption that the man he had seen briefly and taken for Herold, a resident of Washington, would be heading for the bridge to Maryland at that time of night apparently derived from psychic perception. The prosecutors insisted the second rider was Herold, using the assumed name of "Smith."

Holt was trying to interest Sergeant Cobb in stating that he recognized Herold as the second rider. But the Sergeant had studied all the prisoners carefully and stated positively that the man named "Smith" was not among them. So Holt played his ace, the identity substitution trick. In the following portion of the dialogue, all but the two bracketed notations are verbatim:*

Q. How would he [the second man] compare in size with the last man among the prisoners (Harold)?

A. He is very nearly the size, but I should not think he was the man; he had a lighter complexion than that man.

Q. Did you allow him to pass after that explanation?

A. Yes.

Q. What became of the other man [the third rider, Fletcher]?

A. The other man I turned back; he did not seem to have sufficient business to warrant me in passing him.

Q. Did he seem to be a companion of the *prisoner* who had gone before?

A. I do not know.

The sergeant had just stated that the man "who had gone before" was *not* Herold, But, by his final question on the subject, Holt succeeded in offsetting the denial and leaving a *lasting* impression that Herold had followed Booth out of town after the assassination. The only other "evidence" the prosecution had that Herold was in Washington that night was Fletcher's questionable recognition of the young man riding by at a distance after dark while he himself stood under a flickering gas streetlight.

Holt's ruse couldn't be said to have hanged David Herold, since the military court would have found him guilty whether he had been in Washington that night or not. But it added a detail to the story of the Booth "conspiracy" (Herold's presence in Washington the night of the assassination) and illustrates the War Department's technique of legend-making.

Most of the documents in the Archives which refer to Louis Paine during the first few days after his arrest spell his name "Lewis Paine." The reason for this is that at Mrs. Surratt's he handed Detective Richard Morgan his signed Oath of Allegiance, on which his name was spelled that way by the officer who had issued it.[6] Southerners in Union territory were required to carry such a paper, on which they swore allegiance to the federal government,

*Peterson transcript, pp. 51-52.

Very shortly, however, a number of communications were received from persons—some of them law officers—who were sure the young man was a member of a family of Paynes from Union County, Kentucky. This family had six sons who were known as desperados with Confederate sympathies. One of them, a General George B. Payne, was then in prison in New York awaiting trial. The War Department lapped up this "identification" and was very happy with it until about the middle of May, when General Dix in New York obtained proof from George Payne's wife that there was no connection between Louis and the Kentucky Paynes. He sent Mrs. Payne herself to Washington to convince Special Judge Advocate Burnett. But the rumor hung on, and the prisoner's name was spelled "Payne" almost universally in the proceedings, records, and news reports of the Trial.

A curious and possibly significant sequel to this confusion of identities appeared in Lafayette Baker's memoirs, published in 1867. By that time the Trial was history, and in the course of it Louis Paine had been "identified" as Lewis Powell, a Confederate soldier from Florida who had been captured at Gettysburg and had escaped to serve in General Mosby's Partisan Rangers in northern Virginia for a year before becoming involved with John Wilkes Booth.

Baker undoubtedly knew about this final "identification" as well as anyone in the country, but his references to the case of "Payne" ignored it. He stated, "He was one of three Kentucky brothers, all outlaws, and had himself, it is believed, accompanied one of his brothers, who is known to have been at St. Albans on the day of the bank delivery."

The fact that the detective stuck to the discredited story that the prisoner was one of the Kentucky Paynes, in spite of the revelations at the Trial, turned out to be quite significant. It indicated he *knew* the "Powell" label was incorrect! A little farther on we shall consider the evidence that Baker had considerable opportunity to question Louis Paine before he stopped talking. Apparently he said something to convince Baker that he had been in Kentucky at a time when the real Lewis Powell was serving in the Confederate army—a clue known only to Baker, which caused him to reject the later "identification" and stick to his original claim that the prisoner was one of the Kentucky Paynes.

As we encounter more and more evidence that Louis Paine and his fellow defendants were deliberately framed by officials of the War Department, the reader should be reminded that this was not merely a hysterical national situation in which, because of pressure to find *someone* to punish for the murder of the President, several suspicious-seeming individuals were made the scapegoats by biased or overzealous prosecutors at a court martial. Through the latter half of the war, military tribunals had been used nationwide to stamp out opposition to the Union cause. In the occupied areas of the South, in the uncertain border states, in many parts of the North where opposition to the Administration's prosecution of the war took tangible form—especially within the Union Army—military commissions were employed to pass swift, harsh judgments upon dissident elements, judgments from which there was no appeal.

The procedures of these courts had only a vague connection with the established legal processes of the land. Defendants were presumed guilty and, as Colonel Doster remarked in his reminiscences, ". . . were called on to *prove their innocence.*" According to the policies practiced by the War Department under Edwin McMasters Stanton, the accused had no rights. In Washington alone hundreds of persons were arrested and held without charges for periods of many months; they were denied legal counsel; their friends and relatives could learn nothing about them; the writ of habeas corpus was, of course, annulled for the duration of the war.

When the normal machinery of justice gives way to military power in despotic hands, the very methods of achieving justice are naturally corrupted. The engineers and prosecutors of the Conspiracy Trial were all men who had been practicing "law" of this character through much of the war. To them the conviction of a defendant whom *they* believed to be guilty was their obligation. The precise methods employed were incidental to obligatory conviction. That such a situation bred a tolerance for manufactured evidence, suppressed evidence, perjured testimony, and legal sleight-of-hand is logical. And we need not be surprised or shocked when these and many other aspects of corrupted justice are uncovered in our study of the Conspiracy Trial.

6

mechanics of the trial

the scene in court

Now our investigation turns to the actual proceedings of the Conspiracy Trial, which was ordered by Stanton and authorized by President Johnson on May 1, convened on the eighth, and began public sessions on the twelfth.

The weather was very hot during May and June of 1865. The poorly ventilated chambers of the old Washington arsenal, then used as a penitentiary, were grossly inadequate to accommodate the scores of participants—judges, attorneys, witnesses, and prisoners, all of whom *had* to be there—let alone the elbowing crowds of curious citizens who squeezed into every unoccupied inch of the hall. In those days, when it was improper for a gentleman to remove his coat in mixed company, the affair must have been as much of an ordeal for the purveyors of "justice" as it was for the accused, at least in the physical sense.

Nine army officers* had been appointed by Secretary of War Stanton to serve on the commission, and his success in assembling that many notably undistinguished soldiers in such a short time was something of an accomplishment. All but one or two were nearly as unknown then as they are today. There was not a noteworthy war record in the whole group. In fact the two whose names might be recognized by the average reader—Major General David Hunter, presiding officer, and Major General Lew Wallace (later author of *Ben Hur*)—had attained rank by political connections, and their names had been associated with military defeats throughout the four-year contest. All appeared to be qualified

*Major General David Hunter, president. Members: Major Generals Lewis Wallace and August V. Kautz; Brigadier Generals Albion P. Howe, Robert S. Foster, James A. Ekin, and Thomas M. Harris; Colonels Charles H. Tomkins and D. R. Clendenin.

largely by their prejudices, total ignorance of the law, and subservience to the will of the prosecutors. It was common talk in Washington that the military commission was assembled for the purpose of convicting the accused persons—not to weigh the merits of their cases.

The prosecution was headed by the director of the Bureau of Military Justice, Judge Advocate General Joseph Holt. His assistants were Colonel Henry L. Burnett and another special judge advocate, John A. Bingham.

On May 9, only a couple of days before the proceedings began, the prisoners were brought into court and asked if they wanted counsel. All of them did, and they were given one day in which to obtain it. Since they were held incommunicado in irons, and all were ordinary citizens with few resources or connections, they could hardly be expected to attract the interest of outstanding legal talent. Mrs. Surratt was nevertheless able to engage the services of Reverdy Johnson, a distinguished Maryland jurist of national reputation. The rest of defense counsel were young men of brief experience who were no match for Messrs. Holt, Burnett, and Bingham. Frederick Aiken and John Clampitt assisted Johnson in the defense of Mary Surratt; Dr. Samuel Mudd and David Herold were represented by Frederick Stone, Samuel Arnold and Edward Spangler by Thomas Ewing, Michael O'Laughlin by Walter Cox, and Paine and Atzerodt by Colonel William E. Doster.

If other conditions had been more favorable, Louis Paine would seem to have been well represented. Colonel Doster was an attorney of better-than-average caliber, whose wartime experience had given him personal acquaintance with the workings of military justice. He had been provost marshal of the city of Washington in the early years of the conflict and then been transferred to active duty as a field officer. He had no illusions as to the predicament of defendants before a court martial, having participated in too many of them not to know that a defense as such had become a mere formality.

In his reminiscences of the Trial, written some forty years later,[1] he recalled the circumstances of that historic event in language which is notable for its objectivity, yet which still revealed some of his bafflement at what must have been the most memorable defeat in his legal career:

> On May 12, 1865, being at that time engaged in the trial of causes before military courts at Washington, I was retained for the defense of Atzerodt, by his brother, a detective on the force of Marshal McPhail of Baltimore. The prisoner Payne being without counsel, the assistant Judge Advocate General Burnett, requested me to take his case, also, as he had about as much of a chance to get off as the other, that is—none at all.
>
> This I, at first, refused to do, on the ground that I had my hands more than full with one, considering the excited state of public feeling, and that, in fact, this was a contest in which a few lawyers were on one side, and the whole United States on the other—a case in which, of course, the verdict was known beforehand. I finally allowed my name to go down for Payne temporarily,

but with the understanding that as soon as he could secure counsel for himself, I might and would withdraw. He never secured other counsel and I had to do the best I could for both clients.

The circumstances under which, and the place where, the trial began, were not of a character to cheer counsel in their task. The charge in general was assassination—a crime against which modern civilization revolts and a charge unknown to our law books—upon a President and Secretary of State, the first of whom by the downfall of the rebellion stood at the very pinnacle of public idolatry—the last of whom, by the same cause, and by a recent accidental fall from a carriage, enlisted the respectful sympathy of the public heart.

The funeral of the President with its million illuminations, its crowd of mourners, its solemn catafalque and processions had just passed. The armies of the Republic were about to be assembled for a triumphal march through the Capitol. These things and the feelings they inspired bore hard against the accused, in the minds of the loyal North, and could not help dispiriting counsel as much as they encouraged the ardor of the judge advocate, and tended to inflame the minds of the soldiers who composed the court.

. . . More than all, it was the period proper for punishment of the rebellion, and somebody must be hanged for example's sake.

In this case most of the evidence taken [prior to the Trial] at the Bureau of Military Justice had been daily published as it was taken. The court had doubtless read it. The members could not help feeling that the country expected them, on the evidence already known, to find the prisoners guilty. Their business was chiefly to discover the degrees of guilt and impose the sentences in regular form.

They knew that one of the party [Booth] had been shot without any trial, and the country applauded. Was it likely they apprehended trouble for or during the execution of the rest, with all the paraphernalia of a military trial and after six weeks' hearing? The brutal nature of a military court appears in this. After the argument in behalf of Payne was submitted, the court adjourned for lunch. During lunch one of the members of the commission remarked,

"Well, Payne seems to want to be hung, so I guess we might as well hang him."

In that quotation Doster referred to the most mystifying aspect of his case, which in his summation he called "the riddle of Lewis Payne." To the immense satisfaction and convenience of the prosecutors and the lifelong bewilderment of his attorney, this strange young man *wanted to die!*

He apparently had not told Doster so personally, though different ones of his guards had quoted him to that effect. And his failure to say anything that might be used in his defense surely argued in that direction.

What troubled the attorney's legal mind was that this attitude was at odds with the prosecutors' portrayal of the prisoner. He had been depicted as a hired, professional killer, a physical brute with the mental capacities of a moron, so insensitive that he was no more able to feel remorse at the bloody deed he had done than a wild animal might have felt.

In such a type, the overriding impulse would be for survival. Yet

Paine seemed completely resigned to his fate, in spite of the fact that legally speaking the assault of which he was accused was not a capital crime. As Doster summed it up: ". . . the prisoner was never connected directly with a conspiracy to kill Mr. Lincoln and legally could be found guilty only of an assault and battery on Mr. Seward, with intent to kill—a penitentiary offense."

This being the case, why would a nerveless, unrepentent desperado be resigned to dying?

There was nothing about Paine which suggested a brutish man to Colonel Doster. He was the prototype of stoical endurance. Unlike the other prisoners, he never spoke of the injustice of it all, never complained about anything, never asked for anything. He expressed no political opinions—in fact, never spoke at all to most of those who were around him and, except in one or two instances, never originated any conversation with his attorney. He was accused of having slashed and pistol-whipped five persons at the Seward house; yet in his one long interview with Doster, his only direct reference to these brutalities was to inquire anxiously after the health of Frederick Seward, who was still convalescing in the hospital.

Since his client would deny nothing yet plainly was not the type to have committed the crimes of which he was accused, the Colonel was in a quandary and, at a very early stage, grasped at a straw—a plea of temporary insanity.

"Under the plea of not guilty, I had no recourse except to show that he was not the man Seward's Negro took him to be, and I could not show that. Even under the plea of insanity I could not let the court talk to the prisoner, *and find out for itself what a phenomenon he was.*" (Italics added.)

On one hand Doster was sure Louis Paine was not insane; on the other he saw no alternative explanation for the contradictions in his personality. His mystification as he thought back to those perplexing days forty years earlier is summed up in this extraordinary statement: "I have never entertained a doubt myself, that the man was not what is termed *compos mentis,* i.e., a person of average understanding but in that respect a dwarf. Either this *or he played his part very well to the end.*"

To continue with Colonel Doster's general remarks about the Trial:

> There were minor circumstances against the defense. The prosecution had a month, assisted by the whole war power of the Government, its railroads, telegraphs, detectives, and military bureau, to get its evidence into shape. The prisoners did not receive their charges until the day the trial opened and then they could only communicate sitting in chains, with a soldier on each side, a great crowd surrounding them, and whisper through the bars of the dock to their counsel.
>
> Had counsel been closeted with the prisoners for weeks, with the charges

in their hands and the war power of the Government at their disposal, the odds might have been more even.

Counsel were not independent. In all military courts they are only tolerated. Here they were surrounded by bayonets and seated in a penitentiary. Every [news]paper they read abused them. The judges could not be challenged. They were not peers but high military officers. The names of witnesses were not given the prisoners. Tendencies, not facts, were admitted. The court, not knowing anything about the rules of evidence, ruled out practically everything the judge advocate objected to and admitted everything the counsel objected to.

Eisenschiml reduced this handicap of the defense due to the court's bias to a convincing statistic. He found that the prosecution made fifty-four objections, only *three* of which were overruled. The defense attorneys, all together, made twelve objections, *all* of which were overruled.[2]

The witnesses were many of them detectives in the government pay. The judges were dependent on the Executive [the president being commander-in-chief of the armed forces]. The punishment was not fixed, but discretionary. Crimes were not defined by any known rules of law but were vaguely called offenses against the "common law of war" [a term coined by Holt for the occasion, which had no legal basis or meaning whatever].

. . . Under these distressing circumstances there was nothing to do except what lawyers have often tried before, but which no one to my knowledge has done successfully during the war—plead the jurisdiction—that is to say, in language not technical, to demonstrate to the court that the prisoners, being citizens, had a right to be tried in a civil court, before a jury of citizens, which in this case would have been the Supreme Court of the District of Columbia. Judge Carter of Ohio, a personal friend of Lincoln's, was the president judge.

. . . To prove to a military court that they have no right to try citizens should be no great task in a republic. Every school boy who has read the Constitution knows that it cannot lawfully be done in time of peace. Was this a time of peace? Certainly the war was over; the armies had surrendered in May, 1865. The whole North had rejoiced over the peace. And the doors of the civil courts were open, ready to take charge of the prisoners.

There was no danger to anyone by sending them before Carter; nothing to be gained by a military court except a certainty of death, and shooting them as Booth was shot would have accomplished that with far less expense.

Reverdy Johnson, by far the most experienced member of defense counsel, wrote an exhaustive and eloquent plea to the court's jurisdiction in behalf of all the defense attorneys. This was read in court by his younger colleague, Frederick Aiken—not so much in expectation that the court would see its logic and disqualify itself as in the hope that it would influence the President and the public to take a hand in the interest of justice. Doster records the fate of this vain hope:

. . . From what members of the court have since told me, it had no effect on them whatever. They had Stanton's orders, and that was enough for them who were in the service of the United States.

They retired, deliberated in secret, returned, and overruled the plea, that

> is, they decided they had a right to try them, and Judge Carter had none. . . . This was practically the end of my case, as far as any show of legal defense was concerned. The rest was firing pistol shots against siege guns—two men in irons against a dozen major-generals, with a swarm of detectives within the penitentiary and a division of infantry outside.

At the very beginning of the actual proceedings, Colonel Doster relates, the prosecution contrived to rid itself of the astute defense attorney Reverdy Johnson. The War Department's advocates, speaking through General Harris, a pliable member of the commission who was a West Virginia physician and not a lawyer, delivered a gross insult to Johnson's honor by claiming his oath could not be accepted because of some statements he had made a year earlier as to whether the citizens of Maryland would be obliged to respect and be bound by a particular wartime oath they were required to take.

In a furious verbal exchange, Johnson succeeded in defending himself and was accepted by the court. But his resentment was so deep that he soon withdrew from an active part in the Trial. Doster's reaction to this skirmish, though he saw the cynicism of the calculated insult, was more indignation at Mr. Johnson's virtual abandonment of his client, which he felt left grounds for the conclusion that he had withdrawn because he believed Mrs. Surratt guilty—which damaged the widow's chances.

The condensed nature of this attorney's account of the Trial touched only lightly on an aspect of the prosecution which, to many students, is the most infamous feature of the Conspiracy Trial and also the most evident:

". . . The license with which the Government dragged into this trial a thousand details of yellow-fever plots, steamboat burnings, and other things that were utterly foreign to the issue and which had no other effect than to inflame the public against the prisoners, showed a barbarous disregard or rather contempt for the settled barriers of legal inquiry."

These plots and burnings and "*other things*" Doster spoke of involved the prosecution's effort to rekindle all the passions of wartime—against the Confederacy and its leaders, as much as toward the prisoners—by using the witness stand to review all the "atrocities" perpetrated by the South during the hostilities. Plots to burn northern cities, start epidemics, instigate riots, etc. were supplemented by accounts of brutal treatment of Union prisoners at Libby and Belle Isle in Richmond and at Andersonville in Georgia. Under other auspices, such matters were certainly appropriate for inquiry, as is the case after any war. But the prosecution, as Doster pointed out, made no pretense that this inflammatory testimony had any legal bearing on the guilt or innocence of the eight defendants whose lives were at stake.

Another comparable feature of the prosecution, at which Doster only hints, was the unrestrained use of obviously perjured witnesses and of forged and otherwise manufactured documents alleged to have been found on trains, floating in harbors, etc. There were also clumsily planted clues in abundance and articles of clothing bearing Booth's initials said to have been found in the possession of the accused persons. Inversely, there were a number of incidents of critical evidence being either withheld or destroyed.

Doster related a sordid little incident which illustrates the part played by the Baker detectives, four of whom hovered near the prisoners around the clock. It occurred on June 3 while the attorney was trying to lay the foundation for his white hope for Paine, an insanity plea.

"One of the detectives in charge of Payne told me I should call him, –he would swear he [Paine] was crazy. I did so, and he swore Payne said [after he had been "identified" by the Seward house witnesses], 'they are tracking him pretty close.' I dispensed with further detective testimony."[3]

A final consideration, directly related to the prosecution's use of phony evidence of the most transparent character, is the era in which the Conspiracy Trial took place.

America in 1865 was still about ninety per cent agrarian. The great bulk of the population lived on farms, where they had personal contact only with their nearest neighbors during most of a year. They had yet to acquire the worldliness that comes from mingling with other people at close quarters. Illiteracy was so widespread that in both the Union and Confederate armies company commanders commonly signed the muster rolls for their whole units, because such a large percentage of the men couldn't read or write.

This was the era in which P. T. Barnum made several fortunes from the fantastic gullibility of his countrymen. It was the heyday of the pitchman, the medicine show, and the glib promoter of almost anything. The war had brought hundreds of thousands into closer contact, but only recently.

In the 1860's it was quite possible for a few clever lawyers and unscrupulous detectives to stage a treason trial in the nation's Capitol with all the flimflam of a medicine show.

7

mechanics of the trial

records of the proceedings

The fact that we are able to conduct a systematic investigation of the Conspiracy Trial a century later is due largely to a tremendously important development of the nineteenth century. This was the invention and practice of shorthand transcription.

In 1865 the term "phonography" was used rather than "shorthand." At that time its leading practitioner was Mr. Benn Pitman, a Scotchman who had first settled in Philadelphia, then moved to Cincinnati some time before the Civil War and founded a school for the teaching of the skill, both by direct instruction and by mail. Following a short term in the Union Army when hostilities began, Pitman entered the employment of the government as a court reporter. By the time of the Conspiracy Trial his work was so well known and highly regarded that he was called in to serve as official recorder of the proceedings and supervisor of a staff of five assistants.

Thus we have access to a virtually verbatim record of the whole affair. And the efficiency of the recorders was such that we can study the exact words of the witnesses and attorneys, rather than a possibly distorted report of what some observer *thought* they said.

By today's standards the process was laborious. The reporters took down the dialogue in stenographic symbols, then worked late into the night translating them into longhand script. In order to have additional legible copies without delay, the resourceful Mr. Pitman enlisted the help of two soldiers who had been typographers in civilian life. These men set type from the longhand manuscript (a character at a time, since this was two decades before the linotype machine), and copies were then run off on a flatbed press. Each day copies of the previous day's proceedings were available for the attorneys. Since a number of northern newspapers reprinted the proceedings day by day—usually no more than two or three days behind the actual progress of the Trial—it appears to have been the policy to release letterpress copies to the larger daily papers.

The question of whether these shorthand records were accurate is of importance to our study. In determining this, the only seemingly reliable method is to compare the text word by word in the various reproductions of the proceedings—the original longhand transcript, compilations in book form (of which there are three), and the original issues of the newspapers in which the proceedings were reprinted.

This writer's conclusion after having made the comparison was that these early court reporters were very good at their work. Wherever you find a passage which was not edited or interpreted by the publishers, all versions are the same, practically word for word. Punctuation varies often, according to the editors' tastes, and misspellings are corrected in some versions more carefully than in others; paragraphing is not always identical. But by and large the competence of the reporters is impressive and apparently quite reliable.

Of the three principal compilations of the proceedings, all published in 1865, two were used as the basis for this study. But all three deserve mention:

Benn Perley Poore

The Conspiracy Trial by Benjamin P. Poore, a Washington journalist of the day, was published by J. E. Tilton and Company of Boston. It is an exhaustive and seemingly competent work which includes the verbatim testimony of the witnesses, but not the arguments of the attorneys or the findings of the court. Poore's version is in three volumes, now quite rare; due to its bulk and lack of organization, it is not too convenient as a reference work.

Peterson

This compilation, with the imposing title *The Trial of the Assassins and Conspirators at Washington City, D. C., May and June, 1865, for the Murder of President Abraham Lincoln,* was published by T. B. Peterson and Brothers of Philadelphia.

The title page describes the compilation as "complete and unabridged in this volume, being prepared on the spot by the Special Correspondents and Reporters of the Philadelphia *Daily Inquirer,* expressly for this edition."

To all appearances, the body text was reproduced from the type set by Pitman's two soldier assistants—though this would be rather difficult to establish beyond question. If any copies of the original press proofs still exist, this writer has not been able to find them. That this was the case is suggested by the occurrence of some obvious typographical errors which would have been corrected by a typesetter making up a new form from manuscript—but which would be allowed to remain by a publisher who didn't have access to the same type font or was in too much of a hurry to get his book to market to wait until that font could be obtained.

These noticeable errors are mostly in the spelling of names, which in Peterson are generally phonetic—as a stenographer would put them down because he couldn't interrupt to ask for the correct spelling. While no witness at the Trial could possibly be confused with another because of this fault, it has prejudiced many historians against the Peterson compilation and has caused some to overlook its great virtue as a source of historical information:

All versions of the proceedings have the same source—the transcripts made in court by Pitman and his assistants. But unlike all the others, the Peterson version was clearly not edited in any way, even to correct obvious errors. Thus it is not altered or colored by the views or interests of an editor. Its flaws are innocent and unconcealed. The reporters' attitudes to the Trial and its principals are evident in the narrative introduction and conclusion—which are set in a different and larger typeface at the beginning and end *and are meticulously proofread*—indicating that these portions were composed for the edition, while the body text was printed from the original forms or electrotypes of them.

In short, if we can overcome the prejudice created by the misspelling of some names, Peterson is the best place to look for the verbatim proceedings of the Trial.

Benn Pitman

Shortly after the end of the Trial, Benn Pitman applied to the Bureau of Military Justice for permission to publish a compilation of the proceedings for his own profit. Judge Advocate General Holt authorized him to do so, with the provision that the work should be done under the supervision of Assistant Judge Advocate H. L. Burnett. Burnett's function was to assume responsibility for the "strict accuracy" of the record. Pitman was glad to proceed on these terms, since it enabled him to describe his book as the "official" record of the Trial—a potent advantage in the marketplace.

The Assassination of President Lincoln and the Trial of the Conspirators, by Benn Pitman, was published by Moore, Wilstach and Baldwin of Cincinnati in the fall of 1865. For a hundred years it has been accepted and respected as the most reliable record of the proceedings—the "official" one.

Pitman's compilation differs from the others in many respects, but most noticeably in its treatment of the daily interrogation of the witnesses. While the others give the dialogue between attorneys and witnesses in question-and-answer form, Pitman *rewrote* the testimony in narrative style—with the stated purpose of making it easier to read and eliminating repetition. He reproduced verbatim passages only when in *his* opinion the statements made were open to interpretation.

Apparently Mr. Pitman did not think there were any passages of uncertain interpretation in any of the testimony bearing on the case of Louis Paine. Practically all of it is set down in predigested form in the narrative style of the compiler. Thus virtually every word of testimony regarding Paine in Pitman's version was strained through the understanding and viewpoint, not to say the prejudices, of at least one editor.

So now we come to an aspect of the "official" compilation by Pitman which will not please some of the historians who have respected and relied upon this version of the proceedings. To anyone who objects, we can only suggest that he make the comparison among the various versions and see for himself.

In Pitman every statement by a witness which could be interpreted in favor of the accused, Louis Paine, is either altered to make it incriminating or deleted. Whole passages which clearly raise a question as to the guilt of this prisoner are missing. New and most incriminating passages are *added* in Pitman. In some cases the entire sense of a statement is reversed in the rewriting. And alterations to the same end—to support the contentions of the War Department—have also been made in testimony relating to most of the other defendants.

There is absolutely no possibility that the different effect created by the alterations was accidental. There are far too many instances, and the consistency of purpose in the changes is too evident. By the law of averages *accident* would have to work to the advantage of the accused once in a while. But here it never does.

Someone performed major surgery on the "official" compilation of the proceedings, someone with an interest in seeing that no records within control of the War Department would ever support the accusation that it had deliberately hanged the innocent.

This writer is personally convinced that the someone was *not* Benn Pitman. His personal and professional reputation, as far as can be learned, was without a blemish. Moreover he was a technician with no ax to grind. There is evidence that Pitman himself was far from pleased with the results of his work with the Trial records. He was quoted as stating, some years after the Trial, that the mass of testimony transcribed by him and his assistants was "a great heap of rubbish."[1] He didn't amplify this curious remark, and it isn't certain whether he referred to the original material or the manuscript for his compilation after the War Department's Colonel Burnett had finished "supervising" its production in the interests of "strict accuracy." The nature of the finished manuscript suggests that the conscientious phonographer referred to the latter.

the archives transcript

From the very beginning of his assignment as official reporter, Pitman worked under the direction of Colonel Burnett. The special or assistant judge advocate had control of the records from the first day of the Trial to the last. His exercise of control is almost as evident in the transcripts of the proceedings which were placed in the War Department's files as it is in Pitman's volume.

Benn Pitman's own account of the recording procedure made it clear that *only one* original longhand transcript of the shorthand notes was made. Yet this body of documents in the National Archives—the testimony of witnesses at the Trial, written in longhand on legal cap—contains *two* copies of large portions of the testimony. Since these appear to agree with each other in most respects, this circumstance only shows that considerable work was done recopying the longhand draft—which would seem to be an entirely unnecessary undertaking, in view of the fact that typeset press copies had been turned over to Burnett by Pitman's crew and that these represented as accurate and legible a permanent record as one could wish.

The reason for the recopying is indicated by discovery of certain pages upon which an editor had been at work, crossing out whole paragraphs which were undesirable from the War Department's point of view.

Parts of the testimony in these official longhand transcripts agree with Peterson almost word for word. An exact comparison with the Pitman compilation is difficult to make, due to his practice of rewriting the dialogue at the witness stand in narrative form. But large portions are revised to agree with Pitman as to meaning.

The fact that *two* copies of much of the material are on file, plus the clear evidence of editing in the crossed-out paragraphs, raises a question as to why such signs that the record was tampered with were allowed to remain in the War Department's files. There is no way of telling when the recopying was done, but there is every indication that the job was stopped before it was finished—before the single, corrected draft could be completed and filed away.

An analysis of these records in comparison with the Peterson and Pitman compilations might interest a few persons with a taste for research in minute detail. But it would make rather dry reading for most others. So the situation can be summarized in general terms as follows:

Most of the alterations in the original longhand transcript appear to have been made currently—that is, during the Trial. (The following section will touch on this angle.) The changes are not so comprehensive as those in the Pitman compilation and deal mostly with certain subjects which Burnett apparently considered sensitive at an early stage of the proceedings.

For example, there were some very peculiar circumstances in the affair at the Seward house, and there were some gross irregularities in the identification of Louis Paine. There is evidence of *much* editing in such places. The testimony of Margaret Branson at whose home Paine boarded in Baltimore, received a complete face-lifting in Pitman. The offensiveness of this testimony to the War Department had not been realized when the draft of the official longhand record was made. In both words and sense, it conforms closely to Peterson. But on page 3091 of this official record, we find a considerable portion of the text crossed out *just at the point where Miss Branson testified that Paine was arrested by the Baltimore provost marshal after an altercation with their maid, that he signed an Oath of Allegiance, and was sent north.*

Bingham had made a great effort to prevent Miss Branson from testifying on this subject in court. But for once Doster had insisted, and her reference to Paine's Oath went into the record. It appears in full in the Peterson transcript. But in Pitman's compilation *this reference and the important particulars which followed are deleted!*

The War Department had had Paine's signed and dated Oath of Allegiance ever since his arrest. They knew the document could be a potent factor in his defense. Burnett knew that if Miss Branson mentioned it, Doster might realize its importance and insist that it be produced. But Colonel Doster, absorbed with his insanity plea, didn't catch on, didn't ask to see the document. So the prosecution succeeded in withholding the vital evidence—and Colonel Burnett saw to it that Miss Branson's revelations regarding Paine's Oath were omitted from Pitman's "official" compilation of the proceedings.

the newspaper account

The *Daily National Intelligencer* in Washington was one of the newspapers which published the court proceedings from day to day during the Trial, running two or three days behind the actual sessions. The testimony printed was said to be verbatim. In general this version was in line with Peterson, either word for word or as to the sense of the statements.

Here too, in places, we find Burnett's blue pencil had been busy. But at this point there were many fewer instances in which he felt alterations were necessary in the interests of "strict accuracy." The situation at the Seward house was of particular concern to him. Changes in the testimony of William Bell, the houseboy who had opened the front door to the intruder, suggest that the editor was trying to clear up certain questions which had been left unanswered in the testimony as it was given originally: (1) How did the intruder know which room was Secretary Seward's? (2) Why did Major Seward fail to notice his brother Frederick lying unconscious in the hallway? (3) Was this servant experienced enough to be reliable?

We shall study this important testimony thoroughly in the chapter on the attempted murder of Mr. Seward. The point is that the version printed in the *National Intelligencer* was revised to answer these questions—revised in exactly the same way as in the Pitman compilation. Yet further on in Bell's interrogation, as the newspaper reported it, a glaring irregularity in the servant's identification of Paine at the police station was *not* "corrected" as it was later in Pitman.

In the interest of simplifying a discussion which is at best very complex, we shall not attempt to compare testimonies on Louis Paine as they appeared in all four of these sources—Pitman, Peterson, the "original" transcript in the Archives, and the daily newspapers. With regard to the latter two, we can say in general that Colonel Burnett did not, at the time these were edited, feel it was necessary to completely revamp the record. But he had no hesitancy about making any alterations which occurred to him.

Since the Peterson version of the proceedings was compiled, we presume, by normally fallible human beings, we can hardly suppose it conveyed the verbatim testimony with the accuracy of a tape recorder. But there are no signs that it was tampered with in any way—even to correct the errors of spelling. The typographical excellence of the separate introduction and conclusion in a different type face suggests that the publishers acquired the forms for the body text under conditions which made it impossible to make corrections.

Assuming that Peterson is the most authentic compilation available, a comparison with Pitman shows that the latter was completely revamped, under Colonel Burnett's supervision, to support all the War Department's charges against the defendants in minute detail.

8

the arrest of Louis Paine

"A great mystery envelopes this man—a mystery which seems impenetrable." This was the curious remark with which the journalist who wrote the introduction to the Peterson compilation began his profile on the prisoner Louis Paine—or as he spelled the name, "Lewis Payne." [1]

The curious thing about the statement is that the man who wrote it had already sat through the whole Trial, heard the prosecution's detailed exposition as to who Paine was and what part he was charged with playing in the Booth "conspiracy," and heard Colonel Doster's much more detailed explanation of his personal history from early youth to the time of his arrest. Taken together, the revelations of the prosecution and defense attorneys represented about as complete a biography as could be desired. The information given was quite enough to satisfy the military judges, the War Department, the contemporary public, and all historians up to the present date.

Yet this particular journalist's introductory comment made it more than plain that he, at least, perceived there was still much more *unknown* than known about this young giant who *smiled* when Mr. Seward's Negro servant identified him positively as the knife-wielding intruder. This journalist interpreted the smile as "sneeringly defiant" and said the prisoner "looked like a perfect desperado." But the stenographer who transcribed the testimony of the servant on May 19 described the same smile as an enigmatic one.

The journalist was much impressed by the prisoner's demeanor in court: "During the progress of the trial he remained apparently indifferent to all around, and was possessed of a most extraordinary control over his feelings."

In spite of this and other comments on Paine's manly bearing, the writer of Peterson's introduction was not in the least partial to the silent young man on his way to the gallows. He was aware of the mystery which surrounded the prisoner, but had still swallowed the legend hook, line, and sinker. The profile he wrote enumerated all the War Department's accusations and the "proof" of each which had been provided. It closed with this descriptive paragraph:

"Payne is a bad looking man, tall and of huge proportions, neck bare, face smoothly shaven,* a shock of black hair over a low forehead, and fierce eyes with small corner, around which the white is always disagreeably visible. He leans his head straight back against the wall, and when looked at, glares the looker out of countenance."

Mention of Louis Paine's bare neck, in combination with the rest of the reporter's description of his physical appearance, points up a subtle device used by the War Department to characterize the prisoner by means of his attire—and its effect upon one articulate observer: *All* the other defendants appeared in court in their own clothing—the men wearing shirts, ties, and coats in observance of the strict proprieties of the era. Paine's own clothing was taken from him shortly after his arrest and turned over to Major Thomas T. Eckert, Assistant Secretary of War, who signed the receipt for it on April 26.[2]

In consequence, the prisoner was obliged to sit in the dock daily for six weeks wearing trousers and a short-sleeved gray undershirt. In 1865, such a costume was associated with rowdies and hoodlums—and even persons of that order would have hesitated to appear at a public gathering, where ladies were present, in such improper dress. How great a factor this was in creating the extraordinary public prejudice against Paine can't be measured precisely of course. But the epithets used to describe him in *all* contemporary accounts were synonymous with "hoodlum." His costume at the Trial was a major source of that unfavorable image.

Paine's arrest and interrogation

The raid on the Surratt boardinghouse the night of April 17 was conducted by Colonel Baker's detectives. Metropolitan police from Superintendent Richards' office had called in the early morning right after the assassination to search for John Surratt, and left without bothering the other inmates when they failed to find him. With the return of Lafayette Baker from New York on the seventeenth, however, the roundup of Booth's associates proceeded swiftly—for the detectives appeared to know exactly who they were and where each could be found.

Much of the mystery and confusion which surrounds the incident at Surratt's can be attributed to the affiliation of the arresting officers. The

*Paine was not "smoothly shaven." As L. C. Baker noted in his "handbill," the prisoner had "no beard nor appearance of beard." Though he was twenty-three years old, Paine did not *need* to shave.

War Department controlled a force of about two thousand individuals classified as detectives. Most of them took their orders from Colonel Baker, either directly or indirectly. Of these an unknown number—probably under a hundred—were carefully chosen operatives, trained and indoctrinated by Baker, willing and able to play any part he assigned them in any scheme he planned.

It is doubtful that any of these men ever knew the broad design of the project in which he was involved, since it usually served the purposes and pleased the vanity of the self-proclaimed "master detective" to let his final objective be unperceived even by those who helped accomplish it. He liked to boast that his special crews worked with such secrecy that they were not even known to each other. All of which clearly gave the chief ultimate control over the whole situation—and no one else enough sensitive information to be a threat to him.

The secrecy of their activities rules out any close study of Baker's henchmen as individuals. When they appear at all, it is in assumed roles. It can only be supposed that they went about their work in a spirit which conformed to their leader's own definition of their calling:[3] "The work of a detective is simply deception reduced to a science or profession."

The actual number of the officers who made the raid that Monday night can't be established. There appear to have been six. Three of them—Morgan, Smith, and Wermerskirch—took the witness stand on May 19 to give testimony regarding the arrests which were made. One, named Rosch, testified the same day as to the search of Paine's person. Two others, Devoe and Sampson, wrote out depositions on the arrest, search, and interrogation of this prisoner—but did not take the witness stand to testify under oath, though they were anxious to do so and wired Holt to that effect from New York on May 20.[4]

Of the three detectives who testified regarding the actual arrests, only Smith appears to have been fully instructed as to what he was supposed to accomplish in the way of incrimination. Both Morgan and Wermerskirch displayed some independence and consistency in their testimony. Although they were among the same group of New York imports that included Devoe and Sampson (as indicated by Colonel Olcott's statement of expenses in the National Archives),[5] they apparently had no special orders from Baker with regard to this assignment.

Major Smith (many War Department detectives held military rank, as did Baker) was apparently in charge of incrimination, though he delivered far less of it under oath than Devoe and Sampson had earlier in their depositions, *which were not sworn.* The general tenor of the prosecution's case against Louis Paine showed how greatly it had been influenced by the unsworn statements of the latter two—even if these witnesses were not considered reliable enough to be brought into court. Detective Rosch said very little when he testified, and the fact that what he said did not agree with the depositions tends to place him among the uninstructed.*

At the time of his arrest and for a few hours afterward—it may have been as few as three or as many as thirty—Louis Paine answered the questions put to him willingly and with apparent candor. But something happened during that period which caused him to decide to hold his peace. There are no known records which can tell us what brought him to this decision. The nature of his interrogation may have convinced him that he had been elected as a whipping boy no matter what he said. Or there may have been subjects he did not wish to talk about, even to extricate himself from a critical situation. Or he may even have had an aberration which caused him to see a certain justice in the thing which was happening to him. In any case, within a short time after his arrest he entered a stolid silence which he did not break for six weeks.

We shall be giving some consideration to the War Department's efforts to show that no such interval of communicativeness occurred, during which the prisoner may have revealed information about himself which is not to be found in the records. But first, let's examine the version of the arrest brought out at the Trial by three of the detectives.

Since Detective Morgan's testimony, as transcribed in Peterson, gave the most detailed account of Louis Paine's arrest, it is shown in full. It is verbatim, including the peculiarities of punctuation, name-spelling, and capitalization. Omissions indicated by ellipses are dialogue which has no bearing on the case of Paine.

RICHARD C. MORGAN

Testimony May 19, 1865, Regarding Paine

PETERSON TRANSCRIPT *Page 74*

Examined by Judge Holt

Q. State whether or not on the 17th or 18th of April last, you were in the service of the Government, and if so, in what capacity?

A. I am in the service of the War Department, acting under the orders of Colonel Olcutt.

Q. State whether on one or both of these days, you had possession of the house of the prisoner, Mrs. Surratt? A. Yes.

Q. State where that house is? A. Number 548 [541] H Street, city of Washington.

Q. State whether or not you took possession of the house, and what occurred there?

A. About twenty minutes past 11 o'clock on the evening of the 17th of April,

*O. S. Oldroyd (*Assassination of Abraham Lincoln,* Washington, D. C., 1901, p. 88) stated that Smith was paid a thousand dollars for his part in the capture and conviction of Paine, and the others (Morgan, Devoe, Rosch, Sampson, and Wermerskirch) were paid five hundred dollars each.

in company with other officers, I went to the house of Mrs. Surratt for the purpose of seizing the papers that might be found, and of arresting the inmates of the house; after we had been at the house about ten minutes, and Major Smith and Captain Weunerskerch, and some other officers, had arrested the inmates of the house, who were in the parlor all ready to come out, I had sent an officer for a carriage to take them away, when I heard a knock and a ring at the door at the same time; Captain Weunerskerch and myself went to the door and opened it; the prisoner, Payne, came in; he had a pick-axe in his hand; he had on a gray coat and black pants, a hat made out of the sleeves of a shirt, I judged; as soon as he came in and immediately closed the door, he said, "I guess I am mistaken," said I, "who do you want to see?"

He replied, "Mrs. Surratt"; said I, "you are right, walk in."

He took a seat. I said, "what did you come here for, this time of night?" He said he came to dig a gutter; that Mrs. Surratt had sent for him; I asked him when and, he said in the morning; I asked where he last worked, and he said somewhere on Ninth street; I asked him where he boarded, he said he had no boarding house, that he was a poor man, and earned his living with the pick-axe in his hand; I asked him how much he made a day, he said, nothing at all sometimes, sometimes one dollar, and sometimes one dollar and fifty cents; "Have you any money?" "Not a cent."

I asked him why he came at this time of night? He said he came to see where it was to be dug, so that he could commence early in the morning; I said, have you had no previous acquaintance with Mrs. Surratt? He said, No; I said, why did she select you for this work? He replied, that she knew he was working in that neighborhood; that he was a poor man and she came to him; I asked him how old he was, and he said about twenty; I asked him where he was from; he said from Fauquier county, Va.; previous to this he had pulled out an oath of allegiance, handed it to me and said, that will show you who I am; it contained the name of Louis Payne, Fauquier county, Va.; I asked him if he was from the South; he said he was; I asked him when he left there; he said two months ago, in February; I asked him why he left; he said that he had to leave or go into the army; that he preferred to earn his living with the pick-axe; I asked him if he could read; he said no; I asked him if he could write; he said he could manage to write his own name.

Q. Is that the pick-axe he had on his shoulder (producing the pick)?

A. Yes; I then told him he would have to go to the Provost Marshal and explain; he moved a little at that, and did not answer; the carriage had arrived to take up the women; they were sent off, and Payne was also taken in charge of officers; . . .

Q. Did Mrs. Surratt leave the house before Payne came, or afterwards?

A. They were preparing to leave and were in the parlor; . . . they were just ready to go and had started to go when we opened the door; I think they passed out as Payne came in.

Q. Then she did not see him before she left?

A. Yes, she must have seen him as she passed out; I heard no conversation in regard to it.

. . . .

Q. Were you or not afterwards at the provost marshal's office?

A. About three o'clock in the morning I got there; Mrs. Surratt had been there and had been taken to the Old Capitol prison before my arrival.

Q. Did you hear Mrs. Surratt say anything in regard to the prisoner at any time?

A. No.

CROSS-EXAMINATION BY MR. AIKEN

. . . .

Q. State if Mrs. Surratt made any remarks in regard to Payne.

A. As she passed out it now comes to my recollection that she made some remark to Major Smith, but I did not hear what it was.

As Morgan told it, the big prisoner did not sound evasive. The answers he gave to the questions asked him were apparently forthright and prompt enough that the detective's suspicions were not aroused—at least not enough so to mention it.

Assuming, for the sake of argument, that Louis Paine was telling the truth at this point, we now have a number of items of information about him. They don't add up to very much; but *if true,* they are most of the truth we shall hear either *from* Louis Paine or *about* him through the whole course of the Trial testimony. Louis Paine told Detective Morgan that:

He had come north from Fauquier County, Virginia.

The Oath of Allegiance he handed Morgan confirmed that this was his last residence before going north. The prosecution's frantic efforts to keep the document out of court on June 2 suggest that its mention here was a slip on Morgan's part.

He "left there" two months earlier, in February.

The prisoner did *not* say he had come to Washington at that time. The War Department would insist he had, in spite of later evidence that he had gone to Baltimore from Fauquier County.

He had been earning his living as a laborer.

All three officers agreed he carried a "pickaxe," the equipment of a "laborer." The prosecution would insist it was a disguise.

He had no previous acquaintance with Mrs. Surratt.

As mentioned in an earlier section, the initial interrogation of three of the four women arrested at the same time was to the effect that Paine was a stranger to them. But Weichmann would swear the young man boarded at the Surratt house for three days in the month of March. It would not be remarkable if Paine—simply to avoid an awkward situation—had denied knowing a woman who, with her whole household, was under arrest and on her way to prison. At any rate, Paine apparently denied knowing the widow.

He thought that he was "about twenty" years old.

From his photograph he looks a little older. Baker gave his age as twenty-two to twenty-three.

He was "from the South"—that is, a southerner.

He had left Fauquier County as a refugee rather than going into the army.

The only Confederate "army" in Fauquier County during the period in question was Mosby's Partisan command. Thus Paine seems to have stated that he did not want to join the guerrillas.

He could not read, and could only manage to write his name.

At no time during his imprisonment and trial was Louis Paine known to have read or written *anything*. His signature, "L. Paine," appears at the foot of his Oath of Allegiance. The experimental, childish forming of the letters bears witness that the writer was either illiterate or nearly so. In his summation, Doster said Paine was illiterate.

He had no money in his possession—"not a cent."

An assassin who had been so careless as not to have provided himself with money for his escape was so improbable a proposition that the War Department was obliged to forearm itself with "evidence" in this respect.

Except on one or two points, there was no great disagreement among the testimonies of the three arresting officers—unless we count the conflicting statements of Morgan and Smith as to who was in charge of the detail. Each asserted he had led the raid, and so did Devoe in his deposition.

Major H. W. Smith was the troubleshooter for the trio. The identification of Paine made by Seward's houseboy called for Paine to be wearing a newish pair of heavy, good-quality boots. Morgan said nothing about that, but Smith stated that the prisoner had on a "pair of very fine boots." Then Wermerskirch, something of a maverick on the witness stand, messed up the "evidence" by stating that ". . . he was full of mud to his knees."

A little later in his examination he topped it off with this self-willed statement: ". . . the prisoner had taken no particular pains to disguise himself; his face looked as it is now, and I would recognize him if he put another coat on and *covered himself with mud.*"[6]

Captain Wermerskirch added another bit of insurance that he would go down in history as a reasonably honest witness—even though a detective: He said that on the way out Mrs. Surratt asked for a moment to pray. "She knelt down, but whether she prayed or not I can't say."

Major Smith had taken the stand before Wermerskirch. His principal revelation was that he had told Mrs. Surratt to look at Paine in a good light and had asked her if she knew him.[7]

He said she had replied, "Before God I do not know this man and have never seen him." In his turn, Wermerskirch affirmed that the widow had denied knowing Paine in just about those words. The unco-operative Morgan, first of the three on the witness stand, had refused Holt's invitations to remember Mrs. Surratt's denial: He only recollected ". . . that she made some remark to Major Smith, but I did not hear what it was," when pressed with the same question by the widow's attorney, Mr. Aiken.[8] If Smith alone had reported the denial, it might be doubted. But confirmed by Wermerskirch it seems credible.

The importance of whether or not Mrs. Surratt had denied knowing Paine became more obvious a little farther along in the Trial. And in this we see a good example of the sophistry which was evident in so many of the War Department's charges against the defendants. Since Paine was charged with attacking Seward, the fact that he apparently returned to the widow's house three days after the crime was said to incriminate her in a plot with him. Also, since Booth had called at the house a number of times, Paine's asking to see Mrs. Surratt implied that he, as well as she, was a conspirator with the dead actor.

By this method of reasoning, the prosecution claimed to have a strong circumstantial point against *both* defendants—without providing unassailable proof against either of them.

Mrs. Surratt was the more damaged of the two by this legal card trick. Paine's alleged connections with Booth weren't established at all, except by some of Louis Weichmann's more imaginative assertions. But Mrs. Surratt's denial of knowing Paine was about half the case against her. The rest depended altogether upon the unsupported allegations of Weichmann and John Lloyd, the frightened drunkard who was operating her tavern in Surrattsville (now Clinton), Maryland. Weichmann later admitted privately that he had testified for the War Department under the threat of being charged as an accomplice in the assassination.[9]

Doster claimed his testimony and Lloyd's would have been accepted in a civil court only if they appeared as confessed collaborators in the conspiracy who were turning state's evidence.[10]

identification of Paine

Because her denial of knowing Paine was made such an issue, the quality of the widow's eyesight became a preoccupation of her defense attorneys. Every witness who admitted knowing her was asked if he had ever noticed any signs of poor vision on her part. From this rather anemic response to the charge that she had denied knowing Paine, it would seem that her attorneys hadn't been permitted to see the records of the first interrogations of Anna Surratt and Honora Fitzpatrick.[11] They were not defendants at the Trial and were not believed to have any guilty knowledge that would have prompted them to lie. Their positive assertions that *they* had not recognized Paine should have carried more weight than even medical proof that Mrs. Surratt was half blind. The widow saw the young man many times during the Trial in excellent light (in the prisoners' dock they sat only two seats apart for six weeks) but *never* admitted she knew him.

When she was called to the witness stand on May 30, Anna was not asked if she had recognized Paine but was asked about her mother's eyesight, which she said was very poor. By this time the prosecutors, by constant reference to "Payne" and "Wood" as the same man, had this witness and all others—as well as the defendants themselves—using the name "Payne" when they were talking about "Wood." So Miss Surratt's original belief that she did not know the man arrested at her mother's house and that he was *not* "Wood" had been totally obscured.

In the transcript of her interrogation, Foster's effort to remove this inconvenient belief from her mind is obvious, though he didn't seem to be making much progress at the time. She had admitted that a man who she *thought* was named "Wood" came to the house once and said he was a Baptist preacher, but her recollection of him was so vague she didn't "know what kind of a moustache he wore or whether he had moustache or whiskers." Foster persisted: [12]

> Q. When did you see him [Wood] next?
> A. I haven't seen him since.
> Q. Didn't you see him the night you were arrested?
> A. I didn't look at that man that came in at all.
> Q. Not when we thought he was a Surratt?
> A. Oh, I saw him then but I didn't recognize him then because he had changed, or something about him looked as though I had never seen him before.
> Q. He had changed his dress you mean?

A. Well he looked different, but there was something about him—about somebody that I had seen.
Q. Isn't there a conviction in your mind that he was the very man that you saw there who pretended to be a Baptist Preacher?
A. Indeed I would not like to say. I have not thought of him since . . .
Q. Would you ever forget that eye or the look that he had?
A. No sir.
Q. Would you ever forget the eyes, that he had at your house before?
A. They did not look like the eyes of the man who was at our house.

. . . .

Q. How often did Booth call on the man named Wood, or who called himself Wood at that time?
A. If he ever came there it was not to my knowledge.

On the same day that the foregoing dialogue was recorded, April 28, Colonel Olcott wrote a report to Colonel Burnett summarizing the findings of interrogation of several suspects by Colonel Foster and himself.[13] We find him inclined to interpret Anna Surratt's foregoing statements rather loosely. After quoting her as thinking that a "bogus preacher" stayed at the boardinghouse for about one week, he continues as follows:

"States that she didn't like him because of the peculiar *wildness* of his eyes; that the prisoner Paine bears a strong resemblance to him in height, expression, and color of the hair; but she is not sure whether he is the man or not. She was betrayed into an expression of his appearance having changed but suddenly seeming to recollect herself retracted her words in confusion. . . ."

The difference between Anna's recorded statements and Olcott's interpretation of them highlights a basic consideration of this study: There are so many instances in the records of the Trial in which a defendant, suspect, or witness may be falsifying that we need criteria by which to decide whether to believe a particular statement. Although no formula can be set which will apply in all cases, a general rule of thumb can be obtained by determining each individual's personal connection with the situation as far as that is possible.

Anna Surratt offers a simplified example. She can be presumed to have wished to help her mother's case any way she could. No evidence has ever turned up that she had any knowledge of a conspiracy by Booth or anyone else. If the mother was involved in any plot, the daughter knew nothing about it. The prosecutors were so convinced of this that although Anna was technically under arrest, she was not a suspect and was permitted to visit her mother in prison regularly—though the male defendants were forbidden to have *any* visitors other than their counsel. In this case, the young girl could be expected to assume that the truth would be more helpful to her mother's interests than any falsehood. So she would probably tell the truth.

Thus her statement that she didn't know Louis Paine, but that he reminded her vaguely of someone else, may be taken literally.

mrs. Surratt's interrogation

To return to the matter of Mrs. Surratt's veracity as to her non-recognition of Louis Paine:

Miss Fitzpatrick's account at the time of her interrogation on April 28 [14] and her turn on the witness stand on June 9 was comparable to Anna Surratt's in some respects. On the earlier occasion she insisted that, although she "did not think he was disguised at all," she had simply not recognized Paine when they were arrested together. When pressed to say she thought his eyes were "fierce," she said she'd never noticed them. But she did know the man named "Wood" and described him as a tall man with "black hair, smooth face, no whiskers, no moustache." Miss Fitzpatrick added the note that he "didn't look like a 'priest.'"

But in court the young lady showed the effectiveness of her indoctrination by using the name "Payne," whether she was referring to Paine or "Wood." She stated she hadn't recognized him at the Surratt house and didn't until the shirt sleeve was removed from his head at the police station. She said she had not heard Mrs. Surratt deny knowing Paine, but that the widow had asserted that he was *not* John Surratt.

The third young lady arrested that night was Olivia Jenkins, the widow's niece. She did not appear as a witness, and this writer saw no record of her interrogation by the War Department investigators. We shall be referring to this curious circumstance later.

None of the defendants was allowed to testify in his own defense, and their statements that they were innocent were not permitted to be put on the record—though their "confessions" of guilt were. Since all were "presumed to be guilty," the prosecution's view was that only protestations of innocence could be expected from them and these would be considered false. So for knowledge of what Mrs. Surratt had to say for herself our only source of information is the record of her interrogation in the National Archives; and these statements serve to throw the whole subject of her recognition of Paine into a state of confusion rather than clearing it up.

The lengthy record of the widow's interrogation is dated April 17, the very night of her arrest.[15] Some odd pages of dialogue which don't fit in with this series are attached to the document, and the date would seem to be incorrect (Mrs. Surratt having been arrested shortly before midnight on the seventeenth), though the interrogation could have *begun* on the seventeenth. Such peculiarities raise suspicions about the authenticity of the record—as do some of the statements attributed to Mrs. Surratt. But these transcribed interrogations (which apparently required the presence of a stenographer) do not, as a rule, seem to have been tampered with.

When asked about Paine, the lady denied positively that she knew him—and added that her daughter had been much frightened when he came in, and that she herself thought he had come to kill them, and that it was very fortunate the officers were there.

Mrs. Surratt said a man named Wood, who claimed to be a Baptist preacher, came to her house in February. He had come from Baltimore to preach there on Sunday.

Her description of this man "Wood" was curious, since it disagreed with all other descriptions of him which were given by any witnesses at or before the Trial. He was, according to Mrs. Surratt, a short, stout man with black hair and eyes. He was a man of few words, not inclined to talk, who remained in his room most of the time. He seemed to be a young man of "twenty years and odd."

The widow reasserted that she didn't know the man who came the night of her arrest. "I never thought it was the Wood who was at our house."

In another document a War Department investigator's summary of some of Mrs. Surratt's statements clearly misrepresented them: [16]

"Mrs. Surratt repeats substantially the story that she told on her first examination . . . that, calling himself Wood, a man representing himself to be a Baptist Minister and answering in the main to the description of the Seward Assassin occupied rooms there a few days. . . ."

By now the reader will have received the impression that Louis Paine and the mysterious "Wood" resembled each other very closely. This was actually the case. A number of witnesses, including the women occupants of the Surratt house, had seen both men. No one seems to have seen them together, nor at intervals of less than a couple of weeks. But the confusion as to Paine's identity in the statements of these and other witnesses was due to the similarity of his face and stature to those of the other man.

The very idea of mistaken identity due to the similar appearance of two persons has been worn threadbare in fiction. Its occurrence in fact literature is so rare that we read of such instances with tongue in cheek. One feels like apologizing for bringing it up in a serious study of this kind. But there it is. Doster himself appears to have seen both men. He did not think they were the same person, since Paine was in prison and the other man was at large. But he did see a strong resemblance and was willing to believe the two were brothers. The similarity was one of outward appearance only. Thus those who had seen both and confused one with the other had the impression of a very peculiar, self-contradictory person.

With this to go on—that the two men were so much alike in appearance that witnesses who had seen both at different times confused one with the other—Mrs. Surratt's denial that they even looked alike raises some strong suspicions about her.

The investigator's summary ignored the widow's falsified description of "Wood" and said she thought he answered to "the description of Seward's Assassin"—which was to say, he fitted the description in Baker's handbill. Thus she was *quoted* as saying that "Wood" resembled Paine even though she'd denied it.

We have to remember the conditions of Mrs. Surratt's arrest. Weichmann had thrown suspicion upon Atzerodt when he hastened to Superintendent Richards' office the morning after the assassination. But police from that agency had already called at the boardinghouse earlier the same morning in search of John Surratt, whom they *already* suspected. After Weichmann's call they did not return for Mrs. Surratt—so he must have given them no information on her at that sitting. He was then ordered to Canada by Baker and was out of reach as a source of information until he returned at the end of the month.

So the authorities in Washington—civil or military—had no suspicions of the widow during the first three days, and still had none when she was arrested on the night of April 17. Arnold and O'Laughlin were also arrested on the seventeenth, the former where he was working at Fortress Monroe, the latter in his home town of Baltimore.[17] Otto Eisenschiml pointed out that although the prosecutors wished the court to believe these men were implicated and traced by means of the letter signed "Sam," which was found in Booth's trunk at the National Hotel, they had been taken into custody *before* the writer of the letter was identified as Sam Arnold,[18] a friend of Booth's who lived in Baltimore.

The War Department created the impression that they had been tipped off to the whole roster of the conspirators by Louis Weichmann. But while on the witness stand on May 13, he was asked whether he knew either of the prisoners Arnold and O'Laughlin. He answered that he did not.[19]

This adds up to the fair conclusion that *Baker* ordered the arrests of Mrs. Surratt and the two men, not by a conventional process of finding clues and tracing the suspects nor by any information Weichmann might have been able to supply *if* he had been on hand, but by reason of his *own* private knowledge of Booth's associates in the kidnap scheme. The casting of Weichmann as the War Department's only source of information is thus shown to have been a pretence—one which succeeded in obscuring Lafayette Baker's starring role in this drama of deceit.

The nature of Baker's role is clearly of interest to us, but let's stick to the question of Mrs. Surratt for the present. We have no reason to think he would scruple against framing the widow any more than he would against framing Louis Paine. But a stranger in town with no friends was a different proposition from a matron who was a native and lifelong resident of the area and who, if innocent, might be able to produce unimpeachable defense witnesses by the score. This train of thought carries us to another assumption—that Colonel Baker *knew* she was guilty of *something,* and it must have been something he *knew* he could prove. This wasn't a case of picking up suspected subversives and throwing them in Old Capitol for a few months until he could think of something with which to charge them. The crime in question was the assassination of the President, and the whole country was aroused by the tragedy. There would have to be specific charges which the War Department could make in court without long delay, with most of the nation's citizens looking on and much of the civilized world as well.

The only appropriate charge under the conditions would have to be complicity in the assassination of Abraham Lincoln—and Baker must have *known* he could prove it.

It was a fact, as we shall see later, that Paine *had* boarded at Surratt's a couple of days in March. At the trial of John Surratt in 1867, Detective Morgan recalled he had asked the young man where he slept nights and was told "he boarded wherever he could get work."

"I asked him," Morgan continued, "if he expected to sleep there that night. He said he supposed Mrs. Surratt would let him sleep there all night, as he was going to work in the morning." [20]

At any rate, his inopportune arrival and his strong resemblance to the man named "Wood," who *had* visited her house, put the widow in an awkward situation *if she knew "Wood" had attacked Seward or was involved in Lincoln's assassination.* Whether she recognized him as Paine or "Wood," if she *said* she did, the fat was in the fire. For he would be arrested by reason of his connection with her boardinghouse, and the implication that she had harbored and conspired with an assassin would be strong. If she denied knowing him and he were arrested anyway, her connections with "Wood" were sure to be brought out during the investigation of Paine. Her only hope was that Paine would be released as a harmless stranger if she convinced the detectives she didn't know him.

Now, if Mrs. Surratt had had nothing on her conscience and really didn't recognize the tall young man, she would merely have said "no" when asked whether she knew him. But under pressure of a "Hobson's choice" she overdid it. Her denial was too vehement. She answered as if the question had been, "Do you know this murderer?"

The many post mortem defenders of Mrs. Surratt have leaned heavily upon the theory that every incriminating statement made about her was a lie. But this theory has not succeeded in clearing her name. In our investigations we are approaching the subject from a different direction—trying to determine whether her statements and attitudes were those of a guilty person or those of an innocent person who was being framed.

the official depositions

The depositions written out by detectives Ely Devoe and Thomas Sampson may be examined in the original at the National Archives.[21] Neither document adds much to our enlightenment about Louis Paine, but both are educational material in the "Baker Method" of crime detection, which exercised a formidable but invisible influence over the conduct of the Conspiracy Trial. Historian David M. DeWitt, who was one of the leading champions of Mary Surratt, quoted Lafayette Baker's official order to his detectives at the beginning of his "investigation" of Lincoln's murder. It spells out the Method about as concisely as could be desired. Colonel Baker's instructions to his operatives urged them "to extort confessions and procure testimony to establish the conspiracy . . . by promises, rewards, threats, deceit, force, or any other effectual means." [22]

Detectives Devoe and Sampson traveled to Washington from New York on April 15, the day after the assassination. They were with the group which included Morgan, Wermerskirch, and Smith. Some of them stated that they were under the orders of Colonel Olcott, who had accompanied them to Washington as a special commissioner for the War Department and who submitted a detailed report of their expenses during this duty to Colonel Burnett—a document also to be found in the Archives.[23] Since none of them (except Olcott, in the memo to Burnett cited earlier) ever mentioned the name of Colonel Baker, the fact that they were getting their instructions from him has been obscured. The depositions of Devoe and Sampson will help to clarify the point.

Both men claimed to have taken part in the arrests at the Surratt house and to have interrogated Louis Paine at length, either at the boardinghouse or later at General Augur's headquarters, where they also alleged they had searched his person. Both depositions were dated April 19—and *both gave the date of the raid as Tuesday, April 18 rather than April 17.* The updating of the event by one day was hardly accidental, since the effect was to make it possible for Baker's handbill, with its incredibly accurate description of Paine, to have been published prior to his arrest rather than after it.

In the case of Ely Devoe, there is substantial evidence that he was not even in Washington when the raid on the Surratt house took place, although he asserted in his deposition that it was *he* who arrested the occupants of the boardinghouse and took them to General Augur's office.

One of the vouchers in his name which is attached to Colonel Olcott's report on detective expenses is dated April 28. It lists the amount of $18.87—"For expense from N. Y. to D. C. and in pursuit of President's & Seward's assassins *in Md.* April 16 to 28th."

Colonel Baker's written report to Stanton on his activities in pursuit of Booth, dated July 7, 1866 (five months after his dismissal),[24] mentioned his having dispatched six men into lower Maryland "on Monday, April 18, or Tuesday following." So he confirmed that he had sent detectives out in the period covered by Devoe's expense voucher—and also that a year after Paine's execution, he was still interested in updating the night of his arrest, referring to "Monday, April 18," instead of the seventeenth.

Detective Charles H. Rosch testified at the Trial on May 19 that *he* and Sampson had searched "Payne."[25] Devoe's deposition stated that Colonel Olcott had ordered *him* to make the search, with Sampson's help, at Augur's headquarters. Of the arresting officers, he named only Wermerskirch, and a detail of his description of the prisoner—his boots—indicates that Wermerskirch may have been his source of information. He wrote that the prisoner "was a young man about 6′, 2″ in height, weighing about 175 pounds" who wore "muddy black pantaloons and boots." It will be remembered that Captain Wermerskirch was the *only* officer to notice that Paine was "mud to his knees."

Devoe's catalogue of the contents of the prisoner's pockets is interesting in comparison with the list given in Sampson's deposition—and the list recited by Rosch from the witness stand:

Devoe's list of Paine's possessions

pocketbook containing two newspaper clips
box of pistol cartridges
small dictionary
pocket compass in mahogany case
small hair brush
two tooth brushes
bottle of hair grease
several other small articles
$25 in bills

Rosch's list of Paine's possessions

pocket comb
needle case
tooth brush
hair brush
and other articles

Sampson's list of Paine's possessions

pocket compass in mahogany case
hair grease
small hair brush
two tooth brushes
small dictionary
postage stamps
pistol cartridges
a pocketbook without any money in it
$25 in bank notes
some pennies
a large quantity of loose plug chewing tobacco
a new, smallsized pocket knife
several scraps of paper
a newspaper extract from Lincoln's inaugural address
an article about Vice-President Johnson

The partial catalogue of Paine's personal belongings which Mr. Rosch gave from the witness stand on May 19 apparently included all the items the War Department wished to bring into its case against the prisoner at that time. They made no issue of the nature of these articles, and no importance was attached to them by the defense.

Yet Devoe's and Sampson's lists contained certain items which appeared to have a bearing on the prosecution's charge that Paine was an assassin in flight: a compass, a box of pistol cartridges, twenty-five dollars in bank notes. It is, or will be, quite evident that the prosecutors had no compunction about using evidence of doubtful authenticity when it suited their purpose. So their reason for not introducing these articles in evidence is uncertain—as is their reason for not calling either Sampson or Devoe to the witness stand. One plausible conjecture is that others besides those two saw the prisoner searched and might be called by the defense to testify that the incriminating articles were *not* in his possession. Another is that the defense might have been able to prove that Devoe, and possibly Sampson, were not even in Washington at the time.

Though they had no bearing on the case, Devoe's and Sampson's lists do enlighten us as to some of the points Colonel Baker thought it would be necessary to establish with regard to Paine to identify him as the man who had attacked Seward—*about whom Lafayette Baker knew a great deal.* In both depositions elaborate efforts were made to represent the prisoner as being very evasive as to where he worked as a laborer, where he lived in Washington, how long he had been there, etc. Both made a particular point of his having, they said, twenty-five dollars in his possession. Devoe included a long sequence in which he asked, "How is it that you say you could not go to New York because you had not money to carry you there, and now you have $25 in your pocket." Sampson echoed the same general theme in a *different* dialogue he said *he* had had with the prisoner.

In this case, as with much of the vast amount of testimony relating to the Trial—given both in and out of court—our investigation is a matter of sorting through a bushel of falsehood to find a grain of truth. The points these two detectives were trying to make involve aspects of the case against Louis Paine which come to the forefront later in the Trial and are discussed in later chapters, in which they are analyzed in context. It would be a digression to explore them fully at this stage—but they serve to stress the fact that the individual who masterminded the Conspiracy Trial *knew all the facts about the Booth "conspiracy" even before any arrests were made, and after the arrests were made knew just how the eight defendants would have to be misrepresented in order to fit them into the fictitious version of the plot to assassinate Lincoln.*

The items in Devoe's and Sampson's lists which were inserted to establish specific "facts" about Paine—and the "facts" they were supposed to establish—were as follows:

1. *His possession of twenty-five dollars.* First, to prove that he was not a penniless laborer. Second, to contradict the statement that he had been in New York before coming to Washington, in case such a claim were made by the defense. Had Doster not been absorbed in his effort to lay the groundwork for an insanity plea, and had he looked farther into the recent history of Louis Paine, he would have found ample proof that his client had been in New York and had arrived in Washington only a few days before the assassination. Oddly enough, Sampson might have been close to the truth in his deposition when he said the prisoner told him he had been in the city only "six days."
2. *The reading matter of various kinds.* In order for the prisoner to be identified as the man who had attacked Seward and participated in Booth's "conspiracy," it had to be shown that he could *read* and write. But he was in fact illiterate. Presumably a man who carried newspaper clippings in his wallet could read them.

Another important function of Sampson's deposition was to make it a matter of "record" *that the detective detail which raided the Surratt house had seen the description of "Seward's assassin" on Baker's handbill.* He asserted:

"The moment I saw him I was convinced that he answered the description given me by Col. Olcott of the man who attacked Mr. Seward, and I said immediately, that is the man who attacked Mr. Seward. Mr. Morgan coincided with me at once that he was the man."

The fact that the prosecution at the Trial kept very quiet about the handbill seems to indicate they realized that its publication *prior* to Paine's arrest would be very hard to prove—Sampson's deposition notwithstanding. They preferred to let it be testified by Morgan and Smith that Paine was arrested only as a "suspicious character."

Also, bearing on the identification of Paine by Seward's houseboy, which we shall get into soon, Sampson closed his masterpiece of creative writing with this testament:

"He took William Bell over to look at the prisoner and he exclaimed, 'That is the man, there is no use my looking any longer; those are the pantaloons he had on.' "

As we shall see, young Bell may have said those very words—that he "recognized" Paine by his distinctive plain black trousers. Mr. Sampson (or the person who told him what to say in his deposition) seemed to have forgotten that Bell's earlier description of the intruder had sent the War Department in search of a man who looked like George Atzerodt. He closed on this tongue-in-cheek note: "I never saw a more perfect identification in my life."

Although the prosecution made no use of these two depositions during the Conspiracy Trial of 1865, a distant echo of them was heard at the trial of John Surratt in July and August of 1867. After having been allowed to escape prosecution for two years, although his presence in various parts of Europe was known all the time, Surratt was finally apprehended in Italy and, in spite of all the War and State Departments could do to prevent it, was brought back to Washington for trial. The proceeding was a civil one, but the judge and prosecutors were so wholly subservient to the War Department that it was virtually a playback of the Conspiracy Trial in which the prosecution had two objectives: (1) To make sure John Surratt was *not* convicted and (2) to affirm that the sentences passed by the military commission were justified. Many of the same witnesses were called—the honest ones telling their stories about the same as before and the false ones supporting the War Department's charges more forcefully than they had in the first place.

Messrs. Morgan and Smith took the witness stand again. Each was still insisting that *he* had been in charge of the detail which raided the Surratt house. The former stuck very close to his original story:[26]

Major Smith (now Colonel Smith), however, was still pulling stroke oar for the War Department at John Surratt's trial. He now testified as if he had Devoe's deposition in one hand and Sampson's in the other. First he moved the time of the raid back from 11:30 to 10:15 to allow time for the lengthy interrogations those two detectives claimed to have conducted. Then he introduced each of them by name as being members of the detail (although he had not mentioned them at the Conspiracy Trial) and included some of their allegations in his testimony. He said, among other things, that Paine told him he had been "working on the railroad and on the canal" and that he had been in Washington "a week or ten days."[27]

Smith's testimony included one particularly curious example of history repeating itself. At the Conspiracy Trial he had said nothing about Paine's Oath of Allegiance, since Morgan had already related that the prisoner had handed the document to *him.* At the Surratt trial he said the prisoner's "pass" was handed to one of the officers and then to him. "I looked at it; it was an amnesty oath, in which he bound himself not to go south of the Potomac, I think. I looked at it and it appeared as if the paper—" That was as far as he got. The following tells why:[28]

> Mr. Bradley—Where is that paper?
> The Witness—I do not know.
> Mr. Bradley—Then do not say anything more about it.
> Judge Fisher—You cannot speak of the contents of the paper.

Here we have a remarkable switch. Mr. Joseph H. Bradley was *not* a prosecutor, but counsel for John Surratt! Now it appears that mention of the mysterious Oath of Allegiance would be harmful to Surratt's interests! And Judge George P. Fisher, guardian of the interests of the War

Department, didn't want the document brought into the trial either. Why?

In a nutshell, this is the reason why: Surratt's case was that he had taken part in Booth's "conspiracy" to *abduct* Mr. Lincoln but had no part whatever in the assassination. Both Bradley and Fisher apparently knew (as our investigations will show) that if Paine's Oath had been put in evidence in the Conspiracy Trial—or if it had been introduced in the trial of John Surratt—it would have been the key to an entirely different defense for Paine and *all* of Booth's associates. With it, the defense in '65 could have proved that the monstrously magnified Booth "conspiracy" never amounted to anything—never got beyond the conversation stage.

Obviously, in 1867, John Surratt was as much interested in keeping the Booth legend intact as was the War Department. If it were exploded, if it were known that Booth had abandoned the kidnap scheme or *any other* plot weeks before the murder, Surratt would have had to come up with some convincing answers as to just what his connection with Booth was, and why the actor was in constant touch with him and/or his mother during the week before the assassination. Surratt's life depended upon having it believed that the assassination was Booth's idea, and a corollary of the abduction plot, which had been a bona fide undertaking in which Surratt had been involved. Otherwise his flight from the country after Lincoln's murder could mean only one thing—that he had been a party to the *actual* assassination conspiracy.

the prisoner's knife

As far as the records of the Trial proceedings are concerned, none of the items taken from Louis Paine at or shortly after his arrest, either clothing or personal effects, was returned to him. However, one article on Sampson's list was given back to him and was in his possession throughout the whole period of his imprisonment—his knife!

A Baptist minister of Washington, the Rev. Dr. A. Gillette, attended the condemned man the night before his execution.[29] He quoted Paine as having made a "confession" to him which generally parallels the account Colonel Doster gave in his summation before the court.[30] The clergyman stated that he had "a few small articles, a *knife* and a Bible" which he asked be sent to his "people" in Florida.

On the morning of July 7, shortly before the hour set for the executions, Colonel Doster went to the penitentiary to pay final respects to his mystifying client who didn't want to be saved from the gallows. The jailers told him Paine had talked quietly with Dr. Gillette for two or three hours, then slept soundly for the balance of the night. Unlike the other condemned prisoners (so Doster was told), he had eaten a hearty breakfast. However, Doster felt that the young man's rocklike fortitude was somewhat shaken "by the hurried way in which he was to be executed."

The corridor was full of the friends and relatives of the other three who were to be hanged, permitted by the War Department to make their hurried farewells. Paine had had no visitors and was alone now. Doster described their last conversation in a sentence.

"He thanked me heartily for the trouble he had given me, and offered me his jack-knife, as the only earthly thing he had to give, which I declined."[31]

A knife in the possession of *any* prisoner charged with a capital crime is a remarkable circumstance. A knife in the possession of *this* prisoner, notorious in the nation's press as a "perfect desperado" whose stated desire to die had been one of the fascinating rumors of the Trial—a phenomenon!

But there was never any hint that Paine had menaced or even resisted his jailers throughout his captivity. His attitude was described as one of complete resignation. No implications that he had ever *considered,* let alone attempted, suicide had been circulated—except in one instance. This was in Secretary of War Edwin Stanton's official order of April 22, 1865.[32]

The order was signed by Assistant Secretary of Navy G. V. Fox and conveyed Stanton's "request" to the Navy Yard commandant that the male prisoners be fitted with canvas hoods "put over the head of each and tied around the neck with a hole for proper breathing and eating but not seeing. . . ." The purpose of this cruel device which, in the heat of early summer, was a medieval torture, was stated as being "for better security against conversation." The extreme measures taken to prevent the prisoners from talking to *anyone* is one of the principal bases for the widespread suspicions about Edwin Stanton.

Tacked onto the end of the order was this further admonition: " . . . that Payne be secured to prevent self-destruction." This possibility never seems to have occurred to *anyone* responsible for the prisoner or any of those who were in daily contact with him at the time of the Trial. It had occurred to Stanton (or was it suggested to him?) only five days after Paine's arrest. Yet the prisoner had a suitable implement for suicide in his pocket up to the very moment of his execution!

In Paine the War Department had a problem prisoner. Except for a short period after his arrest, he had refused to answer any questions or tell anything about himself for six weeks. In view of the evidence we have found that he was being "framed" from the very beginning, it is fair to assume that the War Department remained in frantic apprehension during that six weeks lest Paine begin talking, provide proof of his own innocence and their fabrication of the Booth "conspiracy," and turn the spotlight of suspicion upon the engineers of the Trial.

The ruthlessness of Lafayette Baker and the fact that the War Department didn't scruple against "judicial murder" are, we believe, well established. Would they balk at murder in a more direct form if self-preservation required it? Stanton could easily have ordered Paine's jailers to keep an eye on him if he had any misgivings—without an official order which would make his fears for the prisoner's life a matter of public record. But that would not have served the same purpose.

With the War Secretary's misgivings a matter of record, Paine could be eliminiated by "suicide" at the discretion of the Trial's engineers when or if they considered it necessary—and with complete impunity.

alterations in the pitman version

Since all the arresting officers were minions of the War Department, their testimony from the witness stand was rather close to what the prosecutors expected them to say. So the alterations in Pitman's "official" version of the proceedings, compiled under the supervision of Colonel Burnett, are relatively minor compared to the major surgery committed by the War Department's official in charge of "strict accuracy" on the testimony of other witness—particularly those who appeared for the defense.

Here as elsewhere, though, all the undertones and shadings of meaning have been eliminated by the compiler's narrative style, which omits all the questions and merely summarizes the answers. Also, in each of the officers' testimonies, there are changes which should be mentioned briefly to show the consistency with which Burnett weeded out even very minor exchanges which could by interpretation raise small doubts that the War Department's case against the defendants was as damning as was claimed.

Morgan actually took the witness stand *before* Smith on May 19. As we have seen, he seemed much less inclined to beat the drum for the prosecution than his fellow officer. In Pitman his testimony is shown as following Smith's which, since it begins with the statement "I was in charge of the party that took possession of Mrs. Surratt's house . . . ," appears as that of the officer in charge. To the casual reader, Smith's testimony therefore is the principal one.

In Morgan's testimony in Pitman,[33] *all* his negative answers to the repeated question as to whether he had heard Mrs. Surratt say anything about Paine are deleted, as are the questions themselves. In Peterson he named only Smith and Wermerskirch in referring to other officers who were present; but in Pitman he says, "I ordered Thomas Sampson and Mr. Rosch to take him [Paine] up to the Provost Marshal's office."

Thus the presence of Sampson was made a matter of "record"—though Devoe is still noticeable by his absence. Morgan's mention of the Oath of Allegiance appears in Pitman.

In Smith's testimony according to Pitman,[34] the officer's quotation of Mrs. Surratt's denial is beefed up a bit, as follows: "Before God, sir, I do not know this man, and have never seen him, and I did not hire him to dig a gutter for me."

During his cross-examination of this witness (according to Peterson)[35] the widow's attorney, Mr. Aiken, won a small moral victory for the defense by trapping Smith very neatly into identifying the wrong coat as the one Paine had worn when he was arrested. After needling him to repeat his identification of the coat about four times, until the detective had become irritated and was getting nasty, Aiken blandly produced the *right* coat. Smith backpedaled with a lame excuse about the light being poor; but it was too late, and Aiken had the pleasure of calling attention to his unreliability.

This entire episode is missing in the Pitman compilation.

The testimony of Wermerskirch in Pitman parallels Peterson very closely as far as the information is concerned. He still says Paine "had taken no particular pains to disguise himself," and his first statement that "He was full of mud, up to his knees" is allowed to stand. This reference to the condition of the prisoner's boots (in combination with Sampson's assertion that the boots were "soaking wet") touches on a situation which came up every so often in the War Department's case against the "conspirators." They didn't hesitate, when it suited their purpose, to try to prove that *two* conditions which were in direct contradiction to each other were *both true*. For example, in one phase of their presentation a given defendant might be represented as being stupid beyond belief. In another he would be shown as a very wily, clever individual.

In the instance of Paine's boots, they undertook to show that their condition supported the charge that he had been wandering and hiding in a swamp for three days. At the same time, they contended that the boots he was wearing when arrested were recognized by Seward's house-boy as the same ones the intruder had been wearing the night of the attack—a fine pair, heavy, nearly new, and in excellent condition.

examination of Paine's clothing

It fell to Colonel H. H. Wells of General Augur's staff to make an examination of Paine's clothing after he had been placed aboard the monitor *Saugus*. This officer testified at the Trial on May 19; since his testimony was brief, we shall reproduce it in full as recorded by both Peterson and Pitman, to show their obvious contradiction.

COLONEL H. H. WELLS

Testimony for Prosecution

PETERSON TRANSCRIPT MAY 19
Pages 77-78

EXAMINATION BY JUDGE ADVOCATE HOLT

Q. State to the Court whether you had Payne in your custody on the 19th of April.

A. Yes sir.

Q. State whether you took his clothes off.

A. Yes; I took his coat, pants, vest and all off him on board the monitor.

Q. State whether he had a white shirt on.

A. Yes sir, and an undershirt minus one sleeve; there is a very distinct mark by which they can be recognized; when I described to him his struggle with Seward I said, "I shall find the blood here," and I found it on the coat sleeve and also on the shirt sleeve.

Q. The white shirt?

A. Yes sir. [Then the witness took the shirt, and said, there it is, pointing to the blood stains.] I called his attention to it and said, what do you say now? and he leaned against the side of the boat and said nothing; I also took from him the boots that have been shown in court, and asked him where he got them; he said in Baltimore and that he had worn them three months; I called his attention to the falsehood apparent from their being so little worn, and sent them to the Treasury Department to see if it was possible to ascertain what the time was.

CROSS-EXAMINATION BY MR. DOSTER

Q. You saw the blood on the coat?

A. Yes, on the sleeve.

Q. On the outside?

A. No, on the inside, on the lining of the left arm.

Q. Did you threaten the prisoner at any time?

A. No sir.

Q. Did you not tell him he was a liar?

A. I think I did tell him so several times; I called his attention to the blood on the coat and asked him how the

PITMAN COMPILATION MAY 19
Page 158

I had the prisoner, Payne, in my custody on the *17th* of April, the night of his arrest. He had on a dark-gray coat, a pair of black pants, and something that looked like a skull-cap.

I took off his coat, shirt, pants, vest, and all his clothing the next day on board the monitor. He had on a white linen shirt and a woolen under-shirt, minus one sleeve; *a pair of boots with a broad ink stain on them on the inside.*

[A box containing various articles of clothing was exhibited to the witness.]

These are the articles. There is a distinct mark on them by which I recognize them. I described to the prisoner at the time what I supposed was his position when he committed the assault, and told him I should find blood on the coat-sleeve in the inside. Spots of blood were found in the position I described.

[The witness exhibited the spots referred to.]

I found spots, also, on the white shirt-sleeve. I called Payne's attention to this at the time, and said, "What do you think now?" He leaned back against the side of the boat and said nothing.

[The articles were offered in evidence.]

I asked him where he got his boots. He said he had bought them in Baltimore, and had worn them three months. I called his attention to this falsehood, as it was apparent the boots had only been slightly worn. He made no reply to that.

I took the boots away with me, and sent one of them to the Treasury Department to ascertain, if possible, what the *name* was.

CROSS-EXAMINED BY MR. DOSTER

I did not threaten the prisoner at any time. I think it is very possible I called him a liar. I saw stains of blood on the coat that was brought to me *from Fort Bunker Hill;* I called the prisoner's attention to the fact, and said, "How did that blood come there?" He replied,

blood came there, and he said he did not know how it came there.

Q. How did you know it was blood?

A. Because I saw it.

"It is not blood." I said, "Look and see, and say, if you can, that it is not blood." He looked at it and said, "I do not know how it came there."

The reader will have noticed some internal peculiarities in this testimony, as well as some glaring differences between the two versions. Right at the beginning, we find a difference of opinion between Peterson and Pitman as to the date on which Colonel Wells took custody of the prisoner. The importance of this point is emphasized by Burnett's anxiety to show that Louis Paine was in Wells' hands immediately after his arrest. He attempted to establish that fact not only by changing the date on which Wells *said* he took custody—from April 19 to April 17—but also by altering the testimony of Seward's houseboy, William Bell (which we shall see later), to make sure there was no doubt about it.

There is very good documentary evidence that Colonel Wells was telling the truth in his statement recorded in Peterson—that the prisoner became his responsibility "on the 19th of April." On the eighteenth, as the following document from the National Archives shows, Paine was turned over to the commandant of marines at the Washington Navy Yard:[36]

NAVY YARD, WASHINGTON
April 18th—4½ A.M.

Received of Lieutenant Sharp—one Prisoner—Lewis Paine—:

THOS. Y. FIELD
Major Comdg. Marines

The above Prisoner has been placed in close confinement on board the "Iron-Clad" "*Saugus*"—lying in the stream; and will not be allowed to communicate with anyone, particularly with other prisoners.

THOS. Y. FIELD
Major Comdg. Marines

The reason for Colonel Burnett's desire to show that Wells had taken *immediate* charge of Louis Paine is not readily apparent. It is related to an internal problem of the War Department which must have caused much anxiety for Messrs. Stanton, Holt, Burnett, Bingham, and others for many months after the Trial, if not for the rest of their lives. Lafayette Baker had handed them Louis Paine on a platter and supplied most of the "evidence" with which they had been able to obtain conviction of him and the other seven defendants. By the latter part of 1865, when Pitman's compilation was published, large segments of their case against the "conspirators" were under violent attack from jurists, the political opposition, and the opposition press. The protest against the hanging of Mrs. Surratt was becoming such a hot potato that efforts were already under way to put the full blame for it on Andrew Johnson's doorstep.

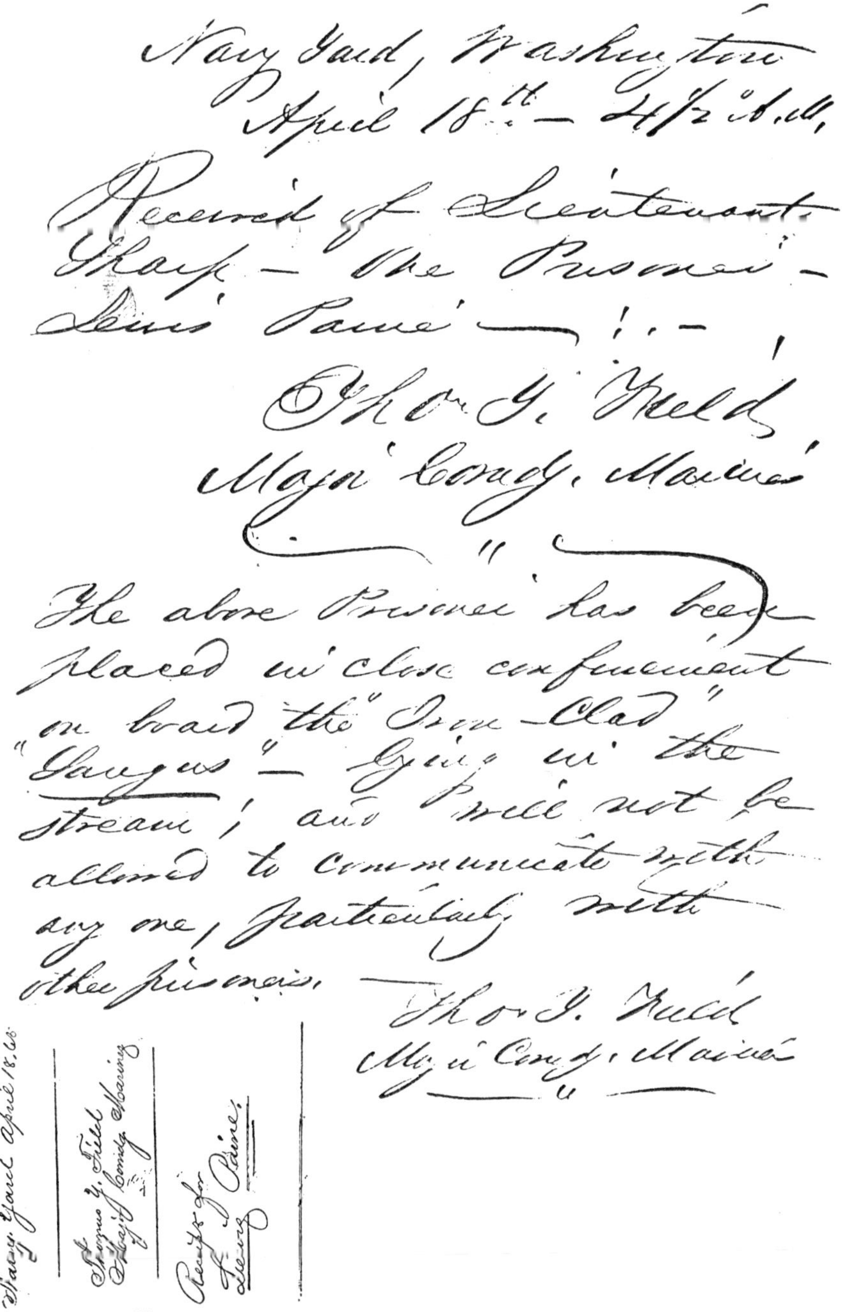

Navy Yard, Washington
April 18th — 2 1/2 A.M.

Received of Lieutenant Sharp — the Prisoner — Louis Paine —!—

Thos. Y. Field,
Major Comdg. Marines

The above Prisoner has been placed in close confinement on board the "Iron-Clad" "Saugus" — lying in the stream; and will not be allowed to communicate with any one, particularly with other prisoners.

Thos. Y. Field
Major Comdg. Marines

Navy Yard April 18, '65

Thomas Y. Field
Major Comdg. Marines

Receipt for Louis Paine.

Fig. 2.–Major Field's Receipt for Paine on the *Saugus*

Also the charges that Jefferson Davis and Confederate leaders had sponsored the "conspiracy" were being questioned openly, not only in the South but by anti-administration politicians in both parties and the northern press.

Within a year the War Department's whole case against the Confederacy would fall to pieces as, one after another, the witnesses to that grandiose pretense would be exposed as paid perjurers engaged by Baker and suborned by the prosecution. One of these star witnesses, Sanford Conover, would be tried and sentenced to the penitentiary.[37]

It is safe to assume that in late 1865 a number of persons in the War Department who had been involved with the Conspiracy Trial had ugly premonitions that an exposure of scandalous methods in one aspect of the Trial might lead to inquiry into their methods in general—a consequence which could bring quite a few top officials into a civil courtroom as defendants, where their infamy would be spread before the whole world.

Anything Burnett could do to shore up the War Department's case against the "conspirators" as seen in retrospect—such as rewriting the "official" record of the Trial—was, from his and his associates' viewpoint, a crying necessity. Baker's ruthless methods were well known to them. They had seen him use them with devastating effect against Confederate sympathizers and opponents of Mr. Lincoln's war policies in the North. They had had firsthand experience with them during the Conspiracy Trial. They knew his penchant for, not to say his pleasure in, artistically conceived blackmail—or to use his term, "entrapment." In brief, he had them over a barrel. None of them would breathe freely until his death under mysterious circumstances on July 3, 1868 (which we shall come to in a later chapter).

It had not been enough to avoid the mention of his name throughout the Trial. It was not enough to omit it from the Pitman transcript. If anything, that had only tended to establish that he had had nothing whatever to do with it—left them no grounds for accusing him of having hoodwinked *them* with perjured witnesses and false, manufactured, and destroyed evidence. The only recourse left to them (Burnett and his associates) was to rewrite the record of the Trial in such a way as to show that Lafayette Baker could have had no *opportunity* to influence its course or to have acquired any information which would contradict the findings of the court martial.

Between Paine's arrest and the date upon which Colonel Wells *said* he took custody of the prisoner and examined his clothing on the ironclad, there was a period of perhaps thirty-six hours during which the young man was *Baker's prisoner*. They had no way of knowing what the detective chief might have learned from him before he stopped talking. He might have given Baker an airtight alibi which had been suppressed without their knowledge to be brought out later with the claim that they had been told about it but had refused to acknowledge it.

Thus Burnett eliminated this inconvenient thirty-six-hour period by the simple means of having the "official" record show Paine in custody of Colonel Wells—not just from 3:00 A.M. on the eighteenth, when he was "identified" by William Bell, but "on the 17th of April, the night of his arrest."

Now we return to the original subject of this section—the examination of Paine's clothing by Colonel Wells.

As mentioned in an earlier chapter, two coats were produced in court: the one Paine was wearing when he was arrested and the one found in the woods northeast of the city, which was believed to have been discarded by Seward's attacker in his flight. Photographs showed the prisoner wearing each of them. The prosecution advanced the theory that the intruder at Seward's had been wearing *both* coats, since it was easier to make the court believe this proposition than that he had been able to acquire a different coat while hiding in the woods for three days. The fact that the prisoner just smiled enigmatically as he tried on both coats at once, and denied nothing, simplified the task of the prosecutors greatly.

In the Peterson version, Colonel Wells doesn't specify which coat he is talking about. But rereading the testimony several times fails to reveal any inkling that the one he referred to was other than one of the garments Paine was wearing when arrested. He says at the opening that he took the prisoner's "coat, pants, vest and all"—and we can only assume these were the clothes he was talking about, and that he had no other coat to examine at that time.

In Pitman a clear reference to the coat found in the woods is tacked onto the last paragraph. This, with the added dialogue—the prisoner's denial that the stains were blood, followed by the statement "I do not know how it came there"—added up to a tacit admission both that the stains were blood and that the coat found in the woods had been his.

In either version, though, Colonel Wells was describing a physical phenomenon in his statements as to the location of the stains. How blood stains on the prisoner's shirt sleeve and "on the inside" of his coat sleeve—on the lining—could have been *anyone's blood but his own,* it is impossible to conceive. Then, in Pitman, mention of blood from the same source—Mr. Seward's wounds—which was also found on the *outside* of the coat found in the woods reduces this testimony to an absurdity.

If the reader will study Colonel Wells' references to the prisoner's boots in the Peterson transcript, he will see that the officer was concerned only with their *newness.* He said he sent them to the Treasury Department "to ascertain what the *time* was"—the length of time they had been worn. It will be noted, too, that he said nothing about the muddy condition Sampson's deposition had mentioned. The boots Colonel Wells examined had either been renovated expertly *or they were not the same boots in which the prisoner had been arrested.*

Pitman's version of this testimony brings in an entirely new factor—an ink smudge on the inside of one boot, which seemed to have been put there to mark out a signature. Pitman quotes the officer as saying he sent this boot to the Treasury Department to ascertain "what the *name* was."

Three officials of the Treasury Department—Messrs. Clark, Jordan, and March—had taken the witness stand *before* Colonel Wells to relate their examination of a boot given them by a Mr. Fields, Assistant Secretary of the Treasury. They said they had removed the ink smudge with oxalic acid and revealed a faint signature which they were reasonably sure read, "J. W. Booth." They did not mention Colonel Wells at all, but said Fields told them the boot had belonged to "Payne." [38]

In their contempt for the defense counsel, the prosecution didn't bother to reconcile the obvious disparity between the statures of Paine and Booth. But it didn't occur to the defense to ask how a man described as a "superbly proportioned giant" could possibly wear the same boots as a man at least six inches shorter. Later, at the Trial of John Surratt, the prosecution introduced some testimony to the effect that John Wilkes Booth's hands and *feet* had been abnormally large—so this point was considered a loose end that needed to be tied up two years later.

From all this it seems rather evident that *someone*—we might as well call him Lafayette Baker—had had time to tamper with Paine's boots in order to establish an evidential association between him and Booth. There is even substantial doubt that the boots placed in exhibit at the Trial were *the same pair Paine was wearing when he was arrested!*

On April 18, Captain D. H. L. Gleason, a fellow employee of Weichmann's in the War Department's Commissary of Prisoners, signed a statement which included this paragraph:[39]

"The pair of boots which were found on the assassin of Secy. Seward [Paine] were shown the witness [Gleason] and he identified them as a pair Mr. Wright [an official in the Commissary] had loaned to Weichmann on Saturday morning. He loaned his boots and a pistol to Mr. Weichman on Saturday morning [April 15] before the other clerks."

So the boots which were shown to Gleason the day after Paine's arrest, and were represented as those he had been wearing when arrested, were really a pair Weichmann had borrowed and left at the boardinghouse when he went to Canada on Monday the seventeenth. They were found by the officers who searched the house in the early hours of the eighteenth. They were shown to Gleason and identified by him on the eighteenth.

Was Paine required to put them on for his examination by Wells on the nineteenth? Or did Baker just substitute them for the prisoner's real boots before they were turned over to the prosecutors as evidence?

A descriptive detail of these boots was mentioned by the dependable Detective Smith when he was called to the witness stand during the Surratt trial to review his recollections of the arrest of Paine two years earlier. He said, "His boots were rather fine, if I remember right; they had red tops."[40]

Why, we may ask, did Smith happen to recall this particular feature of Paine's boots at that late date, although he had not mentioned it when he testified at the Conspiracy Trial? There was a good reason for him to do so, for the objective—one of the objectives—of the prosecution at the Surratt trial was to prove that the War Department's handling of the earlier trial had been above reproach, that the guilt of the defendants had been clearly established, and that the evidence produced against them had been authentic.

One piece of evidence produced by the prosecution at the Conspiracy Trial was such a barefaced fabrication that the defense made bold to express strong objections to the introduction of such obviously counterfeit material. (The objections were overruled, of course.)

This was a cipher letter dated April 15 which a man named Charles Duell (suspected of being a Baker detective) claimed to have found floating near the wharf at Morehead City, North Carolina, on May 1. He mailed it to Secretary of State Seward, who sent it to Judge Holt. The defense called attention to the fact that the paper was very little stained by water and the cipher letters were quite legible, even though it was alleged to have been floating in the harbor for some days.[41]

The letter[42] (see Appendix B, "The Morehead City Letter") was addressed to "Dear John:" and purported to be a message about the assassination and the "conspiracy" behind it, written to some Confederate conspirator and signed "No. FIVE." Along with other penny-dreadful double-talk, it included these sinister phrases:

"I am happy to inform you that Pet has done his work well. He is safe and Old Abe is in hell . . . Red Shoes showed lack of nerve in Seward's case, but fell back in good order. . . ."

Now, the so-called "Morehead City" letter was part of the fabric of falsehood by which the War Department—with Baker's invisible assistance—was undertaking to prove that the Confederacy, John Wilkes Booth, and the eight defendants were all conspirators together in the plot to assassinate Lincoln and other high federal officials. In order to make sure the person called "Pet" in the letter was clearly identified as Booth, the perjurer Sanford Conover testified on May 22[43] that this was the actor's code name among the leaders of the rebel underground in Canada.

"Red Shoes," it seems, was to have been shown as being the code name of the "conspirator" accused of attempting to assassinate Mr. Seward, Louis Paine. But Detective Smith must have forgotten some of his lines and neglected to mention the *red tops* of Paine's boots—the boots *represented* as being Paine's. The best he could do was not to neglect this responsibility the second time around. So he came through, not exactly on cue, two years later at the Surratt trial.

In a case of this kind, where the planning of the crime took place *after* it had been committed and the clues work better in reverse (and lead an investigator to the law enforcement authorities, rather than to the criminals), methods of detection may be expected to seem unconventional, even frivolous, at times. In any other case we would be startled to read Colonel Wells' bland reply to Doster's question, "How did you know it was blood?"

"Because I saw it."

summary of conclusions

Colonel Baker knew all about Booth's activities and associates prior to the assassination. He knew the actual appearance of the man who attacked Seward, and he knew that Louis Paine resembled him.

Louis Paine probably told the truth about himself to the arresting officers.

Paine may have given additional information about himself to Baker or his detectives before he stopped talking, including the item that he had been in Kentucky before arriving in Fauquier County, Virginia.

Mrs. Surratt's false description of Wood and too emphatic denial of knowing Paine make her innocence highly improbable.

Baker's ordering the arrest of Mrs. Surratt indicated he *knew* she was guilty of *something* in connection with the assassination, and could prove it. The metropolitan police, however, had no suspicions of Mrs. Surratt.

John Surratt, as well as Colonel Baker and the War Department, had an interest in keeping the legend of the Booth "conspiracy" intact—suggesting that Surratt knew about and was involved in the plot for which the legend served as a screen.

Stanton's alleged fear that Paine might commit suicide was made a matter of record to make it possible to liquidate Paine if that became necessary.

The Pitman compilation of the Trial proceedings was greatly altered to increase the incrimination of Paine in the testimony regarding his arrest.

Stanton and a number of his subordinates connected with the prosecution, by using the fabricated evidence supplied by Baker and his detectives, became vulnerable to blackmail by the detective chief.

9

witnesses to the crime at Seward's

Three witnesses to the attempted murder of Secretary of State Seward testified at the Conspiracy Trial for the prosecution. These were: William H. Bell, the houseboy who opened the door to the intruder; Sergeant George F. Robinson, the military nurse who was on duty in the sickroom; and Major Augustus H. Seward, eldest son of the victim and an army paymaster.

Newspapers reported that Miss Fanny Seward, daughter of the Secretary, who had been sitting up with her bedridden father (injured in a recent carriage accident), was present in his room and had also identified Payne as his assailant. However, neither Peterson nor Pitman indicates that Fanny was in the room, and she was not called to the witness stand.

Traditional accounts of this affair lead us to believe that the testimony of the witnesses was clear-cut and that all three were in full agreement with each other. The prosecution asserted that the identification of Louis Paine by these people was conclusive beyond all doubt. Although the defense raised some minor questions as to the complete reliability of the testimony, the cross-examination was superficial and didn't impair the War Department's crushing case against the prisoner. If Doster was even aware that interrogation of these people immediately after the crime had prompted the authorities to search for a culprit who wore either a moustache or a goatee or both, his cross-examination did not indicate it.

The statements of the three witnesses, as recorded in Peterson, show some very important differences of opinion among them as to what had actually occurred that night. In each case, their descriptions of the circumstances under which they talked to or struggled with the intruder raise much doubt as to whether any of them saw him clearly enough to know whether or not he wore a moustache. When Seward's physician, Dr. Verdi, took the stand he said he arrived at the house a little before eleven o'clock and found a seriously wounded man in a third-floor bedroom who had not been mentioned in the testimony of these witnesses.

This man's presence in the house and the cause of his injury were never explained by the War Department or anyone else.

Bell, Robinson, and Seward

In addition to the internal discrepancies we find by analysis of the Peterson record, comparison of this with the Pitman compilation brings its usual crop of surprises. For our study of this important phase of the case against Louis Paine, we shall first consider the testimony of Messrs. Bell, Robinson, and Seward, in that order, as Peterson records it—and then study the changes Colonel Burnett thought it necessary to make in the "official" record by Pitman.

William Bell's testimony

per peterson

During the first part of his interrogation young Bell appears to be a very frank and intelligent witness. His answers are simply stated and clear, and his recollections are explicit. Holt's questions do not seem to be calculated to lead the witness in any particular direction, except in one instance:

In his second question, the Judge Advocate tells the witness to "look at the prisoners at the bar and see if you recognize *either* of them."

Now, this could be a mere slip of the tongue or even a stenographic error. Since there were eight prisoners in the dock, the appropriate phrase would be "*any* of them." Even the most collected and articulate person will occasionally use the wrong word inadvertantly and convey a different thought from the one he intended. And just as often the slip is unnoticeable until it is seen in print. However, it is curious that Holt also made the same slip in his opening questions to the *next* witness, Sergeant Robinson.

Peterson's diagram of the seating arrangement in the prisoners' dock shows Paine and Atzerodt seated next to each other, the third and fourth from the right respectively as they faced the court, with a guard standing between and behind them. Holt's use of the word "either," whether he intended to say it or not, gave the witness a choice of *two* men when he pointed out the culprit—rather than a choice of *seven.* The moustached and goateed Atzerodt had been the man the War Department originally thought was the attacker of Secretary Seward. Now the witness was pointing out Louis Paine, who bore not the slightest resemblance to his fellow prisoner in either face or stature.

Under the circumstances Judge Holt may very well have had doubts as to whether such a bald contradiction would escape the notice of

(Continued on page 111)

WILLIAM H. BELL

Testimony for Prosecution

PETERSON TRANSCRIPT MAY 19
Page 72

By Judge Holt

Q. State whether or not on the 14th of April last you were living in the house of Mr. Seward, the Secretary of State, and if so in what capacity?

A. I was in the capacity of a waiter.

Q. Look at the prisoners at the bar, and see if you recognize either of them.

A. *Yes, I recognize that man* [pointing to Paine.]

Q. Did he attempt to come into the house of Mr. Seward on the night of the 14th of April?

A. He did.

Q. State the circumstances connected with his entrance into the house.

A. When he came he rang the bell and I went to the door, and this man came in; he had a little package in his hand, and said it was medicine from Dr. Verdi; he said he was sent by Dr. Verdi with particular directions how he was to take the medicine, and he said he must go up; I told him he could not go up; he then repeated the words over a good while, telling me he must go up, "must see him, must see him." I told him he could not go up, that it was against my orders; that if he would give me the medicine I would tell him how to take it if he would leave me the directions; he said that would not do, and I started to go up, and finding he would go up I started past him and went up the stairs before him; I asked him to excuse me; I thought perhaps he would say that I refused to let him come up. I thought perhaps he might be sent by Dr. Verdi, and that he would tell Mr. Seward that I tried to stop him; he said, "All right;" I noticed that his step was very heavy, and I asked him not to walk so heavy, he would disturb Mr. Seward; he met Mr. Frederick Seward on the steps outside the door, and had some conversation with him in the hall.

Q. If you heard that conversation state it?

PITMAN COMPILATION MAY 19
Pages 154-155

I live at the house of Mr. Seward, Secretary of State, and attend to the door. That man [pointing to the accused, Lewis Payne] came to the house of Mr. Seward on the night of the 14th of April. The bell rang and I went to the door, and that man came in. He had a little package in his hand; he said it was medicine for Mr. Seward from Dr. Verdi, and that he was sent by Dr. Verdi to direct Mr. Seward how to take it. He said he must go up. I told him that he could not go up; then he repeated the words over, and was a good while talking with me in the hall. He said he must go up; he must see him. He talked very rough to me in the first place. I told him he could not see Mr. Seward; that it was against my orders to let any one go up, and if he would give me the medicine and tell me the directions, I would take it up, and tell Mr. Seward how to take it. He was walking slowly all the time, listening to what I had to say. He had his right hand in his coat-pocket, and the medicine in his left. He then walked up the hall toward the steps.

I had spoken pretty rough to him, and when I found out that he would go up, I asked him to excuse me. He said, "O! I know; that's all right." I thought he might, perhaps, be sent by Dr. Verdi, and he might go up and tell Mr. Seward that I would not let him go up, or something of that kind. I got on the steps and went up in front of him. As he went up I asked him not to walk so heavy. He met Mr. Frederick Seward on the steps this side of his father's room. He told Mr. Frederick that he wanted to see Mr. Seward. Mr. Frederick went into the room and came out, and told him that he could not see him; that his father was asleep, and to give him the medicine, and he would take it to him. That would not do; he must see Mr. Seward. He must see him; he

A. He said to Mr. Fred. Seward that he wanted to see Mr. Seward; Mr. Fred. Seward told him that he could not see him; he said that his father was asleep at that time, to give him the medicine and he would take it to his father; that would not do; he said he must see him, he must see him; Mr. Fred. said "you cannot see him, you cannot see him;" he kept on saying he must see him; Mr. Fred. says, "I am the proprietor here; I am Mr. Seward's son; if you cannot leave it with me you cannot leave it at all;" he had a little more talk, and still holding the little package in his hand; Mr. Fred. would not let him see him anyway; he started towards the steps as if to go down, and I started to go down before him; I had gone about three steps, and turned around, saying "do not walk so heavy;" by the time I had turned round he jumped back and struck Mr. Frederick Seward, and by the time I had turned clear around, Mr. Frederick Seward had fallen, and thrown up his hands, then I ran downstairs and called "murder;" I went to the front door and cried murder; then I ran down to General Augur's head-quarters at the corner; I saw no guard there, and ran back; by that time three soldiers had come out of the building and followed me; I had got about half way back to the house when I saw the man run out and get on his horse; he had on a light overcoat, and no hat, but he had on a hat when he came into the house; I had not seen the horse at all before I halloed to the soldiers "there he is getting on his horse;" he got on his horse and started off, and I followed him as far as the corner of I and Fifteen-and-a-half streets; he turned up Vermont Avenue and I lost sight of him there.

Q. Did you see with what he struck Mr. Fred. Seward?

A. I did not exactly see whatever it was; it appeared to be round and wound with velvet; I took it to be a knife afterwards.

Q. How many times did he strike him?

A. I saw him raise his hand twice; I did not wait to see how many times said it in just that way. Mr. Frederick said, "You can not see him." He kept on talking to Mr. Frederick, saying, that he must see him, and then Mr. Frederick said, "I am the proprietor here, and his son; if you can not leave your message with me, you can not leave it at all." Then he had a little more talk there for a while, and stood there with the little package in his hand.

Mr. Frederick would not let him see Mr. Seward no way at all, and then he started toward the step and said, "Well, if I can not see him—" and then he mumbled some words that I did not understand, and started to come down. I started in front of him. I got down about three steps, I guess, when I turned around to him and said, "Don't walk so heavy." Then by the time I turned around to make another step, he had jumped back and struck Mr. Frederick. By the time I could look back, Mr. Frederick was falling; he threw up his hands and fell back in his sister's room; that is two doors this side of Mr. Seward's room. Then I ran down stairs and out to the front door, hallooing "murder," and then ran down to General Augur's head-quarters. I did not see the guard, and ran back again. By that time there were three soldiers who had run out of the building and were following me.

When I got way back to the house, turning the corner there, I saw this man run out and get on his horse. He had on a light overcoat, but he had no hat on when he came out and got on his horse. I did not see his horse when he came to the house, and did not know he had a horse until I saw him get on it. I hallooed to the soldiers, "There he is, going on a horse!" They slacked their running, and ran out into the street, and did not run any more until he got on his horse and started off. I followed him up as far as I Street and Fifteen-and-a-half Street, and he turned right out into Vermont avenue, where I lost sight of him. He rode a bay mare; it was a very stout animal, and did not appear to be a very high horse. He did not go very fast until he got to I Street.

he hit him; he hit him twice and then I ran down stairs.

Q. Did this man say anything as he struck him?

A. When he jumped back again he just said to him, "You," and hit him over the head; that is all I heard him say.

Q. Was Dr. Verdi Mr. Seward's family physician?

A. He was.

Q. Did Payne advise you in talking to you?

A. No, he did not say much to me; he only kept saying "Must see him," and walking very slowly forward all the time.

Q. Had you ever seen this man before that you know of?

A. No, never that I know of.

Q. When you came out did you observe any person about the door or pavement?

A. No sir, no one at all.

Q. You did not observe his horse?

A. I did not see any horse at all.

Q. How far from him were you at any time after he mounted his horse?

A. I might have been as far as from here to that door, about twenty feet.

Q. Did you see the color of the horse?

A. He appeared to be a bay horse, very stout; he did not appear to be a very hardy horse, and did not appear to be going very fast till he got to I street, and then he got away from me altogether.

Cross-examined by Mr. Doster

Q. How old are you?

A. I don't know exactly; I reckon between nineteen and twenty.

Q. How long had you been at Mr. Seward's?

A. Three months.

Q. Have you ever been to school?

A. Yes, four or five years.

Q. Where precisely was this man standing when you had this conversation with him?

A. He was just inside the door.

Q. Did he give you the package of medicine at any time?

A. No he did not hand it to me.

I must have been within twenty feet of him, but at I Street he got away from me altogether.

I do not know what he struck Mr. Frederick Seward with. It appeared to be round, and to be mounted all over with silver, and was about ten inches long. I had taken it for a knife, but they all said afterward it was a pistol. I saw him raise his hand twice to strike Mr Frederick, who then fell. I did not wait any longer, but turned round and went down stairs. When he jumped round, he just said, "You," and commenced hitting him on the head; but I had hardly missed him from behind me until I heard him say that word.

I never saw this man about the door that I know of, nor did I see any person on the pavement when I came out.

Cross-examined by Mr. Doster

I do not know how old I am; I guess I am between nineteen and twenty. I was at school four or five years. I have been at Mr. Seward's nine months, and am second waiter. The talk with the man was inside; he came in and I closed the door. He had a very fine voice.

I noticed his hair and his pantaloons, and I noticed his boots that night. He talked to Mr. Frederick at least five minutes while up there near his father's door, in the third story. He had on very heavy boots at the time, black pants, light overcoat, and a brown hat. His face was very red at the time he came in; and he had very black, coarse hair.

I saw the same boots on him the night they captured him, and the same black pants.

The first time I saw the prisoner after that night was on the 17th of April. They sent for me about 3 o'clock in the morning to go down to General Augur's head-quarters. A Colonel there, with large whiskers and moustache, (Colonel H. H. Wells) asked me to describe this man. I told him he had black hair, a thin lip, very fine voice, very tall, and broad across the shoulders, so I took him to be. There were twenty or thirty gentlemen in the room at the time, and he asked me if any gentleman there had

Q. You say he talked rough to you?

A. He did not talk rough; he had a very fine voice when he came in.

Q. You say you recognize that man as the prisoner at the bar; state what there is about the man that resembles the man you saw that night?

A. I noticed his hair, his pantaloons and his boots; that night he was talking to Mr. Fred. Seward nearly five minutes, he had on very heavy boots, black pants, light overcoat and a brown hat; his face was very red at the time he came in; he had very coarse black hair.

Q. Have you seen the same boots on this man?

A. Yes, the night they captured him.

Q. Have you seen the same clothes on him?

A. I have seen the same pantaloons; he had on black pantaloons.

Q. And would you infer from the fact that he wore black pants that it was the same man?

A. No, I know his face.

Q. What points about his face besides his hair did you notice?

A. I noticed when he talked he kind of raised the corner of his lip and showed a wrinkle in his jaw, as though his teeth were very tight; I knew him the moment I saw him.

Q. Did he talk when you recognized him the first time?

A. He did not talk then, but I noticed the raising of his lip that I had seen when he was talking with me.

Q. When have you seen the prisoner before since the night of the assassination?

A. I saw him on the 17th at General Augur's head-quarters.

Q. How did you happen to go there to see him?

A. They sent for me to the house; Mr. Webster and another gentleman came for me.

Q. What did they say to you?

A. He sent a man up to the room where I was, and asked me to get up; I asked him what they wanted; it was in the night, about two or three o'clock; he said Mr. Webster wanted me; I had been getting up every night since the hair like him, and I told him there was not. He then said, "I will bring a man in here and show him to you." I was leaning down behind the desk so that I could not be seen. The light was then put up, and a good many men walked into the room together. I walked right up to this man, and put my finger right here, (on the lip,) and told him I knew him; that he was the man. Nobody had offered me any money for giving the information, and no threats had been made to me.

When he struck Mr. Frederick Seward, and I ran out, I did not observe any horse; but when I saw him run out of the house, I followed him to I Street; it seems to me he went very slow, because I kept up with him till he got to I Street.

Recalled for the Prosecution—May 19.

[By direction of the Judge Advocate the handcuffs were removed from the prisoner Payne, who put on the dark-gray coat, and over it the white and brown mixed coat, and the hat identified by Colonel Wells.]

When he came to Mr. Seward's he had on that coat, and that is the very same hat he had on; one corner of it was bent down over his eye. He had on a white collar, and looked quite nice to what he looks now. He had the same look as he has now, but he looked pretty fiery out of his eyes at me, the same way he looks now.

(Peterson continued)

thing happened, and I asked him to ask Mr. Webster to come up to my room; I was tired of getting up at night; when I got up and saw Mr. Webster, he told me he wanted me to go down to General Augur's; I went down there; there was a light, very bright, in the Hall at the time; they asked me how light it was at Mr. Seward's that night; I told him it was not light in our hall, that the burner did not give but very little light; they asked me what kind of a looking man the one was who came to see Mr. Seward; I told him he had black hair, thin lips, a fine voice, very tall and broad across the shoulders; there were about twenty or thirty gentlemen in there; they brought in one man and asked me if he was the one, and then brought in another; neither looked like him, and I told them no; they then opened the middle door, and this man came walking in; at the door the light was turned up very bright; as soon as I saw him, I put my finger right on his face, and said, "I know him, that was the man."

Q. Did either of the two men they showed you before look like the man?

A. No, one had moustaches, the other whiskers.

Q. Were they as tall as this man?

A. No, they were short; they didn't look at all like this man.

Q. Had you at that time heard of any reward for the apprehension of the supposed assassin of Mr. Seward?

A. Yes, I had heard of a reward for the different ones, but I had not heard of a reward offered for this one, and have not yet; I saw a bill posted up the next morning from General Augur's head-quarters, offering a reward, but not for this man.

Q. Did any one offer you money before for this man's apprehension?

A. No sir.

Q. Did anyone threaten you?

A. No sir.

Q. When the prisoner struck Mr. Seward and you went down stairs, did you find any soldiers there?

A. No; the passage was free; the door was closed; I went down, opened the door, and kept on down to the corner.

Q. What kind of pace had the horse when he rode away?

A. It seemed as if he went very slow at first, for I kept up with him till he got to I street; then he went off at a rapid rate.

Later the same day William Bell was recalled to the stand. The introduction to the following testimony is part of the Peterson text (page 76):

RE-EXAMINATION OF WILLIAM H. WELLS [BELL] (Colored)

The proceedings of the Court were here delayed by an order from Judge Holt to remove the fetters from the hands of Payne, in order that he might put on both the coats already spoken of in this record. When Payne was unfettered he rose, and there was a hush through the court, as every eye was directed towards him and mingled expressions of admiration and abhorrence could be distinctly heard; abhorrence at his real or supposed crime and admiration for his fine physical development. His face slightly flushed and his lips curled. An involuntary smile revealed the dimples in his cheeks to which the colored boy had alluded in his previous testimony. He first put on the coat of Confederate grey and over it drew the longer cream colored one. The hat was then handed to him and he put it on, and turning towards the young Negro, bent his dark blue eyes searchingly upon him.

Judge Holt then said to the boy—Do you recognize him now?

A. Yes sir; but he had a white collar on, and looked quite nice, and he had one corner of that hat over one eye, turned down like; I tell you his eyes looked pretty fiery; here the boy shook his head as he added, "Oh, he knows me well enough;" in spite of the solemn importance of the words, the homely positiveness of the boy evoked a laugh, to which Payne himself replied by a renewal of his old smile.

---

defense counsel and the opposition press. This accidental use of the word "either" tends to betray the Judge Advocate's uncertainty to the modern student, if not to citizens of that era. In effect, he told Bell to choose between Atzerodt (the suspect "identified" by his original description) and Paine (the suspect he "identified" three days later.)

Doster's cross-examination began to turn up little flaws in the witness's "positive" identification of Paine:

Except for his reference to the intruder's "very red" face and his "coarse black hair"—an odd feature to notice, considering the man had been wearing a wide-brimmed slouch hat—all the distinguishing factors Bell recalled in his *first* answer to the question related to the intruder's clothing. However, when needled by Doster for inferring that Paine was the guilty man because he *also* wore black pants, the witness hastened to declare that he recognized him by his face. It will be recalled that in Sampson's deposition the "black pantaloons" were the *only* feature by which Bell claimed to recognize the prisoner.

Pressed to describe the precise facial characteristic he recognized in Paine, Bell detailed a certain raising of the lip that was noticeable "when he talked." In the next breath he admitted the prisoner had *not talked* when he identified him in Augur's headquarters three nights later.

The witness not only failed to mention the moustache which originally sent the War Department in search of Atzerodt; he now gave a detailed description of a distinctive movement of the suspect's lip, which might have been invisible if he had worn a moustache — as moustaches, in the fashion of that day, were *always* untrimmed and drooped over the upper lip and often the whole mouth.

Next Colonel Doster led the witness into an area of testimony which apparently had not been foreseen in his preparation to testify—for he is suddenly talking very candidly and giving information which the defense, in the more favorable conditions of a civil trial, might have used to discredit his identification altogether: He stated that the light in the hall of Seward's house had been very poor indeed. He revealed that the detectives showed him only *two* other men in addition to the prisoner from whom to identify the guilty man—that one wore a moustache and the other whiskers and, with innocent positiveness, ". . . they didn't look at all like this man."

Finally, he stated that he saw a "bill" posted in Augur's headquarters the *next morning* which offered a reward, ". . . but not for this man."

Until April 20, when the War Department posted its $100,000 reward for Booth, Surratt, and Herold, the *only* offer of a reward had been made in Lafayette Baker's handbill—$30,000 for Booth and "Seward's assassin." It was quite true, as young Bell asserted, that the assailant of the Secretary of State had not been *named.* But by extraordinary coincidence, *every single feature of clothing, figure, or face by which this young man said he recognized Louis Paine as Seward's would-be assassin was also itemized in the description given in Baker's handbill!*

But wait, that is not quite correct. Bell mentioned a *brown hat,* and the handbill did not. The man who attacked Seward lost his *brown hat* in the struggle in the bedroom. It was found there the following morning, and that is where William Bell saw it. When Baker saw Paine in custody at Augur's headquarters he had *no hat*—and therefore none was mentioned in the handbill.

The writer has not found any evidence that Bell received a reward for his part in the conviction of Paine, as did each of Baker's detectives and others. But it may not be necessary to explain William Bell's testimony in terms of financial gain, as was the case with so many prosecution witnesses. The painfully uncertain situation of all members of his race in Washington during the period so soon after the Emancipation Proclamation is quite well known. They were free people by proclamation but were almost universally treated as inferiors whose very features advertised a traditional subservience. Although it was the seat of national government, Washington had been a "southern" community until the Civil War. And Bell must have been fully aware of his novel position, from the traditional southern viewpoint—a Negro testifying against a white man in a criminal case. He was vulnerable to influence.

Sergeant Robinson's testimony per peterson

Sergeant Robinson followed Bell on the witness stand. The cautious nature of his statements gave him the air of an honest man, and he showed a genuine desire to tell the truth, even at the risk of displeasing the prosecution. If his testimony has been construed as a full identification of Paine, this was accomplished by biased interpretation—not by any eagerness of his to finger the guilty party. Not all the state's witnesses were false, it goes without saying, but so many were clearly interested in either money or notoriety, or were lying to save their skins, that an independent-minded one like Sergeant Robinson is noticeable by contrast. Even though he had been a private the night Seward was attacked and now a month later was a sergeant, his promotion didn't seem to be connected with special services rendered to the War Department, as was the case with *General* Baker, *General* Eckert, *Colonel* Smith, and others.

Our particular interest in Sergeant Robinson's testimony will be in its comparison with that of the next witness, Major Augustus Seward. But first we should take notice of a few singular aspects of the nurse's testimony:

The reader who wonders whether Doster was right in his opinion that the assassin's hat was too small for Louis Paine—and why the remark caused laughter in the courtroom—may refer to the photograph (Plate I) which shows the prisoner wearing the hat in question. Slouch hats were, in fact, worn large and low on the head, and this one was definitely on

(Continued on page 116)

SERGEANT GEORGE F. ROBINSON

Testimony for Prosecution

PETERSON TRANSCRIPT MAY 19
Page 73

BY JUDGE HOLT

Q. State whether or not, on the night of the 14th of April last, you were at the residence of William H. Seward, Secretary of State?

A. I was.

Q. In what capacity there?

A. In attendance as nurse upon Mr. Seward.

Q. Look at the prisoners here and see if you can recognize *either* of them as having been at that house that evening?

A. I see one of them who looks like him; the one in his shirt [pointing to Payne].

Q. State the circumstances attending the encounter between the person of whom you speak and Mr. Seward?

A. The first I saw of him I heard a scuffling in the hall; I opened the door to see what the trouble was; as I opened the door he stood close up to it; as soon as it was opened wide enough he struck me and knocked me partially down and then rushed up to the bed of Mr. Seward, struck him and maimed him; as soon as I could get on my feet I endeavored to haul him off the bed and he turned on me; in the scuffle there was a man come into the room who clutched him; between the two of us we got him to the door, or by the door, when he clinched his hand around my neck, knocked me down, broke away from the other man and rushed down stairs.

Q. What did he strike you with?

A. He struck me with his fist the last time; the first time with a knife.

Q. Did he stab you, and if so, where?

A. Yes, here [pointing to about the centre of his forehead].

Q. Did he say anything when he struck you?

A. He did not that I heard.

Q. Did he pass immediately to the bed of Mr. Seward when he first knocked you down?

PITMAN COMPILATION MAY 19
Pages 155-156

On the 14th of April last I was at the residence of Mr. Seward, Secretary of State, acting as attendant nurse to Mr. Seward, who was confined to his bed by injuries received from having been thrown from his carriage. One of his arms was broken and his jaw fractured.

That man [pointing to the accused, Lewis Payne] looks like the man that came to Mr. Seward's house on that Friday night. I heard a disturbance in the hall, and opened the door to see what the trouble was; and as I opened the door this man stood close up to it. As soon as it was opened, he struck me with a knife in the forehead, knocked me partially down, and pressed by me to the bed of Mr. Seward, and struck him, wounding him. As soon as I could get on my feet, I endeavored to haul him off the bed, and then he turned upon me. In the scuffle, some one [Major Seward] came into the room and clinched him. Between the two of us we got him to the door, or by the door, and he, unclinching his hands from around my neck, struck me again, this time with his fist, knocking me down, and then broke away from Major Seward and ran down stairs.

I saw him strike Mr. Seward with the same knife with which he cut my forehead. It was a large knife, and he held it with the blade down below his hand. I saw him cut Mr. Seward twice that I am sure of; the first time he struck him on the right cheek, and then he seemed to be cutting around his neck. I did not hear the man say any thing during this time.

I afterward examined the wounds, and found one cutting his face from the right cheek down to the neck, and a cut on his neck, which might have been made by the same blow, as Mr. Seward was partially sitting in bed at the time; and another on the left side of the neck.

A. He did.

Q. Did you see him strike Mr. Seward?

A. *I did.*

Q. With the same weapon he struck you with?

A. Yes.

Q. How often?

A. I saw him cut twice.

Q. Did he seem to be cutting at his head or where?

A. He struck beyond the head and neck the first time; then he struck him in the neck.

Q. Describe how he held the knife?

A. He held it in this way [raising the hand which held the knife, pointing downwards].

Q. Did it seem to be a large knife?

A. It did.

Q. Did he say anything at all after stabbing him?

A. Not that I heard.

Q. Did you observe the wound that had been inflicted?

A. I did.

Q. Look at this knife and see if it is the same one held in his hand?

A. It was about the length of that. It looked as though it might not be as wide as that, but I only saw it in motion.

Q. Describe the character of the wounds inflicted on Mr. Seward?

A. There was one cutting his face down on the left side, and another one cutting his neck below. I think they were both made by the same blow. He was sitting partially up in bed at the time, his head reclining so that the same blow might have made both. The other cut was on the opposite side of the neck. There were three wounds in all. It was all bloody when I saw it. I do not know but there may have been more.

Q. Was Mr. Seward in his bed at the time?

A. He was.

Q. From what cause?

A. He had been thrown from his carriage.

Q. Were his limbs broken?

A. I was told that one of his arms was broken and his jaw fractured.

Q. While striking him did Mr. Those were all I noticed, but there may have been more, as it was all bloody when I saw it. Mr. Seward received all his stabs in bed; but after the man was gone, and I went back to the bed, I found that he had rolled out, and was lying on the floor.

I did not see Mr. Frederick Seward down on the floor; the first I saw of him was after the man was gone, when I came back into the room he was inside the door, standing up. The man went down stairs immediately after he unwound his arm from round my neck, and struck me with his fist. I did not see him encounter Major Seward.

After he was gone we picked up a revolver, or parts of one, and his hat.

[A slouch felt hat was exhibited to the witness.]

I should judge that to be the hat; it looks like the one found there.

[A revolver was exhibited to the witness.]

That is the revolver picked up; I did not see this part, [the ramrod, which was disconnected.]

[The hat and revolver were both offered in evidence.]

[At the request of the Court, the guard was directed to place the hat on the head of the prisoner, Payne, to see if it fitted him or not, which was done, Payne smiling pleasantly. It was found to fit him.]

Recalled for the Prosecution—
May 19.

[The accused, Lewis Payne, clad in the coat and vest in which he was arrested, and the hat found at Mr. Seward's, was directed to stand up for recognition.]

He looks more natural now than he did before. I am not sure about it, but I think that is the man that came to Secretary Seward's house on the night of the 14th of April, a little after 10 o'clock. The pistol that was picked up in the room after he left was loaded. I examined it.

Seward get out of his bed or remain in bed?

A. He remained and received the stabs in bed.

Q. Did he during the struggle roll from the bed or remain in bed?

A. He rolled out after we had left the bed; when I came back I found he was lying on the floor.

Q. You say that this man, during the whole of this bloody work, made no remark at all; that he said nothing?

A. I did not hear him make any remark.

Q. When he came out of the room had Frederick Seward risen from the floor, or was he still lying?

A. I did not see Mr. Frederick Seward around at all.

Q. Where was he when this man came out?

A. The first I saw of Mr. Frederick was in the room standing up; he had come inside the door.

Q. You say he knocked you down when he came into the room; what did he strike you with?

A. I suppose with a knife; he struck me the last time with his fist, he had his arm around my neck and let go and struck me.

Q. Did he immediately go down stairs?

A. He did.

Q. Did you see his encounter with Major Seward?

A. I did not see that.

Q. After he left was anything picked up which he left behind?

A. There was a revolver and his hat.

Q. Look at this revolver and see if you recognize it as the one he left?

A. I should judge it was; I did not notice this in it (pointing to the rammer).

Q. I understand the Mr. Seward you

(Peterson continued)

speak of to be the Secretary of State, and the house you speak of to be in Washington city?

A. Yes sir.

Q. Do you recognize this as the hat that was picked up?

[A light-brown felt slouch hat was shown. General Wallace requested that the hat produced might be tried on Payne. It was handed to Payne's guard, who placed it on his head to the evident amusement of Payne himself.]

General Wallace said, "Does it fit loosely?" The guard replied, "No, it fits tight."

Mr. Doster, [Payne's counsel], "It is too small for him, I should say," [laughter.]

After Bell had identified the prisoner in the two coats, Sergeant Robinson was also recalled to the stand.

RE-EXAMINATION OF MR. ROBINSON

While this witness was being looked for the Judge Advocate-General said, I wish this witness also to see the prisoner in his present dress, that he may give his opinion as to whether it is the same man or not. Having taken the stand Mr. Robinson said he is more like the man than he was before; I should think that he is, but yet I am not sure about it.

Q. You didn't state precisely the hour when this stabbing occurred, in your previous examination?

A. It was not far from 10 o'clock.

Q. Was it before or after 10?

A. I think it might be after.

Q. Do you know whether the pistol that was picked up there was loaded or not?

A. It was loaded.

Q. Did you examine it?

A. Yes sir.

---

the small side for Louis Paine. Even a century later it may be evident why the fit of the hat and Doster's comment caused laughter in the courtroom, why even the prisoner smiled at this obvious contradiction of the state's claims.

We see from the Judge Advocate's line of questioning here that he was much more interested in bringing out the bloody details of an attack upon an invalid than he was in learning how sure Sergeant Robinson was that Paine was really the culprit. The witness being a nurse, it was logical to ask him to tell about the nature of the wounds. But he had only stated that the prisoner "looks like" the same man. Some further questions on this subject were in order—from Colonel Doster, if not from Holt. The witness had not and did not describe the intruder's features or clothing *at all*.

When both Bell and Robinson were recalled to the stand later in the day to see the prisoner in the coats and hat Seward's assailant was believed to have worn on the night of the crime, each followed the line he had taken earlier: Bell was *more* sure; Robinson was *less* certain than before.

Paine was arrested upon identification by Seward's houseboy *only*. The following day, when Baker had already set the wheels of incrimination in motion, Major Seward identified the prisoner on the *Saugus* —or so he claimed.

Sergeant Robinson did not even see Paine until two weeks later, on May 4. It was a letter from Major Seward to Colonel Burnett[1] on May 3 which suggested that Robinson be shown the prisoner, as he "has sufficiently recovered from his wounds to leave the hospital" and "I think will prove an important witness." Burnett arranged his visit to the *Saugus* on the fourth.

Now, this nurse's wounds, according to his own testimony as to their nature and his condition immediately after the struggle, were greatly exaggerated in the press, partly due to the wording of Stanton's wires. But Major Seward's letter also seemed inclined to leave the impression that Robinson's wounds were serious and that he had been hospitalized for two weeks.

In the following section we shall find evidence that the Major expected the nurse's testimony to be much different from what it was when he suggested calling him as a witness. But the Sergeant's promotion before the Trial apparently didn't persuade him to relate anything other than the truth as he remembered it.

Judge Holt's persistence in trying to find out if Robinson had heard the stranger *say anything* during the struggle—he asked about it three times—has a bearing on Major Seward's testimony, which we shall look at next. The heavy sarcasm of his question as to whether Robinson was talking about the Mr. Seward who was Secretary of State and a house located in the city of Washington will also be more understandable when we have heard from the next witness.

Major Seward's testimony per peterson

According to the Peterson version, Major Augustus Seward took the stand as soon as Robinson left it on May 19. But Pitman has the Major appearing on the following Friday, a week later, May 26. Pitman has the various testimonies grouped by their connection with the cases of individual defendants—rather than chronologically, as in Peterson—and has Major Seward's follow directly after Sergeant Robinson's in his text. If he had separated the two men's recitals so they wouldn't be read in order, the reason for changing the date might be evident. But he did not, so we simply mention this oddity without trying to explain it.

The details of the attack on Secretary of State Seward are ordinarily omitted from textbook accounts of the incident. But the whole dramatic situation surrounding the assassination of President Lincoln—of which this was an exciting episode—has been retold in books for popular reading many times. The basic elements of the affair at the Seward house have, more often than not, been embellished with the writer's interpolation of what is known from the testimony of Bell, Robinson, and Augustus Seward in order to increase the readability for those more interested in a drama of violence than in historical exactness.

contradictions among the three witnesses per peterson

In general, the modern version of this incident follows these lines: The stranger was admitted by Bell and started upstairs over the servant's protest. He met Frederick Seward at the top of the flight and pistol-whipped him into unconsciousness when denied entrance to the sick-room. He then rushed into the room and fell upon Mr. Seward, stabbing at him furiously until pulled off by Sergeant Robinson and Major Seward. He turned upon these two with his knife, stabbing or slashing both men seriously before he broke away and ran downstairs. Some versions say he met a State Department messenger, Mr. Emrick W. Hansell, at the foot of the stairs and plunged the knife into his chest simply because he was in the way. Other versions omit any reference to Hansell. Out in the street he mounted a horse—which we are told was left there by David Herold, who was to have waited to guide the assailant southward by the same route Booth took—and rode off without haste, heading northward by mistake.

The reader has probably noticed that Bell's story, or Robinson's, or

(Continued on page 121)

MAJOR AUGUSTUS H. SEWARD

Testimony for Prosecution

PETERSON TRANSCRIPT MAY 19
Pages 73-74

Examined by Judge Holt

Q. State whether you are the son of William H. Seward, Secretary of State?

A. I am his son.

Q. Were you or were you not at his home on the night of the 14th of April last?

A. I was.

Q. Will you state whether or not that night any one of the prisoners at the bar made his appearance at that house?

A. *Yes, I saw this large man who has no coat on* [Payne.]

Q. State the circumstances attending your meeting with him that evening?

A. I retired to bed about 7 o'clock on the night of the 14th, with the understanding that I would be called at 11 o'clock, to set up with my father; I very shortly fell asleep, and so remained until wakened by the screams of my sister; I jumped out of bed and ran into my father's room in my shirt and drawers; the gas in the room had been shut down rather low, and I saw what appeared to be two men, one trying to hold the other; my first impression was that my father had become delierious, and that the nurse was trying to hold him. I went up and took hold of him, but saw at once from his size and the struggle that it was not my father; it then struck me that the nurse had become delierious and was striking about the room at random; knowing the delicate state of my father's health, I endeavored to shove the person I had hold of to the door, with the intention of putting him out of his room; while I was pushing him he struck me five or six times over the head with whatever he had in his left hand; I supposed it at the time to be a bottle or a decanter he had seized from the table; during this time he repeated with an intensely strong voice "I am mad, I am mad;" on reaching the hall he gave a sudden turn and breaking

PITMAN COMPILATION MAY 26
Pages 156-157

I am the son of the Hon. William H. Seward, Secretary of State, and was at his home in this city on the night of the 14th of April last. I saw that large man, with no coat on, [pointing to the accused, Lewis Payne], at my father's house that night.

I retired to bed at half-past 7 on the night of the 14th, with the understanding that I was to be called about 11 o'clock to sit up with my father. I very shortly fell asleep, and so remained until awakened by the screams of my sister, when I jumped out of bed and ran into my father's room in my shirt and drawers. The gas in the room was turned down rather low, and I saw what appeared to me to be two men, one trying to hold the other at the foot of my father's bed. I seized by the clothes on his breast the person who was held, supposing it was my father, delirious; but, immediately on taking hold of him, I knew from his size and strength it was not my father. The thought then struck me that the nurse had become delirious sitting up there, and was striking about the room at random. Knowing the delicate state of my father, I shoved the person of whom I had hold to the door, with the intention of getting him out of the room. While I was pushing him, he struck me five or six times on the forehead and top of the head, and once on the left hand, with what I supposed to be a bottle or decanter that he had seized from the table. During this time he repeated, in an intense but not strong voice, the words, "I'm mad! I'm mad!" On reaching the hall he gave a sudden turn, and sprang away from me, and disappeared down stairs.

When near the door of my father's room, as I was pushing him out, and he came opposite where the light of the hall shown on him, I saw that he was a very large man, dark, straight hair,

away from me, disappeared down stairs; while in the vicinity of the door of my father's room, as I was pushing him out, when he came opposite the light in the hall it shone on him, and I saw him distinctly; I saw that he was a very large man, with dark straight hair, smooth face and no beard; I noticed the expression of his countenance; I then went into my room and got my pistol which had to be taken out of the bottom of my carpet bag; I then went down stairs, intending to shoot the person if he attempted to return; while standing at the door the servant boy came back and said the man had ridden off on horseback; I then realized for the first time that the man was an assassin who had entered the house for the purpose of murdering my father.

Q. Did you then return to your father's room?

A. I suppose it was five minutes before I got back; there was quite a crowd collected at the door; I sent for a doctor, and made arrangements to keep the crowd out; it may not have been three minutes.

Q. State whether you examined the number and character of the wounds given your father and brother, Mr. Fred. W. Seward?

A. No, I did not examine them that night; I was beaten very badly myself. I found when I got up stairs again; after my father's wounds had been dressed and after my arm had been bandaged, I went in and saw my father; he had one very large gash on his right cheek, besides a cut on his throat, on the right side, and one under his left arm; I did not examine my brother's wounds; I did not know that night how badly he was hurt; the next day he was insensible and so remained, and it was four or five days before I saw what his wounds were.

Q. What did you then discover?

A. There were two wounds about here [pointing to the left side of the head, over the ear]; after the piece of the skull had been taken out it left the brain exposed.

smooth face, no beard, and I had a view of the expression of his countenance. I then went into my room and got my pistol. It may possibly have taken me a minute, as it was in the bottom of my carpetbag, to find it. I then ran down to the front door, intending to shoot the person, if he attempted to return. While standing at the door, the servant boy came back and said the man had ridden off on a horse, and that he had attacked the persons in the house with a knife. I then realized for the first time that the man was an assassin, who had entered the house for the purpose of murdering my father.

I suppose it was five minutes before I went back to my father's room. Quite a large crowd came around the door; I sent for the doctors, and got somebody to keep the crowd off before I went up to his room. It might not have been five minutes, but certainly three, before I got back; I think nearer five.

I was injured pretty badly myself, I found when I got up stairs again. After my father's wounds were dressed, I suppose about an hour, and after my own head had been bandaged, I went in and saw my father, and found that he had one very large gash on his right cheek, near the neck, besides a cut on his throat on the right-hand side, and one under the left ear. I did not examine my brother's wounds; in fact, I went into his room but for a short time that night. I did not know how badly hurt he was. The next day he was insensible, and so remained; and it was four or five days before I saw what his wounds were. I found then that he had two wounds, one on the scalp, that was open to the brain, and another one over the ear. After the pieces of fractured skull were taken out, it left the covering of the brain open. It was such a wound that I should have supposed could have been made with a knife, but the surgeons seemed to think it was made by the hammer of a pistol. I heard that a pistol was picked up in the house, but I did not see it. I saw the hat that was found, and think I should recognize it.

Q. Had he received any stab at all from the knife?

A. I never saw anything of my brother during the whole time.

Q. Did a wound indicate that a knife had been used?

A. I thought myself it was done by a knife, but the surgeon seemed to think it was done by the hammer of a pistol; it was such a wound as I would have supposed might have been done with a knife.

Q. Did you see a pistol picked up in that room?

A. I did not; I know there was one picked up.

Q. Did you see any article of clothing?

A. Yes; a hat.

Q. Would you recognize it? [producing a hat].

A. Yes, I am quite certain that is the hat; I saw the hat after it had been picked up and put in a bureau drawer; it was taken out and shown to me the next day; I did not see it that night.

Q. And you say you supposed it to have been the nurse?

A. Yes; I had no idea who the man was until he was out of the house.

Q. You say that you were struck with a knife?

A. The surgeons think it was with a knife I was struck with; I supposed at the time it was with a bottle or a decanter; that the nurse had become delierious and was striking at random.

Q. *Do you feel entirely satisfied that the person at the bar is the same man?*

A. *I do.*

Cross-examined by Mr. Doster

Q. Be good enough to state whether this is the first time you have seen the prisoner since he was taken?

A. No; I saw him on board the monitor the day after he was taken.

Q. Did you identify him then?

A. Yes.

[A slouch felt hat was exhibited to the witness.]

I am quite certain that is the hat. I did not see it the night it was picked up, but the next day it was taken out of the bureau-drawer, where it had been put the night before, and shown to me.

The surgeons think it was a knife with which I was struck, and after the servant boy told me what the man had been doing, I supposed so myself, though at the time I thought I was being struck with a bottle or a decanter. Not having any idea that it was a man with a knife, I did not think any thing about it.

I feel entirely satisfied that the prisoner at the bar, Payne, is the same man that made the attack on that night.

Cross-examined by Mr. Doster

This is not the first time I have seen the prisoner since the attack; I saw him on board the monitor the day after he was taken. He was brought up on deck of the monitor, and I took hold of him the same way I had hold of him when I shoved him out of the room, and I looked at his face, and he had the same appearance, in every way, that he had the few moments that I saw him by the light in the hall; his size, his proportions, smooth face, no beard, and when he was made to repeat the words, "I'm mad! I'm mad!" I recognized the same voice, varying only in the intensity.

. . . .

(Peterson continued)

Q. Please state the circumstances.

A. He was brought up on the monitor; I took hold of him the same way I did in the room, and looked up in his face; he had the same features, with his size, his proportions, his swarthy face, and no beard that I noticed, and when he was made to repeat the words, "I am made, I am mad," I recognized the same voice, varying only in intensity.

Major Seward's, when read separately, tends to support this version on its major points—though none of them says a word about Hansell nor even hints that there were more than four men, counting Secretary Seward, who were involved in the encounter with the stranger.

When we compare their testimonies, however—particularly those of Robinson and Major Seward—the picture suddenly becomes very confused. The former relates that he was practically run over by the intruder when he went to open the door. When he picked himself up and struggled with the man who was slashing at his patient, *another man* came into the room and helped him drag the attacker to the door, where he broke away and ran downstairs.

He states clearly, without any possibility of misunderstanding his meaning, *that he did not see Major Seward at all* and that he *"did not see Mr. Frederick Seward around at all."*

To Holt's next question as to where Fred Seward was when "this man" came out, the sergeant was even more specific: "The first I saw of Mr. Frederick was in the room standing up; he had come inside the door."

Major Seward, on the other hand, didn't mention the presence of *anyone* in the room other than his father and the shadowy figure he dragged from the bed and, *singlehanded,* "pushed" out the door. He not only failed to acknowledge that Robinson was there and helped eject the stranger; he stated, and then restated, *that he thought it was "the nurse" with whom he was struggling.* He continued to think it was the nurse until he got down to the front door, after stopping in his room to get a pistol.

With regard to his brother, Frederick—who was said to have been beaten unconscious in the hallway in front of the sick room, and whose insensible body must therefore have been lying on the floor near the door —Major Seward said, *"I never saw anything of my brother during the whole time."* He volunteered this information, not in answer to a question as to where his brother was at a particular moment, but in reply to Holt's inquiry whether Frederick had been stabbed with the intruder's knife.

Another obvious contradiction is seen in the Major's repeated statement that the attacker had said, "I am mad, I am mad," in an "intensely strong voice." But Robinson answered Holt's direct question *three* times that he had not heard the man say *anything.*

The reason for Judge Holt's sarcastic remark to Sergeant Robinson—was he talking about the same event Major Seward was going to describe when he took his turn on the witness stand?—begins to come into focus. *All* the prosecution witnesses had previously been interrogated by some official of the War Department, though not necessarily by Holt himself. He was not in the dark as to what each would testify in general. But the impromptu questions he was asking the nurse were bringing out some contradictions to what he *knew* to be the Major's version. Major Seward said *he* had ejected the intruder from the sickroom, thinking he was struggling with Robinson. But Robinson said he had seen *nothing* of Major Seward while *he* was ejecting the stranger.

So there Holt was—and here we are—with only two witnesses to the event in question, and these two in radical disagreement with each other. In a civil court, Holt and the War Department would have been on thin ice. It is almost unthinkable that the defense (one which had not been intimidated, overruled, and nearly silenced by the prosecution's brass-knuckled methods) would fail to force a showdown on the two conflicting testimonies and find out which of the witnesses was lying, or if *either* of them was competent to give evidence that Lewis Paine was the man who perpetrated the crime.

The Judge Advocate's method of getting off the horns was simple, effective, and characteristic of the prosecution's standing procedure. He ignored the contradictions. It was up to the defense to point them out anyway, and his confidence that the defense would not do so was not misplaced. As far as any public or newspaper reaction was concerned, there was a subtle force working in Judge Holt's favor. As between the son of the Secretary of State, an officer and a gentleman, and a lowly private (who had a telling additional count against him), the word of the former carried the greater weight by far. If there were any disagreement between their two accounts, Robinson would have to be mistaken.

If the nurse had anything at stake, anything to gain by pleasing the prosecutors, he didn't make much effort to protect his interests. Holt gave him three chances to recollect that perhaps the intruder had said something or other, but he hadn't heard it clearly in the confusion. If he hoped for a share in the rewards Baker had offered for Seward's assailant—and as one of only four or five persons who might be able to identify Paine as the culprit, he was surely in line—his effort to qualify was certainly halfhearted. He said only that Paine "looked like" the man. When he was recalled to the stand to see the prisoner in the coat and hat on exhibit, he was much less positive.

The War Department, via Stanton's wires from the Peterson house to General Dix, had said "the attendant" (presumably Robinson) had been carved up so badly he wasn't expected to live. But the sergeant was inclined to minimize his injuries. If he, as an enlisted man, were loath to share the credit for ejecting the intruder with an officer, who perhaps had arrived late or not pushed so hard as he had, it would be understandable. But it would be folly to leave the Major out of his story altogether and risk being exposed as a liar—*unless it were true that the Major had really not appeared on the scene.*

Robinson, remember, did not deny the Major could have had an encounter with the man outside the room—which could account for the wound on his arm. He simply said he had not seen it.

Major Seward's testimony is not so readily analyzed.

By omitting Robinson from the struggle in the bedroom, where Robinson's duties as nurse obliged him to be, the Major tended to contradict an established fact. True, the nurse *could* have been cowering in a corner. But then he would have had no wound on his forehead to point to; the first reports from Stanton would not have given him the lion's share of the credit; and his cowardice in not leaping to the defense of his patient would surely have brought him disgrace, if not a court martial.

Then there is the Major's claim that he thought he was wrestling with the "delirious" nurse through the whole course of the incident. He tells how he "shoved" the man toward the door, during which effort he was struck "five or six times over the head with whatever he held in his left hand."

The weapon in the intruder's hand during his alleged struggle with Major Seward was the knife with which he had stabbed the victim in the bed. Sergeant Robinson stated that the man clutched his throat with his free hand; the knife was found out in the street the next day. So the intruder must have dropped the revolver—which was found on the same floor later—*before* he attacked Seward.

Consequently, since the weapon would have to have been the knife, Major Seward should have had more wounds than one cut on the arm after "five or six" blows he said he received on the head. And how could the intruder be clutching Robinson with one hand and punching him and at the same time be cutting at Major Seward with a knife?

The Major related that as they came opposite the light in the hall, "I saw him distinctly." In the previous sentence he had said that on reaching the hall, the man ". . . gave a sudden turn and breaking away from me, disappeared down stairs." But, we'll take his word for it that he had a distinct view of the man's face as he made that "sudden turn." We'll accept his statement that he saw a man with "dark straight hair, smooth face and no beard." We'll note his precise words—"I noticed the expression of his countenance."

For the sake of the reputation of Major Augustus H. Seward, it would have been better if he had said it was too dark to see the man's face. For his own words put a question mark after his testimony and negate his identification of Paine!

The Major said he thought the man was the nurse until he was out of the house and gone. A detail about Sergeant Robinson was never mentioned at the Trial, yet one recent historian of this incident stated it positively:[2] Sergeant George F. Robinson was a Negro.

Is it possible that Major Seward could have seen the intruder closely and clearly enough to notice "the expression on his countenance" without perceiving that he was not a Negro, let alone that he was not the nurse?

The only circumstances under which Major Seward could have been telling the truth would have been if Sergeant Robinson resembled Louis Paine to such a remarkable degree that one could be easily mistaken for the other. The possibility that this was the case is so remote that it is hardly worth considering. Such a phenomenon would surely have aroused comment among reporters and observers of the Trial. Louis Paine's features in all twelve of the photographs of him this writer has seen are clearly Caucasian; his complexion is not noticeably dark. It is not impossible that the Sergeant's complexion was light, but it is improbable that his hair was long and straight. In any case, if Major Seward had mistaken him for Paine, he would not have been the only one, and the prosecution, rather than ignoring the coincidence, would have hastened to point it out as a condition which strongly supported the Major's statements.

Major Seward's gratuitous statement that he had seen nothing of his brother, Frederick, "during the whole time" adds a further complication to his story.

William Bell said the young man was struck down on the landing at the top of the stairs. When Dr. Verdi arrived at a little before eleven, he found Frederick prostrate and unable to articulate, though not yet lapsed into the long coma which appears to have occurred later. Surgeon General Barnes also arrived twenty minutes later, but he testified that he found Frederick "insensible." From statements such as these, we get the impression of the unfortunate young man lying prostrate in the hallway, where the Major would have almost tripped over him on his way to the father's room.

But Sergeant Robinson says the first he saw of Mr. Frederick was when he *walked* into the sickroom after the intruder had run out. So now we picture Frederick struggling to his feet and lurching toward his father's room. How could his brother have failed to notice him when *he* ran out? The light in the hall was strong enough, the Major said, to give him a good view of the stranger's countenance. And even if he didn't notice Frederick on the way out, he testified that he came back to the room in five minutes or less, in which case he would have seen his brother *in* the room.

Before eleven o'clock three or more surgeons had examined Frederick Seward and reported his desperate condition to Stanton and Secretary of the Navy Welles when they arrived.[3] By about 2:30 A.M. General Dix and the Associated Press in New York had the War Secretary's report that Mr. Seward's younger son was not expected to live.

But Major Seward testified, "I did not know that night how badly he was hurt." Everyone else in the house knew, and people as far away as New York. Wasn't *anyone* talking to Major Seward?

The reports of the various individuals who hastened to the Seward house within the first hour after the attack offer a tentative explanation as to why Major Seward remained the only one uninformed about his brother's grave wounds: *Nobody saw him*.

Gideon Welles recorded the event in his diary and only mentioned seeing the father and Frederick, both prostrate and bloody in adjoining rooms. Stanton came in and made inquiries of his own; then he went to the Peterson house in the same carriage with Welles to attend the President.[4]

Stanton may or may not have had any additional information on the situation at Seward's when he sent his first wire to General Dix at 1:30 A.M. In it he said *nothing* about Major Seward. In fact he related an account of the attack that differed from those of both Bell and Major Seward, though it agreed with Sergeant Robinson's very closely. He said the noise of the scuffle in the sickroom ". . . alarmed Mr. Frederick Seward, who was in an adjoining room, and hastened to the door of his father's room, where he met the assassin, who inflicted upon him one or more dangerous wounds." [5]

Now, Stanton was on the scene very shortly after the attack. In his first wire he was evidently reporting the event just as it had been related to him personally. His version of what happened, particularly since it supported the statements of the most reliable of the three Seward witnesses, can't be ignored. And Major Seward didn't figure in it at all.

In his 3:00 A.M. telegram Mr. Stanton told General Dix, "The attendant who was present was stabbed through the lungs, and is not expected to live." Then he added, "The wounds of Major Seward are not serious."

It's apparent the "attendant" the War Secretary referred to was not Robinson—though Robinson *was* the attendant. It also appears that Stanton, just since his last telegram, had learned that Major Seward was in the house during the attack on his father.

Surgeon General Barnes testified to what he found when he went to the Seward mansion. In the Peterson version, he stated he saw only Mr. Seward and his son, Frederick: ". . . the rest of the family I did not see." [6]

Pitman's transcript quotes these exact words from the Surgeon General. But in the last paragraph of his testimony a sentence is inserted which contradicts this statement: "I saw Major Seward in the room." [7]

So Colonel Burnett thought it necessary to make *sure* Major Seward was included in the cast of characters when he edited the testimony of Surgeon General Barnes.

the mystery of Emrick Hansell

All of which brings us to the puzzling case of Mr. Emrick W. Hansell, who was counted among the casualties but *not* among the participants in the fight at Seward's.

One of the more curious aspects is that the Pitman version—though making no effort to explain Mr. Hansell's presence in the house, or the circumstances under which he was injured, described the gentleman's wound in much more detail than Peterson. The testimony in which this information was given was that of Dr. T. S. Verdi, the Seward family physician.

Peterson recorded the doctor's statement on Hansell as follows: [8] "I found Mr. Hansell, a messenger of the State Department, lying on a bed, wounded by a cut in the side some two and a half inches deep."

In Pitman, the wound is apparently the same, but Dr. Verdi is more graphic and detailed in telling of his examination: [9]

> I found Mr. Emrick W. Hansell on the same floor with Mr. Seward, lying on a bed. He said he was wounded. I undressed him, and found a stab over the sixth rib, from the spine obliquely toward the right side. I put my fingers into the wound to see whether it had penetrated the lungs. I found that it had not, but I could put my fingers probably two and a half inches or three inches deep. Apparently there was no internal bleeding. The wound seemed to be an inch wide, so that the finger could be put in very easily and moved all around. It was bleeding then, very fresh to all appearances; probably it was not fifteen or twenty minutes since the stab had occurred.

This elaboration of the doctor's testimony—with particular mention that the wound had been inflicted *fifteen or twenty minutes before he examined it*—seems to be somehow related to an alteration made at the beginning of Verdi's recital in Pitman. In Peterson he wasn't sure when he had been called to the house, but thought it was "perhaps *a little before eleven* . . ." In Pitman, he said he was summoned "about half-past 10 o'clock, perhaps a little sooner."

Peterson said *nothing* about the timing of Hansell's wound. But Pitman (presumably by virtue of Burnett's editing) rewrote the testimony to make sure the reader understood that the wound was inflicted a little *before* 10:15 P.M., the approximate time when the intruder rang the doorbell.

Burnett's care to show Hansell was wounded very early in the episode—before 10:15—also implies that he would have us believe the stabbing of the messenger *preceded* the assassin's entrance at the front door. In other words, he was attacked out in the street.

As we shall see when we compare Peterson with Pitman on the testimonies of Bell, Robinson, and Major Seward, this would be a neat solution to the problem of how to explain the presence of the wounded Hansell. In the Pitman version there was no place for him in the events which took place upstairs. Ergo, he must have been wounded *downstairs.*

Latterday historians, for the most part, have gone along with Pitman and Burnett on this—though they usually have Hansell encounter the fleeing intruder in the first floor hallway, as he (Hansell) entered the house, and receive his wound there—unwitnessed, due to Bell's reported activities out in the street.

The catch is that when Stanton came, the doctors told him this man—whom Stanton thought to be Seward's "attendant"—was so gravely injured from a stab "through the lungs" that he was not expected to survive. Yet Dr. Verdi found him and treated him in a room on the same floor as Mr. Seward's. That was on the *third floor* of the house.

If the reader can picture Mr. Hansell—a mere messenger for the State Department, desperately wounded—dragging up two flights of stairs in the Seward mansion to bleed all over the bed of some member of the Secretary of State's family, rather than remaining downstairs and asking members of the gathering crowd for help, this writer cannot.

Mr. Hansell *must* have received his wound on the third floor. How he happened to be there cannot be found in a literal reading of the record—though we can be reasonably sure it was with the knowledge and consent of Mr. Seward and his family.

We have two accounts of what happened on the third floor. Major Seward's is so filled with discrepancies, and his very presence there during the struggle with the intruder so unconfirmed and uncertain, that there is much doubt he was involved in the fracas at all.

Sergeant Robinson, however, asserted that *someone* (not Major Seward) rushed into the room and helped him drag the knife-wielding stranger out. The only other male on the third floor at the time (other than the unconscious Frederick) appears to have been Mr. Hansell. So the large knife wound in his side is explainable only by assuming that it was *he* who came to Robinson's assistance.

If it *was* Hansell who helped Robinson (and, for lack of another candidate, we are safe in assuming it was he), Robinson must have known he had done so. Though it was quite dark in the sickroom, the nurse's statement that Paine "looked like" the man who attacked Seward was—as we shall see later—quite accurate. Being able to observe this, he would also have been able to recognize Hansell, or at least recognize that he was *not* Major Seward. Even if he hadn't met him until that occasion, he found out who he was very shortly afterward, without a doubt.

So now we have the question as to why Sergeant Robinson didn't name Hansell during his interrogation by Holt. Perhaps it was because Holt was careful not to ask him. But it could also have been because he was aware that Major Seward, when he took the witness stand, was going to say that *he* hauled the intruder out of the room. The Sergeant balked at contributing to this falsehood and stayed within the literal truth by simply saying he had not seen Major Seward's encounter with the attacker when Holt asked him. His reason for avoiding an open disagreement with the Major may be found in their comparative positions in the military. It may also be found in his position as personal servant to the Secretary of State. The War Department clearly needed a witness to the events in the sickroom who would be willing to identify

Paine more positively than Robinson was willing to do. As it turned out, Major Seward served that purpose well. He was an Army officer, a son of the victim—and a white man.

The Major's identification of Paine actually did prove to be the crusher from the standpoint of the defense. The Peterson introduction relates that after a short cross-examination, Doster gave up on his examination of Major Seward, ". . . as a refutation of this evidence was hopeless.[10]

private interests of the Sewards

Why was Seward's son willing to take part in such a gross corruption of justice? He owed his appointment as an army paymaster to Stanton, but the war was over. He would no doubt have been leaving the service shortly in any case. If he had any connection with the Stanton clique, no hint of it has come to this writer's attention. His father's political alliances had not been with the War Secretary—in fact, as the Cabinet member who had supported President Lincoln's moderate reconstruction policies most strongly, Mr. Seward had been on the opposite side of this major postwar issue from Stanton and the Radical Republicans.

There are indications that the Major's perfidy involved a personal or a family situation, rather than a political one—that the events of that night left the Sewards with a skeleton in their closet. The Major's testimony at the Trial kept it hidden during that difficult period. But at least two ruthless men knew the skeleton was there, and they held a club over the head of the Secretary of State long after the victim of the secret, Louis Paine, had gone to his grave.

After Lafayette Baker's dismissal from the government service on February 8, 1866, he went to work on his memoirs. He engaged Phineas Headley to do the ghostwriting and consulted a former printer from Seward's home town of Auburn, New York, about the publishing. This man, whose name was Derby, was currently employed as a minor official in the State Department. It developed that Mr. Seward was very much concerned about what Baker might reveal in his book. He had obtained proof sheets from Derby and took exception to some of the material, managing to have publication delayed for several months until Baker took over the publishing himself and finally went to press.[11]

There is no way of knowing just what revelations Seward wanted suppressed in Baker's writing project. There could have been other matters, in addition to the family skeleton, he wished kept quiet. A study of the volume shows that most of the damaging insinuations it contained were directed at Stanton, and the detective is not known to have had any particular hostility toward Seward, who had in fact given him his start as a cloak and dagger man when internal security was a function of the State Department in the early months of the war. Three weeks after Stanton took office as Secretary of War on January 20, 1862, he had prevailed upon President Lincoln to transfer antisubversion activities to his department. He then engaged Baker, who subsequently built the secret service into the Gestapo-like instrument of power which Stanton wanted and got.

Whatever pressure there was from Seward, Baker was discreet in his description of the carnage in Lafayette Square on April 14. Neither of his two brief comments on the incident tells much. The first [12] says that ". . . Payne, a professional murderer, . . . fought his way over prostrate figures to the sick victim's bed." The second reference only hurts Major Seward's story by neglecting to name him and giving all the credit to Sergeant Robinson: "Payne, having, as he thought, made an end of Mr. Seward, which would have been the case but for Robinson, the nurse, mounted his horse," etc.[13]

As the campaign against Andrew Johnson gathered momentum, Seward kept his role as most influential advisor to the embattled President. Gideon Welles, who was convinced that the worldly Seward knew well that Stanton and his crowd were out to destroy Johnson and reverse his mild reconstruction policies, couldn't understand why ". . . Seward himself defers to Stanton—is becoming afraid of him." [14]

A ground swell of protest against Stanton was developing in the Republican Party, but Johnson—with Seward's agreement, if not his urging—allowed the War Secretary to keep his post until it reached the point when the President finally realized he had been tricked into denying Mrs. Surratt clemency (this had become a political albatross around his neck for two years) and gave the archschemer Mr. Stanton his walking papers.[15]

But before this eventuality was reached, scandal over the government's failure to pursue and extradite John Surratt developed. Eisenschiml's account of this peculiar situation shows Seward meekly deferring to Stanton's wish to keep Surratt from being brought home for trial. Arrangements with foreign governments for the seizure and extradition of Surratt had to be made through the State Department of course. And here there was a history of ignoring reports from abroad as to the conspirator's whereabouts. When the papal government in Rome finally forced the issue by arresting Surratt, every possible tactic was used to delay his return.[16] In short, some circumstance—perhaps Stanton's knowledge of what really happened at Seward's house on the night of April 14, 1865—made the Secretary of State subservient to the War Secretary's wishes as long as the latter remained in office.

As an intriguing footnote to the unresolved mystery of the skeleton in the Seward family closet, here is Colonel Doster's brief mention of a situation which may have had a bearing on it:[17]

> Near the end of the trial a report spread that Mr. Seward, in pursuance of a sagacious and generous policy, would in case Payne was sentenced to death, ask for his pardon, on the ground that it was not right that he [Seward] should outlive his own murderer—and some pretended to predict this with certainty. The prisoner when he heard of it failed to put the slightest confidence in it. He had made up his mind that death was the only door through which he would ever leave the penitentiary. The sudden death of Mrs. Seward at the very time quenched all hopes on that score.

pitman version of the Seward witnesses

In its revision of Dr. Verdi's testimony to show Hansell was wounded very early in the altercation, the Pitman-Burnett version was revamped with such delicacy that the change is hardly noticeable except to the most suspicious reader.

But the testimony of Bell, Robinson, and Major Seward was another matter. Here the stakes were even higher. Burnett rolled up his sleeves, sharpened his pencil, and went to work. He knew exactly what he had to do—remove *every one* of the contradictions which have been pointed out in the present chapter.

The over-all effect of these three testimonies in Pitman is far different from that in Peterson. There is no confusion among the three recitals, no instances in which a witness disagrees with his own previous statements, no uncertainty as to the "facts" of the incident as all three tell it. This renovation may be due in some degree to Mr. Pitman's effort to make the record read sensibly when he changed the form from question-and-answer to first person narrative. But he could not possibly have made all the changes that were made without having discovered that the War Department's whole pretense of the identification of Paine by eyewitnesses was a fraud.

Minor changes such as Pitman might make in all innocence are throughout these testimonies. The revelation of Burnett's purpose is in the major ones, and we shall give our principal attention to these.

William Bell's testimony per pitman

Early in Bell's monologue, the phrase "He talked very rough to me in the first place" was inserted. This reversed the Peterson statement that "He did not talk rough; he had a very fine voice. . . ."

One of the prosecution's potential trouble spots in their case against Paine—though it came to nothing, due to the impotence of his defense—was that the witnesses' descriptions of him were not consistent. Some said he was definitely a rough, uncultured man. Others said he was genteel, both dressed and acted like a gentleman—William Bell left this impression in his testimony recorded by Peterson. Others said he was refined on some occasions and "vulgar" on others. The man on trial apparently fell into the category of the uncultured, as described in Baker's handbill.

In this change Burnett assured the reader that Seward's assailant was *not* gentlemanly, but *rough,* like the man the War Department had hanged.

In describing the stranger's conversation with Fred Seward at the top of the stairs, Pitman had Bell begin as follows:

"He met Mr. Frederick Seward on the steps this side of his father's room. He told Mr. Frederick that he wanted to see Mr. Seward. Mr. Frederick went into the room and came out, and told him that he could not see him; that his father was asleep. . . ."

Here Pitman answered a question which no one had yet asked—though we may ask it later on: *How did the attacker know which room was Mr. Seward's?* Peterson left us to wonder about that. Burnett wrote the answer into the record in anticipation of the question: He knew which room it was because Frederick went in to see if his father were awake.

Several lines farther along Burnett anticipated and answered another question: *How did Major Seward fail to see his brother lying insensible in the hall?* These words were put in Bell's mouth:

". . . Mr. Frederick was falling; he threw up his hands and fell back in his sister's room; that is two doors this side of Mr. Seward's room."

In Pitman, Bell answered Doster that he had worked for Mr. Seward "*nine* months." In Peterson he said he had worked there only *three* months.

Burnett's transformation of Bell's testimony having to do with his identification of Paine at General Augur's headquarters is best appreciated by reading this part of Pitman's text verbatim and comparing it with the same episode in Peterson (which see). Bell's testimony in Pitman is such a far cry from the same account in Peterson, and the distortion so formidable, that it requires little comment. The boy's remark on the poor light at the Seward house was deleted, and here Bell picked Paine out of a veritable crowd of men rather than having a choice of three—a short man with a moustache, a short man with whiskers, and Paine. Its conflict with the description of the same event in Sampson's deposition was also glaring.

The young man's mention of the reward notice he saw posted in Augur's headquarters the next morning was notable by its absence in

Pitman. It must have occurred to Burnett that someone might compare Bell's list of identifying features with Baker's handbill and wonder whether Baker was quoting Bell or vice versa. It will be recalled that on the witness stand Bell sounded as if he were *reading* his description of the intruder from the handbill—from which we judge he *had* read the notice and mentioned descriptive features of Paine it enumerated.

Burnett's introduction of Colonel Wells by name and description at this point, in combination with William Bell, was an adroit bit of psychology. Without saying in so many words that the Colonel was in charge of the identification, it was implied that he was there and ready to take charge of the prisoner as soon as Seward's servant had identified him. Yet Colonel Wells testified (per Peterson) that he took charge of Paine on *April 19.*

Sergeant Robinson's testimony per pitman

In making the comparison between Robinson's testimony in the two transcripts (which see), the reader should keep the questions at issue in mind—the questions Burnett wished to show the witness answering in a way that supported the prosecution's position. These were as follows:

Did the witness identify Paine as the intruder with whom he struggled?

In Peterson the Sergeant was most uncertain *both* times he was questioned on his recognition of the prisoner. In Pitman his uncertainty was reflected fairly accurately at the opening of his testimony. But when he was recalled to see Paine in the two coats and hat allegedly worn by the intruder, his statement quoted in Peterson was changed in Pitman to sound *much less* uncertain:

Peterson: ". . . He is more like the man than he was before."

Pitman: "He looks more natural now than he did before."

Moreover, the Pitman version removed any vestige of doubt raised by Doster's remark that the hat seemed too small for Paine—which brought laughter in the court—or the guard's reply to General Wallace that "it fits tight." The whole exchange was boiled down to this unequivocal statement:

"At the request of the Court, the guard was directed to place the hat on the head of the prisoner, Payne, to see if it fitted him or not, which was done, Payne smiling pleasantly. It was found to fit him."

Did Major Seward take part in the struggle with the intruder in the sickroom?

Robinson's testimony in Peterson made it clear that Major Seward *was not* present in the sickroom during the struggle—though some other man was.

Burnett reversed the nurse's testimony on this point by making revisions at two places: First, by adding in brackets that Major Seward was the "someone" who entered the room and helped Robinson. Second, by stating specifically that the intruder "broke away from Major Seward and ran down stairs."

Toward the end of the testimony, however, Colonel Burnett overlooked a line spoken by Robinson which annulled these efforts to write Major Seward into the action in the sickroom: "I did not see him encounter Major Seward."

Did Sergeant Robinson hear the stranger say "I am mad"?

In Peterson the nurse answered this question in the negative *three times.* In Pitman he said merely, "I did not hear the man say anything during this time" (during the actual attack upon the elder Seward). Phrased in this manner, the denial could be interpreted to mean he had heard the stranger speak earlier or later, but not during the knife attack on the Secretary of State.

In summary, these direct reversals of a witness' testimony in the "official" record of the Conspiracy Trial provide a concise lesson on how to rewrite history.

Major Seward's testimony per pitman

Since it was the *major's* version of the episode which Burnett wished the records to confirm, much of his testimony in Pitman matched that in Peterson almost word for word. But a few alterations were made to "correct" internal contradictions and answer certain questions that might be raised by this witness' recital.

In Peterson Major Seward said he had been struck over the head repeatedly with a heavy object, apparently a knife. But when his presence was finally noticed after the fracas, he was found to have only a minor cut on the arm. In Pitman he stated that he was struck on the head *and* "on the left hand." A little later a reference to having his *head* bandaged was inserted.

His assertions that he thought he was struggling with the nurse, a

Negro, even after he had seen the intruder's features clearly in the hall, were made slightly less absurd by the judicious insertion of a *comma* in his description of the assailant:

Peterson: ". . . a very large man with dark straight hair."

Pitman: ". . . a very large man, dark, straight hair. . . ."

Young Seward had not admitted that Sergeant Robinson was in the room or that *anyone* had helped him eject the stranger. But the nurse's presence was an acknowledged fact—and he had steadfastly denied hearing the intruder say, "I am mad," or anything else. Thus the Major's statement on the loudness of the man's voice had to be qualified: In Peterson he had described it as "intensely strong." In Pitman this was changed to "intense but *not* strong.

Still another good reason for revising Major Seward's description of the intruder's voice was that it had to fit the prisoner in the dock, whom he had identified positively as his father's assailant. The only description we have of Louis Paine's voice was in Colonel Baker's remarkably accurate handbill—in which the detective called it "small and thin, inclined to tenor."

Thus the collective effect of numerous minor alterations of the Major's testimony in Pitman was to confirm his version of the attack upon his father more strongly and make his "identification" of Paine more conclusive.

summary of chapter nine

From the prosecution's point of view, it was absolutely essential that Paine be identified as Seward's assailant. Except for the questionable testimony of Louis Weichmann, which we shall examine next, they had almost *no* evidence with which to connect Paine with the "Booth Conspiracy."

Yet a man answering to the prisoner's description *had* been involved in Booth's kidnap scheme and also in the events immediately preceding Lincoln's murder—as numerous witnesses would testify. The War Department claimed to have *all* the "conspirators" in custody, and their cases against most of them—particularly that against Mrs. Surratt—depended heavily upon "guilt by association" with this unidentified man and with Louis Paine.

Therefore failure to connect Paine with the crime at Seward's would have been disastrous for the prosecution: The cases against the other defendants would be weakened; their conception of the "plot" would be questioned; early steps to frame Paine might be exposed; and it would be evident that a key figure in the conspiracy was still at large.

Analysis of the testimony of William Bell and Major Seward makes it quite evident that these two prosecution witnesses were perjured in their identification of Paine as Secretary Seward's attacker. Alterations made in the Pitman compilation were intended to hide this fact.

Emrick Hansell's serious wound supports the belief that it was he who went to Robinson's assistance. The nurse's testimony and other evidence make it plain that Major Seward did not participate in the fracas in the sickroom. So it follows that Major Seward's credentials as a witness to the crime were borrowed from Hansell—which would not have been possible unless Hansell had been induced to countenance the deception.

From this we can conclude that someone *other than Louis Paine* tried to kill the Secretary of State. Also, since Sergeant Robinson, whom we take to have been an honest witness, stated that the prisoner "looked like" the man he struggled with, Paine's resemblance to the would-be assassin must have been marked.

But the implications go far beyond the question of whether Louis Paine was framed. There was a deliberate effort to conceal the facts of the incident at Seward's. Hansell's part in it was suppressed. Major Seward's role was misrepresented. William Bell's perjury was suborned by *someone.* Could these things have been done without the knowledge and consent of Secretary Seward?

The obvious assumption is that the attack upon Seward was part of the same conspiracy by which Lincoln was assassinated. This was the War Department's contention. Why, then, would two members of Seward's household and an employee in his department collaborate with the War Department in concealing the facts of the crime and incriminating an innocent man as the culprit? Why would Secretary Seward support the efforts of the War Department to advance a false explanation for a conspiracy of which he himself was an intended victim?

At this early stage we can only ask the question, and point out the implication that the attack upon Seward—even though it coincided with Lincoln's murder as to timing—may not have had any connection with the original conspiracy to assassinate the President, *a conspiracy which Secretary Seward evidently did not wish to see exposed.*

10

Paine at the Surratt house

Only one resident of Mrs. Surratt's boardinghouse had more than a hazy recollection that Louis Paine had stopped there—Louis Weichmann. The widow, of course, denied flatly that Paine had ever visited her place or that she had ever seen him before, though parts of her description of "Wood" sounded very much like the tall young prisoner as he was described by his landlady in Baltimore. The other four occupants who testified, in addition to Weichmann, said they knew him only as "Wood" and gave answers about "Payne" merely because the prosecutors kept using that name in their questions. But usually when they said "Payne" did this or that, they were actually speaking of "Wood."

As *types,* all the principal characters in the Conspiracy Trial are universal and can be found under other names in any period of history. But Louis Weichmann, of them all, was probably the most commonplace and understandable—the one whose counterparts are as numerous today as they were in 1865. He was an intelligent young man with a theoretical interest in high purposes, but with a much more compelling urge to take care of number one.

After graduation from high school in Philadelphia, he attended St. Charles College, a Catholic seminary in Maryland. He claimed to have studied for the priesthood; but this was false, according to a friend of his named Brophy, who at the time of the execution wrote a detailed, sworn statement to the effect that Weichmann was, among other unworthy things, a liar and a coward.[1] It was at this school that he met John Surratt. At his graduation in 1863, Weichmann did not enter the priesthood but took a meager job as teacher in a one-horse boys' school. His sympathies appear to have been clearly with the South in the war, but this didn't prevent him from seeking and eventually getting a clerkship (January 9, 1864) in the War Department office where records of Confederate prisoners were kept. When Mrs. Surratt and her two younger children moved from Surrattsville to the boardinghouse at 541 H Street in November 1864, he became the first paying boarder, and on occasion supplied John Surratt with information from the files of his office for transmission to Richmond.[2]

How deeply he was involved in John Surratt's undercover activities was never established. They seemed to be close confidants, though Surratt wasn't inclined to trust his self-seeking school friend too far. It could have been resentment at John's reservations—or just a desire to hedge his bets—which prompted Weichmann to begin hinting his "suspicions" to Captain Gleason at the Commissary of Prisoners.

At any rate, when the assassination took place and the roof fell in on the Surratt family, Weichmann* found himself in the War Department's toils as completely as if he had been an all-out conspirator. The prosecution denied he was under arrest when he testified, and he himself proclaimed he was serving as its star witness purely from a sense of patriotic duty. But he *was* arrested when he returned from Canada on April 30 and taken in irons to Carroll Prison. When he testified on May 13, he was *still* under arrest and under threat of prosecution as an accomplice in the "conspiracy." The next day Judge Advocate General Holt wrote a letter to Stanton recommending the release of Weichmann and Lloyd, "as they have faithfully given their testimony." [3]

In the last hours before the executions, young John Brophy tried desperately to have his sworn statement that Weichmann told him he had testified under duress brought to President Johnson's attention, but Holt prevented it. Later, at the Surratt trial, the prosecutors succeeded in keeping Brophy off the witness stand—though another man, Louis Carland, did get to testify and said the troubled Weichmann had confessed to him that the prosecutors at the Conspiracy Trial had told him exactly what to testify and exactly what would happen to him if he refused to do so.[4]

Louis Weichmann's perjury

As an example of the art of perjury, Weichmann's testimony is far from being a masterpiece, although the sincerity of his manner made an excellent impression on such members of the military commission as General Wallace, General Harris, and others, whose limited intellect and blinding prejudice led them to believe his allegations without understanding what he said.

Where a situation he was describing included parties who might be allowed to testify and show him to be a liar, Weichmann related the facts fairly accurately but attached a sinister interpretation to them.

* Prior to the Conspiracy Trial, Weichmann had spelled his name with an "ie," but later changed to "ei" because all the newspaper reporters spelled it that way (WWLM, page 452). We are using the "ei" to avoid confusion, since all the records and documents cited do so.

A prime example of this was the occasion on December 23, '64, when Booth, Surratt, and Weichmann met Dr. Mudd on the street and all four went to Booth's room at the National Hotel.[5] Weichmann's version (as usual, he had the date wrong) of what was said and done while they were there made it sound as if Mudd were up to his eyebrows in the "conspiracy." Through his attorneys, the doctor denied the meeting had ever taken place, and witnesses were produced to prove it. Though he *was innocent*, Mudd elected to deny any contact with Booth rather than risk telling the truth and seeing it twisted against him by prosecutors who were obviously in search of scapegoats and not particular as to whom they awarded that unhappy distinction.

The doctor's daughter, Nettie, wrote his biography some years later and gave her father's own account of what had occurred that day in Booth's room.[6] The reader is astonished to find that Dr. Mudd told the *facts* of the incident in almost complete agreement with Weichmann, but the significance of them was far different. He was slightly acquainted with Booth prior to that, and when they met on the street and then encountered the other two men (Weichmann and John Surratt), the actor asked for an *introduction* to Surratt, whom Mudd also knew as a distant neighbor in Maryland. That was all Booth wanted of him, and nothing of a conspiratorial nature transpired—which seems logical, since Booth and Surratt had just met. The War Department's rule of thumb—that any statement by a defendant in his own defense was an obvious falsehood—no longer applies of course, and we are at liberty to believe Dr. Mudd if we wish. The point is, when there was a chance of being contradicted or when the statements he was required to make were not pure fiction, Weichmann was not allergic to the truth.

But virtually *all* his statements about Paine were of the unsupported variety. That is, no one else was present to confirm or deny what he said —or those present were defendants, whose statements were admitted or rejected as evidence on the whim of the prosecutors. (Sam Arnold's "confession" to his arresting officer was admitted,[7] but Doster's request to have Atzerodt's read for the record got an indigant refusal from Holt.)[8]

Louis Paine's supposed connection with the Booth "conspiracy" was expounded *solely by Weichmann,* and was virtually the only basis for Paine's role in the legend. Thus examination of Weichmann's testimony on this subject in Peterson, and comparison with the same testimony in Pitman, are basic to the question of the young man's guilt or innocence.

On the following pages the verbatim transcripts of Weichmann's statements about Paine on his three trips to the witness stand are reproduced. The Peterson version is in the left-hand column, and Pitman's is on the right. Series of dots indicate the omission of testimony which does not concern the case of Paine.

(Body text resumed on page 149)

LOUIS J. WEICHMANN

Testimony for Prosecution

First Appearance

PETERSON TRANSCRIPT MAY 13

Pages 24-28

EXAMINED BY JUDGE HOLT *

Q. State whether you remember, sometime in the month of March, a man calling at Mrs. Surratt's, and giving himself the name of Wood, and inquiring for John H. Surratt?

A. Yes, I opened the door for him. He asked if Mr. Surratt was in; I told him no, but I introduced him to the family; he had then expressed a wish to see Mrs. Surratt.

Q. Do you recognize him here?

A. Yes, sir; that's he; that's the man Payne; he called himself Wood then.

Q. How long did he remain with Mrs. Surratt?

A. He stopped in the house all night, and had supper served up to him in my room; they brought him supper from the kitchen.

Q. When was that?

A. As nearly as I can recollect, it was about eight weeks previous to the assassination [Feburary 14]. I have no exact knowledge of the date.

Q. Did he bring a package?

A. No, sir.

Q. How was he dressed?

A. He had a black overcoat on and a black frock coat with grey pants at the time.

Q. Did he remain till the next morning?

A. Yes, he left in the earliest train for Baltimore.

Q. Do you remember whether, some weeks after, the same man called again?

A. Yes. I should think it was about three weeks [March 7], and I again went to the door. I then showed him into the parlor, and again asked his name. That time he gave the name of Payne.

Q. Did he then have an interview with Mrs. Surratt?

* *Dates in brackets are this writer's interpolation from witnesses' statements.*

PITMAN COMPILATION MAY 13

Pages 113-118

I remember going with John H. Surratt to the Herndon House, about the 19th of March, for the purpose of renting a room. He inquired for Mrs. Mary Murray, who kept the house; and when she came, Surratt said that he wished to have a private interview with her. She did not seem to comprehend; when he said, "Perhaps Miss Anna Ward has spoken to you about this room. Did she not speak to you about engaging a room for a delicate gentleman, who was to have his meals sent up to his room?" Then Mrs. Murray recollected, and Mr. Surratt said he would like to have the room the following Monday, I think, the 27th of March, when the gentleman would take possession of it. No name was mentioned. I afterward heard that the prisoner, Payne, was at the Herndon House. One day I met Atzerodt on the street, and asked him where he was going. He said he was going to see Payne. I then asked, "Is it Payne who is at the Herndon House?" He said, "Yes." That was after the visit John H. Surratt had made to engage the room.

. . . .

Some time in March last, I think, a man calling himself Wood came to Mrs. Surratt's and inquired for John H. Surratt. I went to the door and told him Mr. Surratt was not at home; he thereupon expressed a desire to see Mrs. Surratt, and I introduced him, having first asked his name. That is the man [pointing to Lewis Payne, one of the accused.] He stopped at the house all night. He had supper served up to him in my room; I took it to him from the kitchen. He brought no baggage; he had a black overcoat on, a black dress-coat, and gray pants. He remained till the next morning, leaving by the earliest train for Baltimore. About three weeks afterward he called again, and I again went to the door. I had forgotten his name, and, asking him, he gave the name of Payne.

A. Miss Fitzpatrick, myself and Mrs. Surratt were present; he remained about three days, and represented himself to be a Baptist preacher; he said he had been in Baltimore about a week, had taken the oath of allegiance, and was going to become a good loyal citizen.

Q. Did you hear any explanation why he said he was a Baptist minister?

A. No; Miss Surratt said he was a queer-looking Baptist preacher.

Q. Did they seem to recognize him as the Wood of former days?

A. Yes, sir; in conversation one of the ladies called him Woods, and then I recollected that on his previous visit he had given the name of Wood.

Q. How was he dressed then?

A. In a complete suit of grey.

Q. Did he have any baggage?

A. Yes sir; he had a linen coat and two linen shirts.

Q. Did you observe any trace of disguise or preparations for disguises?

A. One day I found a false moustache on the table in my room; I threw it into a little toilet box, and Payne searched for it and inquired for his moustache; I was sitting in the chair and did not say anything; I retained it ever since; it was found in my baggage among a box of paints I had in my trunk.

Q. Did you see him and Surratt together by themselves?

A. Yes; it was on the same day; I went to the third story and found them sitting on a bed playing with Bowie knives.

Q. Did you see any other weapons?

A. Yes, sir. Two revolvers and four sets of new spurs.

[The witness here identified a knife and pistols shown him.]

. . . .

Q. Do you remember having gone with Surratt to the Herndon House to hire a room?

A. Yes, sir.

Q. What time was that?

A. It must have been the 19th of March.

Q. For whom did he wish to rent this room?

I ushered him into the parlor, where were Mrs. Surratt, Miss Surratt, and Miss Honora Fitzpatrick. He remained three days that time. He represented himself as a Baptist preacher; and said that he had been in prison in Baltimore for about a week; that he had taken the oath of allegiance, and was now going to become a good and loyal citizen.

Mrs. Surratt and her family are Catholics. John H. Surratt is a Catholic, and was a student of divinity at the same college as myself. I heard no explanation given why a Baptist preacher should seek hospitality at Mrs. Surratt's; they only looked upon it as odd, and laughed at it. Mrs. Surratt herself remarked that he was a great looking Baptist preacher. In the course of conversation one of the young ladies called him "Wood." I then recollected that on his first visit he had given the name of Wood. On the last occasion he was dressed in a complete suit of gray; his baggage consisted of a linen coat and two linen shirts.

The only evidence of disguise or preparation for it, that I know of, was a false moustache, which I found on the table in my room one day. I put the moustache into a little toilet-box that was on my table. Payne afterward searched round the table and inquired for his moustache. I was sitting on a chair and did not say any thing. I retained the moustache, and it was found in my baggage that was seized.

On returning from my office one day, while Payne was there, I went up stairs to the third story and found Surratt and Payne seated on a bed, playing with bowie-knives. There were also two revolvers and four sets of new spurs.

[A spur, a large bowie-knife, and a revolver, found in Atzerodt's room at the Kirkwood House, were exhibited to the witness.]

That is one of the spurs. There were three spurs similar to that in a closet in my room when I was last there, and those three belonged to the eight that had been purchased by Surratt. The knives they were playing with were smaller than that knife. The revolvers

A. Well, he went in and inquired for Mrs. Mary Murray, and when she came, he had a private interview with her, but said that she did not seem to comprehend, though he thought that a Miss Ward had spoken to her already on the subject, and he said to Mrs. Murray, Miss Ward may have spoken to you about the matter of hiring a room for a delicate gentleman, and Mr. Surratt added he would like to have the room by the following Monday, as the gentleman wanted to take possession on that day; I think that was the Monday previous; it was the 27th of March.

Q. The name of the person was not given?

A. No, sir, no name was mentioned at all.

Q. Did you afterwards learn that Payne was at that house?

A. Yes, sir. I met Atzeroth on the street, and asked him where he was going? He stated that he was going to see Payne. I asked him, is it Payne that is at the Herndon House, and he said yes.

. . . .

CROSS-EXAMINED BY REVERDY JOHNSON

Q. You saw Payne yourself when he came to the house?

A. Yes, sir; the first time he gave the name of Wood; I went to the door, and opened it, and he said he would like to see Mrs. Surratt.

Q. What was his appearance, genteel?

A. Yes, he had on a long black coat, and went into the parlor; he acted very politely; asked Mrs. Surratt to play the piano for him.

. . . .

Q. You say you found upon your own table a false moustache; what was the color of the hair?

A. Black.

Q. Was it large?

A. About medium sized.

Q. This you put into your own box?

A. Yes, in a toilet box and afterwards in a box of paints; it was found in my baggage.

Q. When he came home he seemed to be looking for it?

they had were long navy revolvers, with octangular barrels; that has a round barrel.

. . . .

The first time that Payne came to Mrs. Surratt's, when he gave the name of Wood, he had on a black coat; and when he went into the parlor he acted very politely. He asked Miss Surratt to play on the piano and he raised the piano-cover, and did every thing which indicated a person of breeding. The moustache that I found upon my table was black, and of medium size; it was sufficiently large to entirely change the appearance of the wearer. When I found it I thought it rather queer that a Baptist preacher should use a moustache; I thought no honest person had any reason to wear one. I took it and locked it up, because I did not care to have a false moustache lying round on my table. I remember exhibiting it to some of the clerks in our office, and fooling with it the day afterward; I put on a pair of spectacles and the moustache, and was making fun of it.

. . . .

BY MR. DOSTER

Atzerodt has been frequently to Mrs. Surratt's house, and had interviews with John H. Surratt in the parlor. I knew nothing of what took place between them. On the occasion of Payne's last visit to the house, Atzerodt came to see Surratt, and I saw Payne and Atzerodt together, talking in my room. I do not know of any conversation that passed between Atzerodt and Booth, or Atzerodt and Payne, having reference to a conspiracy.

. . . .

At half-past 2 o'clock, on the afternoon of the 14th, I saw Atzerodt at the livery-stable, trying to get a horse. The stable-keeper, in my presence, refused to let him have one. I asked Atzerodt where he was going, and he said he was going to ride in the country, and he said he was going to get a horse and send for Payne. I met Atzerodt one day on Seventh Street, and asked him where he was going. He said he was going to see Payne. I asked him if it was Payne who was at the Herndon House. He

A. Yes, he said "where is my moustache?"

Q. Why did you not give it to him?

A. I suspected, I thought it queer.

Q. But you locked it up?

A. Yes, I didn't like to have it seen in my room.

Q. But you could have got it out of your room by giving it to him when he asked for it?

A. I thought no honest person had a reason to wear a false moustache. I took it and exhibited it to some of the clerks in the office. I put it on with specs. and was making fun with it.

. . . .

[Shortly after this Reverdy Johnson left the court, and other attorneys cross-examined the witness.]

CROSS-EXAMINED BY COLONEL DOSTER

. . . .

Q. On the 4th of April do you know where Payne was stopping? Do you know anything about Payne on that day?

A. Yes, sir; I remember that Atzeroth and I met and I asked him where he was going, and he said he was going to get a horse for Payne.

Q. But where was Payne?

A. I don't know; I only saw him on those two occasions.

Q. Where then was Atzeroth stopping?

A. I don't know.

Q. Did he not speak of the place where Payne was stopping?

A. No, sir.

Q. Do you know of his having stopped at the Herndon House?

A. I know it because Atzeroth told me; I met him one day on Seventh street; he said he was going to see Payne, and I asked him if it was Payne that was at the Herndon House, and he said yes.

Q. You said Payne paid a visit to Mrs. Surratt and stopped only one night?

A. Yes, sir.

said, "Yes." When Payne visited the Surratts, his business appeared to be with Mr. Surratt. On the occasion of his first visit, I was in the parlor during the whole time. I did not notice any other disguise than the false moustache spoken of, nor any thing else to show that Payne wanted to disguise himself. He appeared to be kindly treated by Mr. Surratt, as if he was an old acquaintance.

I do not know whether the Surratt family regarded him as a man in disguise or as a Baptist minister. One of the young ladies looked at him, and remarked that he was a queer-looking Baptist preacher, and that he would not convert many souls.

(Peterson continued)

Q. With whom did he appear to have business?

A. He appeared to have business with Mrs. Surratt.

Q. Did he have any other dress, going to show that he wanted to conceal himself, that you saw?

A. No, sir.

Q. Have you seen Payne since the assassination until today?

A. No, sir, I believe not.

Q. Was he received by Mrs. Surratt as an intimate friend?

A. He was by Mrs. Surratt; he was treated as an old acquaintance on his first visit.

Q. Now you say he represented himself to be a Baptist minister; did they regard him as a man in disguise, or as a minister?

A. One of the young ladies remarked that he was a queer looking Baptist preacher; that he wouldn't convert many souls.

Q. Did you ever see Payne and Atzeroth in company?

A. Yes; Atzeroth was at the house on the occasion of Payne's last visit.

LOUIS J. WEICHMANN

Testimony for Prosecution

Second Appearance

PETERSON TRANSCRIPT MAY 18
Pages 62-65

On May 18, immediately before Weichmann took the witness stand for the second time, a New York telegrapher named A. R. Reeve testified that John Wilkes Booth had handed him a message at his office in the St. Nicholas Hotel in New York on March 23 and told him to send it to Louis Weichmann in Washington. The text of the telegram was as follows:

NEW YORK, March 23, 1865
To ——— Weichman, Esq.
No. 541 H. Street, Washington, D. C.

Tell John to telegraph the number and street at once.

J. BOOTH

The original draft of the wire in Booth's handwriting was put in evidence.

EXAMINED BY JUDGE HOLT

Q. Look at that telegram and state whether you received it on the day of its date?

A. I cannot say that I received it on the 23rd of March, but I received a telegram of the exact nature of this one.

Q. Who is the person referred to there as John?

A. John Surratt was frequently called John.

Q. Did you deliver the message to him?

A. I delivered the message to him the same day.

Q. What did he say?

A. I questioned him as to what was meant by the number and street; he replied to me, Don't be so ——— inquisitive.

Q. See whether this is the telegram you delivered?

A. It is.

. . . .

Q. Did you know the handwriting of Booth?

A. I have seen his handwriting, and could recognize his autograph.

PITMAN COMPILATION MAY 18
Pages 118-120

[A telegraphic dispatch was handed to the witness.]

I received this dispatch and delivered it to John H. Surratt on the same day. I can not say that I received it on the 23d of March, but it was after the 17th of March.

NEW YORK, March 23, 1865.
To Weichmann, Esq., 541 H Street:

Tell John to telegraph number and street at once.

(Signed) J. BOOTH.

[The original of the above dispatch was offered in evidence.]

This is in Booth's handwriting. I have seen Booth's handwriting, and recognize his autograph. When I delivered the message to John Surratt, I asked him what particular number and street was meant, and he said, "Don't be so damned inquisitive."

During Payne's second visit to Mrs. Surratt's house, some time after the 4th of March, I returned from my office one day at half-past 4 o'clock. I went to my room, and ringing the bell for Dan, the Negro servant, told him to bring me some water, and inquired at the same time where John had gone. He told me Massa John had left the front of the house, with six others, on horseback, about half-past 2 o'clock. On going down to dinner, I found Mrs. Surratt in the passage. She was weeping bitterly, and I endeavored to console her. She said, "John is gone away; go down to dinner, and make the best of your dinner you can." After dinner, I went to my room, sat down, commenced reading, and about half-past 6 o'clock Surratt came in very much excited—in fact, rushed into the room. He had a revolver in his hand—one of Sharpe's revolvers, a four-barrelled revolver, a small one, you could carry it in your vest-pocket.

He appeared to be very much excited.

paine at the surratt house

[The witness was here shown the original telegram purporting to have been written by Booth, and said, that is his handwriting.]

Q. State whether, on or about the 4th of March last, you had an interview in your room with John Wilkes Booth, John Surratt and Payne, the prisoner at the bar?

A. I will state that as near as I can recollect it was after the 4th of March, and the second time that Payne visited the house; when I returned from my office one day at half past four o'clock and went to my room, I rang the bell for Dan, the Negro servant, and in reply to an inquiry which I addressed to him he told me that John had ridden out at about half past two o'clock in the afternoon, with six others, on horseback; on going downstairs I found Mrs. Surratt weeping bitterly and asked her what was the matter; she said to me, "go down and make the best of your dinner, John has gone away;" about half-past six o'clock John Surratt came home and was very much intoxicated; in fact he rushed frantically into the room; he had one of Sharp's small six-barrel revolvers in his hand; I said, "John, why are you so much excited?" he replied, "I will shoot any man who comes into this room; my hopes are gone and my prospects blighted; I want something to do; can you get me a clerkship?" The prisoner Payne came into the room, and about fifteen minutes afterwards Booth came into the room, and was so much excited that he walked frantically around the room several times without noticing me; he had a whip in his hand; the three then went up stairs into the second story, and they must have remained there together about twenty minutes; subsequently I asked Surratt where he had left Payne; he said Payne had gone to Baltimore; I asked him where Booth had gone; he said to New York; some two weeks afterwards Surratt, when passing the post office, inquired for a letter under the name of James Sturdy, and I asked him why a letter was sent to him under a false name; he said he had particular I said, "John, what is the matter; why are you so much excited?" He replied, "I will shoot any one that comes into this room; my prospect is gone, my hopes are blighted; I want something to do; can you get me a clerkship?" In about ten minutes after, the prisoner, Payne, came into the room. He was also very much excited, and I noticed he had a pistol. About fifteen minutes afterward, Booth came into the room, and Booth was so excited that he walked around the room three or four times very frantically, and did not notice me. He had a whip in his hand. I spoke to him, and, recognizing me, he said, "I did not see you." The three then went up stairs into the back room, in the third story, and must have remained there about thirty minutes, when they left the house together. On Surratt's returning home, I asked him where he had left his friend Payne. He said, "Payne had gone to Baltimore." I asked him where Booth had gone; he said Booth had gone to New York. Some two weeks after, Surratt, when passing the post-office, inquired for a letter that was sent to him under the name of James Sturdey. I asked him why a letter was sent to him under a false name; he said he had particular reasons for it.

The letter was signed "Wood," and the substance of it was, that the writer was at the Revere House in New York, and was looking for something to do; that he would probably go to some boarding-house on West Grand Street, I think. This must have been before the 20th of March.

When I asked the Negro servant to tell me who the seven men were that had gone out riding that afternoon, he said one was Massa John, and Booth, and Port Tobacco, and that man who was stopping at the house, whom I recognized as Payne. Though they were very much excited when they came into the room, they were very guarded indeed. Payne made no remark at all. Those excited remarks by Surratt were the only ones made.

. . . .

reasons for it; this must have been two weeks after this affair, before the 20th of March [*therefore the "affair" was before March 6*]; the letter was signed Wood, and the writer stated that he was at the Revere House in New York; that he was looking for something to do, but would probably go to some boarding-house in Grand street; I think West Grand street; this was the whole substance of the letter.

Q. Are you familiar with Booth's handwriting or simply with his autograph?

A. I have seen his autograph at the hotel and have also seen his autograph at the house.

Q. Here is a note signed R. E. Watson—will you look at it and see whether that is Booth's handwriting?

A. No sir, I would not recognize that as Booth's handwriting.

Q. Was there any remark made in their excited conversation on the occasion of which you have spoken as to where they had all been riding?

A. No sir, they were very guarded; Payne made no remark at all; the only remarks made were those excited remarks by Surratt.

Q. Surratt had been riding, you say, and Booth had a whip in his hand?

A. Yes sir.

Q. He appeared to have been with them also?

A. Yes sir, he was much excited.

. . . .

Cross-examined by Mr. Ewing

Q. Do you recollect when it was that Booth played "Pescara," in the *Apostate?*

A. Yes sir; he played it that night; that must have been about the 24th of March.

Q. Was it not the day before or the day after their return from the ride that he played in the "Apostate?"

A. That I cannot say; it must have been after the 4th of March; this man Payne was stopping at the house at the time, and when he came to the house he made some excuse to Mrs. Surratt, saying he would like to have been there before the 4th of March, but could not

By Mr. Aiken

My suspicions were aroused by Payne and Booth coming to the house, and their frequent private conversations with John Surratt, and by seeing Payne and Surratt, playing on the bed with bowie-knives and again by finding a false moustache in my room but my suspicions were not of a fixed or definite character. I did not know what they intended to do. I made a confidant of Captain Gleason in the War Department. I told him that Booth was a secesh sympathizer, and mentioned snatches of conversation I had heard from these parties; and I asked him, "Captain, what do you think of all this?" We even talked over several things which they could do. I asked him whether they could be bearers of dispatches or blockade-runners. I remember seeing in New York *Tribune*, of March 19th, the capture of President Lincoln fully discussed, and I remarked to Captain Gleason, "Captain, do you think any party could attempt the capture of President Lincoln?" He laughed and hooted at the idea. This happened before the horseback ride of Surratt and the six others. I remarked to the Captain, the morning after they rode, that Surratt had come back, and I mentioned to Gleason the very expressions Surratt had used, and told him that to all appearances, what they had been after had been a failure; and that I was glad, as I thought Surratt would be brought to a sense of his duty.

. . . .

By Mr. Ewing

The ride of the parties spoken of, I think, took place after my reading the article in the *Tribune* of March 19th. I also saw in the *Republican*, some time in February, that the assassination of President Lincoln was contemplated, and Surratt once made the remark to me that if he succeeded in his cotton speculation, his country would love him forever, and that his name would go down green to posterity.

I do not know what were his intentions, but he said he was going to engage in cotton speculations; he was going to engage in oil.

get there; by that circumstance I recollect that it was after the 4th of March; whether it was before or after the day that Booth played "Pescara" I can't say.

Q. Did you go to see that play?

A. Yes sir; Booth sent complimentary tickets, at least gave a pass to Surratt for two, and he asked Surratt whether he thought I would go; the pass was a written one, and the doorkeeper at first refused us admission.

Q. State whether the affair of the ride was before or after Booth played in the *Apostate?*

A. To the best of my recollection it was before.

Q. How long before?

A. Well, as near as I can recollect, about two weeks before [*March 4*].

Q. You cannot state positively whether it was before or after the play in the *Apostate?*

A. I would not like to state positively.

. . . .

At this point various defense attorneys cross-examined Weichmann: Doster, as to statements he had made about the "horse ride"—the witness merely repeating what he had said before; Aiken, as to how he happened to be testifying for the prosecution and whether he was under arrest—the witness saying he was NOT *under arrest, had not been induced by threats or promises, was performing a patriotic duty. Then, over Bingham's repeated objections, Aiken confronted the squirming witness with various incidents of his pro-Confederate activities over many months and association with Confederate sympathizers and blockade runners. Mr. Clampitt followed with more in the same vein and inquiry into the reason and nature of Weichmann's disclosures of affairs at the Surratt house to Captain Gleason in his office—and his conjecture that a plot to capture the President was afoot there.*

Q. You did, then, hear of a proposition of that kind?

A. I did not hear, but it was freely discussed in the papers; if you will refer to the *Tribune* of March 19th, you will see it mentioned; it was merely a casual

My remark to Captain Gleason about the possibility of the capture of the President was merely a casual remark. He laughed at the idea of such a thing in a city guarded as Washington was. It was the morning after the ride that I stated to Captain Gleason that Surratt's mysterious and incomprehensible business had failed; and I said, "Captain, let us think it over, and let us think of something that it could have been." I mentioned a variety of things—Blockade-running, bearing dispatches; and we then thought of breaking open the Old Capitol Prison; but all those ideas vanished; we hit upon nothing. I will state that since that ride my suspicions were not so much aroused as before, because Payne has not been to the house since; and Atzerodt, to my knowledge, had not been to the house since the 2d of April. The only one that visited the house during that time was this man Booth.

(Peterson continued)

remark that I made; these suspicions arose in my mind after this horseback ride; I remarked to Captain Gleason that Surratt had come back, and told him that what they had been after had failed.

Q. How came you to connect the matter of the capture of the President, of which you read in the newspaper, with any of these parties?

When this last question was objected to by Bingham, and the objection sustained, Mr. Clampitt turned to the embarrassing subject of Weichmann's apparent willingness to betray his friend John Surratt. The witness countered that it had been Surratt who had betrayed HIM *"by placing me in the position in which I am now."*

Then Mr. Ewing, who seems to have had a suspicion that there was something phony about the "horse ride," took over again and pressed the subject further:

Q. You spoke of reading a publication in the *Tribune*, of March 19th, referring to a plot to capture the President?

A. Yes sir.

Q. Can you not, by connecting that circumstance with the ride which these parties had in the country, fix more definitely the time of that ride—whether before or after the date of that publication?

A. I think it was after it; I would also state that I saw in the Washington *Republican* a statement concerning a contemplated assassination of President Lincoln, and Surratt once made a remark to me that if he succeeded in his cotton speculation his country would lose him forever, and his name would go down to posterity forever green.

Q. You think, then, that this occasion, when they appeared to have come in from a ride in the country, was after March 19th?

A. Yes sir.

Q. Was your remark to Captain Gleason, respecting the probable capture of the President, made after the ride?

A. Yes sir; I said to Captain Gleason that Surratt's mysterious, incomprehensible business had failed, and I added, "Let us think over what it could have been;" we mentioned a variety of things, even the breaking open of the Old Capitol Prison; I would mention that after the ride my suspicions were not so much aroused as before it, because neither Payne nor Atzeroth had been at the house since; the only one of them who visited was the man Booth.

. . . .

LOUIS J. WEICHMANN

Testimony for Prosecution

Third Appearance

PETERSON TRANSCRIPT MAY 19
Page 77

The day Weichmann made his third and final appearance on the witness stand was the one on which Louis Paine had been told to put on both of the coats—the Confederate grey one first, with the "longer cream colored one" on top of it. With several other witnesses, Weichmann was recalled to see if he recognized the prisoner's coat.

EXAMINED BY JUDGE HOLT

Q. Look at the prisoner, Payne, and state whether you ever saw him dressed up with that coat on before.

A. Yes sir, when he last came to the house.

Q. When he remained three days?

A. Yes sir.

Q. State whether you ever saw that vest before.

A. Yes sir; he also had a pair of boots.

Q. State whether he wore a white cravat or not.

A. He wore a black cravat.

Q. Did you ever know him to wear a white cravat?

A. No sir, I never did.

PITMAN COMPILATION MAY 19
Page 120

[The accused, Lewis Payne, was here attired in the coat and vest in which he was arrested at the house of Mrs. Surratt.]

Payne wore that coat and vest the last time he came to Mrs. Surratt's, when he staid three days, on the 14th, 15th and 16th of March, and it was on the 16th that the party took that horseback ride. The next day after that I mentioned my suspicions to Captain Gleason. I had spoken to him previously, on various occasions, about this blockade-runner, and about Mrs. Slater, but I cannot fix the precise date. I am enabled to fix the date of Payne's last visit to the house, from the fact that he went with John Surratt, Miss Fitzpatrick, and Miss Dean to see "Jane Shore" played at the theater. Forrest was playing there at that time, and Surratt had got a ten-dollar ticket. It was the next day that this horseback ride occurred.

. . . .

(Peterson continued)

CROSS-EXAMINED BY COLONEL DOSTER

Q. All this happened when you were

giving information to the War Department, and on intimate terms with Mrs. Surratt and her family?

A. I was on intimate terms for a time; it was on this occasion that Payne went to the theatre with Surratt to see the play of *Jane Shore;* I indicated my suspicions to Gleason at the time, and the very morning after that the horseback ride took place.

Q. I was asking you to fix the date, that's all.

A. It was about the 14th of March; he came to the house on the evening of the 13th and remained there the 14th, 15th and 16th; on the 18th he went to the theatre; it was when Forrest played there four nights in that week.

CROSS-EXAMINED BY MR. COX

Q. So you fix the 16th as the date of that horseback ride?

A. Yes sir; to the best of my recollection.

Weichmann testimony of may 13 per peterson

On Weichmann's first trip to the witness stand, his assignment was relatively simple. He merely testified that a man who went by the name of "Wood" visited the Surratt boardinghouse for one night several weeks before the assassination, and that a man who gave his name as "Payne" stopped there for about three days around the middle of March.

The witness stated that "Wood" and "Payne" were the same individual —and that he could positively identify the prisoner Louis Paine as that man.

Now, this was substantially the same story Weichmann had told Colonel W. P. Wood, superintendent of Old Capitol Prison, on April 30, the day he returned from his trek to Canada and was arrested—except that he hadn't as yet seen Paine the *prisoner.*[9]* Moreover, all the occupants of the Surratt house whose testimony is recorded recalled one or more visits by "Wood," though their recollections as to the dates of his visits varied a little.

When she testified in court, Anna Surratt said he ("Payne") stayed for one night "not very long after Christmas" and called two or three times after that.[10] But during her pre-Trial interrogation, she said "Wood" had stayed at their house—and insisted she didn't recognize Louis Paine as the same man.[11]

Mrs. Surratt, in her pre-Trial interrogation, admitted that "Wood" had visited the house, but denied he bore any resemblance to Paine.[12]

Mrs. Eliza Hollahan, a boarder, testified on May 20 that such a man had stopped at the house twice—once in February and once around "the middle of March," but she "never saw him as Payne." She saw the man "pointed out as Payne," but "he called himself Wood." [13]

* Weichman told Colonel Wood that the man who came in February and gave his name as "Wood" came again "around the middle of March" and "gave his name as *Paine*" and, *on the second visit,* "represented himself as a Baptist preacher."

Her husband, John T. Hollahan, testified, "I saw Payne there once at breakfast under the name of Wood." [14]

Nora Fitzpatrick, one of the three young ladies arrested with Mrs. Surratt by Baker's detectives (but released almost at once), told Colonel Wood she had gone to the theater one evening in March with "Wood," John Surratt, and a young lady named Deane.[15] When interrogated by Colonel Foster on April 28, she stated she didn't recognize the prisoner Paine as "Wood," who had visited the house twice.[16] When she testified at the Trial, she stated she had seen "Wood" first at breakfast "during the winter," that she had been to the theater with him in March, and that she knew him *only by the name of "Wood."* [17]

The collective effect of these various testimonies, including Weichmann's, was general agreement that a man named "Wood" had visited the boardinghouse in January or February or both, and had come again in March to attend the theater (Ford's) with John Surratt and the two girls. Miss Fitzpatrick testified that Booth had come to the box they were occupying.

Then a man whom Weichmann *said* was "Wood" showed up around the *middle* of March and stayed two or three days—though Weichmann was the only one who claimed to have seen him around the house during that visit.

Weichmann described "Wood" as a gentlemanly type of man, very gracious, who had asked Mrs. Surratt to play the piano. And he said the man who came around the middle of March and said his name was "Payne" told them he had been in Baltimore, that he had just signed the Oath of Allegiance—and that he was a *Baptist preacher.* Most of the other occupants also recalled that this man (the second man) had claimed to be a preacher. So did Mrs. Surratt.

"Payne" and "Wood"

The most obvious riddle presented by this collective testimony is this: Does it seem plausible that "Wood," who had met most of the boarders at breakfast in the winter, returned "two or three times after that," and escorted Miss Fitzpatrick to Ford's Theater in March would have returned for a three-day visit shortly after the theater party and expected any of those same people to believe his name was "Payne"—let alone that he was a Baptist preacher?

In spite of the early doubts of all these witnesses that Paine and "Wood" were the same man, the prosecutors succeeded, by using the name "Payne" in all their references to "Wood," in crystallizing the idea that Paine (Payne) *was* "Wood"—even in the minds of most of these same witnesses—and that "Wood" was a "bogus preacher."

The prosecution's claim that "Wood" represented himself as a preacher was a deliberate deception. Two of the earliest documents in their files (now in the National Archives) were precise in recording that it was "Payne," the man who stayed at the boardinghouse in March, who said he was a preacher. These were Foster's undated summary of the initial interrogation of the household members and Colonel W. P. Wood's report on his interview with Weichmann on April 30.

As it happens, we have ample evidence at hand to show beyond reasonable doubt that "Wood" and "Payne" (Paine) were different men—though they apparently bore a strong resemblance to each other in features and stature.

"Wood" made several verified appearances at the Surratt house between late January and early March. *During that entire period, Louis Paine was living at the boardinghouse of Mrs. Mary A. Branson at the corner of Eutaw and Fayette Streets in Baltimore—and had not been absent during the whole time.*

Mrs. Branson was arrested "by order of the Secretary of War" on April 28—two weeks after the assassination—and placed under house arrest, in the custody of Colonel John Woolley, provost marshal of Baltimore.[18]

On May 1, Mrs. Branson was interrogated by Assistant Provost Marshal Wm. H. Wiegel, and a transcript of her statements was forwarded to Burnett through channels. The lady stated that "Lewis Payne" had come to stay at her house "about the 19th of January," introducing himself as a refugee from Virginia. She said he remained at her house as a paying guest until he was arrested by the provost marshal in March, after which he was released and sent north to New York.[19]

The day after Paine's arrest at the Surratt house in Washington, Colonel John A. Foster of the Bureau of Military Justice sent to Baltimore for a copy of the Oath of Allegiance the prisoner had handed to Detective Morgan when he was arrested—to verify that the document was authentic and not a forgery.

Major Wiegel referred to his records and forwarded a copy of the Oath in question to Foster, with a covering letter dated April 18, 1865. The letter stated that "Lewis Paine" had been "detained . . . as a Refugee" on March 12, 1865, and released on March 14 after taking the amnesty oath. He had been ordered to go "north of Philadelphia to remain during the War." [20]

A photographic copy of the Oath of Allegiance Paine handed to Detective Morgan appears here. The original is in the Lincoln Assassination Suspects file in the National Archives.

On June 2, Mrs. Branson's daughter Margaret took the witness stand for the defense. She testified, among other things, that Paine had not been absent from their boardinghouse to her knowledge at any time during his stay until the night of his arrest by the provost marshal. He was arrested,

Head Quarters Middle Department, 8th Army Corps,
OFFICE PROVOST MARSHAL,

Baltimore, Mar. 14th 1865

OATH OF ALLEGIANCE.

I, Lewis Paine Fauquier Co Va Refugee do solemnly swear that I will bear true faith, allegiance and loyalty to the Government of the United States, and support, protect, defend and sustain the Constitution, Government and laws thereof; that I will maintain the National Sovereignty in its integrity, any ordinance, resolution, or law of any State, Convention or Legislature to the contrary notwithstanding. That I will discourage, discountenance and forever oppose secession, rebellion and the disruption or severance of the Union; that I disclaim and abjure all faith, fellowship or sympathy with the so-called Confederate States and Confederate Armies, and pledge my property and my life to the sacred performance of this my solemn Oath of Allegiance to the Government of the United States. And further, I will not attempt to trade or have any correspondence directly or indirectly, or have any business transactions whatever with any person living in the so-called Confederate States, unless under the proper Military supervision and approval.+ And that I do this with a full determination, pledge and purpose, without any mental reservation or evasion whatever, and that I will well and faithfully perform all the duties required of me as a true and loyal citizen of these United States. So help me God.

+ & to go north of Philadelphia & remain during the war.

L Paine

WITNESS:

Edwin Vaughan
Capt. and Asst. Provost Marshal.

Office Provost Marshal,
Baltimore, March 14 186
OATH OF ALLEGIANCE
TAKEN BY
Lewis Paine
Refugee Va

FIG. 3.–Louis (Lewis) Paine's Oath of Allegiance

she said, due to an altercation with an "impudent" maid, during which he struck the woman, being arrested later on the maid's complaint.[21]

In view of the foregoing documentation of Paine's continuous residence in Baltimore from January 19 to March 14, is it possible to believe he was the same man as the "Wood" who made various well-verified visits to the Surratt boardinghouse in Washington in January, February, and early March, 1865?

In addition, the "Payne" who arrived at the Surratt house around the middle of March stated that he had just signed the Oath in Baltimore. When Louis Paine was arrested at Surratt's after the assassination, he handed Morgan his Oath, dated "March 14." Is it not equally clear that the "middle of March" visitor was Louis Paine himself, the prisoner in the dock?

In her interrogation on April 17, Mrs. Surratt—though she gave a false physical description of Paine—said he had introduced himself as a Baptist preacher. He was very reticent, she said, remaining in his room throughout most of his stay. This was so logical that we can assume it was true. He had been given amnesty on the condition that he leave Baltimore and go "north of Philadelphia" until the end of the war. If found *south* of Philadelphia before the war ended, he was liable to be arrested and imprisoned for violation of his amnesty oath.

Paine's business in Washington was apparently urgent enough to warrant the risk of rearrest. His three secluded days at Surratt's suggest he was waiting for someone he expected to find there—someone who did not show up.

The prisoner's refusal to talk to *anyone* or say a word in his own defense made it possible for Weichmann to invent several instances in which he showed Paine in guilty communication with Mrs. Surratt, John Surratt, Booth, and Atzerodt—and to attribute to Paine all the incriminating activities of "Wood."

The significance of his yarn about the false moustache was mentioned earlier. That of his statements about "Payne's" residence at the Herndon House prior to the assassination will be brought out in the next chapter. It should be mentioned in passing, though, that Weichmann's assertion that John Surratt had reserved a room at the Herndon House for "Payne" ("Wood") was probably true, even though the landlady of the hotel denied she knew Surratt on the witness stand. Miss Anna Ward, a local schoolteacher, was involved in the transaction and testified on June 3 that she *had* inquired about a room.

However, Weichmann's claim that Atzerodt told him "Payne" was staying at the Herndon House was a bald-faced lie. As we shall see shortly, Atzerodt *was* in touch with the mysterious man at the Herndon House during the week before the assassination—but he knew him *only* by the name of "James Wood."

Weichmann testimony of may 18 and 19 per peterson

Weichmann's principal duty on May 18 was to expound the alleged incident of the "horse ride," an episode in the Booth "conspiracy" which the prosecutors seem to have conceived since their star witness' first trip to the stand.

The "horse ride" was wholly in the realm of innuendo. Except for the servant Dan's news that Surratt had ridden out with "six others" during the afternoon, Weichmann offered no evidence that Booth, Surratt, and "Payne" had been anywhere together when the three showed up that evening. The implication that they had attempted to kidnap the President and failed was pure supposition, but very cleverly done.

When we consider that this testimony was given in a national tribunal, before judges who were not morons and defense attorneys alert for flaws in it, and later published far and wide for millions of others to read, the universal credence it received is miraculous.

In trying to fix the date of the "horse ride," the floundering Weichmann located it all over the month of March, 1865. He dated it "to the best of his recollection" on *March 4, March 10, March 16,* and "*after March 19.*"

Could an event so elusive in the mind of an intelligent man like Weichmann have had any connection with reality? Many of his dates for other incidents were incorrect, but with respect to the "horse ride" his confusion was on a magnificent scale.

General Thomas Ewing, Jr., defense counsel for Dr. Mudd, had been a field officer during the war. He was the brother-in-law of General William T. Sherman and evidently a competent lawyer. Thanks to his persistence, we have one fixed date by which Weichmann's amazingly confused account of the "horse ride" can be shown to be an invention pure and simple. This is the date of Booth's appearance in *The Apostate.* The witness thought this was March 24—but it was actually the 18th.[22]

Louis Weichmann's ability to talk nonsense from the witness stand and get away with it can hardly be denied. The complaint by one of the defense attorneys that they were not getting transcripts of the testimony in time to analyze the testimony and ask the recall of witnesses before they were released may be the clue to the young man's success. His technique when cornered on a date about which he was unsure or confused was to answer the question briefly, then follow it with a lengthy statement on some entirely different subject, which was calculated to draw the examiner away from the embarrassing line of inquiry. This evasion seemed to work very well in an oral exchange, although it is obvious enough when the printed testimony can be studied.

On May 18, when Ewing asked the date of the "horse ride" in terms of the date Booth played in *The Apostate,* Weichmann almost seemed to throw him off the scent with the business of the free pass Booth gave Surratt, etc. But Ewing came back to his original question; cornered, Weichmann said he thought the "horse ride" had been *two weeks before The Apostate*—which would have been March 4.

Now this put the witness on the spot, because since his first testimony he had evidently received instructions to set the date of the affair much later in the month. He had to resort to Plan B—as he did every now and then refute his own statements by stating just the reverse of what he had said. He said he could not say positively whether the "horse ride" occurred before or after *The Apostate.* On his next turn with the witness the same day, Ewing got Weichmann to say the ride happened *after* he saw the article in the *Republican*—or *after March 19.*

Before the witness took the stand for the third time on May 19, those who were coaching him decided he had overshot the mark by a few days and that the "horse ride" should take place a little earlier. So this time he was ready with their final estimate—Paine "came to the house on the evening of the 13th and remained there the 14th, 15th and 16th." For good measure, he added that Paine had gone to the theater with Surratt on the 18th to see *Jane Shore,* and that "it was when Forrest played there four nights in that week." (See Appendix C, "Dates of Paine's Visit to Surratt's in March.")

The item about Paine's having gone to the theater with Surratt was supposed to have tied in with Miss Fitzpatrick's statement (during interrogation after her arrest, as well as from the witness stand) that she went to the theater with Surratt, "*Wood,*" and a little girl boarder named Deane on an unspecified evening in March. But it didn't work out. He had already said "Payne" left for Baltimore right after the "horse ride." If that had been on the 16th, as he said, "Payne" would not have been in Washington on the 18th to go to the theater. Moreover, Weichmann had said he and Surratt went to see Booth play in *The Apostate.* If both of the witnesses' statements were correct, John Surratt had a full evening on March 18—He saw *The Apostate* with Weichmann *and also* saw *Jane Shore* with "Wood," Miss Fitzpatrick, and Miss Deane.

There were very good reasons for shifting the date of the "horse ride" all over the month of March. The prosecution had to make this event fit in with other events, which had fixed dates. It had to be between March 1 and March 21, during which period Booth was in the city, according to the register at the National Hotel.[23] Sometime in February, Weichmann had gossiped to Gleason about some sort of plot he thought was scheduled for Inauguration Day, March 4, and when he first took the witness stand, he was still trying to put the "horse ride" around that date.

On the same day Weichmann testified for the second time, May 18; Ethan Horner, the officer who arrested Arnold, testified that that defendant had told about a meeting of the "conspirators" around the "middle of March," at which he had said he would withdraw unless the abduction were attempted within the following week.[24] Also, the War Department had a wire Booth had sent O'Laughlin on the 13th of March telling him to "come at once," presumably for the "middle of March" meeting.[25] So the "horse ride" had to be scheduled sometime during the week after the 15th.

Now, the date the prosecutors finally selected for the "horse ride"—and expounded through Weichmann on the 19th—was March 16. This reconciled pretty well with other important dates they had to take into consideration, and it would do for the history books *if they could keep Paine's Oath of Allegiance out of court.* Fortunately (from their point of view) they were able to do so. Paine's documented whereabouts in the Baltimore jail on March 12, 13, and 14 would have wrecked the timetable they had worked out for Weichmann's final statement on the dates of Paine's visit and the "horse ride."

Of all those believed to have been involved in the incident, only John Surratt said *anything* to confirm the "horse ride" or any other actual attempt to kidnap Lincoln. His remarks were made during a lecture at Rockville, Maryland, after he was released following his trial in Washington in 1867.[26] At that trial his position had been that he *was* involved in Booth's kidnap scheme, but not in the assassination plot.

For this contention to be credible (in view of his close association with Booth prior to the assassination), the kidnap plot had to be shown as more than just a conversation piece.

Although Weichmann had intimated that *seven* men rode out that day on some mysterious business, he had named only Booth, Surratt, and "Payne" as participants. (Pitman added Atzerodt to the roster.) In 1867 this turned out to be a blessing to John Surratt. He was able to describe a foray that failed because someone else was riding in Lincoln's carriage when they waylaid it—and *all four* of the "conspirators" alleged to have taken part were dead and couldn't contradict his story.

On their part, the prosecutors also had good reason for wanting to show that the kidnap plot was an *active* project—that it hadn't folded up entirely by the middle of March, the "conspirators" disbanding altogether. They were claiming the assassination plot was a direct corollary of the abduction scheme and that the same group of people was involved in both undertakings. If Booth's "gang" were shown to be nothing more than a drinking and debating club that broke up a month before the assassination, it would have seemed rather obvious that the murder of Lincoln was the product of a *different* conspiracy—which it was.

Further, it is significant that the other defendants at the Trial whose participation in the "horse ride" was intimated evidently had no knowledge of the affair whatever. Both Arnold and Atzerodt, for example, were willing to talk freely about Booth's plan to kidnap the President, and both admitted they had been members of the group. It would have done neither of them the least damage to tell about the "horse ride"—Arnold in his published article after his release, or Atzerodt in his "confession" to the Rev. Butler before the execution[27]—if there had been such an affair. They just knew nothing about it.

Weichmann's testimony according to pitman

One would think the incrimination in Weichmann's three testimonies transcribed in Peterson would have been adequate to satisfy even Colonel Burnett—though their many internal contradictions required his attention. The War Department's censor went to work with his blue pencil and now and then resorted to the bone saw.

A direct comparison between Peterson and Pitman is difficult at best, because of the latter's narrative style. And in this case there was much rearrangement of the testimony to increase the frustration of the investigator. Some readers may wish to make a minute comparison of the verbatim testimony included with this chapter or in the original volumes. For less avid students we shall mention only a few of the more important revisions, additions, and deletions in the "official" record.

At the end of Reverdy Johnson's cross-examination in Peterson, he gave Weichmann a dressing down for his sneaky behavior in finding and keeping the "false moustache."

This line of examination tended to discredit the witness. Again on the eighteenth, Mr. Clampitt worked the witness over for his willingness, not to say eagerness, to betray his longtime friend John Surratt. Burnett handled these passages in such a way as to remove all criticism of the witness.

Burnett made several "corrections" in the "horse ride" story.

In Peterson "Payne" had merely walked into the room after the "ride." He said nothing and was not described—leaving the reader to wonder whether he had even been with Booth and Surratt. Burnett inserted—"He was also very much excited, and I noticed he had a pistol."

In Peterson the servant Dan didn't name *any* of the six men supposed to have ridden out with Surratt. In Pitman we find he names ". . . Booth, and Port Tobacco [nickname for Atzerodt], and that man who was stopping at the house, whom I recognized as Payne."

Some of Weichmann's most abject confusion on the date of the "horse ride" appeared during General Ewing's cross-examination on the eighteenth in which he tried to establish the date of the affair in relationship to Booth's appearance in *The Apostate.* Burnett amputated that whole section.

Weichmann's statements on the nineteenth that "Payne" had arrived on March 13, boarded at Surratt's on the "14th, 15th, and 16th" (night of the "horse ride"), and had gone to the theater with Surratt and the girls on the 18th were clearly false.

That is, to anyone who knew Paine's Oath was dated March 14. Burnett knew it—and made this testimony read better by dropping the reference to March 13 and having "Payne" attend the theater on the 15th (conforming to the actual date of *Jane Shore*), the day *before* the "horse ride."

From the standpoint of our over-all study of the conspiracy—the hidden conspiracy—the most important omission of all is discovered in the Pitman version of Weichmann's testimony on May 18.

At one point in Peterson, Holt showed the witness a note signed "R. E. Watson" and asked if he recognized the handwriting as Booth's. Weichmann said he did not, and Holt went on to other subjects. In Pitman we find *no reference* to the "Watson" letter.

During our research, the original of this letter was discovered in the National Archives. We shall have a full discussion of it in a later chapter, in the course of which it will become abundantly plain why Colonel Burnett removed Holt's reference to the "Watson" letter from the "official" record of the Trial.

summary of chapter ten

The War Department's contention that the prisoner Paine was the same man as the "Wood," who visited Surratt's several times and had frequent contacts with Booth, was found to be false. We conclude that Paine and "Wood" were two different men.

Louis Paine resided in Baltimore throughout the period of the alleged kidnap plot in Washington, but *did* stop at the Surratt house for two or three days after the middle of March, introducing himself to the family as a Baptist preacher. When he left there, he evidently went to New York.

The prosecutors' consistent practice of attributing all the characteristics and activities of "Wood" and "Payne" to a single man—the prisoner Paine—gave him the aspect of a thoroughly self-contradictory personality—both well bred and "vulgar," both expansive and reticent, both brutally violent and non-violent in the extreme, etc. In consequence, Colonel Doster felt that a plea of insanity was well justified, and Paine's image in history is that of an unpredictable, mentally retarded desperado.

11

the man at the herndon house

One of the incidents in Weichmann's testimony regarding Paine was a visit he made to the Herndon House at Ninth and F Streets with John Surratt around March 19. The purpose of the visit was to reserve a room for a mysterious, unnamed gentleman, a friend of Surratt's. He mentioned that a friend of the Surratt family, a local schoolteacher named Anna Ward, was supposed to have spoken to the landlady previously as to whether there were any rooms available in the establishment. Miss Ward testified on this and other matters at the Trial on June 3. She confirmed that she had inquired about rooms at the Herndon House for John, but didn't know for whom the room was intended.[1]

Mrs. Martha Murray, wife of the proprietor, testified on May 19. She was a prosecution witness, but in some respects her testimony in the Peterson transcript gave much less than wholehearted support to the War Department's case. The lady was not under arrest, although, as with everyone who had had anything at all to do with Booth or his associates before the assassination, she clearly felt she was under suspicion for having harbored one of the "conspirators." Her vagueness on some points and flat denial that she knew John Surratt may have been due to her desire to disassociate herself and her boardinghouse from the plot to kill the President, of which she obviously knew nothing.

---

mrs. Murray's testimony per peterson

A century later, in view of many aspects in the case of Louis Paine which we have already explored, it's rather frustrating to see Colonel Doster take his turn at examining this witness and not be able to think of any questions with more bearing on his client's guilt or innocence than one query as to the location of the boardinghouse. Why, for instance, didn't he ask her to give a precise description of her mysterious boarder? Or

(Continued on page 162)

MRS. MARTHA MURRAY

Testimony for Prosecution

PETERSON TRANSCRIPT MAY 19
Page 72

EXAMINED BY JUDGE HOLT

Q. Look at the prisoners at the bar and see if you can recognize any of them?

A. I have not seen any of them, unless it is that gentleman [pointing to Payne, who was directed to stand up]; he has the same appearance of a man I saw.

Q. Was the person of whom you speak a boarder at your house?

A. Yes sir.

Q. Under what name did he pass?

A. I did not hear any name; when Mr. McDevitt came to the house afterwards I showed him the name on the book which I thought was entered when he came there, and Mr. McDevitt cut the name out of the book; I cannot remember what the name was.

Q. How long did he remain there?

A. He came on Friday and left on Friday, two weeks afterwards.

Q. You keep the Herndon House, do you not?

A. My husband does.

Q. Was the Friday on which he left the 14th of April last?

A. Yes; the day the President was killed.

Q. What time in the day did he leave?

A. About 4 o'clock; we had dinner at half-past 4; this gentleman said he was going away, and wanted to settle his bill, and wished dinner before the regular dinner hour; I gave orders to have an early dinner given him; I never saw anything further concerning him.

Q. Did he come to your house as an invalid?

A. No; he said he came from the cars about 11 or 12 o'clock.

Q. Did he come alone, or with others?

A. He came alone.

Q. Was he visited by others while there?

PITMAN COMPILATION MAY 19
Page 154

My husband keeps the Herndon House, corner of Ninth and F Streets, opposite the Patent Office, cat-a-cornered. The only one of the prisoners I recognize as having seen before is that man, [pointing to the accused, Lewis Payne.] I think I have seen him; his features are familiar to me, but I would not say for certain. He was two weeks in our house, and he left on the Friday, the day of the assassination. He left on the 14th day, about 4 o'clock. We have dinner at half-past 4, and this gentleman came into the sitting-room and said he was going away and wanted to settle his bill; and he wished to have dinner before the regular dinner; so I gave orders for the dinner to be cut off and sent up to him. He went into the dining-room to eat his dinner, and I have not seen him since.

I do not recognize either of the prisoners as having visited this man. I remember that he once came in with two gentlemen to supper. I do not remember that any one spoke to me about engaging a room for this man. I am spoken to by so many that I could not remember any particular circumstance of that kind.

The changes in this testimony in Pitman being obvious in both nature and purpose, the text is shown above without comment.

(Peterson continued)

A. I expect he was.

Q. Would you be able to recognize any person who visited him? Look at the prisoners.

A. I do not see anyone I could recognize; I never noticed anyone, but one evening when at the supper table this gentleman came in; I had finished my supper, and got up, and did not pay any further attention; I left them sitting at the table.

Q. Had anyone spoken to you for a room for this man before he came?

A. No, not to my knowledge; some gentlemen have spoken to me for rooms, but I do not recollect anyone speaking for this man.

Q. Do you remember whether John Surratt called at your house?

A. I do not know him; I never heard of him till this circumstance.

CROSS-EXAMINED BY MR. DOSTER

Q. State to the Court the location of the Herndon House.

A. It is on the corner opposite the Patent Office.

---

better still, why didn't he scream for Mr. McDevitt, who she said had *cut the man's name out of the register?* That officer was apparently on the staff of Superintendent Richardson, head of the metropolitan police who, under Baker's order, had sent Weichmann to Canada. Weichmann testified that he had told McDevitt where "Payne" was staying and that the officer's call upon Mrs. Murray was made the day after the assassination.

Any one of the prosecutors could have told him what name McDevitt had cut out of the register; Colonel Foster knew it when he wrote up one of his summaries of the evidence for Colonel Burnett shortly after reading George Atzerodt's "confession." Foster could only have obtained the information from McDevitt, and he wrote, "It appears from the book that he registered his name as *Kincheloe*." [2]

Atzerodt's statement

If we choose to believe it, we have some rather clear statements as to the identity of the man who was Mrs. Murray's boarder for those two weeks prior to the assassination. They are in the "confession" of Atzerodt to Colonel H. H. Wells on April 25.

In deciding whether the statements in this document (National Archives, LAS file: see Appendix D, "Atzerodt's Statement to Wells") are reliable, a number of factors should be considered. Colonel Wells had been one of the most active and eager officers involved in the investigation, though he functioned as a provost marshal and was not directly connected with the War Department clique. He was trusted with various duties in the apprehension and confinement of the prisoners; he interrogated Mudd and had custody of Paine when he was first taken to the monitor. Wells did his duties with some enthusiasm, but this writer has found nothing to indicate that he had any part in the fabrication of the legend or its supporting evidence. The transcript of Atzerodt's statement was not in Wells' handwriting, but in the practiced script of a clerk; it was submitted first to Lieutenant Colonel J. H. Taylor, assistant adjutant general of Wells' military district, on May 2; then it was referred to General C. C. Augur, in command of the Washington garrison, and forwarded by him to Colonel Burnett on May 5. Even allowing for this last officer's lack of respect for the sanctity of official documents, this one had passed through too many hands to be tampered with. And there is no indication it was.

As for Atzerodt, he was an ignorant man who *knew* he had not committed an overt crime, as his behavior the night of the assassination and his failure to try to escape indicate. He could be expected to minimize his association with Booth and the others, but the knowledge that he had not killed anyone, or even tried to, would probably prompt a person of his level of intelligence to tell the truth when he told anything, but to tell no more than seemed necessary. This is what he was evidently doing in his so-called "confession." Before his execution he repeated substantially the same story to his spiritual advisor, Dr. Butler [3]—adding little more than a statement that he had attended a meeting around the middle of March at a restaurant, which seemed to be the same one Sam Arnold told about.[4] On this latter occasion, after having sat through the whole Trial, he referred to Paine as "Payne." In his statement to Wells, he used *only* the name "Wood." Many of the little German's statements were verified by testimony taken at the Trial. But perhaps the strongest argument for the truth of Atzerodt's "confession" is that the prosecutors for the War Department were so violently opposed to having it read in court for the record.

The first part of George Atzerodt's account tells that John Surratt came to Port Tobacco sometime after Christmas of '64 and invited him to take part in a mysterious, undefined scheme which involved running the blockade. He was working at his job as carriage-painter and couldn't leave then; but Surratt came back three weeks later, and they went up to Washington together, where he stayed a few days at the boarding-house. He met none of the group on this visit, though Surratt told him some were in New York and others in Baltimore. He went home for a week, then got a letter from John telling him to come back. This time he stayed at a hotel and was introduced to Booth *at Weichmann's office.* Somewhat later Booth asked him if he would like to go into the "oil business." Surratt and Booth shuttled back and forth between Washington and New York, and Atzerodt tried to sell two horses which the former claimed were his and wanted to dispose of. This was apparently during the period from March 20 to April 8.

Shortly after the fall of Richmond, Booth returned to Washington (April 8, according to the register at the National Hotel) [5] and took Atzerodt to the Herndon House to meet a young man named James Wood. They had actually met before at the "middle of March" meeting. On that occasion the young stranger was presented to the group under the alias of "Mosby," so this probably was the first time Atzerodt had heard the name "James Wood." As usual, Atzerodt was vague about the subject of their discussion and did not mention abduction anywhere in his original statement.

After some rambling references to meetings on the street and in hotels for three or four days, during which Herold was mentioned as one of the group, he said he met Booth at the National Hotel and was told to take a room at the Kirkwood House and try to get a pass to Richmond from Vice-President Johnson. Here we get the impression that Atzerodt was really not being let in on the plot—that the pass, if he could get one, was intended for Booth's use. This was on Thursday the thirteenth of April.

On Friday the fourteenth, at about three in the afternoon, Herold came to the Kirkwood and "said Booth and Wood wanted to see me." They went out together, but got separated when the actor wasn't at the restaurant where he was supposed to be and Herold went to look for him.

At this point the prisoner was asked to give some particulars on the appearance of James Wood:

> Wood is a tall man with black hair. Straight. He is a strong stout made man. No hair on his face, rather poor. He is rather a good looking man. I can't remember faces or features well enough to describe them. He had a wild look in his eyes. Saw him clean his teeth. He carried a tooth brush with him. Think he had long legs. Saw a bottle of hair oil on his stand. Think his arms was long. He was a large well built man. He wore boots. Wore a soft hat, leed (lead?) color I think, not black I am sure.

In this connection it should be remembered that Louis Paine had been placed in Colonel Wells' custody on April 19, and was probably still in his custody at the time of this interview. The officer was trying to determine if the "James Wood" Atzerodt spoke of was the same man as the prisoner on the monitor. Some of the German's comments were evidently in answer to Wells' questions. The phrase "no hair on his face" could apply to either a man with no beard, like Paine, or a clean-shaven man like "Wood."

It is uncertain what Atzerodt meant by "rather poor." By all other accounts, "Wood" looked anything but poor. He dressed well, had plenty of money, and stayed at the better hostelries. Paine, on the other hand, *was* poor-looking. It may have been that the clerk misunderstood Atzerodt's answer to Wells' question.

One descriptive feature Atzerodt mentioned seems to have been the principal distinction between "Wood" and Paine—"a wild look in his eyes." This expression in the eyes was mentioned by others who described "Wood." Anna Surratt was asked about it in her pre-Trial interrogation on April 28 (National Archives document) and, speaking of Paine's eyes, said, "They did not look like the eyes of the man that was at our house."

To return to the "confession," Atzerodt went back to the Kirkwood, and soon Herold came in and "said Booth and Wood wanted to see me immediately." Herold left a knife and pistol in his room and said:

> Let us go and see Booth and Wood. We went to their house on 9th St. (Henderson House) and they then proposed the murder to me. Booth proposed that we should kill the President. Said it would be the greatest thing in the world. This was about half past six or Seven O'clock on Friday. That Wood would go up to Seward's house and kill him—that he and Harrold had been and seen Andrew Johnson and found out where he was. He then asked me if I was willing myself to assist them. I said that I did not come for that and was not willing to murder a person. They said they did not want me to do any act, but only to show them the road into the lower part of Maryland, and if I did not I would suffer for it. I said I would do all I could on the road. . . .

He was told to get a horse and go and wait near the "Eastern Branch Bridge." They parted then, and he saw none of them after that. Around seven he got the rented horse he had left at Naylor's stable and rode out to the Navy Yard and wandered around town until midnight. At "about 12 o'clock" he took a streetcar to the Navy Yard. This aimless trip was covered in the Trial testimony of a man named Washington Briscoe, whose home was at the Navy Yard. He testified that he saw the little German, whom he knew, on the streetcar and spoke to him; that Atzerodt asked to sleep in his store that night, was refused, but got off with Briscoe at Garrison Street still coaxing, then took the car back to the city when it returned from its trip to the end of the line.[6]

Now, considering the circumstances—that the reluctant conspirator had failed to keep his appointment to guide "them" (meaning Booth, Wood, and Herold, apparently) to southern Maryland and was just shuffling around wondering what to do—his streetcar trip to the Navy Yard needs no explanation. But Atzerodt gave one:

"I went up to Woods to the Navy Yard about 12 o'clock after the assassination. Went in a Street Carr. . . ."

Allowing for the lack of an apostrophe to make the "Woods" possessive (the writer rarely used them) and also for the prisoner's German grammatical form, he appears to have said, "I went up to Wood's at the Navy Yard. . . ."

The idea that "Wood" had any residence in Washington, other than the Surratt house for one night in February and the Herndon House from March 31 to April 14, has never been proposed to this writer's knowledge. Yet this statement of Atzerodt's was supported by the testimony of at least one witness at the Trial.

A boy named "Peanuts" Burroughs took the stand on May 16. He was a regular employee at Ford's Theater and told about a small stable Booth had rented on the alley behind the building, in which he kept the little bay mare he had hired and ridden on his flight after the murder. In the course of Burroughs' examination about Booth's horse by Judge Holt, these questions and answers are recorded in Peterson,[7] and similarly in Pitman:[8]

Q. What was the appearance of the horse?
A. It was a little horse; I don't remember the color.
Q. Do you remember whether he was blind of one eye?
A. No sir; the fellow who brought the horse there used to go with Booth very often.
Q. Do you see that man among the prisoners here—I mean the man that brought the horse?
A. No sir, I don't see him here; this fellow, I think, lives in the Navy Yard; I saw him go in a house one day there when I carried the bills down.

Burroughs' statement about the man he had seen often with Booth, who lived at the Navy Yard and brought the horse on which the murderer escaped, has caused a great deal of conjecture among students of the assassination. The very clear import is that there was a man directly connected with the assassination who had not been caught in Baker's dragnet—was *not* among the defendants at the Conspiracy Trial, since this witness couldn't recognize him among the prisoners in the dock.

That one sentence in Atzerodt's "confession" suggests that the unknown accomplice who brought the horse for Booth's getaway to the stable behind Ford's was the man named "James Wood."

To finish up with the "confession," Atzerodt described the route he thought the fugitives intended to take through Maryland—a route which did *not* include a stop at the Mudd farm near Bryantown, which was seemingly occasioned by Booth's leg injury and caused them to take a much more easterly course south and strike the Potomac River at a point farther east then they had planned. At any rate, the route Atzerodt described—calling for the Potomac to be crossed at Maryland Point rather than at Pope's Creek, and then south to the "Confederate lines," *not* toward Richmond via Port Conway and the Garrett farm—was the route the fugitives *intended* to take when they left Washington.

A footnote to Atzerodt's description of the escape route Booth *intended* to take is found in Doster's summation in behalf of this defendant: Atzerodt told him Colonel Wells had promised him "a reprieve" if he would tell by what roads Booth was traveling. He did so, but Wells' promise was quickly forgotten.[9]

The little German had two more comments touching on the identity of "Wood":

"I understand that Woods came from Virginia but don't know the county. I heard him speak of Warrenton and Fauquier Co. . . . Booth and Harold sometimes spoke of Moseby and asked where he was. . . ."

This reference to Mosby seems to have been taken to mean General John S. Mosby, commander of the Confederate guerrillas in northern Virginia; he was suspected of having conspired with Booth in the abduction scheme, though the charge was quite groundless. As it happened, "Mosby" was one of "Wood's" aliases. Sam Arnold, in his "confession" recounted at the Trial by his arresting officer, told about the meeting in March at Lichtau House (it was actually Gautier's) and said those present were "J. W. Booth, M. O'Laughlin, G. W. Atzeroth, John Surratt, and a man with an alias of Moseby, and a small man whose name I couldn't recollect." [10]

From Atzerodt's list of those present at this meeting, given just before his execution,[11] we learn that the "small man" was Herold and "Moseby" was "Wood"—or as the condemned man called him by that time, "Payne."

A final pertinent statement by Atzerodt was this: "Wood was to kill Seward, Booth the President and Harold, V. P. Johnson."

Before the Trial, a marine officer in charge of the prisoners on the *Saugus*, Frank Monroe,[12] signed an affidavit to the effect that Atzerodt said Booth had wanted *him* to kill Johnson. But in his pre-execution statements to the Rev. Butler, the doomed man still said Herold was to have done it. In view of his statement that Herold had a knife and gun but left them in his room at the Kirkwood (these weapons and a coat of Herold's were found in Atzerodt's room by Detective John Lee),[13] there seem to have been some peculiarities in that young man's behavior on the night of the assassination which we will want to study in a later chapter.

discrepancies and withheld evidence

Returning once again to the Herndon House, our point of departure for this chapter, Mrs. Murray's uncertain identification of Paine as the man who had boarded with her was typical of all those who thought they recognized him. Not one—except Weichmann, of course—was ever positive he was the same man he had seen before. Her flat assertion that she didn't know John Surratt contradicts Weichmann, but she may have made it to avoid getting involved. She also said she did not know Atzerodt, although he said he had been to her house to see "Wood"; and she said the boarder had an early dinner and checked out just after 4:00 P.M. the day of the assassination, though Atzerodt said he, Booth, "Wood," and Herold met there in the early evening of that day.

These discrepancies might be explained by saying the proprietor's wife couldn't see *everyone* who came in the house; but a meeting of four men in a room which had been vacated earlier would seem like something to attract the attention of the landlady if she were on the premises. However, there may be a simple explanation of the confusion as to the time of the last meeting at the Herndon House. First, Atzerodt wanted it believed that he had learned of the murder only shortly before it occurred—the later the meeting, the better. Also, the word "evening" to southerners means from midafternoon onwards, not around sundown as with northerners.

Looking back over the testimony of Mrs. Murray and the "confession" of Atzerodt with regard to "Wood's," or "Kincheloe's," stay at the Herndon House, there are indications that this gentleman was much more than an obedient follower of Booth. Herold's message that *both* of them wanted to see Atzerodt implies an equality of status between "Wood" and Booth; a trusted, if subordinate, role for Herold; and a position of relatively uninformed and unreliable also-ran for Atzerodt.

In Doster's summation for Atzerodt before the court, he reviewed his client's role in the "conspiracy" and included a statement in the German's own words, to which his name was signed. The only details in it which were *not* in the "confession" to Colonel Wells were the admissions that an abduction had been planned and that Booth *had* asked him to kill Vice-President Johnson, which he refused to do.

However, the absence of *any* reference to "Wood" in Atzerodt's statement to Doster—and only one reference to "Payne"—makes it clear that Doster had never seen his client's statement to Wells. *Not one* of Atzerodt's several encounters with "Wood" was mentioned.

According to the procedures of the court martial, the defendants were considered guilty until *they* could prove their innocence. But—and this was an important corollary of that peculiar conception of military justice —the War Department was obligated to produce *all* evidence it acquired, *either for or against* the prisoners. In practice it was responsible for gathering any and all evidence pertinent to both the prosecution *and* the defense—even to the extent of paying the expenses for defense witnesses, as well as for those for the prosecution.

Thus there was no question as to the War Department's legal and moral obligation to show defense counsel all documents in its possession bearing on the case. Its failure to acquaint Doster with Paine's Oath, the contents of Atzerodt's "confession" to Wells, and many other species of evidence allows only one conclusion: The War Department deliberately withheld or concealed many items of critical evidence with the express intention of hindering the defense of the prisoners.

So far, most of the activities in Washington attributed to Paine were those of "Wood," "Kincheloe," and "Mosby." In the next chapter the scene shifts to Baltimore, and for the first time we hear some testimony as to the activities of Louis Paine—as Louis Paine.

summary of chapter eleven

The tall dark-haired man who stayed at the Herndon House under the name of "Kincheloe" for two weeks prior to the assassination—in whose rooms the final arrangements for the murder of the President were made —was the same "James Wood" who had visited the Surratt house on several occasions during the early months of 1865.

the man at the herndon house

"James Wood" had come to Washington from Fauquier County, Virginia, in January of 1865 and was first known to Booth and his accomplices by the alias of "Mosby."

"Kincheloe" (alias "James Wood," alias "Mosby") resembled Louis Paine so closely that Mrs. Murray, as well as other witnesses, thought they were the same man.

Colonel Doster, Paine's attorney, was never permitted to see George Atzerodt's revealing statement to Colonel Wells.

12

the men at the Branson house

On June 2, Miss Margaret Branson was called to the stand as a defense witness. She and her family had been under house arrest at their home from April 28 to May 23, when Margaret, her mother, and their maid, Margaret Kaighn, were called to Washington to be available as witnesses. They were not called upon to testify for the prosecution—for reasons which will soon be evident. Colonel Doster had arranged for their summons when he heard Paine had stayed at the Branson boardinghouse in Baltimore. But when he interviewed them, "They were so frightened that nothing could be got from them except that he had nearly beaten the servant to death, because she would not clear out his room. Otherwise they said he had behaved himself with extreme quietness, scarcely ever saying anything." [1]

So Doster called Margaret to the stand, not because he had any need for her testimony in the defense he was planning, but merely because she was one person who really had known the prisoner as Louis Paine.

Throughout his examination of this witness, Doster's line of questioning revealed his interest in laying the groundwork for an insanity plea—rather than eliciting testimony bearing upon his client's possible innocence.

Forty years later he devoted a paragraph of his memoirs to a rather quaint explanation of how he got the idea to plead insanity:

"General Harris, a physician, one of the members of the commission, before I thought of this plea, suggested to me that a person constipated as Paine was well known to be [from testimony of prison officials] must be entirely out of order, and that this was a general accompanying symptom of the early stages of insanity. . . ."

Now and then in his search for evidences of irrational behavior on Paine's part, Doster stumbled into areas of questioning that brought furious objections from the prosecutors—particularly from the waspish Bingham, whom Doster disliked intensely.

(Body text resumed on page 175)

MISS MARGARET BRANSON

Testimony for Defense

PETERSON TRANSCRIPT JUNE 2
Pages 124-125

EXAMINED BY MR. DOSTER

Q. Where do you live?

The witness' first statement was evidently a summary of a number of questions and answers.

A. I live in Baltimore and first saw the prisoner Payne at Gettysburg. I do not remember the time, but it was immediately after the battle of Gettysburg. I was there as a volunteer nurse. He was in my ward and very kind to the sick and wounded. I don't know whether he was there as a nurse or not. I don't know if he was a soldier. He had on no uniform. As nearly as I can recollect he was dressed in blue pants with no coat and a dark slouch hat. He went by the name of Powell and by the name of Doctor.

Q. How long did you know him there?

A. I do not know the time; I was there six weeks, and I do not know whether he was there the whole time or not.

Q. In the hospital, where he seemed to be attending the sick and wounded, were the patients both Confederate and Union soldiers?

A. Yes; I left the hospital the first week in September; I met Payne again some time that fall and winter; I do not remember when; I met him at my own home; he remained there only a few hours; I had very little conversation with him.

Q. Did he state to you where he was going?

Objected to by Judge Bingham on the ground that declarations of the prisoner could not be read in evidence.*

Mr. Doster replied that he intended to set up a plea of insanity in the case

**The description of the debate which follows is verbatim from Peterson, not this author's interpolation.*

PITMAN COMPILATION JUNE 2
Pages 160-161

BY MR. DOSTER

I live at No. 16 North Eutaw Street, Baltimore. I first met the prisoner, Payne, at Gettysburg, immediately after the battle there. I was a volunteer nurse, and he was in my ward. He was very kind to the sick and wounded. I do not know that he was a nurse, nor do I know that he was a soldier. As nearly as I remember, he wore blue pants, no coat, and a dark slouch hat. He went there by the name of Powell, and by the name of Doctor. The hospital contained both Confederate and Union soldiers. I was there about six weeks, and left the first week in September. I do not remember whether Powell was there the whole of that time.

I saw him again some time that fall or winter, at my mother's house. He was there but a very short time; only a few hours, and I had very little conversation with him.

Q. Did he say to you where he was going?

ASSISTANT JUDGE ADVOCATE BINGHAM. The witness need not state; what he said to her is altogether incompetent evidence.

MR. DOSTER. May it please the Court, I intend to set up the plea of insanity, as I have already stated, in the case of the prisoner, Payne. It is very true that, under all other pleas, declarations of this kind are not considered competent evidence for the defense, but the declaration of a person suspected of insanity is an act, and therefore admissable.

ASSISTANT JUDGE ADVOCATE BINGHAM. That is all very true; but the proper way to get at it is to lay some foundation for introducing the declarations in support of the allegation that the party was insane. In this case no foundation has been laid.

MR. DOSTER. I claim that the whole conduct of the alleged murderer, from beginning to end, is the work of an in-of Payne, and that while the declaration of the prisoner would not be admissible to prove his innocence, yet to prove his insanity his declarations were acts, and therefore admissible.

Judge Bingham replied that the counsel had laid no grounds for this course of examination to prove insanity.

Mr. Doster said that the prosecution themselves had laid the ground by proving a series of acts of assassination which he should claim were the work of an insane man.

Judge Bingham remarked that he supposed it was then the theory of the counsel that a man might take a knife large enough to butcher an ox, rush past all the attendants in the house, wounding and maiming them, stab a sick man in his bed again and again, and escape punishment on the ground that the acts were too atrocious for a sane man to commit.

Mr. Doster replied that all the circumstances connected with the assassination bore upon themselves evidence of the work of an insane man. The prosecution had proved that the accused had entered the house by a stratagem very likely to be resorted to by an insane man without the slightest possible disguise, stopping for five minutes to talk to a Negro on his way; after committing the deed making no attempt at concealment, leaving his pistol and hat there in the room and throwing away his knife deliberately where it could be found, in front of Mr. Seward's door, getting on his horse and riding away so deliberately that a man on foot could follow him for a square; then, instead of escaping as he could very well have done on his horse, turning his horse loose, wandering about the city, and finally going to the house of all others where he would be liable to be arrested. He claimed that the prosecution, in proof of these acts, has laid abundant ground for the examination he was now making, and he called attention now to Payne's stolid manner in court, so different from that of the other prisoners.

Mr. Clampitt said that he did not deny the right of the counsel to set up sane man, and that any further declarations I may prove, are merely in support of that theory and of that foundation as laid by the prosecution.

Assistant Judge Advocate Bingham. According to that, the more atrocious a man's conduct is, the more he is to be permitted to make a case for himself by all his wild declarations, of every sort and to everybody, at every time and at every place. If he only manages to get a knife large enough to sever the head of an ox as well as the head of a man, rushes past all the friends of a sick man into his chamber, stabs him first on one side of the throat and then on the other, and slashes him across the face, breaks the skull of his son, who tries to rescue him yelps, "I am mad! I am mad!" and rushes to the door and mounts a horse which he was careful to have tied there, he may thereupon prove all his declarations in his own defense, to show that he was not there at all.

Mr. Doster. It is claimed here that there is no foundation laid for the plea of insanity. In the first place, all the circumstances connected with the assassination show the work of insane men. The entrance into the house of Mr. Seward was by a stratagem which is peculiarly indicative of insane men. Then the conduct of Payne, after he entered the house, without the slightest particle of disguise, speaking to the Negro for five minutes—a person that he must know would be able to recognize him again thereafter; the ferocity of the crime, which is not indicative of human nature in its sane state; his leaving all the traces which men usually close up behind him. Instead of taking away his pistol and his knife and his hat, he walks leisurely out of the room, having plenty of time to take these away, and abandons them; he takes his knife and deliberately throws it down in front of Mr. Seward's door, as though anxious to be detected; and then, instead of riding off quickly, as a sane man would under the circumstances, he moves off so slowly that the Negro tells you he followed him for a whole square on a

the plea of insanity or any other plea for his client, but he rose indignantly to protest against his bringing in the house of Mrs. Surratt, as a place where such a man would be most likely to be arrested; there was no evidence that the house of Mrs. Surratt was a place he would be likely to go to for the purpose of hiding and screening himself from justice.

The objection was sustained by the Court.

Q. How long did he stay at your house?

A. A few hours.

Q. Do you know where he then went?

A. I do not.

Q. When did you see him the third time?

A. In January of this year, at my home.

Q. Describe how he was dressed at the time.

A. In black clothing, citizens' dress.

Q. What did he represent himself to be?

A. A refugee from Fauquier county, Virginia; he gave his name as Payne.

Q. How long did he stay at your house?

A. I think six weeks and a few days; I do not remember the exact time.

Q. Do you remember about the date he came in January?

A. I cannot; I think he left about the beginning of March.

Q. Did he ever see any company while there?

A. Never to my knowledge.

Q. Did you ever see J. Wilkes Booth?

A. No sir.

Q. Do you know whether Payne was ever called upon about that time by J. Wilkes Booth?

A. No sir.

Q. Did he or not take a room in your mother's house?

A. Yes.

Q. What were his habits? was he quiet, or did he go out a good deal?

A. He did not go out a great deal; he was remarkably quiet.

walk; and afterward, instead of escaping either to the north, on the side where there were no pickets at the time (for it was shown he had a sound horse), or instead of escaping over the river, as he had ample opportunity of doing—because if he could not get across the Anacosta Bridge, he might have swam the river at any point—he wanders off into the woods, rides around like a maniac, abandons his horse, takes to the woods and finally comes back to the very house which, if he had any sense, he knew must be exactly the house where he would be arrested—where there were guards at the time, and where he must have known, if he had been sane, that he would immediately walk into the arms of the military authorities.

He goes to this house in a crazy disguise; because who in the world ever heard of a man disguising himself by using a piece of his drawers as a hat, supposing that a sane man would not discover the disguise. Finally, there is the conduct of this person since he has been here on trial—the extraordinary stolidity of this man, as opposed to the rest of the prisoners; instead of showing the slightest feeling, he has displayed an indifference throughout this trial. You yourselves noticed that at the time of that solemn scene, when the Negro identified him he stood here and laughed at the moment when his life was trembling in the balance. I ask you, is that the conduct of a sane man? There are, besides, some physical reasons which go hand in hand with insanity, and corroborate it, of a character more delicate, and which I can not mention now, but which I am prepared to prove before the Court at any time. I say that the most probable case of insanity that can be made out has been made out by the prosecution, in the conduct of this prisoner before the assassination, during the assassination, at the time of his arrest, and during the trial.

Mr. Clampitt. May it please the Court, I do not rise for the purpose of denying to the counsel for the accused, Payne, the right to set up the plea of insanity, or any other plea that he

Q. In what way did his quietness show itself?

A. He was a great deal in his room; he seemed to be reserved and I thought seemed to be depressed in spirits.

Q. Was he or not exceedingly taciturn?

A. He was remarkable for not saying anything.

Q. Have you or not a library in your father's house?

A. No; we have a good many old books; a good many medical ones.

Q. Do you know whether the prisoner can read?

A. I do not.

Q. Did he or did he not give himself up to reading medical works while he was there?

A. He did.

Q. Was not his taciturnity so remarkable as to be commented on by the rest of the boarders?

A. I think not.

Q. Do you know whether the prisoner was at that time in possession of a great amount of money?

A. I do not; he had enough to pay his board.

Q. Do you know how the prisoner happened to leave your house?

A. We had a Negro servant who was exceedingly impudent to him.

JUDGE BINGHAM—You need not state what passed between the girl and that man.

MR. DOSTER—The witness is just to state that.

JUDGE BINGHAM—Why?

MR. DOSTER—It is for you to show why she should not.

JUDGE BINGHAM—Well, let her answer it.

WITNESS—He was arrested by the authorities and sent North to Philadelphia.

CROSS-EXAMINED BY COLONEL BURNETT

Q. He was arrested as a Southern refugee, was he not, and made to take the oath of allegiance?

A. I do not know what he was arrested for, as I never knew the reason why; he was taken to the Provost Marshal's office and was afterwards released and returned to the house.

Q. Do you know whether he came direct to Washington when he left in March?

A. I do not.

Q. Did he make any acquaintance in Washington while he was boarding at your house?

A. Not that I know of.

Q. Was he absent any time while he was at your house?

A. Never but one night to my knowledge.

Q. How many persons boarded at your house?

A. I do not know.

Q. Were there any other Southern refugees boarding at your house?

A. None but him.

BY MR. DOSTER

Q. Was or was not the prisoner, during the month of February, gone long

thinks proper; but I do rise for the purpose of indignantly proclaiming that he has no right to endeavor to bring before this Court the house of Mrs. Surratt as a rendezvous to which Payne would naturally resort. There is no evidence which has shown that he would naturally go to her house for the purpose of hiding or for the purpose of screening himself from justice.

The Commission sustained the objection of the Judge Advocate.

WITNESS. I do not know where he went to from my mother's. In January of this year, he came again to our house. He was dressed then in citizen's dress of black, and represented himself to be a refugee from Faquier County, Va., and gave his name as Payne. He took a room at my mother's house, staid there six weeks and a few days, and left in the beginning of March. He never, to my knowledge, saw any company while there. I never saw J. Wilkes Booth, and do not know that he ever called upon Payne.

(Peterson continued)

enough to have made a journey to Canada and back again?*

**During his long testimony regarding an alleged tie-in between Booth and the Confederate underground in Canada, the perjurer Richard Montgomery testified he had seen "Payne" at the Queen's Hotel in Toronto, where the rebels made their headquarters, and was told by Clement Clay that he was working with them. It was this statement which prompted Doster's question as to whether the prisoner had been away from the Branson house long enough to have gone to Canada.*

A. Not to my knowledge.

Q. If he had been would you have known it?

A. I certainly would.

Q. In what hospital did you see him at Gettysburg?

A. In the General Hospital; Dr. Chamberlain's.

Q. Who did the prisoner seem to be nursing, the Confederate or Union wounded?

A. He attended to different ones in my ward, and I had both in my ward.

Q. Was your mother with you there?

A. No.

Margaret Branson's testimony per pitman

In this case, since the changes in the Pitman transcript of Margaret Branson's testimony can be described without a lengthy digression, we shall make the comparison between the two compilations now and dispose of it:

The initial interrogation, before Judge Bingham made his objection, didn't vary particularly from Peterson. But Bingham's summary of the crime and Doster's description of the extraordinary behavior of Seward's assailant were both completely rewritten in a form designed to show the prisoner guilty in the exact manner the prosecution had charged. The long dialogue with Miss Branson which followed the court's approval of Bingham's objection is pared down to an innocuous paragraph (which see).

It is hardly necessary to call the reader's attention to all the important statements by this witness which were thus deleted from the Pitman compilation. But two very enlightening omissions should be mentioned:

Burnett took the liberty of removing his own reference to the Oath of Allegiance.

But Doster never missed it. In his recollections, written forty years later, he still spoke respectfully of Burnett and favorably of the Pitman transcript—and still spelled his client's name "Payne." The name was spelled "Paine" on the Oath of Allegiance, which had been taken from the prisoner at his arrest and which was in the War Department's possession from the beginning. *Doster never saw the document.*

Doster didn't seem to notice Margaret's statement that Paine was ordered north after his arrest in Baltimore.

He never missed it, although he heard about it later. This not only indicated that he *had not seen* Paine's Oath; it also showed that the prosecutors had succeeded in keeping secret the fact that they had a number of other documents bearing on Paine's associations with the Branson family, some of which are still to be found in the National Archives.

Mrs. Branson, Margaret's mother, wasn't called to the witness stand; but a servant in her household, Margaret Kaighn, testified for the defense immediately after the daughter. If it seems peculiar that this woman's rather negative statements about the prisoner were brought out by the defense rather than by the prosecution, it must be remembered that Colonel Doster was by this date, June 2, completely absorbed in strengthening his client's insanity plea, and this witness' testimony supported that plea. Doster questioned her particularly about Paine's altercation with the maid. The following is from Peterson, but is not much different in Pitman:

TESTIMONY OF MARGARET KAIGANE [KAIGHN][2]

EXAMINED BY MR. DOSTER

Q. State whether you are a servant in the house of Mr. Branson.
A. Yes Sir.
Q. Did you see the prisoner Payne there?
A. Yes; he came there in January or February and stayed till about the middle of March.
Q. Do you remember at any time a controversy that Payne had with the Negro girl there?
A. Yes, he asked her to clean up his rooms there; she said she would not do it. He asked her why, she said she would not do it. He called her some names, and slapped her and struck her.
Q. Did he not throw her to the ground and stamp on her body and try to kill her?
A. Yes.
Q. Did he not strike her on the forehead?
A. Yes.
O. What did the Negro girl do in consequence?
A. She went to have him arrested.
Q. Did he or did he not say he would kill her?
A. He did while he was striking her.

the prisoner's claim that he was Powell

Miss Branson's testimony that she believed Paine to be the same man as a Confederate prisoner named Powell, whom she had met at Gettysburg in '63, was not a revelation to the prosecution—nor to Colonel Doster. For, several days before Margaret took the stand on Friday, June 2, Paine had broken his long, stubborn silence. This appears to have occurred on Saturday, May 27, a couple of days after the Bransons first entered the courtroom. From the attorney's recollections we learn how it happened:[3]

> During the first two weeks of the trial I could get nothing out of Payne either as to his previous history, or as to anything he might have to say in his own defense, or as to whether he wished to be defended at all. During all this time I knew very little more of him than the public generally, and not near as much as the prosecution, and was in great doubt whether to explain his conduct by lunacy, unparalleled stupidity or fear of prejudicing his cause by communications with his counsel. He would sit bolt upright with the back of his head against the wall; his two manacled hands spread out on his knees, staring straight forward at the crowd behind the president of the court. The curiosity to see the prisoners was wonderful and the crowd sometimes so great as to prevent counsel from seeing what the court was doing. The heat too began to be excessive and, as the ventilation was poor, the situation was extremely uncomfortable.
>
> By the time the prosecution had got to the middle of their evidence concerning Payne, and when he had been identified, standing up with his hat and coat on, by Seward's Negro boy, the approaching danger seemed to thaw him out. One Saturday afternoon he asked me what next day was. I answered, "Sunday." He then said if I could get down to the arsenal and could procure a private interview with him he would like to tell me something.
>
> I saw him next day in the court room alone, although sentinels were at each door, outside. He then gave me the history of his life disconnectedly, but kept very still about his share in the transaction [the assassination] at first. He inquired how Mr. Fred Seward was getting along and, when he was told, said he was sorry he had hurt the young man and owed him an apology. This he said often afterwards. His mind seemed of the lowest order, very little above the brute, and his moral faculties equally low. On hearing the narrative, I immediately concluded that the only thing possible to be done on his behalf was to let the court know all that I knew about his mental and moral nature and his previous education.
>
> This, by the rules of evidence which were strictly enforced against the prisoners, but relaxed in favor of the prosecution, could only be done under the plea of insanity, which was accordingly adopted. Under the plea of not guilty, I had no recourse except to show that he was not the man Seward's Negro took him to be, and I could not show that. Even under the plea of insanity I could not let the court talk to the prisoner, and find out for itself what a phenomenon he was. That was to be done by experts. He could not remember for a long time what state or county he was born in or how old he was.
>
> Dr. Nichols [a civilian physician, for thirteen years superintendent of the Government Hospital for the Insane] was called, examined him, and gave me to understand that he had grave doubts of the prisoner's sanity. Just as he was about to testify on that point a messenger arrived stating that his wife was on the point of death. She died, and his testimony could not be had. This was a great blow.
>
> Dr. Hall, another eminent physician of Washington, who was the first

> doctor called in to see Mr. Lincoln after he was shot, also examined him. He also testified that he had doubts about the soundness of his mind. All agreed that his physical system was greatly deranged. It is singular, however, that all the army surgeons who were examined swore the other way, and the prosecution knew better than to call civilians who made insanity a specialty.
>
> I have never entertained a doubt myself, that the man was not what is termed *compos mentis,* i. e., a person of average understanding but in that respect a dwarf. *Either this or he played his part very well to the end.* Neither have I any doubt that before a civil tribunal where the court would have waited until I received my witnesses from Florida * (which this court would not do) and could have inquired into his previous conduct, the physicians would have declared him not an accountable being, on account of his utter dullness, and inability to decide between right and wrong.

The prisoner's "narrative," of course, was his account of the personal history of Lewis Powell, whom he claimed to be—and whom Margaret Branson would testify she had known at Gettysburg. Rather than giving the details of the story in his memoirs, Doster referred his readers to the published compilations of the Trial, in which the biography he read to the court is found.

Before we turn to those pages in Peterson, one observation should be made about the passages from Colonel Doster's recollections of his client which we have just read, while his estimate of the young man's character and mental capacities is fresh in mind.

A century later the question of Louis Paine's guilt or innocence is quite academic. Sympathy—if the study of his case inspires any—is wasted upon a person who has been dead a hundred years. But an irony of human relations is seen in the many wisps of doubt which appear briefly here and there in the attorney's memories of the Trial. Both in the foregoing extracts and in his argument with Bingham he cited contradictory conditions, statements, and actions which could *not* be explained in terms of insanity. The words and actions of Paine—in conversation with his attorney or at the Surratt house—and those of the man who attacked Seward were not irrational at all when studied separately. They only *seemed* inconsistent, and therefore irrational, when associated with *one* man. Doster recited one clue after another that he was dealing with the activities of *two* men rather than one—and one of them "playing a part." Yet his literal, two-dimensional viewpoint made it quite impossible for him to see anything but externals, or find any explanation for the outrageous contradictions evident in his client's personality other than insanity.

A ready example, since he made such an emphatic point about the "utter dullness" of the prisoner:

Doster accepted the young man's statement that, as Powell, he had served in Mosby's Partisan Rangers for most of the year of 1864. Colonel

*Relatives of Lewis Powell whom Doster had tried to summon to Washington.

Doster had been a field officer. With his additional experience as provost marshal and with the Bureau of Military Justice, he probably knew much more about the history and operations of Mosby's 43rd Battalion in northern Virginia than the average well-informed officer. In fact his summation gave a very educated description of guerrilla warfare in the style of Mosby.[4]

He knew that this Confederate command was almost unique in American military history, an elite cavalry organized for the sole purpose of fighting *behind* the "enemy's" lines. True, from the Union point of view it was a diabolically well-led gang of highwaymen and bushwhackers—and there was some truth to that—but the essential qualifications for the individual trooper as to intelligence, daring, initiative, and resourcefulness were probably higher than those in any military unit ever assembled on this continent up to that time.

In a nutshell: A man as dull as Colonel Doster thought Paine to be wouldn't have been trusted to hold the horses in Mosby's Rangers!

summary of chapter twelve

Margaret Branson confirmed that Louis Paine had arrived in Baltimore from Fauquier County, Virginia, in January, 1865, and represented himself as a refugee—and was not absent, to her knowledge, until his arrest after the altercation with the maid.

This witness' startling revelation was her statement that she had known "Payne" two years earlier in a hospital at Gettysburg by the name of "Powell," and that "Powell" had stopped at their house briefly during the winter of '63. The situation she described was an exact counterpart of the extraordinary one the prosecutors had presented two weeks earlier in the Trial—with "Wood," though well acquainted with the Surratt house boarders, showing up a week after his last visit and saying his name was "Payne."

Paine's sudden revelation to Doster that he was "Lewis Powell," son of a Baptist minister in Florida, was made some *five days* before Miss Branson took the stand and claimed to have known him as "Powell." Doster had informed Burnett of the prisoner's statements as to his identity. Therefore Margaret's testimony had the appearance of a planned effort to confirm the story Paine had told his attorney earlier.

Doster, though he accepted this explanation of his client's real identity, expressed a vague suspicion that Louis Paine was "playing a part."

13

the "biography" of Lewis Powell

Louis Paine knew quite a bit about Lewis Powell—enough to satisfy Colonel Doster, the prosecutors, and posterity, if not Lafayette Baker. And Baker didn't object to his hanging under another man's name, as long as he was agreeable to hanging.

The manner in which the narrative was recited was so curious that even Doster noticed it. He gave "the history of his life disconnectedly" but had little to say about "his share in the transaction, at first." "He could not remember for a long time what state or county he was born in or how old he was."

When Dr. James C. Hall testified on June 13 and reported the findings of his examination of the prisoner, these were some of his observations:[1]

> . . . The prisoner answered all questions put to him willingly, but his mind appeared to be very inert; his intellect was of a very low order, and dull and feeble. . . . It seems to me that no man who was perfectly sane could exhibit the same utter insensibility which the prisoner manifests; there was no attempt at deception; he answered my questions, so far as his mind would permit him, without any apparent intent to deceive or mislead me; . . . He was perfectly calm; his memory was very slow, and at times it appeared very difficult for him to answer a simple question; he could not remember the maiden name of his mother.

After that statement Doster, who was examining Dr. Hall, asked:

> Q. Do you think that was sincere or an affectation?
> A. I think it was sincere; his memory is very deficient.

Dr. Charles H. Nichols and his colleague Dr. Hall—both civilians—wouldn't say flatly that the prisoner was insane, but they felt the actions attributed to him, together with his apparently faulty memory and abnormal resignation to death, were grounds for suspecting he was not mentally responsible. In fairness to the military surgeons who were called by the prosecution—though Doster hinted they were subservient to the War

Department's wishes—it should be mentioned that they interviewed the prisoner after the two civilian doctors had questioned him several times about his personal history as "Powell." And Hall had remarked that the prisoner seemed to answer much more promptly the second time a question was asked. By the time the military surgeons examined Paine, most of the questions had already been asked at least once, and he could answer quickly enough to satisfy them that he was not insane, not even of low mentality.

Paine's "narrative" of Powell's personal history is not found in a separate document, but is incorporated in Colonel Doster's summation for the prisoner. That eloquent address to the court on June 21 opened with three "admissions":[2]

1. That the prosecution had established beyond all doubt that his client was the person who had attacked and attempted to kill Secretary Seward.
2. That it had been proved that the prisoner was not insane "within the medical definition."
3. "That he believed what he was doing was right and justifiable."

Doster's plea, then, was a development of the third point—an appeal for the court's sympathy, understanding, and mercy for a young man of good family background, whose moral character had been completely corrupted by the vast corruption of civil war. The attorney's effort was a valiant one—but surely no voice ever cried in a wider wilderness!

In effect, the summation was an emotional indictment of war as the destroyer of everything decent in human nature. The "facts" of Powell's biography, according to Louis Paine, were not listed together but were woven into a rhetorical presentation along with Doster's interpretations of them and conjecture as to how they fitted into and supported the *prosecution's* conception of the "conspiracy." So at this final and crucial stage in the defense of Louis Paine, his attorney was—with the very best intentions—serving as wheel horse for the War Department by doing what it had been unable to do—explaining just how this defendant fitted into the legend of John Wilkes Booth.

the biographical data

It is not always possible to distinguish the particulars provided by Paine from Doster's conjectures and data he may have obtained from other sources. So in order to study the "narrative," we have to segregate the positive statements from the rhetoric and assume that the prisoner either volunteered each "fact" or answered affirmatively when his attorney asked him if such and such were the case. We shall take the biographical data in order from Peterson, point by point, and follow each with some observations.

The complete name of the prisoner was given as Lewis Payne Powell.

Louis Paine's claim that he was Lewis Powell got off to an inauspicious start. He apparently did not know his *own middle name*. Powell's military records in the National Archives are under the name "Lewis T." In Mosby's Rangers he was known to some of his companions by his full name, "Lewis Thornton Powell." Burnett had checked on this and was careful to correct the error in Pitman's transcript.

Lewis Powell was the son of the Rev. George C. Powell, a Baptist minister.

This was correct.

His father was "supposed to live at Live Oak Station on the railroad between Jacksonville and Tallahassee in the state of Florida."

This was not a *home address,* but a *mailing address.* In 1865 it was the universal custom among rural Americans, both North and South, to name their *county* when telling where their home was. There was a village of Live Oak in Suwannee County in northern Florida, and it was a station on the railroad—site of the present town of that name. Paine had evidently not mentioned the county.

In this era, rural mail was not yet delivered to the home of the addressee. Letters addressed to rural dwellers were sent to the nearest postal station—in this case, Live Oak Station. It was up to the rural resident to make a trip to the post office from time to time to see if there was any mail for him. If it was rather far, or if he was not expecting any mail, he might come quite infrequently. Thus it was the practice in many areas for the postmaster to publish a list of his unclaimed letters in the county or district newspapers, and distant farmers often found it expedient to travel to the postal station only when they read in the newspapers that there was mail for them.

Immediately after hearing Paine's "narrative" about Powell late in May, Colonel Doster wrote a letter to the Rev. Powell at "Live Oak Station" asking him to come to Washington to appear as a witness for his "son"—hoping he could testify that there was a strain of insanity in the family. In October, three months after the executions, he received an answer from Powell from "Live Oak, East Florida," dated September 30.[3] Among other things, the minister said he had not received the attorney's letter until July 6, some five weeks after it was written, though it could hardly have taken more than two weeks to reach the local post office. He said he had been ill when the letter came—which would not have delayed his receiving it *if* the family lived in or even near the village. Consequently, the Rev. Powell must have lived far enough from Live Oak so that he went for the mail rarely and only when he was well enough to travel. The fact that he datelined his reply "Live Oak" may only indicate that he had gone to the postal station, as many rural people did in a day when paper and ink were not ordinary household articles, to get stationery and a stamp and *write* the letter as well as mail it.

He was born in the State of Alabama "in the year 1845."

The Rev. Powell's letter called Doster's attention to the fact that his alleged son had been mistaken about his age—and wrote that his birth date was April 22, 1844. Then, as now, it was unusual for a literate person with normal family ties not to know the year of his birth. Powell was literate himself and came from an educated family. *He* was born in Alabama, though Doster noted that Paine wasn't able to remember it for a long time—and was *never* able to remember the county of his birth (Randolph County), which in those days a person would know as well as he knew his birth state.

His father had six daughters and two sons in addition to Lewis.

The Rev. Powell did have six daughters, but he had *three* sons in addition to Lewis. The names of the three other sons, all older than Lewis, were Benjamin, George, and Oliver. George had married and moved to Orange County, Florida, around 1857, about two years before the rest of the family also migrated from Georgia to northern Florida. Louis Paine didn't know about this third brother, who had not lived with the family for some seven years. If he had really been Lewis Powell, he would surely have remembered George as well as Benjamin and Oliver. He did not *name* any of them.

The family lived for a time in Worth and Stewart Counties in Georgia.

The Powell family did live in Stewart County and was listed there in the 1850 census—the Rev. Powell having been called to serve as pastor of Beulah Church in that county in 1848, in which year he moved there from Russell County, Alabama, with his family. However, the most reliable records of the father's long career as a Baptist minister state that he moved directly from Stewart County to Florida. He may have stopped briefly in Worth County and other Georgia counties on his way to Florida, but exhaustive research has failed to unearth any confirmation of Paine's statement that either Lewis or the Rev. Powell *ever* lived in Worth County.

The Powell family then moved to Florida in the year 1859.

Correct. The Rev. Powell's obituary,[4] which has proved to be accurate in every respect which can be checked, says Lewis' family moved to the vicinity of Belleville in Hamilton County, Florida, in that year. They were not listed in that county or in the neighboring counties in the 1860 census, so may have been in transit during that census. But the Rev. Powell was living somewhere in the environs of Live Oak in 1865.

Lewis Powell was sixteen when "war broke out."

Literally speaking, this was correct. Lewis *was* sixteen (born April 22, 1844) on January 10, 1861, when Florida voted to secede, and on April 12, when Fort Sumter was fired upon. But he enlisted in the Jasper Blues of Hamilton County on May 30—by which date he had become seventeen. It does not refute Paine's statement as to Powell's age when we find that the muster-in roll of the 2nd Florida Infantry on July 13, 1861, lists Lewis T. Powell as having joined for one year as of June 4—and gives his age as *nineteen.*[5] Lewis merely lied about his age in order to enlist, or because he looked older than he was and wanted to be considered as more nearly a man.

Until enlisting, Lewis had been "engaged in superintending his father's plantation and a number of slaves."

The 1830 census for Crawford County, Georgia, and the 1840 census for Randolph County, Alabama, show the Rev. George C. Powell owning a few slaves. He had been licensed to preach in Talbot County, Georgia, in the 1830's, but was not ordained until 1847 at Liberty Church in Russell County, Alabama. The 1850 census for Stewart County, Georgia, shows he no longer owned slaves at that time* Thus Powell seems to have freed his slaves before Lewis reached the age of *three.*

At this point, then, Paine's account of Lewis Powell's boyhood activities showed a particularly glaring flaw—there being no slaves "on his father's plantation" for him to superintend. But to know the history

*1850 census, Stewart County, Ga.—Slave schedules. The Baptists denounced slavery early in the century and generally required prospective ministers and missionaries to dispose of any slaves they owned before they could be ordained. Powell evidently did so in 1847.

of the Powell family even as well as he did, Paine would almost have to have known the Rev. Powell didn't own slaves. The next passage in Doster's argument for his client indicates it may have been *his* idea to represent the Powells as slave-owners. His central theme was the various southern institutions which had combined with wartime experiences to destroy the good character of Lewis Powell. The very first of these was his misfortune to have been reared in a slave-owning society—which provided the first of his four reasons for going to war: defense of that social system. Obviously Doster couldn't have made his point if he had had to add that the Rev. Powell had abolished slavery as far as his family was concerned not long after Lewis was born. Paine either misinformed him or said nothing about slaves, leaving the attorney free to improvise.

Powell enlisted in "Captain Stuart's Company, 2nd Florida Infantry, commanded by Colonel Ward and was ordered to Richmond."

Correct to the degree that the Hamilton Blues (or Jasper Blues), in which Powell *had* enlisted, subsequently became one of the companies in the 2nd Infantry, which was ordered to Richmond in the fall of '61.

The 2nd Infantry was attached to A. P. Hill's corps, with which Powell "passed through the Peninsula campaign and the battles of Chancellorsville and Antietam."

According to *Soldiers of Florida,*[6] official state record of the participation of Florida units in the Civil War, this was largely correct. However, it is not stated in the above record that the 2nd Infantry was engaged at Antietam, though A. P. Hill's corps participated, and it *is* stated that the regiment took part in the battle of Fredericksburg. Private Lewis Powell, according to the muster roll, was with his unit at that time, December 13, 1862, and would surely have listed that bloody battle, which *both* sides agreed was a thumping Confederate victory.

"Here (after the battle of Antietam) he heard that his two brothers had been killed at the battle of Murfreesboro."

The battle of Antietam (near Sharpsburg, Maryland) was fought on September 16-17, 1862, and the one at Murfreesboro, Tennessee, December 31, 1862, to January 2, 1863. So, if Doster quoted Paine correctly, Powell learned of his brothers' deaths *three and a half months before they occurred.*

Although Louis Paine knew about only *two* of Lewis Powell's three brothers, Benjamin and Oliver, all three (including George) served in the Confederate Army. The two Paine knew about were both killed in the war—Oliver at Murfreesboro and Benjamin at a time and place unknown. George was wounded seriously at Petersburg on September 15, 1864, but survived to return to his family in Orange County, Florida, after the war.

The official service records of Oliver and George reveal the following:[7] Oliver was a private in Company C, 4th Florida Infantry; he enlisted September 5, 1861, at Madison. George was a private in Company B, 10th Florida Infantry; he enlisted May 12, 1862, at Rico's Bluff. Benjamin's service record has not yet been located, but correspondence with the Florida State Library at Tallahassee indicates that he is believed to have served in the army and lost his life.

Colonel Doster, quoting Paine, stated that Lewis Powell enlisted *after* his older brothers (Oliver and Benjamin). Yet the records show he enlisted three months *before* Oliver. The date of Benjamin's enlistment is as yet unknown.

"Finally, the 3rd of July, 1863, in the charge upon the Federal centre at Gettysburg, he was wounded, taken prisoner. . . ."

The assault Doster refers to is evidently Pickett's Charge, in which elements of A. P. Hill's corps did participate. On the muster rolls of Company I, 2nd Florida Infantry, for the three two-month periods from July through December, 1863, Lewis T. Powell is listed as "Absent—wounded at Gettysburg, Pa., *July 2,* 1863." Subsequent muster rolls for the regiment carried Powell as a "prisoner of war" through February, 1865.[8]

Thus, if the Confederate records are correct, Powell was wounded and captured a day earlier than Paine said—and did not participate in Pickett's Charge.

His wound was the result of a "gunshot" in the right wrist. He was admitted to a Union 12th Corps field hospital on July 4.[9] On July 6 he was transferred to a general hospital and subsequently assigned duties as a nurse.

Since the length of time Powell was hospitalized and the date his nursing duties began can't be determined, there is no way of judging the seriousness of his wound. But the Union medical staff had the staggering task of caring for more than 21,000 patients, and "walking wounded" were turned over to the provost marshal as quickly as possible to make room for more gravely wounded men. The point is that Doster might logically have looked to see whether Louis Paine had a scar on his right wrist. We can only conclude, since he makes no mention of it, that it didn't occur to him to investigate. The fact that no member of the court brought this up—and that neither Doster, the nine military judges, nor any of the military men involved noticed the attorney's glaring error in the comparative dates of Antietam and Murfreesboro, shows that all concerned were satisfied to believe the prisoner guilty by his own admission—regardless of the truth or falsity of his statements.

"From Gettysburg he was sent to West's Buildings Hospital, Pratt Street, Baltimore, and remained until October, 1863, when . . . he deserted."

Union records show that Powell was remanded to the provost marshal on September 1 and admitted to West's Buildings General Hospital on September 2. He was not listed as a patient, so was evidently still a nurse. He escaped from this hospital on September 7 rather than in October.

In Doster's address to the court, no cognizance was taken of the stop at Branson's in Baltimore, in the winter of '63, of which Margaret Branson had testified. He pictures the escapee as making his way southward to try to rejoin his regiment.

Not being able to get through the lines, he joined Mosby's command.

With some exceptions, the veterans of Mosby's Rangers who wrote their memoirs were inclined to de-emphasize the fact that the notorious Lewis Thornton Powell had served with that select organization. But enough of them did mention his part in various encounters with "the enemy" to establish beyond doubt both that he served with Mosby during most of 1864 and that his comrades considered him a particularly aggressive cavalry fighter.

However, he doesn't appear to have joined up until sometime in the spring of '64, leaving a period of some months unaccounted for between that time and his escape from Baltimore in September of '63. Paine's so-called "confession" to the Rev. Dr. A. Gillette the night before his execution, which contains a few items Doster didn't mention,* asserted

*One of the most interesting revelations in Dr. Gillette's account of Paine's "confession" to him was that the prisoner had finally recalled his (Powell's) mother's first name *correctly* as "Caroline." But he *still* couldn't remember her *maiden* name. Strange enough in itself, this becomes even more so when genealogical research reveals that the mother's maiden name was the same as her married one *Powell*. She was apparently a cousin of her husband, a fact which was notable enough to have been very well known to the real Lewis Powell.

that Powell first joined the guerrilla forces of Harry Gilmore (whose scene of operations was to the west of Mosby's stamping ground in Fauquier and the neighboring counties), "but became dissatisfied and deserted." [10] We shall refer back to this statement of Paine's when we attempt to reconstruct the actual career of Lewis Powell.

Powell deserted Mosby on January 6, on which day, as a Mrs. Grant had testified, "he saved the lives of two Union soldiers."

With respect to this event, Colonel Doster was citing court testimony rather than quoting Paine. On June 12 he had called Mr. and Mrs. John Grant of Warrenton, Virginia, as defense witnesses—not to the innocence of Paine, but on the theory that the incident they described was at such variance with his later conduct as an assassin as to imply that his attack upon Seward occurred during a period of insanity. The wife's testimony, as condensed in Peterson, was as follows:

TESTIMONY OF MRS. L. GRANT, JUNE 12 [11]

EXAMINED BY MR. DOSTER

I reside in Warrenton, Va.; I recognize the prisoner Payne as a man I saw on the road in front of my house, having three Union soldiers in his charge; an attempt was made to kill the prisoners, and the man called Powell [meaning Payne] tried to prevent it, and I heard him say that he was a gentleman and wished to be treated as such; that if they attempted to kill the man he had captured he would defend the prisoner at the peril of his life; one of the prisoners was killed, when the party left the road, and I did not see them afterwards; the affair occurred last Christmas.

CROSS-EXAMINED BY JUDGE ADVOCATE HOLT

I was speaking of the affair to a citizen, and telling him this man tried to save the Union soldiers, when I was informed that his name was Powell; I had not seen him before, nor have I seen him since until today, but I am certain he is the man.

QUESTIONED BY THE COURT

He was dressed as a Confederate, and I thought they called him lieutenant; there were the marks of an officer upon him; he looked more genteel than the common soldiers.

When Mr. Grant took the stand, he confirmed his wife's story of the incident, though stated he hadn't seen it himself, as he was approaching the house when the firing started and was still some three hundred yards away. However, the last few lines of his statement leave the impression that this citizen of Warrenton—who may well have been with Mosby himself—knew Lewis Powell by more than hearsay:

". . . All I heard was that the prisoner at the bar, who went by the name of Powell, had tried to save the lives of two Union soldiers; the prisoner was not an officer, so far as I am aware." [12]

Mr. Grant was right; Powell was a private throughout his service with Mosby. And Mrs. Grant put her finger on one of the differences between Lewis Powell and Louis Paine when she said, "He looked more genteel than the common soldiers."

There is no way now of checking the date on which Powell deserted Mosby and went to Washington. Paine said he (as Powell) took the Oath of Allegiance at Alexandria on January 6, "as a refugee from Fauquier." Doster could easily have checked it with the provost marshal there, since these officers kept a record of all persons to whom they administered the Oath. He apparently didn't do so. Since taking the Oath was the easiest way of getting past the Capitol's ring of defenses *legally*, Powell probably did so—using any one of his half-dozen aliases.

Powell "took a room at Mrs. Branson's, the lady he had met at Gettysburg, and resolved to wait for the return of peace."

Doster obviously meant to say Margaret Branson, not her mother, was the lady Powell met at Gettysburg.

Here Paine attributed his own activities to Powell, rather than vice versa, as he did in the foregoing portions of the "biography." The remarkable thing is that Colonel Doster failed to notice that this version of Powell's history ignored not only the soldier's first visit to the Branson house in 1863 but also the verified appearances of "Wood" at the Surratt house in February and March of '65, even though the War Department had gone to great pains to establish that "Wood" and Doster's client were the *same person.*

The attorney proceeded to picture the unfortunate "Powell" brooding in his room at Branson's, whiling away the time reading medical books, and watching the little money he had left from the sale of his horse melt away.

"The fracas occurred . . . by which he was arrested, brought before the Provost Marshal and ordered north of Philadelphia."

Later passages of Colonel Doster's summation make it clear that he had no notion as to the date in March on which Paine was arrested—though someone had *told* him about the special condition under which the young man was granted amnesty—"To go north of Philadelphia and remain there during the war."

Lafayette Baker, probably all the members of the prosecution, and a number of other persons knew that *Louis Paine had gone north to New York.* But the literal Colonel Doster took his client's "narrative" about his experiences as Powell at face value. He described the pitiable plight of the "refugee," stranded, "penniless and friendless" in a strange city, "without a trade or profession . . . unused to manual labor." Homeless and starving!

The attorney's lack of insight, his failure to see any of the dozens of outrageous contradictions in Paine's yarn, is phenomenal. As a soldier himself, how could Doster have made the statement about Powell's being unused to manual labor without being struck by its absurdity? *Any* man who had spent two years in the infantry under Robert E. Lee—a general with an absolute fixation about the necessity of field fortifications—was as much a laborer as he was a fighting man. Powell might not have *liked* manual labor—in fact it may have been one of his prime motives for joining the Partisan cavalry—but he was far from being "unused" to it. The inspiration for this nonsensical statement was undoubtedly the fact that *Paine's* profession had not called for the exertions of a laborer, and *his* hands, as Baker had noticed at his arrest, were well kept and "showed no signs of hard work."

"At the beginning of the war" Powell saw Booth perform in a play in Richmond, and after the show he "gained an introduction to the actor."

This item in Paine's "narrative" is not impossible, though it is most improbable. The prosecution had produced several witnesses to support its theory that Booth had been considering assassinating the President since early in the war, though all of this evidence turned out to have been perjured. They had no positive knowledge of when and how Booth made connections with John Surratt and his mother—and not even an inkling of how he had gotten together with "Payne." *Paine's* yarn was a windfall. It solved the problem of how Powell had met Booth, yet was quite impossible to check.

Booth may very well have performed in Richmond "at the beginning of the war"—and during the few months prior to the assassination, when he was trying to assemble a supporting cast for his debut as a kidnapper, he was known for being hail-fellow-well-met with all classes. But prior to that late period, he was not known to have cultivated people like George Atzerodt and David Herold, or raw country boys such as the Lewis Powell of 1861 whom Doster described.

Doster's description of both parties at the time of their supposed first meeting was enlightening. Of Booth, he said, "The actor was of delicate mould, polished, graceful, subtle, with a brilliant fancy and an abundant stock of reading."

Of Lewis Powell, he said, "The soldier was tall, awkward, rough, frank, generous, and illiterate."

Even allowing for a metamorphosis during his wartime experiences, only the first of these six characteristics belonged to Powell. Either by nature or deliberate cultivation, he was by 1865 the type of worldly individual who was described as a "gentleman" by every witness who encountered him.

Obviously, though, Colonel Doster was giving his own impression, not of Lewis Powell, whom he had not yet met, but of the prisoner Louis Paine—and his description tallies with those of the witnesses who had also met *only* Paine.

The last descriptive adjective of the six is probably the most important one in connection with our study—"illiterate." Colonel Doster, without having seen his client's Oath of Allegiance with its painfully executed signature, apparently *knew* Louis Paine could not read and write. The fact that neither he nor Margaret Branson concluded the prisoner could read just because he was known to have borrowed her family's medical books while in Baltimore, shows only that both of them knew medical books were *illustrated.*

One day in March, after having been arrested and ordered north and having left the Branson house, "Powell was dragging himself slowly along the street past Barnum's Hotel [in Baltimore], a poor creature, overcome by destiny," when he met John Wilkes Booth.

Doster's hearts-and-flowers description of this scene in Peterson doesn't specify the date in March when the meeting occurred, and no reference is made to the fact that the protagonist was liable to arrest and imprisonment if the authorities found him south of Philadelphia before the war ended. Both oversights were "corrected" in Pitman, which gave the date of the reunion as "in the beginning of March," and emphasized the young man's fear of being picked up by "Government detectives." [13]

Powell says, "Booth, I want food; I am starving," and the villainous actor promises him ". . . as much money as you want, but you must swear to stick by me; it is the oil business." So the desperate victim "swore that fatal oath binding his soul as firmly to Booth as Faust to Mephistopheles, and went in and feasted. Next morning Booth gave him money enough to buy a change of clothing and keep him for a week."

In the space of what appears to have been a week, by Doster's account, Booth brainwashed the ignorant, impressionable boy (who seems to have regressed wonderfully in the three months since he had been one of the most swashbuckling of Mosby's troopers, of whom Mrs.

Grant had said, "There were the marks of an officer upon him"). He informed him that the plan was to capture the President and turn him over to the rebel authorities.

In Peterson, Doster doesn't say that this plan was ever implemented—but Pitman assures us that it was and that it failed.

"On the evening of the 14th of April, at 8 o'clock," the attorney said, "Booth told him the hour had struck, placed in his hands the knife, the revolver, and the bogus package of medicine, and told him to do his duty. . . ."

Poor, gullible "Powell" felt he was bound by his Oath, whether the undertaking were the "oil business" or the murder of the Secretary of State. "He went and did the deed."

comments on the biography

Colonel Doster's scenario was probably a pretty good one by the standards of that era, but its chronology was faulty. Since March 14 was a fixed date, whether the counselor knew it or not—the date of Paine's release by the Baltimore provost marshal—the week's delay in Baltimore for Powell's indoctrination by Booth would have made him several days late for the "middle of March" meeting of the "conspirators" at Gautier's, and even caused him to miss the exciting "horse ride" which Weichmann had told about.

Also, since Booth had to be in Baltimore on the evening of the fourteenth to meet Powell in front of Barnum's Hotel and begin corrupting his morals, why did he wire O'Laughlin from Washington on the thirteenth and tell him to "come at once?" Why did he want O'Laughlin in the Capitol if he himself were going to be in Baltimore? From this chronology, even Booth might not have been at Gautier's for the "middle of March" meeting.

All these problems of timing are solved in Pitman by Burnett's care in stipulating that the meeting in front of Barnum's was "in the beginning of March"—even though he had Paine's Oath in his own files and knew perfectly well that March 14 was a fixed date, the date of Paine's release from jail by the Baltimore provost marshal.

The whole yarn, as narrated by Paine and set to violin music by Colonel Doster, shows that Louis Paine had a broad, if often faulty, knowledge of Lewis Powell's personal history—yet knew nothing about the Booth "conspiracy" except what he had heard in the courtroom.

Forty-two years later—though his reflections in the interim since the Trial had brought a faint suspicion that Louis Paine had "played his part well to the end"—Colonel (then Brigadier-General, retired) Doster apparently still believed the "narration" of his client. He recollected a few details which were skipped in his argument to the court:

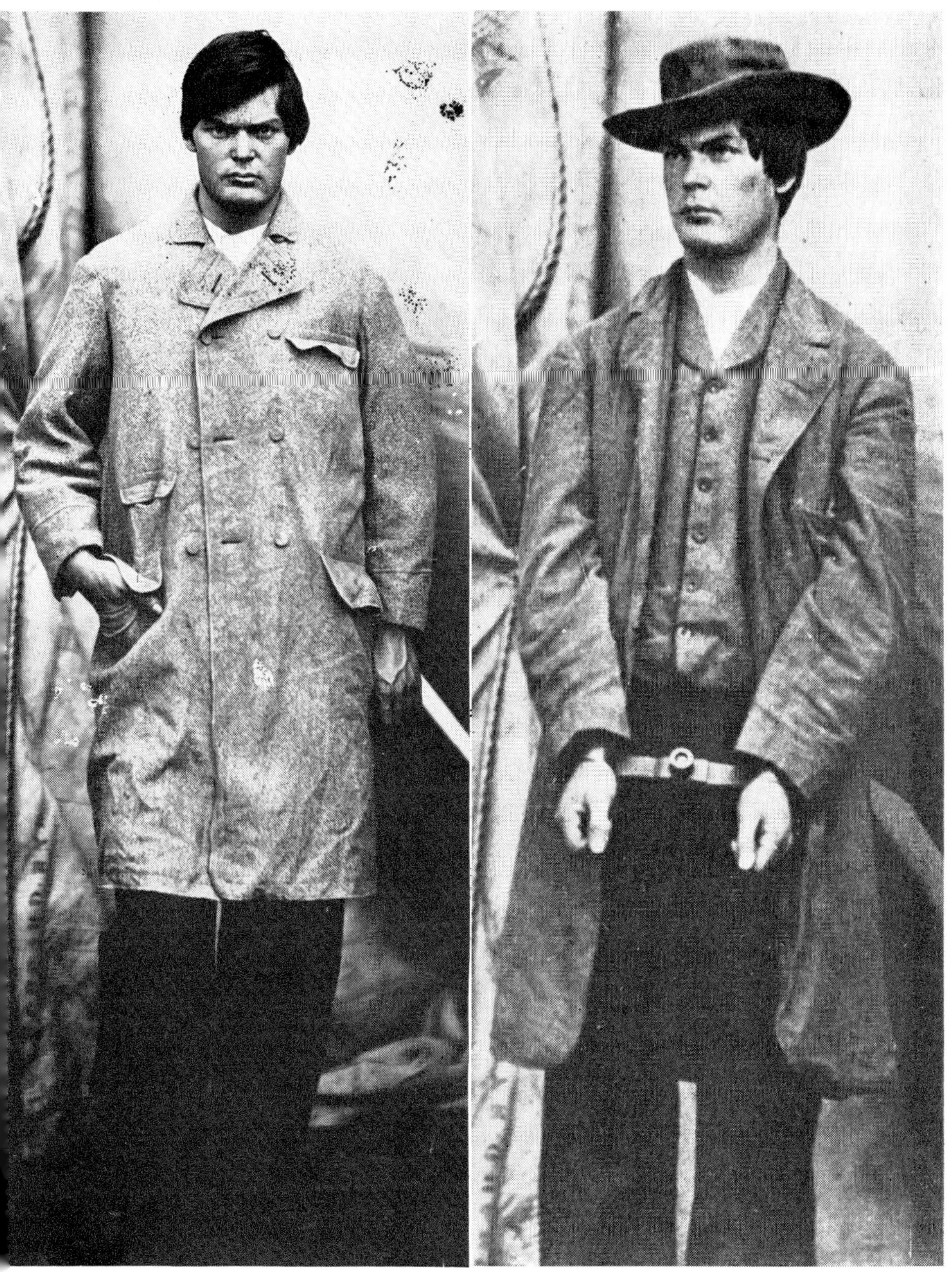

Library of Congress *National Archives*

LOUIS PAINE

Plate I-A.—Wearing the coat in which he was arrested. Compare the above photo with the description in Colonel Baker's "handbill."

Plate I-B.—Wearing the coat found near Fort Bunker Hill and the hat said to have been left at Seward's house by his attacker.

Library of Congress

PLATE II.—COLONEL LAFAYETTE C. BAKER
Head of the War Department Detective Bureau

Library of Congress

PLATE III.—EDWIN McMASTERS STANTON

Secretary of War in Lincoln's Cabinet

MRS. MARY E. SURRATT

HUGH LOUIS PAINE

DAVID E. HEROLD

GEORGE A. ATZERODT

PLATE IV.—THE DEFENDANTS SENTENCED TO HANG

All Library of Congress

Samuel B. Arnold

Michael O'Laughlin

Ned Spangler

Dr. Samuel A. Mudd

Plate V.—THE DEFENDANTS SENTENCED TO PRISON

All Library of Congress

National Archives

PLATE VI.—JOHN WILKES BOOTH

Library of Congress

Plate VII.—JOHN HARRISON SURRATT

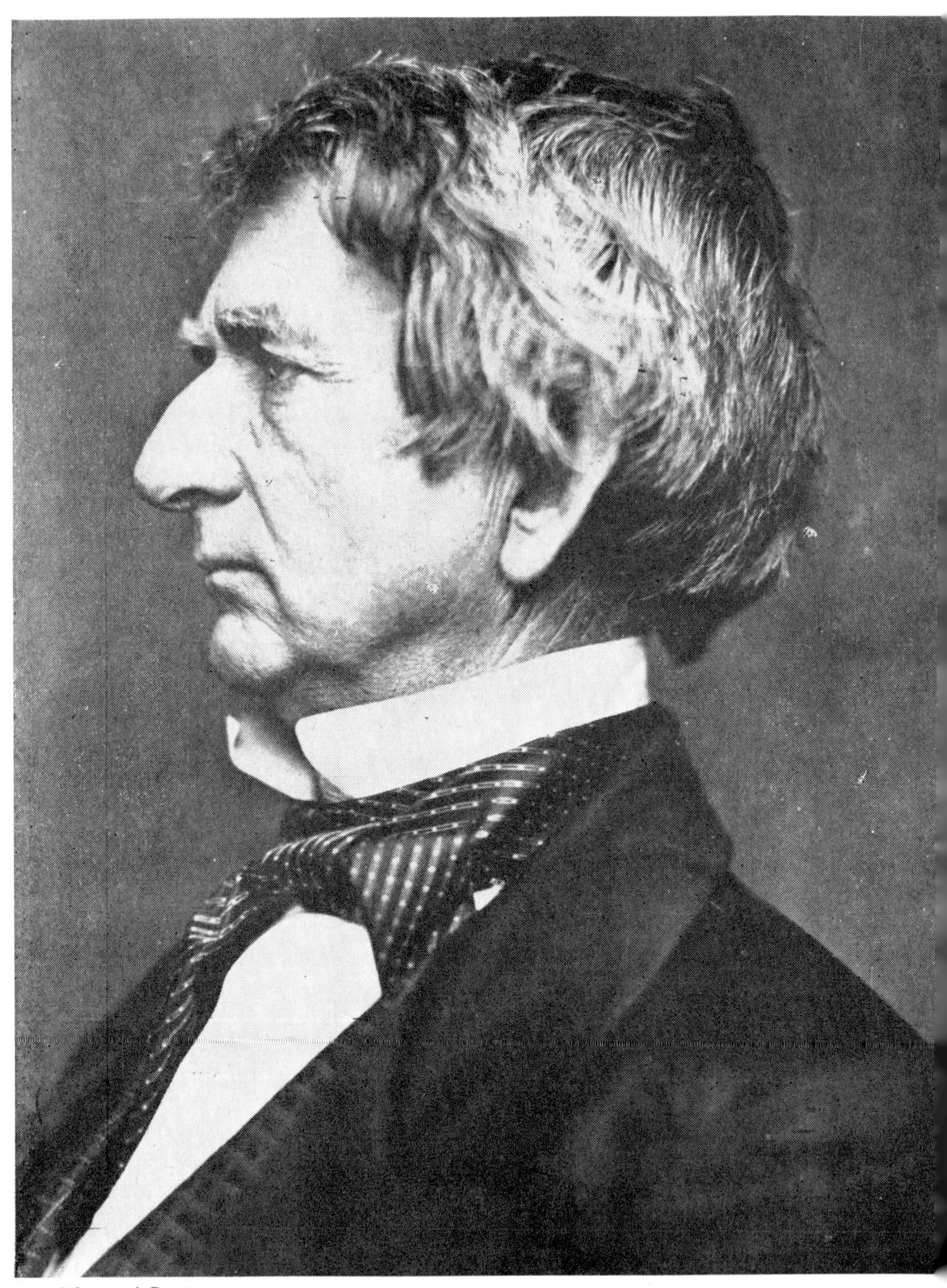

Library of Congress

Plate VIII.—WILLIAM H. SEWARD
Secretary of State in Lincoln's Cabinet

> Some things should be added. He said he was a member of Mosby's Gang, and on deserting changed his name from Powell to Payne in Alexandria, where he took the Oath of Allegiance. The plan about medicines, and the pretext that he was a messenger from Dr. Verdi, Seward's physician, he got from Herold, who was an apothecary's boy.
>
> After abandoning his horse he took to the woods north of Fort Lincoln and stayed there three days, in the top of a cedar tree. The skirmishers passed right below him—backwards and forwards. The blood on his sleeve came from his own finger, which was hurt in the struggle with Frederick Seward. He wiped the blood there after leaving.
>
> He threw away his coat, disguised himself with his drawers, and pick, and came to town because he could not stand hunger any longer. Came to Mrs. Surratt's because she was the only person he knew in Washington, to get something to eat. Booth never told him what his plans were until 8 o'clock of the evening of the assassination. Mrs. Surratt was innocent. . . .[14]

In the light of our study of the basic "narrative" as it was embellished by Doster in his summation, the unreliability of these footnotes nearly a half-century later need not be belabored. But a few points are worth mentioning.

Paine's statement (or was it an affirmative answer to Doster's question?) that the pretext of the medicine was Herold's idea sounds a little out of character. A notable feature of the prisoner's account, as Doster originally related it, was its complete lack of references to *any* of the other defendants except Mrs. Surratt, whom he declared was innocent. The fact that Herold had worked for a druggist was brought out in court, so there was no mystery about how Paine knew it. Yet this—if Doster recollected it correctly—was the only instance in which the prisoner said anything which implicated any of his fellow defendants. It would appear that all of them but Mrs. Surratt were total strangers to him, in which case he would have known nothing he *could* say about them. But Herold's behavior at the Trial was very strange. He had been captured in Booth's company and was, of all eight on trial, the one most clearly involved in the assassination. Yet he was so unconcerned and flippant in court that puzzled observers thought him either "reckless" or mentally retarded. It seemed from his deportment as if he had advance information that the proceedings were just a formality and he would be found not guilty at the end. Paine, we would judge, considered Herold guilty.

Paine's alleged behavior in abandoning his horse and hiding in the woods till he was starving will not ring true, even to persons who have yet to acquaint themselves with the talents of only a run-of-the-mill member of "Mosby's Gang" with respect to self-preservation.

The explanation of how the blood got on Paine's shirt may have been the literal truth—from a cut on his own finger.

Since Louis Paine was not Lewis Powell, as he claimed to be, who was he? How did he acquire his extensive knowledge of Powell's personal history? Why was he not only willing but determined to be hanged in Powell's place? What part did Powell play in the Booth "conspiracy?"

These are a few of the riddles we shall be trying to solve in chapters to come.

summary of chapter thirteen

Louis Paine had enough knowledge of Lewis Powell's personal history to indicate that he knew him quite well. But his ignorance of many facts Powell would obviously have known about himself was virtual proof that *he was not Lewis Powell.*

Paine looked like Powell; Paine looked like "James Wood"; therefore Powell looked like "James Wood." Both Powell and "Wood" had left Fauquier County, Virginia, early in 1865; both had been associated with Mosby's Rangers; therefore we have the proposition that Lewis Powell *was* "James Wood"—alias "Kincheloe," alias "Mosby."

14

the frightened Branson ladies

The master key to the dual mystery of Louis Paine and Lewis Powell was at the Branson house in Baltimore. And the ladies of that household were as careful to conceal the fact from Colonel Doster as were Louis Paine and the War Department.

There was evidently collusion between the prosecution and the ladies—Mrs. Mary A. Branson and her daughter Margaret, that is. They had been "arrested on April 28 by order of the Secretary of War on charge of complicity with Payne and others charged with assassinating the President of the United States."[1] From that date until the twenty-third of May, while the Trial had ground through its grim first two weeks and scores of witnesses had been heard, the ladies were kept under arrest and under guard at their home in another city. Since they were the only persons known to have had a bona fide acquaintance with the alleged "conspirator" Paine, it would have been logical to call them to the witness stand at the very beginning of the proceedings, or at least by May 19, when the testimony against Paine was heard. Considering the charge upon which they were arrested, it might have seemed even more logical to find them among the prisoners in the dock.

On May 26, Colonel John Woolley, provost marshal of the city of Baltimore, wrote a rather acid letter to Colonel H. S. Burnett, judge advocate, complaining about the irregular procedure by which, although the prisoners were his responsibility by order of the Secretary of War himself, they were released to travel to Washington without even a guard, in compliance with a summons signed by Burnett and Assistant Provost Marshal Major Wiegel without prior arrangement with the writer, Colonel Woolley. The summons had not been served through his office, and he was "not aware of the source from which they were received." The indignant provost marshal asked to be informed promptly "if it is intended they shall be kept under guard or are they fully released?"[2]

Doster was the cause of their being brought to Washington at all. The prosecution had no plans to call them as state witnesses. In his book the attorney said, "In addition to the physicians I had early summoned Mrs. and Miss Bronson [sic] of Baltimore, at whose house he had stayed, in the hope of learning something about him." [3] The statement indicates that he had heard of the Bransons before Paine broke his silence, but he knew nothing about them, or even that they had been charged with complicity and were under arrest.

When he finally did interview them, "They were so frightened that nothing could be got from them except that he had nearly beaten the servant to death, because she did not clear out his room. Otherwise they said he had behaved himself with extreme quietness, scarcely ever saying anything." So this and the few generalities he obtained from Margaret on the witness stand were the sum total of his information about the Bransons. Someone must have told him the mother knew nothing, since he didn't ask her to testify. And he only half listened to what the daughter said—as indicated by the statement in his summation that Powell had met *Mrs. Branson* at Gettysburg, though Margaret's answer to his final question had been that her mother was *not* there with her.[4]

Burnett, on the other hand, knew a great deal about the family. There was reason for his reluctance to bring them into court. When he finally agreed to do so, it is highly probable he took every possible precaution to make sure they didn't knock the props from under the War Department's case. Their evident fear of telling the defense attorney *anything* suggests they had been impressed that it wasn't too late for Burnett to write them into his script as accomplices in the "conspiracy" and defendants in court. They would not have needed to be guilty to have been horrified at that possibility. But the *nature* of the information they withheld from Doster suggests there were other eventualities which seemed even more frightening to them.

The precise points at which Bingham interrupted Margaret's interrogation tell us a little about the facts the prosecution didn't want revealed, though they don't tell us *why*. The first time was when Colonel Doster asked Margaret if Powell had said where he was going from there when he stopped at the Branson house after escaping from the hospital. The second time was when the witness was asked how "Payne" happened to leave the boardinghouse after his long stay in the spring of '65. Would a discussion of the young lady's connection with Powell have raised the possibility that the wrong man was on trial? Would the airing of the real cause of Paine's argument with the maid have brought out enough intelligence on his actual identity to refute the War Department's charge that he was a "hired killer" sent to Booth by Confederate agents in Canada?

These are questions which cannot be answered categorically from the evidence presented so far. But the vital importance of the information the Bransons had to offer is implied by Burnett's precaution of reducing Margaret's testimony to a few harmless sentences in the "official" records of the Trial.

The first of several important facts Burnett withheld from Doster and posterity was that *three* Branson ladies, not just two, were arrested on a charge of complicity with the "conspirators." Colonel Woolley enumerated those arrested by Stanton's order as "Mrs. Branson and her daughters, Mary A. and Maggie." [5] It was his understanding that all three had been summoned to Washington by Burnett. But only the mother and "Maggie" arrived—*and Doster never even knew of the existence of "Mary."*

the two "lost" documents

Next we find that Woolley's assistant provost marshal, Major W. H. Wiegel, had interrogated *all three* of the ladies on May 1, drawn up written reports on the statements of each one, and forwarded them through channels to Secretary of War Stanton, who passed them along to the Advocate General's office on May 4. Clearing first through Colonel Woolley's office, the documents were then sent to the headquarters of the 8th Army Corps in Baltimore. The commanding general—after reading them, we assume—signed the order for their transmission to the Secretary of War. This officer's name was Major General *Lew Wallace!*[6]

In other words, one of the judges on the military commission had read this evidence personally. He was present when the watered-down testimony of Margaret Branson was heard. He must have known that the lack of any other references to the Bransons during the proceedings meant that vital evidence was being suppressed by the prosecution. He didn't open his mouth on the subject during or after the examination of Margaret on June 2. Thus the bulk of evidence from this quarter was withheld with his knowledge and tacit consent.

The communication from Woolley to the Secretary of War regarding the Bransons contained *four* enclosures. Each of the officials who forwarded it on its way to the Bureau of Military Justice signed for the whole group of documents—and all four were finally received by Holt and company. The group consisted of the separate depositions of the three Branson ladies and the statement of a man named Henry Shriver, an occupant of the Branson boardinghouse, made to one James L. Stevens of Baltimore.[7] These became, or should have become, a part of the documentation of the Trial in the files of the Bureau of Military Justice, which were later a part of the War Department Archives, which were later transferred to the present National Archives, which has custody of most of the existing records of the Conspiracy Trial.

Two of the four documents Holt and company received from Colonel Woolley on May 4, 1865—probably the two most important—*vanished.* Their contents were never mentioned during or after the Trial, and they are not to be found in the National Archives. These were the depositions of the daughters, "Maggie" and Mary Branson. The other two enclosures —the statements of Mrs. Branson and Henry Shriver—are in the Archives. Their value compared to that of the "lost" documents is small, but they do provide a few clues to the situation in the Branson household during Paine's stay:

Head Quarters, Middle Department, 8th Army Corps,
Office Provost Marshal
Baltimore, May 1, 1865

Examination of Mrs. M. A. Branson

I keep a Boarding House, Cor. of Fayette & Eutaw Sts. (No. 16).

I first saw Lewis Payne about the 19th of January, 1865—I never heard of him before—my daughters have never told me who this man Payne is—Payne said he was a Refugee from Virginia—I had but very little conversation with him—he never told me that he had been North before— I never heard him say *why* he came to Maryland. I never heard Payne mention anything about Gettysburg—

My daughter Mary went out often with Payne—

Don't know where they went—I don't ask my children where they go when they go out.

Don't know that one person ever called to see him while he was at my house—

Never heard him say anything about his acquaintances here or elsewhere. Never knew him to receive any letters—never heard him make use of any disloyal language—

I never heard of the families of *Payne* or *Powell* before he came to my house. Never heard of the name of *Powell* of Virginia—

I never took the Oath of Allegiance. I consider myself loyal.

He was arrested by Col. Woolley. After his release he came to my house and took dinner & went away—after that my daughter Mary received a letter from him in New York. I have not seen him since he left to go to New York, and only heard from him through Mary's letter. I never saw any intimacy between him and any of the boarders.[8]

In the consideration of Mrs. Branson's statement as evidence, the date upon which it was made is a factor. It was taken down on the *third* day after she was placed under house arrest. We can imagine that she and her daughters had discussed their predicament and that the prospect of being indicted for harboring an alleged assassin was horrifying. But the fact that they had not been carted off to prison at once was a hopeful sign. The Trial would not begin for another ten days. The newspapers had published accounts of Paine's arrest and "identification" as Mr.

Seward's attacker, but they had no conception of the version of the "conspiracy" the War Department would promulgate at the Trial. On May 1 the War Department didn't either. The detailed testimony regarding "Payne" would not be heard in court or reported in the newspapers for three weeks.

In other words, as of May 1 Paine was just a reticent young man who had boarded at Mrs. Branson's house for several weeks, had gone out "often" with her daughter Mary, had struck a maid, then been arrested and sent north to New York. Since leaving he had got himself into a lot of trouble.

Mrs. Branson, it appears, had only heard the name "Powell" in the last day or so. Her practice of not inquiring into the doings of her daughters had left her in the dark on a number of matters—and the daughters still had not thought it necessary, as of May 1, to take her into their confidence. Perhaps they *never* did. So we can assume that her deposition was either the truth or very close to it. She did not yet know what should be said or not said for the best interests of herself and her family. She only knew it would be better to make it clear that she knew almost nothing about the young man's affairs or antecedents, though Mary's association with their boarder was common knowledge around the neighborhood and there was no use trying to hide that.

The statement from Henry Shriver was in a letter to "Lieut. Col. Saml. B. Lawrence" from "James L. Stevens," dated April 27, 1865. It was written on 8th Army Corps stationery, so the writer must have been a Union officer, though he did not give his rank or organization. This communication contained no vital data on Paine or the Bransons which we don't have from other sources, but its information clearly led to the ladies' arrest. It also injected a new and apparently unrelated element of mystery into the situation at Branson's.[9]

The writer explained that, at breakfast on that morning, his uncle, a "Mr. Armstrong," told him a rumor "that some of the inmates of Mrs. Branson's boarding house . . . were in confidence with the assassins of our late President. . . ." He happened to know a Mr. Henry Shriver, who was one of the boarders, and hastened to his office to inquire about the matter. Shriver told him the following:

> "Paine, one of the assassins of the President now in custody, was formerly a resident of Mrs. Branson's boarding house, S. W. Corner of Fayette & Eutaw Streets. Joseph Thomas was also a boarder with Mrs. Branson at the time. Paine reported himself at the house as a refugee from Virginia—One day Paine took offense at some act of a colored woman, servant in the house, and knocked her down, whereupon she immediately reported his conduct to the Provost Marshal. Upon taking the oath, Paine was permitted to go North.
>
> "After Paine's departure for the North (March, 1865) Joseph Thomas still remained at Mrs. Branson's. A few days since, upon hearing of the arrest of Paine he, with his wife, removed from Mrs. Branson's to the Howard House."

The writer, still quoting Shriver, said another boarder, named Mr. Ward, met Thomas on the street and asked why he had left without saying goodbye. " 'Thomas replied that he was fearful they would have trouble at Mrs. Branson's house.—Thomas had contemplated leaving Mrs. B's three months ago and was waiting for a certain room in the Howard House to be vacated which he wished to occupy.' "

"Thomas committed suicide Monday afternoon, 24th inst."

Although Stevens' letter closed with a dramatic and intriguing punch line, there is no evidence so far that the suicide of Mr. Thomas had anything to do with the Bransons, Louis Paine, or the assassination of the President. It seems to have been an unrelated tragedy which crossed wires with the one we are studying.

Shriver's spelling of the name "Paine" is interesting, since it suggests the young man was known to his fellow boarders by the name as he spelled it on his Oath—which harks back to our assumption that the War Department changed it to "Payne" during the time when they were trying to connect him with the reckless Payne brothers of Kentucky. Paine's spelling of his name becomes an important detail when we begin tracing him back to his origins as a separate person from Lewis Powell.

We may also note that Shriver, along with all concerned in Baltimore, had the impression Louis Paine had gone to New York immediately after his release by the provost marshal on March 14.

The military police officer who arrested Paine after his altercation with the maid was named H. B. Smith. On April 21 he forwarded some letters he had confiscated at Branson's to Major W. H. Wiegel, together with a covering letter. The letters are not now attached to this document, and a notation says they were of "no importance." It's unfortunate we can't see them to decide for ourselves. Some of Smith's comments, however, are interesting:[10]

"Mrs. Branson," he wrote, "is a notorious rebel. . . . Paine made his home at this house . . . and the intimacy between Miss B—and him would be remarked under ordinary circumstances. When I arrested Paine some two months since, I took him from this house."

As early as April 18—the day after the raid on Surratt's in which Paine was arrested—Colonel Foster queried the Baltimore provost marshal on the amnesty oath the young man had handed to Detective Morgan. Major Wiegel's answer, which was cited earlier, is reproduced herewith:[11]

News accounts of the Trial elicited a considerable number of crank letters from citizens in all sections of the country. The ridiculous nature of many of these, and in some cases the writers' obvious desire to implicate acquaintances they didn't like, cast suspicion on any communications in which bias or personal spite seemed to be a factor. Yet this was a period of widespread hysteria; many official documents written before

Head Quarters, Middle Department, 8th Army Corps,
OFFICE PROVOST MARSHAL,

Baltimore, April 18th 1865

Col John A. Foster
Judge Advocate
[illegible] Staff

Col

I have the honor to forward the Copy of Oath required. Lewis Paine was detained at this Office March 12/65 as a Refugee on the 14th he was permitted to take the oath of Allegiance & was ordered North of Philadelphia to remain during the war. I know of no authority permitting him to return south of the above named City

Respty
Your most obdt Servt
W. H. Wiegel
Maj & Asst Pro Marshal

W. R. B. J. A. G. 31—1865
Pro. M. Baltimore
April 18th 1865
Major W. H. Wiegel
Sends copy and original oath of Lewis Paine
Provost Marshal's Certificate of Oath, found upon person of Lewis Paine at time of his arrest, is herewith enclosed

FIG. 4.—Major Wiegel's Letter Confirming Paine's Oath and Restriction to Northern Territory

and during the Trial (most of those penned by Colonels Foster and Olcott, for example) showed a violent prejudice toward one or another of the persons who were being held as suspects. Thus indications of bias in a document are a secondary consideration—less important than the question of whether its writer was or had been in a position to know whereof he spoke. In citing this final letter relating to the frightened Branson ladies and their mysterious boarder, it should be noted that the writer appeared to be well qualified to give the information he offered, and that he wrote under the official letterhead of the military agency to which he was attached:

SURGEON GENERAL'S OFFICE
WASHINGTON CITY, D. C.
June 3rd, 1865

COLONEL,

I perceive by reading the proceedings of the trial on Saturday the 3rd inst. that a Miss Margaret Branson was a witness for the defense;

Desiring that all evidence adduced shall tend to the conviction of the guilty, and acquital of the innocent, I feel it my duty to inform you as one of the prosecuting officers in the trial, that Miss Branson while a female nurse in the General Hospital at Gettysburg, together with several others was always considered as a strong sympathizer with the rebellion, coming to the Hospital for the purpose of caring for the wants of the rebel wounded therein;—About the time of her departure from the Hospital, or a day or two previous, a first sergt. of the rebel army who was nearly recovered from his wounds, a man of unusual intelligence and one of the most unyielding of all the rebels we had, in company with some eight or nine others made their escape from the Hospital and were never heard from afterwards; it was the general belief that they were assisted in their escape by this Miss Branson, and another of the same stripe, who left about, or at the same time; this lady was always considered as devoted to the interest and success of the rebel cause, and associated only with those of the same proclivities; the loyal lady nurses refusing to associate with them; there are some others now in this city, who will bear me out in these statements I have no doubt, they having been on duty in the hospital at the time,

I was the Chief Steward of the Hospital above referred to,

I have the honor to be,
Very Respectfully Yours,

SAMUEL S. BOND,
Hospital Steward, U. S. Army—
Surg. Genls. Office[12]

To Col. Burnett
Judge Advocate

The foregoing letter to Colonel Burnett, in a cultivated style, form, and penmanship, brings an abrupt change of perspective to our view of the Branson ladies. On the basis of her testimony, Margaret Branson is usually assumed to have been a *Union* war nurse who had taken particular notice of a certain attendant at her hospital who was kind to the wounded men of both armies, though she knew him only casually as "Powell" or "Doctor." Her account of his visit to her home "sometime that fall and winter"—since she was only slightly acquainted with him—was far from satisfactory. According to her story, *she* was the only person in the household whom he knew; he stayed "a few hours"—yet she had "very little conversation with him." With whom, then, did he converse during those few hours?

The mother's deposition indicates she hadn't known about Powell's visit in '63 at all—hadn't heard the name of "Powell" until her interrogator brought it up. So, if she told the truth, it couldn't have been *Mrs.* Branson who entertained the visitor—whom Margaret didn't admit knowing was a soldier at all, let alone an escaped Confederate prisoner.

From Mr. Bond's letter we gather that she not only knew who and what he was but might even have helped him to escape. Lewis Powell, his army record shows, made his escape from the West's Buildings Hospital in Baltimore on September 7.[13] Margaret says she left the General Hospital in Gettysburg "the first week in September." Moreover, she said he came to her house in "that fall *and* winter," which implies more than one visit—which points to the conclusion that Powell either remained in Baltimore for some weeks after his escape or made a risky trip back to the Branson's after he had joined the Partisan cavalry, an exploit which would not have been out of the ordinary for either Gilmore's or Mosby's men. In either case, he would have to have had an unusually strong incentive for visiting the boardinghouse of a lady whom the provost marshal described as a "notorious rebel" and therefore under suspicion by the federal authorities.

the other miss Branson

The *incentive* was not Margaret but her sister, Mary. But how did Powell meet Mary? Interpretation of one of Mr. Bond's sentences offers an answer: "It was the general belief," he wrote, "that they were assisted in their escape by *this* Miss Branson, and *another* of the same stripe. . . ." Not *another person*, but *another Miss Branson!*

Mr. Bond continued, ". . . and another of the same stripe, who left about, or at the same time; *this* lady was always considered as devoted to the interest and success of the rebel cause, and associated only with those of the same proclivities; the loyal lady nurses refusing to associate with them; . . ."

At the first reading it seemed that Mr. Bond was *repeating* his statement about Margaret Branson's rebel sympathies. But he was evidently talking about the *other* Miss Branson, whose first name he did not remember. Both sisters, then, were at Gettysburg as nurses, and both left at about the same time—a fact which Margaret, with the approval and co-operation of Colonel Burnett, was keeping a very deep secret when she testified. But why?

Confirmation of the thesis that Lewis Powell and Mary Branson were romantically involved will come a little later from an unexpected source. So let's proceed on that assumption. The reason Mrs. Branson's deposition was allowed to remain in Burnett's files may have been that it contained no direct contradiction of Paine's story, which Doster had revealed to the court—undoubtedly via Burnett—before Margaret Branson was called to testify on June 2. When the mother was interrogated on May 1, she was asked, not if Paine and Powell were the same man, but whether she had heard her daughters *or Paine* speak of a man named "Powell" who had been at Gettysburg. She answered in the negative, and also said her daughters hadn't told her "who this man Payne is"—a rather positive sign that she thought both her daughters *knew* who Paine was.

The mother, having been kept in the dark by Margaret and Mary, saw no harm in mentioning that "Mary went out often with Payne."

We have already had many indications that Paine and Powell bore a close external resemblance to each other. But it is impossible to believe that Mary could have had romantic connection with Powell beginning in the fall of '63 and have kept frequent company with Paine in the spring of '65, and yet have had any illusions that they were the same man. Unlike *any* of the witnesses the state called to "prove" they were the same person, Mary knew both young men intimately enough to *know* they were not. And Margaret knew what Mary knew!

It is possible that the two girls' depositions on May 1 revealed their knowledge on this subject. But that would not have become a complication for the prosecution until much later in the month, when Paine told Doster he *was* "Lewis Powell" and Doster told Burnett and the court. Though he could and did refrain from bringing the Bransons into court for the prosecution, Burnett could not refuse Doster's demand that they be called as defense witnesses, since Doster might have known—or could easily have found out—that the War Department had them under arrest.

Fortunately, from Burnett's viewpoint, Paine had not mentioned Mary to his attorney. So the prosecution could get away with producing only Margaret and her mother *if* they could be so terrified by threats of prosecution that they could either not testify (as with Mrs. Branson) or say only as much as Burnett told them to say (as with Margaret)—in other words, say nothing to contradict the yarn Louis Paine had told.

There may have been even more to it than that. Later on we shall attempt to establish that the Trial's invisible engineer, Lafayette Baker, and a confederate of his who was also an active but invisible participant in the prosecution, knew very well who Lewis Powell was and what role he had played in the conspiracy. It seems certain that Colonel Burnett would have known it too. As Powell's girl friend, Mary might have been told what he was up to. But even if she hadn't been, the War Department had Mary and her mother and sister under its thumb—with the threat to prosecute and hang Mary as consort and accomplice with Seward's would-be assassin. Margaret's concern on the witness stand, we thus assume, was to protect the reputation or the life of her sister, Mary, or both.

Since Mary had been associated with *both* men, the War Department had her coming and going. To deny complicity with "Payne," the *confessed* culprit in the dock, she would have to reveal Powell's separate identity—in which case (so the prosecution could argue) they could put a price on Powell's head and proceed to try her as *his* accomplice, and of course mistress.

It may not have been necessary to spell out the threat that clearly to the Branson ladies. But a fair guess at the nature of Burnett's proposition to Margaret can be made. It would have been couched in the persuasive, oblique language of the polished lawyer whom Colonel Doster still admired half a century later, but it would have boiled down to this: "Let us keep Payne, and you can keep Mary."

No wonder Doster found mother and daughter so frightened that "nothing could be got from them. . . ."

If Margaret's testimony in Peterson is now reread in the framework of the foregoing considerations, much of what she left unsaid can be read between the lines: Her unequivocal statement that she had first met "the prisoner Payne" at Gettysburg; that he was the same man who came the same fall and again in '65; the lack of any mention that she even *had* a sister; the desire to say *something* favorable to the prisoner that might possibly work to his advantage. Behind all this we may even sense her rationalization that, after all, this was the way Louis Paine *wished* to represent himself.

summary of chapter fourteen

Margaret Branson and her sister Mary had known both Louis Paine and Lewis Powell well and *separately,* and knew beyond all doubt that they were different men.

Margaret, though appearing as a witness for the defense, was induced by prior threats to support the War Department's (and the prisoner's) claim that Paine and Powell were the same person.

The transcripts of both girls' pre-Trial interrogations were destroyed by the prosecutors. Attorney Doster never saw them, and the very existence of Mary Branson was concealed from him.

15

the career of Lewis Powell

Lewis Thornton Powell was born in Randolph County, Alabama, on April 22, 1844. He was the seventh of the ten children of George C. and Caroline Powell, the youngest of their four sons. At the time of Lewis' birth and for three years thereafter, the father was employed as assistant tax collector for the county and later as tax assessor. In 1847 the elder Powell was ordained a Baptist minister at Liberty Church in Russell County, Alabama. In 1848 he was called to Beulah Church at Green Hill in Stewart County, Georgia, and moved there with his wife and (at that time) eight children.

There are no records of Lewis' boyhood between the ages of four and fifteen in Georgia. We can assume that the family of a country preacher in that time and place lived a life which was far from affluent. The Rev. Powell, with the help of his sons and a son-in-law who lived with them, cultivated a small rented farm to augment his income. It would have taken some exertion, management, and self-denial to feed the dozen or more mouths, and this without the help of slaves. The subsequent activities of Lewis Powell suggest an attitude of protest against Christian austerity, and an impatient pursuit of the material advantages a country minister's son had to do without.

The second oldest brother, George, married and moved to Florida in 1857; his good reports on conditions there, now that the Indian wars were over, may have had something to do with the Rev. Powell's decision to follow with the rest of the family in 1859 and settle near Belleville in Hamilton County. His next congregation, however, appears to have been in Bradford County, not far to the southeast.[1]

the infantry and the partisans

When war came, Lewis was first of the four brothers to answer the call of the drums. Doster said he enlisted over his father's protest. Lewis signed up with the Jasper Blues, Captain Stewart's company, on May 30, 1861.

At seventeen, the young man had the unusual height and commanding appearance of his father. He was aggressive, articulate, and handsome, in spite of a rather intense cast to his prominent, dark eyes. His prospects for becoming an officer in a regiment largely filled with uneducated country boys must have seemed excellent.

But life as a foot soldier didn't agree with Lewis from the beginning. On July 13, '61, when the Blues were shipped to Jacksonville and became Company I of the 2nd Florida Infantry, he was already sick in the hospital and missed his unit's departure for Richmond.[2] He caught up with it sometime in October and by June 23, '62, was sufficiently adjusted to soldier life to re-enlist for the duration and collect a bounty of fifty dollars.[3] By November 5 of the same year he was sick again and spent a period in the Florida Hospital in Richmond.[4]

Powell's participation in any of his regiment's many battles—with the exception of Gettysburg—doesn't appear in his records. The word "present" next to his name on the muster rolls of Company I from December, '62, to July 2, '63, indicates he was involved in some of them. Yet he remained a private through the two years before his capture, so presumably was not among the more zealous warriors of the notably valorous 2nd Infantry. One of the afterthoughts on Powell's biography which Paine mentioned to Dr. Gillette on the eve of his execution was that the long marches were hard for him and that he frequently "became faint and fell to the ground."[5]

The somewhat confused accounts of Lewis' capture at Gettysburg leave room for more speculation as to whether he was as dedicated to the work of killing Yankees as latterday historians insist—or whether he was as willing a student of organized murder on the battlefield as Doster claimed. The type of wound he received—a gunshot in the wrist—was looked upon with suspicion in both armies, since any injury to the hands was valid reason for withdrawing from combat, though not ordinarily dangerous to life. There was always the implication that the wound might have been self-inflicted.

Also, the records of Company I state that Lewis was wounded and missing on July 2, the second day of the great battle. But Union medical records are just as clear that he turned up in a field hospital two days later, on July 4. Louis Paine's version was that "he" had been wounded and captured in the assault on the federal center—Pickett's charge—on July 3, which leads us to believe that he had been so informed.

From these peculiarities—together with reports of Powell's reckless courage while with Mosby—we get the impression of a soldier who considered it foolish to risk his life for such abstractions as honor and homeland, but became a ferocious fighter when personal gain was involved.

The character of Powell's wound presumably led to his being detailed as a nurse. His wrist required medical care but didn't incapacitate him When he was transferred to Letterman General Hospital on July 6,[6] the harried doctors, with their legion of torn and broken bodies to care for, were glad to find a husky rebel who could function as a nurse. There is no reason to doubt Margaret Branson's statement that he was good at the work and "very kind to the sick and wounded."

Margaret and Mary arrived sometime after July 15, according to her testimony. Her statements that she didn't know whether he was a soldier or a civilian, or whether he was there during the whole time she was, were merely efforts to make it seem they were scarcely acquainted. By the time Lewis was transferred to the Baltimore hospital on September 2,[7] his intimacy with both girls—but particularly with Mary—was firmly established. Bond implied that their departure in the first week of September was due to the growing suspicion among hospital officials that the young ladies were using their status as nurses to help Confederate enlisted men escape. This may have been the case, though the transfer of Powell—which would not have been voluntary—probably helped Mary decide to go home to Baltimore. She would not have been in a position to help him escape from the West's Buildings Hospital; but if she were at home in the city to provide a hiding place, food, civilian clothing, and money, his chances of a successful getaway would be much better than if he slipped out of the Gettysburg hospital and tried to make his way south through a countryside crawling with federal soldiers. So Powell's "desertion" from West's Buildings on September 7[8] was probably the end product of careful prearrangement with the Branson girls—an escapade not confided to the garrulous Mrs. Branson.

The idea of joining the Partisans was probably one of the objectives in Powell's plan for escape. In any case, a return to his regimented, half-starved, vermin-infested life in the infantry was the last thing in his mind. He was a good horseman and had the foot soldier's brainset about the cavalry—that to be horse-borne in any capacity was the ultimate privilege, and that the mounted guerrillas lived in a quasi-military paradise, with a minimum of discipline, a maximum of physical comfort and excitement, and—for good measure—a license to steal for their personal profit.

By the time Powell was able to arrange his "transfer" to this favored arm of the Confederate service, Partisan units had fallen into great disrepute with the top leadership of Lee's army. It was felt that the accomplishments of the many guerrilla bands in harassing Union supply lines was offset by the damage their existence did to the morale of the regular troops. These free-ranging, independent horsemen with a way of life so different from the unrewarding misery of the line infantry were a real detriment to discipline, and an invitation for any spunky young soldier to slip off in the night to join the Partisans and get his share of the fun and the loot.

The official viewpoint on guerrillas at the beginning of 1864 was expressed in Brigadier General Thomas L. Rosser's (commander of the Valley District) letter to General Lee:

"Without discipline, order or organization, they roam broadcast over the country, a band of thieves, stealing, pillaging, plundering and doing every manner of mischief and crime. They are a terror to the citizens and an injury to the cause. They never fight; can't be made to fight. Their leaders are generally brave, but few of the men are good soldiers and have engaged in this business for the sake of gain."[9]

The judgment of this school of thought was that Partisan units should be incorporated in the regular army and deserters from other branches sent back to their original organizations.

General Lee agreed in principle with this view—although in detail it was not fair to the many dedicated men who served in the Partisans along with the scoundrels General Rosser had in mind. Lee made a list of the independent battalions which should be disbanded, but made an exception in the case of Mosby, who was highly regarded by Stuart and other influential officers. On his recommendation, the Confederate Congress later repealed the act authorizing such independent units. But with things going from bad to worse for the South as the war dragged on and on, a soldier in the field was a soldier in the field, and the guerrillas continued to operate much as before.[10]

The only authority for the belief that Powell first made his way to the Shenandoah Valley and joined Major Harry Gilmor's unit was Louis Paine. It was probably quite true, considering the remarkable accuracy of much of the prisoner's information about the man he claimed to be. And it offers a reasonable explanation for Powell's whereabouts until he showed up with Mosby in Fauquier County in the early spring of '64. Paine said "he" became *dissatisfied* with service under Gilmor after a while and took the first opportunity to join Mosby's command. That may have been a sufficient explanation, but there were certain conditions and events which could have helped him decide upon another change.

Unlike Mosby, Gilmor was not an independent commander operating at his own discretion. His outfit was on detached service from the regular cavalry but subject to the orders of General J. E. B. Stuart, from whom he received his assignments, which included very few from which the troopers could improve their financial situations.[11]

Sometime in early February, 1864, Stuart sent Gilmor to cut the B & O Railroad in West Virginia, to hamper the transportation of Union reinforcements from the western armies. The Partisan leader took twenty-eight men up the valley to a point on the tracks near Martinsburg and set up obstructions. Presently the westbound Baltimore express arrived, loaded with civilians, convalescent soldiers, and a number of notables from Washington, and slid to a stop at the barricade. Gilmor's men leaped aboard with their pistols drawn and, as the northern newspapers described the outrage, went through the cars robbing the passengers and crew at gunpoint until a following train filled with Union infantry arrived and drove them off.

On the way back to the valley, seven of these same men of Gilmor's waylaid a caravan of neutral Jewish merchants near Strasburg, Virginia, and robbed them of their valuables, including some six thousand dollars, mostly in twenty-dollar gold pieces.

These two incidents took Harry Gilmor before a court martial and almost ended his career in disgrace. But he was able to convince the court that his men robbed the civilians against his express orders, and his brother officers were kind enough not to ask what connection the stopping of a passenger train had with orders to cut the rail line. The upshot was acquittal, but Major Gilmor surely had a list of the troopers whose blatant thievery had put him on such a spot. Whether or not the name of Lewis Thornton Powell was on that list, the party was over for hustlers in Harry Gilmor's battalion.

There is at least a possibility that Lewis Powell used the name of "Payne" when he went with Mosby. He had reason to hide his identity—if only to avoid being sent back to the 2nd Florida Infantry, due to the growing sentiment in official circles to disband all Partisan units and send their members back to their original organizations. Company I of the 2nd Florida Infantry carried him on its rolls as a "prisoner-of-war" through February, 1865, its last bimonthly muster before the regiment surrendered with Lee at Appomattox. And this writer has not yet found the name "Lewis Thornton Powell" on the rolls of any company in Mosby's 43rd Battalion, though there were "Paynes."

Former members of the command who wrote their memoirs, of which there were several, did the writing *after* Lewis Powell (alias "Payne," or vice versa) had been identified as a deserter from the Rangers at the Conspiracy Trial. Some didn't refer to him at all. Those who did called him "Powell," either because they knew that was his real name when he was with the command or, more likely, because everyone called him that *after* the Trial—after publication of the Pitman compilation the same year, that is. They remembered that he had lived with a family named Payne near Warrenton when he was not in the field, and quoted Louis Paine to the effect that he (Powell) took the Oath as "Payne" at Alexandria when he deserted. Mr. and Mrs. Grant, who testified about the incident in front of their farm near Warrenton six months earlier, seemed sure that they had been told the Confederate soldier's name was "Powell"

—though after that lapse of time they might have remembered it as "Payne" just as readily, since their point was that "Powell" was the same man as the prisoner on trial.

There is one clue to the identity of the family of Paynes with whom Lewis Powell boarded while he was with Mosby.

Lewis Powell, as with most other human beings who practice deception on a large scale, developed a pattern in his technique which became almost a trademark. When he chose a new alias, which was quite often, he *always* used the name of someone with whom he had been associated earlier—rather than picking a new name at random. It wasn't a bad idea, actually, since the connotations of the name probably helped him remember which one he was using currently.

To Sam Arnold and the other "conspirators" at the "middle of March" meeting, he was "Mosby." At the Herndon House he was "Kincheloe," the name of a popular officer in Mosby's Command. A little later we shall look at evidence that he used the name "Payne" throughout his hitch with Mosby.

Upon learning that Atzerodt and the Surratt house inmates knew Powell as "James Wood," curiosity prompted the writer to look for a person by that name in Fauquier County, Powell's last stamping ground before Washington. As expected, a farmer named "James Wood Payne" was found near Warrenton—possibly Powell's host during his career as a Partisan.[12]

Life in the 43rd Battalion must have suited Powell to a T. Its commander was a magnetic leader, whose men followed him cheerfully or went wherever he told them to go without the need for rigid discipline. They had no drill, no camp chores, no inspections. They lived like private citizens until called to duty by messenger or signal. They usually operated in small groups under superbly qualified officers or non-coms, rarely assembling as many as two or three hundred men in one place, even for a major foray. Individual qualifications (in addition to the essential ability to ride like an Indian and handle a pistol, their only firearm) were unusually high in terms of resourcefulness, audacity, and skill at deception. In combat they were invariably outnumbered, and they so often undertook missions by pairs or threes in country crawling with Union patrols that only the more quick-witted and daring survived.

Mosby himself was their model. By precept and example he taught them always to be where the enemy least expected to find them, and always to do the *last* thing he would expect them to do *first.* When encountering an enemy patrol or a battalion of his cavalry unexpectedly, never run away—ride at and through them. Mosby's personal application of such principles of warfare on many occasions made him sort of an unbelievable legend to his own men, and they idolized him.

John W. Munson was as close to his leader as any of the ordinary troopers. Mosby often picked young John as a traveling companion, because he didn't talk much and the guerrilla chieftain liked to make his battle plans in the saddle, sometimes riding for miles without saying a word to those with him.

Unlike some of the other veterans who published their recollections,[13] Munson didn't romanticize the life of the guerrilla. At times it was easy, and then again brutally hard and dangerous. Along with the heroic exploits, he remembered the dandies with tailored gray uniforms and with flowing feathers in their hats, who always found some equipment needing adjustment until the front ranks for a charge had been formed. He remembered the occasions when Mosby called the whole battalion together to answer roll call—and give the captains a chance to sort out malingerers for shipment to the regular army in Richmond. The General, he said, never accepted a penny's worth of booty, nor did most of the officers. But the rules permitted a trooper to relieve a captured Yankee of everything he owned—money, watch, clothing, etc. The loot from a raid was divided equally among all the enlisted men who participated. On one expedition the strong box of a Union paymaster was captured, and each Ranger involved got over $2,500. Those who were willing to take the risks could reap a handsome profit. Munson remembered the men who were corrupted by the life and those who weren't. Among others, he remembered Powell:[14]

> . . . In the autumn of 1864 . . . Lt. Ed. Thomson with about thirty men rode over to the neighborhood of Salem, now called Marshall, and stopped in a little ravine. Thomson wanted to draw the enemy out of the town so that he could get at them on some sort of fair basis as to numbers, and he thought the best way to get them out was to . . . send in and invite them out by firing at them. He asked for three volunteers to undertake the rather risky job, and Louis Powell, Tom Benton Shipley, of Baltimore, and Bowie of the Northern Neck [as distinguished from the more famous Walter Bowie of Maryland] stepped to the front before others could answer. They were first class men, always ready for any duty, and game.
>
> Poor Powell ran amuck after the war and paid with his life for his mistake. While in our Command he boarded with a Mr. Payne, and in some unaccountable way, certainly in a moment of temporary insanity or mistaken loyalty to the South, he joined in the assassination of President Lincoln, *taking the name of his old host.* [V.S. italics] . . . It was he who attacked and stabbed Mr. Seward, the night that Booth killed the President. I have never heard how he became one of that crowd of crazed conspirators, but I have always held that it was the original purpose of Booth and his associates to try and kidnap Mr. Lincoln, and perhaps other prominent officials, and get them across the upper Potomac and into our part of the country, and hide them in the mountains until terms for their release could be made with the authorities at Washington. If Powell suggested it I would not be surprised, for he was always keyed up for any new sensation. When he left our Command to go to Washington he became a deserter, and our connection with him ceased.
>
> But to our story. Powell and Shipley and Bowie galloped into Salem and fired on the pickets, while Thomson and his men were concealed in the bushes,

> watching for the enemy to come out, and ready to signal to John Puryear to charge them, with Thomson in the rear, as they passed. Our men got them in a lane between Utterback's and Shumate's and killed, wounded or captured all but one of them.

Mosby's hit-and-run tactics continued to make him a thorn in the side of the Union army as one scheme after another failed to run him to earth. In the fall of '64 Sheridan approved a suggestion by General Crook for the formation of a hand-picked company of cavalry veterans from his division, armed with the newest seven-shot repeating rifles and led by Captain Richard Blazer, a former Indian fighter. It was a crack outfit, well officered and confident—but after some weeks of ranging up and down Fauquier County, it hadn't been able to make contact with Mosby. The Partisans simply ignored Blazer until he ambushed a small party of them around the middle of November and killed two. Then Mosby, who was sick at the time, sent his A and B companies on the warpath under Captain Adolphus Richards.[15]

Richards trailed Blazer to Kabletown and set up the standard Mosby trap—luring the Union force into a charge by having one company show itself while the other lay in hiding to pounce from behind. It was a bitter, close fight in which the guerrillas' pistols were more effective than the Spencers. It ended with the few Union survivors riding for their lives. Captain Blazer was run down and captured by Syd Ferguson, aided by Sam Alexander, Cab Maddox, and Lewis Powell.

The same four troopers were assigned the agreeable duty of taking Blazer to Richmond under guard on November 18. This Union officer was rather admired by his captors, and he was treated with special consideration on the journey. A letter now in the National Archives, written only six days after Louis Paine's arrest (before the War Department changed his name to "Payne"), shows how easily Captain Blazer could have altered the Trial's course by proving that the prisoner was *not* the man who had guarded him on the way to Richmond. It also reveals how little interested the prosecutors were in establishing Paine's real identity:[16]

> WINCHESTER, VA., Apr. 24th, 1865
>
> *Brig. Gen. W. H. Seward**
> *Washington, D. C.*
>
> SIR
>
> Capt. "Dick" Blazer of the Blazer Scouts was captured last summer and taken to Richmond by one Paine, belonging to Mosby's Gang. He thinks from the description it is the same Paine arrested with the Surratt family and supposed to be the assassin who attempted the life of your honored father, the Secretary of State. Capt. Blazer is very well acquainted with the man and

* General William H. Seward, Jr., son of the Secretary of State.

would recognize him at once if he were the same. He has made inquiries of Mosby's men as to this Paine and they say he went away some time ago, but where they could not tell. I send you this note thinking that the testimony of Capt. Blazer might throw further light upon the history of this man. Capt. Blazer belongs to the 91st O. V. I. [Ohio Volunteer Infantry], 1st Brig., 4th Prov. Divis., Army of the Shenandoah.

I am Sir

Very Respect. Your Obt. Serv't.

A. N. Windsor

Chaplain, 91st O. V. I.

It might not have brought Lewis Powell to justice, but how easily Captain Blazer's testimony could have checkmated Paine's story that *he* was Powell. There is no record that Blazer was ever called to Washington, either during the prisoner's six weeks of silence, in which his identity was a complete mystery, or during the following six weeks, in which he was "identified" to the world as Lewis Powell, formerly of Mosby's Command.

When this letter was written, many news reports were still spelling the prisoner's name "Paine," which *sounded* exactly the same as "Payne" to Captain Blazer. And it was by that name he knew the Ranger who had helped conduct him to Richmond the preceding November. This gives substantial support to the theory that Powell was using the first of his many aliases (Payne) during his service with Mosby.

contacts with the Bransons

The date of Powell's desertion from Mosby's battalion is unknown. It may or may not have had a connection with the argument over killing prisoners in front of the Grant house in Warrenton. He might logically have taken the Oath at Alexandria on his way north—though more likely under the name of "James Wood," since that was what he called himself when he appeared next at the Surratt house.

Witnesses placed the time of his first appearance at Surratt's at anywhere from "not long after Christmas" (per Anna Surratt) to "about the last of February" (Weichmann to Colonel W. P. Wood).[17] There may have been more than one visit in the winter, before he showed up again in March to go to the theater with Surratt, Miss Fitzpatrick, and Miss Deane. About the middle of March he attended the meeting of the "conspirators" at Gautier's, using the alias of "Mosby." At this time he was not staying at Surratt's, and may have been lodging in the Navy Yard district at the address where "Peanuts" Burroughs saw him—the place Atzerodt referred to as "Wood's." Between March 19 and 30 he was in New York at the Revere House, until he moved. During the first two weeks of April he was registered at the Herndon House under the name of "Kincheloe."

This was a much different young man from the furtive escapee who had slipped out of Baltimore in the fall of '64 with the help of the Branson girls. Life in Mosby's Gang had developed him into an experienced desperado; well dressed in the flashy style of a southern gentleman; the proceeds of a year's industrious looting in his pockets; geared to the building of his fortunes through the practice of guile and impersonal violence. In civilian life he appears to have applied the lessons in deception, elusiveness and surprise that he had learned in the Rangers. After his four months of coming and going in Washington, Baltimore, and New York, no witnesses could be found who were *sure* they knew him—and the only witness at the Trial who knew him by his real name, Margaret Branson, said he was Louis Paine.

We can assume Powell kept in touch with Mary Branson, possibly even had lodgings somewhere in Baltimore. There was one possible hint that he may have arranged to meet her in another city, either Washington or New York. It will be recalled that the bloodstained coat found in the woods northeast of the Capitol on Easter Sunday after the assassination was first reported to have had a card in one pocket, as well as riding gloves and a false moustache. These items were turned over to Major Thomas Eckert, Stanton's assistant, and were never seen or mentioned again. The fact that such important clues were whisked out of sight so quickly raises the suspicion that one or all of them might have helped to identify someone the War Department didn't wish to have identified. The *someone* could only have been Lewis Powell.

A name and a number were written on the card. As the *Missouri Democrat* of April 19 reported it, the writing said, "Mary J. Gardner 419."

Now, "Mary" being about as common a girl's name as could be found, it's just a guessing game beyond the assumption that a girl named Mary sent, gave or left Lewis Powell the card, and that the number may have been that of a hotel room.

Under what conditions would it have been unnecessary for her to write down the *name of the hotel?* If the card was left for Powell at *his* hotel, while he was out, by a young lady who was also registering at that hotel and wished him to get in touch with her. And why the formality of a first and last name and middle initial? Either because her acquaintance with him was so slight he might not know who she was if she just wrote "Mary"—or to tell him the full name under which she had registered, because the last one wasn't her own.

Such speculation isn't discouraged by recollecting that Colonel John Wooley's letter of protest to Burnett on May 26 mentioned Mary's full name, with a middle initial which sounded so much like "J" that it could have been misprinted in the *Missouri Democrat*—"Mary A. Branson." Also, there was the young lady's care to conceal her relationship with Powell from her mother. She told her mother she had had a letter from

"Payne" from New York, but it was probably from Powell, and would have been signed "Lewis" or "Louis" in either case. But more important, Louis Paine *couldn't write!*

It isn't vital to establish the exact nature of Powell's connection with Mary Branson, except in so far as it may throw light on some other aspect of the mystery—such as the part played by Thomas T. Eckert, confidant of Stanton and head of the Office of the Military Telegraph.

This Major Eckert, in whose possession the "Mary J. Gardner 419" card was last seen, was an eager unofficial helper in the War Department's campaign to convict and hang Louis Paine. The Trial had not the least connection with his regular duties; but Stanton, according to Eckert, put this prisoner in his personal custody. For several weeks before and during the proceedings the Major spent most of his time hovering around Paine, allegedly trying to get a confession from him. He was called to the witness stand four times, yet never with reference to what he had been able to learn from his prisoner. Years later, however, he recited a whole list of statements he claimed Paine had made to him,[18] all confessional, all incriminating, and mostly pure hogwash. But he did throw in a detail which was probably true—that Paine (as Powell) had fallen in love with "his nurse" at Gettysburg, an unnamed young lady who was later referred to as the soldier's "sweetheart."

Now, Louis Paine was extremely careful not to mention *any* associations between Powell and any member of the Branson family when he told Doster his "narrative" and when he talked to Dr. Gillette the night before the executions. Thus Eckert—unless he was just guessing or got the idea from Mary's missing deposition—could have known about the affair only from Lewis Powell himself. We shall have more on the devious major a little later.

the weeks preceding the assassination

Powell's activities during the weeks prior to the assassination can't be pictured in detail from the few instances in which he allowed himself to be seen and recognized. But enough pieces of the puzzle are at hand to get a fair general idea of what he was up to. From these we can put together a rough outline. It began with John Surratt.

Surratt was the catalyst of Booth's kidnap scheme. Of the eight persons believed to have been involved in it, including Booth himself, five were brought into the group by the enterprising Confederate dispatch-bearer. He had excellent contacts in both capital cities. Baker claimed he knew both John and his mother in Surrattsville for at least two years prior to the assassination.[19] He knew their place was a way station on the route the Confederate couriers traveled between Richmond and Canada, and he said his men frequently caught messengers leaving the tavern. He claimed to have both mother and son caught in his web and at his mercy. But it's more likely that John was in exactly the position he wanted to be in at that time—a perfect position to play both ends against the middle.

Before December 23, 1864, John Wilkes Booth had been dabbling with the idea of abducting the President. He was serious enough about it to have taken a trip down through Maryland to survey the roads, buy a couple of horses, and try to make contact with people along the Confederate mail route. He met Dr. Mudd on such a trip but probably didn't take him into his confidence, though either Mudd or someone else told him young John Surratt knew all the right people in Richmond and Washington. The day before Christmas he met Mudd on Seventh Street; while they were talking, Surratt walked by with Weichmann.[20] Booth asked the doctor to introduce him, and he did—thereby stumbling into the trap which took him to Dry Tortugas and very nearly got him hanged.

Booth told Surratt what he had in mind, and Surratt took it under advisement. But no one else of any capability wanted to play. The actor's boyhood friends Arnold and O'Laughlin, each of whom had had his fill of soldiering in the rebel army after only one year, were willing to listen to Booth *talk* about getting rich and famous via derring-do so long as nothing really illegal transpired. Baker said the actor was turned down by various former army men;[21] but this is doubtful, since even in later years when it was quite safe to do so, no such persons ever claimed to have had a proposition from him—except for a fellow actor who testified at the Trial. So there the matter stood, to Booth's deep frustration, until sometime in February of '65.

When Powell showed up at the Surratt house in January or February, he wasn't just knocking on doors looking for a rooming house. He had come to Washington to see John Surratt. He had met him sometime the previous year—possibly on his trip to Richmond as Captain Blazer's guard, or perhaps through some of Mosby's many contacts in Maryland. The former is the most likely, since the Surratts moved to Washington on November 1, 1864, and John was out on the road through most of that month. If he had met Powell prior to that, he wouldn't have been able to give him the address of the boardinghouse.

It appears that the kidnap plan seemed feasible to Powell at first, at least in theory, since undertakings as audacious as that had been accomplished by Mosby and his men on many occasions. Powell had probably been in on some of them. But he must have had misgivings as soon as he met Booth (possibly at the "*Jane Shore*" theater party), and even more so when he met the other "conspirators" at the "middle of March" meeting.

For Booth, however, the effect was just the reverse. His dead fancy of starring in a grand drama of abduction that would make the name of John Wilkes Booth immortal suddenly sprang to life again with the entrance of a bona fide gentleman of fortune fresh from service with Mosby, whose name was a synonym for high adventure. Powell had a few days in which to estimate the chances for success, while Booth described his master plan with gestures and sent notices for the meeting at Gautier's on March 14 to his supporting players.

The meeting at midnight in the private room of the restaurant had possibilities as a notable scene in Booth's drama. But it fizzled. If Powell thought of coming right out and telling the leader that such a third-rate collection of bumblers (with the exceptions of Surratt and himself, of course) couldn't kidnap Mr. Lincoln on the streets of Richmond, let alone from a Washington theater, Sam Arnold saved him the trouble. Even Sam realized the thing was ridiculous. But rather than offend his boyhood friend by saying so, he insisted the coup take place within a week or he would withdraw. The haggling went on through the night. Powell, as a newcomer introduced only by the nickname of "Mosby," let the others argue. The meeting broke up toward dawn—and so did the "gang."

Right after this meeting on March 14, Powell left Washington. Weichmann said Surratt told him the ex-Ranger had gone to Baltimore, and perhaps he did make a stop there. But his destination was New York, to which city the scene of activity had been shifted.

It's unfortunate we have to take all Weichmann's statements with reservation unless they are easily verifiable or are confirmed by some reliable witness. Because his assertion that he saw a letter to John Surratt from "Wood" in New York sometime around this date fits neatly into the puzzle. In the letter, which was not produced in evidence of course, "Wood" told Surratt he was looking for something to do and was staying at the Revere House, but was moving to a different address.[22]

Booth checked out of his hotel on March 21; on the twenty-third he sent Weichmann a telegram from New York saying, "Tell John to telegraph the number and street at once."[23] Now, Weichmann *said* he delivered the telegram to John the same day, but this was probably untrue. Somewhere around the twenty-first, a letter addressed to Surratt from New York reached Washington, and it would have caused him to take the next train to New York, if he had received it then. It was the letter Holt showed Weichmann on May 18—signed "R. E. Watson"—asking if the witness could identify the handwriting as that of Booth. Weichmann could not, and there was no more mention of the document in Peterson. In Pitman *all* mention of it was carefully deleted. The original is now in the National Archives. It reads as follows:[24]

NEW YORK, March 19th, 1865

Mr. J. H. Surratt

DEAR SIR

I would like to see you on important business, if you can spare the time to come on to New York. Please Telegraph me immediately on the reception of this whether you can come on or not and much oblige

Yours tr—

R. D. WATSON

P.S.
Address Care Demill (?) & Co.
178½ Water St.

Discussion of the authorship of the foregoing letter at this point would take us off on a tangent. But it was surely a factor in Surratt's activities from the date he received it to the date of the assassination.*

Powell remained in New York until March 31, when he returned to the Capitol and registered at the Herndon House as "Kincheloe." Booth shuttled back and forth between Washington and New York. From there Surratt wrote Atzerodt to try to sell two horses which belonged to Booth and were being kept at Howard's stable.[25] One, a small bay, was sold to a stage contractor on April 12; the other, a heavy, dark bay, blind in one eye, remained at another stable for the time being.[26]

In this period Booth's activities didn't seem to be related to those of his erstwhile confederates—except in the selling of the horses, which implied an end, rather than a beginning, of conspiracy. On March 27, a Monday, he wired O'Laughlin in Baltimore to get Sam Arnold if he could, but to come to Washington on Wednesday with or without Sam, because "We sell that day sure."[27] O'Laughlin ignored the wire; Arnold was applying for a job at Fortress Monroe and was through with plotting;[28] Herold too was out of the picture, having found a clerkship at the Base Hospital, Army of the James, on March 21.[29] Only Atzerodt appears to have been on hand for whatever project the actor had in mind for Wednesday.

---

* Atzerodt's "confession" to Colonel Wells indicated that Surratt returned to Washington from *somewhere* "about a week" before the assassination, but he said he didn't know whether Surratt was a party to the crime. Weichmann and other, more reliable, witnesses at the boardinghouse said Surratt returned to his mother's house for a few hours on April 3, got Mr. Holahan to give him greenbacks in exchange for some twenty-dollar gold pieces he had acquired, and went on to New York. (Peterson, p. 147, Holahan testimony.) No evidence available now, and nothing brought out at the Surratt Trial in 1867, proves him to have been in Washington again after April 3. But Atzerodt said he had a letter from Surratt from New York after he hastened there (on April 3) telling him to sell two horses—which the German attempted to do on April 12. So Surratt was in New York sometime between April 4 and 13.

Booth left Washington again on April 1,[30] the day after Powell returned, and went to New York. On the seventh he had lunch with a fellow actor named Samuel Knapp Chester (whom he had formerly tried unsuccessfully to enlist in his scheme for abduction) and made a comment which revealed a new trend in his conception of a grand gesture: "What an excellent chance I had, if I had wished, to kill the President on inauguration day; I was on the stand as close to him nearly as I am to you.[31]

He had in fact occupied a seat on the speaker's stand, using a ticket obtained for him by a young lady named Bessie Hale, to whom he was supposed to have been engaged, the daughter of Senator J. P. Hale of New Hampshire.[32] His curious remark to Chester a month later—to say nothing of his activities in the interim—made it rather clear that the idea of killing the President had just been planted in his mind around April 7. Yet Colonel Burnett, in a speech delivered years later, shored up the legend with the statement that Booth had planned to stab Mr. Lincoln during the inaugural ceremony.[33]

An objective view of the circumstances leads to this conclusion: Booth, not knowing Powell had returned to the Capitol on March 31, went to New York the following day, probably with the idea of finding him. Surratt arrived in Washington from Richmond (he said) on April 3, then immediately followed Booth to New York. Shortly thereafter we find that Booth's thoughts had turned from abduction to murder. When he went back to Washington on the eighth, Powell was waiting for him, and the preparations for the assassination moved swiftly.

the final arrangements

During his lecture in Rockville, Maryland, Surratt intimated he left Washington for Richmond right after the "horse ride," following which Booth's "gang" broke up. He added, "I never after saw any of the party *except one,* and that was when I was on my way from Richmond to Canada on business of quite a different nature."[34]

When Surratt stopped in Washington on April 3, he apparently *was* on his way "from Richmond to Canada."[35] Since he was no longer in jeopardy on a treason charge when he told of meeting one "of the party," is it possible he felt safe in hinting at his real role in the final plot? In Washington on the third he had seen his mother. She could have been the "one" he meant—though he never admitted she had any part in *any* plot. He could have seen Powell—or have read the "Watson" letter for the first time. At any rate, it was after Surratt's arrival in New York that he surely encountered *Booth* again. The actor began thinking murder, then hurried back to Washington to do it.

All of which leaves the impression that New York City, rather than Washington, was the geographical birthplace of the assassination plot. The "Watson" letter came from there. Powell came from there to set up his headquarters in the Herndon House. Booth went to New York on April 1 thinking abduction and returned from there on the eighth primed for murder. Surratt hastened to New York on April 4. Baker was in New York through the whole spring of '65, including the crucial period from March 19 to April 9.

One of the numerous truths which Lafayette Baker wove into his self-glorifying version of the "conspiracy" was that the man he called "Payne" was *a "hired assassin" dispatched from New York.*[36] This was in direct contradiction to the version of the Booth-Payne relationship which emerged from the Trial. But Baker couldn't resist implying that, by the brilliance of his deductions, he knew more about the mystery than anyone else. In this case as in most others, it wasn't deduction. He *knew* who in New York had hired Powell.

Atzerodt was apparently not drawn into the final preparations until Wednesday, April 12. His account to Colonel Wells of what happened that day and the following ones before the assassination is coherent and well supported by evidence from other sources. Booth looked him up that day and took him to the Herndon House to see Powell.[37] He had met the young man a month earlier at the "middle of March" meeting, under the name of "Mosby." Booth now introduced him as "James Wood." He was told they intended to go to Richmond, now that the city had surrendered, and open a theater if they could get passes. After a brief conversation in that vein, Booth and Atzerodt walked down the street together; when they parted, the actor told him to come back to the Herndon House that night.

The German didn't mention it in his "confession," but this was the same day he went to Naylor's stable and took away the big one-eyed horse he had been trying to sell for Booth on Surratt's orders. Later in the day he tried to sell the horse to another stableman named Matthew Pope, but without success.[38] Later he told Fletcher he had sold the horse "in Montgomery County,"[39] but it ended up in the possession of Powell.

That Wednesday evening at about half-past seven Atzerodt went back to Powell's room and found Powell, Booth, and Herold there.[40] He was received rather coolly. He had made a date to go to the theater with a young man who was waiting for him down in the street. Booth told him not to bring anyone near the house again. Before he left, he learned that the actor and Herold were going to the theater too, though they didn't leave when he did.

This statement, made before Atzerodt had any clear idea of what had happened at Ford's on Good Friday—except that Booth had shot Lincoln—offers a plausible explanation as to when and by whom the preparations for the crime were made in the presidential box. After the murder it was found that a hole had been chipped in the wall of a small passageway leading into the box, to make it possible to wedge a wooden bar across the first of its two doors. Before shooting the President, Booth had put this bar in place, jamming the door shut so that no one else could enter the box without breaking down the door. *When* the hole in the wall was made and *by whom* has always been a matter of much conjecture. It is usually assumed that the actor slipped into the theater the afternoon before his crime and made his preparations in the box. Interpretation of Atzerodt's account suggests this was done on the previous Wednesday evening by Booth and Herold.

That evening before Atzerodt left to join his friend—suggesting, by the way, that he was not deeply involved in the plans of the others—Booth told him to look him up the next day, either at the National Hotel or at Powell's room. He did so and found Booth at the National around 10:30 A.M. He was told to go to the Kirkwood House, where Andrew Johnson lived, and try to get a pass to Richmond signed by the Vice-President. Booth said he would come there with "another man" to recommend him. This proposal was not quite so nonsensical in 1865 as it sounds to us now. The Vice-President lived like any other citizen, without formality or a bodyguard, accessible to any citizen who wished to speak to him.

Atzerodt went obediently, registered at the hotel under his own name, paying one day's board, and spent the rest of the day drinking, as usual.

On Friday, April 14, the little German seems to have resumed his drinking where he had left off the previous evening. He could carry an almost limitless quantity of liquor, but it must have distorted his conception of time on this particular day. The events he told about ran two or three hours behind the same events related by other observers.

Early in the morning Herold asked him to go down to Surrattsville to "see after" some "things" Booth had left there with Mr. Lloyd several weeks earlier. Atzerodt hired a horse for the trip but then decided not to go, giving Wells the explanation that he was to have seen Booth that evening and, if he had done as Herold asked, would not have been able to.[41]

Around noon (Atzerodt said it was 3:00 P.M.) Herold came to the hotel and said Booth and "Wood" wanted to see him. They were to have met at a restaurant. Powell was there, but Booth was not; so Herold went to look for him. The German said he got tired of waiting and drifted off to drink at various restaurants. He thought it was nearly six when he got back to the Kirkwood, but it was probably just after three. The clerk said a young man had called for him, so Atzerodt sat down in the lobby to wait.

Herold came in again presently and said Booth and "Wood" wanted to see him immediately. But before they left, Herold asked for the key to his room and, in Atzerodt's presence, left a large knife and a pistol there. At the Trial it was charged that these weapons were given Atzerodt to use in killing Johnson. But when Herold left them in the room at the Kirkwood, the other man (according to his "confession") did not yet know of the proposed murders. Also, Atzerodt was apparently given a pistol by Booth or Powell when the idea was broached to him later. The morning after the assassination he gave it to an acquaintance, John Caldwell, as security for a loan of ten dollars.[42] The night before his execution he told the Lutheran minister Mr. Butler that Booth had wanted *Herold* to kill Johnson because he believed him to have more nerve.[43] In other words, Herold left his own weapons in the other man's room simply because he did not expect to need them for the part in the conspiracy which had already been assigned him, not by Booth, but by Powell.

According to the "confession," when the four men met, Atzerodt was not asked to kill anyone, only to "show them the road into the lower part of Maryland," which he agreed to do. He went so far as to rent a horse for the journey before changing his mind about taking any part at all. There is a very good possibility that Atzerodt omitted many details from his original "confession" which he considered incriminating. But the numerous details which can be confirmed make it, in this writer's opinion, the best available record of the conspirators' activities during the last two or three days before the assassination.

After the meeting at the Herndon House, where Booth and Powell told the German what was afoot, he went outside with Herold, who asked him for the key to his room at the Kirkwood. He didn't have it, so they parted there. He never saw any of them again and didn't return to his hotel.

Atzerodt set the time of the parting at around 6:30 or 7:00 P.M. Another, somewhat more reliable, testimony suggests it was near to 4:00 P.M.

On April 27, about two weeks after the assassination, a man named Matthew J. Pope was interrogated by a War Department investigator.[44] He said he lived in the Navy Yard and kept a stable on K Street between Eighth and Ninth Streets. He knew Herold because he had sold a horse for him two or three weeks before the President was shot. On the afternoon before the murder Herold and another, taller man left their horses at his stable. Herold was riding a medium-sized roan, the big man was mounted on "a large bay horse, blind in one eye." He thought the other man was dressed in light clothes. In a couple of hours they came for their horses, riding off at between 4:30 and 5:00 P.M.

Mr. Pope was called to the witness stand on June 2 for the defense. From the statement above, it appears he could have contributed some useful information on the movements of the conspirators just prior to the crime. But Doster only asked him about Atzerodt's offer to sell him the one-eyed horse on April 12, and the prosecution didn't cross-examine.[45]

The man who rode off with Herold between 4:30 and 5:00 P.M. was obviously Powell. Mrs. Murray at the Herndon House testified that her mysterious boarder for two weeks, who looked like the prisoner in the dock, had asked for an early dinner around four and had checked out as soon as he finished eating. She knew nothing about a meeting of four men in the vacated room between seven-thirty and eight—which would surely have attracted her attention. Since her testimony agrees with Pope's as to Powell's departure, it seems the final meeting was sometime before four o'clock.

On April 27, after his capture, Herold was interrogated by Colonel Bingham, one of the War Department's prosecutors.[46] Among other things, he said he took his horse from Shreve's stable at about four o'clock that Friday afternoon, stopped at his mother's house in Washington for ten minutes around six, then rode out of town. He said he had been out in the country trying to sell a horse owned by Atzerodt. He said he stopped at Lloyd's tavern in Surrattsville on the way back, that he was there only about ten minutes, and that on the way back to Washington he met Booth, seven or eight miles out of the Capitol at the foot of Soper's Hill.

The prosecution, basing its charge on the stableman Fletcher's yarn about having seen Herold in the city after 10:00 P.M. the night of the assassination (a reasonably careful study of the chronology of Fletcher's story shows it to have been the clumsiest of fabrications), claimed Herold had been assigned to wait at Seward's to guide the incredibly stupid "Payne" out of town after he had murdered the Secretary of State. It was a fanciful explanation for "Payne's" inexplicable return to the Surratt house, and also worked Herold into the plot in what the War Department considered a convincing manner.

But Herold was both a glib talker and an astute liar. In almost every instance in which a statement of his could be checked without difficulty, he told the truth. His departure from the stable around 4:00 P.M. was easily verifiable, as was the stop at his mother's house at about six. He apparently expected John Lloyd to confirm his story about stopping at the tavern for a drink in the later evening, possibly around eleven o'clock. But Lloyd, like Weichmann, was testifying for the War Department under threat of prosecution as an accomplice and hanging, and did not (if he was asked about it) confirm this statement of Herold's.

Since the last thing Powell needed was someone to guide him out of town (we can be sure he had his escape planned down to the last detail; that it went exactly as he intended it to; that no matter what impression Atzerodt had about the whole quartet fleeing south together, Powell had planned to go north from the beginning), the idea of Herold's waiting for him in front of Seward's is unbelievable. But the mystery of Powell's *and* Herold's whereabouts from the time they rode away from the stable at, say, 4:30 P.M. is anyone's guess.

The Mosby technique, in general, was to ride boldly into an occupied village or Union encampment, do what one came to do before the "enemy" realized what was happening, and make one's escape in the resulting confusion. Thus Powell would not have been likely to park his big, one-eyed horse in a city stable and sit around watching the clock and attracting attention until ten. He would more likely have ridden out of town in *some* direction, making sure that everyone he encountered saw him riding *away* from the city. At a prearranged time and place he would have turned and headed back to Washington at a good clip, gone directly to Seward's, done his bloody work in exactly the time he had allotted for it—and ridden off so slowly that no one would believe that William Bell's cries of "murder!" applied to him.

Two circumstances which make it seem plausible that Powell may have ridden out of town, then back on schedule to the Seward house are: (1) that the War Department was unable to find even a hint as to how "Payne" spent the time between the final meeting at the Herndon House and 10:15 P.M. that evening,[47] and (2) that the one-eyed horse, when found less than a mile from Seward's, was lame, dripping with perspiration, and so exhausted it was close to foundering—in other words, far more exhausted than one would expect after that short a ride, even if ridden hard.[48]

The fact that Herold's whole evening is not accounted for by a ten-mile trip to Surrattsville leads to speculation that he would have been doing something similar to avoid suspicion, something prescribed by Powell—such as riding *with* Powell to the turning-back point, then cutting across to Surrattsville and leaving there in time to meet Booth on the road from Washington.

There were a couple of other interesting and possibly true statements in Herold's interview with Bingham: He was shown the photos of nine men who were, as of April 27, suspected of being involved with Booth. He readily and cheerfully identified Surratt, Atzerodt, O'Laughlin, and "the carpenter at Ford's" (Spangler). Louis Paine's photograph was certainly one of the nine. But Herold either failed to see his resemblance to Powell or denied knowing him to shield Powell. The former seems the more likely, for later in the interview he intimated that "a man from Mosby's Command" was supposed to have murdered Seward—which he would not have mentioned if he had wanted to conceal Powell's identity. He *claimed* that all information he had on the assassination was given him by *Booth*.

The rest of his story amounted to a denial that he knew anything about Booth's crime until the next day, when the actor threatened to implicate him in it if he refused to accompany him on the escape southward. He quoted Booth as saying there were important people back in Washington who were involved in the assassination and that if Herold didn't stick by him, they would "put him through."

evidence of Powell after Paine's arrest

Any history of Lewis Thornton Powell beyond July 7, 1865, is considered apocryphal of course, as far as the accepted legend of the John Wilkes Booth "conspiracy" is concerned. For that matter, so are accounts of his experiences after April 17, the date of Louis Paine's arrest. The conviction that the War Department's husky young prisoner was Seward's attacker and Booth's closest accomplice—later identified as the Florida soldier Lewis Thornton Powell—was so universal during and after the Trial that the real Lewis Powell was virtually immune to detection from April 17 onward.

True, there were certain parties—and they may have been numerous—who knew that he had not been arrested that evening at the Surratt house and that he continued to live on after the hangings on July 7. But this was guilty knowledge which none of them could reveal without also telling what *he* knew about the real conspiracy to murder Abraham Lincoln. We can imagine that some may have been uneasy in the fear that Powell might be recognized by some miracle, perhaps arrested and persuaded to talk about the assassination. But unlike the spiteful Baker, who found it hard to keep the secret of his greatest deception, Powell seemed satisfied to quit while he was winning—and it may have spared him an end like Baker's, hunted down by assassins hired by mysterious men who couldn't live in peace until the superdetective's barbed tongue was silenced.

But this is getting ahead of our story. With the arrest of Louis Paine, Lewis Powell ceased to exist for all practical considerations. So evidences of his existence were not taken to be such. There may have been dozens of these around the time of the Trial. A hundred years later we are fortunate to be able to find three.

The big bay horse, blind in one eye, which Powell was riding when he left Pope's stable around four-thirty or five in the afternoon of Good Friday was found about three-quarters of a mile northeast of the Capitol.

It was discovered by a Lieutenant John Toffey shortly after midnight. At the Trial the young officer testified (May 17) that he had found the animal near his station, Camp Barry.[49] It was much exhausted and a little lame. On the instructions of his superiors, he took it back to the city and turned it over to the grooms at General Augur's headquarters.

Several days later General Augur received the following letter from a farmer in Howard County, due north of the Capitol in Maryland:[50]

SANDY SPRING, April 19, 1865

General Augur

SIR;

I was requested to write to you by two men who professed to have been sent to my farm by you for purpose of getting information in regard to a horse which was stolen from me on Sunday night in Howard Co. They requested I should write on return of my Brother. He has returned, having tracked the horse about two miles above Unity in Montgomery Co. on the road that leads to mouth of Monocacy River. They went on to Barnesville examining all the bye roads and could not find any track of the horse off the main roads which had been that day used very much in consequence of a *Sale* near and was much used.

This man who stole the horse I described to the man whom you sent to me. He was seen by a boy near my place, the first time on Saturday morning coming out of a woods and on the boy's approach he remarked, Boy have you heard any news? The boy answered in the negative and passed bye being frightened at his pistols one of which he had his hand on. The boy describes him as rather a tall person, large eyes, not sunburnt, without beard (shaved) dressed rather handsomely in a gray suit and light-colored hat, answering to the description given by the little girl who saw him in my barn secreted.

My Brother was arrested at Barnesville and taken together with his companion to Monocacy Junction where he prevailed upon the commanding officer to have pickets doubled and some roads guarded although they suspected him strongly of being the *veritable* Booth. The horse he stole from me was a dappled roane in fine condition, two shoes off behind and small with waving mane and tale, very light color would go any gate rack pace or loaf but seldom trotting. My brother could assist no further in detection of this person whoever he may have been as he was not known there and could not gain confidence of the highest officer at the place who was a Lieutenant.

Hoping he may be caught ere you receive this, still I write as it may possibly give some clue if these parties were concerned in the assassination of our President, everything corresponding, time, etc. it may possibly have been persons concerned in it.

Yours truly

SAMUEL HOPKINS

Clarksville

Howard County, Maryland

Mr. Hopkins' letter speaks for itself as to the possible identity of the man who stole his horse two days after the assassination. His description of the stranger's features, stature, and dress can be taken for an adequate description of Lewis Powell by anyone who entertains the idea that the real attacker of Seward escaped into the country after his crime. In view of the uncertainty of William Bell's identification of Paine, it is not particularly necessary to reconcile Hopkins' statement that the stranger wore a gray suit with Bell's statement that the intruder had black trousers. Likewise, the finding of a brown hat and a pistol at the Seward house—considering how readily the prosecution acquired any physical clues it needed—doesn't offset Hopkins' mention that his stranger wore a light gray hat and carried pistols.

Clarksville, Maryland, and the area mentioned in Hopkins' letter is about fifteen miles from Lafayette Square in Washington, and almost due north of the city.

General Augur forwarded the letter to Colonel Burnett, who took no cognizance of it whatever.

On Thursday, April 20, three men disembarked from the lake steamer "Canada" at Burlington, Vermont, and having missed the train for Montreal, slept in the depot of the Vermont Central Railroad all night.

They did not appear to be acquainted, just traveling in the same direction. The next morning they took the 5:05 train for St. Albans, from which town they were believed to have traveled by stage to Canada. After they had left the Burlington station, a night watchman was said to have found a handkerchief with the name "J. H. Surratt, No. 2" written in the corner.

This incident, due to the disappearance of John Surratt prior to the assassination and the wide belief that he was an accomplice of Booth's, was investigated in great detail, and all persons who had seen the three strangers were interrogated. Some of them stated that the tallest of the three men resembled a photograph of John Surratt they were shown. No conclusions were reached at the time, but the identity of the strangers became a large issue at the Trial of John Surratt in 1867, at which proceeding the prosecution charged that Surratt had been in Washington on the day of the assassination and attempted to trace his escape route to Canada.

The only aspect of the affair which concerns our present subject is the physical description of the tall stranger given by Mr. Carroll T. Hobart, conductor on the train from Burlington to St. Albans, who had several conversations with him during the journey. Here is his description:[51]

> . . . a very tall man, six feet one inch, or more (being taller than the conductor, who is five feet eleven and a half inches), broad shoulders, otherwise slim, straight as an arrow; did not look like a laborer, although dressed rather poor; had on a loose sack-coat, colored; cassimere shirt, all one color; collar some turned over; an old spotted scarf, long, which hung down and was held by the vest, which was light color, buttoned half way up, old style; light colored pants, being loose, had the appearance of having no suspenders on; had on a light-colored, tight-fitting skull-cap. His entire outfit was rather dusty, dirty, and seedy. His hair was black as jet and straight; no beard, nor the appearance of any; was young, not more than twenty-one or twenty-two. He left the train at St. Albans.

The other man (the third one had allegedly stolen the money of his two companions and disappeared) was very short, stout, sandy complexioned, with whiskers and a goatee. He and the tall man claimed to be laborers returning to their home in Canada.

Mr. Hobart was sure he could identify the tall man as John Surratt—though his description didn't conform to Surratt's appearance in any respect. It did, however, sound like a playback of the descriptions of Louis Paine given by the officers who arrested him at the Surratt house. Hobart's idea that the man was Surratt, we suspect, has to be related to the fact that since he had seen the tall stranger the War Department had posted a reward of $25,000 for Surratt's apprehension. It was posted on April 20, the day before the suspicious men rode on Hobart's train to St. Albans.

At the Surratt trial the conductor was called as a witness for the prosecution.[52] His description of the tall man was about the same as originally, except that he added some more details. The man, he said, sometimes affected a "Cannuck" accent, but dropped it occasionally and "spoke good square English." "His hands were not like a laboring man's, were not like a Canadian's that had been used to hard labor by any means; they were white and delicate."

When asked to identify the prisoner (Surratt) as the tall stranger on the train, he said he "resembles the man I saw very much. I should not recognize his face. He had at that time a *mustache,* but no whiskers on his chin."

It was finally determined—as we would expect—that the tall man was not Surratt. But the handkerchief with his name on it which was found in the Burlington station has continued to perplex students of the assassination. If the tall stranger was indeed Lewis Powell trying to make his way to Canada, it's conceivable he might have had one of Surratt's handkerchiefs. But this writer is inclined to take all such *obvious* clues—so many of which were featured in the Conspiracy Trial—as reflecting the heavy-handed "Baker Method" of incrimination.

The Surratt Trial brought out a plausible if rather pat explanation for the handkerchief—that Weichmann and Holahan also passed through the Burlington station on their way to Canada a day or so earlier, and the latter testified that in his hasty departure from the Surratt house he had picked up one of John's handkerchiefs and later lost it in the Burlington station.[53]

Was the tall young man Mr. Hobart saw Lewis Powell or just someone who bore an extraordinary resemblance to him and behaved suspiciously? The reader may take his choice. But at least we can be sure the conductor's description of the man, both originally and at the Surratt trial, was authentic. He was not, like so many witnesses at the Conspiracy Trial, being influenced to make his description fit that of Louis Paine or—in this case—Lewis Powell.

Lewis Powell may have been seen but not recognized, after making his escape from Washington, by Paine's attorney, Colonel William Doster.

Now we have the appearance of a formidable irony. Colonel Doster, the only person in Washington who was endeavoring to save Paine's life, spending part of an evening with the real criminal without the faintest suspicion who he was.

He tells it in his own words:[54]

> Between the end of the trial and the publication of the sentence on the 6th of July, at a time when the newspapers were full of descriptions of the prisoners and their defenses, I was startled one evening by the appearance in my office of a tall, muscular, and well dressed gentleman, who said he was from the eastern shore of Maryland, and who asserted with great emphasis that Payne was his younger brother, an insane man, who had escaped from a private lunatic asylum the year before, and of whom his family had lost all traces, until reading a description of Payne in the newspapers, they felt sure that he was their fugitive brother. The family physician had already visited the commission and identified him beyond mistake. I scrutinized him closely and there certainly appeared to be in the height of the two, complexion, and general air a resemblance.
>
> I told him he could see the prisoner in the morning, when the court opened, but his anxiety of mind was so great that he must have an interview with him that very night. I must jump into his cab and see the Secretary of War about a pass. Having to do with a member of an insane family, I yielded. The Secretary, of course, refused. Not baffled, the stranger drove to the arsenal, and tried to prevail on General Hartranft to admit him, but without success. Next morning, long before the hour of opening, the stranger was on hand, sitting before the dock. When Payne entered he at least did not recognize the other staring him in the face. After an attentive examination he came to the conclusion that everything was his brother except the shape of the nose, and left greatly disappointed.

But could this have actually have been Powell? The alternative to believing so is to accept the possibility that there were not just one but *three* other men who resembled Louis Paine closely enough to be mistaken for him—or at least to be taken for his brother. Also, there were internal weaknesses in the insistent stranger's story which are more apparent to us than they would have been to Doster. Paine's picture and description had been published in the newspapers for at least ten weeks, since a day or so after his arrest. Why would his "brother," living only a short distance from Washington, have waited until the end of the Trial to inquire about him? If his attorney's plea that the prisoner was insane prompted the stranger to think Paine was his "lunatic" younger brother, why had he not made inquiries around June 2, when this line of defense was made public? On that same date the prisoner was identified in all the country's newspapers as Lewis Powell, a man known to have been a resident of Florida whose service with the Confederate Army was verified by *Union* hospital records. In the face of such positive identification, why would the man think Paine was his idiot brother from Maryland a month later? And for that matter, why did *Doster* consider the possibility, unless he had great doubts that his client had told him the truth?

Of all the conspirators, Powell was the only one who might have been operating under a firm agreement as to his compensation. Unlike Surratt, his escape was permanent—not just a temporary evasion of arrest and a life of hiding. After the conviction of Paine, he was free to come and go as he pleased, though under another name, of course. He had either collected his fee beforehand and banked it in a safe place—or was in an excellent position to collect his fee, and then some, from those who had hired him. If he turned up again, he would surely be in the character of an affluent, well-dressed gentleman who rode in cabs. Moreover, the very audacity of the call upon Doster would seem to be true to type for Powell—even if what he hoped to accomplish by it was rather obscure!

Assuming this *was* Lewis Powell, it seems impossible that he could have had any idea of spiriting Paine out of a prison filled with detectives and surrounded by a division of infantry. This would have been too big an order even for Mosby, the master of deception under whom Powell had studied, though the application to Stanton and the call upon General Hartranft would have been a credit to Mosby himself.

The man's willingness, when refused a personal interview with the prisoner, to appear in court the next day would seem to have been the ultimate recklessness. For he could hardly be certain that the other defendants—at least five of whom had known Lewis Powell as "Wood," "Mosby," et al.—were convinced it was he who was on trial with them. They apparently were (or were keeping the secret), but how could he be sure of it?

Mr. Hobart's afterthought at the Surratt trial—that the man on his train wore a *moustache*—may have been an explanation. Doster didn't mention a moustache, but he left the impression that the stranger in his office was *older* than Paine, an illusion that might have been due to the stranger's moustache and Paine's complete beardlessness.

If this man was Powell, he must have had some objective in trying to see Paine, other than to try to effect his escape. We can't assume that even Powell was immune to the gnawing of conscience, that he wasn't just presenting himself to give Paine a chance to denounce him—though a confession to Doster would have been the most positive remedy for a guilty conscience. The explanation may have been in the realm of curiosity. Not having seen Paine since well before the assassination, he may have been almost unbearably mystified as to why the prisoner was determined to die in his place.

This is as far as documentation can take us in tracing the career of Lewis Powell. That he lived on under another name is certain. In another context, we shall have a theory as to where he lived and whose name he borrowed.

16

John Wilkes Booth

A number of conditions have combined to prevent any genuine understanding of John Wilkes Booth as a historical figure. While many other famous or notorious personalities whose careers were longer, more complex, and not nearly so well documented have been explained fully and convincingly by means of historical research, Booth is almost as much a mystery today as he was on the evening of Good Friday, 1865, when his seemingly pointless crime shocked the world. No attempt to explain his deed has ever succeeded. Neither his temperament nor his heredity, nor his public or private life prior to that date, seemed to have qualified him for the role of assassin. We do not presume to be able to explain him completely, and have found nothing in the way of justification or extenuation. But we do believe that someone properly qualified for psychological analysis could find a plausible, if pathetic, human being behind that disgraced name—when the legend which surrounds it is dismantled and set aside.

In the first place, those who wrote original commentaries on Booth fell into one or the other of two extreme classes. They were either immensely fond of him, or else they despised him. The former category was made up largely of members of his closely knit family or friends of his family who had known him prior to April 14, 1865. Since early boyhood he had been their darling, the sunniest, most effervescent member of a highly emotional kinship of theatrical people—his mother's favorite and greatly spoiled. The latter category knew him only as a member of a profession which was considered at least disreputable and frequently immoral in those days. In general, they judged the crime rather than the man and felt that propriety obliged them to speak of the assassin only with the most exaggerated contempt. Many of those who had been Lincoln's most bitter political enemies were among the loudest in their denunciation of Booth, the most resourceful in finding colorful new phrases with which to heap scorn upon his dead body and befouled name. There were some who called attention to themselves by protesting too much.

This class of commentator would seldom admit that Lincoln's murderer may have been insane—since that implied a small degree of extenuation. To them he was a political fanatic, infuriated by the defeat of his beloved South, figuratively thirsting for the blood of the man who had led the Union to victory.

Some years after the crime, when the public temper and prejudice against Booth had subsided somewhat—partly due to the retirement or death of those who had been most active in whipping up the frenzy against Lincoln's assassin and his "accomplices"—members of the actor's still-grieving family and wide circle of friends felt able to put their recollections of him in print. They made it quite plain that they did not approve of what he had done, and they asked neither understanding nor forgiveness—just a chance to tell about the immensely charming young man he had been before whatever happened to him happened. They were backed up by great numbers of his legion of acquaintances in the theatrical profession—particularly after it became evident that a former association with John Wilkes Booth could be turned into a gold mine of free publicity.

Allowing for the expansiveness of stage people, the picture they gave us of Booth in his earlier years was apparently authentic (restrained as they still were by the fear of seeming to defend what he did) and about as accurate as biographies ever are. Taken together, they portrayed a young man of exceptional attractiveness and sensitivity, an extrovert, a great lover of applause and approval—busily earning it by exertions in charm, whether on a stage, in a saloon, in a drawing room, or in the company of just one young lady. Men liked him, and he was quite at ease with them—an unusual facet in a man who appears to have been the prototype of a matinee idol, with an almost aphrodisiac effect upon women. Booth, to judge by the large numbers of attractive young ladies who embellished his acquaintanceship, felt a rather normal sense of obligation to the most smitten of these and did not create artificial barriers to warm friendship if his Juliets sometimes turned out to be professionals. The female biographers, however, insisted that his were the instincts and behavior of a perfect gentleman—from which we can gather that he was also discreet.

The first twenty-five years of his life were, or seemed to be, a lighthearted epic which had no connection with the events which brought about his crime and death.

Those who felt they knew John Wilkes best thought of him as a harum-scarum young fellow, feasting on the cream of life with nothing on his mind but practical jokes, girls, and applause—certainly not capable of deep feeling on any subject so complex as politics.

Booth's last two weeks, spent largely alone and in hiding except for the company of one devious young man, produced little in the way of a rational explanation for his crime. With the exception of one brief comment he made at the Garrett dinner table the day before he was found and shot, his conversations with people on the road and with his captors indicated the state of mind of a man playing a corny part in a melodramatic dream sequence. When he argued with the detectives from inside the barn, for example, he didn't talk in the manner his desperate situation called for; he recited his lines as if he were reading from the tag end of a really miserable script.

This was the predicament of his biographers, those who had known him fondly: It was as though their fascinating young rake of the years before April 14, 1865, had died by the same bullet which killed Lincoln. And that caricature of him lived on just long enough to complete their mystification. At the same time came the deluge of wild denunciations—the practiced, artistic vilification in the press; the methodical, calculated, documented damnation of the War Department—accomplishing the dual purpose of elevating Abraham Lincoln from awkward, unappreciated humanity to artificial sainthood, and reducing John Wilkes Booth to the level of the rattlesnake.

The real problem for Booth's original biographers was the *legend* of his "conspiracy." As a deliberately created fiction superimposed upon the skimpy framework of his crackbrained scheme for abducting the President, it had very little connection with what he had been or done before. It created an entirely new identity for him which had no authentic history prior to April 14. Projected into the public mind with the full authority of the federal government behind it and a flood of documentation to overwhelm all questions, it became for all practical purposes the *truth* about John Wilkes Booth.

Whether this representation of "Johnny" seemed rational or not, those who had known him could do nothing about it. To refute even the most minor of the War Department's allegations was impossible. He *had* done the deed. The few hints he had given them that he was up to something—such as the "To whom it may concern" letter he entrusted to his brother-in-law, comedian John Clarke, hinting at a plan to strike a blow for the Confederacy—only made the legend more credible.[1] Far from refuting it, they were almost obliged to believe it. It was they, rather than those who damned Booth, who fell back on the explanation of madness. How else to explain what he had done—so out of character, it seemed to them—other than by sudden, complete insanity?

Edwin, for instance, knew all about his younger brother's sophomoric pleasure in spouting pro-Southern clichés in pro-Union company. "We regarded him," he wrote to a friend, ". . . as a good-hearted, harmless, though a wild-brained boy, and used to laugh at his patriotic froth whenever secession was discussed. That he was insane on that one point no one who knew him well can doubt." [2]

the actor's thirst for fame

Booth's father, the gifted but eccentric English actor Junius Brutus Booth, had migrated to the New World in his twenties with his mistress, Mary Ann Holmes, to put an ocean between them and his legal wife in London. He bought a farm north of Baltimore in Harford County, Maryland, to house his family and took to his adopted country's sprawling theatrical circuit to support them. He was a hardy, hard-drinking professional and a master of his trade, specializing in Shakespearean roles. American audiences applauded his art and chuckled at his bibulous escapades. At work he was a colorful, somewhat notorious character; in his brief periods home from the road he was an earnest farmer and devoted family man, and his brood increased in carefree illegitimacy.

The elder Booth, for all his success on the stage and love of the gypsy life, didn't want his sons to become actors. But it was in the blood. Junius Brutus, Jr., the eldest son, followed in his father's steps both professionally and in his private life and made a name for himself as actor and manager on the West Coast. Edwin, also senior to John Wilkes, barnstormed the country with his father while still a youth—principally to try to keep the old rascal out of trouble—and graduated from bit parts to starring roles in his own right, by virtue of having the most brilliant and fully developed talent in the family.

While Johnny was going to school in Maryland and reciting Shakespeare for an adoring audience of mother and sisters, Edwin was serving his long, brutal apprenticeship in the mining camps of California, making up in harsh experience for his lack of formal education. He had inherited his father's taste for the bottle and the fleshpots, and in earlier years was criticized for not applying himself to the mastery of his profession. Overcoming these weaknesses gave his performances and reputation a burnished brilliance; he was a national favorite and clearly the greatest of the Booths even before his younger brother took to the boards.[3]

As far as native ability and inherited weaknesses went, Edwin and John Wilkes seem to have been comparable. The latter also had to contend with the temptations of drink and women, which were occupational hazards for handsome leading men in that lusty era of the American theater. But indulgences of this kind don't seem to have become a professional stumbling block for Johnny, except to the degree that the gay life was an alternative to the long, heartbreaking regimen of learning his business in the way Edwin had learned it.

In this we may find the clue to what made Edwin an all-time great of the American stage and John Wilkes a despised assassin. From his youth, the younger brother appraised the acting profession in terms of its rewards—those which Edwin had earned by years of effort and sacrifice and was reaping when John reached the age to follow in his steps. His was an inbred, lifelong ambition to be, not just an actor, but a star of first magnitude—a star brighter than Edwin.

His sister Asia knew of this devouring ambition. "I must have fame!" she quoted him, "fame!"[4] His first bit part in *Richard III* in Baltimore at seventeen, arranged by Asia's suitor John Clarke, was a humiliating flop. But far from discouraging Johnny, it crystallized his ambition. In October of '58 he acted a minor part in *Hamlet* in Richmond, with Edwin starring and completely overshadowing him. This unfavorable comparison, coupled with the knowledge that Edwin could earn $5,000 for a single month's engagement, made Edwin's mark the one to be bettered. The doting mother encouraged Johnny's obsession that *he* was the Booth chosen by destiny to be the greatest.

Sister Asia, looking back over the many years which included her favorite brother's shooting-star ascent and abrupt descent into infamy, remembered the words of a gypsy who, she said, read the palm of John Wilkes while he was still a boy in Maryland:[5]

"You've a bad hand, the lines all cris-cras! It's full of sorrow—full of trouble—trouble in plenty. You'll break hearts, they'll be nothing to you. You'll die young, and leave many to mourn you. You'll make a bad end, and have plenty to love you. You'll have a fast life—short, but a grand one. Young sir, I've never seen a worse hand, and I wish I hadn't seen it, but if I were a girl I'd follow you through the world for your handsome face."

Whether Asia's recollection of the prophecy was accurate, and whether John Wilkes remembered it or not,* his career seemed like a deliberate attempt to see it fulfilled. He felt that Nature had made him a free gift of dramatic skill even greater than Edwin's or his father's. He was basically a young man steeped in make-believe, with an exalted conception of his possibilities—and either too lazy or too much in a hurry to earn the prize the hard way.

After a couple of years of promising engagements in the East—with the great advantage of being billed as the son of Junius Brutus and the brother of Edwin—he found he wasn't satisfied with fame by relationship. Most critics granted his potential, though some of them noted an overly dramatic, overly physical quality to his acting as compared *always* with Edwin's style or his father's. Some, such as the British actor and physician Sir Charles Wyndham, felt he showed the lack of willingness to study and learn his art, and an inclination to use leaps, gestures, and other violent action as a substitute for solid artistry.[6] Also, and very

* In *The Unlocked Book* (New York: G. P. Putnam's Sons, 1938, p. 57), Asia stated her brother often referred to the prophecy in later years.

important, he found himself received much more warmly by sentimental, uncritical southern audiences than by those in the more cosmopolitan North.

In October of 1860 he made his first starring appearance with no mention of his family connections in the billing. This was in Montgomery, Alabama, in the role of the sinister "Pescara" in *The Apostate,* a spine-tingler which both his father and Edwin had played with great success. The performance was a sensation.[7] John Wilkes Booth had shown he could make the grade in his own right.

He headed north in February of the fateful year of 1861 and played "Pescara" with particular brilliance in Albany, the heart of Edwin's northern domain. His target, to outdo Edwin and be known as the greatest of the Booths, must have seemed within range. His father had died on a Mississippi steamboat in 1852 and was now only the memory of a great tragedian, unavailable for accurate comparison. Edwin's star was still climbing steadily; he seemed in no fear for his laurels, even helped his arrogant younger brother when he could. Somewhere along the line—there's no way of telling the exact point—it must have dawned upon John Wilkes that the applause he received in the North was response to a charming personality and an illustrious name, rather than acclaim for his talent. And the evolutions of civil war were building a wall of steel between him and his appreciative southern audiences.

Those who like to mark the beginning and end of things may see some significance in the fact that John Wilkes Booth's brief, spectacular career as a star in his own right was a four-and-a-half-year span between two performances as the evil "Pescara" in *The Apostate.* In his final appearance in character at Ford's Theater on March 18, 1865, he portrayed the same role which had launched him on a tragic course in October of 1860 in Montgomery, Alabama.

superficial political fervor

Many aspects of Booth's career have been and still are subjects of controversy. One of these was his dedication to the Southern cause. The prosecutors at the Conspiracy Trial went to great lengths to prove he had been a bitter political fanatic since the early days of the war and had been involved in subversion of one kind or another almost from the beginning.

In retrospect, in their search for an explanation for his murderous act, his family and friends recalled many conversations in which he argued violently in defense of the Confederacy. He even told Asia on one occasion that he was smuggling quinine across the lines. Yet prior to the assassination none of his close associates was excessively concerned about his political views or what he might do about them. Later they helped to verify the charges of fanaticism with these recollections; but the student of this subject gets the clear impression they didn't take him seriously beforehand, because they knew him too well—his love of notoriety and the center of the stage, even in conversations with his family and friends, and his inclination to dramatize and romanticize everything he did. Southern sentiments were not the least unusual among Marylanders, but in Booth they were voiced in a manner consistent with his flamboyant personality. Edwin, a staunch Union man, could express his views with quiet, reasoned logic. But John Wilkes delivered himself of high-sounding, eloquent phrases of southern wartime oratory which revealed very little deep thought on the issues of the conflict. His "To whom it may concern" letter [8] is a good example of self-conscious, self-glorifying, superficial sentiments.

The superficiality of Booth's political fervor is borne out by his attitude to armed participation in the war. In December, '59, he joined the Richmond Grays temporarily and, in a borrowed uniform, stood with the guard which under Robert E. Lee officiated at the hanging of John Brown in Charles Town, Virginia. Far from taking pleasure in the execution of the old abolitionist, as so many southerners did, the sensitive young man wrote his sister Asia; "Brown was a brave old man; his heart must have broken when he felt himself deserted." [9]

Such feelings were very much in character for a boy who had always been so tenderhearted he couldn't hunt game and, in the absence of his older brothers at their farm, couldn't butcher fowl or meat animals for the table.

Physically John Wilkes was a fine specimen and noted for introducing athletics into almost all his theatrical roles. He would have been well able to stand the rigors of campaigning if he had been prompted to take up arms for his beloved South. But he was never in uniform except for that one occasion; and when Edwin asked why he didn't enlist, since he felt so strongly, he said he had promised their mother not to go into the army.

Another circumstance which argues against Booth's sincerity as a Southern Partisan, as well as against the political motivation of either the abduction plan or the assassination, was the almost total lack of political statements in any of the conversations attributed to Booth and his fellow "conspirators" in any reliable record. Arnold, Atzerodt, Herold, and Surratt all quoted Booth in connection with the abduction plot—in which all willingly admitted they had been involved—yet none attributed convincing statements of political opinion to the actor. The actor Samuel Knapp Chester testified in detail on Booth's repeated efforts to get him to join in the kidnapping, and said he was promised money and fame, not urged to take part for political considerations. Atzerodt quoted as Booth's argument to him for assassination that "it would be the greatest thing in the world."

Likewise with Doster's contention that Booth had been a forceful and magnetic leader with an almost hypnotic control over the minds of his henchmen, particularly "Payne." A study of the comments about him by his accomplices reveals no trace of blind devotion to their leader or irresistible force of mind and purpose in his makeup. On the contrary, it appears to have been his extravagant promises of rewards that kept them interested at all, and Arnold said they all voted him down at the "middle of March" meeting, because his plan for kidnapping the President from a theater in the middle of a performance was so obviously absurd.[10] Anna Surratt remembered her brother had told her Booth was "crazy."[11]

It would have helped if Colonel Doster had explained why he decided *not* to make defense witnesses of Edwin Booth or of Ella Turner—the Washington prostitute who was Booth's mistress in that particular city. He interviewed both of them. Both knew the actor very well, but the attorney decided they wouldn't help and might hurt his plea that "Payne," being of very low intelligence, had come under the mental and spiritual domination of the cunning, persuasive actor.[12] He still made this claim in his summation for Paine, but offered nothing in the way of evidence to back it up.

Still another point bearing on the sincerity of Booth's devotion to his ravished Southland: On April 1, when his loose-knit band had scattered and his kidnap plan was clearly on the rubbish heap—and when Richmond's fall was expected in a matter of hours—the "fanatic" took a train for the North on a mission with clear non-political aspects. On April 3—the very day the Southern capital surrendered to the Union armies—he registered at a hotel in Newport, Rhode Island,* and signed his name "J. W. Booth and Lady."[13] The lady's name and identity are unknown and probably unimportant. But even the War Department wouldn't have claimed that "J. W. Booth and Lady" were there to discuss the surrender of *Richmond*.

Finally, the War Department's resort to perjured testimony to represent Booth as a rabid secessionist who had the backing of the Confederate government indicates it was unable to find bona fide evidence to that effect.

Being a very vain, superficial person, then, and too self-centered to

* In *The Day Lincoln Was Shot,* by Jim Bishop (p. 94), the hotel at which "J. W. Booth and Lady" registered on April 3 was given as the Aquidneck Hotel, New York City, Room 3, which was probably correct.

embrace any cause unless it would result in spectacular self-aggrandizement, Booth must have had some motivation other than Southern patriotism for both his abduction scheme and the assassination.

Booth's career and finances

The question of whether the actor's stage career had begun to falter before he became involved in his kidnapping scheme has been a subject of debate. An excellent source of information on the topic is found in the book *John Wilkes Booth,* by Francis Wilson, a member of the theatrical profession and a friend and admirer of the Booths. This writer was unusually objective in presenting all the available evidence, both pro and con, and did not consider himself an apologist for Booth. But in reaching the conclusion that the actor was a Southern Partisan of deep sincerity, who suddenly became insane when Richmond fell and murdered the President as an act of vengeance, Mr. Wilson's unquestioning belief in the legend caused him to ignore most of his own data, which argued strongly against the conclusion.

Also, in analyzing Booth's motives and his personal history, Wilson used the self-justifying scribbles in the "diary" found on his body as a guide—which obviously resulted in considerable distortion of his reasoning.

On the face of it, Booth's earnings as an actor had plummeted since the early years of the war, in one of which he claimed to have earned $20,000. Wilson called attention to a peculiarity of the American theater in that day—that popular performers tended to build their strongest followings in one particular section of the country, and to consider that section their "domain" until some competitor came along who could top their popularity and box-office pull. "There was a saying in the dramatic world," he wrote, "that Edwin Booth was supreme in the East and Junius Brutus, Jr., in the West, but that John Wilkes Booth ruled in the South." [14]

He points out that the drawing of the battle lines practically closed this exclusive and lucrative field to the young actor. He still played engagements in northern cities—but there reviewers inevitably compared his performances with those of his father and Edwin, more often than not unfavorably or with allowances for his comparative youth and inexperience. When playing in Edwin's domain, he could hardly expect anything else and could look for no change in the situation, with or without the war. From this standpoint alone, a source of deep frustration can be seen for a young man obsessed with the ambition to be "the Booth."

Aside from the possibility of a deep-seated emotional disturbance on this score, which the actor undoubtedly concealed with great skill, his earning power from acting was declining during the later war years. He performed in a number of northern cities but rarely had return engagements. During 1864 he became interested in the western Pennsylvania oil lands and a boom developing there which seemed to promise wealth for investors. He gambled and lost several thousand dollars in the venture, but was still claiming to be in the "oil business" through the early months of '65, using it as sort of a cover for his negotiations with prospective accomplices in the kidnapping scheme.

The introduction to the Peterson transcript of the Trial proceedings includes a profile of Booth which was apparently based upon pre-assassination newspaper reports and theatrical reviews. It has the virtue of having been written by a competent journalist rather than by one of the stage fraternity, whose judgment was conditioned by deference for the Booth family:[15]

> Booth . . . was well known to theatre-goers and the public generally as a very fine-looking young man, but as an actor of more promise than performance.
>
> He is best remembered, perhaps, in "Richard," which he played closely after his father's conception of that character, and by his admirers was considered superior to the elder Booth. He was quite popular in the Western and Southern cities, and his last extended engagement was in Chicago.
>
> Excellent actors say—and actors are not over-apt to praise each other—that he had inherited some of the most brilliant qualities of his father's genius. But, of late, an apparently incurable bronchial affection made almost every engagement of his a failure. The papers and critics apologized for his 'hoarseness,' but it was long known by his friends that he would be compelled to abandon the stage.
>
> In the winter of 1863 and '64 he played an engagement in the St. Charles Theatre, in New Orleans [the city then being occupied by the Union armies], under the disadvantage of his "hoarseness," and the engagement terminated sooner than expected on that account. He had many old friends in that city, but this was his first appearance there since the inception of the rebellion. . . .

Since his family biographers gave little emphasis to a throat difficulty which may have hampered Booth's career, it may not have been so major a factor as the reporter assumed—though the actor himself would have been greatly depressed by the fear of losing his stage voice, and it can be noted that his engagements during '64 were generally short ones. His last appearance in New York was for one night at the Winter Garden on November 25, 1864. It was a "benefit" for the "Shakespeare Statue Fund" in which all three Booth brothers performed in *Julius Caesar,* with Edwin as Brutus, Junius Brutus, Jr. as Cassius, and John Wilkes as Mark Antony. This was one of the last of his engagements. He had already taken up residence at the National Hotel in Washington and had, earlier in November, made a trip into lower Maryland, ostensibly to buy land and horses but really, it was charged, to try to make connections to carry Lincoln to Richmond by the route used by Confederate couriers.

Wilson stated that managers were still anxious to arrange bookings for Booth in the spring of 1865, but that the would-be kidnapper turned them down in order to concentrate upon his grand plan. However, he didn't name any managers whose offers were refused, so this must be considered only as his personal impression. And whether by his own wish or the lack of opportunity, Booth did very little professional acting in either 1864 or 1865.

The student of this period in the assassin's career wonders how he was able to afford his affluent way of life during the five or so months in which he was dabbling with abduction but not earning much, if anything, at his profession. He stayed at good hotels, owned horses, traveled around in style, dressed and drank expensively, and supported mistresses in at least two cities.

At the Trial (May 13) Booth's business agent in his oil speculations, Jos. H. Simonds, testified the actor had disposed of his $6,000 land holdings in Pennsylvania on September 27, 1864—deeding part to his brother Junius, without compensation, and part to Simonds in payment for his services.[16]

No reliable proof was discovered that he had financial backing for his kidnap plot from interested persons in either the South or the North. He may have had some savings—did have a few hundred in a Canadian bank, the War Department said—but the rarity of his engagements for at least two years previous and his penchant for free spending make this unlikely.*

Latterday historians of the assassination usually portray Booth as keeping his accomplices on call by giving them handouts for living expenses. This writer has found no evidence that he gave them anything but grandiose promises. Arnold, O'Laughlin, and Herold were shiftless young men dazzled by hopes of a quick killing, and living off their families in the meantime. Atzerodt had a trade as carriage-painter when he worked at it. John Surratt's income was apparently derived from his duties as courier and whatever deals he could pull off now and then. On one occasion he borrowed some money from Atzerodt, of all people.[17]

The notion that Booth paid the living expenses of the destitute "Payne" was Doster's, who got the idea from the prisoner Paine. Since the attorney didn't try to work the mysterious Mr. "Wood" who visited the Surratt house into his summation at all—even though that well-dressed, refined gentleman had been prominent in the testimony of the residents—it indicated that he *did not* believe "Payne" and "Wood" were the same

* Evidence to be presented later will show that Booth made large amounts of money throughout 1864 by smuggling quinine to the South.

person, even though the prosecution made a great show of proving they were. Thus the financial status of "Payne" in the legend is based upon Paine's "narrative," rather than on the evidence the prosecution had at hand that "Wood," or Powell, was quite comfortably fixed for cash. In New York, Powell stayed at the Revere House, a good hotel with its own restaurant. Judging from Atzerodt's "confession," he (Powell) maintained *two* places of residence in Washington during the two weeks before the assassination—one at the Herndon House and one down in the Navy Yard district. He was so well, if flashily, dressed that his costume became an identification feature mentioned by most of the persons who tried to describe him. He bought the one-eyed horse from Booth. If he was the stranger who came to Doster's office in the night just before the Trial ended, he was still notably affluent three months later. All of which suggests that if anyone was financing the remaining conspirators during the last few days before the assassination, it was probably Powell rather than Booth.

Without exception, all of Booth's accomplices were penniless when they were apprehended. Booth himself—though Herold told Bingham the actor had a little money during their flight—was not found to have any when he was caught.

This adds up to the probability that the so-called Booth "conspiracy" was a pathetically threadbare proposition, which came to nothing as much because the "conspirators" couldn't afford to be kidnappers as for any other reason.

the kidnapping "conspiracy"

The early periods of Booth's absorption with his project are much obscured by misinformation and misinterpretation of such information as there was.

The prosecution dated Booth's active efforts in the direction of abduction from his trip into lower Maryland in November, 1864. He did make such a trip, though no testimony at the Trial indicated that he did anything but circulate in the neighborhood of Bryantown, where Dr. Mudd lived, and let it be known he wanted to buy land and horses. He bought two horses from a neighbor of Dr. Mudd's named Gardiner,[18] the two which John Surratt wrote Atzerodt to try to sell from the stable where Fletcher worked, in early April of '65.

Late in November, 1864, Booth gave his "To whom it may concern" letter to Clarke in Philadelphia.* Though its references to abduction were veiled and would have had little significance if Clarke or anyone else had

* In *The Unlocked Book* (p. 126) Asia said John left the letters with her; that she burned one and gave two to Clarke after the assassination. He in turn gave them to the police.

read it before the assassination, it did sound like a statement of his kidnapping plan when read in the light of Booth's eventual crime.

But at this time he had not yet met John Surratt, Mrs. Surratt, or Atzerodt. In his statement to Bingham, Herold said he had met the actor months earlier (which this writer doubts) and had later had some conversations with him about "oil lands." Since Arnold didn't know Herold by name when he listed those present at the "middle of March" meeting at the restaurant, it seems Herold didn't join the "conspiracy" until about that time.

Booth didn't meet Powell until late February or early March, 1865. Thus, of the whole group later identified as his "accomplices," he knew only Arnold and O'Laughlin, boyhood friends, in late November of '64 when he gave the letter to Clarke. He was slightly acquainted with Mudd from his trip into Maryland and probably knew Spangler at the theater. But neither of these ever belonged to his "gang."

It would appear, then, that the young actor began writing the script for his make-believe abduction—and hinting to his friends that he was involved in something big—before he had lined up more than two accomplices, if any at all.

Early in January Booth went to Clarke's house in Philadelphia, opened the mysterious envelope, apparently signed the letter and enclosed some bonds, then sealed the envelope again and returned it to Clarke's keeping.[19]

The tradition is that Booth had some sort of operation worked out to kidnap the President sometime in January, 1865. The basis of this idea appears to be the fact that he signed his "To whom it may concern" letter early that month. He was in the Capitol from January 12 to 28,[20] but still had only Arnold, O'Laughlin, and Surratt on hand as accomplices. If there were any other unknown parties involved at that time, none of the three ever mentioned it. At any rate, nothing happened either then or later, if we believe Arnold's account given to the newspapers a number of years afterwards. Since he was entirely in the clear after his release by Johnson's order in 1869, and had always admitted he was a party to the abduction idea, he would have had no reason to hide the activities of the group if there had been any.

After the failure of anything to materialize in January, he said,[21] "we seldom saw each other," because rumors of kidnapping were circulating freely in Washington by that time. He also said Booth ignored several good chances to attempt an abduction (elsewhere than in a theater)—"and thus the only favorable opportunities were permitted to pass by without the slightest notice being taken."[22] It seems that Booth's obsession with the idea of doing the thing in a theater was the great obstacle, since the others thought it nothing but folly.

In the face of the War Department's steamroller strategy, the defense was able to do little more than strike back feebly at the hail of allegations. They seemed to realize there was a sound line of defense in the possibility that Booth's "conspiracy" was nothing but a conversation piece which came to a final end sometime in March. In fact Mr. Cox, attorney for Arnold and O'Laughlin, stated as much in his summation.[23] To make any real progress on this point, though, it would have been necessary to discredit much of Louis Weichmann's testimony, since he was the chief source of information about the activities of the "conspirators" in general and the "horse ride" yarn in particular. Several efforts were made to throw doubt on his reliability, and each time the prosecutors rushed to the defense of their star witness, usually with personal counterattacks upon the ethics of the defense lawyers. They were always supported by the court, and Weichmann's perjured version of the "conspiracy" became its accepted proof—and the basis for its history in later years.

If the case had been tried in a civil court and the prosecution had adopted the same line—that the assassination was a corollary to, and a result of the failure of, the kidnap plot—the defense might have been in an excellent position to prove the kidnap plan was a stone-dead issue by late March and had no connection with the assassination, except that its failure helped to put Booth in a frame of mind which made him susceptible to the influence of a stronger personality, through whom he became the tool of political interests that wanted Lincoln eliminated.

For one thing, the prosecutors would not have been able to protect Weichmann from exposure without the scandalous collaboration of the judges and freedom to corrupt procedures in any way which served their own ends. For another, the defense, with a clear objective of showing the superficial character of Booth's kidnap scheme, would have made much more of the considerable evidence to that effect—particularly the testimony of the New York actor whom Booth tried unsuccessfully to enlist, Samuel Knapp Chester.

This man's recital for the prosecution on May 12[24]—the first day of testimony—was virtually a chronological history of Booth's brainchild. In it we have an illustration of how the significance of testimony depends greatly upon the point of view of those who hear it. Those who heard Chester's account in the arsenal courtroom—spectators and participants alike—had already been indoctrinated by a propaganda campaign in which Booth was portrayed as the sinister, brilliant leader of a murderous "conspiracy." So the words of the witness seemed to confirm that belief.

When the same testimony is read from the point of view that John Wilkes Booth was a frustrated actor with nothing but a daydream in which he pictured himself as the star and leader of a desperate band of supporting players, Chester's words carry a much different meaning. We shall review the more pertinent of his statements.

Under examination by Judge Holt, the witness said he had known Booth quite well for six or seven years. One day in the early part of November, 1864, they met on the street in New York, "and I asked him why he was not acting, and he told me that he did not intend to act in this portion of the country again; that he had taken his wardrobe to Canada, and intended to run the blockade."

On the twenty-fourth or twenty-fifth of the same month, when Booth was in the city for his appearance in *Julius Caesar* (in which Chester was also appearing) he asked the witness if he knew of a costumer from whom he could get "dresses" for his part. Asked again where his *own* wardrobe was, "he said it was still in Canada in charge of a friend, and I think he said, named Martin . . . I think he said it was in Montreal. . . ."

The witness said Booth told him he had a "big speculation on hand . . . one they [his friends] would not laugh at." It was not "the oil business," which was never mentioned to him, but Booth would not be specific as to its nature. "Some time after that I met him again and he again talked of this speculation, and asked me how I would like to go in with him; I told him that I was without means, that I could not; and he said it did not matter, he always liked me and would furnish the means."

Booth returned to Washington, and from there wrote Chester several letters "telling me he was speculating in farms in lower Maryland and was sure to coin money; that I must go with him to Virginia, and still telling me that I must join him. . . . I paid very little attention to it. . . ."

"Late in December or early in January, he came to New York. . . ." The two spent an evening together, eating and drinking at different saloons and restaurants; Booth frequently mentioned his "speculation" but declined to say what it was until Chester said he had to go home. Then he took his friend to an unfrequented section of Fourth Street. "He stopped and told me then that he was in a large conspiracy to capture the heads of the Government, including the President, and take them to Richmond; I asked him if that was what he wished me to go in; he said it was; I told him I could not do it; that it was an impossibility; only to think of my family; he said that he had two or three thousand dollars that he could leave them. . . ." After half an hour of coaxing and threatening on Booth's part, Chester still refused and finally agreed only not to betray the plot.

"He said that he could implicate me in the affair, any how; he said that the party were sworn together, and that if I attempted to betray them I would be hunted down through life. . . ."

Holt asked the witness what part Booth wanted him to play in the conspiracy, to which he answered, "That I was to open the back door of the Theatre at a signal." Holt continued to question along this line (see following pages).

(Body text continued on page 258)

SAMUEL KNAPP CHESTER

Testimony for Prosecution, May 12, 1865

PETERSON *Page 46*

Q. Did he indicate at what theatre this was to occur?

A. Yes, he told me Ford's Theatre; because it must be someone acquainted or connected with the Theatre who could take part in it.*

Q. Did he urge you upon the ground that it was an easy affair, and that you would have very little to do?

A. Yes, he said that; that was all I would have to do, he said. He said the thing was sure to succeed.

Q. What preparations did he say, if any, had been made toward the conspiracy?

A. He told me that everything was in readiness; that it was sure to succeed, for there were parties on the other side ready to cooperate with them.

Q. Did you understand from him that the Rebel Government was sanctioning what he was doing?

A. He never told me that.

Q. What do you mean by parties on the other side?

A. I imagined that they were on the other side, but he did not say who they were; I mean they were those people; he said on the other side.

Q. Did he mention the probable number of persons engaged in the conspiracy?

A. He said there were from fifty to a hundred; he said that when he first mentioned the affair to me.

Booth continued to write to Chester, urging him to join the plot. In one letter he enclosed fifty dollars. Holt's interrogation continued:

Q. Did he at the time he sent you the first $50 mention any more?

A. In the letter he did not.

Q. Did he speak of having plenty of funds for the purpose?

A. Not in his letter.

Q. Did he in his conversation?

A. In his conversation after he came to New York again.

Q. What did he say then?

A. When he came to New York he called on me again and asked me to take a walk with him, and I did so; he told me that he had been trying to get another party to join him named John Matthews, and when he told him what he wanted to do that the man was very much frightened, indeed, and would not join him, and he said he would not have cared if he had sacrificed him; I told him I did not think it was right to speak in that manner; he said no, he was a coward, and was not fit to live; he then asked me again to join him; he told me I must do so; he said that there was plenty of money in the affair; that if I would do it I would never want again as long as I lived; that I would never want for money; he said that the President and some of the heads of the Government came to the theatre very frequently during Mr.

* *In spite of Chester's refusal to take any part in the "conspiracy," Booth made an effort to have him engaged by Ford's, assuming that a good offer might entice his friend to come to the Capitol. In December, 1864, stated theatrical agent Matthew W. Canning, Booth urged him to speak to John Ford about hiring Chester, and the theatre owner agreed to do so. But the actor wisely declined the offer and stayed at the Winter Garden in New York (Archives document, quoted by Eisenschiml in WWLM? pp. 451-2).*

Forrest's engagements; I still urged him not to mention the affair to me; to think of my poor family; he said he would provide for my going with him; I still refused; he said he would ruin me in the profession if I did not go; I told him I could not help that, and begged of him not to mention the affair to me; when he found I would not go, he said he honored my mother and respected my wife, and he was sorry he had mentioned this affair to me, and told me to make my mind easy, he would trouble me about it no more; I then returned him the money he sent me; he said he would not allow me to do so, but that he was very short of funds—so very short that either himself or some of the party must go to Richmond to obtain means to carry out their designs.

Q. He said, however, that there was plenty of money in the enterprise?

A. Yes sir.

Q. When did this last conversation occur?

A. That, I think, was in February.

Q. Did he have any conversation with you at a later period, after the inauguration, as to the opportunity which he had for the assassination of the President? Did he speak of that?

A. Yes sir, on Friday, one week previous to the assassination, he was in New York.

Q. What did he say then?

A. We were in the House of Lords at the time, sitting at a table, and had not been there long before he exclaimed, striking the table, *"What an excellent chance I had to kill the President, if I had wished, on Inauguration Day";* that was all he said relative to that.

Q. Did he explain what the chance was?

A. No; he said he was as near the President on that day as he was to me; that is all he said.

Q. Can you tell at what time in February he said it would be necessary to send to Richmond for money?

A. No sir; I cannot tell positively.

Cross-examined by Mr. Clampitt

Q. Did he mention any names of those who were connected with him in this plan as communicated to you in reference to the assassination of Mr. Lincoln?

A. No, sir, not that I am aware of.

Q. You never heard him mention any names?

A. I never did.

Cross-examined by Mr. Ewing

Q. Do I understand you to say that he spoke to you of a plan to assassinate the President and to capture him?

A. To capture him.

Q. Did he say anything to you as to how he would get him off?

A. No.

Q. As to where he would take him?

A. To Richmond.

Q. By what route?

A. He did not say.

Q. He spoke of there being persons on "the other side?"

A. Yes, sir.

Q. Did he use just simply that expression, or did he explain what he meant by "the other side?" What did you understand him to mean?

A. He did not explain it at all, but I supposed it was in the South.

Q. Across the lines?

A. Yes, sir.
Q. Across the river?
A. Across the Potomac.
Q. Did he say nothing to you as to the means he had provided or proposed to provide for conducting the President after he should be seized?
A. No, sir; on one occasion he told me that he was selling off horses after he had told me that he had given up this project.
Q. When did he say to you that he had abandoned the idea of capturing the President?
A. In February, I think.
Q. Did he say why he had abandoned it?
A. He said the affair had fallen through owing to some of the parties backing out.
Q. On what day was it that he said to you what an excellent chance he had for killing the President?
A. That was on a Friday, one week previous to the assassination.
Q. On what day of April was that?
A. The 7th.
Q. Did he say anything to you as to his then entertaining, or having before that entertained, the purpose to assassinate the President?
A. No, sir.
Q. Did he say anything to you then as to why he did not assassinate the President?
A. No, sir; that was the only exclamation he made use of relative to it.
[Two questions asked earlier were repeated here and answered the same].
Q. Did he ever indicate how he expected to get him [the President] from the box to the stage without being caught?
A. No, sir.
Q. Did he say how many were to help him in seizing the President?
A. No sir.
Q. Did he name any other officials who were to be seized besides the President?
A. No; the only time he told me, he said *"the heads of Government, including the President."*

BY THE JUDGE ADVOCATE [HOLT]

Q. I understood you to say that he stated that the particular enterprise of capturing the President and heads of the Government had been given up, and that in consequence he was selling off the horses he had bought for the purpose?
A. Yes sir.
Q. He did not state to you what mode of proceeding had been substituted for that, but simply that that one had been given up?
A. He told me he had given up the affair.
Q. That it had fallen through?
A. Yes sir.

In this particular Trial it is always necessary to learn something about a witness and his connection with the parties and issues involved before we decide how much credence to give to his testimony. Those who were testifying under duress or with hopes for a share in the rewards, or for the love of public attention, were numerous. And much of the confusion in historical treatments has been due to uncritical acceptance of the statements of perjurers. Before we draw any conclusions from the testimony of Samuel Knapp Chester, we shall examine his credentials:

When the news of the assassination reached New York, this young actor seems to have realized that his association with Booth was bound to come to light and that he might even be under suspicion as an accomplice. He therefore reported to the authorities and was taken to Washington.* He was interrogated by Colonel Foster and made such a good impression that Foster recommended him to Burnett as a desirable witness for the prosecution, pointing out that he was particularly intelligent, articulate, and forthright.[25] Though Chester apparently thought his information showed Booth's plot as something entirely in the realm of conversation, the War Department saw it as supporting its allegation that the assassin had been conspiring against the government for months, if not years.

Chester testified voluntarily to clear his own name. But unlike the numerous actors who reaped a harvest of publicity from real or fictitious contacts with the assassin or his crime in later years (see Appendix E, "Actors Who Claimed a Connection with Booth"), this one told his story under oath at considerable risk. Public feeling had been whipped up to such a frenzy that men were being arrested merely because they wore a moustache like Booth's, had performed in the same theaters he had, or had some family relationship to him. Erstwhile friends were finding it discreet to deny they knew him. By giving himself up and making a favorable first impression, Chester may have earned a seat on the witness stand rather than one in the dock—but it was the kind of publicity he would have been happy to forego.

On the stand his performance was highly convincing. He was brief, factual, and somewhat independent, refusing to be drawn into conjecture beyond the literal statements Booth had made to him. He was equally sure what he did *not* know and what he *did* know. He exhibited the trained memory of an actor. The chronology of his account was almost perfect—dates and events conforming to those established later by other means—yet known to *him* only by accurate recollection of his meetings and conversations with Booth.

From this writer's point of view, posterity is greatly indebted to this forthright young man who looked for safety in the truth, and had a very good memory for it.

The War Department's evaluation of Chester's testimony is seen by the

---

* In *The Unlocked Book* (p. 127) Asia Booth Clarke related that one of the two envelopes Booth had left with her and which she gave to her husband after the assassination was addressed to "S. K. Chester." This letter may or may not have led to Chester's arrest. Archives documents referring to him gave the writer the impression he had surrendered voluntarily. In any case, Booth's letter must not have implicated his friend in any way, since the War Department did not consider Chester a suspect.

label given it in the index of the Pitman compilation—"Booth's confessions to Chester."[26] Obviously the statements to Chester were anything but *confessions*. They were, as we have seen, his efforts to "sell" Chester on joining the abduction scheme by an outrageously exaggerated description of a plot which was far more imagination than substance. When the testimony is studied in this light rather than literally, it confirms our belief that the kidnap scheme was little more than a daydream.

Points confirmed by testimony of Samuel Chester were:

Booth had virtually terminated his stage career by November, 1864.

He had taken his wardrobe to Canada and left it with "a friend."

In that month he was talking about a "big speculation," though all Chester was told was that his (Booth's) friends "would not laugh" at it.

This could be taken as showing that his failures, first as an actor and then in the oil business where he had hoped to get rich, were rankling in the actor's mind, prompting him to search for some dazzling achievement which would impress his friends and the theater-going public by whom he thought he had been belittled. Until very late in November he had no concrete idea for a grand gesture.

His trip into Maryland early in November may have been, as he said, to speculate in farmlands, rather than to prepare for the abduction.

The idea for the kidnapping had occurred to him by late December, but he was not yet sure whom he wanted to kidnap.

He told Chester he was in a "large conspiracy to capture *the heads of the Government, including the President,* and take them to Richmond."

Booth's plan for making the capture in a theater was like the script for a blood-and-thunder melodrama, in which practical considerations were incidental and the dramatics all-important.

The thing was to work out the way the dramatist wanted it to, just like a stage play. For instance, he wanted Chester in the cast at Ford's, so he could "open the back door of the Theatre at a signal," yet he had no idea how the President and an unspecified number of "heads of the Government" were to be overpowered and dragged through the door without embarrassing interference from the audience of hundreds.

This knotty question was raised at the Trial during the testimony of Ethan Horner, the officer who arrested and interrogated Sam Arnold.[27] During cross-examination of Horner by Mr. Ewing on May 18, he was asked:

> Q. Did he [Arnold] say anything as to what had been the purpose of parties [to the abduction] after the time he withdrew?
> A. He said the purpose of the party when he was a member of it, was to abduct *the heads of the Government* [author's italics], so as to force the North to have an exchange of prisoners, or something to that effect; I asked him, also, what his part was to be in the conspiracy, and I think he said that he was to catch the President when he was thrown from the box of the theatre.

The court reporter had time to add this comment of his own: "With the exception of O'Laughlin and Mrs. Surratt, all the prisoners joined in the laugh which the idea of Arnold catching Mr. Lincoln in his arms naturally induced."

Since Arnold was referring to the plans discussed at the "middle of March" meeting, which broke up in an argument when he and others refused to go along with Booth's nonsense about staging the abduction in a theater, it seems that at that late date the actor was still babbling about hauling off several officials in addition to the President. Also, after posturing and boasting for at least three and a half months, he still hadn't faced the realities of his project. Even the less intelligent members of the group realized it, and Powell must have had a hard time to keep from laughing.

Booth's conversations with Chester were innocent of any references to politics or his devotion to the Southern cause.

The only inducement he offered when urging his fellow actor to join him was repetition of vague promises of future wealth from an unspecified source.

In late December or early January, when he revealed his plan to Chester, he claimed that "there were parties on the other side ready to co-operate."

Yet at this time it is extremely doubtful that he had even *discussed* the plan with more than three potential accomplices—Arnold, O'Laughlin, and Surratt.

He did not claim he had the backing of the Confederate Government.

Although he was still bragging of having access to unlimited funds, he was broke in February and was glad to have Chester return the fifty dollars he had sent him.

He hastened to add darkly that he or some of his party would have to go to Richmond for "means to carry out their design." His gesture of sending Chester fifty dollars as an inducement to abandon his career, job, and family showed a state of mind far removed from reality.

The "middle of March" plans, which Weichmann expanded into the "horse ride" episode, "had fallen through [never been attempted], owing to some of the parties backing out."

Chester related this incident to Booth's statement that he had given up the kidnapping idea after that and "was selling off the horses he had bought for the purpose." By the association of these statements, we know Booth was referring to the collapse of the plot in March, after which Atzerodt was instructed to sell the two horses Booth had bought the preceding November.*

On Friday, April 7, in New York, when the two men were talking about something not connected with the kidnap plot which had been abandoned in March, Booth blurted out his surprising statement about a lost opportunity to kill Abraham Lincoln.

This was the first reference to assassination on his part of which there is

* At the Trial (May 22, Peterson, p. 82) a stableman named William Cleaver said Booth sold his one-eyed horse to Sam Arnold on February 8; but it was back in Booth's possession in March, being kept at Howard's stable, with Surratt as reputed owner but Booth paying the livery costs. Thus it appears, if Cleaver was correct about the sale to Arnold, that it was only a temporary deal with his friend and not the "selling off" in April, in which Atzerodt disposed of the other horse to a stage contractor and tried unsuccessfully to sell the one-eyed animal. Also, a D. C. boardinghouse keeper named Mary Van Tine testified (Peterson, p. 32) that Arnold and O'Laughlin took a room together at her place around February 10 and lived there during the week days until March 20, going home to Baltimore on week ends. This circumstance indicates that the sale of the horse to Arnold was not connected with the *termination* of the kidnap plot but was merely a temporary deal by Booth to raise a few dollars. O'Laughlin at that time was acting as Washington agent for his brother's feed company in Baltimore.

any authentic record. It suggests that the idea had just recently been planted in his mind in New York. The contrast between his activities for months past—much talk about abduction but no action—and his purposeful, organized preparations for the assassination which began when he returned to Washington on April 8 tends to confirm our earlier assumption: That someone in New York (whom we believe was John Surratt) introduced him to the idea of murder and sent him back to the Capitol, where Powell was waiting to take him in hand.

the assassination

Chester's account of his conversations with Booth over a period of some five months—the whole course of Booth's preoccupation with kidnapping—gives us material for understanding the man's transition from a harmless though deeply frustrated actor to a well-organized, efficient assassin.

There may be technical terms to define Booth's mental state during the period from November '64 to April 7, when he dabbled with abduction, and from April 8 to April 14, when he prepared for and then committed a senseless murder. A study of all his associations and reported conversations prior to the act makes it plain that *no one* who had any dealings with him *thought* he was insane, disturbed, or anything but normal (if immature) in his conversations and actions.* Later recollections by his friends and family brought out evidences of mental unbalance in the light of what he had done. But if he had *not* murdered Lincoln, the question of his sanity might never have been raised.

Booth had grown up in an atmosphere of make-believe. His natural taste for applause had been whetted constantly since early youth by the successes of his father and brothers—and the assurances of a doting mother that he could have as much and more. When he launched on his acting career, his relationship to three famous Booths brought much quicker and more favorable reaction to his genuine but undeveloped talents than he could have enjoyed if his name had not been Booth. It was not surprising that he was deceived into believing he was on a shortcut to fame and fortune. A different type of young man might have appreciated the advantage he enjoyed yet realized it would be a temporary one; that within a given period his appeal to audiences due to relationship would wear off; that then he would have to compete on a more equal basis with other actors—standing or falling according to the quality of his performance.

But that was not John Wilkes Booth's type. He was a lazy young man and loved the good life. Rather than setting himself to the task of

* We assume John Surratt was not speaking literally when he told Anna Booth was "crazy."

learning his business, he rode the gravy train in the lighthearted delusion that fame and fortune were his birthright, while others must spend years earning theirs. Before he realized what was happening, he found himself nearly at the end of the line.

Contemporary comment upon his acting style makes it clear how he reacted to the dilemma. He resorted to gimmicks—exaggeration of emotions, violent and often incongruous physical activity, volume rather than quality of voice. And more dangerous than these, subjectivity in his roles—identifying himself with the characters, trying to make his performances more authentic by *living* the parts rather than *portraying* them. Wilson mentioned the common conjecture that the murderous characters Booth had played conditioned him for the role of assassin, but pointed out that he appeared as often in frothy, romantic parts as he did in those like the tyrannical Richard III,[28] the evil Pescara, and the like.

The point was that *all* the characters in his repertoire became intermingled with his own personality. In conversation, in letter-writing, in any of the ordinary communications of living, he was never offstage and just himself. A study of his language in any dialogue, such as those with Chester, shows he was always theatrical, always spoke as if he were reading a script. In this manner the necessary boundary between art and reality was gradually erased, and he was unable to distinguish between the two. This was demonstrated in the extraordinary impracticality of his kidnap scheme and his absorption in dramatic effects, with no conception of the mechanical problems involved.

As long as the scheme could be kept in a state of suspended animation, he lived the soul-satisfying part of leader in a magnificent conspiracy, and no harm was done. But the daydream had a time limit. According to Arnold, the others would suggest alternatives to kidnapping the President from a theater, such as waylaying his carriage as he returned from one of his frequent visits to the Soldiers' Home or the hospitals. But Booth always turned these down, usually with the excuse of "the pressure of business," and sulked when they wouldn't play along with his fantasy of doing the thing in a theatrical setting. Arnold thought he had become "a monomaniac on the subject."[29]

Anyone who saw something of himself in James Thurber's delightful character "Mr. Mitty" may also see a little of himself in John Wilkes Booth. Because until the middle of March, 1865, Booth was a reasonably contented "Mitty," living a splendid fantasy that pushed his failures and thwarted ambitions far into the background. In time he might have wakened, realized the long hard effort it would take to become the great actor he conceived himself to be, and settled down to earn his laurels.

Unfortunately he wouldn't let go of his dream, and there were those who realized how susceptible a man in his mental state would be to direction into a more sinister role and what a perfect tool he would be for the elimination of Abraham Lincoln. He had already rehearsed the scene himself a thousand times—the casual entrance by the front door of Ford's, the joke with an attendant, the quick ascent to the balcony, then down the hallway to Box 7 unnoticed. Rewrite the script a little, put a loaded pistol in his hand, and presto! his hopeless daydream would become a successful tragedy. By writing an escape sequence into his role, his flight from the city would be assured, and steps could be taken to make certain he wasn't captured alive and talking.

John Nicolay, secretary to the President and one of his many biographers, put into words the idea that has occurred vaguely to quite a number of historians of the assassination:[30] *"The murderer seemed to himself to be taking part in a play.* Hate and brandy had for weeks kept his brain in a morbid state."

Of course the "play" was the one in which he had been starring, in his own imagination, for several months. His obsession to perform it on a stage before an audience was well known to his confidants in the "conspiracy." The mystery is why the rewriting of the ending, to climax in murder rather than a gay, romantic kidnapping, didn't shock him back to his senses.

The change in the script must have been made with great subtlety. It may be that the key to this mystery is in Nicolay's second sentence above. Not "hate"—since there is no convincing evidence that Booth hated Lincoln or, for the most part, thought of him otherwise than as a suitable candidate for abduction (and, during that last week, for assassination), due to his high office. The word is "brandy."

John Wilkes Booth was known to have inherited the taste for strong drink which was common to all the male members of his family. He was normally a discreet drinker, too aware of his public image to risk being drunk in public, but could "absorb an astonishing quantity, and still retain the bearing of a gentleman." A longtime friend of his named John Deery was a national billiard champion and operated a saloon and billiard parlor over Grover's Theater on E Street at Pennsylvania Avenue. His article in the New York *Sunday Telegraph* (May 23, 1909)[31] recalled the character of Booth's imbibing during the week before his crime:

> For a period of about ten days before the assassination, he visited my place every day, sometimes in the afternoon, sometimes in the evenings. At this time he was out of an engagement and drinking quite freely, noticeably so, even for him, I thought. At times he seemed a bit crazed, apparently on account of the frequency of his potations. But there was a deeper cause, as I was to know later. . . .
>
> That Booth was unquestionably laboring under some undue excitement was apparent to me a week before the fatal shot was fired. As I now clearly recall, he seemed to be crazed by some stress of inward feeling, but only one who was very intimate with him could have told it. As I afterwards remarked to friends when speaking of that experience, "Booth was crazy, but he didn't

show it." Still I had no real conception of the tumult that was working in his breast for, excepting in purely social matters, John Wilkes Booth always kept his own counsel. He never used to gossip about his professional work, nor boast of his stage career as is the general custom of actors. The particular thing that attracted my attention, and what seemed out of the ordinary, was the amazing quantity of liquor he drank in my billiard parlors. . . . He would sometimes call for a second glass of brandy and toss it off when he had barely drained the first one. This was far from his usual way, for, while a steady drinker, I had always found Booth to respect the amenities and "drink square," as we used to say in those days.

During that last week at Washington he sometimes drank at my bar as much as a quart of brandy in the space of less than two hours of an evening. . . . It was more than a spree, I could see that, and yet Booth was not given to sprees. He was a steady dram-drinker, and sometimes overstepped the bounds and got intoxicated, but he was a sober man the next day.

I believe Booth was as much crazed by the liquor he drank that week as by any motive when he shot Lincoln. . . .

Deery, of course, was going along with the popular belief that Booth's act was due to a sudden, inexplicable seizure of insanity. But his description of the actor's heavy and continuous drinking during that week argues more strongly that the inner conflict the saloonkeeper suspected was the tug-of-war between his passionate desire to perform what he had been led to believe would be his greatest role (one which would be applauded by the South and the legions of Lincoln's bitter critics in the North) and the revulsion against killing that stemmed from a normally gentle nature. No effects of this heavy drinking were noticed by any of the numerous persons who testified to having seen Booth or had dealings with him during those several days. His external demeanor was apparently not altered in the least; but the events of the evening of Good Friday suggest that the effects of liquor upon his mind and conscience were formidable and fatal.

From testimony of witnesses at the Trial, the later recollections of persons acquainted with Booth, such as Deery, and the "confession" of George Atzerodt, a fair picture of the assassin's activities in the days before the murder can be drawn. He made at least two visits to the Surratt house, though John was not there; so he must have had business to transact with the widow—and his only business that week concerned the plot. On Thursday he visited Grover's Theater and inquired of the manager, Mr. C. Dwight Hess,[32] whether Lincoln was invited to attend the performance of *Aladdin* the next evening. On learning that an invitation was to be sent to Mr. and Mrs. Lincoln, Booth went upstairs to Deery's place and asked him to reserve the right-hand front box for him—the one next to the President's—for Friday evening. As his reason for not having made the reservation while he was with Hess, he said the manager might give him the ticket free, and he didn't want to be under an obligation to him.

This, in combination with Atzerodt's hint that Booth and Herold were at Ford's on Wednesday evening, suggests that *both* theaters were being considered as possible scenes for his performance, since it would not be known until Friday which theater the President might attend. Also on Thursday Atzerodt was told to register at Vice-President Johnson's hotel, the Kirkwood, and try to get his signature on a pass to Richmond. If he had been able to do so—though it doesn't appear that he made any effort to carry out this instruction—Johnson might have been labeled indelibly as an accomplice in the assassination (it is this writer's belief that that was the intention of the real conspirators), for the pass bearing his signature was probably intended to be found on John Wilkes Booth's *dead body.*

Friday morning Booth loitered in the lobby of Ford's, where he always picked up his mail, and learned that the President had accepted Mr. Ford's invitation to occupy the presidential box, Number 7 on the right, that evening. He also hired the little bay mare from a stableman named James Pumphrey around noon,[33] telling the man (witness, May 15) he wanted to take the horse out at about four that afternoon. He also said he was on his way to Grover's Theater to write a letter.* He did return between four and five o'clock, and rode off.

In the late afternoon, either before or after this, he was said to have left a card at the Kirkwood addressed to Vice-President Johnson. It read, "Don't want to disturb you. Are you in? J. W. Booth"

It has only been *assumed* that it was Booth who left the card in the mailbox of Johnson's private secretary, *William A. Browning*[34] (witness, May 16). No one saw Booth put the card in the box right next to the Vice-President's. Herold was also at the Kirkwood looking for Atzerodt that afternoon. This card has puzzled historians, because there seemed to be no reason for it. In the conception of the conspiracy we are developing, it can be equated with Atzerodt's instructions to get a pass signed by Johnson. Like the pass, which was not obtained, the card from Booth would imply that Johnson had knowledge of the intended crime and was a party to it. And this was precisely the conclusion reached by Johnson's political enemies.

Through these days of the last week, Booth made an unknown number

---

* The letter referred to was evidently the one to the *Intelligencer* which actor Matthews claimed was given him by Booth. By "Grover's Theater," Booth meant John Deery's saloon on the second floor. Deery was in Booth's confidence to such a degree that Booth asked him to buy a ticket for the box next to the President's at Grover's for the night of the assassination, and Deery did so. We have only the saloonkeeper's explanation that the actor's reason for not buying the ticket himself was to avoid being obligated if the manager of Grover's gave him a free pass. The letter having been written in Deery's place, it is much more likely Booth entrusted it to him than to Matthews—and its disappearance, plus the matter of the ticket, in this writer's opinion, places John Deery under very serious suspicion.

of visits to Powell's lodgings at the Herndon House, just around the block from Ford's, in the daytime as well as in the evenings. Powell, it would seem, remained in his room much of the time. He was out at least once when he, Herold, and Atzerodt were to have met Booth at a restaurant but didn't make connections. No witness at the Trial, of course, mentioned having seen Powell *anywhere,* and no one answering his description was seen with Booth—though he was probably the man "Peanuts" Burroughs saw putting Booth's horse in the stable behind the theater—and *was* the man on the one-eyed horse who the stableman Pope said rode off with Herold late in the afternoon.

In other words, Powell was careful to keep himself out of sight. He was also careful to let Booth believe *himself* to be the organizer of the whole thing. But the decisiveness and thoroughness that were evident, the quick adjustment to changes in the situation, and above all the attention to all the practical details of the preparation, were definitely *not* consistent with Booth's type as a conspirator (as demonstrated so well during his several months of bumbling with the abduction idea). The efforts to implicate Johnson simply would not have occurred to Booth, if only because he had nothing against Johnson—but more logically because if the implication were successful, it would only detract from Booth's conception of himself as the arch-conspirator and star.

So these embellishments were Powell's, and they serve as clues to at least the general identity of his employers. They also suggest that there was no serious intention to kill Johnson—since he could hardly have filled the roles of both accomplice and victim at the same time.

The possibility that Booth (whose political views were invariably expressed in broad generalities which showed he knew almost nothing about politics) could have conceived the idea of assassinating Seward is too remote to consider. The Secretary of State was, with the exception of Stanton, the most influential member of Lincoln's cabinet. He was an ambitious man, who had been disappointed in his hopes of being nominated to run against Lincoln in the election of 1860. As a politician, his great asset was his adaptability to the existing situation. After the failure of his subtle campaign to make himself a sort of European prime minister in Lincoln's government—with the President a figurehead—he followed the policy of supporting Mr. Lincoln strongly and thereby gained greatly in political stature during the course of the war. In April, 1865, his position on reconstruction policies supported the President's generous attitude toward the conquered South, aimed toward a rapid return of former Confederate states to full participation in the political life of the nation, and gradual integration of the freed slaves into the fabric of American society.

Thus Seward's position was as distasteful to the Radical Republicans as was Lincoln's. That segment of the Republican party favored Stanton's vengeful attitude toward the South, as seen in his plan to make the seceded states an occupied area in perpetuity, under military governors and under a form of martial law—which would of course be administered by Stanton's War Department. Also, the Radicals saw a frightening political possibility in Lincoln's (and Seward's) tolerant attitude toward the defeated Confederacy: That the seceded states would become a solid Democratic block which, combined with the strong Democratic elements in the northern and border states, would quickly overwhelm the Republican party and rob it of the dominant position it enjoyed at the war's close.

Dr. Eisenschiml's estimate of the situation which was the background for the assassination was along these lines.[35] But he was too cautious a historian to draw the conclusion that there were politicians fanatical enough in their opposition to Lincoln to resort to sponsoring his murder. Our investigation, however, has ruled out Booth personally as the instigator of the crime—or so we believe—and presented a considerable body of evidence and reasoning to the effect that he was merely the tool of concealed interests who were represented in Washington by Lewis Powell, and in New York by other parties. The only other possible instigating agencies were the Confederate government and Vice-President Johnson personally. This first conception—which was the one offered by the War Department during the Conspiracy Trial—was exploded completely within only a year or so after the Trial. The second—the charges against Johnson—was a part of the Radicals' efforts to discredit him, especially after he broke with them on the question of reconstruction and reverted to the general policies of Lincoln, the result of which was the unsuccessful impeachment headed by the Radicals—and possibly in connection with the assassination itself, since he inherited the presidency by it.

Thus by process of elimination, whether we like to believe American politicians once condoned murder or not, we find ourselves with no other reasonable explanation for the attack upon Seward than that it was encouraged and approved by some of the Radicals—paid for too, since Lewis Powell had no other motive but gain. And behind Powell there was a prime mover with even more complex motives.

The identity of the individuals who supported the real conspiracies against Lincoln and Seward may sometime be revealed by research. Our present investigation was not intended to cover that aspect, and mere suspicions are not enough basis for naming any persons beyond those we feel are indicted by our findings. For those interested in the political background of the assassination, we recommend Chapter XXVI of *Why Was Lincoln Murdered?*, by Otto Eisenschiml. The title of this scholarly chapter in an excellent book is "The Case Against the Radicals." From it we take the liberty of quoting one pertinent paragraph:

> Julian, one of these Radical leaders, boldly stated that the accession of Andrew Johnson to the presidency would prove a blessing to the country. In this sentiment he was not alone. On April 15, only a few hours after Lincoln's death, a caucus of Republican leaders was held, at which the tragedy was described as a gift from Heaven, and it was decided to get rid of Lincolnism. *Ben Butler was chosen to be Secretary of State.* Unfortunately for that plan, Seward's injuries were not fatal, and his position did not become vacant. Blunt Senator Wade told the new President: "Johnson, we have faith in *you.* By the gods, there will be no trouble now in running the government!" Johnson had been ranting for weeks past that secession was treason, that treason must be made odious, and that all Confederates should be hanged.

On March 26, 1867, during a debate in the House of Representatives on the recently revealed text of Booth's suppressed "diary," an interesting footnote was added to the conception we have been considering—that Booth was *not* the instigator of the assassination, but merely a foil who was organized and supervised by an agent of parties in New York—an agent named Lewis Powell.

This "footnote" occurred in a tirade by Benjamin Butler directed at Judge Bingham, in which it was charged that the suppression of the "diary" concealed a plot inside the government (directed, Butler was implying, by Johnson.)* Specifically, Butler was belaboring Booth's notation that he had "almost a mind to return to Washington, and in a measure clear my name, which I feel I can do." Ben Butler orated as follows:[36]

> I believe that piece of evidence would have shown what the whole case, in my judgement, now shows: that up to a certain hour Booth contemplated to capture and abduction, and that he afterward changed his purpose to assassination *on consultation with the conspirators about him.* . . .
>
> How clear himself? By disclosing his accomplices? Who were they? If we had only the advantage of all the testimony, Mr. Speaker, we might have been able . . . to find out who, indeed, were the accomplices of Booth; *to find out who it was that changed Booth's purpose from capture to assassination;* who it was that could profit by assassination who could not profit by capture and abduction . . . who it was expected by Booth would succeed to Lincoln if *the knife* made a vacancy. . . .

The italicized phrases revealed something Butler may not have intended to reveal to his contemporaries—*that he knew Booth was the foil of one of his "accomplices,"* just as we have deduced. In the light of the fact that he (Butler) had been named as Seward's successor when Seward was expected to die, his final sentence above suggests that *his* connection with the attempt upon Seward's life might be investigated to good purpose. For rhetoric does not explain General Butler's curious intimation

* *There were no serious differences between Butler and Bingham. This pair of devious politicians were bedfellows, and became the two principal managers of the campaign to discredit and impeach President Johnson.*

of the "succession" he had in mind: Lincoln's office was made vacant with a pistol; the assassin who tried to make Seward's office vacant used *"the knife!"*

To return to the mesmerized Booth—some of his remarks made to different persons during the early evening of the assassination have become standard elements in the "legend." They were told in retrospect and both rather pat. But a couple are worth repeating, because they were consistent with the frame of mind in which we believe Booth anticipated his starring performance in the tragedy at Ford's Theater that night.

As he was leaving the National Hotel around 7:00 P.M. the evening of Friday the fourteenth, Booth stopped to chat with the desk clerk. He asked him if he intended to go to Ford's Theater that evening, to which the clerk replied he had not thought to. The actor said he should, because "There will be some good acting there tonight."[37]

Just before entering the theater on Tenth Street, where the entertainment was already in progress, Booth stopped at a saloon nearby to brace himself for the great "performance" with a final glass of brandy. Some of the patrons were acquaintances of his, and there was some banter on the subject he had come to detest. Someone needled him with, "You'll never be the actor your father was." Nettled, Booth snapped back: "When I leave the stage I'll be the most famous man in America."

He was right.

The circumstances of the actual assassination are well known, and there is no serious controversy about them. Just before 10:00 P.M. Booth got his horse from the stable in the alley, led it to the rear door of the theater, and asked unsuspecting Ned Spangler to hold it for him. Spangler did so until his duties called him inside, then asked "Peanuts" Burroughs to hold the horse. Booth went around to the front entrance,* had his drink, and conned the ticket-taker into letting him enter the theater without a ticket. He idled downstairs a moment or two before slipping up the stairs to the balcony. There he stood against the wall apparently looking for a seat. He was actually waiting for the place in the comedy when Harry Hawks, alone on the stage, would say a line that always rocked the house.

As the progress of the scene told him the funny line was soon to be spoken, he slipped down the right-hand hallway to Box 7 and into the short passageway to it, barring the door behind him as planned. He listened at the inner door until Hawks recited the line. Laughter filled the house as usual, and Booth stepped into the box with the cocked derringer in his hand. Lincoln sat in an armchair to the left facing the stage, with Mrs. Lincoln on his right, and to her right Major Rathbone and his

* He is believed to have used a passageway under the stage.

fiancée, Miss Clara Harris. The assassin took a step forward, aimed the pistol, and fired. Even those in the box were not immediately aware what had happened and why the President's head had slumped forward on his chest. In the pause Booth dropped the derringer, pulled a knife from his belt, and pushed past Mrs. Lincoln to the railing above the stage. Major Rathbone lunged for him and received a slash as Booth tore free and vaulted over the railing. It was a ten- or twelve-foot drop—no feat at all for the athletic actor. But his spur caught in the American flag draped across the outside of the box, and he landed off balance, his left ankle turning.

Chances are he did shout "*Sic Semper Tyrannus,*" either before he jumped or when he regained his feet, much too excited to notice the pain. Then he raced for the rear door across the stage and was mounted and riding wildly down the dark alley before the astonished people in the theater realized what had happened.

Some convincing evidence has been presented[38] to show that all the exits from Washington were closed immediately, except the one Booth took over the Navy Yard bridge. But this was before the introduction of the telephone, and Booth would have been able to ride the three miles to the bridge and cross it before orders closing it could have arrived there, even if they had been sent immediately. He did cross, giving Sergeant Cobb his own name, and continued on the road to Surrattsville—while the shock and hysteria at Ford's Theater spread through the city, and the next day gripped the whole country.

flight and the "field glass"

The facts of Booth's crime and his flight were greatly hidden in the subsequent confusion—but most of all by the distortions and misrepresentations of those who were determined to sell the public an explanation of their own choosing. It is known that Booth and Herold arrived in Surrattsville around midnight and stopped at Lloyd's tavern. Herold took one of two carbines John Surratt had hidden there several weeks earlier. Herold also took two bottles of liquor which Mrs. Surratt had instructed Lloyd to have ready when she drove out with Weichmann that afternoon. He took one of the bottles to the injured actor, who stayed on the porch. Booth talked with Lloyd, refused to carry a carbine, and drank heavily of the liquor.[39]

The pair moved on southward but detoured to the Mudd house, near Bryantown, which they reached at four o'clock in the morning. Dr. Mudd set Booth's ankle and made him a crutch. Booth was ill all day, but later on shaved off his moustache with a razor Herold had borrowed from the doctor. They left around four in the afternoon and went to the farm of a Confederate sympathizer named Samuel Cox, about ten miles from Bryantown. Here they remained hidden in the woods nearby until the evening of Friday, April 21, being provided with food by Cox and his stepbrother, Thomas A. Jones. That night, the twenty-first, they crossed the Potomac into Virginia in a boat provided by Jones.[40]

Next morning Herold appeared at the home of a Mrs. Quessenberry, who refused to take them in,[41] but a certain Mr. Bryan came along and took them to the farm of a Dr. Stewart. Here they got a meal but no other comfort, and spent the night in the cabin of a Negro named Lucas.[42] Next morning, the twenty-fourth, Lucas drove them in his cart to the Rappahannock ferry at Port Conway. They met three Confederate soldiers who had been with Mosby (Jett, Ruggles, and Bainbridge) and crossed the river to Port Royal, then were taken to Garrett's farm three miles farther south. Herold left Booth there and went on to Bowling Green, but returned to Garrett's the next afternoon.

The Garretts, having been told Booth was a wounded Confederate soldier named "Boyd," treated him as a guest. The second night there, the twenty-fifth, Booth and Herold slept in the tobacco barn behind the farmhouse, because Union cavalry had passed down the road in the early evening and Booth didn't want to sleep in the house.

On the morning of the twenty-sixth around 2:00 A.M., two of Lafayette Baker's detectives (Colonel E. J. Conger and Lieutenant Luther B. Baker, cousin of the chief detective) rode up with a cavalry detail under Lieutenant Doherty. They had arrested Willie Jett in Bowling Green and had him with them. The terrorized Garretts presently admitted there were two strangers in their barn. The building was surrounded, then set afire when the actor refused to surrender. Over Booth's scornful protests, Herold gave himself up, but the defiant actor still refused to do so, and Sergeant Boston Corbett pushed his carbine through a crack and shot him in the neck. He died on the Garrett porch after having made a number of theatrical statements to his captors. His wound was very similar to the one he had inflicted upon Lincoln, and his death occurred about 7:00 A.M., within minutes of the same time of morning the President had expired.[43]

The ramifications to the story of Booth's crime, flight, apprehension, and death are almost endless. Literally scores of aspects are and have been matters of controversy. Those which concern our study in this chapter are the ones which bear on the assassin's motivation.

Booth's choice of an escape route is usually explained in terms which conform to his alleged devotion to the Confederate cause, which prompted him to commit the murder as an act of revenge for the defeat of the South. In view of our thesis that patriotism or political fanaticism had very little to do with either his scheme to abduct the President or the ultimate resort to assassination, that the causes rather were deeply personal—a combination of thwarted ambition, vanity, self-pity, and drink—his reasons for fleeing southward through Maryland are far from obvious.

The route he took—if he had not been injured—would have taken him into an area where the concentration of Union troops was heavier than anywhere in the country. Those Confederate units which had not yet surrendered were in such desperate straits that any protection they could offer the fugitive—if he could have reached them and they had been foolish enough to prejudice their own cause by harboring him—would have been of very short duration. He could, and actually did, get a little help from Southern sympathizers through Maryland, which was not occupied or conquered territory. But he could have had no realistic expectation of help from private citizens south of the Potomac—even without Stanton's proclamation that persons aiding the fugitives would be "treated as accomplices in the murder of the President." Most intelligent southerners would have assumed that that would be the penalty. Also, the majority were well aware of Lincoln's forgive-and-forget policies and would have had little sympathy for the man who had destroyed their white hope for a generous peace.

On the other hand, escape in any other direction was as impossible, or more so. It was a common assumption in the North during the several days in which Booth's whereabouts was unknown to the public that, being an actor, he would have assumed a disguise and possibly even remained in Washington. The horse sense of the average nothern citizen told him this was the *only* way a man whose features and stature were as well known throughout the country as Booth's could possibly hope to avoid capture. The logic of it was almost impregnable.

By borrowing a razor at Dr. Mudd's place and removing his moustache, the fugitive made a belated and superficial effort at disguise—and that not according to any prior plan, since he hadn't even brought a razor of his own. Then he proceeded on his route southward in the same clothing he had worn on the night of the murder, which had been seen more or less clearly by hundreds of witnesses in the audience. In addition, he was riding a rented horse whose owner would give the authorities the animal's description as soon as he learned of the crime.

According to Atzerodt, who was well acquainted with the lower portions of Maryland, he (Atzerodt) was not even consulted about the best escape route in that direction until the late afternoon before the assassination. From this we would judge that the direction of Booth's flight had not been chosen until just before that final conversation at the Herndon House.

A document in the National Archives[44] implies that, as of April 12, Booth intended to head for New York after his crime rather than fleeing southward. A letter signed "Etta" and dated "New York, April 13," was from a young lady who, by her own words, was of easy virtue and living on funds furnished by the actor, whom she addressed as "Dear Wilkes." The first sentence reads:

"I received your letter of the 12th (stating you would be in this city on the 16 inst.) this morning, and hasten to answer it."

The second paragraph appears to be in answer to Booth's statements in his letter to the effect that he was upset over the fall of Richmond and felt like "doing something desperate." Then there are hints that she has promised to do her part in some unspecified venture, and the paragraph ends, ". . . and Wilkes hath said *vengeance* is mine." (See full text in Appendix F, "The 'Etta' Letter.")

In this writer's opinion, the letter is an obvious plant. One-day mail service between Washington and New York seems very unlikely in 1865. Also, the opening sentence and the oblique second paragraph are clearly contrived to tell the reader that on the twelfth Booth was plotting to kill the President and expected to be in New York to meet a female accomplice on the sixteenth. This fits too neatly into the War Department's conception of his motives—and might also have been designed to direct the search for him toward New York rather than toward the South.

The most unavoidable conclusion from a study of the culprit's flight is that no current preparations of any kind were made for it—other than Mrs. Surratt's trip to Surrattsville with Weichmann the same afternoon, to leave a small parcel with John Lloyd and instruct him to have two bottles of liquor ready.[45]

Lloyd opened the package after Mrs. Surratt had gone and found it contained a "field glass." Since the widow saw Booth in front of her house on H Street just as she entered the carriage to drive out to the tavern—according to the testimony of her daughter Anna[46]—*but did not give him the package,* we can assume both that the package was not intended for him and that he wasn't supposed to know about it. The package was intended for Herold, and Lloyd stated under oath that he gave it to *him.*[47]

Booth had no baggage, not even a razor or a blanket or any change of clothing. True, life in general was very primitive in 1865 by the standards of today, and comfort while traveling had yet to be invented. But the average person setting out on a long trip, and particularly a man as vain as Booth, could be expected to take toilet articles and a change of socks and linen with him at the very least.

He didn't even have much money, hardly more than sixty dollars, one would judge. His reported expenditures during the flight ($25.00 to Dr. Mudd, $10.00 to Herold, $10.00 to the Negro who took him to the Cox farm, $2.50 to Dr. Stewart for food, and $10.00 to Jack

Garrett) amounted to only $57.50. And if any money was found on his body by the detectives, none was turned in with his belongings. Lest it be argued that he had money but that it was stolen, his reproachful note to Dr. Stewart for his lack of hospitality enclosed the $2.50 for food served him with reluctance and mentioned that pride prompted him to make payment, though the money was "hard to spare." [48]

Lack of preparation on the part of such a remarkably impractical conspirator as Booth is not surprising. But Powell, who we believe was supervising the arrangements for the assassination, would not have overlooked anything so necessary to a successful escape as an ample supply of money. So it follows that a long journey and a successful escape for John Wilkes Booth after the crime was not one of Powell's objectives.

Powell was clearly responsible for the uncharacteristic efficiency and thoroughness with which Booth prepared for his starring performance at Ford's on the night of the fourteenth. And Booth's attitude to his role in the drama was just as clearly that of an actor who reports to the theater to perform his part in a play and, after the applause is over and the curtain rung down, goes home to bed like everyone else. His script for that night ended with his wild ride through the city. If there had been anything after that, he would hardly have told the guard at the bridge his real name.

Herold's statement to Bingham was that he met Booth *by accident* on the road to Surrattsville. But his actions from that point onward, beginning with the stop at Lloyd's tavern to pick up the liquor and rifle, make it evident that the meeting was carefully planned rather than accidental—that it was his *business* to take charge of the actor at that point. It is noted that Herold was even less prepared for a long journey than Booth. He had no money at all, in fact no personal effects nor any arms, though he had been carrying the rifle. We get the impression that he had expected to return to Washington almost immediately.

The fact that neither Booth nor Herold was prepared for a long journey, and doubts that Powell would have taken any chances of having Booth captured alive before he had time to make his own escape to the North, led this writer to the conclusion he had not intended that the actor should live out the night—and that Herold had been sent to meet him to make *sure* he did not.

This view of Herold's function in the plot is clearly at odds with the familiar idea that the young man went with Booth to aid him in his flight. But it is strongly supported by certain aspects of the situation, and not refuted by the fact that he remained with the actor *most of the time* until they were apprehended at Garrett's farm—in spite of having many opportunities to desert him and *apparently* having nothing to gain from remaining in the company of the nation's most wanted criminal, a penniless fugitive, and everything to lose if they were caught together.

The package which Mrs. Surratt took out to the tavern and gave to Lloyd with instructions that it be given to Herold *was* given to Herold—and he still had its contents, the field glass, at the Garrett farm. It was found there by a member of the Garrett family after the Conger-Baker party had left for Washington with Booth's body and Herold a prisoner.

Now why would Mrs. Surratt take the long carriage ride to Surrattsville to leave an article as innocent as a "field glass" for David Herold when she could have handed it to Booth in front of her own house? Her champions say she really went out to the tavern on private business and that John Lloyd was frightened into giving incriminating testimony against her by threats of prosecution as an accomplice in the assassination. The private business described—a sum of money owed her by one John Nothey for two years—could have been transacted by mail quite readily, as a member of the court pointed out, since it was set forth in a letter to Nothey which she entrusted to one B. F. Gwynn for delivery.[49]

Booth's mysterious illness

The "field glass" might not have been so innocent as it seemed. If Herold's function in the program Powell had arranged was to serve as Booth's executioner, the latter might have had trouble persuading the young man to shoot Booth, who was armed and known to be an exceptionally good shot with a pistol. But Herold had been a druggist's clerk. He might have agreed to the more subtle agency of poison—particularly since Booth could be counted upon to drink heavily at every opportunity. And a field glass, or its case, would be a suitable container for a small quantity of poison in pill or powder form.

It may have been due to the actor's injury that he sat on the porch at the tavern while Herold went inside and told Lloyd to get "those things" Mrs. Surratt had told the tavernkeeper to have ready. It's also possible Booth didn't *know* they were to pick up anything, but had just stopped to get a drink. While Lloyd went upstairs to get the two carbines which Surratt, Herold, and Atzerodt had left there six weeks earlier, Herold went into the bar. Lloyd had returned to the porch when Herold came from the bar with one of the bottles and handed it to Booth, who drank deeply. Booth refused to carry one of the carbines, Lloyd said, "because his leg was broken." And he already had two pistols. The fugitives stayed only a few minutes and then rode on.[50]

To continue with the history of the "field glass": After Booth's death,

Lieutenant Baker displayed an extraordinary interest in this commonplace object. It was Miss L. K. B. Holloway, sister-in-law of farmer Garrett, who found what she referred to as a pair of "opera glasses" after the arresting party had left. She showed them to Mr. Garrett, and he said to get rid of them, that he wanted nothing around to remind him of that dreadful night. So Miss Holloway sent them to her mother at their farm eight miles away.

As soon as Booth had been pronounced dead, Colonel Conger gathered up the dead man's effects and hastened back to Washington alone to break the news to Colonel L. C. Baker. Lieutenant Baker was left to find a cart in which to transport the corpse and then follow more slowly with the prisoner Herold and young Jack Garrett, whom he had ordered to accompany him to the Capitol as a material witness.

The next afternoon, after conducting the caravan to Washington, Lieutenant Baker returned to the farm with Jack Garrett and asked if a field glass had been found. "They did not know really that they [the glasses] were there," wrote Miss Holloway (see her letter, Appendix G), "but simply supposed that Booth had them and thought they might be there." She told Lieutenant Baker she had sent them to her mother's place. He immediately left, with Jack Garrett as his guide, and rode to the other farm, demanded and received the glasses. He and young Jack returned to the Garrett place, stayed there for the night, and rode off to Washington the following day.[51]

All Booth's effects and arms—except for his "diary"—were presented as exhibits at the Trial on May 17, the day Colonel Conger testified.[52] The "field glass" was not among them.

It is evident that Lieutenant Baker went to a great deal of trouble and inconvenience to recover the glass. Yet he did not even know it existed when he left the farm to accompany Booth's body and Herold to Washington. He learned about it upon his return to the Capitol—from whom else than his boss, L. C. Baker? Its apparent value as evidence relating to Booth's crime was nil. But Lieutenant Baker was acting under the direct, secret orders of Lafayette Baker, his cousin. When he made the long return trip to Garrett's, he felt it was necessary to recover the glass at all costs—not as evidence, but to make sure it was *not* presented in evidence. The glass vanished. And in Lafayette Baker's account of the chase and capture, he mentioned neither the "field glass" *nor* his agent's return to the Garrett farm to recover it.

The theory that the "field glass" or its case was used as a container for poison is only relevant and important if combined with evidence that poison was actually administered to Booth. Otherwise speculation as to whether Herold had poison in his possession during the flight would be pointless and lead to no valid conclusions.

As it happens—and this is an aspect of the episode which seems to have been minimized or overlooked by students of the assassination—Booth *was* taken violently ill after leaving the tavern at Surrattsville, and he arrived at Dr. Mudd's farm in a state of prostration. Although the fugitives moved on to the Cox farm some ten miles from Bryantown after staying at Mudd's for twelve hours, Booth was still very ill and remained so during the six days that the pair stayed in hiding at the Cox place. These two incongruous delays—twelve hours at Mudd's and six days at Cox'—at the very beginning of a desperate flight for their lives can hardly be explained otherwise than by Booth's illness, which made it impossible for him to travel.

The subject of Booth's illness is studied best in terms of his physical condition during the three-week period from his return to Washington from New York on April 8 to the hasty and secret burial of his body in Washington on April 27. There are ample and authoritative reports on this at several points in the twenty-day span. We shall look at them in order:

Throughout the week prior to the assassination.

In the course of the investigation of the crime and the Trial, literally dozens of persons made statements as to their dealings with Booth during this period. Though none was medical in character, the collective impression is that the actor was in vigorous good health and high spirits. Saloonkeeper John Deery thought he was under mental and emotional strain, however, and noted that he drank heavily—a quart of brandy each evening. His physical condition, from all other evidences, was excellent.

At Lloyd's tavern in Surrattsville two hours after the crime (testimony of John Lloyd, Peterson transcript, pages 29-30).

Booth sat on the porch, due to his injured ankle, but did not mention being in great pain when he talked with the tavernkeeper. He drank deeply from the bottle of liquor brought to him by Herold. The two fugitives mounted their horses and rode southward together.

At Dr. Mudd's farm near Bryantown six hours after the crime.

Mudd's description of the assassin's physical condition is extracted from his full statement made April 22, 1865 (reproduced in full in *Why Was Lincoln Murdered?*, by Otto Eisenschiml, pages 254-58. Italics added).

Last Saturday morning April 15, about four o'clock, two men called at my house. . . . One on a horse led by the other man who tied his horse to a tree nearby. I aided the man in getting off his horse and into the house . . . I assisted him in getting upstairs where there were two beds, one of which he took. *He seemed to be very much injured in the back, and complained very much of it. . . . He seemed to be tremulous and not inclined to talk . . . and seemed inclined to sleep, as I thought, in order to ease himself; and every now and then he would groan pretty heavily. . . .*

On examination I found there was a straight fracture of the tibia about two inches above the ankle. . . . I did not find the adjoining bone fractured in any way. *I do not regard it as a peculiarly painful or dangerous wound.* There was nothing resembling a compound fracture. . . .

He continued still to suffer and complained of severe pain in the back especially when being moved. In my opinion pain in the back may originate from riding, *as he seemed to be prostrated.* [Booth was an experienced and expert rider.] *He sometimes breathed very shortly and as if exhausted. . . .*

He had a pretty full forehead and his skin was fair. *He was very pale when I saw him. . . .* I do not know how to describe his skin exactly, but I should think he might be classed as dark, and *his paleness might be attributed to receiving this injury . . .* [Herold ate breakfast with the family] *but the other man remained upstairs in bed. . . .* I judge that between four and five o'clock on Saturday afternoon [same day] they left my house. . . .

Dr. Mudd added that he did not think the injury to Booth's ankle would be made more painful by riding, as long as he did not strike it on anything.

At the farm of Samuel Cox near Bryantown from Saturday night, April 15, until the evening of Friday, April 21 (John Wilkes Booth, by Francis Wilson, Chapter XIV).

The pair was given refuge at the Cox place, only ten miles from Bryantown, a few hours after they left Mudd's. Their reason for remaining hidden in the woods there for six days and five nights, rather than trying to escape, has never been explained. The only person known to have observed Booth during this period of hiding (other than Herold) was Thomas A. Jones, foster-brother of Cox, who took food and newspapers to the men in the woods. The following is his description of his first meeting with Booth:

"He was lying on the wet, cold ground, his head supported by his hand . . . . An old blanket was partly thrown over him . . . *he was exceedingly pale, and his features bore traces of intense suffering. . . .* I visited them daily, giving them food, newspapers . . . for six days."

Booth spoke to Jones and shook his hand, but did not rise. Though in his "diary" he said he was starving, Jones brought food regularly. The War Department later attributed his "wasted condition" to starvation, but he does not seem to have been without food for long at any point in his flight, if he was able to eat. It is notable that Herold lived under identical conditions during the eleven days but showed no signs of physical depletion. The evident reason why the two men *hid* rather than riding for their lives is that Booth was too ill to travel.*

At the Garrett farm near Port Royal from the afternoon of April 24 to the early morning of April 26, when Booth was shot (John Wilkes Booth, by Francis Wilson, Chapter XVIII).

See Miss Holloway's full statement in Appendix G. Miss Holloway did not mention that Booth looked ill, though he seemed very subdued and depressed. He ate at the table with the family and conversed with them, and sat on the porch between times. When Mrs. Garrett offered to change the dressing on his ankle, he declined, saying "it did not give him the slightest pain."

From the foregoing it is clear that John Wilkes Booth was in excellent health during the week before his crime and was still well when he reached Surrattsville, except for the discomfort of his injured ankle, though Dr. Mudd did not regard the wound as "peculiarly painful or dangerous." After drinking from the bottle Herold gave him and riding away from the tavern, he suffered a sudden inexplicable and very serious seizure. At Dr. Mudd's he was prostrated and remained in bed for twelve hours.

Booth managed to make it the short distance to the Cox farm, but was ill and unable to travel until Friday the twenty-first. By the time he arrived at Garrett's he had recovered somewhat. Miss Holloway, not having seen the actor in the flesh before, would not have noticed that his physical condition was *wasted* in comparison to his normal appearance.

In view of the evidence, we can probably agree that the question is not *whether* Booth became gravely ill after the drink he took at Surrattsville—but *from what cause?*

Without any other attending circumstances, the illness might be explained away as a sudden seizure from unknown but not necessarily suspicious causes. However, when we relate the illness to the matter of the "field glass" and the secretive actions of Mrs. Surratt, Herold, and Lieutenant Baker in connection with that suitable container for poison,

* An article from *The Century* reprinted in *The Unlocked Book* (pp. 177-80) quotes an interview with Thomas Jones which was much more specific about Booth's health at the Cox farm. Jones said the actor remained "pale at all times" during the six days and, as far as he knew, didn't rise from the ground until he was helped onto Jones' horse to be taken to the river to cross. He made no references or inquiries about the welfare of his mother or family, nor about the fate of Mrs. Surratt and his other associates. "Booth's first solicitude," Jones said, "seemed to be to learn what mankind thought of the crime."

we have what appears to be a matched set of related circumstances representing cause and effect.

The conclusion that Booth was ill from poison delivered to the tavern by Mrs. Surratt and administered by Herold is further strengthened by events in Washington after the actor's body was brought back there:

Booth died of a bullet wound in the neck at 7:00 A.M., April 26. His body was transported to the Capitol wrapped in a blanket—the first twenty miles or so by wagon and the balance of the distance by river steamer. It reached Washington around midnight of the same day. Next morning Secretary of War Stanton ordered an "inquest" to establish the "identity" of the corpse. The members of the committee he appointed were, with one or two exceptions, all individuals who were associated with his clique.* Dr. John Frederick May, an eminent physician of Washington who had removed a small tumor from Booth's neck two years earlier, was brought to the *Montauk* in the Navy Yard and identified the actor by the scar on his neck. He was also identified by a tattoo on one hand.

The same night, about forty hours after Booth's death, the body was buried hastily and secretly in an unmarked grave under the direction of L. C. Baker. This action brought widespread suspicions that the corpse identified as Booth's was not really his. Stanton's flimsy explanation for the hasty secret burial was "preventing him being made the subject of rebel rejoicing."[53]

It's so obvious that the *location* of Booth's burial place or the lapse of time until he was interred could have nothing to do with southern reaction to his crime—even if *all* ex-Confederates had applauded it—that Stanton's explanation must be considered a substitute for the *real* one. There was virtually no reason to question the identification made by Dr. May and others. *But* the *condition* of the body which, according to Dr. May, was greatly wasted, with the "facial expression sunken and sharpened by the exposure and starvation it had undergone,"[54] might very well have raised some questions, in view of David Herold's unchanged appearance after the same "exposure and starvation."

Also, Dr. May was puzzled to find the skin very much "freckled," although Booth was not inclined to freckle and had not been exposed to the sun to any extent during his journey. In later years, Dr. May referred to the strange skin condition as "yellow and discolored."[55] We can probably assume his knowledge of his profession was broad enough that he would not have been so puzzled by the condition of Booth's skin *unless that condition were most unusual.*

---

* Surgeon General Barnes, Judge Advocate General Holt, Colonel Bingham, Major Eckert, William Moore (of Stanton's staff), Colonel L. C. Baker, Lieutenant L. B. Baker, Colonel Conger, a photographer and his assistant, and Charles Dawson, clerk at the National Hotel (SOLD, Eisenschiml, p. 34).

If one entertains the idea that Booth was poisoned, as this writer does, and that the wasted condition of his body and strange discoloration of the skin may have been medical evidences of his poisoning, the *real* explanation for his hurried secret burial may have been to avoid an autopsy which might have been demanded by influential persons who viewed the remains.

The question of what poison could produce the physical effects testified to by Dr. Mudd and the skin condition after death reported by Dr. May is a technical one. On this subject we refer the reader to Appendix H, "Professional Study of Booth Poisoning Data."

Further evidence that the genuine conspiracy called for Booth to be poisoned by Herold immediately after the assassination will appear when we consider Lafayette Baker's activities with regard to the pursuit of the fugitives in the following chapter.

In fairness to Colonel Burnett, it must be mentioned that he did *not* delete the references to the "field glass" from John Lloyd's testimony in the Pitman compilation. This can be interpreted in various ways: That he was unaware of the phase of the conspiracy which concerned the liquidation of Booth. That he knew there was no phase of the conspiracy which might be revealed by Lloyd's mention of the "field glass" (but Lieutenant Baker's zeal to recover the glass and the fact that it vanished after he did recover it argue against this interpretation). That *all* of Lloyd's allegations about Mrs. Surratt were important to the circumstantial case against her. It was the widow's case which became the focus of controversy after the executions; thus it would be unwise to omit any incrimination from the Trial record, both because all of it was needed to confirm her guilt and because her conviction was the one most likely to be re-examined, in which case the absence of references to the "field glass" in the "official" compilation would be glaring. Finally, Burnett might have known the function of the mysterious glass in the real conspiracy but reasoned that it couldn't possibly be connected with a plan to poison Booth, since the actor had obviously not died of poisoning.

for notoriety's sake

Throughout this study we have found that documents relating to the assassination frequently convey a much different meaning from their former one when they are reread in the light of our findings—that is, when we acquire a new conception of the viewpoint of the person who wrote a given letter or statement. The notations John Wilkes Booth made in his "diary" while hiding at the Cox farm are usually interpreted as confirming the legend of his "conspiracy." When we study his plaintive afterthoughts on the terrible crime he had committed—his own appraisal of what he had done and why—we find considerable confirmation for the version of his role in the real conspiracy to murder Lincoln which has been presented in this chapter.

We have pictured Booth as a frustrated young actor with delusions of grandeur, who had entertained the daydream of a grand conspiracy in which he would amaze the world by kidnapping "the heads of the Government including the President" from a theater in the nation's Capitol. He planned to harm no one. The daydream itself was so satisfying to his ego that his impatient accomplices were unable to persuade him to consider any other locale than a theater or, in fact, to take positive action even in that locale. With the collapse of his fantasy around the middle of March, his despair was unbearable. Heavy drinking brought no consolation. And there were those present who realized that a man in Booth's state of mind could be directed toward murder and used as a foil to accomplish the elimination of Abraham Lincoln. Lewis Powell, a subtle, persuasive, and unprincipled man, was selected to aim Booth at the target. He performed his task with such skill that Booth, his pathetic instrument, never realized how bitterly he had been tricked until the last day of his life, only a few hours before his death in Garrett's barn.

Aside from the fact that Booth's own moral standards and grip upon reality were so defective as to allow him to be drawn into murder, his betrayal by those whom he thought to be his friends and accomplices is also part of the situation he speaks of in his "diary"—as is the ironic circumstance that he was in hiding and greatly dependent upon his own would-be murderer, who apparently lacked the nerve to finish the job.

In short, the "diary" text which follows was written by a man still under the influence of a delusion—but a delusion already beginning to weaken under the assault of conscience.

The first entry, though referring to the three days in which preparations for the assassination were made—with the dates incorrect and the term *Ides* misused—was written sometime during the six days at the Cox farm, judging from the references to newspaper stories (italics are added):

> *April 13, 14, Friday the Ides*—Until today nothing was ever thought of sacrificing to our country's wrongs. For six months we had worked to capture. But our cause being almost lost, *something decisive and great* must be done. But its failure was owing to others, who did not strike for their country with heart. I struck boldly and *not as the papers say.* I walked with a firm step through a thousand of his friends, was stopped, but pushed on. A colonel was at his side. I shouted *Sic semper* before I fired. In jumping broke my leg. I passed all his pickets. Rode sixty miles that night, with the bone of my leg tearing the flesh at every jump.
>
> I can never repent it, though we hated to kill. Our country owed all her troubles to him, and God simply made me the instrument of His punishment.

> The country is not what it was. This forced Union is not what I have loved. I care not what becomes of me. I have no desire to outlive my country. This night (before the deed) I wrote a long article and left it for one of the editors of the *National Intelligencer* in which I fully set forth our reasons for our proceeding. He or the gov'n—

The entry ended abruptly at that point, due to some interruption. On Friday the fugitive made another rambling entry, beginning with an unsuccessful attempt to cross the Potomac the previous night:

> *Friday, 21*—After being hunted like a dog through swamps and woods and last night being chased by gunboats till I was forced to return wet, cold, and starving, with every man's hand against me, I am here in despair. And why? For doing what Brutus was honored for—what made William Tell a Hero; and yet I, for striking down an even greater tyrant than they ever knew, am looked upon as a common cutthroat. My act was purer than either of theirs. One hoped to be great himself; the other had not only his country's, but his own, wrongs to avenge. I hoped for no gain; I knew no private wrong. I struck for my country, and her alone. A people ground beneath this tyranny prayed for this end, and yet now see the cold hands they extend to me! God cannot pardon me if I have done wrong; yet I cannot see any wrong, except in serving a degenerate people. The little, the very little, I left behind to clear my name, the Government will not allow to be printed. So ends all! For my country I have given up all that makes life sweet and holy—tonight misfortune upon my family, and am sure there is no pardon for me in the heavens, since man condemns me so. *I have only heard of what has been done (except what I did myself), and it fills me with horror.* God, try and forgive me and bless my mother. Tonight I will once more try the river, with the intention to cross, *though I have a greater desire and almost a mind to return to Washington, and in a measure clear my name, which I feel I can do.*
>
> I do not repent the blow I struck. I may before my God, but not to man. I think I have done well, though I am abandoned, with the curse of Cain upon me, when, if the world knew my heart, *that one blow would have made me great,* though I did desire no greatness. Tonight I try once more to escape these bloodhounds. Who, who, can read his fate? God's will be done. I have too great a soul to die like a criminal. Oh! may He spare me that, and let me die bravely. I bless the entire world. I have never hated nor wronged any one. This last was not a wrong, unless God deems it so, and it is with Him to damn or bless me. And for this brave boy, Herold, here with me, who often prays (yes, before and since) with a true and sincere heart, was it a crime in him? If so, why can he pray the same? I do not wish to shed a drop of blood, but I must fight the course. 'Tis all that's left me.

The wandering, overdramatized, self-pitying character of these reflections and the vague motives mentioned in connection with the crime reveal a greatly disoriented personality and a thought process more like that of a romantic youngster than of a man of twenty-six.

The expression "something decisive and great" recalls Atzerodt's statement that Booth said the assassination would be "the greatest thing in the world." These theatrical lines still dominated his thought, fighting against the admission that he had, in a bad dream it seemed, committed a cowardly crime.

Reason was breaking through slowly, like the wakening from that dream, as shown in the curious statement "I have only heard of what has been done (except what I did myself), and it fills me with horror." This obvious denial that he knew Seward was to be assassinated until he read it in the papers is rather convincing evidence that he didn't remember that minor incident of the drama in which he had starred. The sequence of thoughts here is interesting—First, horror at the *second* crime, which the newspapers described in gory terms; then an anguished cry for God's forgiveness; then the notion that he could return to Washington and clear his name. Did these comprise a flash of understanding that scheming men had used him as their unsuspecting agent? If so, the illumination was only brief, since he returned at once to self-justification —"I do not repent the blow I struck." And again, the central motive for those fantasies of abduction and then assassination—"that one blow would have made me great."

We need not belabor Booth's exaggerated description of his injured leg, in view of Dr. Mudd's diagnosis of the break as a simple, not a compound, fracture. The actor was clearly not in a frame of mind to minimize his afflictions.

His favorable references to Herold tell us he had no suspicions as to the young man's loyalty as yet, though these suspicions would become very concrete indeed as his tragic adventure drew to a close. Herold's frequent prayers, obvious enough for Booth to notice them, inform us that by April 21 David had begun to realize that the one night's work which Powell had said would make him rich had entangled his fortunes with those of the doomed actor, and he was deeply concerned for his own skin.

A vast change had come over Booth by the time he reached the Garrett farm. They found him quiet and courteous, almost self-effacing, as their guest for two days under the name of "Boyd." None of them suspected him of being other than what Willie Jett said he was—a wounded Confederate soldier making his way home.

But at the last it seemed he had meant the prayer "Oh! may He spare me that [the death of a criminal], and let me die bravely." When the detectives and soldiers surrounded the barn, then set it afire, and Booth refused to come out and surrender, all the defiant statements attributed to him were in the best theatrical tradition and language.[56] He seemed to be doing his best to get them to shoot him and at the same time providing colorful dialogue as grist for the newspaper accounts of how John Wilkes Booth had died—bravely.

Miss Holloway's account of their two days' acquaintance with "Mr. Boyd" contained one very positive indication that, though he went into eternity in true Shakespearean style as he intended, Booth had come to an understanding of himself and his crime before he died.

On the afternoon of his second day with the Garrett's, Tuesday, April 25, he was eating dinner with the family when Jack Garrett came in with the first reports they had heard of Lincoln's assassination. Miss Holloway remembered the conversation at the table as follows:

"While at dinner the tragic event was commented upon, as to the motive which prompted the deed and its effect upon the public welfare. At this time Boyd remained silent, but upon hearing one of the daughters remark that she supposed that the perpetrator had been paid, he turned to her with a smile and said:

" 'Do you think so, Miss? By whom do you suppose he was paid?'

" 'Oh,' she replied, 'I suppose by the North and the South.'

" 'It is my opinion,' rejoined he, 'he wasn't paid a cent, but did it for notoriety's sake.' "

17

Lafayette Baker

We have had a number of glimpses of the behind-the-scenes influence of Lafayette Baker throughout the whole episode of Abraham Lincoln's murder and the arrest and trial of Booth's alleged accomplices. Most of these implied an intimate knowledge on his part of the circumstances leading up to the assassination. His reaction to the unexpected arrest of Louis Paine, for example, indicated that he knew at once that the tall muscular prisoner bore a close resemblance to Lewis Powell. Publication of his "wanted" notice for the man already in custody—in addition to being a classic piece of treachery—would have been fantastically risky unless he were *sure* that the prisoner's appearance was very close to that of the man he *knew* had been associated with Booth. But knowing this, the risk was small. If Lewis Powell had been apprehended by some accident, Baker could have explained Paine's arrest as an understandable case of mistaken identity. From his point of view, the holding of Paine was a stroke of genius. It called off the search for Seward's assailant and made Powell's escape almost a certainty.

It's interesting to speculate what course of action Baker and the War Department might have taken if Paine hadn't happened along. It's anyone's guess, but Dana's notice to the police chiefs naming and describing Atzerodt as the one who had attacked the Secretary of State leads us to believe that Atzerodt was originally selected as the whipping boy, before a more suitable candidate happened along—after which the "identification" was tailored to fit the man in custody.

Baker claimed to have masterminded the Trial and supplied most of the evidence against the "conspirators," although the War Department gave him very little credit for it. Our findings have supported his claim in detail. We even noted that he refused to recognize the variation in his master plan resulting from Paine's belated claim that he was really Lewis Powell. It would have been discreet for him to have gone along with the almost universal credence of Paine's story, one would think. But up to the day of execution, there had been no absolute confirmation that the two men were the same. It was not at all impossible that Powell's family would make an issue of the matter when they were finally heard from and furnish proof that he had not been hanged. By sticking to his story that Paine was from Kentucky and a hired killer who was sent from "the North" just a few days before the assassination, Baker would have appeared to have been as brilliantly right as usual in this eventuality.

Here we have one of the dominant forces in Baker's complex personality: his vanity. He was absolutely obsessed with his own cleverness, his genius for outwitting others and putting them helplessly at his mercy. In his biography he constantly repeated charges of treachery which were made against him, as if he considered them the most gratifying statements of appreciation. A good example might be ". . . That General Baker had the machinery of his bureau so thoroughly organized, that his espionage over the acts of public men was so complete, that he could ruin almost any one whom he chose to sacrifice."[1] He didn't deny this was true—merely asserted that throughout Lincoln's administration no one had dared to sign his name to such charges for fear of his vengeance.

the art of treachery

Dr. Eisenschiml quoted two descriptions of Baker by individuals within the federal government during the war years who spoke for the many who deplored the kind of corruption this man had introduced by means of his detective bureau. The opinions they express may be taken as authoritative, both because the writers were public servants, in excellent position to know the facts, and because the objection to Baker's methods in both instances was on moral grounds, and by implication voiced a moral axiom—that even winning a civil war does not justify the abandonment of all principles of justice and honor in dealing with the opposing forces within and without.

The first opinion was that of Mr. L. E. Chittenden, Register of the Treasury in the Lincoln administration—who was, oddly, an admirer of Stanton:

> Baker wore the uniform, and probably had the authority to assume the rank, of a colonel in the army. He took into his service . . . men who claimed to have any aptitude for detective work, without recommendation, investigation, or any inquiry, beyond his own inspection. . . . How large his regiment ultimately grew is uncertain, but at one time he asserted that it exceeded two thousand men.
>
> With this force at his command, protected against interference from the judicial authorities, Baker became a law unto himself. He instituted a veritable Reign of Terror. He dealt with every accused person in the same manner; with a reputable citizen as with a deserter or petty thief. He did not require the formality of a written charge; it was quite sufficient for any person to suggest to Baker that a citizen might be doing something that was against the law. He was immediately arrested, handcuffed, and brought to Baker's office, at that time in the basement of the Treasury. There he was subjected to a

> brow-beating examination, in which Baker was said to rival in impudence some heads of the criminal bar. This examination was repeated as often as he chose. Men were kept in his rooms for weeks, without warrant, affidavit, or other semblance of authority. If the accused took any measures for his own protection, he was hurried into the Old Capitol Prison, where he was beyond the reach of the civil authorities. . . .
>
> Corruption spread like a contagious disease, wherever the operations of these detectives extended. . . . Honest manufacturers and dealers, who paid their taxes, were pursued without mercy for the most technical breaches of the law, and were quickly driven out of business. The dishonest rapidly accumulated wealth, which they could well afford to share with their protectors.[2]

Chittenden said he once caught Baker red-handed in the act of committing a forgery. He described the detective's response to being caught as follows: "Perfectly unabashed, without a blush, the fellow smiled as he looked me in the face and said, 'That game didn't work, did it?' "[3]

The second sample of opinion on Colonel Baker was written by the author of the minority report of the judiciary committees in 1867:

> And there can be no doubt that to his many previous outrages, entitling him to unenviable immortality, he has added that of wilful and deliberate perjury; and we are glad to know that no one member of the committee deems any statement made by him as worthy of the slightest credit. What a blush of shame will tinge the cheek of the American student in future ages, when he reads that this miserable wretch for years held, as it were, in the hollow of his hand, the liberties of the American people.[4]

Baker's was the frustration of a master craftsman in the treachery business. The artist in almost any other line has a double satisfaction of both expressing his creative genius and enjoying the admiration his work engenders in those who see it. But accomplishments in the art of treachery run counter to the mores of our society and are rarely appreciated, and never approved. Baker knew his achievements in his chosen field of expression far outshone those of any competitor. But simple self-preservation kept him from proclaiming them. The most he could do was boast of his exertions in stamping out traitors, subversives, profiteers, and assassins—piously chanting his hatred for evildoers of all kinds—and scattering hints that his methods of defeating them had been brilliant beyond belief.

His biography actually had three main objectives:

1. To tell as much about his unappreciated wartime achievements as he could, without putting a rope around his neck, and let his readers' imaginations fill in the rest. "In the narration of my official experience . . .," he leered, "much was left out of the book, whose interest was equal to anything included in it, because the time has not yet come for its publication."[5]
2. To cast suspicion upon Stanton, Johnson, and other former associates

in the government who had by either action or inaction, he felt, been responsible for his dismissal in disgrace. Johnson was his most apparent target—the innuendo quoted above was aimed at him—but Stanton was number one on his list. He was not successful in scuttling the career of the former, since he had no real evidence against Johnson. But he did surround the latter with such a web of suspicion that Lincoln's War Secretary has been the prime suspect as the engineer of Lincoln's assassination for a hundred years.

3. To prove that he alone was responsible for the apprehension of John Wilkes Booth and should have received all the credit for it and, if not the whole of the $75,000 reward offered by the War Department for the capture of Booth and Herold, at least the lion's share, instead of the mere $3,750, which belittled him both financially and professionally. His indignant application to Stanton minced no words: ". . . General L. C. Baker apprehended both Booth and Harrold, within the words and meaning of the proclamation of the Secretary of War promising rewards for that service, and is entitled to the reward primarily. . . . Next to him stand Colonel Conger and Lieutenant Baker. . . . Lieutenant Dougherty and the cavalry were subordinate, though necessary, instruments . . . Under what view of the case can others be permitted to share in the reward for the capture of Booth and Harrold?"[6]

Lafayette Baker didn't actually need the money, though he wished it to be believed that he had left the service of the War Department a poor man and wrote his memoirs to earn bread. It was his vanity that was injured. The relatively tiny share of the blood money awarded him by a special committee of the House of Representatives on April 26, 1866—with Conger getting $15,000 and Doherty $5,250[7]—implied a disbelief in what he proclaimed as his crowning achievement as a master detective—his pinpointing of almost the exact geographical location of Booth and Herold on Monday, April 24, and sending Conger and Lieutenant Baker to pick them up, accompanied by Lieutenant Doherty and twenty-five cavalrymen of the 16th New York.[8] Immediately upon the return of Booth's body to Washington, Stanton is said to have made Baker a general.[9]

Unpopular as he was with many classes of people in Washington, this feat of Baker's had brought him a great deal of grudging acclaim (which was manna to his ravenous ego) as well as numerous hints that there was something very phony about the transaction.

When he came to that incident in his biography, he found himself unable to resist gloating over how Lafayette Baker, detective supreme, had sat in Washington and solved the riddle which had stumped the War Department, the U. S. Army, and half the country's police agencies for ten days.

This investigation of ours is deeply indebted to the egotism of General Baker. Up to this point *most* of the evidence we have found of his involvement in the conspiracy to assassinate Abraham Lincoln has indicated that Baker possessed a lot of inside information on the background of the crime—information which he could conceivably have accumulated from his pervasive network of spies and informers. But analysis of this incident—the flight and capture of Booth and Herold—enables us to relate him to the conspiracy in more specific terms.

the search for Booth

Judging by the fact that one of Baker's first measures upon returning to Washington in response to Stanton's telegram was to send six detectives, headed by Lieutenant Baker, into lower Maryland to look for Booth,[10] he apparently expected these men to find the assassin easily in the area to which he sent them. Unlike the army of soldiers which was combing the state of Maryland inch by inch, Baker's detectives weren't just beating the bushes. They were looking where Baker *told* them to look.

Their chief's seemingly remarkable feat of sending them to the part of the state where Booth and Herold were actually hiding at that time wasn't fully appreciated, due to their failure to find the fugitives. But Baker's knowledge of where to look was a phenomenon *which can hardly be explained otherwise than that he knew the plan called for Booth to be liquidated immediately after the assassination, not far south of Washington.*

This writer finds it difficult to believe that Baker could have acquired knowledge of such a plan *without having been a party to it—if not the instigator of it.* And this was the core of the actual plot to murder Lincoln—to close the case immediately, by reason of the death of the obvious culprit.

But in "four or five days" the detectives came back empty-handed. So something had gone wrong in the situation Baker had anticipated. The "liquidation" had been bungled. For the next two or three days he was as much in the dark as everyone else as to Booth's whereabouts. Then came the light!

His *second* inspiration as to where Booth and Herold might be found dawned on him sometime during the afternoon of Monday, April 24—the day the fugitives crossed the Rappahannock to Port Royal with Jett, Bainbridge, and Ruggles, and at about the time they and Herold deposited Booth at the Garrett farm under the name of "Boyd." Baker really did obtain a cavalry detachment from General Hancock, and sent it with Colonel Conger and Lieutenant Baker to Belle Plain, seventy miles down the Potomac.[11] Sometime after midnight on Tuesday they located Booth and Herold at Garrett's—in the very area to which they had been sent, *or so Baker claimed; and Conger and Lieutenant Baker backed him up.*

So the question comes up a second time—how did Baker know where to look?

The facts are hard to come by. Baker's biography contains no less than three versions of the episode: The one written by the reporter Townsend after an interview with the detective chief;[12] Baker's written report on it to Stanton, dated July 7, 1866;[13] and the sworn joint statement of Conger and Lieutenant Baker addressed to Stanton on December 24, 1865.[14] The many discrepancies found among these three accounts suggest that Baker wished the *precise* facts to be obscured.

In addition, certain other principals in the affair also left recollections of it in writing, and their statements differ from Baker's quite radically. Some of them, like Baker, were obviously lying, and those who seemed forthright knew only part of the situation.

During the Conspiracy Trial the question of how Booth's apprehension transpired was not particularly germane, except perhaps in the case of Herold. But Holt's desire that the subject *not* be brought up was obvious in his examination of Colonel Conger, Boston Corbett, and Lieutenant Doherty. The first witness (Conger) was instructed to begin his statement "at the point where you met the Confederate soldier Jett."[15] The second (Corbett) was told to begin "at the point where you arrived at the house."[16] Doherty was told to confine his story to the circumstances of Herold's capture.[17]

Thus, not a word about this matter was allowed to come out at the Trial. And whenever the prosecution was careful to skirt a subject or conceal a document, it was invariably a clue that something was rotten in Denmark.

One report was written by G. A. Townsend after an interview with Baker.

Of the several available versions, Townsend's* is complete enough to serve as a point of departure:[18]

> . . . the district suspected being remote from the railway routes, and broken by no telegraph station, the Colonel [Baker], to place himself nearer the theatre of events, ordered an operator, with the necessary instrument, to tap the wire running from Point Lookout, near Chappell's Point, and send him prompt messages.
>
> The same steamer which took down the operator and two detectives, brought back one of the detectives and a Negro. This Negro, taken to Colonel Baker's

* Miss Holloway's mention that a New York reporter named "Waters" was with the pursuit party, combined with G. A. Townsend's apparent "scoop" of the story, encourages the theory that "Waters" was actually Townsend.

office, stated so positively that he had seen Booth and another man cross the Potomac in a fishing boat, while he was looking down upon them from the bank . . . that Baker knew at last that he had the true scent.

Straightway he sent to General Hancock for twenty-five men, and while the order was going drew down his coast survey maps, with that quick detective intuition amounting almost to inspiration. He cast upon the probable route and destination of the refugees, as well as the point where he would soonest strike them. Booth, he knew, would not keep along the coast, with frequent deep rivers to cross, nor, indeed, in any direction east of Richmond, where he was liable at any time to cross our lines of occupation; nor, being lame, could he ride on horseback, so as to place himself very far westward of his point of debarkation in Virginia. But he would travel in a direct course from Bluff Point, where he crossed to eastern Maryland, and this would take him through Port Royal, on the Rappahannock River, in time to be intercepted by the outgoing cavalrymen.

When, therefore, twenty-five men, under one Lieutenant Dogherty, arrived at his office doors, Baker placed the whole under control of his former Lieutenant-Colonel, E. J. Conger, and of his cousin, Lieutenant L. B. Baker . . . and bade them go with all dispatch to Belle Plain, on the Lower Potomac, there to disembark and scour the country faithfully around Port Royal, but not to return unless they captured their men.

Quitting Washington at two o'clock P.M., on Monday, the detectives and cavalrymen disembarked at Belle Plain, on the border of Stafford County, at ten o'clock, in the darkness. Belle Plain is simply the nearest landing to Fredericksburg, seventy miles from Washington City, and located upon Potomac Creek. . . . here the steamer *John S. Ide* stopped and made fast, while the party galloped off in the darkness.

The narrative says the detectives spent the whole night inquiring for the fugitives at various farmhouses and arrived at Port Conway on the Rappahannock on Tuesday morning. After ferrying across to Port Royal they encountered a fisherman named Rollins, who directed them to a Negro named Lucas, who had carried two strangers, one with a crutch, a short distance toward Bowling Green in his wagon. From the informative Lucas they learned all about Booth's arrival at the ferry, the meeting with Jett and his friends, and that Jett was going to see his sweetheart in Bowling Green and had loaned his horse to Booth. Next, *with a fine disregard for the time element,* the narrative has the search party arrive at Bowling Green, only fifteen miles from Port Royal, in the dead of night and stop at the darkened tavern.

. . . Here they hauled from his bed the captain aforesaid [Jett], and bade him dress himself. As soon as he comprehended the matter, he became pallid, and eagerly narrated the facts in his possession. Booth, to his knowledge, was then lying at the house of one Garrett, which they had passed, and Harold had departed the existing day with the intention of rejoining him.

Taking this captain along for a guide, the wornout horsemen retraced their steps, though some were so haggard and wasted with travel that they had to be kicked into intelligence before they could climb to their saddles. The objects of the chase thus at hand, the detectives, full of sanguine purpose, hurried the cortege so well along, that by two o'clock early morning all halted at Garrett's gate. . . .

Except that the whole day of Tuesday was accounted for only by a fifteen-mile ride from Port Royal to Bowling Green—which left the cavalrymen utterly exhausted—this story hangs together pretty well, at least internally. But when its separate elements are examined carefully, some interesting flaws appear.

In the second of Baker's three versions of this story—his report to Stanton[19]—he tried to make it quite clear that he had the foresight to send a telegrapher to the southern tip of Maryland on Sunday, April 23.

Baker reprinted what purported to be Major Eckert's reply to his request for a telegrapher.

OFFICE UNITED STATES MILITARY TELEGRAPH
WAR DEPARTMENT, WASHINGTON, D. C.
April 23, 1865

COLONEL BAKER:

This will introduce to you Mr. Beckwith, a cipher operator, of great scouting experience, who may be of great service to you, in addition to his telegraphing.

I also send with him Mr. Cheney, a repair man, to make speedy connections wherever it may be found necessary. Please furnish him a side-arm.

Yours truly,
THOMAS F. ECKERT

On Sunday, April 23, by his own account, Baker had *no* men in the field looking for Booth, and was for the time being not even a participant in the pursuit. He would not get his extraordinarily lucky break in the discovery of the Negro who was supposed to have seen the fugitives crossing the Potomac until the afternoon of the following day, Monday the twenty-fourth. So what plans had he on Sunday the twenty-third for using the services of a telegrapher?

Mr. Beckwith, the telegrapher in question, wasn't just *any* telegrapher. He was General Grant's personal *cipher operator,* able to send top secret messages to the War Department in code that could only be deciphered there by an operator or official who knew that special code.

Baker said *he* sent Beckwith to Port Tobacco on the steamer *Keyport* on Sunday evening in the company of two of his detectives, Hubbard and Woodall.[20]

Beckwith said *Stanton* sent him to Port Tobacco, and that he rode down with an escort of soldiers departing Sunday morning.[21] He said nothing about Hubbard and Woodall being along.

Anyhow, by one means or another he got there—and the messages he sent back to the War Department in code were addressed to *Major Eckert.*

Only one of the several messages Beckwith sent (some are still in the Archives) appears to have been important. On Monday he met Major James R. O'Beirne, a provost marshal of the District of Columbia, who had been in the field for a week with a force of cavalry searching for Booth in southern Maryland. The major had big news. The day before this he had heard a report that two men had been seen slipping away from Dent's farm near Port Tobacco and were believed to have crossed the Potomac into Virginia. O'Beirne had given chase, but his exhausted troops straggled, and he hurried back to Port Tobacco to collect his forces.[22]

Beckwith listened to the major's story, then insisted he stand by until the information had been sent to the War Department. The wire was sent, and a reply came back ordering O'Beirne to remain *north of the Potomac.* The pursuit was then turned over to Colonel Baker, so he said.[23]

The provost marshal was furious, feeling he had been robbed. When he returned to Washington after Booth's apprehension, he encountered Secretary Stanton, who told him in the presence of witnesses, "If you did not succeed in capturing Booth, it was, at all events, certainly the information you gave that led to it."[24] Later the House committee on distribution of the reward money awarded Major O'Beirne $2,000, in spite of the fact that he had no proved connection with the capture of the fugitives.[25]

So *this* was Stanton's and Eckert's explanation of how Baker happened to pick up Booth's trail. But was it true? Baker related this version in the first of his *three* accounts of the pursuit in his biography—then turned around and gave an entirely different explanation in the third one!

A third version, the Conger-Baker report, plays up the Negro informant.

The first two of Baker's three versions of the pursuit were quite vague as to when Hubbard and Woodall were supposed to have arrived at Port Tobacco and had the amazing luck to find the well-informed but nameless colored man who hadn't told his story to any of the thousands of other searchers in the area. They were even more vague as to how Woodall managed to get him to Washington—eighty or more miles up the Potomac—so fast. His third version, however—the joint report by Conger and Lieutenant Baker—was specific:[26]

> On Monday, the 24th, General Baker, steady in the opinion he had formed [that Booth would attempt to escape across the lower Potomac], sent one of

Library of Congress

PLATE IX.—MAJOR THOMAS T. ECKERT

Head of the War Department Telegraph Bureau. Made Assistant Secretary of War just prior to the assassination and Brigadier General afterward.

Library of Congress

PLATE X-A.—FORD'S THEATER

Situated on 10th Street between E and F. The Herndon House was around the block at the corner of 9th and F Streets.

Library of Congress

PLATE X-B.—WAR DEPARTMENT BUILDINC

Located on Pennsylvania Avenue at 17th Street. Photo taken from 17th Street in the 1870's after alterations to front portico. The building was torn down in 1879.

Library of Congress

PLATE XI-A.—THE WASHINGTON ARSENAL

The Trial was held in the barracks-like building seen here across the artillery park.

National Archives

PLATE XI-B.—THE COURTROOM SCENE

Contemporary sketch of the Arsenal chamber where the Trial was held. By all accounts it was much more crowded than this.

Library of Congress

PLATE XII.–THE JUDGES AND PROSECUTORS

These members of the Military Commission, from left to right, are:

1. Col. D. R. Clendenin
2. Col. Charles H. Tomkins
3. Brig. Gen. Thomas M. Harris
4. Brig Gen. Albion P. Howe
5. Brig. Gen. James A. Ekin
6. Maj. Gen. Lew Wallace
7. Maj. Gen. David Hunter (Pres. of the Court)
8. Maj. Gen. August V. Kautz
9. Brig. Gen. Robert S. Foster
10. Col. John A. Bingham, Asst. Judge Advocate
11. Col. H. L. Burnett, Special Judge Advocate
12. Joseph Holt, Judge Advocate General

PLATE XIII.—PAGE FROM BOOTH'S "DIARY"

The little appointment book (which is usually referred to as a "diary") in which Booth wrote his reflections on the crime during his week in hiding at the Cox farm. When its existence was exposed by Baker in his book in 1867, Stanton was forced to produce it and it was discovered that eighteen pages prior to the date of the assassination had been cut out. Stanton could not or would not explain their removal. In all probability the missing pages contained memoranda on the actor's appointments during the preparations for the assassination, and would have been highly incriminating for anyone named or otherwise identified.

MONDAY, JUNE 20, 1864.

TUESDAY 21

WEDNESDAY 22

THURSDAY, JUNE 23, 1864.

After being hunted like a dog
through swamps, woods, and last
night being chased by gunboats till
I was forced to return wet cold
and starving, with every mans hand
against me, I am here in despair. And
why? For doing what Brutus was
honored for. What made Tell a
Hero. And yet I, for striking
down a greater tyrant than
they ever knew, am looked
upon as a common cutthroat.
My action was purer than either
of them. One, hoped to be great
himself. The other had not only
his country's but his own wrongs
to avenge. I hoped for no gain.
I knew no private wrong. I
struck for my country
and that alone. A country that
groaned beneath this tyranny
and prayed for this end, and
yet now behold the cold hand
they extend to me. God cannot
pardon me if I have done
wrong. Yet I cannot see any
wrong except in serving a
degenerate people. The

FRIDAY 24

SATURDAY 25

Lincoln Museum

Library of Congress

PLATE XIV.—THE SURRATT BOARDINGHOUSE

1865 photo of the house at 541 H Street where Paine was arrested with Mrs. Surratt and the three girls.

Library of Congress

PLATE XV.—THE SURRATT TAVERN

The tavern at Surrattsville (now Clinton) where Herold gave Booth whisky two hours after the assassination.

Library of Congress
PLATE XVI-A.—LOUIS PAINE IN PROFILE

Mrs. A. G. Bassett
PLATE XVI-B.—THE REV. DR. A. D. GILLETTE

Library of Congress
PLATE XVI-C.—THE EXECUTION SCENE

The condemned, from left to right: Mrs. Surratt (seated), Louis Paine (in white hood), David Herold, George Atzerodt.

> his men, Theodore Woodall, with a telegraph operator, into Lower Maryland with his instruments, to be attached to the wire at given points, and thus enable him to communicate, without loss of time, with that region. Woodall, while on this duty, fell in with ———, an old Negro, whose statement so impressed him, that, instead of sending it by telegraph to Washington, he took and delivered him bodily to his superior.
>
> The examination of the colored man satisfied General Baker that he had at last struck the trail of the fleeing murderers. That they had crossed the Potomac, near Matthews Point [Mathias Point], on Saturday night, the 22nd of April, and that Booth was lame.

There are a number of gaping holes in Baker's fable about his Negro informant: The incredible coincidence by which Detective Woodall encountered the man almost the moment he stepped off the steamer is one. His failure to use the services of Beckwith (who went down with him for the very purpose) to *wire* news of his discovery to the War Department is another.

But the greatest flaw is in the statement that Woodall brought his informant back to Washington so quickly that Colonel Baker had completed his illuminating interview with the Negro and had Lieutenant Doherty and his troopers at his doorstep by two o'clock the same afternoon.

Even supposing Woodall had been able to make immediate arrangements for passage up the Potomac by steamboat, the distance to Washington was *eighty miles*. We have no accurate knowledge of how fast riverboats traveled such a distance in that day, but five hours for the downstream journey is probably a conservative estimate. *Upstream*, even though the Potomac is not a swift-flowing river, would have taken longer. We'll give Baker the edge and call it a seven-hour trip. We'll also concede that Woodall and his prize re-embarked as early in the morning as 9:00 A.M. Arithmetic does the rest. They couldn't possibly have landed in the Capitol before *four o'clock in the afternoon*—two hours after the Townsend story said the search party boarded the *John S. Ide* on its way to Belle Plain!

Yet Baker really did organize the expedition sometime during the afternoon of Monday, April 24. And many people doubted that a mysterious Negro informant had anything to do with his sudden decision to do so.

Albert G. Riddle, a noted Washington attorney who later took part in the prosecution of John Surratt and also represented Lafayette Baker in the legal action which preceded his dismissal, had this to say about it:[27]

> The old Negro informant is to be relegated to the realm of myth; all the means taken to reproduce him were futile; he was never again heard of or found, and became the theme of unsparing gibes and sarcasms of Baker's rivals and enemies.
>
> He was a pure creation of the genius of L. C. Baker. . . . The old Negro

> was a necessary creation, to give color to a *real informant* [author's italics], and to make seeming ground on which the expedition could rest; . . .

The House committee on the distribution of reward money [most of the material Baker published on this and other aspects of the pursuit of Booth was in connection with his claims for the rewards and glory of the capture] was equally unimpressed:[28]

> In the first place, upon what information Colonel Baker proceeded in sending out the expedition which, on April 26, overtook and seized the two fugitives, is in no manner disclosed or intimated in his official report.
>
> In a paper, however, filed by Messrs. Conger and Baker, it is stated that the information in question was derived, on April 24th, from "an old Negro," from whom it was obtained and reported on the same day to General Baker by Theodore Woodall, "one of his men;" and that this information was to the effect that Booth and Herold had crossed the Potomac near Mathias Point on the night of Saturday, April 22. But the name of this Negro is not made known, nor has any claim whatever been filed by such a person. . . .

The report of the committee proceeded to state that they didn't believe any information obtained from Major O'Beirne could have tipped off Baker either. It seems the congressmen didn't even believe in *Woodall,* let alone the unnamed Negro, and logically so. Woodall, if he existed and was involved in the manner stated, would have had an excellent claim for reward. But he made none.

So we must look further for Baker's "real informant," to use Riddle's term.

pursuit by the Conger-Baker party

In his report to Stanton, Colonel Baker quoted himself as having said to Conger and Baker (who, incidentally, had returned to civilian status and were recruited by their former boss specifically for this undertaking)—"You are going after Booth, and have got the only reliable information concerning his whereabouts."[29]

Lieutenant Baker later quoted him as saying, "Lieutenant, we have got a sure thing."[30]

We return to the story of the pursuit as related by Conger and Baker in their joint statement:

> A hasty interview with the Secretary of War, and Colonel Conger was sent with a note from General Baker to General Hancock for a commissioned officer and twenty-five cavalry, to report immediately to General Baker, for duty under his command, while Lieutenant Baker made the necessary arrangements with the Quartermaster's Department for transportation down the Potomac. Upon

> their return from these duties, General Baker fully explained to them the information on which he was acting, and, with the aid of a map, pointed out with care the place of Booth and Harrold's crossing and their probable course and plans . . . that the expedition was to start the moment it could be got ready. It was to go down to Belle Plains, and, if there was no dock for landing at that point, to go to Aquia Creek, and if the dock had been destroyed there, that the horses must be made to take the water, for in no event must they go below; once on land they must act on their own judgement and descretion. . . .
>
> About two P.M. of the 24th, Lieutenant Dougherty of the Sixteenth New York Cavalry, reported to General Baker for orders.
>
> The party left Washington about sundown on the evening of the 24th, on the steamer *Ide;* arrived at Belle Plains about ten in the evening and landed. . . .

Through the night and next morning the detectives searched the farms in the neck of land between the Potomac and the Rappahannock, arriving at Port Conway about twelve noon, when they halted for thirty minutes. They encountered the fisherman Rollins and, taking him with them, rode off toward Bowling Green. They arrived at a tavern called "Half-way House," midway between Port Royal and Bowling Green, "about nine in the evening." They were told that five men, one of them lame, had stopped there the day before, then left, and that they all came back but one.

On the supposition that Booth had been left at Bowling Green, "the command pushed forward and reached Bowling Green between eleven and twelve o'clock."

At "Half-way House," which would have been perhaps four miles *beyond* the Garrett farm in the direction of Bowling Green, they were told that five men, one answering to Booth's description, had come in to drink the previous day, Monday the twenty-fourth, and that the other four had returned later without him—which led the detectives to believe Booth had been left in Bowling Green. In other words, according to their story, they went to Bowling Green expecting to find Booth there.

Now, when he took the witness stand on May 17,[31] Colonel Conger was told to begin his story at the point where he met young Jett. He said that when they arrived at Bowling Green, a Negro told him Jett was at a nearby tavern. In other words, he implied he was looking for Jett rather than Booth. He went into the tavern by himself and found a room in which a man was sleeping, who was roused when he entered. He said, "Is that you, Jett?" and the man said yes.

In the Peterson transcript of Conger's testimony, he added this curious comment to his account of finding Jett in bed: *"I expected to find somebody else."*

Judging from the fact that he went into the room alone at Bowling Green—though they were extremely wary in approaching the supposedly desperate, well-armed, and dangerous Booth at Garrett's—we would

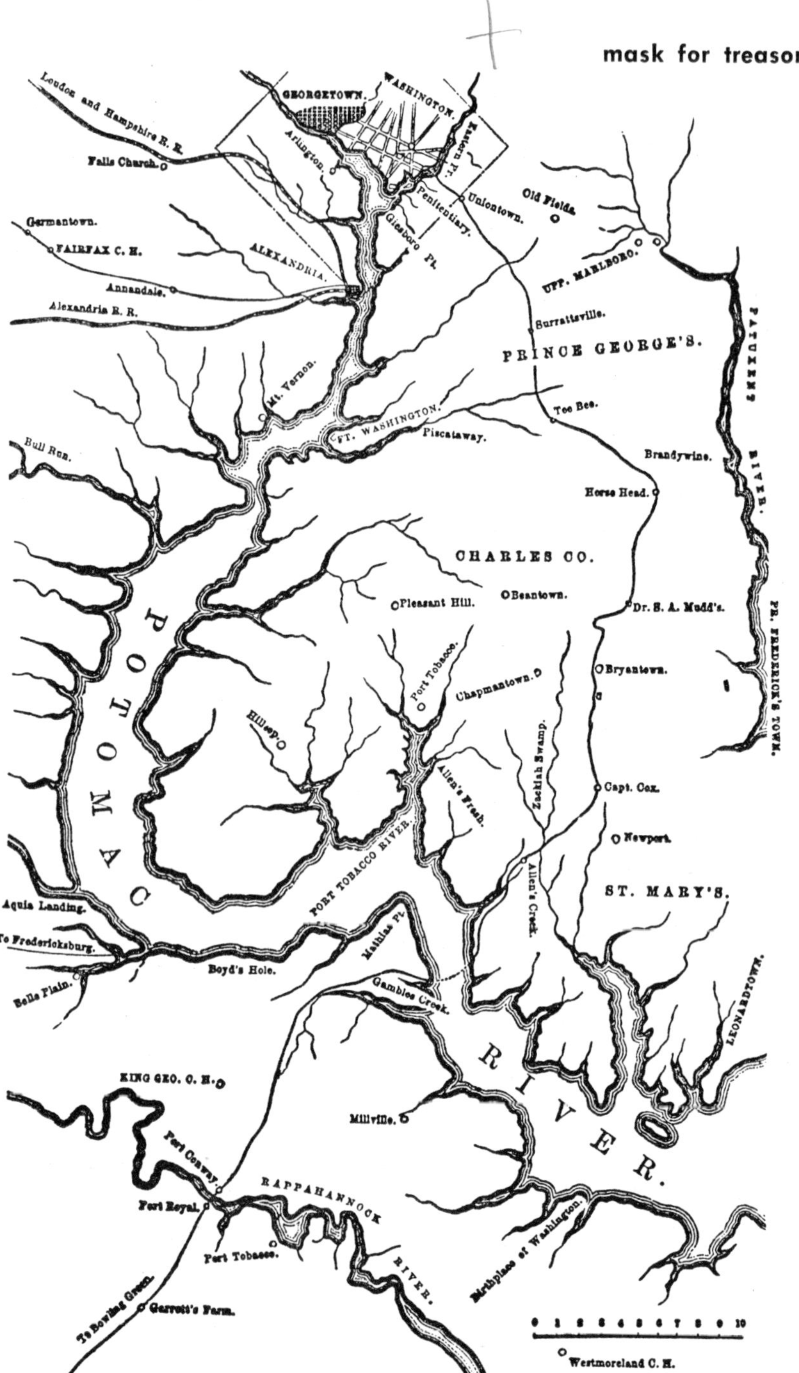

FIG. 5.–Map of Booth's Flight to the Garrett Farm

gather that the "somebody else" Conger expected to find was *not* Booth. But who was it?

Pitman, we are not surprised to discover, deletes this suspicious sentence from the witness' testimony.[32]

While Conger was talking to Jett, telling him to get dressed, Lieutenant Baker and Lieutenant Doherty entered the room. Jett asked to speak to the Colonel alone, and Baker and Doherty were ordered to withdraw. Then the young man said he knew what they wanted and could tell them where Booth was—at Garrett's farm. But Conger said they had just passed there, implying that Booth could not be there. It developed then that Jett thought the search party had come *from Richmond,* rather than from Washington—and he said that if Booth wasn't at Garrett's, he didn't know where he was.[33]

Here we have four pieces of a jigsaw puzzle:

1. That when they started out from Washington, the pursuit party *did not have precise information* as to where Booth could be found.
2. That the yarn about Booth's having been with the party of five men at "Half-way House"—*beyond* the Garrett farm—was probably false, the only plausible reason for it being to explain why the party went directly to Bowling Green from that point.
3. That Conger went to the tavern looking for somebody *other than Jett* and also *other than Booth.*
4. That Jett was expecting a search party to arrive *from Richmond,* not from the North.

While these four pieces create a suspicion, we will need more elements of the puzzle to assemble anything like a clear picture of what really happened. By backtracking, we shall find some others.

It seems significant that Lafayette Baker, though claiming to have deduced that Booth and Herold crossed the Potomac near Mathias Point (see map), told his detectives to disembark several miles upstream at Belle Plain, rather than putting them on the trail at the fugitives' crossing point, where there would be a much better chance of tracking them by questioning the natives. They were told specifically *not to go beyond* Belle Plain; if they couldn't land there they were to go *back upstream* to Aquia Creek to disembark, which would have taken them *away* from Booth's route by several miles.

The Townsend version of the pursuit gives a puzzling reason for the choice of Belle Plain as debarkation point: "Belle Plain, on the border of Stafford County . . . is simply the nearest landing to Fredericksburg . . . and after a futile ride on the Fredericksburg road, they turned shortly to the east and kept up their baffled inquiries all the way to Port Conway on the Rappahannock."[34]

This is just a more specific description of the party's itinerary after leaving the boat at Belle Plain—with the interesting detail that the route along which they were inquiring at farmhouses was *westward*—away from Booth's assumed line of travel between Mathias Point on the Potomac and Port Royal.*

According to George Atzerodt's "confession," the route "they" *intended* to take was one turning west at T. B. (or Teebee) to strike the Potomac at Maryland Point; it appears that the initial route of Lafayette Baker's search party showed it was proceeding on the assumption that the fugitives had traveled in the direction *Atzerodt* said.

But Atzerodt had been in custody since the twentieth and confined on the monitor *Saugus*. Would Baker not have known about his "confession" and the escape route he talked about before the twenty-fourth? Not necessarily. One of the prime themes of his biographical account of the pursuit of Booth was the lack of co-operation he received from other agencies—and his success in spite of them, by virtue of sheer genius. Colonel Wells didn't get the stenographic record of his interview with Atzerodt transcribed as a report for two or three days, as he was also involved in lower Maryland getting statements from witnesses regarding Dr. Mudd's case. When he finally did get it transcribed, he headed the report "Port Tobacco, April 25, 1865." It may be that the hot tip Woodall brought Baker *or sent him,* on the twenty-fourth from that town was simply George Atzerodt's revelation of the escape route Powell and Booth talked about the afternoon before the assassination.

In any case, the party's fruitless ride toward Fredericksburg—away from Port Tobacco and away from Booth's actual line of travel—indicates (1) that there was no connection between Beckwith's information from Major O'Beirne and Baker's dispatch of Conger and Lieutenant Baker, and (2) that Baker had *no* "reliable information concerning Booth's

---

* Lieutenant Doherty's version of the pursuit of Booth was related in an article in *Century Magazine,* January, 1891, pp. 446-49. It differed from those of L. C. Baker, Conger, and Lieutenant Baker in a number of details—notably in that Doherty claimed *he* had led the pursuit from start to finish.

Doherty stated specifically that Colonel Baker had ordered the detail to search in the direction of *Fredericksburg,* since no troops had been sent there yet. During the night, after several hours of inquiring at farmhouses on the road leading to that town, they met a Negro who told of seeing a Union cavalry regiment ride toward Fredericksburg the previous evening, on the same side of the Rappahannock —the *north* side.

Assuming from this information that other cavalry had already searched on their present route, Doherty headed eastward for Port Conway, in order to cross the river on the ferry and *approach Fredericksburg* on the southern side of the Rappahannock.

However, at Port Conway they met Mrs. Rollins, the ferryman's wife, and learned that Booth had crossed there the day before and headed toward Bowling Green with Willie Jett and his friends. They hastened to follow this lead rather than proceeding to Fredericksburg.

whereabouts" on April 24. Thus we can see that the whole story of his sending a party to the exact point where Booth was caught was a brazen fiction concocted *after* the capture, in which certain measures of his on the twenty-fourth were placed in a causal relationship with *later events* which led the search party to Garrett's farm.

The problem narrows down considerably. We see that both Conger and Lieutenant Baker knew very well that the amazing "intuition" of the chief detective was a hoax. There were two probable reasons why they didn't expose it. First, they had been brought back into service by their boss on the prospect of a large share of the reward money. Second, they were "company men," so to speak; and the circumstances of the apprehension and capture of the fugitives may have put them in possession of information so detrimental to the War Department that they wouldn't dare reveal what really happened.

When Conger got Jett out of bed in Bowling Green, the young man asked to speak to him alone. To grant his request at all was unjustifiable under the circumstances and out of character for Baker detectives—and Conger pulled rank to do so. Lieutenant Doherty was the one he really wanted out of the room; but to avoid arousing his suspicions, he told him and Lieutenant Baker to leave.

Now, what did Jett have to say to Conger that the other officers shouldn't hear? And how did he get the idea their party had been sent out from Richmond? And why was Jett upset to learn Conger and his group had come from Washington? To form any opinions on these questions we will have to look into the activities of Jett, Ruggles, and Bainbridge, who were supposed to have been returning home from Mosby's recently disbanded Rangers—but who first found a farmer willing to keep Booth "until Wednesday morning" and then spent nearly two days in the company of his alleged "accomplice" David Herold.

Jett, Bainbridge, and Ruggles

Jett, Bainbridge, and Ruggles were probably all enlisted men rather than officers, and all mere boys under twenty.[35] According to Miss Holloway, Willie Jett was only eighteen at the time of this incident and "had never been in the war."

One major difficulty in fitting these three into clear roles in the capture of Booth is that almost everyone involved with them had an interest in distorting the truth of the situation in some respect. They themselves must have come very close to being prosecuted for their admitted activities in helping to hide Booth at the Garrett farm. Yet, though arrested and taken to Washington, they were not charged with anything, and Jett took the witness stand for the prosecution. The period in their association with Booth and Herold which interests us is that between the time they left Booth at Garrett's on Monday afternoon and Conger's discovery of Jett at the tavern in Bowling Green on Tuesday at midnight. All three, as far as we can discover, were residents of Port Royal. But throughout the period in question they were hustling around the countryside on *some* business which involved the two fugitives they fell in with at the Rappahannock ferry. They may have had very good reasons of their own for not revealing what that business was.

The one articulate witness to this episode who had no serious ax to grind was Miss L. K. B. Holloway, sister-in-law of farmer Garrett, who was at the farm throughout Booth's stay there. Her written statement on the affair appears in full in Appendix G. The reader of it will notice that the only biased remarks she made were those regarding Willie Jett, whom she blamed for bringing trouble upon the family by asking Mr. Garrett to care for Booth, yet telling him the stranger was a wounded Confederate named "Boyd." It was her opinion that Jett had slipped over to Ashland, "a telegraph office," and sent a wire to Washington informing the authorities of Booth's whereabouts. And this was not without logic, since it was *he* who asked Mr. Garrett to take care of "Boyd" until Wednesday, on which day he would return for him. This particular arrangement, coupled with the fact that Jett *did* return with the Conger-Baker party at 2:00 A.M. on Wednesday, surely justified her belief.

Before taking issue with this idea, though, we shall note that Miss Holloway was objective in all other respects in her account of the incident. Being at the scene at Garrett's through the whole business, and having no reason for making any false statements, she was more likely than anyone else to know the sequence of events, the entrances and exits of the various characters, and the time of day or night when these occurred. Thus we shall refer to her letter in these respects with considerable confidence.

As to Miss Holloway's theory that Jett had wired Washington from Ashland: The first argument against it is that there is much doubt that commercial telegraph service between northern Virginia and the Capitol had yet been resumed, the war having been over for hardly two weeks. The second is that Jett couldn't have sent a message of such sensational nature over public wire facilities—with the whole nation searching for Booth—without setting off a publicity bombshell which the War Department could not have concealed. The third is that Jett, if he *had* wired the news of the fugitives' exact whereabouts to Washington, would have been free from any suspicion of having *helped* Booth and would have had an ironclad claim for a big slice of the reward money. It might have aroused the scorn of some of his neighbors, but that would be a risk to which he would have resigned himself before sending the wire.

Also, by Conger's account, Jett wasn't expecting an arresting party to arrive from *Washington.* So much for Jett for the moment.

As a native of the region, Miss Holloway may have known what she was talking about when she said the three men who crossed on the ferry with Booth and Herold were *not* Jett, Bainbridge, and Ruggles. She even knew the names of the three other passengers—William Rollins, Mr. Green, and Richard Wilson. According to her, the three ex-rebel soldiers were just hanging around Port Royal. Baker's version that they were young warriors homeward bound from battle, and all officers—who drew a pistol to force the boatman to take the fugitives over—makes a more dramatic story. But since they were probably residents of the area and neighbors of the ferryman, a resort to such threats is most unlikely. The only importance in the distinction is in the new perspective in which the youths begin to appear.

Jett went along with the version Baker told when he testified at the Trial on May 17.[36] He stated that Herold came up to him and said his companion was the assassin of the President, and that when Booth learned about Herold's revelation, he said, "I didn't intend telling that." In spite of being "so shocked that I did not know what to say," Jett admitted he and his friends escorted the fugitives to Garrett's, "Booth riding on Ruggles' horse."

Up to this point the witness was communicative—then his memory for details vanished: "Harold and the rest of us went on within a few miles of Bowling Green; the next day Harold returned towards Garrett's, and that was the last I saw of him till after he was captured."

Holt asked two more questions on this—and they were notably unsearching ones:

> Q. Did I understand you that Booth went alone to Garrett's?
> A. No sir; Ruggles, Booth, Bainbridge, and I rode up to Garrett's and we left Booth there and Harold came on with us to Bowling Green and had dinner.
> Q. Do you know where Harold went to from Bowling Green?
> A. No sir; he left us the next day at two or three o'clock.

This was just about the sum total of what young Jett had to offer on a period of over thirty-six hours during which he and his friends were very cosy with David Herold—the period in which Conger and Baker finally learned where Booth could be found and which ended with the death of Booth and the capture of Herold. Now let's see how Miss Holloway accounts for the time of these five men.

All arrived at Garrett's farm about three o'clock Monday afternoon.

Herold waited at the gate, which was far enough from the farmhouse that they didn't recognize him when he came the next day. The three Confederates brought Booth to the house and arranged for him to be kept there, as "Boyd," until Wednesday, when Jett said he would come for him. Jett did all the talking.

The farm was three miles from Port Royal. Jett testified at the Trial that they tried one other farm first, where their request was refused. They had three horses for five men, all but Booth taking turns walking. This rules out Booth's having been at "Half-way House," several miles farther along (as the Conger-Baker report had claimed). Getting out to Garrett's by three would have consumed most of the two hours, since they left Port Royal at a walking pace.

Jett's movements the balance of Monday afternoon were uncertain. Those of Bainbridge and Ruggles were not accounted for. Jett took Herold to the house of Mrs. Clark near Bowling Green that night, and both stayed there.

Jett testified all four "went on within a few miles of Bowling Green." This could have been the "Half-way House." He then told Holt that "Harold came on with us to Bowling Green and had dinner." He and Herold slept at Mrs. Clark's that night—apparently the same house where Conger found Jett the following night. What Bainbridge and Ruggles did that evening is not explained, but Bainbridge was with Jett and Herold the next day.

After dinner on Tuesday the twenty-fifth, Bainbridge, Jett, and Herold rode up to the distant gate, the latter dismounting from behind Jett and walking toward the house. Jett and Bainbridge "rode on" toward Port Royal.

This may have been around four o'clock, and after the Garretts and Booth had been sitting on the porch for some time.

"It was *then* [when he saw Herold coming] that Boyd asked Jack Garrett to go upstairs and get his revolver." There was no question whether Booth recognized Herold; and asking for his revlover when he saw him at the gate with the other two leaves an impression he thought Herold dangerous to him—an impression which is not dispelled by his explanation to young Garrett that Herold was "one of our men."

The desire to arm himself suggests that he had not expected to see Herold again, and that his unexpected return aroused suspicions of possible betrayal.

In this we can see *why* Booth would be suspicious. None of the descriptions of Herold—not even those of his defense witnesses at the Trial—represented him as a mature, loyal young man or one who would stick with a friend in time of danger. He was portrayed as "a light, trifling boy of very little reliability,"[37] the spoiled, slightly retarded son of a family consisting of mother and six sisters.

To this add Lafayette Baker's succinct description of him as "a youth of inane and *plastic* character," and Booth's suspicions would seem to have been well founded. He knew the young man better than we do and surely had enough insight to realize that, with a price of $25,000 on his head and a full twenty-four hours to escape unhindered by a cripple on borrowed time, it was just not in character for David to show up again and put his head in a noose with nothing to gain.

Booth went to meet him, and they talked for a long time, midway between the gate and the house. Then they came up to the house together. We must assume Herold had an explanation the actor was willing to accept.

"Not long afterwards" Jett and Bainbridge came back hurriedly "to see, as Jett professed, how his friend Boyd was getting along."

At the same time, Miss Holloway supposed, they were telling Booth and Herold they had better escape because federal troops were understood to be crossing the Rappahannock. Jett then rode off in the direction of Port Royal—to meet the federal troops he had summoned by telegraph, Miss Holloway conjectured.

The lady didn't *hear* Jett's conversation, nor did she say whom he talked to—Booth or Herold or both. Judging from the behavior of the Garrett's guests, though, they had *not* been given any warning. They showed no signs of alarm and made no preparations to hide or depart.

Miss Holloway must also have been mistaken in thinking Jett went to Port Royal to meet the troops. If he had, they would not have ridden *past* the house and all the way to Bowling Green about twelve miles away—where, around midnight (as witnessed by Lieutenant Doherty), they found Jett asleep in bed.

"About an hour before sundown" the federal troops were seen dashing along the road in the direction of Bowling Green.

Even when he saw with his own eyes that his pursuers were at hand, Booth did nothing decisive. He hid in the bushes but, after they had passed, sat on the porch again. Later in the evening he asked Jack Garrett to take him (just *him,* not Herold) to Guinea's Station, a few miles to the west. Jack wouldn't go that night but was willing to do so in the morning. So Booth agreed to that and advanced the young man ten dollars. The only precaution the actor took that night was to sleep in the barn rather than in the house.

Booth was apparently not ill, nor was his leg bothering him. His extraordinary lack of action after having seen the pursuit party on the road can be explained, this writer believes, in only two ways. Either he was sick of running and knew that capture was just a matter of time—or else Herold had assured him that steps had been taken to send the pursuit party off on a false scent and there was nothing to worry about. His leisurely arrangement with Jack Garrett for transportation the next morning argues for the latter explanation.

These are all pieces of the jigsaw puzzle which, in this arrangement, tell us more about what did *not* happen than about what did. But the reader has no doubt been fitting them together and may already have arrived at a conclusion. There are a couple of other pieces which may be helpful:

The Conger-Baker report[38] included an incident which occurred as their party was leaving Port Conway on the road to Bowling Green. No importance was attached to it. It seems to have been mentioned merely because Lieutenant Doherty and his troopers saw it and would have wondered why it was omitted:

"After passing the river a short distance, two men were discovered on horseback, as if observing the party, to whom Conger and Baker gave chase. After pursuing them about two miles, they plunged into the woods and disappeared."

The identity of these men is at least suggested by Miss Holloway's statement that Jett and Bainbridge rode on toward Port Royal after letting Herold off at Garrett's, then returned at a gallop to speak to the fugitives briefly—about the approach of federal troops, Miss Holloway thought.

Herold's behavior while on trial puzzled a number of observers. He gave every appearance of enjoying the attention he was getting, and smiled often as if he hadn't a worry in the world. When Weichmann was on the stand and was asked if he knew Herold, he pointed him out, and the prisoner inclined his head smilingly in acknowledgment of the recognition. Edward V. Murphy, one of the official court reporters, wrote later that "Herold seemed entirely unaware of the gravity of the situation in which he was placed, or of the probable fate that was before him." [39] This was more than strange, because the case against him was more clear-cut than that against any other defendant, not excluding Louis Paine.

Doster wrote[40] that "The prisoner Herold was the most reckless and boyish of the party and seemed considerably pleased by the attention he attracted. He was frequently calling one or the other of the counsel to him to make suggestions that were puerile. When the defense of Mrs. Surratt appeared to be making out a tolerable case in her behalf, by showing the real character of the witnesses against her, he appeared jealous of her good luck and said: *'That old lady is as deep in as any of us.'*" The poisoning incident suggests that Herold knew whereof he spoke.

Herold's predicament

This is the way the puzzle fits together in this writer's opinion: The failure of his effort to poison Booth left Herold in a quandary. Getting away from the hunted actor was no problem, but the posting of a reward for him by the War Department made him an outcast; and even if he could have returned to Washington, the individual who had promised to pay him for disposing of Lincoln's assassin would refuse to do so (if *he* were still there), since he had bungled the job. He still had the "field glass" with him at Garrett's and may not have realized the poisoning wasn't going to work until they were across the Rappahannock. But even so, he felt he still had a financial stake in Booth and a chance to come out of the affair a hero rather than a villain. If he could find a way to turn Booth in, he could claim the credit for his capture and the $50,000 on his head. His story that the fleeing actor "forced" him to accompany him would be hard to disprove—and he wouldn't have known he would be labeled as an accomplice in the assassination (and present in Washington when it was committed) by the War Department's interpretation of Fletcher's testimony.

The meeting with Jett and company was his chance to try Plan B. He told them he had Booth in tow and that he was worth $50,000 cash. If they helped him redeem his prize he would cut them in, and it sounded like a good proposition to the three youths. The first thing was to find a place to hide the actor until contacts with the authorities could be made. Jett arranged that at Garrett's. The next thing was to decide whom to notify. It wasn't just a matter of sending word to Washington and waiting for half the Union Army to converge on Garrett's farm. Herold wanted to make a deal for the reward *and his own immunity* before Booth was delivered up.

As of Monday night, they didn't *know* there was any search for Booth going on south of the Potomac. There was no great rush, and the four talked it all over during dinner in Bowling Green. They decided a telegram was out of the question. Some federal authority would have to be contacted quietly—and the nearest such authority was the Union Army in Richmond, some forty miles due south. Not only was Washington many miles further, but most of the country between that city and Bowling Green was infested with Union soldiers and detectives.

So Ruggles agreed to go to Richmond and try to reach some high officer, and he left early Tuesday morning. After he had gone, the other three began to wonder if Booth would stay put at Garrett's without some reassurance that Herold was making arrangements for his escape and hadn't just deserted him. Herold, of course, was the only person Booth was likely to believe, the only person who could persuade him to remain at Garrett's until the sell-out could be arranged. He agreed to go back and stay with Booth and let Jett be the spokesman when Ruggles returned with someone in authority.

Jett and Bainbridge left him at the farm; and Booth, though suspicious, swallowed the story about a plan to smuggle him south. Herold's willingness to stay with him was fairly convincing, but he decided later not to put his faith in the fast-talking young man—and paid Jack Garrett to cart him off alone in the morning.

After leaving Herold at the farm, Jett and Bainbridge scouted over toward Port Royal and were surprised to see Yankee cavalry crossing the Rappahannock. Once in the village, the troop posted pickets on its exit roads and settled down to rest and eat after its hard night of searching toward Fredericksburg. The boys were satisfied the cavalry intended to stay there for a while. They stopped back at the farm to tell Herold and Booth that soldiers would be approaching on the road and warn them to take cover when they passed. They then separated—not expecting to hear from Ruggles until the next day—and Jett went back to spend the night at the Bowling Green Hotel, operated by the parents of his girl friend.

Late Tuesday afternoon, after many futile inquiries around the village, Conger and Baker had the good luck to run into Rollins, who had seen Willie Jett and his friends give Booth and Herold a lift toward Bowling Green the previous afternoon. He knew Jett had a girl there and might still be found at Mrs. Clark's. This new lead got the whole troop into the saddle in a hurry and sent it pounding past the Garrett place "about an hour before sundown."

At the "Half-way House" the detectives found "four or five young women" who wouldn't tell Yankee soldiers the time of day, let alone give information about local boys who had fought for the Confederacy.[41] After much time had been wasted, one of the men hinted they "were looking for a party that had committed an outrage on a girl." Then the young women said Jett and his friends had been there twice the preceding afternoon and that there was a strange young man with them who answered to the description of Herold. Since Booth had not been with them, they could hardly have mentioned him; so the detectives assumed the others had left Booth *somewhere* nearby. When they pushed on for Bowling Green it was with the expectation of finding *Herold* with Jett and, from the former, obtaining news of Booth's whereabouts by whatever methods proved necessary.

When Conger burst into the bedroom and found Jett alone, the young man's attitude surprised him. Rather than denying he had ever seen the fugitives he asked to speak to the Colonel privately. When they were alone, he blurted out that he knew whom they were looking for and was authorized to make a deal. Conger said he promised the young man immunity in return for information. The treatment of the aged Mr. Garrett—threatened with hanging in his own front yard in the presence of his family if he didn't talk—suggests the detective drew a pistol and gave Jett one minute to tell all he knew.

Willie talked, revealing that he thought the party had come from Richmond, where Ruggles had gone. When Conger said he had just passed the Garrett place, Jett guessed the plan had misfired and that Booth and Herold had left there. He was taken along, and of course that's where the fugitives were cornered. Willie Jett thought things were working out all right, since he could now claim the rewards for both Booth *and* Herold. But Conger and Baker, who were in this for the money themselves, soon put him straight. If he made *any* claim at all, they would arrest him and his friends as accomplices with Lincoln's assassins, and they could not disprove it. According to the conditions of Stanton's proclamation, all three of the boys would surely hang for aiding the fugitives. So Willie and his friends got the message and forgot all about the reward money.

Herold, however, still thought he held a good hand. Indirectly he had been responsible for the capture of Booth. That was one point in his favor. More than that, though, his mission to dispose of Booth had now been accomplished, if not according to the original plan, by circumstances he himself had set in motion. He could now claim his fee for the original job and expect the influential person who had masterminded the assassination to see to it he went free. Simple-minded David Herold didn't realize he was playing with the big boys who made their own rules.

His attitude throughout the Trial indicated he was encouraged to believe his claim would be honored and that he had nothing to worry about. But at some point before he walked up the steps to the scaffold, he realized he had been tricked. The real mystery is how he was kept from screaming "foul" and naming names when he realized they were really going to hang him. This is also the real mystery of Mrs. Surratt. Both had plenty to tell but remained silent to the end.

An answer may be found in understanding what Colonel L. C.

Baker meant by *entrapment*—an activity at which he was the self-proclaimed past master. "Entrapment," as Baker used the word, did not mean trapping a criminal and bringing him to justice. It meant placing a person in a situation—usually through knowledge of some wrongdoing on his part—in which he was absolutely at the mercy of the entrapper.

Both Herold and Mrs. Surratt, according to our findings, had been involved in a crime *other than the one for which they were tried and sentenced*—the attempted poisoning of Booth.

They had not succeeded in this; but to use it as a defense, they would have to (1) reveal unknown information that actually confirmed their roles as accomplices in the assassination of Lincoln, and (2) reveal to their families that they had been guilty of murderous acts and intentions rather than being, as they appeared to so many, innocent victims of injustice.

Lafayette Baker was in full control of the situation. Having succeeded in fixing the whole responsibility for Lincoln's murder upon Booth and the eight hapless defendants at the Trial, he was not likely to take any chance that one of the four sentenced to die might speak up and ruin his masterpiece in treachery.

He would have secured the silence of Mrs. Surratt and Herold by any and every means at his disposal—false promises of reprieve, threats against their families, even the administration of drugs prior to the executions. There are strong indications that all three recourses may have been used.

The Trial was over. Four were to hang. The military had taken over at the direction of President Johnson and was in full charge of the executions. Yet Baker, Eckert, and several of Baker's detectives haunted the death cells during all the final hours. Detectives conducted the condemned persons from their cells to the gallows and stayed near them until they swung into eternity.

Regardless of Mrs. Surratt's and Herold's personal reasons for holding their tongues, the governing factor was Colonel L. C. Baker's determination that they must die without contradicting his tailormade legend.

Mrs. Mary E. Surratt

The case against Mrs. Surratt presented at the Conspiracy Trial was an extremely weak one and highly circumstantial, depending largely upon innuendos and the obviously perjured testimony of Louis Weichmann. In our conception of the actual conspiracy, her connection with it becomes much more specific by reinterpretation of three phases of evidence produced against her:

She denied that she had ever known Louis Paine before.

We have proposed that her reason for denying she knew Paine was due to the fact that he *looked like* Powell, or "Wood," who had stayed at her house, had been closely associated with her son John, and had supervised the assassination of Lincoln. Her denial of knowing Paine, then, amounted to a denial that she knew Powell.

She had frequent private consultations with Booth, not only while the abduction scheme was afoot but also during the week in which the murder of the President was being activated.

According to our proposition that Booth was skillfully brainwashed in preparation for his crime, Mrs. Surratt's contacts with him during the final week suggest she had some responsibility for keeping him in the desired state of delusion.

She made a trip to the tavern in Surrattsville the afternoon of the crime; she left a "field glass" for Herold and told Lloyd to have two bottles of whisky ready.

Within the proposition that the "field glass" was a suitable container for poison, and that after drinking the whisky Booth became ill in a manner toxicologists say conforms to the symptoms of poisoning with white arsenic, it is possible to connect the widow more directly with the attempted murder of Booth than with the assassination of the President.

Therefore we conclude Mrs. Surratt had a choice between *possible* conviction upon weak, circumstantial evidence or *certain* conviction as a party to the assassination of Lincoln *and* the attempted murder of Booth. In the latter case, her daughter Anna would know her mother to be, in terms of intention at least, a double murderess—and would have to carry the knowledge and the stigma through life. In the former, Anna could *believe* her mother an innocent victim if the worst came to the worst and she were executed. The choice, then, was not a difficult one, and may explain why Mrs. Surratt went to her death without telling what she knew of the real plot and those behind it.

the Watson letter

All the radials in the web of treachery we have been studying lead to

Lafayette Baker. The evidence presented so far shows that he had an extraordinary knowledge of the events which preceded the assassination of Lincoln, including the plot to poison Booth; that he played a leading role in the conviction of the eight defendants at the Conspiracy Trial; that he was the principal author of the "legend" of John Wilkes Booth; and that one of the main objectives of his biography was to focus suspicion upon Secretary of War Stanton and Andrew Johnson as the instigators of the murder of the President.

It could be argued that Baker could have been involved in the assassination and its repercussions in all these respects *without having been the instigator of the crime.* But such a great degree of guilty knowledge and such unremitting efforts to prove *others* had engineered the plot—John Wilkes Booth and the Confederate government being only the *first* he accused—can be disregarded as evidence of Baker's guilt only by a rather unreasonable insistence upon positive proof, which ordinarily means *documentary* proof.

We contend there is no such thing as *positive proof* in a situation of this kind—that only the collective weight of evidence and logic constitutes proof, and *that* only relatively when compared with a theoretical *absolute* truth. In dealing with events so far in the past, even a sworn confession by the alleged perpetrator of a crime couldn't by itself fix the guilt beyond all possible doubt.

It so happens that in this case there is a highly incriminating document which, combined with the numerous other indications that Lafayette Baker was deeply involved in the conspirary to murder Lincoln, points to the chief detective as the *prime mover.*

The document in question appeared very briefly during the court proceedings in the Conspiracy Trial as recorded by Peterson—though reference to it was carefully deleted from the Pitman compilation. It was the letter which Holt showed Weichmann on May 18 to see whether the witness recognized the handwriting as Booth's. Holt clearly thought the letter's message should incriminate *someone.* It was written from New York to John Surratt and signed "R. E. Watson."[42]

This letter is now in the files of the National Archives in Washington, among the documents relating to "Conspiracy Trial Suspects." In the original, the middle initial in the signature is "D" rather than "E," but it is clearly the same letter Holt showed Weichmann.

A handwriting authority of unusual competence made a searching comparison between the "Watson" letter and authentic samples of Lafayette Baker's script—and stated positively that he was its author. The identification was later confirmed by a second handwriting expert. (See Appendix I, "Handwriting Analyses.")

The text of the letter is as follows:

NEW YORK, March 19th, 1865

Mr. J. H. Surratt
DEAR SIR

I would like to see you on important business, if you can spare the time to come on to New York. Please telegraph me immediately on the reception of this, whether you can come on or not & much oblige

Yours tr—
R. D. WATSON

P. S. Address Care Demill & Co.
178-½ Water St.

It is hard to imagine any innocent reason why the chief of the War Department detectives would have written to John Surratt. It is even harder to imagine an innocent reason why Baker would have written to Surratt under a fictitious name. The letter would be incriminating regardless of what it said. Being dated March 19, 1865—just after the collapse of Booth's kidnap scheme, and just before the events preceding the assassination began to unfold—there is no reasonable alternative to believing the "important business" Baker referred to was the murder of President Lincoln. For further evidence that L. C. Baker was the author of the "Watson" letter, see Appendix J, "Supplementary Evidence."

Any candidate for the role of instigator of the crime must qualify by the three standard criteria: (1) opportunity, (2) capability, (3) motive. The burden of our study to this point has, we believe, made it clear that Baker had every *opportunity* to mastermind the assassination, and was by nature and inclination *capable* of such treachery. His *motive,* however, has not yet come into clear focus. In other words, how would he have gained if he had been the instigator and the plot had worked out exactly as planned?

Lafayette Baker's love of power—that is, being able to exercise an advantage over others—was pretty evident. But it would seem that the type of power he enjoyed could only be practiced in time of crisis, such as wartime; that it would have terminated with the close of the Civil War in any case—unless the state of crisis could somehow be continued, or the country's return to the normal political climate of peacetime could be prevented.

Two members of Lincoln's cabinet had solutions to that problem, *either* of which could have effectively prevented the nation's return to the conditions of peacetime democracy:

War Secretary Stanton's solution was to turn the defeated Confederacy into a huge conquered province occupied by federal troops and governed by martial law in perpetuity, the administration being under the jurisdiction of the War Department.[43]

Secretary of State Seward, in spite of widely disseminated claims that his statesmanship had succeeded in keeping the country *out* of war with England while the Civil War was in progress, had urged Lincoln that a war with England was the most reliable means of unifying the country. Lincoln's ruling—"One war at a time, Mr. Seward."—had put Mr. Seward's proposal on ice, but only until the end of the domestic conflict.[44]

According to one biographer, Seward's interest in fostering war with England was to acquire for himself the national power which such a crisis would bring to the office of Secretary of State[45]—the power which, in civil war, fell into the hands of the War Department.

Since Baker was currently associated with the War Department, his personal ambitions were linked more closely to those of Secretary Stanton than to those of Seward. The realization of his own dreams of future power—a permanent national detective force modeled after the wartime bureau he and Stanton had created[46]—depended upon the adoption of Stanton's ominous program for the nation's future. The towering obstacle to the adoption of that program was Abraham Lincoln.

Baker's motive, then, would have been to remove the obstacle to Stanton's plan for making himself a virtual dictator, thus setting the scene for the achievement of his own (Baker's) ambitions. How long Baker would have been satisfied to be the *second* most powerful man in the country is a question. If all this had succeeded, there would surely have been an eventual showdown between these two devouringly ambitious men—since neither was the type to settle for less than top dog.

Lafayette Baker's mode of living and what is known of the operations of his bureau in wartime don't reveal an unusual love of wealth on his part. He was accused of extortion, blackmail, and outright theft, along with most other familiar crimes, but was widely believed to have left office a poor man.

However, there were persistent newspaper insinuations that he had amassed a fortune by shaking down war contractors and pocketing some of the money his bureau collected from the sale of contraband property it had seized.

His latterday biographer cited an article in the Washington *Star* of July 6, 1868—three days after Baker's death—which attempted to spike reports that the detective had enriched himself in the government service: [47]

> The newspaper statements that General L. C. Baker died worth 200,000 are entirely incorrect. So far from having that amount, he left nothing whatever, and his family are in destitute circumstances. His unfortunate hotel enterprises in Lansing, Michigan, swept away the profits from his book, and the copyright of the same. He has been in declining health for more than a year, and his

> spirits have been much depressed by his pecuniary embarrassments, and the failure of his expectation to receive what he considered justly due him [the reward money] for his services in the arrest of the assassins of Lincoln.

In effect, the journalist who wrote this moving tribute informs us that Baker didn't have the avarice we would expect to find as a strong secondary motive in a person of his type. Fortunately, there is a much more reliable source of information on the point.

examination of Baker's codicil

In 1960 a New Jersey chemist named Ray A. Neff picked up an old volume in a Philadelphia bookstore for fifty cents. As he was browsing through it several months later, he discovered it contained what appeared to be a cipher message in a code which utilized letters in the body text. In the margin of one of the pages he found a faint signature—"L. C. Baker." Translation of the message—or rather, two messages—with the help of a professional crytographer revealed them as communications by Baker which referred directly to the plot against Abraham Lincoln's life.

This exciting find launched Mr. Neff on a search of the old files in Philadelphia's City Hall which eventually turned up the transcript of a hearing before the Philadelphia Register of Wills in 1872. The purpose of the hearing was to determine if a *suppressed* codicil to Baker's original will should be probated.

The transcript of the hearing disclosed many hitherto unknown facts relating to the last few months of Baker's life and the circumstances of his death. It also furnished solid corroboration that the cipher message Mr. Neff found in the old volume (Colburn's *United Service Magazine*, Series II, 1864) was authentic and had actually been composed by the detective, part of it only a few days before his death.

The historical magazine *Civil War Times** (which is being quoted here with the publishers' permission) saw Mr. Neff's discovery as one of extraordinary importance. The editors co-operated in his further inquiries and, in the August 1961 issue, presented the particulars in great detail. Comment by professional historians was cautious and sometimes inclined to question the value of the evidence. This was not altogether unexpected of course, since the "legend" of the Booth "conspiracy" has never been challenged except in minor details. And while it remained intact, no other instigators of the assassination except Booth could be exposed with any success. The "legend" provided pat answers to nearly all questions.

---

*Now published as *Civil War Times Illustrated* in Gettysburg, Pa.

Our research, however, has indicated an entirely different framework for the plot against Lincoln's life, in which Booth is relegated to the role of a mere tool in the hands of others. As a proposition, this is neither new nor original. The theory was expressed publicly many times during the couple of decades following the assassination. It was inevitable that someone would eventually have the time, resources, and curiosity to explore it.

Mr. Neff's discoveries fit neatly into this different framework, both confirming our findings and being confirmed by them. We feel his discovery should and will be recognized as the product of one of the most significant and scholarly instances of basic research ever made in the field of American history.

The decoded text of Baker's two cipher messages can be studied to best advantage against the background of his last few months of life, which was revealed in considerable detail during the hearing before the Register of Wills on October 14-15, 1872. For this reason we shall first look at the testimony taken in that court.

Baker's home in Philadelphia was at 1739 Coates Street. His next-door neighbor was Mrs. Mary Baker, widow of John F. Baker, a cousin of the detective. She died of tuberculosis in 1870, at which time her daughter Elizabeth found an unprobated codicil to the will of Lafayette Baker, who had died July 3, 1868. The codicil, dated "June 31, 1868,"* provided that "all books, diaries, and personal papers not of a financial nature" should be given to "my longtime friend Laura Duvall of Washington, D. C."

Laura Duvall was a demimonde who had appeared as a witness for Baker in his sensational exposé on the seduction of girl employees of the Treasury Department by certain of its officials.[48]

Upon the advice of her attorney, Elizabeth turned the codicil over to Orphans Court, and the hearing was scheduled to determine whether it should be probated. Several interested parties presented themselves with counsel. Baker's heirs, who had received nothing under his original will, since there was nothing of value to distribute, were represented. They suspected he had owned a large amount of money which had not been produced by the executor. Laura Duvall was represented by her attorney but was not present. The executor, Joseph E. Stidfole, was there with his lawyer. And finally, a detective named John P. Smallwood was on hand to represent the interests of the U. S. War Department—or so he said.

---

*June having only thirty days, this date is taken to be July 1.

The first revelation from Elizabeth Baker's examination was that her mother, Mrs. Mary Baker, was in the house at the time of Baker's death and had arranged for two men to carry a number of heavy boxes from the house to her own attic.

She also testified that her mother spent a lot of time with Baker during his last months and that Laura Duvall had called on him frequently, bringing flowers.

From the heirs' viewpoint, her most important news was that although her family had always been poor, her mother had left an estate valued at *$275,000!*

The next witness was Dr. William Rickards, Baker's longtime friend and personal physician. The doctor had attended Baker throughout his illness and was present at his death, having diagnosed his fatal seizure as virulent meningitis and arranged to have the remains buried immediately in a sealed coffin and the house fumigated for the protection of its next occupants.

When the examination turned to the cause of death, it came out that there had been several attempts upon the detective's life beginning December 23, 1867, and continuing into February of 1868.

On the first date he was stabbed in the side by a stranger on his own front porch. Later he was shot at twice, though missed, and once beaten up on the street by three or four men who tried to drag him into a carriage. A police guard had been kept at the house for several weeks.

Baker's illness began on January 12, 1868, after a dinner with friends. He came down with what appeared to be ptomaine poisoning, though no one else at the dinner party—including his wife, Jennie—was ill. The doctor thought he alone had been affected because of his run-down condition. On February 14 Dr. Rickards was called and found Baker suffering from what appeared to be typhoid. He seemed to recover, but had several recurrences of the fever during the months until his death. A searching cross-examination by Mr. Rogers, attorney for Laura Duvall, brought a reluctant admission from the doctor that the symptoms of the ailment were *more* clearly those of *arsenic poisoning* than typhoid, and that he had suspected the former during his treatments and practically proved it by testing with leeches. Yet he denied the detective could have been poisoned, because he felt "no one had the opportunity."

On July 1—evidently the same date he wrote the codicil in favor of Laura Duvall—Baker developed severe headache, muscular spasms, paralysis, and constriction of the throat. Under the doctor's care he seemed to recover, but died at about noon on July 3. The newspapers carried the story that the notorious detective had died of "typhoid"—but the death certificate, signed by Dr. Rickards, gave the cause as "Meningitis," necessitating immediate sealed burial.*

Dr. Rickards' opinion was that Baker was "perfectly sane," and that it was "unthinkable" that he could have committed suicide.

On the second day, two women who had nursed General Baker during his illnesses were questioned.

Mrs. Bridgit McBane revealed the following:

1. That Mrs. Jennie Baker, his wife, hardly ever stayed at the house at night, because "she was afraid."
2. That she (Mrs. McBane) was sure Baker was insane. "He was always talking about how somebody was tryin' to do him in and as how he had papers to prove it and as how he had a lot of money hidden and they was after it." She had not seen any money.

Miss Kathleen Hawks testified:

1. That she had worked as nurse from February 1 to June 1.
2. That a bullet fired through the window at Baker in February almost hit her.
3. That Baker was in deathly fear of being murdered. When she asked him by whom, he said, "My old friends." Asked if she meant "enemies," she said the word was *"friends." Baker told her he had papers "which would send them to prison."*
4. That a certain "Mr. Cobb" visited her patient on different occasions, after which Baker was greatly upset. Once she heard "Cobb" say, "Our patience is running short, Baker, you haven't much time."
5. That on June 1 she asked "the General" for her back pay of about eight dollars, since she wanted to go to New York. He sent her to the attic to get a tin box out of a trunk and, when she brought it, opened

---

*The conclusion that Baker died from arsenic poisoning follows logically from a review of Mr. Neff's statements on the effects of that poison in Booth's case (see Appendix H).

The symptoms of Baker's illness following the January 12 dinner party, as described by Dr. Rickards, are quite similar to those Neff associates with white arsenic. Also, there was the partial recovery—similar to Booth's—and the several recurrences during the next six months, the one in July being the fatal seizure.

Neff pointed out that the effects of arsenic poisoning are "cumulative" and that Booth was "doomed" and would have died within a period of weeks or months from the poison's delayed action if he hadn't been shot to death before this could occur.

With Baker, the aftereffects seem to have appeared on schedule, creating a terminal condition which Dr. Rickards evidently didn't relate to the illness in January—which he admitted had all the earmarks of arsenic poisoning—prompting him to attribute Baker's death to meningitis.

the box with a key which hung around his neck. The box was full of money, brand-new bills in denominations of from five to a hundred dollars, wrapped in bundles with little bands of paper around them. She had never seen so much money at once. He gave her twenty dollars and told her to put the tin box back in the attic. She did so.
6. That she had seen ten or twelve boxes in the attic.
7. That she believed Lafayette Baker "was as sane as you or I."

The next witness was a traveling salesman named William Carter, who had been a national detective under Baker during the war. He stated that he visited his old boss at his home on June 30, 1868, and found him in bed. There was a stack of books by his bed, and he was busy "making marks in" one of them. Asked by his visitor what he was doing, he said, "I'm writing my memoirs." Then ". . . they are going to have to get up early to get ahead of old Lafe Baker."

Carter picked up one of the books and noticed an article which interested him. He also noticed cipher marks on some of the pages. He described the books as bound volumes of "an English military journal." "General Baker" told him to take the volume he had picked up along with him, and also wanted him to take "about a dozen boxes of books and papers." Carter took the one volume, but said he had no place to store the boxes, so declined to take them.

The object in the questioning of this witness was to determine whether Baker had been sane when he wrote the codicil. Asked if he thought his former boss "strange or insane," Carter said, "No, he didn't seem insane but he didn't seem hisself. . . . He seemed sort of funny. He kept laughing and kind of cackling. All the time that I was there he kept writing in the book."

Miss Elizabeth Baker was recalled and cross-questioned as to whether she thought her mother had taken the money from Baker's house. She admitted her mother had suppressed the codicil, but denied that she would steal.

Mr. Marshall, attorney for Mr. Stidfole, executor of Baker's original estate, asked the Register of Wills to note the testimony to the effect that Baker had a large sum of money as late as June 30; that Mrs. Baker had access to his house and was alone there with the corpse until the undertakers arrived; and "that there is no apparent source of the large estate left by the late Mary Baker."

Dr. Rickards was recalled, and he restated that General Baker had died of meningitis, "a very dread and dangerous disease," and that "a magistrate signed the order for sealing the coffin." He was not questioned as to whether any other physician had verified his diagnosis as to the cause of death. But since the implication that the hasty burial in a sealed coffin was most suspicious had been made quite clearly, the doctor would surely have mentioned corroboration by another physician if there had been any.

Finally, Detective Smallwood submitted a motion that the contents of the boxes inventoried in Mary Baker's estate [those she had taken from Baker's house] "be released to the War Department. These documents were pilfered from War Department files many years ago, and they are important to the Government. I am here prepared to take charge of them for the Government."

The Register ruled Smallwood could pick out the documents he wanted from the boxes and turn them over to the clerk. "I will have them read into the record," he said, "and upon presentation of proof [of Smallwood's status as a representative of the War Department, presumably] I will have them turned over to you."

Smallwood protested that it was the desire of the Government "to have these documents kept secret." He withdrew his motion.

There was no ruling on the codicil until January 6, 1879, on which date it was rejected by Orphans Court. Mary Baker's estate was finally settled the following July, $80,000 being awarded to the heirs of Lafayette Baker. In the meantime, profitable investments had increased the estate to nearly half a million dollars. The mysterious documents were not awarded anyone and were evidently impounded by the court.

This summary of the testimony at the 1872 hearing makes the following points bearing on our investigation:

1. That Baker *did* have a large fortune when he died—a fortune accumulated during his modestly paid career as chief of the War Department's detective force. (Also see Appendix J, "Supplementary Evidence.")
2. That repeated attempts were made upon his life for at least five and a half months by persons identified only as his "old friends."
3. That he was well aware of the threats to his life and that his cipher messages were conceived, at least in part, as a means of striking back at the person or persons who were trying to have him murdered.
4. That the circumstances of Baker's fatal illness can be interpreted to support Dr. Rickards' diagnosis of meningitis. On the other hand, we are informed by pathologists that the symptoms of meningitis are quite similar to those of some types of poisoning, particularly arsenic and strychnine. Thus the possibility that the death accurred by either murder or suicide exists. Of the two, the latter theory would find better support from the nature of Baker's activities immediately before his death. Both the effort to give his secret records

to William Carter on June 30 and the writing of the codicil giving them to Laura Duvall on July 1 suggest anticipation of death. It would seem that he could know his death was imminent only if he planned to take his own life—*OR,* if he was familiar with the "cumulative effects" of arsenic poisoning.

This point has little bearing on our study and is raised merely as an incidental riddle.

into the second echelon

The strong possibility that Baker wrote at least the *second* of his cipher messages in anticipation of death brings us back to the question of whether a man about to die and making a final statement can be assumed to be telling the truth. Let's examine the two cipher messages and see what conclusions can be drawn in the case of Lafayette Baker. The first was:

> I am constantly being followed. They are professionals. I cannot fool them. 2-5-68.
>
> In new Rome there walked three men, a Judas, a Brutus and a spy. Each planned that he should be the king when Abraham should die. One trusted not the other but they went on for that day, waiting for that final moment when with pistol in his hand, one of the sons of Brutus could sneak behind that cursed man and put a bullet in his brain and lay his clumsy corpse away.
>
> As the fallen man lay dying, Judas came and paid respects to one he hated, and when at last he saw him die, he said, 'Now the ages have him and the nation now have I' But Alas as fate would have it Judas slowly fell from grace, and with him went Brutus down to their proper place. But lest one is left to wonder what has happened to the spy, I can safely tell you this, it was I.
>
> LAFAYETTE C. BAKER 2-5-68

And the second cipher message was:

> It was on the tenth of April, Sixty-five when I first knew that the plan was in action. Ecert had made all the contacts, the deed to be done of the fourteenth. I did not know the identity of the assassin but I knew most all else when I approached E. S. [Edwin Stanton] about it. He at once acted surprised and disbelieving. Later he said, "You are a party to it too. Let us wait and see what comes of it and then we will know better how to act in the matter." I soon discovered what he meant that I was a party to it when the following day I was shown a document that I knew to be a forgery but a clever one, which made it appear that I had been in charge of a plot to kidnap the president, the vice-president being the instigator. I then became a party to that deed even though I did not care to.
>
> [The editors of *Civil War Times* point out there is no punctuation in the cipher Baker was using, and that the next to the last sentence could have been intended to read: ". . . that I had been in charge of a plot to kidnap the

president, (and) the vice-president. Being the instigator then, I became a party to that deed . . ."]

On the thirteenth he discovered that the president had ordered (that) the Legislature of Virginia be allowed to assemble to withdraw that states troops from action against the U. S. He fermented immediately into an insane tyrade. Then for the first time I realized his mental disunity and his insane and fanatical hatred for the president. There are few in the War Department that respect the president or his strategy but there [are] not many who would countermand an order that the pres[ident] had given. However during that insane moment he sent a telegram to Gen. Weitzel countermanding the presidents order of the twelfth. Then he laughed in a most spine chilling manner and said, "If he would to know who recinded his order we will let Lucifer tell him. Be off Tom (Eckert?) and see to the arrangements. There can be no mistakes."

This is the first th[at] I knew that he was the one responsible for the assassination plot. Always before I thought that either he did not trust me, for he really trusted no one, or he was protecting someone until it was to his benefit to expose them. But now I know the truth and it frightens me no end. I fear that somehow I may become the sacrificial goat.

There were at least eleven members of Congress involved in the plot, no less than twelve Army officers, three Naval officers and at least 24 civilians, of which one was a governor of a loyal state. Five were bankers of great repute, three were nationally known newspaper men and eleven were industrialists of great repute and wealth. There were probably more that I know nothing of. The names of these known conspirators is presented without comment or notation in the first volume of this series. Eighty-five thousand dollars was contributed by the named persons to pay for the deed. Only eight persons knew the details of the plot and the identity of the others. I fear for my life. LCB.

The editors of *Civil War Times Illustrated* vouch for the accuracy of the foregoing translation from the cipher, it having been rechecked by other cryptologists in addition to the late Mr. Leonard Fousche of New Jersey, who did the original deciphering.

From Baker's messages, as well as from our own investigations, it appears that those, shall we say, *interested* in the assassination of Lincoln were in three echelons. The last two chapters have discussed the activities of the first, or forward, echelon, which included John Surratt, Mary Surratt, David Herold, and possibly some unknown parties in Washington—all under the immediate direction of Lewis Powell or a local agent of the second echelon. Of these, it is unlikely that any but Powell, John Surratt, and possibly Mrs. Surratt knew the identities of any persons in the other echelons.

The cipher messages take us into the second echelon, which included Lafayette Baker, his two top-level associates mentioned allegorically in the first message, and any others in official circles who knew what was planned and participated either actively or passively.

Since the managers of the Trial could hardly have conducted the proceedings without knowledge of what they were supposed to conceal—while fixing the blame and punishment upon certain members of the first echelon and an assortment of patsies—Holt, Burnett, and Bingham can be assumed to have been at least *honorary* members of the second echelon. Those who assisted them—Olcott, Foster, and others—would have been liabilities to the cause unless they also knew or learned the score. So we assume they did.

Colonel Conger and Lieutenant Baker appear to have had more than a little knowledge of the plot behind the plot, though they may rate only as the obedient creatures of Lafayette Baker.

Baker's revelation that a large number of individuals both in and out of official circles supported the conspiracy was an idea expressed often by the political opposition in Congress and the press during the postwar years. Historians as a rule do not reject the possibility. That the group was as large as Baker said is very hard to believe, since the proposition that such a secret could be kept by more than fifty conspirators is incredible. It's more probable Baker's list included a few bona fide backers (comprising the third echelon) and most of the many highly placed men against whom the detective held a grudge.

The identity of some of these invisible backers of the conspiracy in the third echelon might very well be discovered by research. But the course of inquiry would lead into the labyrinth (*sewer* would be a better word) of national politics during the postwar years and go far beyond the limits of our present investigation.

In evaluating the information presented by Baker's messages, we should first make an effort to understand his point of view. The statements of such a notorious liar can't be taken literally, of course. But a certain amount of truth may be strained out of them if we can grasp what he was trying to accomplish.

Baker's principal target was evidently Stanton.

Revenge upon his former boss had been one of his main objectives in the publication of his biography in 1867—and this appears to be a continuation of the same vendetta. We get the impression that the former detective considered Stanton to have been deeply in his debt for *services rendered* in connection with the assassination and the masking of the conspiracy by means of the Conspiracy Trial. Yet Stanton had not supported Baker's demands for the lion's share of the blood money for Booth and Herold and, worse still, had not lifted a finger when President Johnson caught Baker spying on him (in Stanton's behalf, Johnson said) and drove him out of Washington in disgrace on February 8, 1866.[49]

Thus, from Baker's viewpoint, Stanton had thrown him to the wolves and gone merrily ahead building his political fortunes in the new situation which had resulted from the removal of Lincoln by murder.

Early in 1867 the House judiciary committee held hearings on the questions raised by Baker's insinuations that either Stanton or Eckert or both had withheld Booth's "diary" from the Conspiracy Trial. All concerned in the incident were called to testify, including Baker and Stanton. Eckert left the War Department on February 28, a couple of weeks after Baker first took the stand. But Stanton brazened it out and came up smelling very little worse than before.[50] The detective's disappointment would be understandable. And the fact that the attempts upon his life began in December of the same year suggests that the next phase of his campaign to "get" Stanton was less subtle and more dangerous. It should be noted that these attempts to have Baker killed were probably responses to the "get Stanton" campaign Baker himself was conducting. As far as can be discovered, every one of the known and unknown conspirators against the life of Abraham Lincoln—with the single exception of Baker—was satisfied to let sleeping dogs lie. They made no charges against each other. But *all* were endangered by the vengeful detective's campaign against his former boss.

Now the attempts upon Baker's life from December 23, 1867, until his death on July 3, 1868, seem to have a relationship to the progress of Stanton's career during that time. On August 12 of 1867, Johnson fired Stanton as Secretary of War and appointed General Grant to fill the office on an interim basis. On January 14, 1868, Grant betrayed the trust Johnson had placed in him and vacated the position. Stanton moved in immediately and took over again, literally barricading himself in his office to avoid being removed. The impeachment trial of Johnson which followed was Stanton's bid for the jackpot. If it had succeeded, the War Secretary would have been the most powerful politician in the country, with his eye on election as president in 1868.[51]

On February 21, 1868, President Johnson fired Stanton for the second time and ordered him to turn his office over to Major General Lorenzo Thomas. On February 24 the House of Representatives resolved to impeach Johnson. On March 4 the articles of impeachment were presented to the Senate by a house committee headed by two congressmen with whom we have become acquainted during this study—John A. Bingham and Ben Butler.

On March 24 the House denied President Johnson's request for thirty days in which to prepare his defense and ordered the Senate to begin the impeachment trial on Monday, March 30. On May 26 the Senate failed to impeach Johnson by one vote, and that ended the matter.[52]

From this date onward Stanton was out of office and in poor health, though not out of politics. He campaigned for Grant and saw him elected, but Grant found no place in his cabinet for Lincoln's secretary of war. His health continued to fail and he died on December 24, 1869.

Thus the five-and-a-half-month period in which *someone* made a determined effort to have Lafayette Baker killed embraced the final preparations for the impeachment trial and the trial itself—Stanton's last bid for power. Yet the efforts to kill Baker and obtain whatever incriminating documents he had in his possession began prior to January 14, 1868, and continued *after* May 26, when Stanton's political house tumbled down. So unless we merely *assume* Stanton was the one who was trying to have Baker killed—and that he continued the effort even *after* his political fortunes had been demolished—we would have to guess that someone *other than Stanton* was interested in Baker's extermination.

At the hearing before the Register of Wills in October, 1872, Detective Smallwood's attempt to get hold of Baker's secret records showed that interest in them by persons unknown had not ended with Baker's death in 1868 or Stanton's in 1869. Since Smallwood withdrew his petition hastily when told that any documents he took would be read into a public record *and* that his credentials as a War Department representative would have to be confirmed, we can't be sure which stipulation discouraged him the more. But he represented *someone* who, seven years after the assassination, didn't want Baker's documents publicized—either the Grant administration or someone no longer in the government, who was hoping to hijack Baker's papers from the Philadelphia court to protect his *personal* reputation.

From all the foregoing we find ground for supposing that it was *not* Stanton who was trying to have Baker murdered, even though while he lived he was the prime target of the detective's vendetta.

Assuming that any sane individual conducts himself in a manner consistent with his type in most circumstances, we have three rather compelling arguments against Baker's charge that Stanton was the instigator of Lincoln's assassination:

1. Dr. Eisenschiml's well-supported case that Stanton was a physical and moral coward showed him as a basically timid type, for all his bluster[53]—one unlikely to *instigate* such a monstrous crime for fear of the consequences. Thus one would judge him to have been lacking in the element of *capability.*
2. Our own thesis was that Stanton, though devious, aggressive, and treacherous in politics, was more inclined to capitalize on an *existing* situation—to assume a posture which would enable him to end up on the winning side—than to create a *new* situation on his own initiative.
3. Regardless of which was the instigator, *both* Stanton and Baker possessed guilty knowledge concerning Lincoln's murder which would have destroyed both men if it had been discovered while they lived. But the events which transpired immediately after the assassination (Chapters 2 and 3) revealed a vast difference in the degree of such knowledge each possessed.

Baker appeared to know the background of the crime in minute detail—exactly who had done what, how, and when. The only time he was really mystified was when his detectives failed to find Booth where Baker expected him to be found, in lower Maryland.

But Stanton's bewilderment after the crime was profound. He seemed unable to take any effective measures until Baker appeared on the scene. In short, he behaved like a man who knew a crime was to be committed but had only a vague idea as to how and by whom. If he *had* instigated the murder he would hardly have neglected to make careful plans as to just what he would do and how he would behave afterward—and would probably not have called Baker in to bail him out.

Both of the cipher messages—apparently written at different times and also in different types of codes—contained clear statements of Baker's own complicity in the assassination of Lincoln.

Thus his plan could hardly have been to have them deciphered and publicized while he was still living, since he would have succeeded in exposing himself along with his "old friends." Yet he went to so much trouble to prepare the incriminating messages that he must have intended his bombshell to burst shortly after his departure. Giving the records to his former subordinate William Carter, who had experience with wartime ciphers, was one way of lighting the fuse shortly after his death. The codicil awarding all his papers and documents to Laura Duvall may have been another—though it seemed like trying to hand *her* a lighted bomb.

Carter apparently didn't get the point and wouldn't accept the boxes of records. And the codicil was suppressed under circumstances which Baker didn't foresee—the transfer of his money and papers by Mrs. Mary Baker, who probably only wanted the money. A judgment on the codicil hung fire until 1879, by which time Laura Duvall was also dead, having been killed by a runaway team of horses in Philadelphia in the summer of 1876.[54] Her death was one reason for rejection of the codicil by Orphans Court.

As a consequence, Baker's revenge misfired. The "legend" of John Wilkes Booth, which his cipher messages would probably have demolished, remained intact. *All* members of the second echelon went into history with relative honor. Baker's collection of incriminating records disappeared. The cipher messages themselves reappeared only by the most remarkable coincidence—the purchase of the volume in which they were written nearly a century later, by someone with historical and technical knowledge and the curiosity and persistence to find out what they said and who wrote them: Mr. Ray A. Neff.

Ordinarily when a confession is made in anticipation of death, the possibility that it is the literal truth has to be considered. In the case of Lafayette Baker we can safely disregard the rule. We have a report on this man's attitude from Dr. Rickards[55] given during his testimony at the hearing on the codicil.

Rickards was a longtime friend and admirer of Baker, but obviously not a confidant. He testified ". . . I knew Lafayette Baker and can tell you this, he was a very kind and generous man. Much of the false things which had been written about him gave him worry. It made no difference whether it was good or bad, if it was untruthful, it worried him. He was very apprehensive about what history would say about him. He wanted it to be accurate. He often told me of his concern about this." Asked if he believed all General Baker wrote about himself in his biography, the doctor said, "Yes, he was a truthful man."

The doctor didn't know about the confession his patient had written in which he admitted having helped to murder Abraham Lincoln. And the same document was an indirect confession that he had masterminded the judicial murder of four persons as accomplices in the assassination, at least two of whom—Paine and Atzerodt—had taken no part in it whatever. We find not a vestige of regret or repentence in Baker's view of posterity according to Dr. Richards. But we do find support for our previous estimate of the detective's attitude to his profession. It galled him to think that his masterpiece of treachery would never be known or appreciated as a masterpiece. He "wanted it to be accurate." Now there is a truth within a lie! There was only one thing which took precedence over his desire to be known as the arch deceiver of all time, only one thing which would prompt him to give the "credit" for having planned a *perfect murder of a U. S. president* to anyone else: His obsession to take vengeance upon Stanton.

Baker was so delighted at newspaper accounts of his accomplishments in treachery that he published them verbatim in his biography, sometimes with pious though half-hearted denials, but more often with the comment that extreme measures were necessary in his war against subversives. His fixed practice was to take credit for anything his subordinates or associates did which he thought was an accomplishment. He must have had a long battle with himself before deciding to give Stanton the leading role in the plot against Lincoln.

As a matter of fact, he must have reached that decision during the period between the writing of his first and second messages—providing the longer one in simple cipher was written last, as seems to be the case. Thus, having been written at different times—possibly months apart—the two messages can be taken as *separate revelations which didn't necessarily supplement each other.*

The first and shorter of the two messages, dated 2-5-68 (a month before the impeachment trial began), is a statement of the general origin of the assassination in the form of an allegory.

Baker was so wholly absorbed with methods of revenge in the two years between his dismissal and the date of this message that the allegory was surely not a spur-of-the-moment creation, but the product of concentration over a period of weeks or months. Thus it was not sloppy, but said exactly what its author wanted to say.

In the cases of both Baker and Stanton, the assertion that "each planned that he should be king" seems accurate in a figurative sense. Whether this also described the ambitions of the *third* conspirator remains a question, since we have no clue to his identity from Baker (see Appendix K, "The Unknown Conspirator").

The implied charges against Stanton are limited to (1) his having had advance knowledge of Lincoln's assassination and (2) his having taken advantage of the situation that act created. *This message does not say Stanton was the instigator.*

When we reread the allegory apart from the later and longer cipher message, its meaning is much different from when both are read together and the statements in the second are used to interpret the allegory written much earlier.

In the first place, it does *not* say that "a Judas, a Brutus and a spy" conspired *together* to bring about Lincoln's death. It merely says there were three individuals in Washington who knew but did not trust each other—and that each hoped to become the ultimate power (king) in the nation when that death occurred. "They went on for"—they *waited* for—the day when the President would be killed.

The expression "one of the sons of Brutus" seems to associate Booth with the person characterized as "Brutus." But the fact that John Wilkes Booth happened to be one of the sons of Junius *Brutus* Booth was a coincidence which merely added an extra twist to Baker's riddle. If he had wanted to identify "Brutus" as a particular politician—as he did with "Judas" and Stanton—he could have found a way to do so. Evidently he did not.

The process by which both "Judas" and "Brutus" fell from grace was not shown as having been connected with the assassination in any way. Their political fortunes simply declined in the new, postwar situation.

Summarizing the allegory, then: It doesn't say who was the instigator. It intends to cast suspicion on Stanton without giving him "credit" for planning the murder. It intends to *conceal* the identity of "Brutus." It intends to assert that he (Baker) had a hand in the seemingly perfect crime.

The second cipher message appears to have been written *after* May 26, when Stanton was out of office, yet in hopes of recouping his fortunes by promoting the election of Grant and being appointed to high office in that administration. In spite of the denunciations of his critics, Stanton enjoyed considerable popularity in the North. His political ties with Grant and the Radicals were still intact. His career had taken a drastic turn for the worse, but as of that date neither he nor Baker would have assumed he was washed up.

Baker evidently felt he would have to be more direct in his accusations in order to deal Stanton a fatal blow—having already resigned himself to being destroyed by the same blow. His second message spelled out the charge that the War Secretary had organized the assassination and that Eckert had made the arrangements at Stanton's bidding.

When this message and the allegory are read together, there seems to be an implication that Eckert was the person characterized as "Brutus," simply because this was the only other name mentioned. But references to Eckert show him only as following Stanton's orders and not as a principal conspirator. In addition, Thomas Eckert's actual position in the government rules him out as "Brutus" who, if Baker's allegory was a sound one, would have to have been a close associate of Lincoln who held a high enough office to hope to step into the President's shoes when he died. The relationship between Caesar and Brutus was one of friendship between men on nearly the same political level. Lincoln *was* friendly with Eckert, but as an amiable chief executive would be with a subordinate far down in the hierarchy, whose function in the telegraph office brought them into daily contact.

So Baker, when the second message was composed, still had no intention of identifying "Brutus"—and allowed him to remain the *unknown* member of the triumvirate which wanted Lincoln dead.

The really glaring omission from Baker's coded messages was the lack of any reference to the attack upon Seward.

At the Trial, this had been an integral part of the alleged "conspiracy." The detective's failure to include the Seward attack in his exposé may be equated with Stanton's initial reaction to the incident—a baffled curiosity which absorbed his interest far beyond the more staggering news of the President's murder, at which he showed only small surprise. One would judge from the similar reactions of these two that the attempt to kill Seward was an unexpected postscript to the other crime, not anticipated by either of them.

So we find ourselves again with the unavoidable conclusion that Seward's attempted assassination was a side transaction between Lewis Powell and some so-far unknown member of the second echelon. As background for such a theory, we have this undeniable fact: It was open season on cabinet officers on Friday, April 14, 1865—for *anyone* who had advance knowledge that Abraham Lincoln was to be shot at Ford's that night. If timed to coincide with Lincoln's murder, the Seward attack was *sure* to be taken as the work of the same assassin or assassins.

The detective's direct accusation of Stanton, as the editors of Civil War Times pointed out, would have been more convincing if he had been more careful about his dates.

His yarn that the furious Stanton sent a telegram to General Weitzel on April 13, countermanding Lincoln's order with regard to assembly of the Virginia legislature, apparently refers to a telegram Stanton sent Weitzel on April 9, telling him to clear all negotiations with the Virginia committee headed by Judge John A. Campbell through the War Department. Lincoln *had* agreed to a parley with this committee. But on the twelfth, undoubtedly due to the hornet's nest the idea had stirred up—with Stanton the noisiest hornet—Lincoln countermanded his *own* order of April 6 and called off the parley.[56]

Thus, any such countermanding order by Stanton on the thirteenth would have been superfluous, and there is no official record of one.

When we recall that Baker returned to Washington from New York on April 9 and left again for New York on the morning of the 13th, we see that he *might* have witnessed "an insane tyrade" by Stanton on *April 9*, if there was one, in connection with his telegram to General Weitzel. But his accusation goes on to say that, after countermanding Lincoln's order on the thirteenth, Stanton told "Tom" to "be off . . . and see to the arrangements." So if this incident took place at all, it would have to have been on the ninth—*the day before* "the tenth of April, Sixty-five when I first knew that the plan was in action."

Since Baker's knowledge that Lincoln was to be assassinated appears to have its beginning date on March 19, 1865—the date of his "Watson" letter to John Surratt—it's probable that April 10 was the day *he* informed Stanton of the project, rather than vice versa.

By interpretation, then, the cipher messages, rather than implicating Stanton, further strengthen our belief that Lafayette Baker both conceived and directed the assassination of Lincoln.

general conclusions

Abraham Lincoln's murder, in principle, was the result of a philosophical error on his own part. His desire for the preservation of the Union with as little bloodletting as possible was so intense that he accepted the fallacy that *the end justifies the means.*

It was Seward who urged the suspension of habeas corpus and introduced the practice of arbitrary arrests to preserve internal security. Stanton appropriated these secret police powers for his War Department and, with Baker as his agent, built a political terror instrument for his own use which was free of any effective restraint—as long as Lincoln would tolerate it. First one and then the other of these cabinet advisors impressed upon the President that such a weapon was essential to the defeat of the Union's opponents.

An organization of this kind—a secret police bureau—was contrary to Lincoln's personal and political creed, regardless of necessity. He had the authority to reform or abolish it at any time he was so inclined. But he was prevailed upon to accept it as a necessary evil of civil war. His assassination was a direct result of the moral corruption of those associated with this alien institution and its inevitable corollary—the perversion of justice by military tribunals.

The essential truth of a situation—even one as artfully veiled as the assassination conspiracy—is readily apparent when the X-ray of logic is not short-circuited by prejudice. As evidence we submit two paragraphs from an editorial written exactly two weeks after the assassination by a logical journalist who was not emotionally involved in the event:*

> The results of the victories gained by the Union Army may now all be nullified!—that is, from the political point of view. The hopes which the South had taken from Mr. Lincoln's first declarations may now all be disappointed forever. These hopes were alive, and you have seen how gladly we hailed them. But Mr. Lincoln's death came at a time propitious to the glorification of his memory. He died at a time when he was preaching reconciliation and the forgetting of the past, *when he was nobly repressing the blameworthy exultation of the victorious faction.* [Author's italics]
>
> Is it not possible that the assassin may have arisen from the ranks of this very faction, foiled in its dreadful schemes? Who knows? One may well wonder. Civil wars have this horrible aspect—that they bring to the surface from the very depths of society creatures whose unleashed passions know no limit whatever. The re-establishment of peace in America meant the ruin of those newly created generals, of those agents whose powers, augmented even more by the suspension of the habeas corpus, had brought about such excesses.

*From an editorial by Ernest Dréolle in *La Patrie*, Paris, April 28, 1865. Reprinted in *Lincoln As They Saw Him*, edited by Herbert Mitgang (New York and Toronto: Rinehart & Co., Inc., 1956), pp. 490-91.

18

major Thomas T. Eckert

The name of Thomas Eckert has come up often during our study of the assassination conspiracy, suggesting that he was deeply involved in it—apart from Lafayette Baker's direct accusation that Eckert "made all the arrangements." We do not, as yet, have enough concrete evidence on the Major's activities prior to and after the assassination to be able to take Baker's charges against Eckert at face value. Also, if the theory that Baker himself initiated and directed the President's murder is correct, it would seem that any arrangements Eckert might have made would have been at the behest of *Baker,* rather than Stanton—whom the detective accused as instigator, with "Tom" as his agent.

On the other hand, we have noted an opening in the roster of the genuine conspirators which has not yet been filled—that of a "local agent" of the second echelon to keep an eye on the members of the forward echelon in Washington and see that they completed their assignments. The presence of such an overseer would have been particularly necessary in connection with Lewis Powell. Even if it were possible for one scoundrel to trust another, Baker hadn't known Powell long enough to have had implicit confidence in him. He may even have hired the ex-soldier solely on the recommendation of John Surratt. A small-time hoodlum like Herold might have been willing to work for *promised* rewards, but Powell was one to insist upon substantial hand money in advance. Thus Baker would have *needed* a trustworthy agent in the Capitol to see that Lewis Powell didn't skip out without earning the blood money in his pocket.

In addition, the thesis that the attack upon Seward was *not* a part of Baker's original plan—that it was a separate arrangement Powell had made with someone else—creates still another opening on the conspiratorial roster: the individual who closed the deal with Powell for the assassination of Seward.

Logically, the person who hired Powell to kill Seward would have been someone who knew all about the young man's contract to arrange for the murder of Lincoln and realized that Friday, April 14, was a perfect opportunity to liquidate any other high officials whom *someone* might wish to have liquidated. If a second assassination were arranged to occur shortly after the first one, John Wilkes Booth, the expendable murderer of Lincoln, would be blamed for *both* crimes—exactly as Stanton's first wire to General Dix suggested. With the capture of Booth a following day—dead, of course—by Lieutenant Baker and the six detectives, *both* crimes would have been solved and both cases closed.

Now, we could speculate that Lewis Powell, having agreed in New York to supervise the President's murder, shopped around in political circles to see if anyone else wanted any cabinet members disposed of in the same operation. But the idea is frivolous on the face of it. Powell being a Confederate deserter with no logical entrée to Northern political circles, the Seward deal would have to have been arranged by an intermediary who (1) was in touch with a person or persons who could gain by Seward's death and (2) was in close touch with Powell in the preparations for the murder to take place at Ford's on April 14.

The Number One suspect as this intermediary, then, would be Lafayette Baker's "local agent" in the original plot, who would have qualified on both counts. As to the *identity* of the "local agent" for Lincoln's murder and the "intermediary" for the assassination of Seward, Baker's second cipher message provides us with a suitable candidate for investigation in Major Thomas T. Eckert who, according to Baker, "made all the arrangements."

Without ignoring the possibility that Major Eckert *might* have been an innocent party against whom Baker held a grudge, due to his close association with the hated Stanton, the Major's behavior on some occasions we have seen was suspicious enough to justify our checking him out more thoroughly.

To begin with, Eckert and Baker were involved *together* in some of the most suspicious incidents of the pursuit of Booth and the framing of Louis Paine.

On April 26, Stanton ordered *both* Baker and Eckert to intercept the steamer *John S. Ide* returning to Washington with the body of Booth and the prisoner Herold and take her direct to the Navy Yard. There they were to transfer the assassin's corpse and the prisoner to the *Montauk* and place a guard over them.[1]

On April 27, *both* Baker and Eckert were appointed by Stanton to serve on the committee (largely composed of the War Secretary's satellites) which identified the body as Booth's.[2]

That same night, according to a most reliable source, *both* Baker and Eckert participated in the clandestine burial of Booth's body—which was for the purpose, we have proposed, of preventing an autopsy.[3] In his biography, Baker said *only his cousin,* Lieutenant Baker, was with him during the secret burial, thereby denying his cousin had returned to Garrett's for the "field glass" that night. So at the time his biography was written he apparently had no intention of implicating Eckert. But in 1867, before the house judiciary committee, he hinted that he might have given Booth's suppressed "diary" to Eckert,[4] though he had made quite a point in his book about having given it to Stanton.

There was a unity of purpose between Baker's use of his "handbill" to entrap Louis Paine and Eckert's receipt of the Bunker Hill coat "with the contents of the pockets"—which contents vanished thereafter.

During the period in which the preparations for Lincoln's assassination were being made, a faint shadow that may have been Major Eckert's was seen in a couple of suspicious instances:

Mrs. Murray, landlady at the Herndon House where "Wood" was staying, testified that a "gentleman" had visited her mysterious boarder once at dinnertime and remained talking with him at the table after she and the other diners had left.[5] She did not see him among the prisoners in the dock, so if he was a conspirator, he was an unidentified one. One would suppose that *anyone* who visited Powell at his assassination headquarters during that period was connected with the project in some way. And then again, a Major "Somebody" was a visitor at the Surratt house shortly before the assassination.[6]

During the whole course of the Trial, from the original arrests to the executions of the four who were hanged, Major Eckert was constantly though unobtrusively involved in the affair. Numerous statements describing affairs at the arsenal where the prisoners were confined mention the presence of Major Eckert with or near the prisoners. He was on the scene there practically all the time—and this, in itself, was singular in view of his official capacity in the War Department: head of the Office of the Military Telegraph. Just which of his official duties in connection with military communications he was performing at the arsenal is not evident.

In short, even these bits and pieces of information on Eckert's actual and possible activities show him to have been closely associated with Colonel Baker and the prosecution of the alleged "conspirators."

the bates account of Eckert

Thanks to the literary efforts of a young man who worked under Eckert as manager of the telegraph office, then followed his wartime boss to Western Union when he became president of that firm, we have an excellent source of detailed information on Major Thomas T. Eckert's activities relating to the assassination and Trial. In 1907, David Homer Bates—who by then been an executive and associate of Eckert's in Western Union for over forty years—published his wartime recollections in a book titled *Lincoln in the Telegraph Office.* His subject was represented as the history of the Military Telegraph Bureau of the War Department during the Civil War. But since Eckert had been the head of that department, the book was in effect his biography.

In 1907 Eckert was an old man of eighty-six, though still active as Chairman of the Board of Western Union. Bates was in his middle sixties. The reader of his book receives the impression that the two men had been friends as well as business associates over the years, since all references to Eckert were uniformly complimentary. In presenting information about the older man's wartime experiences, Bates quoted official documents of the period in abundance, but made it quite clear he was quoting Eckert himself with regard to the gentleman's personal connection with certain events. In other instances he told things Eckert wouldn't have admitted—let alone have asserted.

Bates didn't claim his book was written with the collaboration of Eckert, nor that his firm's chairman of the board had been consulted during the writing. If he had, the reader might suppose the older man was far gone in senility. For this book is one of the most extraordinary publications dealing with the Civil War period. David Homer Bates was evidently a man in whom secrets had been fermenting for almost half a century, secrets he would rather not have told while Eckert was still living. But time went on, and Bates himself was getting up in years, while Eckert—ten years older—showed no inclination to retire, let alone shuffle off this mortal coil. If he were ever going to tell his story, Bates may have reasoned, he would have to get on with it, because the biographical subject of his book, Thomas T. Eckert, might very well outlive him.

On the title page of *Lincoln in the Telegraph Office,* underneath the author's name, Bates presented his credentials: "Manager of the War Department Telegraph Office, and *cipher-operator,* 1861-1866."

The key words are "cipher-operator." *Cipher,* according to the dictionary, is "A method of secret writing that substitutes other characters for the letters intended. . . ." The substance of the book is such that Bates found repeated opportunities to remind his readers that he had been a "cipher-operator," one whose wartime service consisted of sending and receiving top secret messages in code. He also devoted two entire chapters to explaining how cipher codes and cryptograms were developed, used, and occasionally broken. And he added that he, Eckert, and two other men who had also followed Eckert to Western Union had helped to develop the Cipher System used by the Union Army during the Civil War.[7]

In short, by the time the reader of Bates' book reaches Chapter XXVI, entitled "The Assassination," he has acquired a great deal of information about the author, as well as about other things. He has found Mr. Bates to be worldly, articulate, and a thoroughly competent writer; careful, not to say meticulous, in his documentation; very well acquainted with Thomas Eckert from fifty years' association; *intimately* acquainted with the behind-the-scenes affairs of the Lincoln administration, due to his wartime function as cipher-operator; devoted to the memory of Abraham Lincoln as a man and as a statesman; and finally, qualified by his long experience with cipher codes and cryptograms to think and speak obliquely, to express himself in such a way as to convey two meanings with the same words—one an obvious meaning, the other literally *written between the lines*. In addition, he kept a private journal of his wartime experiences.

So much for the introduction to David Homer Bates, biographer of Thomas T. Eckert. Now we shall see what Mr. Bates had to say about the assassination of Abraham Lincoln.

lack of protection for Lincoln

The narrator began his account with the arrival of General Grant in Washington on April 13 and the illumination of the city that night in celebration of the Union victory.

"Extra precautions were taken by the authorities to protect the President and Lieutenant-General against expected attempts to kidnap or kill them," wrote Bates, "because of secret service reports that plans had been made to accomplish such evil designs during the excitement of that occasion."

He went on to illustrate the effectiveness of these "extra precautions" on Thursday night by noting that Grant had attended a reception at Stanton's house and, *"but for the safeguards provided,* it is more than likely that the efforts of O'Laughlin, one of the conspirators, to enter Stanton's house and execute his murderous task, might have been successful.

"John C. Hatter, now of Brooklyn, one of the War Department telegraph staff, testified at the trial of the conspirators in May, 1865, that one of them—Michael O'Laughlin—was in the crowd at Stanton's house the night of the illumination, and had tried to enter. In fact, he reached the front hall, but Hatter, who was uneasy over his presence, induced him to leave."

The absence of any *safeguards* whatever is evident in a stranger's being able to walk into the front hall of the house without being stopped by anyone until he encountered an off-duty *telegrapher* who happened to be there. In looking up the testimony of Hatter at the Trial, Bates would surely have refreshed his memory (if it needed refreshing) that the defense had produced no less than six reliable witnesses, including a Union naval officer, to account for virtually every minute of O'Laughlin's time on both Thursday the 13th *and* Friday the 14th and prove beyond any reasonable doubt that he had not been within a mile of Stanton's house during that period. The evidence that all three witnesses who claimed to have seen O'Laughlin at Stanton's that night (Hatter, Major Knox, and Stanton's son David—all three connected with the War Department) were lying in their teeth was overwhelming.[8]

Bates was just warming up for his larger task with a veiled thrust at one of the employees in his office who had sold his soul to the military commission. Hatter, still alive and living in Brooklyn, must have winced to read Bates' conclusion as to the consequences of his perjury:

"It was mainly on the strength of Hatter's testimony that O'Laughlin was found guilty. He died in prison at Dry Tortugas, Florida, September 23, 1867."

The narrator next turned his attention to the now famous incident of Friday afternoon when Lincoln walked over to Stanton's office to invite him to attend the theater party at Ford's that evening—General Grant having broken his engagement to attend with the Lincolns at the urging of *Secretary Stanton.*

In telling this story, the first cat Bates let out of the bag was that Stanton *knew* Lincoln's life was in danger beforehand—that he made a vigorous protest against the theater party, "having in mind the numerous threats of assassination which had come to his notice through secret service agents and otherwise." Then came the details of how Stanton persuaded Grant to back out at the last moment with the argument that newspaper reports that both Lincoln and Grant would attend the theater would attract a large crowd "and evil-disposed persons would be better able to carry out their plans."

Bates' statement that it was Stanton who persuaded General Grant to commit an outrageous breech of etiquette by canceling his acceptance of the President's theater invitation was confirmed by the General's cipher-operator, Samuel Beckwith, in a newspaper article he wrote in 1913.[9] It should be noted, though, that the article was written five years after Bates' book was published, and Beckwith may just have been echoing Bates.

More to the point, Washington *evening* newspapers *did* print announcements on Friday, April 14 that General and Mrs. Grant would attend Ford's Theater with the Lincolns that night,[10] and the Grants *did* leave Washington for Burlington, New Jersey, on the 6:00 P.M. train rather than keeping their engagement with the President.[11] The time of day when Grant was prevailed upon to send his excuses to Lincoln is not known, though Bates implies it was fairly early in the morning. Thus, in spite of Stanton's alleged fears that the General's presence would swell the crowd at Ford's and increase the danger to the President, he must have made no effort to have the newspaper announcements canceled after he knew Grant wouldn't attend.

The upshot of Bates' revelation, then, was an obvious conclusion most damning to Stanton—whom he professed to admire: That Stanton knew of the danger to Lincoln's life; and that the absence of Grant without cancellation of the newspaper announcements would protect Grant, but not the President, from the supposedly increased danger. Bates might have expected his readers to relate this situation to one of the best-known and most scandalous aspects of the assassination—that President Lincoln was allowed to attend the theater that night accompanied only by John F. Parker, a notoriously unreliable member of the Washington police force, who left his post in front of Box 7 to watch the play from the balcony, leaving Lincoln entirely unguarded.[12] Consequently, Bates' implied accusation (unconfirmed by any other evidence, as of 1907) was that Stanton, with full knowledge that Lincoln was in great danger, failed to lift a finger to protect him.

This was only the opening gun of Bates' barrage at Stanton and Eckert, the pop of a cap pistol compared to the blast he delivered next. We'll let him continue in his own words (italics added by this author):

> On the morning of the 14th, Lincoln made his usual visit to the War Department and told Stanton that Grant had canceled his engagement for that evening. The stern and cautious secretary again urged the President to give up the theater-party, and when he found that he was set on going, told him *he ought to have a competent guard.* Lincoln said: "Stanton, do you know that Eckert can break a poker over his arm?"
>
> Stanton, not knowing what was coming, looked around in surprise and answered "No; why do you ask such a question?" Lincoln said: "Well, Stanton, I have seen Eckert break five pokers, one after the other, over his arm, and I am thinking he would be the kind of man to go with me this evening. May I take him?"
>
> Stanton, still unwilling to encourage the theater project, said that *he had some important work for Eckert that evening, and could not spare him.* Lincoln replied: "Well, I will ask the Major myself, and he can do your work tomorrow." He then went into the cipher-room, told Eckert of his plans for the evening, and said he wanted him to be one of the party, but that Stanton said he could not spare him. "Now, Major," he added, "come along. You can do Stanton's work tomorrow, and Mrs. Lincoln and I want you with us."
>
> Eckert thanked the President but, knowing Stanton's views, *and that Grant had been induced to decline,* told the President he could not accept *because the work which the Secretary referred to must be done that evening, and could not be put off.*
>
> "Very well," Lincoln then said, "I shall take Major Rathbone along, *because Stanton insists upon having someone to protect me; but I should much rather have you, Major,* since I know you can break a poker over your arm."
>
> It is idle to conjecture what might have been the result if the alert and vigorous Eckert had accompanied Lincoln to Ford's Theater that night. *Had he done so, the probabilities are that in view of Eckert's previous knowledge of the plot to kidnap or kill the President, Booth might have been prevented from firing the fatal shot, and Lincoln spared to finish his great work.*

The setting in which Bates told this story—in a late chapter of a book in which both Eckert and Stanton had been discussed in terms of unvarying respect and admiration—may explain why it has become an accepted part of the *history* of the assassination. It was simply not a setting in which one would expect to find any statements detrimental to its two principal characters. That was the genius of David Homer Bates, cipher-operator and expert in cryptograms.

Here we read the story with its camouflage of praise removed—and see that it is virtually impossible even to *interpret* the words in any other terms than those of denunciation:

First, Stanton's insistence that the President should have a competent guard because of the apparent danger. Second, his refusal to let Eckert act as guard on the pretext that "he had some important work for Eckert that evening." Third, Eckert's refusal in view of the fact "that Grant had been induced to decline" and his echoing of Stanton's pretext in his statement that the *work* in question "could not be put off." And finally, Bates' conjecture as to the different outcome if Eckert had gone to the theater with Lincoln—*not* that Eckert's strength and alertness would have enabled him to overcome the assassin and thus save the President's life; rather, "that *in view of Eckert's previous knowledge of the plot to kidnap or kill the President, Booth might have been prevented* from firing the fatal shot. . . ."

If Eckert's *previous knowledge* of the plot was so precise that he would have been literally poised by the door, ready to pounce upon Booth when he entered, his refusal to go to the theater can only be interpreted as showing that he himself was a party to the plot and wanted Lincoln dead. It would follow, perhaps, that Booth would have been prevented from *attempting* the assassination with Eckert on hand, because Eckert would be held responsible if Lincoln were killed—thus would have to make more than a mere show of thwarting the assassin.

The implied connection between Grant having "been induced to decline" and Eckert's refusal to go to the theater is two-edged. If urging Grant to stay away was an indication that it would be *dangerous* to be in the President's box that night, Eckert was indicted as a coward. If Eckert was assuming Stanton didn't want him at the theater *either*, it followed that Stanton knew Lincoln would be in danger and *didn't want him protected from it.*

When we consider the actual words Bates used in 1907, in view of what had happened that night at Ford's forty-two years earlier—and the suspicions of Stanton that had been voiced abroad in the interim—the expressions "important work" and "work which . . . could not be put off" would have to have been chosen with great care to convey the desired incrimination. A writer who had no intention to incriminate would realize he had better choose other words.

Moreover, on the second page following, Bates stated that he had been on duty in the telegraph office that night and made it entirely clear that Major Eckert was not at the office during the evening to do any "important work" for Stanton.

Another consideration is that David Homer Bates was the *sole* authority for this story. Eckert had never referred to Lincoln's visit to the War Department and request for his company at the theater. In fact, in the second chapter earlier, the narrator had made a point of saying that "Eckert's reticence in regard to all confidential Civil War matters with which he had to do has been so marked as justly to entitle him to the sobriquet of 'Silent Eckert' . . ."[13] A few days after the assassination Stanton told General James B. Fry that Lincoln had stopped at his office the afternoon of *April 14,* but only to exchange affectionate congratulations on the end of "bloody fratricidal war." Later, before a congressional committee, he declared under oath that the President visited his office for the last time on *April 13* to write out a telegram.[14]

There were no other witnesses to the incident—unless Bates witnessed it himself, which he did not claim specifically in his book. In 1895 he had written an article about the assassination for the New York *Independent;* and in 1900 he wrote a paper on the subject for the Ohio Society of New York. He did not mention the episode of Stanton's and Eckert's refusals in either of these earlier accounts. But he did say he was on duty at the telegraph office on the afternoon of the assassination and that Lincoln had "made his accustomed call."[15]

We would judge from this that he didn't feel the time was ripe for his revelations at the earlier two writings, but had changed his mind by 1907 and decided to fire away. If he did witness the scene, the request and refusal of protection—even the words in which the refusals were couched—may not have impressed him as sinister until long after the assassination. But the self-incrimination in the quoted words of Eckert and Stanton was so greatly increased by Bates' interpolation of them—the *thoughts* he said prompted the words—that his intention to incriminate can hardly be doubted.

The author's timing of Mr. Lincoln's visit to the War Department—"On the morning of the 14th"—was probably incorrect, since Lincoln, Stanton, and Grant all attended a long cabinet meeting from 11:00 A.M. to 2:00 P.M. that day. According to Frederick W. Seward, who presided at the meeting as Acting Secretary of State in place of his injured father, Lincoln asked Grant to the theater right after the meeting and the General declined "as he had a previous engagement."[16] Seward's omission of Grant's earlier acceptance which was announced in the newspapers and to Ford's Theater before 11:00 A.M. may have been because he had not heard of the acceptance.

In any case, a difference in the time of day (easily misplaced in memory) does not impair Bates' story. The memoirs of William Crook, one of Lincoln's bodyguards, stated that he conducted the President to the War Department late in the afternoon, so this may have been the visit in question, though Crook didn't go inside to witness the exchange Bates described.[17]

The bodyguard did, however, repeat a curious remark of the President's on the way over which might have had a connection with Mr. Lincoln's request for Eckert's company that night.

Lincoln had turned to him suddenly and said, "Crook, do you know, I believe there are men who want to take my life?" Then, after a pause, "And I have no doubt they will do it."

Taken off guard by the positive manner in which this comment was made, Crook was at a loss for words, but presently asked why the President thought so. The answer was not enlightening.

"Other men have been assassinated. . . . I have perfect confidence in those around me. . . . I know no one could do it and escape alive. But if it is to be done, it is impossible to prevent it."[18]

The possibility of his own death by murder wasn't new to Lincoln. He had had dozens of threats during the war years. A number of his close associates had expressed anxiety over rumors of assassination quite recently, but Lincoln hadn't seemed to take them seriously. Only a few days previously his friend Ward Lamon, before departing for Richmond, had begged the Chief Executive to promise not to visit a theater in his absence.[19] The arrangement of the party at Ford's for Friday evening didn't suggest that Lincoln was greatly concerned for his safety.

That comment to Crook sounded like a new train of thought, perhaps set in motion by something he had heard in the last hour (or perhaps by Grant's strange behavior), something which raised a question as to the loyalty of those around him. If these remarks to Crook—particularly the one about the impossibility of preventing his murder "if it is to be done"—preceded the dialogue Bates described, the President's request for Eckert's attendance at the theater because he could break a poker over his arm appears in a new light. Lincoln could be quite oblique upon occasion. Strength had nothing to do with thwarting an assassin with a pistol. If someone had warned him not to trust Eckert, the danger from that quarter might be less if he had Eckert where he could keep an eye on him during the theater party.

"Very well, I shall take Major Rathbone along, because Stanton insists upon having someone to protect me; *but I should much rather have you, Major. . . .*"

Support for the theory that Lincoln *knew* he could not trust those around him is found in a recent work on the assassination. According to this account, a friend of Robert Todd Lincoln visited him shortly before his death in 1926. The visitor found President Lincoln's son burning some of his father's private papers and remonstrated. He received the reply that "the papers contained documentary evidence of the treason of a member of Lincoln's cabinet, and he thought it best for all that such evidence be destroyed."[20]

Eckert on the night of the assassination

Bates continued his account of how he received the dreadful news at the telegraph office where he was on duty—the shooting of Lincoln and wild rumors of attacks or threatened attacks upon Seward, Johnson, Stanton, and others. When he turned to the subject of Major Eckert's activities on the night of the assassination, he slipped into the technique he had used in earlier portions of his book—making it clear that he was repeating the story *Eckert* told in later years, not the established facts of the situation.

". . . After an hour of this awful suspense, we received word from Major Eckert, who had gone quickly to Secretary Stanton's house on K Street, and from there with the Secretary to the house on Tenth Street, opposite the theater, to which the President had been carried after having been shot by John Wilkes Booth. This message merely assured us of the present safety of Stanton, while confirming our worst fears concerning the President."

Bates added that two men from his office had been in the audience at Ford's. One, Thomas A. Laird, "ran to Eckert's house on Thirteenth Street." The other, George C. Maynard, reported to the telegraph office.

Now, Bates had a message to convey, in addition to the obvious sense of his words. But it was a message addressed to students of the Civil War episode centered around the assassination of Lincoln—not to the casual reader who would accept what he said uncritically. In other words, he expected some of the more glaring inaccuracies he inserted from time to time in his account of the assassination to cause someone to stop and wonder—why had he suddenly lapsed into errors of fact toward the end of a work distinguished by careful research and thorough documentation?

His account of Eckert's movements right after the assassination, related to those of Stanton, was startlingly incomplete and incorrect. He said, in effect, that Eckert was notified of Lincoln's shooting by Laird and went immediately to Stanton's house and from there "with the Secretary," to Ford's Theater—or rather, to the Peterson house across the street from it. He omitted the fact that both he and Stanton had *first* stopped at Seward's, though they did not arrive there together.

The thoroughly established facts were that Stanton had been notified of the attack upon Seward while he was preparing to retire at his own home on K Street. He went directly to the Seward house on Fifteenth Street. He learned of the shooting of Lincoln later, probably at Seward's.[21] It was there he met Gideon Welles and agreed to go to Ford's with him in the same carriage with Judge Carter and General Meigs.

"At this moment," wrote Mr. Welles in his diary,[22] "Major Eckert rode up on horseback beside the carriage and protested vehemently against Stanton's going to Tenth Street; *he said he had just come from there* (this author's italics) and he considered it very unsafe for the Secretary of War to expose himself." Stanton appeared to hesitate, but Welles insisted it was their duty to go; so the carriage moved off with an escort of two soldiers.

Stanton's stop at the Seward house wasn't an obscure detail of the known story. It was a *fact* of the situation, if only because the War Secretary had referred to it in his first wire to General Dix which was published in all the nation's newspapers.

Bates, by his omission, was revealing Eckert's desire to disassociate both himself and Mr. Stanton from the events at Secretary Seward's house that night. In Stanton's case, this was pointless, since Stanton had been *summoned* there. But Eckert's arrival, fully dressed and on horseback, at around eleven o'clock was a much different matter!

The exact time of Lincoln's shooting isn't established, but 10:20 P.M. is a common estimate. The audience didn't realize immediately what had happened; there was great confusion; Thomas Laird would have had to wait some minutes—possibly ten or fifteen—to know certainly that the President had been hit in a vital spot and that his condition was critical. At the very earliest, he couldn't have left to inform Major Eckert before half-past ten—and it was several blocks to Eckert's house *on foot.*

When he arrived there, perhaps by 10:40 P.M., though probably later, he found Eckert in his dressing room *shaving,* so the story goes.[23] Laird's news was that Lincoln had been shot at Ford's; he could not have known about the attack on Seward far uptown. In any case, Eckert had a mere fifteen or twenty minutes in which to dress, acquire a saddled and bridled horse, ride at least four blocks to Ford's, fight through the frantic mob around the theater to make inquiries, and ride some six blocks back to Seward's to be there when Stanton and Welles came out to their carriage.

The time element is such that Eckert's itinerary, indicated by his loud assertion which Welles heard—that he had already been to Tenth Street—is very hard to believe. One would judge that if Laird really did find him at his house shaving, he would have to have ridden directly to Seward's to be there around 11:00 P.M. And having been notified that *Lincoln,* not Seward, had been attacked, his behavior in riding to Lafayette Square—in the opposite direction from Ford's—would take a lot of explaining.

The uncertainty as to what Major Eckert was doing that evening when he was alleged to have been performing some "important work" for Stanton may be related to the fact that the commercial telegraph lines serving Washington were put out of commission for two hours that night, beginning fifteen minutes after the crime at Ford's. Consequently no news of the assassination or alarms for the assassins could be sent out until after midnight—except over the military lines, which were under the control of Major Eckert. Stanton's first wire to General Dix wasn't dispatched until 2:15 A.M.

Dr. Eisenschiml covered this situation with his usual thoroughness[24] and cited the Major's testimony on the subject before the house judiciary committee in 1867. He admitted under oath that the lines had not been *cut*, as originally believed, but had been short-circuited at the main batteries by a ground wire thrown over the main wires. Service could thus be restored simply by removing the ground wire and the interruption effected without the least damage to equipment.

In other words, this was the work of a technician in telegraphy, not an amateur. Also, since the main batteries could not be approached by an outsider, the job would almost have to have been done by someone who had normal access to the installation. Eckert stated he had been "too busy" to investigate that night; yet, his function being the supervision of the telegraph system, investigation of the matter during *and* after the interruption would appear to have been his prime responsibility.

Considering the mystery as to what Major Eckert *was* doing that night, Mr. Bates' revelation about the "important work" for Stanton, his incredibly prompt arrival at the Seward house, and implied denial that either he or Stanton was there at all, the Major is a fair target for suspicion.

Could his unconcern about the communication blackout have been because he already knew *by whom* the wires were short-circuited, as well as *how*? Did he wish to disassociate himself from the scene of the Seward attack because investigation might reveal his connections with Seward's tall, black-haired assailant—not Paine, but Powell? Might we have found the answer to the puzzle of how the intruder knew on which floor and in which room to find his victim?

interest in convicting Paine

Bates' explanation of how the dispatch of a search party from Washington, upon receipt of a wire from Beckwith, resulted in the capture of Booth conformed to the ridiculous explanation advanced by Stanton and Eckert. Here again was *Eckert's* version of the story—with no mention of Colonel Baker, Lieutenant Baker, or Colonel Conger; and Stanton credited with sending Lieutenant Doherty in pursuit. The *complete absence* of Baker's name in Bates' account of the assassination—which is to say, Eckert's—may be significant, since we know those two henchmen of Stanton worked practically as a *team* during the pursuit of Booth and the Trial of the "conspirators." When we recall that by '68 Baker's animosity toward Eckert was so intense that he accused him of making "all the arrangements" for the assassination, the possibility that Eckert was at least one of the "old friends" who wanted Baker dead seems well worth considering.

David Homer Bates' second and last chapter on the assassination concerned Major Eckert's extraordinary interest in the conviction of Louis Paine for the attack upon Seward—an interest which seems to have absorbed the chief of the telegraph office to the exclusion of everything else, from the night Paine was arrested to the hot July noon when he watched the tall prisoner walk to the gallows with fortitude and dignity that awed his executioners and left his spiritual counselor, the Rev. Dr. Gillette, heartbroken. Perhaps it was because so many were moved to wonder by the doomed man's manly bearing—inconsistent with the cowardly attack upon an invalid for which he was convicted—that Major Eckert felt it necessary to keep offering new "proof" of his guilt long after he was dead and in his grave.

This remarkable chapter (XXVII) is recommended to serious students of the assassination for careful analysis. For our purpose, the highlights will suffice. Bates' glowing description of the prisoner was quoted earlier. It began with, "Payne was a remarkable man, mentally and physically," and went on to portray him in a manner almost directly opposed to that popularized at the Conspiracy Trial—a bloodthirsty moron. He was believed, so Bates asserted, to be the only "conspirator" who enjoyed Booth's full confidence. But "he was silent and imperturbable, answering no questions. . . ."

"Might not others of our rulers be struck down?" asked the narrator. "Great fear and anxiety were felt by everyone, *and chiefly by Stanton* (V. S. italics), who deemed it a matter of vital importance to unravel quickly the thread of the murderous plot, and thus prevent further trouble." Not knowing where to begin, Stanton sent Assistant Secretaries Dana and Eckert to the *Saugus* in hopes that "Payne" might be led to talk.

"Dana soon tired of the task, but Eckert persevered in his efforts to break down the barriers between them. . . ."

The break came one day when the provost marshal was having Paine photographed, and the officer struck him on the arm because he kept moving his head. Eckert remonstrated officially, and Stanton upheld him and "directed that Payne should be placed in Eckert's custody, and he so remained until the day of his execution."

At the next meeting Paine expressed appreciation for Eckert's kindness, Bates said, and his custodian found other opportunities to do little favors for him and –

"It was after one of these incidents that Payne broke down, and confided many details of Booth's plot, which were of such a character as to lead to the belief that, with the exception of John H. Surratt . . . all the conspirators were then under lock and key, and that no further trouble might be expected from that source."

Let's pause for a moment to take cognizance of the skepticism of many who are so far unconvinced that Bates' chapters on the assassination may be taken other than literally—that the double meanings we have read into his account are imaginary, and that the discrepancies are due merely to faulty research or an elderly writer's inaccurate recollection on events long past.

In Chapter IV on "Cipher-Codes and Messages" Bates explained the method of setting up a cipher message to prevent its translation by unauthorized persons (pp. 49-50). A "key word" was inserted to indicate to the receiver which chart of substitute words should be referred to and the order of the words in the message. One or two "blind words" would be added at the end of each line to further confuse anyone trying to break the code. "The key-word and the blind words would be discarded by the cipher-operator when translating the despatch into English."

Thus, if Bates had written his two chapters on the assassination in a form of literary code, in which he wished to convey some intelligence beyond the literal meaning, he would have used a particular paragraph or incident as a key to translation. By his own definition, this key passage would be fictitious and would be discarded after it had served its purpose of revealing that parts of his account should not be taken literally.

We submit the following passages (p. 381) as the "key" David Homer Bates inserted to tell the reader to study his book as a cryptogram:

> Under instructions from the Secretary of War each of the conspirators on the *Saugus* was fitted with a hood over the head, with an opening for the nose and mouth, so that they might not communicate with each other. . . .
>
> Payne had asked for some tobacco, which Eckert did not have, but he obtained some before his next visit, and then in Payne's presence cut off a piece and put it into his own mouth, meantime watching Payne, whose eyes were fixed on the coveted morsel. Eckert then cut off a liberal piece and slipped it through the opening in the hood into Payne's mouth. The prisoner said that he never had anything to taste so good as that piece of tobacco.

In the following paragraph Bates told another incident in which Eckert guided Paine during his transfer from the monitor to the arsenal prison, because the hood he was wearing was a complete blindfold. He added this paragraph to make sure the reader wouldn't miss the point in the foregoing one—*that the hoods Stanton had ordered had no eyeholes.*

Paine was wearing a hood without any eyeholes; yet his eyes were fixed on the plug of tobacco Eckert was cutting!

If this was *not* the key to Bates' cryptogram telling of his suspicions that both Eckert and Stanton had been conspirators in the assassination of President Lincoln—if he could have written down such an incident without being aware of the absurdity it contained—he wouldn't have had the intelligence to *deliver* messages for Western Union, let alone discharge his executive responsibilities for half a century!

Since we contend that Louis Paine had nothing to do with Booth or the assassination plot, we shall refer the reader to *Lincoln in the Telegraph Office* for the details of the revelations Eckert claimed to have obtained from "Payne," and mention only the more fanciful samples here.

"Payne" named a gambling place in Baltimore as one rendezvous of the "conspirators" and mentioned a meeting conducted by a physician whose office was on Fayette Street. Eckert went there on the pretext of having indigestion and stole a picture of the doctor from the mantelpiece. He showed it to "Payne," who identified it.

Checking on another alleged rendezvous in Washington, Eckert found scraps of paper in the fireplace which he fitted together and discovered to be a "resolution" in Booth's script pertaining to abduction. He also found Dr. Mudd's name on a bit of paper.

The prisoner related three occasions on which he was close enough to the President to have killed him, but refrained—twice in the winter of '65 and once with Booth in the spring. Eckert claimed to have found some incriminating papers on a ferry on November 26, 1864, and "Payne" obligingly admitted they were his.

We know Louis Paine made a "confession" to Doster when he finally decided to talk around the end of May, so the possibility exists that he might also have used Eckert for purposes of self-incrimination. But the incidents Eckert described were quite incompatible with the "narration" Doster repeated—suggesting, most improbably, that the prisoner told each an entirely different story. Also, the yarn about the Baltimore physician contradicted Bates' *own* repeated assertion that *it was believed* all the conspirators had been captured.

The most damning implication, of course, was that although Eckert said he went to great pains to gather information on Paine's connection with the "conspiracy," he did not confide his findings to the prosecutors. He made four trips to the witness stand and breathed no word of all this when he was testifying under oath.

To wind up his story of Eckert's wartime services to Stanton and the nation, Bates went into great detail about the circumstances under which his boss left the War Department (Chapter XXVIII). The subject seemed to deserve no more than a couple of paragraphs, but he belabored it from page 402 through 408. The section began with:

"Eckert always commanded the full confidence of President Lincoln and Secretary Stanton, and was intrusted with military and state secrets and charged with special commissions *not at first disclosed to the cipher-operators,* who were justly proud of their Chief." (V. S. italics.)

Bates mentioned a number of peculiarities about Eckert's appointment as Assistant Secretary of War and his separation from the government—but seemed only to wish to emphasize that there *were* peculiarities.

"His appointment as Assistant Secretary of War really took effect in March, 1865 [the month in which Lincoln's murder was instigated, according to our findings], although the official date is given as July 27, 1866."

Washington newspapers began using this title for Eckert toward the end of the Trial. Also, Bates started referring to Eckert as "the General" in this context on page 402—though without stating *when* the promotion was awarded. As in L. C. Baker's case, it appears to have been *after* the assassination, during the Trial.

Two letters from Stanton accepting his assistant's resignation were reproduced, one a photocopy of the document. *Both* omitted the *year* in which the resignation became effective. Bates updated the separation by some seven months—July 31, 1866, rather than February 28, 1867.[25]

Both letters dripped with praise, but some paragraphs sounded like *denials of disloyalty:*

"You have had and well deserved my unlimited confidence. To your discretion and patriotic fidelity the most important and confidential interests of the Government were often entrusted, and the trust reposed in you was never betrayed or perverted . . ."

The description of Eckert as he was in 1907 was equally cryptic:

"While he is stern and at times implacable toward those who have deviated from the path of rectitude, below the surface there beats a heart full of warm affection for his chosen friends and of unswerving loyalty to whatever cause he may espouse."

This tribute was followed immediately by the mention that Messrs. Tinker, Chandler, and himself. the surviving members of Eckert's staff of wartime cipher-operators (who had been in such excellent position to know the deepest secrets of the War Department) had been executives under Eckert at Western Union ever since the war. He had been their meal ticket for forty years! Could Bates have used the term "chosen friends" with tongue in cheek?

His book closed with this parting thought: " . . . the only regret being that the limits of this volume have made it necessary to leave out so much that would have been of general interest."

David Homer Bates' method appears to have been to make *negative* statements in such *positive* language that his charges were veiled.

When earlier chapters of *Lincoln in the Telegraph Office* are read in the light of this method (and the suspicions aroused by his last three chapters), the veil is withdrawn entirely in some instances. Chapter XXIV becomes practically a direct accusation that Eckert scuttled the Hampton Roads Peace Conference in February, 1865, under orders from Stanton—and was paid $100,000 by an unidentified Northern politician for the accomplishment. It may be that students of Civil War history can find other revelations in other chapters.

From the oblique manner in which Bates revealed his secrets, it would seem he had a collection of strong suspicions, rather than clear evidence, of treason. He appeared to think *Stanton* had masterminded the assassination of Lincoln and Eckert had merely done the leg work. It might be noted that his job in the military telegraph office gave him a view of the activities of these two superiors, but no insight into those of L. C. Baker. Thus, since he suspected a plot in which Stanton was involved, he might have assumed the War Secretary would be its ringleader, rather than one of his subordinates.

In any case, Bates' airing of his suspicions is helpful in our problem of determining the identities of L. C. Baker's "local agent" and the "intermediary" who made a side contract with Lewis Powell to kill Seward.

Bates was emphatic about Eckert's intense interest in the conviction of Louis Paine—which is readily equated with an intense interest in the escape of Lewis Powell.

After the assassination, Powell represented a far greater danger to the "local agent" and the "intermediary" than even Booth himself. If apprehended and induced to talk, he could have identified and denounced these accomplices beyond all possible denial. But the mesmerized actor was probably unaware that there *was* a "local agent" in the plot to kill Lincoln, or an "intermediary" in the Seward deal.

The conviction of Paine and the escape of Powell was the prime concern of both these participants throughout the Trial and later. By making it clear that this was also the prime concern of Thomas T. Eckert, Bates gives substance to our suspicion that Eckert filled *both* roles in the actual conspiracy to murder Lincoln and the corollary plot to kill Seward.

19

Louis Paine

How do you begin tracing the career of a man who never existed?—On a Sunday late in May, 1865, Paine had his voluntary interview with Colonel Doster and told the attorney his real name was Lewis Powell. Doster listened to his story and passed the information along to Colonel Burnett.

Up to that day the prisoner had been a real, if mysterious, person. His picture had been published far and wide over the caption "Lewis Payne." There must have been a number of people in Virginia, Baltimore, and other places he had visited who read the news stories about Seward's attacker, studied the drawings and photographs of him, and wondered if he could possibly be the Louis Paine (or Lewis Payne) they knew. None is known to have come forward and claimed to recognize him. So if any thought they did, they must have shrugged it off as improbable. Or perhaps they thought it wiser not to admit knowing a man so completely "identified" as a vicious assassin.

After June 3—the day Doster stated in court that his client was really the son of the Rev. George C. Powell of Florida—Louis Paine ceased to exist. His name became just another of the several aliases of Lewis Thornton Powell.

The big prisoner, who had demonstrated his rather grim sense of humor by smiling when Seward's house boy identified him in two coats and a hat too small for him, must have been amused at the towering irony of the situation. No one had believed a word he said until he told that fantastic lie!

Not quite everyone believed him. But it was too late to do anything about it when the Reverend George C. Powell learned that the doomed young man claimed to be his son.

Lafayette Baker wasn't deceived; nor were Stanton, Eckert, Holt, Burnett, Bingham, Olcott, or Foster. Neither was Weichmann. Neither were the Branson girls. As we shall see later, there's good reason to believe that Secretary Seward knew Paine was not Powell and not the man who had attacked him.

Mrs. Surratt wasn't fooled; she had known both Powell *and* Paine. It's a good bet that Herold knew the prisoner wasn't the tall, flashy young man who had hired him to dispose of Booth. Finally—though his name should stand first among those who knew the truth—there was Lewis Thornton Powell.

The legend was built to last. Each of those who knew that Paine and Powell were different men went to his grave without telling, each for reasons of his own. Yet the managers of the Trial couldn't look ahead into the future and know whether someone—the Rev. Powell, perhaps—might come forward to prove Paine's assumed identity was a false one. The masquerade was extraordinarily convenient for their purposes, and they were glad to countenance it. But there was no change in the prisoner's name so far as the court records were concerned, and we have a curious situation in which the history books and an official document of the federal government are in disagreement.

On July 5, 1865, Assistant Adjutant General E. D. Townsend drew up the death warrant ordering the execution of "*Lewis Payne. . . .* By command of the President of the United States."[1] Yet nearly every *history* of the assassination and Trial informs us that the man who was hanged was named Lewis Powell!

Not that it dilutes the guilt of those who conspired to take his life, nor excuses the hate-blinded generation that consented. Louis Paine's personal history and identity were erased from the human record by no one but *himself*. Strictly speaking, this was a case of judicial suicide—or should we say *judicial obliteration?* Paine played a key role in the process of injustice by which he was hanged. He quite evidently *wanted* to die. The real mystery is *why?*

information from the trial

In earlier chapters we presented the three-part proposition that Paine was not Powell, that the attacker of Seward was a different man from the one who was hanged, and that Louis Paine had taken no part in either the real or the fabricated conspiracy to murder Lincoln.

The obvious first step in a search for Paine's personal history was to collect such information as we had about him and see whether it pointed in any particular direction. Information of various kinds was found in the record of the Conspiracy Trial. During that proceeding it was assumed that any statements by or about Paine which didn't agree with his admission that he was Lewis Powell, attacker of Seward and accomplice of Booth, were false. Historians have proceeded on the same assumption. But our premise that he was an entirely different person, whose first involvement in the episode was on the night of his arrest at the Surratt house, called for a re-appraisal of all the testimony about him, as well as of the few recorded statements he made about himself.

When questioned by Detective Morgan in Mrs. Surratt's parlor, Paine said he was a refugee from Fauquier County, Virginia, and had been living in Baltimore since the early weeks of the year. He had arrived in Washington only recently and, being destitute, had been doing odd jobs as a laborer to feed himself. He gave certain other particulars about himself to Morgan and the other detectives. Since he produced his Oath of Allegiance to identify himself, he was not trying to conceal the fact that he had been detained briefly by the military police in Baltimore around the middle of the preceding month. The notation on his Oath that he had been ordered north of Philadelphia, "to remain there during the war," made it clear that his presence in Washington was legal—since the war was over.

Thus the young man would have had no evident reason not to answer Morgan's questions truthfully. Moreover, nearly all his statements were confirmed later by Mrs. Branson's deposition and the testimony of her daughter Margaret. They also revealed a few more details about their boarder's behavior during his six or seven weeks' stay at their house; and the mother asserted her belief that Paine had gone to New York when he left there on March 14 or 15.[2] The Baltimore provost marshal also believed he had gone "north."[3]

Before going to New York, as he apparently did, Paine went to Washington and lodged at the Surratt house for two or three days. In spite of the confusion in the statements of the landlady and boarders there regarding his stay at the house, they helped us to piece together some important particulars about the young man.

Weichmann, confirmed by the young ladies, made it clear that Paine bore a strong resemblance to a man named "Wood" who had visited there during the winter and again in the month of March. Weichmann asserted that "Payne" *was* "Wood," but the young ladies, initially at least, were quite sure he was not. *Only* Weichmann, who was carrying the ball for the prosecution, testified he had seen "Payne" around the house at all after the evening he arrived.

On his arrival he had asked for Mrs. Surratt. He told those present that he was a Baptist preacher, that he had been in Baltimore and had taken the Oath of Allegiance[4]—thereby dating his visit to Washington after March 14, when he signed the Oath.

The effect of Weichmann's testimony was to leave the impression that "*Wood*" had stopped in at this time and represented himself as a Baptist preacher. But our analysis of this and other testimony on the subject resulted in the conclusion that it was Paine, not Wood, who said he was a clergyman. He had evidently not told the Bransons he was a preacher, but Margaret testified that he was wearing "black citizens' dress" when he first came to their house in the winter of '65. Though clergymen had no patent on black clothing as such, it was worn so universally by ministers of the period as to be almost a professional uniform—particularly the "black frock coat." During his first session on the witness stand, when Weichmann was describing "Wood" as a visitor who *claimed* to be a Baptist preacher, he said he had been wearing a "black frock coat" on one of his visits.[5]

Some of the characteristics Mrs. Surratt attributed to "Wood"—the "bogus preacher"—apparently applied to Paine and explained why none of the boarders except Weichmann mentioned seeing him around the house. She said he was "a man of few words," "He didn't seem inclined to talk," and "He remained in his room most of the time."[6]

These descriptions tally exactly with those of the Bransons regarding Paine. Moreover, it's quite logical that regardless of whether his natural disposition or current mood was unsociable, Paine would have remained out of sight as much as possible when he visited the Surratt house in Washington around March 15. The military authorities in Baltimore had just ordered him to go north of Philadelphia, and he was liable to arrest and imprisonment if found south of that city before the war ended.

Such considerations as this bring us to two preliminary conclusions about Louis Paine, in view of our earlier conclusion that "Wood" was Lewis Powell:

First, Paine and Powell resembled each other so closely in features and stature as to suggest a family relationship of some kind.

Second, we have the coincidence that Paine stayed at the Branson house in Baltimore and later visited the Surratt house in Washington—*at both of which Lewis Powell was known and had visited earlier.* The rather obvious assumption is that Paine chose those two boardinghouses out of the hundreds in operation in the two cities *at Powell's recommendation.*

Going back a little further, we find that Powell and Paine both left Fauquier County, Virginia, in the same month—January, 1865. Since the former made his first appearance at the Surratt house at almost the same time the latter arrived at Branson's in Baltimore, we may even assume they left northern Virginia together.

Now, recalling that Powell was said to have stayed with a man named "Payne" near Warrenton while he served with Mosby, the researcher was somewhat justified in concluding that he had traced both young men back to their point of departure—the parental home of Louis Paine near Warrenton, at which Lewis Powell had been a guest during most of 1864.

Anyway, the theory that Paine lived in Fauquier County and Powell was a guest in the home went on the rubbish heap after a few hours study of census schedules and genealogy books on Fauquier County in the 1860's. There were "Paynes" by the dozen—even a few "Lewis

Paynes." But none had the right age and other qualifications in 1865 to have been the one hanged in Washington.

So back to the beginning of the trail again, not much wiser than before, except for the suppositions that *both* Powell and Paine had been merely visitors in Fauquier County, and that the latter could have been born in any state of the Union or any of the territories yet still have been in Fauquier County in 1864 to become acquainted with Lewis Powell.

the Paine family

The next available line of inquiry into the antecedents of Louis Paine didn't seem to be a particularly promising one at first: The possibility that the prisoner might have revealed some clues to his own family background in his "narration" of Powell's personal history to Doster.

We concluded that Paine's information on the man he *claimed* to be was too incomplete and too often incorrect for him to have *been* Powell. On the other hand, he knew much more about Powell than he could have learned in a brief acquaintance. It was clear that the prisoner was gifted with a remarkable memory; yet he had virtually no knowledge, correct or otherwise, on the other man's early years, before the Powell family moved to Florida, which he said occurred in 1859.

From 1859 onward, however, he knew quite a bit about Lewis Powell's family, and much of what he told was fairly accurate, except on subjects he was deliberately falsifying—such as the item that the Rev. Powell's son managed slaves on his father's plantation. This apparent beginning date for the young men's acquaintance encouraged speculation that Paine himself must have been living in Florida in 1859, when the Powells moved there.

One piece of information Paine gave Doster supported the theory. In this instance he was remarkably precise and absolutely correct—yet there was no good reason why he should have been, since he *wasn't* Powell. He recalled that the commander of the volunteer company in which Powell enlisted was Captain Stewart—who was undoubtedly a resident of the county in which the unit was recruited. He also remembered that the 2nd Florida Infantry was *originally* commanded by Colonel (George T.) Ward—even though that officer was killed in one of the regiment's first engagements, at Williamsburg, on May 5, 1862, and was replaced by Colonel E. A. Perry after a general election in the regiment on May 10.[7]

Paine's accurate recollection of the names of these two officers was the more curious because *these were the only two proper names the prisoner mentioned* in his initial "narration" to Doster—other than that of the Reverend Powell and such well-known ones as Booth, Seward, and General A. P. Hill. Some very interesting conclusions can be drawn from Paine's clear memory of these two names. For the present, let's just say it tended to confirm that he had been living in Florida when Lewis Powell joined the army.

Now, the prisoner had located the Powell family home at "Live Oak Station," which is in Suwannee County in northern Florida. Thus, on the assumption that Louis Paine and his family were living there when the Powells arrived in 1859, there was an excellent possibility that *both* families would be found listed in the 1860 census for Suwannee County. Colonel Baker, who had interrogated the big prisoner before he stopped talking, said his age in 1865 was twenty-two or twenty-three (Baker's Handbill). And the young man had signed his Oath of Allegiance on March 14, 1865, "L. Paine." Therefore the 1860 census for Suwannee County should list a Lewis (or Louis) Paine, aged seventeen or eighteen. It did not. Neither did it list a Rev. George C. Powell and family.

Two gentlemen in Florida (for whose interest and collaboration the writer is deeply indebted) discovered a record which supplied the key to the Suwannee Country riddle, as well as to a number of others encountered during the tracing of Louis Paine. This was the obituary of the Rev. George C. Powell, published in an obscure volume known only to a few historians of the Baptist Church.[8]

Among other things, the obituary stated that the Rev. Powell had moved to Florida in 1859 and settled at Belleville in *Hamilton County,* just across the Georgia line. This fact reduced the target supplied by logic to a distinct bull's eye. Now we could expect the 1860 census for *Hamilton* County to list a Lewis (or Louis) Paine, aged seventeen or eighteen—*in the little farming community of Belleville, in the northwest corner of the county.*

He was there! "Louis Paine, aged eighteen, born in Georgia"—but living in the household of one Jeremiah Smith and his wife, Catherine.*

The Smith home in 1860, as the census listed its occupants, had the appearance of a boardinghouse. In addition to Mr. and Mrs. Smith and

---

*Louis Paine was the sole source of information to the effect that the Rev. George C. Powell was a resident of "Live Oak Station" in Suwannee County—which we have assumed the clergyman used only as a mailing address. All the available evidence indicates that the Powell family home in Florida was in Hamilton County from 1859 until 1868, when the Rev. Powell moved down to Orange County (obituary).

The prisoner was also careful to leave the impression that Lewis Powell not only *lived* in Suwannee County but joined the army there. In referring to the company of volunteers Powell joined in 1861, he called it "Captain Stewart's Company" rather than using one of its official designations, the *Hamilton Blues* or the *Jasper Blues*—either of which would have directed any contemporary investigator to Hamilton County (Jasper is the county seat), where almost any native could tell him that Payne and Powell were different men who looked much alike.

Louis Paine, a man named Jackson McNeese lived there with his two children: John, fourteen, and Drucilla, seven. There was also a "Taylor Sowell (or Powell)," aged twenty-four, and "Susan C. Smith," apparently the host's thirteen-year-old daughter.

As against the evident fact that Louis was merely a boarder or a guest in the Smith home in 1860, there was the possibility that the *1850 census* would enlighten us further—perhaps by listing a "Louis Paine, aged 8" who was a permanent member of the Smith family, possibly an adopted child.

Referred to, the 1850 census for Belleville read as follows:

#77	*Name*	*Age*	*Occupation*	*Born*
	Jeremiah Smith	46	P. B. Minister	N. Carolina
	Catherine "	46		Georgia
	Jacob "	20		"
	Nancy "	15		"
	William W. "	17		"
	Sarah "	13		"
	Martha "	11		"
	Hugh L. "	8		"
	Susannah C. "	4		"

In addition to the foregoing information, the census-taker noted that Jacob Smith could neither read nor write, and that William W. was the only child who had attended school in the preceding year. The *1860* census had stated that Susannah C. had been born in Florida, rather than Georgia. And the *1870* census added another detail on Jeremiah Smith—that he could neither read nor write.

Rather than subject the reader to the lengthy and often intricate process of analysis by which Louis Paine's early history and his connection with the Smith family was reconstructed from these and other records and documents, we shall summarize his boyhood and youth in narrative form.

Catherine Smith was Louis' mother, he being a child of her first marriage, to John W. Paine of Gwinnett County, Georgia. Although no record of her maiden name has been located as of this writing, the genealogical data gathered in the course of this study indicates that she was a Payne and that her family had moved to Georgia from Virginia before 1800. In any case, she is believed to have been the granddaughter of William G. Cox, brother of Ichabod Cox—who was grandfather of the Rev. George C. Powell's wife, Caroline. This connection would have made the mothers of Louis Paine and Lewis Powell second cousins—and the two young men third cousins. It is the writer's opinion that *both* parents of both families were related by mutual connections with the lineage of Thomas Coxe, a Welsh immigrant who settled in Jamestown in 1614. Some of his descendents migrated southward during several generations and established the widespread Cox clan in the deep South.*

Somewhere in the neighborhood of 1845, Catherine separated from John W. Paine, by reason of either divorce or his death. Shortly afterward she married Jeremiah Smith. When this family moved to Belleville in Hamilton County, Florida, five of Catherine's younger children went with them. These were Nancy (Jacob Smith's wife), William W. (Wilder), Sarah, Martha, and Louis. Catherine's oldest son, Linsey, remained in Gwinnett County (1850 census, p. 222) and married Mary Driver (county court record). The two older daughters had left home before Catherine's marriage to Jeremiah Smith. A new child, Susannah, was born to the couple in Florida.

The last name of *all* the children in the household was given to the 1850 census-taker as "Smith." At the time of the Civil War William Wilder Smith was still using his stepfather's name.

By 1860 the composition of the family had altered greatly. All the older children had moved out. Only Hugh Louis and Susannah remained—the former having by that time elected to use his blood father's name, Paine. It is assumed that the McNeeses and Taylor Sowell (Powell) who were present in 1860 were relatives of either Smith or his wife, living with them temporarily.

In 1861, Louis, his mother, and Susannah all left the household of Jeremiah Smith. The son left first to enter an activity we shall discuss separately. Evidence to be brought in later will show that Catherine moved to northern Virginia to live with relatives. Since Susannah was only thirteen or fourteen at the time, the mother may have taken this daughter with her.

A search of the court records in Hamilton County has not produced a record of Catherine's divorce from Jeremiah Smith. However, there must have been a divorce, perhaps initiated by Catherine elsewhere. The 1870 census shows that Jeremiah married *again* shortly after her departure. This later poll shows him still living in Belleville, now aged sixty-five—with a young woman aged thirty-two and four small children ranging in age from six to one.

Normal scepticism on such matters at first made it difficult to believe that the elderly Smith could have been married to the woman half his age or have been the father of the new brood of four children. It was more logical to assume he had taken in a daughter-in-law who had lost her husband.

The discovery of Jeremiah B. Smith's last will and testament probated

---

*The Rev. Henry Miller Cox, *The Cox Family in America* (New York, 1912).

in Hamilton County in 1879,* settled the question. Jeremiah left all of his substantial estate to "my beloved wife Sarrah C. Smith and her children by me lawfully begotten."

In this writer's opinion, the *name* of Jeremiah's third and last wife provides a plausible, if somewhat sordid, answer to such questions as: Why did Louis in his later teens discard the family name of his stepfather, "Smith," and adopt the name of his blood father, whom he may never have known? Why did his mother, Catherine, leave her husband's prosperous plantation at Belleville to live as a poor relative on some farm in northern Virginia?

An answer is found in the name and census statistics of Jeremiah's third wife, Sarah C. Sarah's name, age, birthplace, and geographical location conformed exactly to those of Catherine's *daughter* Sarah!

calvinistic influence

In addition to the moral contrasts of his home life, there were other, more subtle influences in Paine's formative years that may have had a bearing on his determination to end his life on the gallows. They relate to the question of whether or not he was, as he stated to several persons in Mrs. Surratt's parlor at a time when he had no reason to falsify, a Baptist minister.

We can probably take it for granted that he was *not* ordained. Paine was too young to have attained such status. Moreover, if he *had* been ordained, there would be a clear, indisputable record of it in the archives of the Baptist Church. But it was still possible for him to have been a properly certified preacher according to the practices of that denomination.

An aspirant to the ministry could, upon convincing his pastor and the congregation of his sincere desire to preach the gospel, be issued a certificate which authorized him to conduct religious services from the pulpit or wherever he found an audience. If he wished, he could also take his certificate to a county judge and be issued a license to perform marriage ceremonies. These were preliminary steps for a young man who desired to enter the ministry. It was assumed the licentiate would eventually feel he was sufficiently prepared and committed to apply for ordination before a presbytery of elders. But there was no fixed time limit for his apprenticeship. He could go on for years supporting himself and his family, if any, by some other occupation, and preach the gospel in the time he could spare from breadwinning. During this whole interim of work and practical experience he was entitled to call himself a Baptist preacher.

*Located and certified copy supplied the author by County Judge John H. McCormick of Jasper, Hamilton County, Fla.

Now, as to the religious influences of Paine's early life: Details are lacking of course, but there are some items of information at hand that enable us to draw certain general inferences. The first item is found in the 1850 census—the notation that Jeremiah Smith, Louis' stepfather, represented himself at that time as a Primitive Baptist minister. This is coupled with the fact that the 1870 census-taker marked him as "unable to read or write."

The Primitive movement originated in North Carolina, Jeremiah Smith's home state, in 1827.[9] Its doctrine was fundamentalist in the extreme, and its positions on many church issues of the day reflected the views of the isolated rural Baptists, as opposed to the more progressive outlook of those who inhabited the long-settled areas on the eastern seaboard.

Among other things, Primitives objected to the payment of salaries to ministers, believing that those who preached the gospel should do so in response to the call of the Spirit, not to earn money. Pastors, they believed, should earn their livelihood by any honest work they could do in the time they could spare from their ministry. They objected to *all* educational requirements for ministers, on the theory that literacy or formal education were no criteria of a man's ability to exhort his neighbors by the inspiration of the Creator:

"God commissions all Christians to exhort their fellow men—and paid, educated ministers sent out by missionary societies imply that God overlooked something necessary to achieving his kingdom. Why send a man to school '*after God has called him to the ministry?*' "[10]

The Primitives also objected to Sunday schools and—on doctrinary grounds—to sending missionaries to the "heathens." Their position on the latter issue was that God had placed the heathen in benighted circumstances for excellent reasons known only to himself, and efforts to change their circumstances in any way were interference with the divine plan for their salvation.

". . . Only by the direct action of the Holy Spirit, without human intermediary, could a man foreordained for salvation be brought to God."[11]

In short, the key word in the Primitive vocabulary was *foreordained.* And, as a whole, the Primitive viewpoint of a century ago was "based on the ultra-Calvinistic belief in the absolute *predestination* of all things."[12]

It's probably safe to conclude that these were the general views of Jeremiah Smith at the time he married Catherine, and that they were still his views in 1850, several years later. In view of the sacrificial economic position of a Primitive minister, we can also assume that no woman would marry one for reasons of security and that a comparable religious zeal on the part of the bride is implied.

A gradual change in Jeremiah's religious outlook between 1850 and 1860 is indicated by various information at hand, not the least of which would be his later marriage to a young woman who was evidently his stepdaughter.

To this add the fact that in 1860 and 1870 the census-taker recorded his occupation as "farmer," rather than clergyman. His growing interest in material well-being between 1850 and 1860 was shown by his purchase of about a hundred acres of additional land bordering his plantation in 1857.* In other words, he was abandoning his Primitive role of a clergyman as a *ragged prophet.*

These few bits of information tell only a little about what must have been a complex domestic situation in the years prior to the breakup of the Smith home. But they do hint at the deterioration of a marriage begun on an ultrareligious note, during which the stepson Louis would have witnessed an apparent backsliding on his stepfather's part, coming after several earlier years of intense fundamentalist indoctrination by both parents. His renunciation of the name "Smith" can be interpreted as protest—though whether against backsliding or some other human frailty of his stepfather's, we can only surmise.

Louis Paine's deportment during his imprisonment and unjust trial—which we shall study in more detail presently—had the character of long-suffering usually associated with religious martyrdom. He didn't resist, strike back, or display any signs of anger. He simply *endured,* like one emulating the "patience of Job." When he finally began talking, he was representing himself as another man whom he knew to be a desperado who had apparently committed a vicious attack upon an invalid. While enacting that *assumed* role—if he was, in fact, a Baptist preacher—he would have avoided statements and expressions that might reveal his religious outlook and training. But Dr. Gillette, a Baptist minister of Washington, spent all of the last night and morning with the condemned man, and "He impressed the clergyman as a person of correct religious ideas."[13] Dr. James Hall testified: "We asked him . . . whether he believed in a God; he said that he did, and that he was a just God; he also acknowledged to me that at one time he had been a member of the Baptist Church."[14]

Predestination involves the belief that human experiences—the temptations, the errors, and the penalties—are foreordained by a stern God for the sinner's ultimate salvation. Paine's manner, as described by dozens of observers, was that of a man wholly resigned to an inevitable fate. Which still leaves us with the question—of what did he consider himself guilty, since he was evidently not guilty of any crime covered by human law?

Paine's apparent lack of any personal knowledge of Lewis Powell's acti-

*Deed on file at Hamilton County Court, Jasper, Florida. Certified copy supplied the author by County Judge John H. McCormick.

vities prior to his army career suggests that it wasn't his cousin's arrival at Belleville in 1859 that made the year memorable—but the arrival of the Reverend George C. Powell, with whom he *did* appear to be well acquainted.

The Rev. Powell may very well have made a strong impression upon Jeremiah Smith's intense young stepson. Elder Powell was the prototype of a frontier minister and rather celebrated in both the states where he had served.* Just fifty years old in 1859, tall, vigorous, commanding in appearance and manner, Brother Powell was a veteran of thirty years' campaigning for the Kingdom in the rude hinterlands of Georgia and Alabama. His official statistics were as impressive as he himself; in 1852, one of his years as pastor of Beulah Church in Stewart County, Georgia, he had baptized forty-one persons—twelve per cent of all those immersed in his association (Columbus) of forty-two churches![15]

The records of Elder Powell's church in Hamilton County have not been located, though there must be references to it in some regional Baptist publications of the day. In view of the sparse and widely scattered population of northern Florida in the early sixties, the Rev. Powell may have acted as pastor for two or more churches in the region, serving them as a circuit rider. One of his congregations was at Providence in Bradford (now Union) County, according to his obituary. He served there "one year at least, during which a number were added to the church, *five of whom became ministers.*"

Was Louis Paine one of these five young men? Extensive efforts have been made to learn the answer to that question, but without success. No minutes for Providence Church can be located. The scanty official records of the early Baptist Church in Florida don't refer to it. An inquiry as to whether Louis Paine made application for a license before a county judge in Bradford County brought the reply that the courthouse burned to the ground in 1875, destroying all records.

So we still have only Paine's statement in Mrs. Surratt's parlor in March and considerable inference to support the theory that he was a certified Baptist preacher.

In the next chapter we shall study certain letters the Rev. Powell wrote after the execution of Louis Paine, and find some positive clues to the puzzle of whether his dead nephew had been a clergyman.

in the confederate army

The next known phase in the career of Louis Paine will seem incon-

*The Rev. Powell was so well known in Georgia that, when he died in Orange County, Fla. in 1881, a union memorial service was held at Antioch church in Talbot County, Ga., where he had been licensed to preach just half a century earlier (Obituary).

gruous with the one we have just discussed. But it may remove any remaining doubts as to whether he and Lewis Powell were different men.

Paine served nearly four years in the Confederate Army.*

He enrolled in Captain D. A. Lee's Company, Harkie's Regiment, Georgia Infantry, on May 6, 1862. His name was recorded on the payroll as "H. L. Paine." Lee's Company subsequently became Company I, 55th Regiment, Georgia Infantry.

(There were some curious ramifications to Paine's military history as shown in the Confederate Army records—and the reader is entitled to assurance that Private H. L. Paine was the same Louis Paine—or Lewis Payne—who was hanged in Washington on July 7, 1865. Both of these subjects, being too complex for discussion at this point, are covered fully in Appendix L, "H. L. Payne.")

At the time of his enrollment in the 55th Georgia—rather, on May 14, to be exact—Louis was paid a bounty of fifty dollars. This indicated he had already served twelve months in another regiment.

A discussion of this first enlistment is a broad subject that comes up in the next chapter. So we shall stick to his career in the 55th Georgia for the present.

In passing, though, it can be noted that his initial enlistment in the army in the spring of *1861* reduces the period in which he *may* have followed the calling of a preacher to the brief span between the Rev. Powell's arrival in Florida in 1859 and his *voluntary* entry into the army in the spring of 1861, unless he had been preaching since his middle teens. His enlistment a year prior to the April '62 draft also implies the failure—or at least the suspension—of his preaching career, since presumably he would not have enlisted if his career in the ministry had been going well, or at least he would have entered the service as a chaplain.

The 55th Georgia was sent to the western theater of operations and attached to Kirby Smith's division, based at Knoxville, Tennessee. The various pay and muster rolls which comprise Paine's records (on all but one his name is spelled *Payne*) don't show whether he was involved in any of the large or small engagements of late '62 and early '63. But he was in a good position to have reliable information that Lewis Powell's two brothers were killed at Murfreesboro, as he told Doster.

Late in February, 1863, he was detailed to the quartermaster in Knoxville to work as a shoemaker and remained in that occupation for the balance of his recorded service, being transferred to the Atlanta shoe shops after the fall of Knoxville. He drew the regular infantry private's pay of eleven dollars a month until the 55th Georgia was captured at Cumberland Gap on September 9, 1863. After that the quartermaster

*We are greatly indebted to Mr. Elmer O. Parker and his associate Mrs. Sarah Jackson of the National Archives for locating the compiled service records of "Private H. L. Payne (Paine)" and providing us with complete photocopies of the file.

paid him for making or "bottoming" shoes at varying rates of compensation.

In August and September, 1864, Private H. L. "Payne" was listed as being "absent without leave" from Atlanta, Georgia. And there his records end. Sherman's armies entered the city in the first days of September. Since Paine was not taken prisoner, he either escaped from the city on his own or was swept along with other retreating Confederate troops.

Paine *may* have deserted at this time—there's no proof one way or the other. But his next known appearance was in Fauquier County, Virginia, around the close of 1864 or early in '65. The obstacles to his having made a safe exit from the beleaguered city and traveled direct to Fauquier—passing through the several Union lines and occupied areas between—were so great as to rule out such a journey.

A much better possibility is suggested by Lafayette Baker's insistence that he—Paine—had come to Washington from Kentucky. The certainty that Baker interviewed the young man personally before he was placed under arrest and remanded to Colonel Wells' custody allows us to assume that Baker *knew* Paine had been in Kentucky, because the prisoner had told him so.

The most plausible means by which Paine could have reached Kentucky from Atlanta at that stage of the war was to have been scooped up along with other able-bodied, unattached soldiers by General Hood's provost marshals and to have made the long, circuitous march to Nashville—where Hood's tattered army was smashed and scattered over a wide area of northern Tennessee.

Our research has uncovered tentative evidence that young Paine had close relatives in Scott County, Kentucky. Baker's statement that the prisoner was "one of *three* Kentucky brothers" tends to confirm this, since there were *six* brothers in the Payne family of Union County, to which it was *proved* he didn't belong. (Paine was in fact one of *three brothers.*)

At any rate, the theory that Louis Paine was with Hood's army at the Nashville disaster works out well as to timing. On December 16 he would have been fairly near the Tennessee-Kentucky border and, whether or not he stopped to look for relatives in the latter state, would have been in a geographical location to make his way east to Fauquier County, Virginia, through areas behind the Union lines.

mr. Seward's information

We are presuming his incentive in going east to Fauquier—arriving there about the turn of the year—was his mother's presence there, coupled with the fact that he no longer had a family home in Florida or anywhere else.

Our source of information to the effect that Paine's mother was living in northern Virginia at this time is the National Archives letter of which Secretary of State Seward was identified as the author (see Appendix I, "Handwriting Analyses"). The full text—the last two pages of a multipage letter—reads as follows:

> *Lewis Payne* is a native (?) of Fauquier County, Va.—in the neighborhood of Manassas Junction. His mother resides there. His family is respectable and [many of] his connections have been killed in the war. You told me you thought he was the hired assassin of the Conspirators—I think he was more. By sending a prudent detective to Warrenton you will be able to trace him. My information is reliable, but I do not desire to put it in writing and will tell you all (which is not now important that you should know for the purposes of justice) when we meet, which will be when I return from N. York where I am compelled to be this week.
>
> Addie will hand you this, which you will please destroy after reading.
>
> [signature obliterated]

It may not be necessary to point out that this was not a letter from some busybody repeating gossip he had heard, but a top-level communication from one of the most astute and worldly members of Lincoln's cabinet to a high official of the Bureau of Military Justice—probably Colonel Burnett. It is presumed to have been written around the middle of May, before Paine "identified" himself as "Powell."

After being obliged to relinquish his secret police functions to the power-ravenous Stanton, Seward didn't retire from the cloak-and-dagger business. He continued to maintain his own system of informers and investigators so that he did not have to rely entirely upon the secretive War Department for his information on undercover matters. His private intelligence activities were largely *private* of course, but hints of them are seen several times in the Lincoln Assassination Suspects file in the National Archives—such as in the April 28, 1865, letter from W. W. Emmons of Detroit to General Joseph Holt regarding the "yellow fever plot" and in the "Morehead City" letter, which was originally mailed to Seward by the reputed detective Charles Duell.

Mr. Seward was well able to obtain "reliable" information on "Lewis Payne." And apparently he had considerably more that he didn't want to put in writing—leaving himself open to suspicion of concealing intelligence vital to the prisoner's case.

True, Manassas Junction being in Prince William County rather than Fauquier, we assume his informant wasn't a native of the region. But the coincidence that he said "His *mother* resides there," rather than referring to Paine's family home, his parents or his father, even though he thought the young man was a "native," has the ring of truth—considering we already know Paine's mother was alone, except perhaps for her daughter Susannah, and no longer had a husband and a home of her own.*

There is one very convincing evidence that Seward—or the "prudent detective" he suggested—did investigate further on the matter of Paine's mother and discover that the uncommunicative prisoner could *not* have been the man who stabbed him, nor a party to Booth's "conspiracy." This was the widely current "report" Doster said circulated "near the end of the trial" that Seward intended to ask for Paine's *pardon* if he were sentenced to death—on the facetious pretext that "it was not right that he should outlive his own murderer."[16] Doster understood that only the untimely death of Seward's wife prevented his intercession for Paine—but we can be sure the War Department would have prevented it if Mrs. Seward's death had not.

On the assumption that Seward's information was correct, we conclude that Louis found his mother at Warrenton. He also renewed his acquaintance with Lewis Powell, not long before Powell had the altercation over the shooting of prisoners, which probably had little to do with his decision to go to Washington and look up John Surratt. When he was arrested at the Surratt house, Paine told Morgan he had left Virginia because he would have had to go in the army if he'd stayed. The only Confederate "army" in Fauquier County at that time was Mosby's Command. Since Paine was completely unknown in that county—suggesting that his stay there was *very* brief—we might wonder who was pressuring him to join the Partisans, unless it was the family with whom his mother was staying. Perhaps he just assumed that a big, able-bodied young southerner couldn't settle there *without* being shamed into fighting for Mosby.

If Louis had made up his mind to return to preaching, he would have found the calling was not recognized as grounds for military exemption in Fauquier County that winter. One of the most embittering events of the long war had occurred on October 14, when Union General W. H. Powell had hanged Albert C. Willis in reprisal for the shooting of a federal spy by Mosby's men. Willis was a licentiate of Crooked Run Baptist Church in Culpeper County and had been riding with Mosby for many months.[17]

Anyway, having seen the war lost at Atlanta, and probably at Nashville as well, the young man's decision to accompany Lewis Powell to Baltimore was understandable. Later he told Doster that *Powell* sold his horse at Alexandria and used the money to pay his board at Branson's. But the chances are it was *he* who did so. He had made good money—but Confederate money—at shoemaking in Atlanta. Just about

*Some progress has been made toward identifying the family with whom Catherine was living—first in Warrenton, then near Manassas after the end of hostilities. Her relationship to them should emerge from further genealogical studies.

the *only* way he could have exchanged his Confederate currency for greenbacks was to buy a good horse from some unwavering rebel in Kentucky and sell it in the northern market.

He turned up next at Mrs. Branson's in Baltimore, about January 19, 1865, the lady said.

Paine in baltimore

The suit Louis was wearing when he arrived at Branson's—which Margaret described as "black citizens' dress" and Weichmann called "a black frock coat"—becomes evidence of a sort, in view of where he had been and what he had been doing for the past four years. Obviously this was not the costume he had worn as an army private, in spite of the necessary broadmindedness as to uniform in that threadbare organization. And it would have been difficult to buy a frock coat—or even a plain black suit to fit a man of his huge proportions—anywhere in the South in January, '65, let alone in war-drained Fauquier County.

A reasonable theory would be that Paine's mother had packed away his black suit and the fine circuit-rider's boots when he joined the army and she went to Virginia in 1861. If he got them from her and wore them to Baltimore, it could have been either because he intended to return to preaching or because they were the only decent clothes he had, or both.

At Branson's he seems to have just waited for the war to end. Any notions he may have had for studying the three R's came to nothing. Books, as such, fascinated him, but the only ones in the Branson library he could begin to comprehend were the illustrated medical ones. A relationship of some kind developed between the lonely young refugee and his landlady's daughter Mary. But this, like every other enterprise in the ill-fated career of Louis Paine, went nowhere. The controversy with the maid occurred, followed by his arrest and release two days later on March 14. He was off on his wanderings again.

In modern parlance Louis Paine would be called a born "loser." He was a wanderer, apparently marked for adversity and destined never to find a solid footing. But he was not a drifter. There were demonstrations of unusual mental capacity and a tempered strength of character in his prison ordeal. There was also a forward motion and an unquenchable hopefulness about him, which we saw most clearly when he stopped at the Surratt house in March, fresh from his most recent disaster at Branson's.

Weichmann was twisting the story of his arrival at Surratt's in March in order to identify him as "Wood" and show that he had been available for earlier plotting with Booth, rather than having been anchored at Branson's since January. But the informer stated that Miss Fitzpatrick, Mrs. Surratt, and probably Anna Surratt were present when he answered the doorbell and brought Paine into the parlor. His account of what Paine said to them was therefore basically accurate, since other witnesses *might* agree on another version and show him to be lying.

Paine said he had "been in Baltimore about a week [Pitman made it 'in *prison* in Baltimore'], had taken the Oath of Allegiance, and was going to become a good, loyal citizen."[18]

In other words, he was confiding in them and telling the truth. When we read this statement of his earlier we didn't know he had been in the Confederate Army for nearly four years, and his assertion that he intended to "become a good, loyal citizen" sounded like an admission that he had been engaged in some sinister, disloyal activity. That was the impression Weichmann *intended* to create. What Paine actually told them—perhaps in so many words—was that he had been a soldier in the rebel forces, but now intended to renew his loyalty to the Union, since the Southern cause was as good as lost.

As to his reason for visiting Surratt's in March, we assume he was looking for Powell with the hope of obtaining some money from his affluent cousin.

His accompanying assertion that he was a Baptist preacher revealed something of his plans for the future. He was going to pick up the pieces of the calling he had fumbled and abandoned in Florida, and begin again.

Apparently he did go to New York from there, and arrived back in Washington flat broke a few days before the assassination. Just how much Mrs. Surratt helped him when he turned to her as a last resort, and some contradictory reports on the circumstances of his arrest at her house, will be discussed a little later.

Anyone who has read only the violently prejudiced contemporary descriptions of the prisoner "Payne"—and particularly the more recent ones that call him a "Neanderthal" type and a moronic brute, able to kill with the same impersonal relish as a wild beast and feel as little remorse afterward—will be surprised to know that those who had a close association with the prisoner and wrote about it were profoundly impressed by his intelligence, manhood, and good character—*in spite* of their belief that he was guilty. They were so impressed with his forthrightness that they believed everything he told them about himself *as Powell.*

Henry Kyd Douglas was a Confederate officer, then under arrest, who was called as a defense witness to refute the perjured testimony of an unsavory character named H. von Steinacker who had appeared for the prosecution. Douglas was confined in the arsenal during several weeks of the Trial, but enjoyed a privileged status and the freedom of the building. He described the proceedings in detail as a cynical, calculated corruption of justice with the scarcely concealed purpose of convicting the innocent. Yet, oddly enough, the only one of the defendants he conceived as an *innocent* victim of all this legal dirty work was Mrs. Surratt.*

A few of Colonel Douglas' remarks about the prisoner "Payne" are worth noting, since his was an inside view of the Trial:

> Although the Court was organized to convict, the trial need not have been such a shameless farce . . . Lewis Payne, and all the men in the conspiracy with Booth, merited death, and they would have been convicted in any court in the land . . . The prisoners, with the exception of Mrs. Surratt, were not a comely-looking set, and with the exception of Payne the men were generally a sorry lot, low enough to be capable of any crime . . .
>
> Payne was a remarkable and desperate man. One day I observed that he seemed to recognize me. I asked General Hartranft to find out in his next visit to his cell who he was. He reported that Payne's name was Powell, that he was the son of an Episcopal or a Baptist clergyman; that he had been a private in the Second Florida regiment, wounded at Gettysburg as I was; a prisoner in West Buildings Hospital at Baltimore when I was, and that he had seen me there; that he subsequently had escaped and never returned to the army.
>
> I saw that Hartranft had taken a great interest in him as a character study. He said Payne seemed to be a man of iron will, cool and fearless, a typical desperado and singularly truthful. He told me one day that Payne had said he had taken his life in his hands when he agreed to go into the affair with Booth; that he had lost and expected to die; that he asked neither pardon nor mercy; and then, he said, Payne paused and solemnly concluded,
>
> "In the presence of Almighty God I swear Mrs. Surratt is innocent of the crime charged against her."
>
> General Hartranft unquestionably believed Payne spoke the truth, as the world believes now. . . ." [19]

Rath's impressions of Paine

Lieutenant-Colonel Christian Rath was the provost of the prison and had the duty of conducting the executions. In 1911 *McClure's Magazine* published an article by a writer named John A. Gray, based on a recent interview with Rath, who was well advanced in age.[20] The subtitle explained that the executioner "had taken an oath not to tell what he knew of the Lincoln conspirators until permitted to do by the War Department." For forty-six years, until this interview (so the writer said), he had remained "reticent."

Colonel Rath's mention of his "oath" to keep silent until the War Department gave him permission to talk about the "Lincoln conspirators" raises some questions—in view of the fact that he kept his oath until October, 1911. By that time, almost half a century after the assassination, nearly everyone connected with Stanton's War Department was dead.

*Douglas also believed that the War Department had corrupted the published transcript of the Trial. He said Reverdy Johnson told him the government had bought up and destroyed all the copies of it which could be found (*I Rode with Stonewall,* p. 342).

Ten or more administrations had held office in the meantime, and surely no one in the War Department in 1911 knew anything about Rath's "oath" or could have been responsible for releasing him from it at that late date.

To whom, then, had Rath made his oath of silence? And who released him from it in 1911? Only one official of Stanton's War Department who has been implicated in the assassination plot by our study survived this far into the twentieth century. This one was Thomas T. Eckert. He died on October 20, 1910!

Rath and Eckert were in close communication throughout the Trial. Was it Eckert to whom he had made the oath of silence? Was it Eckert's *death*, rather than his permission, that released the hangman from his oath?

Analysis of some of Rath's statements which conflict with the legend suggests that he may have had some accurate inside information—as well as some of a questionable nature that he had received from Eckert or the detectives who haunted the arsenal during the Trial. Whether or not all his recollections of "Payne" were accurate (he recalled him as a blond-haired man), he still had a surprisingly favorable opinion of the prisoner forty-six years later.

Rath said he took over as provost in the prison just as the Trial was about to begin, which would have been around May 9. His summary of the conspiracy goes like this—suggesting that he was *still* under an oath of secrecy (the writer has italicized some of Rath's statements which merit special attention).

> John Wilkes Booth alone was behind the conspiracy.
>
> The actor made his plans to kill all the heads of the departments on the same night. Lewis Payne (Powell) was to kill Seward, *John Surratt was to kill Grant,* and Booth was to murder Lincoln. He called the conspirators together and revealed his plot. . . .
>
> Payne, on the night of Lincoln's death, knocked at the door of the Seward mansion, and found that the old man, *having retired early,* was in bed. The attendant refused him admittance, but Payne pushed him aside, forced his way upstairs to the hall, and encountered Seward's son Frederick. A scuffle ensued, in which Payne, who was a giant, forced his way to Mr. Seward's room and stabbed him as he lay on the bed. He thought he had killed him, but he had only succeeded in inflicting a wound in his breast. There was great excitement, and in the confusion *Payne escaped by the back door.* He made his way out of the city, and hid in the trenches for some days; but, finding himself in danger of starving to death, *he came in the night to Mrs. Surratt's house, and hid in the cellar,* where he found plenty of food. *He was found there by the officers when they came to look for him. Upon being brought up out of the cellar,* Mrs. Surratt cried to the officers, "So help me God! I don't know the man, and didn't know he was in the house. I never set eyes on him before." Payne also denied that she knew him, and maintained it to the last. He was taken to the prison under heavy guard, and placed in one of the cells on the main floor of the prison.

This portion of Rath's account has been included in order to call attention to an interesting angle of it relating to Paine. The executioner was one of relatively few persons connected with the Trial who believed Mrs. Surratt to be guilty of something. A little earlier he had stated she "had kept a rebel house for the enemy during the war [which was L. C. Baker's story] and whose home was a rendezvous for the conspirators."

Rath's account of the attack upon Seward and "Payne's" activities afterward has obvious discrepancies in a number of its details—including the item that Paine hid in Mrs. Surratt's cellar and was *found there* by the officers who had gone to the boardinghouse looking for *him*. This is a very different version of how the young man was captured. But it reminds us that the only sources of the information that he rang the front doorbell—presumably having just arrived at the house—were (1) the Baker detectives of the search party, whose statements are always open to question, and (2) three of the four women in the house—Mrs. Surratt, who was obviously embarrassed by Paine's presence, and Misses Surratt and Fitzpatrick who could surely *see* the widow didn't want to be identified with him and might be expected to back her up.

The testimony of the *fourth* woman—Mrs. Surratt's niece Olivia Jenkins—is unrecorded, either in the form of initial interrogation or as a witness at the Trial. It is virtually certain she was questioned at the police station as were the others, and that a transcript was made of it. Transcripts of the other three women's interrogations are still found in the National Archives. What became of the record of Olivia Jenkins' statements? Was it removed and destroyed in the same way as the recorded interrogation of the Branson girls? Did it perhaps contain some confirmation for Rath's curious variation in the story—that Mrs. Surratt had allowed Louis Paine to sleep in her cellar—not just since the night before, but for the past week or so, making it impossible for him to have been the "gentleman" at the Herndon House. For what it's worth, the detectives did say that Paine gave conflicting stories as to where he had been sleeping nights—as he might have when he realized his presence there was an embarrassment to his benefactress.

Another thing, 1865 photos of the Surratt house (which see in Plate 14) show us that the door to the front hallway was on the *second* level, at the top of the flight of steps outside. Below the landing, at street level, there was another front door. To the left as you faced the house there was a doorway in a high fence which led to the back yard and, presumably, the back door of the house.

Now, the personnel of the detective detail must have been experienced and competent for Baker to have trusted them with such a delicate mission. Yet *all* their testimony and depositions relate that they were *all* in the house at the same time. They first saw Paine when he knocked and

Morgan opened the door of the front hallway. No one testified to seeing him come down the street and approach the house.

If they *were* efficient detectives, would they have all gone in the front door on the second level and closed the door—leaving at least two exits on the street level unguarded? Or would they have left one man out on the sidewalk and sent another around to the back door to make sure no one slipped out either of the ground floor exits?

Logic argues that they must have taken these normal precautions, and that the outside man's statement regarding Paine's approach—from which direction, whether furtive or not, etc.—would have been part of the testimony on the raid—unless the prisoner was actually found inside, in the cellar.

All Colonel Rath's information on the raid was secondhand. But he had stated earlier that he was on duty at the penitentiary from the beginning of the Trial. Lafayette Baker, Major Eckert, and several of the former's detectives were around the building constantly. Rath had plenty of opportunity to get the inside story of what had occurred at Mrs. Surratt's that night. Perhaps there were parts of his account which weren't so cockeyed as they seemed!

The reason for pursuing this question at all (though we can't pursue it very far) is the abundant testimony from *everyone* who had any close contact with Paine that the young man's *only* anxiety was for Mrs. Surratt. He apparently told everyone who would listen to him that she was innocent—and in the most emphatic terms. One of the court reporters told of Paine's request to dictate a statement to be taken down by an official reporter clearing Mrs. Surratt of "any connection near or remote, with either the conspiracy to abduct or kill the President."[21] He asserted the same conviction to Doster.[22] He impressed General Hartranft so greatly by his plea for the widow that the general wrote a letter to Holt conveying his statements in Mrs. Surratt's behalf.[23] We will read Rath's recollections on this, also Dr. Gillette's.

Paine's deep anxiety to help Mrs. Surratt was hardly consistent with their brief and casual acquaintance, as the records represent it. The revulsion of a Southerner at the hanging of a woman is one explanation of course, though the repetition and vehemence of his appeals for her life were out of proportion with such a motive. If she *had* been very kind to him and sheltered and fed him when he was destitute—and then was implicated in the "conspiracy" because he was found at her house—his urgent desire to see her freed would be very understandable.

Back to the puzzling recollections of Colonel Christian Rath after the passage of forty-six years—with the notation, probably unimportant, that he was only a captain at the time of the Trial:

> One night the guard heard some commotion in Payne's cell, and creeping up

> quietly and looking in, he found the man lying on the floor, bathed in blood. Upon investigation, he found that Payne was not dead, but had tried to beat his brains out against the bars of his cell; a cotton cap heavily padded with batting was put on his head, and a pair of handcuffs with a fourteen inch bar were put on his wrists. The other prisoners, with the exception of the woman, were hooded in the same way. In a few days the effect of this began to tell on the men. The summer was warm and the heat told on the prisoners. Major Porter, the prison physician, was afraid they would lose their reason, so he ordered the caps removed, and then the men felt better.

Here Rath was relating an incident supposed to have taken place at least two weeks before he assumed his duties as provost of the prison, the hooding of the prisoners being dated exactly by Stanton's order of April 22.[24] Also, the prisoners were not in cells at that time, but were kept below decks on the monitors, and had been manacled from the beginning. We find no other testimony that Paine ever tried to take his own life. Since such an action could be construed as evidence of the prisoner's guilt, the prosecutors would have made it a major point in the case against him if he *had* tried to beat his brains out. Also, Doster would have known about it. The executioner was merely repeating the *excuse* he heard for placing hoods on all the prisoners.

> Payne never complained—no matter what you did to him, he never said a word; and I grew fond of the fellow, and was sorry for his predicament. He had been a Confederate soldier, and was wounded at the battle of Gettysburg, taken prisoner on the field, and sent to the hospital at Washington. When he became convalescent, he was paroled—upon taking an oath that he would never bear arms against the Union again. He loafed around the city and finally fell in with Booth, being willing to do anything for the sake of the cause which he loved and believed in. . . .
>
> John Surratt was a coward, and when the time came to kill Grant, he lost his nerve. Before the murder of Lincoln, he escaped from the city. . . .*
>
> The men were allowed to go into the yard, and we listened to their conversation and learned many things that we could have never learned otherwise. They never denied their guilt among themselves, only disagreed upon dates. Payne held himself aloof from the others, although they all knew each other.

Considering what we know about the positive innocence of Arnold, O'Laughlin, Mudd, and Spangler with regard to the assassination—and our supposition that Louis Paine knew nothing about either the plot or the plotters—Rath's statements that "they never denied their guilt" and that "they all knew each other" place him under sudden suspicion, since he is not repeating rumors in this instance, but reporting what he himself observed.

> There was a mystery about Payne. He was a great big fellow, and as brave as a lion. One day General Hartranft said to me: "There is a colored woman

*See Appendix *M;* "Colonel Rath on John Surratt."

> here who comes from Florida and claims she knows Payne; and she says his name is Powell, and that his father is a Baptist minister there. I will seat her in the courtroom and you bring Payne up and perhaps we can identify him." When I took Payne upstairs, the old woman who had been a slave, was sitting in the center of the room. As soon as she saw the prisoner, she ran to him, embracing him and calling him by endearing names. But he repulsed her, looked at her with a stolid look, and said: "I don't know you, woman; go away." She wept and crooned over him, and there was no doubt in my mind that he was really Powell.

Well, there is doubt in this writer's mind about Colonel Rath. It is quite well known that *no one* was permitted to see any of the prisoners without Stanton's personal permission. Moreover, it is a matter of public record (census schedules) that neither the Powell nor Smith families owned slaves as of 1850 and 1860. The only apparent excuse for this yarn is that it seemed to allay any post mortem suspicions that Paine was not really Lewis Powell. But why should Rath bother to tell it forty-six years later? Had he been accused—or was he afraid someone might yet accuse him—of knowingly hanging an innocent man?*

> Payne thought he had killed Seward, and when he was confronted by Mr. Seward in the courtroom he was amazed. . . .
>
> Payne had a grim sense of humor. One day we were discussing our nerve, and afterward I threw myself on the bed for a little sleep. Suddenly I awakened, feeling as if an icy hand had gripped my heart. There was Payne, looking down at me, with an ugly expression on his face. I wondered how he had got out of his cell, and just then saw Lieutenant-Colonel McCall in a corner, laughing. Payne laughed, and I knew they were only trying my nerve. I was not afraid, though I was startled for a time.
>
> Payne's grim humor could come pretty close to being gruesome. On the death-march to the gallows, Payne, who was bare-headed, took McCall's straw hat off his head and put it on his own. His head was large and the hat was too small, and he wore it until it was time to adjust the noose on his neck. It was not because of his lack of reverence, but because of his great sense of humor. He was a good fellow. We used to pitch quoits in the yard together; he was always good natured. . . .

Fortunately, we have a much more reliable witness to the incident of the hat, and will give his version of it presently. The quoit games in the yard show the prisoner as having much more freedom of movement than would be expected, but another account of Paine's last hours confirms

*There is one other possibility which should be raised here—that the former "slave" woman was sent by Baker to introduce an idea which stemmed from the resemblance between Paine and Powell, but had not yet been brought out in court—that Paine *was* Powell. This incident, if it occurred at all, took place *before* the prisoner had "identified" himself as his cousin, possibly even before it had occurred to him to do so. We might conjecture, then, that it was the colored woman's assertion that he was Lewis Powell, son of a Baptist minister in Florida, that suggested the masquerade to him and prompted his "narration" to Doster.

that he could wander about the prison yard during at least part of his confinement. "In the Bible were some flowers he had pressed—white convolvolus and blue larkspur—that had grown in his prison-yard."[25]

> That night Payne sent for me and said: "Captain, if I had two lives to give, I'd give one gladly to save Mrs. Surratt. I know that she is innocent, and would never die in this way *if I hadn't been found in her house* [V. S. italics]. She knew nothing about the conspiracy at all, and is an innocent woman." He knew that the sentence of death had been read to her an hour before, as it had been read to all those who were to die.
>
> I hurriedly conferred with Major Eckhart (sic), telling him what Payne had told me. We hurriedly sent word to the War Department, and in an hour had orders to take Payne's statement. Then I was filled with a great hope, and thought that the woman would be saved after all.

The executioner's description of the scene at the gallows:

> . . . Last of all came Payne. He walked like a king about to be crowned, his fearless blue eyes roving carelessly over the scaffold and his yellow hair shining like a golden halo in the sun. He, too, was attended by a minister and guarded as were the others. . . .
>
> Payne was dressed in his trousers and a close-fitting jersey shirt, open at the throat and showing his powerful neck. When the nooses had been adjusted and the caps pulled over the heads of the condemned, before I gave the signal to the men below to knock the posts from under the drop, I stepped up to Payne, tightened the noose around his neck under the cap, and said: "Payne, I want you to die quick;" to which he replied in a soft voice without a single tremor: "You know best, Captain." That was the last word he ever spoke.

Whatever the flaws and peculiarities in Colonel Rath's story, his opinion of Louis Paine as a man was apparent. It was from a soldier's viewpoint, with the focus on courage. It showed how completely the prisoner had *become* the man he was *pretending* to be—or rather, his idealized conception of how Lewis Powell *should have been* in his last hours and minutes. In short, he had performed a mental tour de force in the space of five or six weeks: He traded in the old Louis Paine, the wretched, hoodooed backslider whom he despised, for a brand new, custom-made model of Lewis Powell, able to walk to his death with the *sang froid* and elegance which Southerners of the old school liked to believe were standard equipment in a Southern soldier and a gentleman. A grandstand play; a waste of precious life and opportunity. But a good performance!

A soldier's reactions to a masterpiece in the art of dying would of course be much different from those of a gentle servant of God whose cardinal impulse was compassion. Louis Paine was an unknown and mysterious quantity to the Rev. Dr. A. D. Gillette, as he was to Colonel Rath. Yet through his eyes and emotions we see the condemned man in broader, and perhaps truer, perspective.

dr. Gillette's impressions

The pastor of Washington's First Baptist Church had evidently not been following the newspaper accounts of the Trial. He didn't know Paine had "revealed" himself to Doster as "Lewis Powell" nearly six weeks earlier. He had no preconception of the prisoner formed by reporters' descriptions of him as a dull-witted cutthroat with ice in his veins. The clergyman was carried into the vortex of this tragedy suddenly and without preparation by Paine's request for his services, to which he responded without hesitation. Of the two, the man about to die and his comforter, the latter seems to have suffered more from the experience. Dr. Gillette noted the event briefly in his journal:

> WASHINGTON, July 9, 1865
>
> Thursday of last week the Asst. Sec'y. of War, Major Eckert called with his carriage and asked me to visit the doomed in the cells who he said were to be executed tomorrow between the hours of ten and two o'clock.
>
> I said yes, and spent the afternoon and all night and was talking and praying with and for them all that time. General Neasheft [Hartranft] and all officials evaporated (sic) kindly. God keep me if I ever have such a trial again.
>
> Payne or Lewis Thornton Powell, as his true name is, was by nature and early culture fitted for eminence and usefulness—son of a good Baptist clergyman in Florida. I had hope of his salvation and told him so a few minutes before he swung into eternity. My God, what a sight! Three young men and one woman old enough to be the Mother of them all—hung by the neck until dead!
>
> Lord's day [same day as this entry] I preached and read, gave the cup and even gave a narrative of my eighteen hours in the cells and on the gallows.[26]

The clergyman's granddaughter, Mrs. Amy Gillette Bassett, wrote—"The family said that for days he seemed incapable of work, and his nights were sleepless. Frequently he would bury his face in his hands, go off by himself."[27]

Although he accompanied Major Eckert to the prison immediately and willingly, Dr. Gillette was greatly puzzled to learn that the condemned man had asked for him by name—he being a staunch Union man whose sons had fought in the Union Army. One of his first questions to Paine was how he happened to know him by name and why he had asked for his services, rather than for those of some clergyman sympathetic to the Southern cause. He received this reply:

"Do you remember, Doctor, a cold and bitter Sunday when you preached in the Reverend Dr. Fuller's church in Baltimore? It was there I heard you as I sat with two ladies in one of the end pews to the right of the pulpit. I thought you might remember that day as you frequently turned toward us."[28]

The "narrative" Dr. Gillette mentioned in his journal was delivered from his pulpit on Sunday, just two days after his harrowing experiences at the penitentiary. The next day's edition of the Washington *Chronical* (Monday, July 10, 1865) published a news story on it. This being the most detailed and reliable report on the last hours of Louis Paine, the portion which concerns him is reproduced in full, as follows:

> Rev. Dr. Gillette, pastor of the First Baptist Church, improved the solemnities of the past week by an appropriate discourse, especially for young men.
>
> He had never been more impressed with the importance of this duty than during the sixteen hours which he passed with the convicts in the penitentiary between Thursday afternoon and that of Friday.
>
> On Thursday Dr. G. was called upon by Assistant Secretary of War Eckert, who invited him to visit the cells of the doomed convicts for the purpose of administering to them such spiritual consolations as were needed. Stepping into the Secretary's carriage, he at once accompanied him thither. On their arrival Mr. Eckert introduced him to other officers, and then to the convicts.
>
> Their first call was upon Payne, whose real name he soon ascertained to be Lewis Thornton Powell, his middle name being after the Rev. Dr. Thornton, a Presbyterian clergyman of Charleston, South Carolina.
>
> Powell welcomed him, and at once proceeded to relate his early history. His father was a Baptist minister. The convict had been from infantcy brought up under religious influence. At twelve years of age he was by his own father consecrated to God in baptism, and became a member of the church. In direct opposition to the wishes of his family he entered the rebellion. For a time he endeavored to retain his religious character, but became connected with Gilmor. This was his second great step downward. That was followed by his getting into Mosby's Gang, which was far worse. His next companion was Booth.
>
> Dr. Gillette found Powell to be a young man of cultivated mind, ingenuous, frank, candid, and an earnest supplicant for Divine favor.
>
> In conversation he referred . . . to his sisters—to the pleasant seasons once enjoyed by him in the church, the Sabbath school and the social circles.
>
> Powell frankly stated his conviction of the enormity of his crime. The moment he fled from the house of Secretary Seward and leaped into the saddle of his horse, his mind was quickened into a realizing sense of the horror of the damnable deed which he had perpetrated, and he became miserable, wretched—life itself became loathsome.
>
> The Doctor here corrected two points in the published statement. It was reported that he wore "a jaunty hat." That hat was placed on his head by the advice and hands of Dr. G., when Powell's hands were pinioned behind him. Dr. G. suggested the hat on account of the intense heat of the sun.
>
> Secondly. It was said on the morning of his execution he ate heartily &c. On that morning he positively declined taking any food; and he was equally persistent in refusing stimulants of any kind.
>
> His last prayer was, as suggested by his friend, the Doctor, "Lord Jesus, receive my spirit."

When Dr. Gillette's "narration" is read as applying to Louis Paine, whose career we have been studying, rather than to Lewis Powell, the assassin hired by Lafayette Baker to supervise the murder of Lincoln and the liquidation of Booth by poison, the account acquires new shades of meaning.

Evidently, without disrespect for Dr. Gillette or lack of appreciation for his devoted services as comforter and *friend*, the condemned man used him as a medium of communication with someone he wished to know a different version of how and why "Lewis Payne" had died—the Reverend George C. Powell.

Paine's "narrative" to Colonel Doster had contained more than enough discrepancies to inform his uncle that it was he, not his son, who was hanged. The attorney had written, but had no reply. Also, Paine could not be *sure* Doster had related the "biography" in enough detail to convey his message to the Rev. Powell.

Dr. Gillette, on the other hand, could be counted upon, he believed, to write his fellow clergyman minute particulars, particularly regarding his spiritual preparation for the hereafter—"that he had repented and had his hope in heaven"; that "He was entirely resigned to his fate, and . . . would never enjoy life, even if he were pardoned."[29]

One of the precautions he took to guarantee delivery of his message was in asking Dr. Gillette to send the Rev. Powell "his Bible and *autograph.*" The Bible, of course, was merely the agency—the sacred object Dr. Gillette would surely send to his "father." The *autograph,* inscribed on the flyleaf, would tell its own story to the Rev. Powell, who knew his son's signature—and knew that his nephew could hardly write his *own* name. How, then, could he write "Powell?" He couldn't! The only name he knew how to write was the one under which he was tried and executed —"L. Paine" or "H. L. Payne."

There was another message for the Rev. Powell—an enlightening clue, rather—in the prisoner's statement that his middle name, "Thornton," was after the Rev. Dr. Thorton, "a Presbyterian clergyman of Charleston, S. C." It seems that Louis had heard of, or possibly met, the Rev. Powell's old friend and mentor from Talbot County, Georgia—Elder Reuben Thornton, who had encouraged George's aspirations to the ministry, and eventually served on the presbytery which approved his ordination at Liberty Church in Russell County, Alabama, three years after Lewis Powell was born—and given the middle name "Thornton."

Because he hadn't followed the news reports of the Trial and apparently knew nothing about Paine, except that he was one of those sentenced to hang for the "conspiracy" against Lincoln, Seward, Johnson, Grant, et al., Dr. Gillette described the prisoner largely in terms of the kind of person he found him to be—without even coloring his viewpoint with any personal judgments upon the crime he was supposed to have committed.

The resulting effect was probably the *only* unbiased description of Louis Paine by an observer whom we know was really talking about *him,* and had no reason nor desire to misrepresent him. Allowing for the fact that Dr. Gillette found the young man behaving himself admirably in a tragic situation, his comments endowed the prisoner with the qualities of a spiritual as well as a physical giant.

"By nature and early culture fitted for eminence and usefulness. . . . a young man of cultivated mind, ingenuous, frank, candid, and an earnest supplicant for Divine favor." In another interview with the press: "He impressed the clergyman as a person of correct religious ideas.[30]

Integrate these qualities with the remarkable self-control and strength of will (however sadly misapplied) which Colonel Rath noted, and we see a young man with unique potential, oriented for religious leadership. But there were also some weaknesses of flesh which Paine evidently despised in himself—for which he condemned *himself* to death.

Dr. Gillette reported the only instance in Louis Paine's three-month ordeal in which he is known to have given way even briefly to emotion. "He referred to his mother and wept bitterly."

Shall we assume the young prisoner wept for his *own* mother, rather than for Lewis Powell's? (See Appendix N, "Dr. Gillette's Journal.")

For the final moments in the short life of Louis Paine, we refer again to Dr. Gillette's account, as told by his granddaughter:[31]

> On the scaffold there was no scene, no theatrics. Payne kept asking if any word of a reprieve had come for Mrs. Surratt. "She does not deserve to die with us, Doctor," he told my grandfather. Bound about the arms and ankles he sat quietly during the final operations.
>
> The horror of the long three-hour wait [due to General Hancock's delayed arrival] took its toll, and my grandfather was ill for a long time after that day. He had done his best to shield Payne with an umbrella, and in the Brady photograph I can pick out the Doctor's tall figure in the frock coat he wore as a sort of uniform in those days in the pulpit, but whether he was holding the umbrella over Mrs. Surratt or Payne I cannot be sure. The heat was terrific, and when some movement dislodged Payne's hat he [Dr. Gillette] put it back on his head. With a faint glimmer of a smile Payne looked up and said, "Thank you, Doctor, I won't be needing it much longer." A few moments more and he was dangling with the others, at the end of a rope. It was a dishonored death for a most unsoldierly crime, but in the final picture there was something of dignity in the calmness and the silence.

20

the reverend George C. Powell

an epilogue

The bloodshed and destruction of civil war passed by well to the north of Hamilton County, Florida. But its shock waves rolled outward in all directions. They rolled over the Rev. George C. Powell and ground him into the earth.

He was sick when Doster's first letter brought word of his "son's" predicament as a defendant at the Conspiracy Trial. Or did the news with its staggering implications *make* him sick, coming as it did on top of the earlier blows the war had dealt him and his family?

The minister had lost two of his four sons—killed in battle. His eldest was gravely wounded twice and possibly crippled. His youngest had been captured at Gettysburg, and his whereabouts was unknown. Two of his sons-in-law had lost their lives.* The mortality in his wide relationship had been heavy. That Lewis Thornton might return home safely was the Rev. Powell's only hope of salvaging one whole son from the wreckage.

correspondence with colonel Doster

It seems that Colonel Doster's first letter was mysteriously delayed. He had mailed it in the latter part of May, but it didn't reach Powell until July 6. As soon as he was able, he took a train for the first leg of the journey to Washington. At Jacksonville he learned that it was already too late. His "son" had been executed on July 7. The same newspapers which brought him this tragic news carried articles identifying him as the father of the assassin. The descriptions of his "son" were quoted from

*Obediah and James Newman were the husbands of Powell's daughters Elizabeth and Mary. They were two of four Newman brothers who enlisted at Bowling Green, Ky. on Sept. 24, 1861. All four died of wounds or disease in the western theater (Adjutant General's Report, Confederate Kentucky Volunteers).

Northern newspapers and pictured the prisoner "Payne" as the very incarnation of evil:

> After Herold comes Payne, next to Mrs. Surratt the great character of the party. He is tall, straight, stout—the perfection of physical form. It would be hard to guess whether keen activity or muscular energy predominates in him. . . . His large head is thickly covered with black hair; his forehead is almost entirely wanting; his face has no beard; his neck is as immense as a bull's, and yet smooth and fair; his lips thin and firm; his nose small; but his eye—the characteristic feature—reminds you of the man who said "Our name is legion," only you can see that the said legion has not entered. It is an eye of deliberately rolling fire—a pair of perdition-lighted torches; when they move they flash and glare, rather than look. This is not a mere reading of the man's crime, already known, in his look; it is a reasonably sober description of the reality. As you look at his great form, sitting calmly erect and seemingly reckless, you think of a modern boxer or a Roman gladiator. When you meet his eye, you think of Lucifer; but when, in the light of that eye, you regard the whole face, you are reminded of Satan in the swine—a possessed brute. Nothing moves him; without looking defiant, he is imperturbed and perfectly at home. His nerves appear to have gone into muscle.
>
> *Florida Times Union,* July 24, 1865, quoting the Rev. B. H. Nadal in the *New York Methodist*

It is hard to determine how great a factor the notoriety was in the collapse of the Rev. Powell's career. His burden of sorrow, without outside help, was enough to crush him. In 1868 he made the first of a number of changes of residence, which showed him trying to outrun the stigma, and moved down to Lake Jessup in Orange County.[1] The 1870 census-taker found him in Orlando with his wife—who was now using her middle name, *Patience,* rather than Caroline—and his youngest and only unmarried daughter, Anna. He gave his occupation as "blacksmith."

By 1871 he had moved again, this time to the little town of Oviedo, a few miles north of Orlando. This was the year he made a vain effort to return to the ministry. In March he was called to Orlando to re-organize the Bethel Baptist Church, which had been dissolved ten years earlier when the war began. The outcome of this undertaking was described with as much compassion as Mr. W. H. Brack, the clerk, could manage and still tell the truth:

"Brother Powell was a good preacher and a very earnest Christian but addicted to whisky. He was strict in his discipline and had some of the members turned out for non-attendance. The church became tired of his strict discipline and in October 1872 they called Rev. A. C. Tinall as pastor."—*History of Orlando Baptists,* E. H. Gore

By the time of the 1880 census, Rev. and Mrs. Powell, now seventy and sixty-five respectively, were living in a cottage on the farm of their son-in-law Isiah D. Hart in Orange County. Mr. Hart had married their next-to-youngest daughter, Minerva. The elderly couple had one other member of their household, a young colored man named Peter Williams, who cared for them.

Early the following year, Patience Powell was granted the peace of death.* Powell, stooped with his burden of years and heartbreak, followed his life companion quickly. He died in November 1881, "aged 72, less one month" (Appendix O, "Elder George C. Powell: Obituary and Eulogy") at the home of his son-in-law H. L. Meeks in Apopka, Orange County.

The special quality of the Rev. Powell's tribulation was the knowledge that although the young man who was hanged was *not* his son, the man who had participated in the assassination of President Lincoln *was*—and had escaped. Thus he had a Hobson's choice. He could deny that the man executed was his son—and thereby trigger a sensational investigation which would reveal that Lewis Thornton Powell was the guilty man and was at large. By doing this, he would condemn his own son to the life of a hunted criminal.

Or he could accept the stigma and not deny that it was Lewis Powell who had conspired with Booth and been hanged. By doing this, he could relieve his own son of all possible suspicion—allowing him to be completely free, except for the slight inconvenience of having no name or history of his own.

Since he started for Washington when he first heard the news—or said he did, at least—Powell may have made the hard first choice originally. But Paine's execution before he could get there changed the picture. The father's decision to take the second alternative would be understandable, particularly since he was a minister of the gospel and might have had hopes that Lewis Powell's soul could be redeemed by the scourging of conscience.

Two persons involved in the trial and execution of Louis Paine felt an obligation to communicate with the Baptist minister who the prisoner *said* was his father. One of these was Colonel Doster, who apparently hoped Powell would be able to save his client's life by helping to prove him insane. The other was the Reverend Dr. Abram Gillette, whose only wish was to keep faith with the doomed young man he had befriended and offer a grieving father what little comfort he could.

If only for the sake of research, it's a great pity we don't have the letters these two men wrote to the Rev. Powell. But the burden of their messages can be conjectured. And far greater enlightenment is found in the clergyman's answers, which fortunately *are* preserved.

---

*No record of Mrs. Powell's death can be located in Florida, but Mrs. W. O. Richey of Boyce, La., who contributed much to our genealogical research, wrote of a Powell family tradition which indicated Patience preceded her husband in death.

Powell wrote one answer to *two* letters the attorney sent him. It was dated nearly *three months* after the Colonel's first one had arrived.

> LIVE OAK, EAST FLORIDA, Sept. 30, 1865
>
> DEAR SIR: On my return home some days since, I found your very welcome letter, which brought me some *interesting items* in reference to my unfortunate and lamented son. Be assured, sir, that your kindness both to him and myself are highly appreciated. At the time your first letter reached me I was confined to my bed, and it was received only the day before the execution. I did not answer it, for I intended to come to Washington as soon as possible, and started as soon as I could travel. At Jacksonville I met the sad intelligence of his execution and returned home in sorrow, such as is not common for human hearts to bear.
>
> As to his early history, he was born in the state of Alabama, April 22, 1844 (I see by a statement of his that he was mistaken by one year in his age). In the twelfth year of his age he made a profession of religion, and from that time he lived a pious life up to the time of his enlistment. He was soon ordered to Virginia. From that time forward I know nothing of him only by letter. He was always kind and tender-hearted, yet determined in all his undertakings. He was much esteemed by all who knew him, and bid fair to usefulness in Church and State. Please accept the warmest thanks of myself and family for the services rendered the unfortunate youth.
>
> Very truly and sincerely yours,
> GEORGE C. POWELL

Was the letter the Reverend Powell wrote to Colonel Doster consistent with these *supposed* circumstances?

Several aspects impress us with the fact that it was *not*. The tone was impersonal, not to say *unfeeling*. The term "interesting items" with reference to the statements and confessions of the dead "son" suggested an academic, rather than a personal interest in him. Most of the first paragraph was devoted to excusing the "father's" astonishing behavior in failing to respond in any way for nearly three months. Correction of the birth date showed an incongruous interest in statistics. Statements as to the "pious" early life of the dead assassin were *not* followed by expressions of regret for the "son's" monstrous crime which we would expect to find in a letter from the "father" to a Union officer. The grief-stricken "father's" final reference to his youngest "son" as an *"unfortunate youth"* seemed remarkable from any viewpoint. We wonder if the term didn't stir Colonel Doster to indignation. *Unfortunate* to have been caught and convicted as one of the assassins of President Lincoln? Not a word in the Reverend Powell's letter questioned the guilt of the "unfortunate youth."

Of course, these observations are applicable only if the clergyman's letter was written under the *supposed* circumstances. If the letter was written with full knowledge that the young man who had been executed was *not* the writer's son, these several peculiarities show only that the Reverend Powell wasn't greatly distressed by the fate of Louis Paine.

The important consideration is whether Powell was talking about his *son* or his *nephew* in the second paragraph. The birth date he mentioned was obviously Lewis Thornton Powell's, since we know Paine was born in 1842. But from there on his information could apply to either young man.

As it happens, one statement in Powell's letter carried a strong implication that *all* of his second paragraph after the item of the birth date was with reference to Louis Paine rather than his son. He said his "son" enlisted and was soon sent to Virginia. Then—*"From that time forward I know nothing of him only by letter."*

Confederate Army records show this statement by Powell to have been false beyond reasonable doubt—*as applying to his son Lewis.* A muster roll of patients at the Florida Hospital (General Hospital No. 11) in Richmond, Virginia, dated November 14, 1862, listed Private L. T. Powell, Company I, Second Regiment, Florida, as a patient. This roll carried the notation that Private Powell had enlisted (re-enlisted) for the "War" on May 8, 1862, in *Jasper, Florida.*

These official records make it clear that Lewis Powell received the two-month furlough authorized by the "Bounty and Furlough Act" for twelve-month men who re-enlisted for the duration. He spent his furlough at his home in Hamilton County, Florida, and during it the Rev. Powell could hardly have failed to see him.

Thus, he was saying that *Louis Paine* was sent to Virginia and that he knew nothing more of him except by letter (from other persons who wrote of him.)

This implication that Paine may have joined a Florida regiment and been sent to Virginia in 1861 seems less incredible when we recall that he remembered the names of the original commanders of the 2nd Florida Infantry and its Company I. But that company's roster didn't list either a Private Louis Paine or a Private H. L. Payne. Records of Paine's first twelve-month enlistment have not yet been found, and some signs point to the possibility that they were destroyed by the War Department. (See Appendix P, "Louis Paine's Army Records.")

correspondence with Gillette

Dr. Gillette, according to his granddaughter, "was a sick man for weeks [after the executions] and never spoke of the matter to the family for years after . . ."[2] Two months passed before he could face the distressing task of writing to the "father" of the young man he had attended in the death cell and on the scaffold. Although his letter is not preserved, its contents can be assumed from the other entries in his journal and from Powell's answers.

The first of Powell's replies was written in November, 1865. When he received no answer to it, he wrote again in March, 1866. Both documents were handed down to Mrs. Bassett and placed in the custody of the Library of Congress. They are being quoted in full here, with the lady's gracious permission, from photocopies of the original letters.

Our only liberty in transcribing the first letter which follows has been to reduce the number of capitalized words, which Powell used profusely, in accordance with the old style.

LIVE OAK STATION, E. FLA.
Nov. 7, 1865

Revd. Dr. A. D. Gillett

DEAR BROTHER—

Your kind favor of the 12th Sept. last was duly rec'd. and I assure you the contents were read with great interest by myself and family. Pray except (sic) my Dear Brother my most sincere thanks and my humble gratitude for the many kind services and faithful religious instructions rendered to my dear son Lewis Thornton. Such acts of kindness my Dear Brother will ever be remembered with heartfelt gratitude by myself and family.

You will confer a favor by presenting my kind regards to Major Eckert and return him my thanks for his kindness and good will toward our son Lewis Thornton, also to all others who were kind enough to assist my son, to those I shall ever remain under a debt of gratitude.

Lewis left home to enlist in the war much against the wish of all the family. Previous to and up to the time of his leaving home he was very pious and consistent, was much respected by all of his associates and took great interest in the Young Men's Prayer Meeting and all other religious services. His favorite hymn he often sung to the family commences

"Farewell, farewell to all below;
My Saviour calls and I must go;"

Please write to me as early as possible as I am anxious at all times to hear from you being assured that everything in reference to my son is very interesting to us.

We will regard it as a special favor if you will please forward those articles you stated that Lewis left.

I remain in great affliction most respectfully your faithful Brother in Christ.

GEORGE C. POWELL

P. S.

You will confer a favor upon me and also upon one of my friends and Sisters in Christ by making enquiries of Major Eckert and elsewhere if you deem it proper in regard to John F. Butler, Company (B,) 18th Geo. Bat., Capt. Styles Comdg.

He was wounded and supposed to be taken prisoner. Any information of him thankfully rec'd by his distressed wife—

Your &c G. C. P.

The much greater warmth of this letter—compared to the one to Doster—was undoubtedly a response to the kindness and sympathy expressed by Dr. Gillette. Also, the Union clergyman had apparently gone into some detail about the evidences of religious outlook and training he had noticed in the prisoner during their long conversations. Powell felt able to speak almost freely on this subject, and mentioned his "son's" intense interest in church affairs and services—adding particulars on this aspect of the dead man's background which were *altogether out of character* for Lewis Powell, but very much *in character* for Louis Paine.

This writer receives the very strong impression that Powell misinterpreted Dr. Gillette's favorable comments on the prisoner's spirituality (perhaps exaggerated, with the intention of comforting his clergyman "father") to mean that the Washington minister suspected the condemned man's religious impulses were too authentic for him to have committed the crime for which he was hanged.

Dr. Gillette's reticence about discussing the subject even with his own family after that, and his failure to communicate with Powell again, suggest that this letter affected him most adversely. In addition to suspicions it might have aroused that the *guilty* man had gone free, the intimation that he had assisted in hanging an intensely religious, *innocent* young man would have served only to compound the pain of a memory which was already almost unbearable.

Doster's book wasn't written and published until 1915. Dr. Gillette could not have known that Powell learned of his "son's" plight only the day before the executions. The attorney's statement that he had "sent for" the prisoner's father late in May had been made in open court and published in the newspapers and later in the Pitman and Peterson transcripts of the Trial. If Powell's letter made him suspect the Florida minister *knew* that the man hanged was *not* guilty, it was only a step to this conclusion: That Powell had *ignored* Doster's summons, had abandoned the innocent Paine to his fate in order to let his guilty son go free!

This may seem to suggest a grotesque misunderstanding—too fanciful to have really happened. We cannot submit it as more than a plausible theory at this point. But it is a theory *very* strongly supported by discovery of the *verses* to what Powell referred to as his "son's" "favorite hymn he often sung to the family."

Farewell, farewell to all below,
My Jesus calls and I must go;
I launch my boat upon the sea,
This land is not for me.

CHORUS: This world is not my home
This world is not my home,
This world is all a wilderness,
This world is not my home.

I found the winding path of sin
A rugged path to travel in;
Beyond the chilly waves I see
The land my Savior bought for me.

O sinners, will you not go?
There is room enough for you I know,
Our boat is sound, the passage free,
And there is a better land for thee.

Farewell dear friends, I cannot stay,
The home I seek is far away;
Where Christ is not, I cannot be.
This land is not the land for me.

Praise be to God, our hope on high,
The angels sing, and so will I;
Where seraphs bow and bend the knee,
Oh that's the land, the land for me.*

Perhaps the quotation of the first two lines was the method Powell chose to explain the doomed man's puzzling resignation to his brother Baptist minister—on the assumption that Dr. Gillette would either *know* the rest of the verses or would take the trouble to look them up. The point of view of the hymn was too compatible with the behavior of Louis Paine for Dr. Gillette to have missed the point—that the man who was hanged was a man incapable of conspiring to commit one murder and attempting another with his own hand.

Five months later, not having heard from Dr. Gillette in the meantime, Powell wrote again as follows:

Live Oak, East Fla.
March 4, 1866

Revd. Dr. A. D. Gillette
Washington, D. C.
Dear Sir & Brother—

I recd. yours of 12th Sept. some time in November last and immediately answered it and have been most anxiously awaiting a reply, but as yet I have not heard from you, the reason why I am at a loss to imagine.

You stated that my son left his Bible, autograph and other articles with you, also a few articles with some money which was in the hands of the Asst. Secty. of War.

In my last I requested you to please forward these articles to me but as they have not yet arrived I presume something has occurred to prevent your

*After many, many hours of searching in old Baptist hymnals, these verses were found by Mr. W. J. Berry, editor of Primitive Publications, Elon College, North Carolina. The hymn, which has no title, is No. 506 in a Collection by Elder E. D. Thomas; published by Arrowood Brothers, Wayne, W. Va. Mr. Berry informed us that "the author's name is not given in this book."

compliance with my request, or perhaps you have not received my letter. I hope my Dear Sir you will please get the articles from the Secty. of War and send them with the articles you have by Express to me. Make them in as small a package as possible and direct to me at Live Oak Station, Penn & Geo Rail Road, Florida. Also please inform me if it is possible I would be permitted to get and remove the remains of my son from Washington, D. C., to my home in Florida and if so would I be safe in so doing and what would be the best plan to remove him.

I would not make any effort to remove his remains unless it was perfectly agreeable with the Government Authorities.

You will please accept the sincere thanks of myself and family for your past kindness as we shall ever be under a great debt of gratitude to you that time can never efface from our memories and you will confer a lasting favor by complying with the above request at your earliest possible convenience, and any other information you may be pleased to give will be thankfully received by most

Respectfully
Your afflicted Brother
and most obt. servt.
George C. Powell

Direct to
Revd. George C. Powell
Live Oak Station
Penn & Geo Rail Road
Suwannee County
East Florida

We have no way of knowing whether the Bible, "autograph," and other articles were finally sent to the Rev. Powell. Mrs. Bassett told the writer that her grandfather's journal made no further reference to the subject, nor was he known to have received any other letters from the Florida clergyman. She stated that the Bible was not handed down through her family, and she felt that Dr. Gillette would surely have sent it to Powell.

The final disposition of Louis Paine's personal belongings remains a matter of uncertainty. But there is no uncertainty as to the disposition of his earthly remains, or whether Powell was able to get permission from the War Department to have them removed to Florida. He was *not*.

The National Archives have records of applications by the relatives of Mrs. Surratt, Atzerodt, and Herold for possession of the remains of these three "conspirators." There is no record of an application for the remains of "Lewis Payne." Officially they were unclaimed.

Paine's body remained in its initial grave in the courtyard of the arsenal until 1869, when it was moved to Holmead Cemetery, near Nineteenth Street and Florida Avenue.[3] In later years the cemetery was discontinued to make way for an office building. All remains were exhumed and buried elsewhere at an unknown location.[4]

the real Lewis Powell

Research at any unexplored level of human experience produces more new questions than new answers. The residue of unsolved problems at the close of our study is more than desired but less than expected. Some can be solved fully or partially by those who have access to private or obscure records which have been unavailable to us. Others are beyond the reach of inquiry by any recognized means. Yet, in principle, *nothing* is beyond the reach of the human mind.

One question is too tantalizing to be swept into the corner along with the others for which we have no reasonable answers. It is a corollary of Louis Paine's masquerade as Lewis Powell—the real accomplice and supervisor of John Wilkes Booth. The reader will have asked it, as we did:

What became of Lewis Powell?

The logical first thought is that he placed as much distance as he could between himself and everyone who had ever known him; went to Europe or South America; settled in some dusty, incurious little community west of civilization in his own country, using an assumed name; perhaps wandered from place to place, never safe from exposure.

This might be his destiny from *our* point of view. But the governing factor was *his* point of view.

Can we assume he thought of himself as a criminal? He had been a soldier in a movement dedicated to the dissolution of the Union. The Confederacy had idolized its military heroes who had killed scores of the "enemy" with their own hands. The people of the North had done the same. Lewis Powell had merely outdone all his countrymen by supervising the execution of the Confederacy's Number One "enemy." It so happened that there was an official of the Union government so corrupt as to pay him for doing this. The blood on his own hands—Seward's—was also that of an enemy of the South.

Powell had planned to escape, naturally, and did so. We assume he had not *planned* that his cousin should be arrested in his place. The cousin's professions of guilt were his own idea, and surely they must have been as puzzling to Lewis Powell as to anyone else. Having made a successful getaway, was he obligated to go back and put his neck in a noose because his misguided kinsman refused to clear *himself*? Powell would have thought he had done more than honor required by sitting in a courtroom face-to-face with Louis Paine—giving him a chance to point a finger and say, "There's the guilty man."

When it was all over, his position was unique. A man who resembled him closely enough to have *been* he had been executed with the "identification," if not under the name, of "Lewis Thornton Powell." In effect, "Lewis Payne" had never existed, and Lewis Powell was dead. He was a completely free member of society with only two defects, both of which were mere inconveniences: (1) He had no personal history, and (2) he had no name.

If Powell wanted to go home, either from a troubled conscience or from mere preference, what was to prevent it? *No one* in Florida who had known him before had seen him more recently than the spring of 1862, when he had just turned nineteen. Since then he had done a lot of living. *Everyone* in Florida, except for his immediate family, *knew* he was dead. Even if he were to go there and *say* he was Lewis Powell, no one would believe him.

The final lines of the Rev. George C. Powell's obituary state that his death "occurred at West Opopka, Orange County, *at the residence of his son-in-law, H. L. Meeks,* November 1881. . . ."

Ordinarily, the theory that Lewis Powell would have gone home to Florida would present a most discouraging prospect for research. That he would have assumed a new name goes without saying. Even the knowledge that he usually borrowed the names of men he had known, rather than inventing new ones, would help very little, since he'd known hundreds of people or might have decided to vary the pattern.

Mr. H. L. Meeks of Apopka emerged as the prime candidate. There was the coincidence that his first initials were the same as Louis Paine's —as revealed by our research, but otherwise known only to the immediate Powell family. Also, "Meeks" was a familiar name in Georgia and Florida, and Powells had intermarried with some of them. By Lewis' formula for choosing aliases, "H. L. Meeks" filled the bill—since both initials and name could be connected with persons Lewis Powell had known previously.

Much more to the point, *all* of the documentary material collected supported the conclusion that H. L. Meeks was *not* Powell's *son-in-law.* (The analysis of records and documents by which this theory was supported is presented in Appendix Q, "H. L. Meeks.")

Lewis Thornton Powell—H. L. Meeks. The evidence favors their single identity. To date, the chief argument against it is mere disbelief. And remember, we are talking about a man whose later years may very well have been within the early memory of persons still living. In 1900 H. L. Meeks would have been only fifty-six (if he was Lewis Powell). There may be some who, as children in Orange County, Florida, knew him as a neighbor or local citizen and can describe him.

The possibilities for research are excellent. A comparison of signatures may be possible. A document bearing the signature "Lewis T. Powell" may yet be found. And H. L. Meeks must have signed his name to dozens of public and commercial papers if he lived the normal life of a farmer.

The answer to this riddle is in a faded letter stored and forgotten in someone's attic—or in a mundane public document in an old file that has no remote connection with the murder of Abraham Lincoln.

addendum

author's conception of the conspiracy

Like Seward, Stanton, and many others, Colonel L. C. Baker, chief of the War Department detective bureau, had exploited the Civil War crisis to attain a position of personal power in the federal government. The war was drawing to a close. Peace would bring an abrupt and inevitable end to the powers in his grasp and his ambitions for more.

President Lincoln, with his asserted policy of reconciliation and return to normalcy at home and abroad, was clearly the agency through which Baker's fortunes would be eclipsed. The detective knew that certain others in government, whose lofty positions were equally endangered, favored the elimination of Lincoln and the perpetuation of crisis. They might not collaborate in assassination, but they would give it their tacit approval.

John Surratt was a double agent, and Baker was his contact in the North. For months he had kept Baker informed about Booth's bizarre scheme to kidnap the President from a theater. The thing had possibilities for Baker. At the very least, he could add to his laurels by exposing Booth and his "gang" if an abduction ever materialized.

But nothing happened, and nothing was likely to happen. With Baker's approval, Surratt brought in the professional Lewis Powell to get the action started. Powell made a deep impression on Booth, but the Confederate deserter saw at once that the actor was a posturing, prating egotist, obsessed with the idea of a grand gesture before an audience—but wholly incapable of bringing it off.

After the quarrelsome March 15 meeting at Gautier's in Washington, Booth's "gang" dispersed, and the kidnap scheme was dead. Lewis Powell went to New York to report to Baker and try to line up something else. The murder plot was hatched as a result of this interview.

It may have been Powell who saw the possibilities for converting the would-be kidnapper into an assassin, but the full-blown plan had the Baker touch. Booth was already primed to do *something* dramatic during a theatrical performance. Under Powell's skillful direction the something would become *murder*, rather than abduction. The actor was so well known to Washington audiences that his identity as Lincoln's assassin would be known at once to everyone. Arrangements could be made to liquidate him immediately after the crime—and that would be the end of it. No search for the culprit, no further investigation; case closed!

Surratt, being the older acquaintance of Booth, was called to New York by Baker (The R. D. Watson letter) and given instructions for introducing the actor to this new plan to make him famous. Powell returned to Washington and set up his headquarters in the Herndon House. Execution of the scheme was his responsibility, and he had various arrangements to make before he'd be ready to take Booth in hand.

Powell enlisted the help of two persons formerly connected with the kidnap plot—Mrs. Surratt and David Herold. The widow had the actor's confidence and agreed to help mold his state of mind to the theme that Lincoln was the cause of all the nation's woes, and his death would be a blessing applauded by millions.

Herold would take Booth in tow after the crime and see that he joined Lincoln in eternity the same night. Booth could be counted on to accept a drink and to drink greedily. It was a simple matter to put a killing dose of white arsenic in the liquor.

While these preparations were being made, Baker gave his attention to the possible repercussions.

Baker's estimate, probably confirmed by Eckert, was that Stanton would see the vast political advantages to be reaped from Lincoln's death and, if forewarned, wouldn't interfere. On April 10 Baker went down to Washington to call on the Secretary of War. He expressed his "fears" that a plot was afoot to kill the President at one of the city's theaters on the coming Friday evening, April 14. Stanton professed to doubt the rumor but got the message. Baker returned to New York on the thirteenth, sure of his boss' static co-operation.

Bates' account of Lincoln's visit to the War Department on Friday afternoon showed Stanton virtually *ordering* the President not to go to the theater—a neat bit of negative psychology that made Lincoln determined to go. But no specific warning was given, and no effective steps were taken to protect the victim during the performance.

The plot was sound, relatively simple, and—under Powell's deft and subtle supervision—organized down to the last detail, Booth being led to believe that *he* was the leader and star of the company. It should have worked and it *would* have worked, but two unforeseen circumstances upset its delicate balance.

First, someone in the know (apparently Major Eckert) saw an opportunity to kill at least two birds with one stone. He made a side contract with Powell to kill William H. Seward in the same operation, timing the second attack to make it look like the work of the same assassin who killed Lincoln. The timing was too close, and the double crime suggested the involvement of more than one assailant—thus a conspiracy.

Second, Booth was a brandy-drinker. He accepted the bottle of liquor from Herold at Lloyd's tavern, drank some, but didn't like the taste. He didn't drink enough—got deathly sick but was able to make it to Dr. Mudd's and then to the Samuel Cox plantation ten miles away. For a whole week Herold sat there helpless, waiting for his victim to die. But Booth seemed to recover somewhat, and they moved on.

In the meantime Powell was safely on his way to Canada. He was completely free of suspicion, due to Baker's accidental arrest of Paine —a substitute suitable for framing, since he looked like Powell's twin.

Baker, Eckert, Stanton, and others who knew the score were living a nightmare in fear of imminent exposure. If Booth were found alive and talking, they would be ground zero for the greatest political explosion of modern times. Fortunately from their point of view, one of their number was more than a hand-wringer.

Colonel Baker went into action. His first move was to take every possible precaution against Booth's falling into any hands but his. His detectives failed to find the actor in the area south of Washington where Baker expected him to be found. It was sheer blind luck that the Baker-Conger party picked up the trail and traced the fugitives to Garrett's farm. Sergeant Corbett evidently shot Booth in the expectation that the act would make him a public hero. But, in any case, the assassin wouldn't have been brought back to Washington alive.

L. C. Baker's second and concurrent measure was surely one of history's great achievements in treachery. The situation, with public hysteria over the crime and the escape of the known culprit mounting, called for immediate, dramatic steps in the direction of *punishment*. Explanation and expiation must be prompt and convincing.

The detective's solution was the Conspiracy Trial—ordered by Stanton but engineered by Baker. Eight handpicked "accomplices" with Booth must be arraigned, tried, sentenced, and hanged in the shortest possible time and with maximum publicity. In the process, the country must be given a plausible explanation for Lincoln's murder and the satisfaction of seeing someone punished.

The chances against the success of such an audacious undertaking, conducted in the spotlight of world attention and interest, were too great for calculation. But unvarying human nature equalized the odds. This was the sequence of crime and punishment the people *wanted* to see. These were the explanations they *wanted* to believe. L. C. Baker, the supreme psychologist, won the gamble.

appendix

appendix

A— the Sam letter

The following was presented in evidence against Samuel Arnold, in the Bingham argument (Peterson, page 195).

March 27, 1865

DEAR JOHN:—

Was business so important that you could not remain in Baltimore till I saw you? I came in as soon as I could, but found you had gone to Washington. I called also to see *Mike,* but learned from his mother that he had gone out with you and had not returned. I concluded, therefore, he had gone with you. How inconsiderate you have been! When I left you, you stated that *we would not meet* in a month or so, and therefore I made application for employment, an answer to which I shall receive during the week. I told my parents I had ceased with you. Can I, then, under existing circumstances, act as you request? You know full well that the Government suspicions something is going on there. Therefore the *undertaking* is becoming more complicated. Why not, *for the present,* desist? For various reasons, which, if you look into you can readily see without my making any mention thereof, you, nor any one, can censure me for my present course. You have been its cause, for how can I now come after telling them I had left you? Suspicion rests upon me now from my whole family and even parties in the country.

I will be compelled to leave home any how, and how soon I care not. None, no not one, were more in favor of the enterprise than myself, and today would be there, had you not done as you have. By this, I mean manner of proceeding. I am, as you well know, in *need.* I am, you may say, in rags, whereas, today, I ought to be *well clothed.* I do not feel right stalking about with *means,* and more from appearances a beggar. I feel my dependence. But, even all this would have been, and was, forgotten, for *I was one with you.* Time more *propitious* will arrive yet. Do not act rashly or in haste. I would prefer your first, query, "Go and see how it will be taken in Richmond," and, *ere long,* I shall be better prepared *to again be with you.* I dislike writing. Would sooner verbally make known my views. Yet your not waiting causes me thus to proceed. Do not in anger peruse this. Weigh all I have said, and, as a rational man and a *friend,* you cannot censure or upbraid my conduct. I sincerely trust this, nor aught else that shall or may occur, will ever be an obstacle to obliterate our former friendship and attachment. Write me to Baltimore, as I expect to be in about Wednesday or Thursday; or, if you can possibly come on, I will Tuesday meet you at Baltimore at B.

Ever, I subscribe myself, your friend,

"SAM"

B— the morehead city letter

The following is a cipher letter alleged to have been found floating in the harbor at Morehead City, North Carolina, on May 2, 1865 by Charles Duell. The text, which Duell claimed to have deciphered, was read by him from the witness stand on June 5 (Peterson, page 143). The letter was said to have been addressed to "J. W. Wise."

WASHINGTON, April 15, 1865

DEAR JOHN—

I am happy to inform you that Pet has done his work well. He is safe and Old Abe is in hell. Now, sir, all eyes are upon you. You must bring Sherman. Grant is in the hands of old Gray ere this. Redshoes showed a lack of nerve in Seward's case, but fell back in good order. Johnson must come. Old Crook has him in charge. Mind well that brothers' oath and you will have no difficulty. All will be safe and enjoy the trust of our leaders. We had a large meeting last night; All were bent on carrying out the programme to the letter. The rails are laid for safe exit. Old L——, always behind, lost the list at City Point. Now I say again, the lives of our brave officers and the life of the South depends upon the carrying this programme into effect. Number Two will give you this. It is ordered no more letters shall be sent by mail.

When you write sign no real name, and send by some of our friends who are coming home. We want you to write us how the news was received there. We receive great encouragement from all quarters. I hope there will be no getting weak in the knees. I was in Baltimore yesterday. Pet had not got there yet. Your folks are well and have heard from you. Don't lose your nerve.

O. B. No. 5

C— dates of Paine's visit to Surratt's in march

On his third and last trip to the witness stand on May 19, Weichmann's project was to make some sense out of the jumble of dates he had given in trying to connect Paine's visit to Surratt's around the "middle of March" with Booth's kidnap scheme, which the prosecutors knew had *ended* at the meeting of the "conspirators" at Gautier's on March 14. The undertaking was particularly delicate because they also knew that Paine had been in jail in Baltimore from March 12 through the late afternoon of March 14.

Weichmann went to the witness stand with a prefabricated chronology that would clear up all the confusion—*if* Paine's amnesty Oath could be kept out of court, and *if* he could keep the story straight at the final telling.

The Oath was kept out of court, but Weichmann managed to get mixed up again!

1. He and Surratt went to see Booth perform at Ford's in *The Apostate.*
2. Surratt, "Payne," and the girls went to Ford's together one night in March.
3. "Payne" had taken part in the "horse ride" another night.
4. "Payne" had left Washington the morning after the "horse ride."

All these events had to be squeezed into the three-day period in which Louis Paine *did* board at the Surratt house. In addition, the prosecutors had *legitimate* witnesses standing by to testify concerning the meeting of Booth's "gang" at Gautier's on the night of March 14.

Now, before Weichmann's final testimony, his puppeteers looked up the date on which *The Apostate* was performed, and found it was March 18. So far so good.

The theater party Miss Fitzpatrick had attended with "Wood" and Surratt had to be worked in during Paine's three-day visit too. Weichmann hadn't said a word about this important incident in either of his earlier testimonies, but the prosecutors seem to have remembered that the young lady would appear as a state witness later on and was going to testify that she had been to Ford's Theater with "Wood" and John Surratt "one day in March." If this were shown to have occurred *before* Paine's arrival, it would be self-evident that "Wood" and Paine were different men.

The "horse ride" had to be on the *last* of the three days of Paine's visit, in order that Weichmann's statement that he (Paine) had left Washington right after the alleged foray would be correct.

In spite of the difficulties, the prosecutors worked out a chronology that covered everything: the meeting at Gautier's on Tuesday the 14th; the "horse ride" on Thursday the 16th; "Payne's" departure on Friday the 17th; Weichmann's attendance at *The Apostate* with Surratt on Saturday the 18th. This arrangement left Wednesday, March 15, open for the theater party at Ford's which included "Wood" and Nora Fitzpatrick.

It was an easy matter to determine that the play performed at Ford's on March 15 was *Jane Shore*. To help him remember the date and name of the play, Weichmann was primed with the additional information that the celebrated Edwin Forrest had performed there the other four nights of that week—Monday and Tuesday, and Thursday and Friday.

When Weichmann recited the prosecutors' calendar of events from the witness stand at his final appearance, he remembered everything correctly but the date of *Jane Shore*.[22] Rather than fitting it in on the 15th, he tacked it onto the end of his list, saying, ". . . on the 18th he ("Payne") went to the theatre." Then he added the detail that was supposed to have helped him remember the date: ". . . it was when Forrest played there four nights in that week."

With this one slip, the unhappy perjurer again made nonsense of his testimony—since *The Apostate* had played at Ford's on March 18, and by his own statement he had attended with Surratt.

Defense counsel never noticed the contradiction! And Burnett corrected the date of *Jane Shore* to March 15 when he edited Weichmann's testimony in Pitman, the "official" record of the Trial.

As for Miss Fitzpatrick, she had not named the play she saw with "Wood" or given its date in her pre-Trial interrogation. When she took the witness stand three days after Weichmann's last appearance, Holt was careful not to ask her for this information.

From her court testimony that she had known "Wood" only as "Wood" and had seen him only twice—once at breakfast in the winter and once at the theater party—we gather that the party at Ford's was late in the preceding week. She stated that she left for Baltimore early the morning after the party and stayed away about a week—and that the man she knew as "Wood" was gone when she returned. We assume Louis Paine arrived and departed again while she was away.

Although Weichmann stated she was present in the parlor when "Payne" came to the house in March, Miss Fitzpatrick did not confirm it even by implication. When interrogated after the raid on the Surratt house, she insisted she did not know Paine. By the time she took the witness stand a month later, the girl had evidently accepted the prosecutors' endlessly repeated pretence that Paine *was* "Wood." But she still insisted upon calling him "Mr. Wood" and stuck to her story that she hadn't recognized him when they were arrested together at the Surratt house.

From all this we conclude she had never seen Louis Paine before that night, and that the theater party she attended with "Wood" was prior to Paine's arrival for his three-day visit in March.

Finally we find confirmation for the probable chronology of Paine's visit in March (the evening of March 14 or 15 through Friday, March 17) in an unexpected quarter—the interrogation of Mrs. Surratt, dated April 17 (LAS file). Though she stated that the visitor was a "short, stout man" who said his name was "Wood" and that he was a Baptist preacher, the widow remembered he arrived "some day during that week" and "on Friday evening he left saying that he was going to preach there [in Baltimore] on Sunday."

D— Atzerodt's statement to colonel Wells

The following is quoted from the original document, in the Lincoln Assassination Suspects file, National Archives.

PORT TOBACCO, April 25, 1865

GEORGE A. ATZERODT says

I live at Port Tobacco. John H. Surott [sic] came after me in the winter. I was at work and could not leave. it was after Christmas. he said he was going to get a great prize and he wanted me because I was acquainted with the Potomac to go with him. said he was going to run the Blockade. came again three weeks after, we came to Washington together he took me to his Mothers and I staid one week. told me the other parties were over in New York and others in Baltimore. gave me no names there. I returned home again. went home and stayed one week and he wrote for me to come on. I came up in the Stage. Stopped at Kimmel House and Pa House 357 C. St. John Surratt came to the Hotel to take me to his Mother's House. here I was introduced to Booth in Com. Genl's of Prisoners Office. nothing of importance was there said. we were to meet again at an early day. the day was not fixed.

We met again but Booth went to New York before I saw him again. as I understood after he came back he came to Penna. House and asked me how I would like to go into the oil business. I said I would like it if I had the Capitol. he said dont mind the Capital. I have that. I said I would as soon not go into the business. I was drinking hard and he asked me not to drink so hard. He then went to New York again.

J. Surrott came and borrowed some money of me. He was going to New York with a Lady. Surrott had two Horses at Howard's Stable. one or both of the Horses came from down near Bryantown. he claimed to own them. one of them had a blind eye. it was a large bay Horse. the other was a smaller bay Horse. Surrott wrote to me from New York to sell the Horses this was I think in March. I sold the small Horse about a week after I got the order. Booth then returned from New York. and he took me to a Lady's House. near the Patent Office. it is on the Corner of 9th & F St. it is a Hotel or Boarding House (Probably the Herenden House) he took me into the room and introduced me to a young man he called James Wood. this was after the fall of Richmond and two or three days before the President was killed and proposed to go to Richmond to open a Theatre if we could get passes. after that was over we took a walk on the Avenue. he told me to meet him that night. at the same place.

David L. Harrold [sic] came there that night. I came in at half past 7. Oclock and told them. I wanted to meet a young man on the Street who wanted me to go to the Theatre. I took him to the Street by the House, left there and went in alone. they said they were going. Booth told me. I ought not to bring any person near the House. we did not have much to say. we went out, parted and went to the Theatre. Booth and Harrold said they were going out. dont know whether they did go or not. before we parted we agreed to meet the next day at the National. where I could call or he would meet me. at this house again. I went to the National. at ½ past 10. Oclock A. M. I think it was Thursday. he took me in his room. he then spoke to me again about drinking so much, I asked him what he meant by it. he laughfed [sic] and said never mind. he then told me to go to the Kirkwood and get a Pass. from V. President Johnston. he said he would be there with a man to recommend me. I went there registered my name and got a room and paid for one days board. that was on Thursday. about 3 Oclock Harrold came there after me. He said Booth and Wood wanted to see me.

Wood is a tall man with black hair. Staight [sic] He is a strong stout made man. no hair on his face. rather poor. he is rather a good looking man. I cant remember faces or features well enough to describe them. he had a wild look in his eyes. Saw him clean his teeth. he carried a tooth brush with him. think he had long legs. saw a bottle of hairoil on his stand. think his arms was long. he was a large well built man. He wore Boots. wore a soft Hat. leed [sic] Color I think not black. I am sure: we walked down the St. we were to have met in a Resturant but Booth was not there. and we met down at the National. he was not there. Harold went off & said he would find him. we were to wait. I got tired of waiting and left aterwards [sic] into Seventh St. and stopped and drank at different Resturants.

About half past five or near Six Oclock, I went to the Kirkwood House. and they told me a young man had called there for me. I took a chair and Harold came in and said Booth and Wood wanted to see me immediately. He then asked me if I had my key. he wanted to go to my room and show me something. He went to the room and drawed a large Knife and a large Postol out of his Boot. and said let us go and see Booth and Wood. We went to their House on 9th St. (Henderson House) and they then proposed the Murder to me. Booth proposed that we should Kill the President. said it would be the greatest thing in the world. this was about half past Six or Seven Oclock on Friday. that Wood would go up to Seward's House and Kill him—That he and Harrold had been and seen Andrew Johnston. and found out where he was.

He then asked me if I was willing myself to assist them. I said that I did not come for that. and was not willing to murder a person. They said they did not want me to do any act, but only to show them the road into the lower part of Maryland. and if I did not I would suffer for it. I said I would do all I could on the road. they said will you and I promised that I would. Booth then told me to get a Horse and stop near the Eastern Branch Bridge. we then came out: Harrold wanted me to go to the Kirkwood House. and asked me if I had the Key. of the room. I told him no. I did not go to the Hotel and we parted then. & I have never seen them since.

Some time in the morning Harrold came and wanted I should go down to Surrattsville. he said he Booth had some things there and wanted me to see after them. they were in Mr. Surratts old House. kept by Lloyd. and I agreed to go. I went and hired a Horse. at 1 Oclock. I got a small Bay Horse at a stable on 8th St. above Franklin St. about one Oclock and rode him till about three Oclock and then put him in Nailor's Stable and left him there till between Six & Seven Oclock. then I took him and rode out to the Navy Yard. then back again to the Avenue. where I got some oysters. and rode down to the Kimmel House. he took the Horse away from the Stable about ½ past 7 or 8 Oclock. and did not take him back. I did not go to Surrattsville because I could not see Booth that evening

They wanted I should show them the road to Indiantown on Maryland Point. they were to go to Sairottsville around Piscotoway and to strike the Potomac. they were to go through Bumpy Oak. To go to Bumpy Oak you take the road leading from Washington to Bryantown at Terbe [T.B.] which is about six miles from

Sariottsville. you turn off to the right. It is about 25 or 30 miles from Turbee to Maryland Point the road leading from Turbee is not much traveled. I dont know any one at Maryland Point that would aid them to cross. I suppose after they got to Virginia they would go to the Confederate lines. Sanjemoy (?) Creek runs down by Maryland Point. Harrold was well acquainted with the Shores of the Potomac and I think if he got over to Piny Church or the Bridges on the Port Tob'o. road near Bryantown. I would go to Maryland Point. for it is the most direct and there are many Cross Roads.

I understood that Woods came from Virginia but dont know the County. I heard him speak of Warrenton and Fauquier Co. Wood was to kill Seward. Booth the President and Harold V. P. Johnston. I last saw Sarrott about a week before the Murder. dont know where he is but think he has gone to New York. I went up to Woods to the Navy Yard about 12 Oclock after the assassination. went in a Street Carr got in near the National & went up to the end of the road and then road back to the Depot. and then. walked up 4½ St. and there met a Stranger who asked me where he could find a Hotel. to stop at and I told him to come to the Pa. House and he did so. he was a Stranger to me and I never seen him before. and have not since. do not know his name. I dont know whether Mr. Sarrott was in this business or not. I stopped in Mrs. Sarrott House for three or four days. I think they called me Port Tobacco. Booth and Harold sometimes spoke of Moseby and asked where he was. they also spoke of going to Canada. after the assassination. when Booth went to New York last. he said he was going to Canada—

E— actors who claimed a connection with Booth

The actor John Matthews, whom Booth mentioned contemptuously to Chester, was arrested after the assassination and made a statement to Colonel Foster on April 30 (Archives, LAS file) in which he admitted knowing the assassin only slightly. The gist of his statement was merely that Booth met him on the street the afternoon of the crime and offered him his wardrobe box, saying he was quitting the stage and wouldn't need it any more.

Two years later, however, at the trial of John Surratt, Matthews' memory was greatly improved. He now said Booth gave him a letter around 4:00 P.M. that afternoon and asked him to leave it at the office of the *Intelligencer* the next morning. Booth had been about to mail it; and his reason for not doing so, but handing it to Matthews, whom he considered a coward, is obscure. On the morning after the crime, said Matthews, he tore open the letter, read its message with horror, and —after "committing it to memory"—burned it. Two years later he claimed to have forgotton most of the text, but remembered the last paragraph and signature as follows (Wilson, pages 107 and 250):

> The moment has at length arrived when my plans must be changed. The world may censure me for what I am about to do, but I am sure that posterity will justify me.
>
> Men who love their country better than Gold or Life
> (Signed)
> JOHN WILKES BOOTH, PAYNE, ATZERODT, AND HEROLD

This entirely *undocumented* recollection of Matthews promptly became part of the legend of the Booth "conspiracy," being quoted with as much confidence as if the original letter were in War Department Archives. Yet one might ask how this message could implicate the frightened Matthews, or why he didn't tell Booth just to drop the letter in the mailbox as he had first intended. According to Booth's "diary," which had been in Stanton's possession since the Trial and the text of which had been made public earlier in the year of 1867, the actor had written "a long article and left it for one of the editors of the *National Intelligencer* in which I fully set forth our reasons for our proceeding."

One very strong indication that Matthews' belated recollection that Booth had handed him a letter on the day of the crime was inspired by having read the "diary" text nearly two years later in the newspapers is found in the names he recalled as being listed at the end of it. The second name was "Payne"—but the genuine conspirator, whose identity was confused with that of the man who was hanged, was known to Booth as "James Wood." He would have used *that* name in listing his accomplices.

Either Matthews' memory was not very reliable, or he was making the most of an opportunity to get national publicity by inventing the incident of the letter.

W. J. Ferguson's account

In the late 1920's an aging actor named W. J. Ferguson suddenly recalled that as a boy of thirteen or fourteen, he had been employed as a bit player and prompter at Ford's Theater in 1865 and was present in the wings on the night Booth shot Mr. Lincoln. He parleyed his recollections into a *Saturday Evening Post* article, a book based on the article (*I Saw Booth Shoot Lincoln,* Houghton Mifflin Co., 1930), and a testimonial dinner at the Lambs Club.

Ferguson purported to give the actual facts of the murder, to "correct" the record, but had little to say of importance except that the assassin had shouted "sic semper tyrannus" from the box rather than from the stage—a distinction which Booth himself had noted in his well-published "diary." The book did have some interesting material about the construction of stages in those days and some particulars about production procedures. It is often quoted as an eye-witness source of information on minor points of the assassination.

Among other things, the elderly actor recalled being invited to join Booth, James Maddox (a property man at Ford's), and another man for a drink at a nearby "restaurant" on the afternoon of the crime, between four and five o'clock. He mentioned rather primly that *he* drank only a non-alchoholic beverage.

Our study has turned up two men who recalled the incident: one who went into the saloon to look for Maddox, and one who was a member of the group. The assistant property man at Ford's, John F. Sleichmann, testified at the Conspiracy Trial on May 15 (Peterson, page 41; Pitman, page 73) and said he went to the "restaurant between four and five that afternoon and found Booth drinking with Maddox, Spangler, a man named Mouldy, and a *boy* from the theater."

After his death from tuberculosis at Dr. Mudd's farm, poor Spangler's possessions were sorted out by the family. They found a long statement he had written, listing all his activities the day of the assassination and giving his oath that he had not the slightest idea what Booth intended to do. He also remembered the drinking group in the saloon in the late afternoon—that those present were Booth, Maddox, himself, and a boy from the theater (*Life of Dr. Samuel Mudd,* by Nettie Mudd).

The curious thing was that both Sleichmann and Spangler had clear recollections of that occasion—but *both* said the boy present was "Peanut John" Burroughs, a *genuine* employee at Ford's.

Mr. Ferguson said people sometimes asked him why he wasn't arrested along with all the other employees of the theater after the assassination, and why his name didn't come up at the Trial. He said it was because he was just a boy and "didn't count." "Peanuts" was also a boy, of nearly the same age, but *he* counted and was called as a witness in court.

F— the Etta letter

The following is taken from Eisenschiml's *Why Was Lincoln Murdered?* (page 377), referring to the original in "War Dept. Archives" (National Archives).

NEW YORK, April 13th.

DEAR WILKES

I received your letter of the 12th (stating you would be in this City on the 16 inst.) this morning, and hasten to answer it. On account of a misunderstanding between my Landlady and your humble servant, I have been obliged to leave her hospitable mansion, and am now for the time being, stopping at the New York Hotel, after your arrival, should you not approve of my present location, it can easily be changed to suit your convenience.

Yes, Dear, I can heartily sympathize with you, for I too, have had the blues ever since the fall of Richmond, and like you, feel like doing something desperate. I have not yet had a favorable opportunity to do what *you* wished, and *I* so solemnly promised, and what, in my own heart, I feel ought to be done, I *remember* what happiness is in store for us if we succeed in our present undertakings, therefore, do not doubt *my* courage, have faith, "for even as you put your faith in me, so will I in you" and Wilkes hath said *vengeance* is mine.

My removal has consumed the means you gave me when we parted, take this as a gentle hint and bring a good supply, "for money makes the mare go" now a'days. I do as you desired and keep as secluded as a nun, which is not agreeable to me as you have found, but ere this, but anything to oblige you, darling. If anything *should* happen (as I trust there will not) to prevent your coming to the City, please let me know, and I will join you (as agreed upon) at the house of *our* friend A——s. "Don't let anything discourage *you*."

believe me *yours*
and *yours* only
ETTA

P. S. Annie who is acting the maid to perfection, wishes to be remembered to her dear ahem!!! Sam.

Au revoir
ETTA

G— miss Holloway's letter

A letter written by Miss L. K. B. Holloway, sister-in-law of Richard H. Garrett, at whose farm John Wilkes Booth was shot. It is reproduced in full in *John Wilkes*

Booth, by Francis Wilson (chap. XVIII), by permission of the Confederate Museum in Richmond, Virginia.

The capture and death of John Wilkes Booth— by an eyewitness

The war had been over several weeks. A number of days had passed since the tragedy in Washington had been enacted. The assassin had made good his escape from the Capitol and his whereabouts were unknown; but as yet the intelligence of the calamity had failed to reach a large portion of Eastern Virginia.

Such was the condition of affairs when on Monday, April 24th, 1865, at about half-past noon, a boat containing five men crossed over from Port Conway to Port Royal, Virginia, two villages on the Rappahannock River, opposite to each other.

Three of the men proved to be men by the name of William Rollins, Mr. Green and a colored man named Richard Wilson, but the other two were total strangers.

Immediately upon landing, one of the unknown men inquired of the bystanders for a Confederate officer. No sooner was inquiry made known than a young man named William Jett, dressed in a Confederate Captain's uniform, introduced himself as Captain of Mosby's Command. (Jett was a boy of only eighteen years of age and had never been in the war.) His curiosity was such as to prompt him to tell a falsehood to find out why they wished to see an officer.

Whereupon the strangers engaged him in close conversation for several minutes, after which, being joined by his companion, he said to him in the presence of the pretended officer, "I have told this officer who we are and what we have done."

To which his companion replied: "Ah, indeed! I didn't intend to tell anybody that."

The three men conversed quite earnestly for some time, after which young Jett, leading the way, they all left the village in company with two Confederate officers; Lieutenant Bainbridge and Ruggles following.

The search leading in the direction of Bowling Green, one of the unknown men —the one who had inquired for the officer at Port Royal—was left [at the gate to the Garrett farm], while the rest of the men rode on to the house.

On arriving they were met by Mr. Richard H. Garrett, who was the owner of the house. Upon which Jett addressed him saying, "This is Mr. Garrett, I presume?" and on securing an affirmative answer, introduced to him this second unknown as his friend John William Boyd, "a Confederate soldier who had been wounded in the battles around Richmond, near Petersburg." At the same time he requested Mr. Garrett to take care of him until Wednesday morning at which time he would call for him. Complying with this request, Mr. Garrett consented to receive him.

By this time it was about three o'clock in the afternoon, so taking leave, Jett and the officers returned to the gate where the stranger (who was none other than Harold, one of the Conspirators) was awaiting them.

How far Harold was conveyed, or how far the two Lieutenants accompanied Jett, is not known. It has been conjectured, however, that Jett was concealed somewhere along the road, and that Jett, leaving the officers, proceeded on to Ashland, a telegraph office, where he had sent intelligence to the authorities at Washington as to the whereabouts of the two men, and then, retracing his steps, recovered Harold and conveyed him to the house of Mrs. Clark in the neighborhood of Bowling Green, where they spent the night. Harold was also taken to Mr. Garrett's where he remained until Wednesday.

In the meantime, Mr. Garrett had extended to his strange guest all the hospitalities of his house. Everything had passed off quietly. Nothing of consequence had occurred until Tuesday at dinner time when Jack Garrett, the eldest son, returned from Port Royal and reported the news of President Lincoln's death.

While at dinner the tragic event was commented upon, as to the motive which prompted the deed and its effect upon the public welfare. All this time Boyd remained silent, but upon hearing one of the daughters remark that she supposed that the perpetrator had been paid, he turned to her with a smile and said:

"Do you think so, Miss? By whom do you suppose he was paid?"

"Oh," she replied, "I suppose by both the North and the South."

"It is my opinion," rejoined he, "he wasn't paid a cent, but did it for notoriety's sake."

Soon after, they arose from the table, and as he started out Mrs. Garrett (my sister) asked if he would like to have his wound dressed. He replied by saying that it did not give him the slightest pain. Then he thanked her, and with several others went out on the porch commanding full view of the public road and sat down upon the steps.

They had been sitting there for some time when Bainbridge, Jett and Harold rode up to the gate. Harold was seen to dismount from behind Jett and begin walking toward the house, while Bainbridge and Jett rode on. It was then that Boyd asked Jack Garrett to go upstairs and get his revolver. When asked why he wanted it, he said he always felt safe when armed.

Then he was asked who was approaching, to which he replied:

"Oh, that is one of our men."

"What do you mean?" asked Jack.

"Why, one of those who crossed over with us," he said; and walking off, he met Harold about midway between the gate and the house, where they remained in close conversation for fully half an hour, after which they both came to the house.

Not long afterwards Jett and Bainbridge rode up hurriedly to the house to see, as Jett professed, how his friend Boyd was getting along; at the same time telling them that he and Harold had better make good their escape, for he had understood that the Federal troops were crossing over from Port Conway to Port Royal. They then galloped off, *Jett going in the direction of Port Royal to meet, as it is conjectured, the troops who were coming in answer to his telegraphic summons.* [Italics by Miss H.]

About an hour before sundown the Federal troops were seen dashing along the road in the direction of Bowling Green. While they were passing, Boyd and Harold hid themselves in the thickets which were some distance from the house, and did not emerge until they had passed. Then upon being asked why they, ex-Confederate soldiers, should hide themselves from these now that the war was over, Boyd replied that he did not care about meeting any of them.

Failing to comprehend the action of these two men, Jack Garrett resolved to institute some investigation. Upon inquiry he learned that the Federal troops were in pursuit of two Confederate soldiers, one of whom was wounded, and the description they gave corresponded exactly with those of the two men at home. So returning home he asked Boyd if they had gotten into trouble; saying; "You know what you have done. Now, if you have gotten into any difficulty, you must leave at once for I do not want you to bring any trouble upon my aged father."

To which Boyd replied that they had gotten into a little brush over in Maryland, but it was all over.

In the evening as they were sitting on the porch, Boyd requested Jack Garrett to take him up to Guinea's Station that night, offering him ten dollars. When asked why he wanted to go there, he said that he had heard that there was a Confederate Maryland battery near Louisa Court House which hadn't disbanded and if he could reach that he would be safe.

Jack told him he could not take him that evening, but would do so the next morning, giving as his reason that he had only one horse. Being refused, he agreed to be taken the next morning, and gave him ten dollars in advance.

When the hour came to retire, Boyd saw no place in which he could be made comfortable. He said that anywhere would do rather than go upstairs.

Then he and Harold were conducted to a large tobacco house in which was stored away a lot of valuable furniture belonging to the people of Port Royal, covered with hay and other provender.

After they had entered, Jack Garrett locked the door and took the key to the house and gave it to me, saying he would leave it in my care and that I must not let anyone have it, as it was his opinion that they intended trying to steal their horses and escape. Then, assuring themselves, he and his brother Willie went out into a shed opposite the tobacco house to spend the night.

About two o'clock the next morning (Wednesday) the family was aroused by the loud barking of dogs, the clanking of arms, and the heavy tread of sentinels pacing up and down the porch. Soon it was discovered that a sentinel had been placed at every door and window and that the whole yard was full of soldiers.

All at once there was heard a rush for the porch at the end of the house, followed by a violent battering against the door, with frequent demands that it be opened. Hearing the racket, Mr. Garrett arose, partially dressed himself, and hastened to the door to inquire the cause of the tumult.

Instantly he was seized and asked what he meant by harboring Booth, the murderer of their President. He answered that he was not harboring the murderer of their President. Upon which, notwithstanding the entreaties of his wife and little two-year-old daughter, he was taken by force from the house half-clad and threatened with handcuffs and the rope and a pistol placed at his breast.

He was carried into the yard and set upon a block where he remained until eight o'clock in the morning with two soldiers guarding, thereby contracting a severe cold from which he never recovered. Again and again he was importuned with threats of hanging to disclose the whereabouts of Booth, the murderer of their President. Again and again did he profess his ignorance.

Colonel Conger, Lieutenant Baker, the detectives, and Waters, a New York reporter, had come to arrest Booth. It then dawned upon him (Garrett) that this Boyd must be Booth, and also that these men must have been directed by Jett, who, when brought forward in the morning and accused by Mr. Garrett of piloting the soldiers and of deliberately bringing that trouble upon him, made no reply but hung his head.

At this juncture of affairs, Jack Garrett came up from the shed and, perceiving his father's perplexity, said:—"Gentlemen, if you want to know where those men are, I will take you to the place. They didn't sleep in the house tonight, but are in an outhouse."

At once they compelled him to pile lightwood around the building. Then he was sent in after Booth, who warned him not to come in any more, and said to those without: "Who are you and what do you come for?" The reply was: "We want you, we came for you!"

Booth answered: "Then prepare a stretcher, for I will never surrender!"

Jack said: "There are nearly fifty armed men, and escape is impossible. Act like a man and surrender."

"The word surrender is not in my vocabulary. I have never learned the meaning of that. There is one here, however, who will surrender."

Then Jack was sent in after Harold, who was brought out and placed under guard. The lightwood being set on fire, Booth called out: "Now I can pick off eighteen of you before I stop, but I have accomplished all that I want to."

At once the fire was put out. Again Booth cried out: "Give me fifteen steps and I will make good my escape."

The rejoinder was: "No! we will not give you any."

Then Booth said: "I want you to take notice of one thing. The gentleman with whom I am stopping knows not who I am, nor what I have done."

After this a lighted torch was thrown into the barn, which soon set fire to the hay and other combustibles, making a great conflagration.

Then, taking advantage of the light within and the darkness without, Sergeant Corbett placed his revolver through a crack and shot Booth, the ball passing through the jugular vein and taking in one of the cervical vertebra.

As soon as it was discovered that Booth had been shot, Jack Garrett was sent in to bring him out. Then he was carried to the house by four men and laid upon the front porch, to all appearance dead.

At once a matress upon which to place him was asked for. But he said: "No, no, let me die here! Let me die here!"

Then one of the officers ejaculated, "The damn Rebel is still living!" and immediately dispatched a messenger for Dr. Urquhart of Port Royal. A pillow was asked for and I brought it and placed it under his head. Wine was offered, but he refused it: then water was presented, but he wouldn't drink it.

Presently he protruded his tongue. I took my handkerchief and dipped it in water and moistened his lips; he said:

"Tell my mother I died for my country. I did what I thought to be best."

I again moistened his lips and he repeated the message to his mother. Soon he gasped, and I again moistened his lips and tongue a third time and the pulsations in his temples grew weaker and weaker.

It was then Lieutenant Baker asked me to rub his temples and forehead. I did so. The end was near. Then, gasping three times and crossing his hands upon his breast, he died just as the day was breaking and the doctor was reaching the house.

A stray curl that had fallen over my fingers while I had soaked the dying man's temples was cut off by Dr. Urquhart and given to me. A portion of this curl I have in my possession now.

About eight o'clock that morning, the body of Booth was sewed up in a U. S. Army blanket belonging to Lieutenant Baker and together with Harold and the Garrett boys was conveyed to Washington.

After all had left and the family had become a little composed, I went to the bookcase to get some books for the children, as I was teaching school in the family at the time.

The first thing that greeted my eyes were the opera glasses. I knew they did not belong to any of the family. I concluded they must be Booth's, so I took them to Mr. Garrett and asked him what I must do with them. He replied by saying: "Take them out of my sight. I do not wish to see anything that will remind me of this dreadful affair."

I told him I would send them up to my mother's in a day or two. I took a pin and marked "J. W. B." under the buckle on the strap. And during the day my brother came to Mr. Garrett's and I gave them to him to take up to my mother, thinking they were too valuable to be destroyed as Mr. Garrett had directed me to do.

The next evening Lieutenant Baker, in company with Jack Garrett, came to Mr. Garrett's in pursuit of them. They did not know really that they were there, but simply supposed that Booth had them and thought they might be there. Lieutenant Baker asked Mr. Garrett if they were not, and without any hesitancy he told him I had them.

He then came to me and asked where they were. I very reluctantly told him where they were. Lieutenant Baker and Jack Garrett went up to my mother's, which was about eight miles, and got them. They came back to Mr. Garrett's about four o'clock in the evening, and spent the night and returned to Washington the next day.

Such was the close of the eventful career of John Wilkes Booth on the morning of April 26, 1865, a career that was luminous with frequent flashes of brilliant genius, but whose final splendor was obscured by its misdirection.

(Signed) Miss L. K. B. Holloway
Bowling Green, Caroline County, Virginia

This is a true copy:
Susan B. Harrison
House Regent Confederate Museum
Richmond, Virginia

H— professional study of Booth poisoning data

The historical evidence cited in Chapter 16 regarding the physical condition of John Wilkes Booth during the first week of his flight leaves very little room for doubt that after drinking the whisky Herold gave him at Surrattsville, he became violently ill. The question, then, is not *whether* Booth was sick, but *from what cause?*

In addition to the several circumstances which pointed to poisoning, there were numerous symptoms reported prior to death and peculiarities in the condition of the corpse which suggested that the evident illness was not from natural causes. Analysis of these conditions being a technical matter, the problem was referred to Mr. Ray A. Neff of New Jersey, whose organization specializes in the technical aspects of historical research.

Mr. Neff was sent a list of the statements regarding Booth's health during his flight and the reported condition of his body after death. As a point of departure for his study, he had the author's question as to whether the poison, if any, might have been strychnine, with the fatal effects nullified by that poison's tendency to crystallize in combination with alcohol. The investigators' verbatim report follows:

RAY A. NEFF
Historical Investigator
61st Street and Dune Drive
Avalon, New Jersey 08202

Consultant Chemist and Toxicologist
Document Restoration and Analysis
Ultra Violet and Infra Red Techniques

In Reply Refer to: 1416 C
October 28, 1963

INVESTIGATION REPORT Toxicological Data

PROBLEM Was John Wilkes Booth poisoned with Strychnine by David Herold at Lloyd's Tavern at Surrattsville (now Clinton) immediately after the assassination of Abraham Lincoln?

RESULTS A review of the accounts of Booth's capture, both published and unpublished, indicate that he was seriously ill during his flight. He was certainly not in a state of health consistent with a simple fracture alone. While his state of health might be consistent with an infection as a result of the fracture, this is practically ruled out by the testimony and statements of several physicians who saw him after the fracture but prior to death.

There are several things which substantiate your poison theory though not conclusively. John Wilkes Booth was a connoisseur of brandy and he seldom drank anything else, professing and showing great disdain for whiskey. Lloyd's tavern was a well-stocked tavern in an area where many patrons drank brandy and there are indications that brandy was in adequate supply on the night of the assassination. (The testimony of a Herbert Jenks states that the following morning he had a brandy at the tavern.) Yet when David Herold brought out two bottles to Booth he brought whiskey. The reason could possibly be that he was afraid that Booth would detect an off-flavor in brandy but was not apt to do so in whiskey.

As to the theory of a delayed Strychnine poisoning, this is not consistent with all toxicological data reviewed (see bibliography) and with the author's experience. The following is a direct quote from "HANDBOOK OF POISONS" by Robert H. Dreisbach, Lange Medical Publications, Los Altos, Calif. 1955:

A. *Acute Poisoning* (from ingestion) Strychnine and related compounds and derivatives cause first an increase in deep reflexes followed by noticeable stiffening at the knees, especially when going up and down stairs; single extensor spasms then involve the arms and legs. As poisoning progresses, spasms increase in severity and frequency until the patient is in almost continuous opisthotonos. Any sound or movement will elicit a spasm. Death is from respiratory failure.

B. *Chronic Poisoning* Doses less than necessary to cause acute poisoning are without toxic effect.

(End quote)

It is the author's opinion that crystallization from alcohol or other similar treatments would not appreciably alter the clinical manifestations of strychnine. If a sufficient dosage to cause death or even serious symptoms was administered and not treated, death would occur within from ten minutes to one hour, with at least some of the classical symptoms.

After a careful review of the historical as well as the toxicological literature, the author is inclined to believe that if Booth was poisoned at Lloyd's Tavern, it was carried out by the use of Arsenic Trioxide (White Arsenic) in whiskey. This is based on both historical statements and clinical symptomology. I have already described the substitution of whiskey for brandy and its significance. It is this substitution which probably prolonged Booth's life, but if this theory is correct he was still a doomed man. Since Booth did not like whiskey he probably drank less than he would have had it been brandy. This probably made it a chronic poisoning instead of killing him in several hours. (Death time with white arsenic is from about thirty minutes to several weeks or even months; arsenic is cumulative.) This would explain the "yellow and discolored" condition of his skin; it is known as arsenic bronzing and is due to jaundice discoloration, the liver being greatly damaged as well as the kidneys (explaining back pain). In addition the symptoms include anorexia, weakness, diarrhea, (or sometimes constipation) and occasional nausea and vomiting, selective edemas (ankles, eyelids), conjunctivitis, sore nose and throat, dermatitis, including bronzing and jaundice. As you can see, this is similar to the Booth symptoms.

It must also be stated that similar symptomology could be presented by poisoning with Antimony, Barium, Bismuth, Thalium, and several other metallic poisons, including phosphorus but this is unlikely since they all have properties which would not be conducive to their use, i.e. taste, odor, color, etc.

The reason Dr. May did not recognize this as poisoning could be explained by the fact that the physicians of that day were not nearly so well versed in toxicology as are today's, and under the circumstances where poison was not readily obvious but the cause of death was (shooting) a modern medical coroner might not call for toxicology.

appendix

TOXICOLOGICAL BIBLIOGRAPHY

1. *Handbook of Poisons,* Robert H. Dreisbach, Lange Medical Publications, Los Altos, Calif. 1955.

2. *Pharmacology in Medicine,* Victor A. Drill, McGraw-Hill, New York, 2nd Ed. 1958.

3. *Dangerous Properties of Industrial Materials,* N. Irving Sax, Reinhold, New York. 1957.

4. *Emergency Toxicology,* Sidney Kaye, Thomas, Springfield, Ill. 1954.

5. *Pathology,* Peter A. Herbut, Lea & Febiger, Philadelphia, 1950.

RAY A. NEFF

October 28, 1963 License Number A-111

I— handwriting analyses of Eckert, "Watson," "mr. X," and Booth

Identification of L. C. Baker as author of the "R. D. Watson" letter to John Surratt was made by the conventional method of comparing the mechanical characteristics of the "Watson" script with an authentic sample of Baker's handwriting—in other words, by the method recognized in the law courts in this country. The identification was later confirmed by a second expert.

In the course of the original study and identification—and the analyst's report to this writer—another approach to handwriting analysis came up which led into one of the most interesting phases of the overall research. It happened that the analyst, Mrs. Klotho M. Lattin of Santa Cruz, California, had been interested in a less familiar school of the subject—graphology—for many years and had been a licensed practitioner since 1953.

Graphology—in case the reader is not familiar with the term—is the science of detecting and interpreting the personality traits revealed by an individual's handwriting. In Europe, where the science seems to have originated, it has been a respected field of study for many years. Numerous scholarly books have been written on its various methods and it is taught to advanced students of psychology in some German and French universities. In this country, although there are numbers of respected practitioners and the subject has been taught at New York City's New School for Social Research for years, graphology—due undoubtedly to its exploitation by unscrupulous and unqualified sellers of handwriting "fortunes"—is greatly misunderstood by the average citizen and widely and erroneously associated with fortune telling.

A genuine, trained graphologist such as Mrs. Lattin denies flatly that it is possible to tell the future by handwriting analysis—that it reveals *anything* but *tendencies* and the dominant traits of personality or character of a writer at the time a given sample is written. Thus, anyone who pretends to tell the future by graphology or, in fact, uses it to reveal any knowledge beyond a simple character study, is an obvious fraud, she says.

So much for definition. If graphology is considered controversial in any quarter it does not concern this writer, whose interest is confined solely to Mrs. Lattin's startling demonstration of her *personal* capability in connection with this research. The particulars of that demonstration are as follows:

The question of handwriting analysis came up quite late in the investigation when it became apparent that either or both of two letters from the National Archives might have important bearing on the conspiracy to murder President Lincoln—if their authorship could be established. One appeared to have been signed with an assumed name. The other, the last two pages of a multi-page letter, had no date or salutation and the signature had been thoroughly obliterated with opaque ink. The writer thought he saw some similarities to the handwriting of Major Thomas Eckert in both documents—and sent the following four samples to Mrs. Lattin to see if she could determine whether he had written the two in question. Photocopies of all four documents are reproduced on the following pages.

1. Two official receipts for possessions of Louis Paine signed by "Thomas T. Eckert."
2. A copy of the letter to John Surratt signed "R. D. Watson."
3. A copy of the 2-page letter without date, salutation or legible signature which contained what was said to be authoritative information on the identity of "Lewis Payne."

It should be emphasized that Mrs. Lattin was asked only to determine if Eckert were the author of the "Watson" letter and the one regarding "Payne," the writer of which will be referred to as "Mr. X" for the present. If Mrs. Lattin knew the *traditional* version of the "conspiracy," it was not evident from her comments. She did not know who "Eckert" was, and it wouldn't have helped her in any way if she had. She was not told any of the findings of the investigation up to that point.

Much to the writer's disappointment she reported that, although there were certain similarities between Eckert's script and that in the "Watson" and "X" samples, conventional analysis indicated that Major Eckert had not written either of the letters—nor were those of "Watson" and "X" written by the same person.

Evidently fearing that the admitted similarities among the three handwriting samples might make her report seem something less than final, Mrs. Lattin included a graphological character analysis of each of the three individuals to support her conclusion that the handwriting was that of a different man in each case. The character analyses were detailed and somewhat technical. Students of graphology would be greatly interested in the complete analysis but, in the interest of brevity, we will quote merely the descriptions of the three men.

major Thomas T. Eckert

Mrs. Lattin was inclined to dismiss Eckert as an egotistical lightweight, admirably suited by nature to act as somebody's "front man." He did not exert enough discipline over his mental processes or emotions to be able to conceive and carry out long range plans. Yet he was devious and self centered and showed some persistence in pursuing his immediate goals. Here are some of the analyst's comments on Eckert, stated in the present tense:

"The important thing for Major Eckert is prestige, and importance, and public recognition. He is both logical and intuitive. Ruled by his feelings and emotions; rash, impulsive; with a devious mind and definite self interest. An extremely rapid thinker, but not to be trusted; his path is like that of a snake in the grass, as you can see. Probably a good cultural background."

Referring to the sample on War Department letterhead—"Everything on this page tends in the same direction. It is basically false. He is saying something, but his purpose for saying it is to impress others with his own importance and prestige. . . . He was in some haste in writing this, but somewhat triumphant . . . adds to the impression we have of insincerity, affection, vanity and triviality of mind; as well as self centeredness.

"In the second sample, the one on plain paper . . . He is, of course, a highly

Received from Col. H. S. Olcott the package of clothes taken from the person of Lewis Payne on board the gunboat, also the over coat found near Fort Bunker Hill, with ~~its~~ contents of pockets.

Thos. T. Eckert.

Washington, D.C., Apr. 26th, 1865. Maj & A.D.C.

Time ....

Office U. S. Military Telegraph,

WAR DEPARTMENT,

Washington, D. C., April 26th 1865.

Received of Col Jno. A. Foster, Judge Advocate, the Hat & Pistol left by Payne in the house of Secty Seward on the night of the assassination.

Thos. T. Eckert.

Maj & Add'l A.D.C.

Fig. 6.–Eckert's Receipt for Payne's Hat and Pistol *(shown with Fig. 1)*

"evidence" of Paine's "guilt" to the end of his own life. (See Chapter 18, "Thomas T. Eckert.")

"R. D. Watson"

"I am sure," reported Mrs. Lattin, "neither of the others could use any such force of will (as "Watson") . . . a resolute, diligent, close-knit and organized person."

"I do not see 'R. D. Watson' as the same man as Major Eckert. He is more forceful, determined, aggressive. And he has a clear indication of altruism; this being an unusual trait in any case. He is more direct, determined and frequently is persistent in following out his plans. He is a positive person, without making any fuss about it. He likes to show authority, partly because he has been frustrated in doing much that he desired; *so he is rushing forward with the intention of being what I might perhaps describe as a benevolent despot.* I do not think he has actually lacked importance, but he has not felt himself to be adequately fulfilled in his life. *He tends to conceal his purposes, even when he seems most open. On occasion he may say more than he intended, and more than would be discreet;* but he is not exactly frank, or quite truthful in spite of this. He is a careful planner, with good attention to details, and much industry. *He is not exactly what he seems,* though logical in his own way: probably narrow-minded or even intolerant. Actually, *he was under stress when he wrote this, and highly emotional.*

"Rather a dignified, animal sort of person, probably with a strong looking body, but possibly some neurotic symptoms. Perhaps some lack of love life, for which he compensates, and which he hides."

". . . *He* [*Watson*] *seems to me the perfect picture of one who would have done this* [planned the assassination of Lincoln]. He has a very strong will. He feels things deeply. He is definite, clear-thinking, industrious, with critical acumen; more concerned with immediate, objective reality than is 'Mr. X.' 'Watson' does not have so wide-ranging a mind as 'Mr. X'; is more concerned with what is close to him. But 'W' does tend to conceal what he thinks. He talks freely enough, but keeps his own counsel, too. In other words, he does not impart his actual designs . . ."

When the analyst wrote the foregoing descriptions, remember, "R. D. Watson" was merely an unknown man in New York (as far as either this writer or Mrs. Lattin knew) who had written a note to John Surratt on March 19, 1865. The text of the letter said nothing whatever about a conspiracy. It was *assumed* to have some connection with the assassination simply because Judge Advocate General Holt had produced it in court, then whisked it out of sight; also, because Surratt was known to have been involved with Booth earlier in the month of March. The name "Watson" was only *assumed* to be an alias, for no very adequate reason. Lafayette Baker had not been considered as the possible author of the letter.

However, the analyst's description of "Watson" did suggest Baker to this writer, as it no doubt does to the reader. Having authentic samples of Lafayette Baker's handwriting in his files, the writer forwarded them to Mrs .Lattin in California and asked her to compare them with the "Watson" letter. Her report on the comparison was positive:

"I say that Baker *is* 'Watson.' A positive, hard driving person." And, "I can certainly see Baker-Watson masterminding; in spite of the open a's, there are concealing strokes in both; secrecy, desire to deceive without being caught."

"Mr. X"

The analyst had stated unequivocally that "Mr. X" was not the same man as either Eckert or "Watson." But, finding him an interesting personality, she gave an analy-

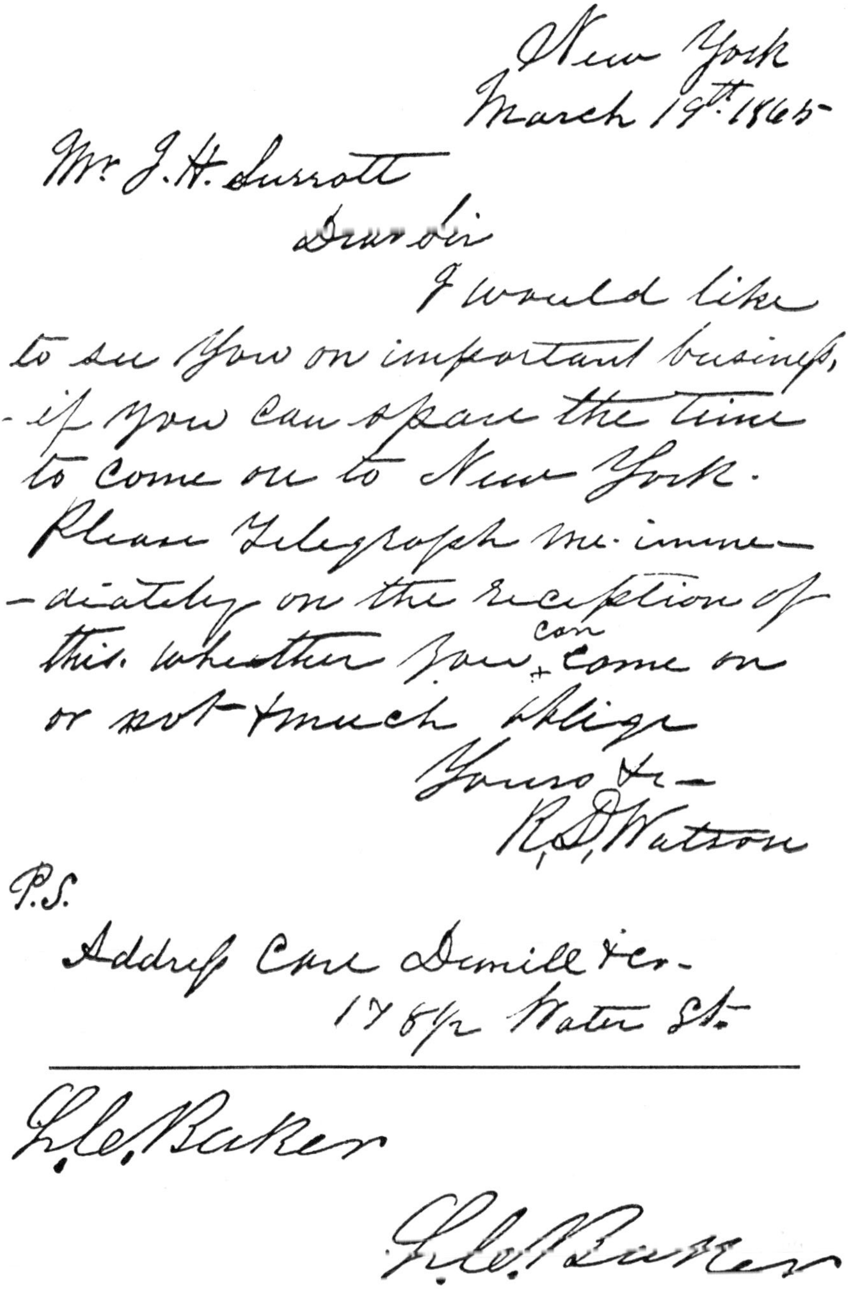

New York
March 19th 1865

Mr. J. H. Surratt

Dear Sir

I would like to see You on important business, if you can spare the time to come on to New York. Please Telegraph me immediately on the reception of this whether you can come on or not & much oblige

Yours &c—

R. D. Watson

P.S.

Address Care Demill & Co.
178½ Water St.

L. C. Baker

L. C. Baker

FIG. 7.—The "R. D. Watson" Letter, with L. C. Baker's Signatures for Comparison

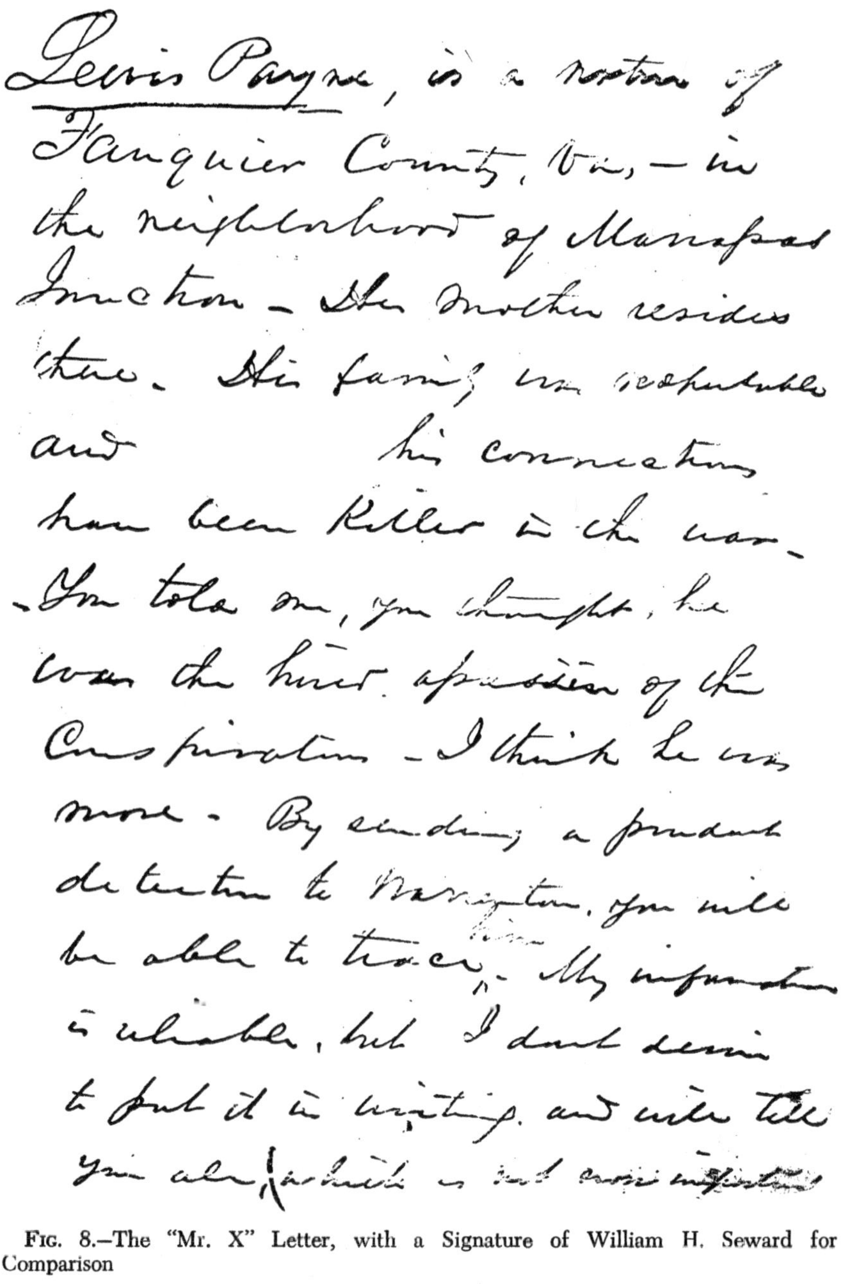

Lewis Payne, is a native of
Fauquier County, Va., — in
the neighborhood of Manassas
Junction — His mother resides
there. His family is respectable
and his connections
have been killed in the war.
— You told me, you thought, he
was the hired assassin of the
Conspirators — I think he was
more. By sending a prudent
detective to Warrington, you will
be able to trace him. My information
is reliable, but I don't desire
to put it in writing, and will tell
you also (which is not [illegible]

FIG. 8.—The "Mr. X" Letter, with a Signature of William H. Seward for Comparison

emotional person, meaning that his feelings predominate and take precedence over his mental processes . . . a hasty, superficial thinker. Yet . . . also shows logic, purposefulness and premeditation; . . . the opportunist . . . The diplomat whose diplomacy covers shrewdness . . . *In this sample he is too much pressured by circumstances* to give rein to his nobler aspirations, except feebly, until he writes 'Washington.' . . . Washington is a sort of heaven to him.

"Note how unimportant is the name of Lewis Payne, compared to the name, Col. H. S. Olcott. The former was unimportant as a man—to him."

We have italicized the phrases which show an insight into the situation involving Eckert's receipt for Paine's clothing—although the analyst knew only what she found in the handwriting. Eckert was indeed under the "pressure of circumstances" when he wrote this receipt—circumstances which he felt made it necessary to devote himself unremittingly to the conviction of Louis Paine, whom he knew to be innocent, until the prisoner was condemned and executed—and to continue to advance

sis of the character traits she saw in his handwriting in even more detail than the other two. The only clue she had from *this* writer was the misleading comment that both "Mr. X" and the person to whom he was writing must have been officials of the War Department:

" 'Mr. X' is the more brilliant, subtle, and intellectual. I do not believe that Eckert could ever leave his ego behind and be the sensitive, intuitive, devious, flexible, evasive person that 'Mr. X' seems to be."

"This is a sensitive, perceptive, cultivated man of hardly less than brilliant intellect. His mind is subtle, devious, and inclined to diplomacy instead of open and direct action. He has little patience with slow thinkers. He is, in fact, rather easily irritated. He is frequently intuitive, but he is also capable of logical organization of his thoughts, so that he has a good deal of executive ability; but he would prefer to work behind the scenes; to act without seeming to act would greatly appeal to him. He might, in fact, in some sense, have a double life; both one before the public, and in another field of action that does not appear. He actually has a high degree of idealism. And also a combination of personal pride and modesty. He is refined and no doubt gently bred, with a preference for elegant simplicity. There is generally a barrier between himself and others, not so much of his own choosing but perhaps due to the disappointments and frustrations he has found in life.

"He would probably make enemies, and in modern times he might be considered somewhat neurotic; in any case he is a very able and very unusual man. But one who has not been able to cope easily with life as he found it. He would be, in fact, a philosopher; too restless and driven to live only in his philosophy."

"I can well suppose he was a Virginia aristocrat; in a sense something of a weakling, but what is now called an egg-head. . . . I might also say he was something of a defeated man, but a very proud man, too. His reasons for action would be very different from those of the others. He was subject to moods, of courage and depression, and very intense. My own personal feeling is that I would not wish to hurt him. On the contrary, while I myself might be baffled by him, as I think many were, I would respect his dignity. That seems funny in speaking of a conspirator, as I suppose he was. He was by no means truthful. Yet there is a spiritual elevation that made him far from ordinary.

"I keep thinking of Machiavelli, if I spell him right; one who believed in power in the right hands; not in the populace. . . . I do not see why he would be in the War Department; he is almost effeminate; not an aggressive or warlike person. I'd look for him in the list of the F. F. V.'s [First Families of Virginia]. An outsider, a gentleman, safe in his mantle of respectability; hence, still not caught in his 'nefarious' schemes."

The writer found this description of 'Mr. X' intriguing but not enlightening. Among the many public figures of Lincoln's era who might be suspected of having even remote connections with the assassination plot, there was no one who seemed to fit such a description. And yet this profile of an unknown man was familiar, and surely must ring a faint bell to some of the many students of the Lincoln epic who are more scholarly than this writer.

The more tangible and immediate considerations of the research and writing pushed the riddle of "Mr. X's" identity into the background. In spite of the fact that Mrs. Lattin's graphic description of "Watson" had led to his identification as L. C. Baker, the writer's confidence in graphology was not sufficient to prompt a diligent search for some member of the Lincoln administration who fitted the analyst's description of "Mr. X." It was nearly three weeks after the profile had been received, read and filed away before a name popped into mind as a possible "Mr. X."

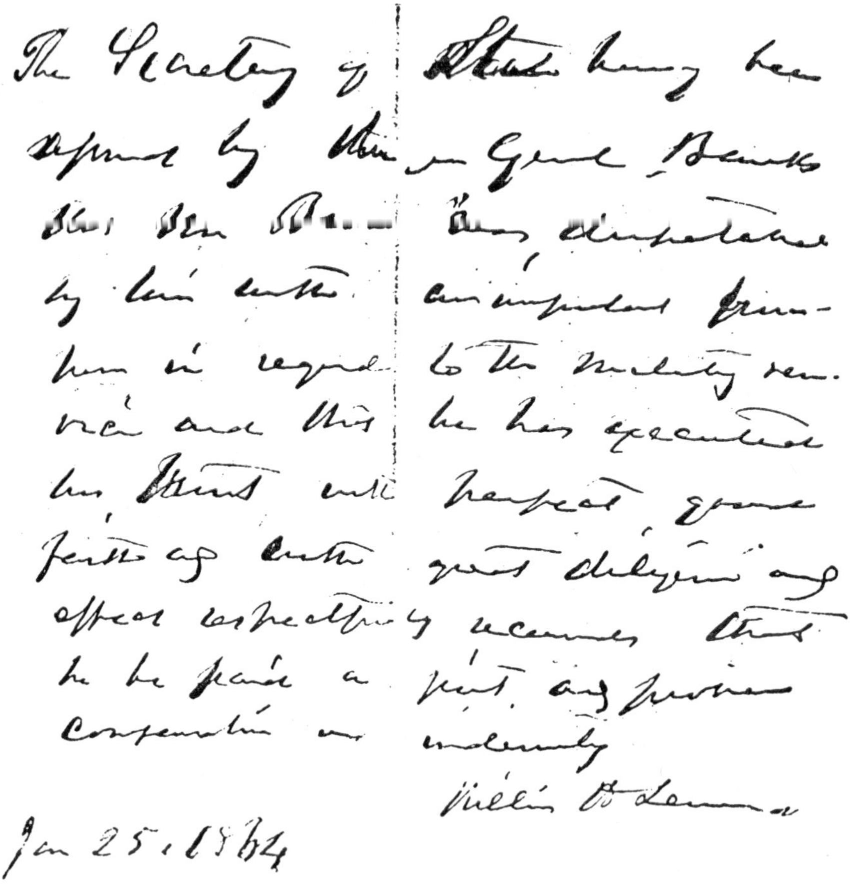

The Secretary of State having been
informed by Major General Banks
that Mr. Brown was dispatched
by him with an important operation in regard to the military service and that he has executed
his trust with perfect good
faith and with great diligence and
effect respectfully recommends that
he be paid a just and proper
compensation and indemnity
William H. Seward

Jan 25. 1864

FIG. 9.—Memo from National Archives Bearing William H. Seward's Signature. "The Secretary of State having been informed by Major General Banks that Mr. Brown was dispatched by him with an important operation in regard to the military service and that he has executed his trust with perfect good faith and with great diligence and effect respectfully recommends that he be paid a just and proper compensation and indemnity."

In response to an urgent request, Mr. Elmer O. Parker, one of the National Archives' authorities on documents of the Lincoln administration, found and forwarded a verified sample of the handwriting of the official in question. This was airmailed to Mrs. Lattin for comparison with the "Mr. X" letter.

While waiting for the analyst's verdict, the writer referred to biographies of the *supposed* "Mr. X" and was able to find the probable identity of the person referred to in the last paragraph as "Addie." Thus it was no great surprise to read the opening lines of Mrs. Lattin's report on her study of the "X" letter compared with the sample supplied by Mr. Parker:

"I can give you your answer at once; this 'Mr. X' is indeed William H. Seward. There is no question about it."

Rather than quoting the analyst's detailed explanation of the mechanical similarities which convinced her of this identification, we reproduce the sample letter from the Archives (which see) written and signed by Lincoln's Secretary of State, and invite other handwriting experts to make their own comparisons with the "Mr. X" letter.

In addition, we refer the reader to the most recent and one of the best biographies of William H. Seward * for a description of the warm personal friendship during the post-war months between Seward and Henry Adams (Addie?), son of Charles Francis Adams, a longtime friend of the Secretary's who was ambassador to Great Britain during the Civil War. Young Adams had been his father's secretary at the British court. With the close of hostilities, he returned to Washington and became "about the closest companion" of Mr. Seward.

John Wilkes Booth

One of the many incidental theories which were investigated in the course of this research was the notion that John Wilkes Booth's "diary" might have been a forgery. This idea was prompted in part by the text, which sounded a little like the kind of message which might have been planted in the pocket of the corpse—if death had occurred by poisoning—to make it appear Booth had committed suicide when he found himself despised as an assassin, rather than acclaimed as a hero. The fact that the notebook never left the hands of persons who were all deeply implicated in the conspiracy—Conger, Lieutenant Baker, Lafayette Baker, Stanton, Eckert and Holt—encouraged the theory.

A photocopy of a page from the "diary" was mailed to Mrs. Lattin with a note to the effect that a verified sample of Booth's script had been sent for and would be forwarded as soon as received. But the analyst's report arrived before the sample could be located. She was unaware of our conclusions that Booth was *not* the mastermind, but merely a pathetic dupe. Yet she wrote as follows:

"Absolutely no one could use a handwriting like that when he was writing a forgery. It had to be genuine. Because no forger could be in such a state of turmoil as this writer was. This writer, when he was writing, was at the actual breaking point. His emotions were wildly desperate. He might have been writing simply because he needed an outlet for his feelings; it was that or scream—or something of the kind. It pains me to look at such writing as this, for I respond to it unavoidably and unintentionally."

Referring to a book in which she had found the reproduction of an autographed photo of Booth—"His signature, two words of writing, in this book is almost normal, though badly cramped, as he did not allow for the smallness of the space available. *Not allowing* is one of the clues; he did not see the obvious. Starting out with a large 'J. Wilkes,' his 'Booth' had to be squashed to get it on the photograph at all. Yes, symbolism, even in this trifle. The narrowness of line to line spacing also indicates a lack of mental clarity, even here. On the full page of writing the spacing is very good; it really did indicate more mental ability than one would expect. But his emotions were then very immature, with intense inner conflicts of feeling and attitudes.

"The signature in this other book [*Collecting Autographs and Manuscripts*, by Charles Hamilton—University of Oklahoma Press] was written with a rather fine pen, but the forms were similar. It expressed pretentiousness, and weakness, and some eccentricity of a rather ugly kind. And a general lack of purpose and, I would

* *The Governor and His Lady* by Earl Conrad, p, 402, G. P. Putnam's Sons, N. Y., 1960.

say, some vagueness of mind. The main purpose, of course, was to be impressive, to compensate for his frustrations.

"I wonder as to the page of writing [from Booth's 'diary']; did he have someone to whom he would turn with his troubles, whom he might have been addressing? Or was he just talking to himself? If the latter, *something of a split personality;* schizophrenic, perhaps? I know nothing of this. I am just wondering. Anyhow, these are good examples of how differently a man can write at different times, yet still be obviously the same man."

Our analysis of the actor's state of mind shortly before, during and just after his crime (see the chapter on Booth) was not dealing with the subject in psychological terms, so the expression "split personality" did not occur. But Mrs. Lattin's study of his handwriting in the "diary" gave her an impression of Booth's mental state which paralleled ours closely. The term she used—"split personality"—offers about the only reasonable explanation for an instance in which a normally gentle man behaved in a diametrically opposite manner when another aspect of his character was brought to the surface by frustration, self-pity, excessive drinking, subjective acting—and subordination to a stronger will by means of flattery.

J— supplementary evidence

From time to time new evidence bearing on the assassination of Lincoln is discovered and publicized. Yet the *traditional* version of the conspiracy has remained largely undisturbed. This is because, being fabricated, it has lacked a logical framework into which new evidence could be fitted. For the same reason, important findings have probably not been recognized as having any connection with the conspiracy.

One objective of this project is that the new concept of the plot presented here may stimulate research on many aspects of the case which the *legend* has obscured in the past. With a new background for research, it is hoped that subsequent studies will help to fill out the large gaps in our version and supply evidence to correct any erroneous conclusions.

Even prior to publication, two examples of the manner in which pertinent discoveries can be evaluated in the light of the new version were furnished through the courtesy of Mr. Ray A. Neff. This professional investigator became interested in our study in its later stages and was kind enough to allow us to cite two items turned up in his current work with the important "Chaffey Papers."

These are a collection of business papers and accounts kept by the Nova Scotia shipping firm of J. & J. Chaffey. Mr. Neff states that L. C. Baker worked for the Chaffeys from 1844 to 1849.

item number one

The fact that L. C. Baker had undercover dealings with this firm during his employment as head of the War Department detectives is established beyond all doubt by a page from a Chaffey account book, a copy of which Mr. Neff supplied to the author.

The page in question lists cash payments to "L. C. Baker" for each of the last six months of 1864—totalling almost $150,000!

Analysis of this and other records in Mr. Neff's possession will no doubt reveal whether these payments to the detective represented his rakeoff from the sale of contraband merchandise seized by his bureau in 1864, as charged in newspaper articles of the period.

From the viewpoint of *our* investigation, the most important information to be found in the ledger sheet is the address at which the monthly payments were made: *178½ Water Street, New York City.*

The reader will recall this was the return address given in Baker's March 19 letter to John Surratt signed "R. D. Watson."

At first glance it appears Baker must have set up a dummy firm (DeMill and Company) at that address, from which to conduct his undercover business and political activities. But the *second* document furnished by Mr. Neff indicates much more strongly that 178½ Water Street was the New York office of J. & J. Chaffey—where L. C. Baker received mail and wires he did not wish sent to his own office or hotel in the city.

item number two

The second document is a letter dated November 4, 1864, which is also headed "178½ Water Street," and is signed by "Thomas Caldwell" for "James and John Chaffey."

The addressee is *"Mr. J. W. Booth, National Hotel, Washington City, D. C.*

After acknowledging Booth's letter of October 28 the letter writer lists four credits to the actor's account between August 24 and October 5, totalling $14,548.40. The accounting deducts $10,000 for "advanced payment for services." It is stated that the balance of $4,548.40 can be drawn upon "any time after the turn of the year on British banks by the payment of nominal discount rates."

Against the background of the *traditional* "conspiracy," the natural assumption is that these payments to Booth represented some secret financial backing for his plot to kidnap or murder the President. But, in the light of *our* conception of the conspiracy and Booth's role in it, this document confirms the ruin of his acting career and his serious plans for leaving the country weeks before the kidnap plot entered his mind.

Booth's situation in the early part of November, 1864 comes into clearer focus. It was around that time he told Samuel Knapp Chester he intended to "run the blockade" and leave the country. The transfer of funds to "British banks" by arrangement with the Chaffey firm surely shows that was his intention. Additional evidence to the same effect is found in the trial testimony of Robert A. Campbell, first teller for the Ontario Bank in Montreal. This witness told of Booth's purchase of a 'bill of exchange" for "sixty-one pounds and some odd shillings" with the explanation that "he was going to run the blockade." [1]

It was November 25, 1864 before the actor made his first vague remarks to Chester about a mysterious "speculation" he had in mind that his friends "would not laugh at." [2]

As to the source of these funds he deposited with Chaffey, the first three were relatively small and *could* have been money Booth earned on the stage. But the deposit dated October 5 was for $12,449.28 in the form of a letter of credit from the Bank of Montreal. Still another document copy furnished by Mr. Neff [3] shows that this precise amount was deposited in the Bank of Montreal on July 1, 1864 by a man in Owensboro, Ky. *all in gold and silver. Apparently* the same amount was transferred to John Wilkes Booth by the letter of credit he deposited with the Chaffey firm on October 5, 1864.

Booth had no engagements that year from which he could have earned such a

[1] Peterson, pp. 80-81.
[2] Peterson, p, 46.
[3] National Archives, File No. 3416, Turner-Baker Papers.

sum. And, even if he had, he would have been paid directly with greenbacks or a bank draft, rather than through a Canadian bank by the deposit of hard money or bullion, whichever it was.

We recall the actor told his sister Asia he was engaged in smuggling quinine to the Confederates[4]—and smuggled goods were invariably paid for in either Northern greenbacks or metal, preferably the latter.[5] Further study of the Chaffey Papers may reveal if smuggling was one of the firm's activities, and whether Booth was engaged by them for this purpose.

No date was given for the "advanced payment for services" of $10,000. But we can theorize that this was where Booth got the money for his investment in oil lands in the early part of '64, which his business agent testified he had sold out in September of the same year "at a total loss to himself." [6]

Booth evidently had spent his balance with Chaffey before he revealed his kidnap plan to Chester in January of '65—or else was still entertaining the idea of going to England and didn't want to disturb the funds. He often mentioned that large amounts of money were available, but remained quite embarrassed financially through the whole period of make-believe plotting.

K— the unknown conspirator

In all probability there were several persons in Washington and elsewhere who were involved to some extent in the murder of Abraham Lincoln and whose identities are unknown. The numerous incidental questions, such as the source of the poison administered to Booth, the disappearance of his "letter to the Intelligencer" which may have named names, the curious circumstance that Booth spent all or part of each evening during the week of preparation in Deery's saloon, etc. hint at the existence of other parties to the plot.

These people, if there were any, managed to keep entirely free of suspicion. But the allegory in Baker's first cipher message was evidently referring to the *instigation* phase of the conspiracy, rather than the period of several days in which it was organized and executed. He was speaking of three individuals in Washington—one of whom was himself—whose personal ambitions for power helped to crystallize the *idea* of assassination. He did not say these three sat down together and planned the thing, or even that all three discussed the advantages of Lincoln's removal together. In fact, since "Each planned that *he* should be the king . . .," any agreement among them before the event is almost ruled out.

In effect, Baker's allegory is an explanation of where *he* got the idea to proceed with the arrangements. He knew that two top officials in the government—both in line to step into Lincoln's shoes if they should become vacant—wanted the President dead. Obviously, this wasn't common knowledge, so Baker would have learned their views from private, separate conversations with them, possibly in very oblique terms, yet not so oblique as to make the understanding uncertain. It may have been that the idea for assassination originated with "Brutus" or "Judas" and was planted in *Baker's* mind, rather than that of someone else, for the very reason that he was the type to translate it into action. If so, then someone else was the

[4] Asia Booth Clarke, quoted in *Prince of Players*, by Eleanor Ruggles, p, 175.

[5] In *The Unlocked Book* (New York: G. P. Putnam's Sons, 1938), which presents the original text of Asia Clarke's manuscript, Booth's sister gives numerous enlightening details of her brother's activities and method of operation as a smuggler of quinine to the Confederacy. See pp. 116-120.

[6] Peterson, p. 45. Testimony of Joseph H. Simonds.

instigator of Lincoln's murder at the level upon which all action begins—the mental level.

In the active sense, then, neither "Brutus" nor "Judas" was a *conspirator* by definition, though both were conspirators in spirit—and we will use the term with that connotation for lack of a more applicable one. Baker left no doubt about Stanton's identification as "Judas" by relating him to an incident everyone knew about—the deathbed scene in which Stanton was said to have coined the lofty phrase, "Now he belongs to the ages." The detective could have identified "Brutus" in the same way if he had wished. In the interests of "accuracy" he included him in the allegory—but allowed him to remain the 'unknown conspirator." *If* Baker's cipher messages had been discovered and publicized immediately after his death, as he planned, the sky would have fallen on Stanton. But "Brutus," the "unknown conspirator," might have escaped public suspicion—but have had to live with the *fear* of exposure and the absolute certainty that *Baker had known.*

The detective's allegory—which we are presuming to have been a sound one—set certain requirements which any candidate for the role of "Brutus" must meet, as follows:

1. He would have been someone so well acquainted with Baker and so influential in his own right that an oblique discussion would both convey his approval of assassination and *not* place him in jeopardy. For the first purpose he would need unusual subtlety; for the second he would have to be more powerful than Baker.
2. To have the same relationship to Lincoln as Brutus did to Caesar, the "unknown conspirator" had to be both a close acquaintance, an intimate, of the President in the official family, and be the holder of an office from which he might hope to move directly into Lincoln's position of power—without the formality or uncertainty of a national election. In short, he would almost have to have been a member of the cabinet—or vice president—since, otherwise, the established order of succession would have put the office of president far beyond his reach, except by a military coup, which is not worth considering.
3. The political history of the "unknown conspirator" had to reflect his love of power and ambition to be president. Without such a background, regardless of his *secret* ambitions, we can hardly imagine Baker taking his aspirations to be "king" seriously. He *could* have been a powerful general, with a personal following among high army officers, who visualized a military dictatorship. But Stanton's pre-eminence in the military hierarchy in 1865 rules this out—and Stanton was a contender himself, according to Baker.

Condensing the requirements for the role of "Brutus" to more concise terms, the candidate had to be—

1. well acquainted with and superior to Lafayette Baker;
2. a close associate of Lincoln of at least cabinet rank;
3. a person whose love of power was well known.

Most students of Civil War politics who are willing to accept these three requirements for "Brutus" will agree there is no need to screen the whole membership of Lincoln's cabinet in 1865 to find the most likely candidate. That body was dominated by only two of its members, and one of these, Stanton, is already labeled as "Judas." The other was Secretary of State Seward. So the choice narrows very quickly to either William H. Seward or Vice President Johnson.

If Baker's cipher messages had been made public right after his death in July, 1868, Andrew Johnson might have had a worse time of it than he did. The Radicals, whose political lynch party in Johnson's "honor" had failed by only one vote in the spring, would have hailed Baker's "confession" as confirming their wildest accusations against Lincoln's successor. They had already defaced Johnson's public image with so many direct and insinuated slanders that he could hardly have avoided the label of "Brutus." Surely he could never have proved he was *not* "Brutus."

From our perspective in the twentieth century, however, and in view of the conception of the conspiracy we have been developing, Andrew Johnson can hardly be considered a candidate for the role. The list of reasons why he couldn't qualify might cover several pages, but numbers One and Two settle the matter to this writer's satisfaction:

1. Johnson was #2 on Lafayette Baker's blacklist. It was *he* who had thrown the detective out in disgrace. The *second* cipher message included a charge that he had instigated the plot to *kidnap* the President; if Baker had him in mind in the *first* cipher message in the role of "Brutus," he would have identified him as clearly and with as great relish as he did Stanton.
2. Johnson, according to our conception of the actual plot against Lincoln's life, was to have been the scapegoat, the one upon whom suspicion as instigator was to have fallen. That he could have played either an active or a passive role in a conspiracy of which he himself was to be a victim is, of course, ridiculous.

By process of elimination, we find ourselves with only one candidate for Baker's "Brutus." Ironically, that one candidate, William H. Seward, was *clearly* a victim of the violence on April 14, 1865—though the victim of a different plot than the one to assassinate Lincoln. We have concluded that neither Baker nor Stanton knew anything about this parallel conspiracy, so the attack upon Seward, presumably by Lewis Powell, need not eliminate the Secretary of State as one who had knowledge of and a passive interest in the assassination of Lincoln.

The possibility that Baker was lying when he said a "Brutus" was one of three ambitious men who wanted Lincoln dead is remote. His making it a trio, rather than a duet of conspirators was actually prompted by a desire for historical "accuracy"—as confirmed by his lack of any effort to reveal who "Brutus" really was. Why include a fictitious conspirator to clutter up an otherwise tidy allegory? Both of Baker's cipher messages were written in the spirit of a man about to die. If, at such a time, he went to the trouble to compose and write messages in cipher, it's a fair guess he did so because he wanted to get something off his chest. It need not have been the literal truth—but he would hardly have injected any elements in his allegory which might confuse the message he wanted to leave behind him. Therefore we can assume there *was* a man involved in the assassination whom he chose to characterize, but not identify, as "Brutus."

Aside from the question of Mr. Seward's qualifications for the role of "Brutus" in the allegory—but very pertinent to the subject—there were two situations connected with the assassination and trial in which the statesman appeared to be greatly compromised by his own behavior.

We have already discussed the first of these—his curiously secretive letter to someone associated with the prosecution of the "conspirators" which he asked the addressee to destroy after reading. He stated that he had "reliable" information on "Lewis Payne" which he didn't desire to put in writing but which he would tell his correspondent all about when he returned from New York the following week. Doster's mention of the widely believed report to the effect that Seward was going to ask for Paine's pardon if he were sentenced (not clemency, mind you, but a *pardon*), suggested he had checked his information and was convinced the prisoner was innocent.

His failure to make a public issue of this, even if it amounted only to grounds for reasonable doubt, cannot be explained in any terms which would enhance his reputation. His inaction, coupled with the conspiratorial tone of his letter and desire that it be destroyed, stamp an indelible question mark upon the image of William H. Seward.

The second situation was the coincidence that his carriage accident occurred a few days before the assassination of Lincoln. The accident may have been just what it seemed, a coincidence, but it had the effect of making it a matter of general knowledge across the country that Seward was a bedridden invalid during the week in which the assassination was organized.

Now, just what was the nature of Mr. Seward's injuries from that accident? The first witness to testify on this subject at the Conspiracy Trial was Sergeant George Robinson on May 19.[1] The Negro soldier had been serving as Mr. Seward's male nurse since his accident. On the stand he was a most reluctant witness, unwilling to make a positive identification of "Payne," and several of his answers contradicted the version of the affair the prosecutors were advancing. His conception of the incident—particularly regarding Major Seward's part in it—was so far from what Holt expected of him that it elicited some stinging sarcasm from the Judge Advocate in the question as to whether he was talking about the same Mr. Seward and an event which took place in the city of Washington. We had the impression that Robinson was crossing up the prosecutors by his perverse desire to tell the truth.

The pertinent dialogue was as follows:

Q. Was Mr. Seward in his bed at the time?
A. He was.
Q. From what cause?
A. He had been thrown from his carriage.
Q. Were his limbs broken?
A. I was told that one of his arms was broken and his jaw fractured.

In Sergeant Robinson's case, the exact wording of this last reply was probably intentional. The phrase, "*I was told,*" could hardly have been accidental. He had been attending the patient for several days, yet he didn't know from his own observation just what the patient's injuries were. Declining to say flatly that an arm was broken and the jaw fractured, he made it clear that this was *what he had been told.*

Next day Dr. Verdi, the Seward family physician, took the stand. His testimony, when related to Sergeant Robinson's, revealed some surprising aspects of the patient's condition. Holt asked him this question:[2]

Q. Was, or was not Mr. Seward at the time of this attack in a critical condition?

A. No sir; he had improved very much from his former injury, when his jaw was broken.

The student may search Dr. Verdi's testimony for any reference to a broken arm. There was none. Moreover, the question of whether Mr. Seward had a broken arm was pretty well settled by the physician's picture of his patient's response to the news that his condition wasn't serious:

". . . I examined him, and immediately reported to the family that his wounds were not mortal, upon which Mr. Seward *stretched out his hands,* manifesting evident satisfaction."

Holt's next questions and the doctor's answers confused the issue further:

Q. State what the effect of these wounds were upon Mr. Seward in reference to his former condition.

A. The effect was to debilitate him and to make it still more difficult for him to rally.

Q. Have you not at some time before this trial stated that the wounds received by Mr. Seward had a tendency to aid in his recovering from the former injury?

[1] Peterson, p. 73.
[2] *Ibid.*, p, 82.

A. No sir; I have heard that such an opinion was expressed, but I do not know by whom; that was not my opinion.

There seems to have been a crossing of the wires on reports of Seward's condition. *Someone*, not Doctor Verdi, must have felt it necessary to explain the Secretary's rapid recovery from wounds on top of injuries which had prompted early announcements that he was not long for this world—and had informed Holt or *his* informants that the stabbing had speeded the healing of his fractures. Dr. Verdi said he didn't agree.

There was no mention that Seward was wearing any appliance or other dressing to set his "fractured jaw." Latterday historians have assumed that some sort of metallic brace would have been required and picture him wearing a ponderous framework to hold his jaw in place—and conclude the knife was deflected by the brace, saving the victim's life.

None of the descriptions by Trial witnesses support this theory—at least, none in the Peterson transcript. None mentioned bandages of any kind. Robinson stated that Seward was slashed on the left cheek and on *both* sides of his neck. Surgeon General Barnes confirmed this, but not precisely:[3]

"Mr. Seward was wounded by a gash in the *right* cheek, passing round the angle of the jaw; by a stab in the right side of the neck, passing into the large muscle; and by a stab on the left side of the neck, passing into the body of the same muscle. . ." We will not belabor this difference of opinion as to which cheek had been slashed, since both testimonies had the same larger implication:

The surgeon's and the nurse's descriptions not only mentioned no bone-setting appliance, they made it clear that Seward's whole face and neck were exposed and wounded in such a manner that it is difficult to imagine he even had a napkin tied around his head to support his jaw. One may ask—was the jaw *really* broken?

In addition to the clear indication that *someone* had felt it necessary to explain Mr. Seward's rapid recovery, we have ample evidence that he *was* up and around in record time. By the middle of May—as his letter from New York regarding "Payne" confirms—he was able to make a long journey and spend a week away from home.

One of the many ways in which Colonel Rath's account differed from all others was in his reference to Seward's situation on the night he was attacked.

"Payne," he said, ". . . knocked at the door of the Seward mansion, and found that the old man, having retired early, was in bed."[4]

So Rath didn't remember the Secretary of State had been injured at all before that night. His recollection of the damage done him by the intruder was also original, amounting to only a "wound in his breast."

Louis Paine, we can be sure, knew only what he had heard in the courtroom regarding Seward's frightful injuries from the knife of his assailant, which makes this comment of Colonel Rath's particularly thought-provoking: "Payne thought he had killed Seward, and when he was confronted by Mr. Seward in the courtroom, he was amazed."

Evidently the arm Robinson was *told* was broken was *not*. Dr. Verdi's reference to Seward's "broken jaw" was plain enough, but no evidence of any measures having been taken to set the patient's jaw can be found in the testimony. And then there were the other tangled and conflicting accounts about the affair at Seward's that night—the uncertainty as to the *appearance* of the intruder by all the witnesses to the attack; conflicting statements on Major Seward's part in it, if any; the entirely unexplained presence of the wounded man, Mr. Emrick Hansell; the failure of the soldiers on the street to even try to stop the escaping assassin; etc.

---

[3] *Ibid.*, p. 75.

[4] *The Fate of the Lincoln Conspirators*, by John A. Gray, *McClure's Magazine*, Vol. 37 (October, 1911), pp. 632-33.

The affair at Seward's was and *still is* an enigma. Perhaps it always will be. But the possibility that Seward knew his attacker was not Paine and kept the knowledge to himself—plus the *fact* that *no one else was accused of the crime*—leads to a further possibility: That he knew the identity of his assailant and the reason for the assault, and didn't want the matter made public.

Most of the features of Seward's public career which have a bearing on his possible identity as Baker's "Brutus" have already been mentioned in the course of our study. So we will cite them only briefly in reviewing his credentials as a possible "unknown conspirator."

first—was he well acquainted with and superior to Lafayette Baker?

L. C. Baker's first regular employment as a detective was under Secretary Seward, during the period when the power of making arbitrary arrests was the prerogative of the State Department. The chief source of information on Baker's service for this agency was his own biography (chapters 7 through 10), and here we learn much about the intrepid detective's triumphs over traitors but very little about his relations with his boss. He speaks of Seward with elaborate respect and no breath of criticism—and covers the whole subject of his transfer to the War Department in a seven-line note from Seward to Stanton on February 15, 1862, in which the Secretary of State commended him to the Secretary of War as "a capable and efficient officer." The impression is made that Baker enjoyed a confidential and cordial association with Seward and remained on good terms with him throughout the war.

second—was he a close associate of Lincoln of at least cabinet rank?

Upon Lincoln's arrival in Washington to assume his office Seward took him in tow and became a sort of general manager for the awkward new president. It was his apparent intention to make himself a sort of European prime minister and Lincoln a figurehead. He even wrote a note to Lincoln suggesting that he turn over the major responsibilities of his office to him, Seward.[5]

Mr. Lincoln managed to assert his intention to fulfill the office of president himself tactfully enough that Seward could back pedal without losing face. Thereafter the Secretary of State adjusted himself to the unexpectedly strong will of the Chief Executive and made himself a commendable record during the war by supporting Lincoln's policies. He is pictured as treating Lincoln with considerable deference and the gulf between the personalities of the two men seemed to rule out a warm, close friendship. But they functioned as political allies and the term "close associate" would certainly apply. Seward's position as Secretary of State was near enough to the top to make him a contender for the President's powers in the event of his death, particularly if a war with England were to develop.

third—was he a person whose love of power was well known?

The most convenient source of information on William H. Seward's consuming desire for power is Mr. Conrad's recent biography of Lincoln's Secretary of State, in which this passion is illustrated over and over in the course of Seward's rather

[5] *Reveille in Washington*, by Margaret Leech, p. 52.

frustrated career. The example of his urging war with England with this very aim has already been cited.[6]

Dr. Eisenschiml mentioned Seward's reported boast to Lord Lyon, the British ambassador, during the period when the Secretary of State was exercising the Gestapo powers against subversion which were later appropriated by Stanton:

"My Lord, I can touch a bell on my right hand, and order the arrest of a citizen in Ohio; I can touch a bell again, and order the imprisonment of a citizen of New York; and no power on earth, except that of the President, can release him. Can the Queen of England do so much?"[7]

J. M. Crawford, a contemporary of Seward's and one of General Mosby's several biographers, cited the *Congressional Globe* as authority for an explicit example of Seward's contempt for democratic processes. A Frederick Stanton (not related to the War Secretary) went to the State Department to protest the imprisonment of his brother, Colonel Stanton, without charges. Seward's curt reply in the presence of witnesses was—"I do not care a d—n whether they are guilty or innocent. I saved Maryland by similar arrests, and so I mean to hold Kentucky."[8]

This may be taken as an example of the moral and political climate at that time in the department of government where Lafayette Baker took his basic training.

Even if we had documentary evidence that William H. Seward was Baker's "Brutus," and therefore the "unknown conspirator," the incrimination could hardly go beyond the detective's *informed opinion* that the Secretary of State knew Lincoln was to be assassinated and approved of it. It follows quite logically that, if this were the case, Seward would have committed a passive act of treason by failing to expose the conspiracy and prevent the assassination. This is a serious charge, of course, but being based only upon one man's opinion of what another man was *thinking*, it's as impossible to prove it *true* as to prove it *not true*. We may be wholly convinced that Baker meant "Seward" when he wrote "Brutus" and that his charge was well founded. The matter, by its very nature, is beyond the scope of human judgment—but well within the bounds of legitimate conjecture.

L— H. L. Payne

A check of the compiled service records of Confederate soldiers in the National Archives produced a list of five soldiers with variations of the name "Hugh Lewis Payne" who *might* have been the same young man who was hanged in Washington in 1865.[1] Four of these were eliminated by one criterion or another—leaving *Private H. L. Payne* (or Paine) as the only likely candidate. He was the *only* one with the letter "H" as one of his initials. Also, he enlisted in Gwinnett County, Georgia *where Louis Paine was born.*

The information given in this soldier's individual records fitted him neatly into the gap in Paine's history between 1860 and January, 1865, when he arrived in Baltimore from Virginia. But a preliminary study revealed some startling peculiarities in his records—and opened one of the strangest phases of the research on the career of this ill-starred young man. It now appeared that pure coincidence was abetting the efforts of the prisoner, Colonel Burnett, Major Eckert, L. C. Baker and others to hide the fact that Louis Paine had ever existed.

[6] Conrad, p. 351.
[7] SOLD, pp. 191-92.
[8] *Mosby and His Men*, by J. Marshall Crawford (New York, 1867), p. 87.
[1] The indispensable help of Mr. Elmer O. Parker, Mr. John E. Taylor and Mrs. Sarah Jackson of the Army and Air Corps Branch in the search for Paine's army records is acknowledged with gratitude.

At first reading, the records showed H. L. Payne as having enlisted in Company I of the 55th Georgia Volunteer Infantry in May, 1862, at Lawrenceville, Gwinnett County, Georgia. His regiment was sent to the Army of Tennessee and, early in 1863, he was detailed to work as a shoemaker in the government shops at Knoxville. He later performed the same duties at the quartermaster depot in Atlanta. In August of 1864, the month in which Sherman's forces laid seige to Atlanta, H. L. Payne was listed as "absent without leave." His records ended there.

The soldier's file included four pay vouchers which bore his signature. Comparison of two of these with the signature "L. Paine" on the Oath of Allegiance of the man hanged in Washington indicated very strongly that "H. L. Payne" and the defendant at the Conspiracy Trial were the same man.

But—reference to a History of Gwinnett County, Georgia[2] brought out the fact that a man named H. L. Payne who had served in the 55th Georgia Infantry applied for and obtained a veteran's penison in 1902 in that county.

The thorough anaylsis of H. L. Payne's records prompted by this contradiction brought to light a coincidence that could only have happened in real life; no fiction writer would dare strain his readers' credulity to such a point: H. L. Payne's army file contained the partial records of *two* men by that name.

Proof of this was found in three different varieties of information conveyed by the documents. We will list them first, then discuss each one separately. These are the data bearing on the presence of two "H. L. Paynes" in the 55th Georgia:

1. A muster roll dated *May 7, 1862* recorded the fact the *"Pvt. H. L. Payne"* had "joined for duty and enrolled" on that date for a period of 3 years. A pay roll dated May 14, 1862 stated that *"Pvt. H. L. Paine"* had "volunteered" on *May 6, 1862* for "three years or during the war"—and had received a bounty of $50. On subsequent records the date of enlistment shown on all rolls was May 7.
2. The file of 24 compiled extracts from payrolls, receipt rolls and muster rolls contained two clear duplications of pay and four clear duplications of information as to the whereabouts and duties of the soldier during a given period—in addition to the discrepancy as to enlistment date.
3. It was evident from even a casual glance at the signatures on the four pay receipts that they were not all written by the same man, though the name and initials were the same and the general forming of the letters was similar. Analysis of the signatures by a handwriting expert confirmed that two were written by one man and two by another.

first—*the fifty-dollar bounty*

In the first category above, the differences in dates of enlistment and in the spelling of the names do not, by themselves, serve as reliable evidence that the records were those of *two* soldiers. Both discrepancies are too readily explained in terms of clerical error.

The important distinction is the payment of a $50 bounty to "H. L. Paine."

During the winter of 1861-62, the Confederate authorities in Richmond were faced with a critical manpower problem. Major military confrontations were shaping up on both the eastern and western fronts and decisive battles were anticipated for the coming spring and summer. But great numbers of the troops then serving in Southern armies had enlisted for only 12 months. Reports of mass disillusionment with the romance of war convinced legislators that a large percentage of the veterans would leave the army at the end of their enlistments. Their solution was passage of

[2] This information supplied by Mr. John A. Smith, attorney at law, Talbotton, Georgia.

the "Bounty and Furlough Act" intended to entice 12-month men into re-enlisting for "the War" when their time expired.

The act offered veterans three inducements to re-enlist for duration: A $50 bounty, a 2-month furlough, and the privilege of rejoining any regiment they chose.[3]

When it became clear that the Act was not going to change the minds of many veterans about getting out—and that there were thousands of ablebodied men who had not and did not intend to *volunteer*—the Confederate Congress passed the first Conscription Act, making all men between the ages of 18 and 35 subject to obligatory service. This law took effect in April, 1862.

Thus, the payment of a bounty to H. L. Paine confirmed that he was a different man than the "H. L. Payne" who enrolled on May 7—*unless* it turned out that the man who applied for a pension in 1902 had served in another regiment before joining the 55th Georgia Infantry.

Records of the pension application obtained from Atlanta showed that the applicant, H. L. Payne, claimed to have served in the Confederate Army *only* from May 7, 1862 to the "surrender of Atlanta" in September, 1864. Thus, the volunteer who got the bounty was a different man, and had served a year in some other regiment before joining the 55th.

second—*the duplications*

Duplications as to the receipt of pay were as follows:

1. Two signed vouchers dated June 1, 1863 (both referring to the same disbursement) showed a payment of $44, which represented four months' pay at $11 per month. This amount covered the period January 1 to May 1, 1863. The paymaster was Quartermaster Captain H. T. Massengale. The payment was made and signed for in Knoxville, Tennessee.

   A muster roll covering the two months of July and August, 1863 bore the notation that the soldier had been paid last by Captain Persons, a company officer, *to February 28, 1863. This* payment covered a *two-month* period since the soldier's previous pay on January 1. Obviously, if these records concerned only one soldier, they would show he had been paid *twice* for the first two months of 1863—in each case by a different officer.
2. The 55th Infantry Regiment was captured at Cumberland Gap on September 9, 1863.[4] After this "H. L. Payne" received no pay through his company, but was paid for making and "bottoming" shoes by the quartermaster in Atlanta. A variety of piecework and daily rates was used.

   A receipt roll made out in Atlanta on February 29, 1864 showed a payment of *$28*—for "bottoming" 80 pairs of shoes at 35¢ per pair—during the period *February 1 to 29, 1864.*

   Another receipt roll, also dated February 29, 1864 in Atlanta, showed a payment of $75—covering the period *February 1 to 25, 1864*—25 days work at $3 per day. It is reasonable to suppose that the hard pressed Confederate Army would not have paid the same private both a piece rate and a daily rate during almost the same pay period.

Duplications of information as to the soldier's whereabouts and duties:

1. Four muster rolls in 1863 noted the soldier's assignment to work in the "Government shop" at Knoxville. Two showed he was *"detailed" February 22, 1863;* one of these mentioned that the assignment was ordered by Assistant Quartermaster Captain Lewis DeLaigle. Two showed he was *"Detached at Knoxville*

---

[3] *The Land They Fought For,* by Clifford Dowdey, c. 1955, p. 100.
[4] From H. L. Payne's pension application—Georgia Department of Archives and History, Atlanta. Courtesy of Mrs. Mary Givens Bryan, Director.

February 28, 1863." The precise wording of each notation, carried forward to a later muster roll in the same words, demonstrated that these were consecutive entries on the records of two different men, and not at that time a confusion of two sets of records.

2. Two separate rolls referred to "Pvt. H. L. Payne's" period of service as a "*shoemaker*" from December 1 to 31, 1863—and to his term of service at "*bottoming shoes*" from December 1 to 29, 1863.
3. Two separate rolls listed the soldier *AWOL from Augusta* (evidently meant Atlanta) and *AWOL from Atlanta* in August, 1864.
4. Two separate rolls listed the soldier as *AWOL from Atlanta* in September, 1864.

It should be mentioned that this and most other infantry line companies took a muster roll about every two months, at which a soldier was marked "present" or a notation made as to any change in his status or duties which had occurred in the preceding period. The quartermaster, however, took a roll of men detailed from the regiments for special duty *once a month.*

A lengthy, special study would be needed to determine why only *parts* of the records of two soldiers were in this file—though the situation was not particularly unusual. In this case, a contributing reason was the capture of Company I with its headquarters at Cumberland Gap in September, 1863. Records seized here were taken to Ohio. The quartermaster records appear to have been captured at Atlanta—and possibly some at Knoxville, as well. Many years later, when all records were consolidated and compiled in Washington, the copyists combined everything they found on "H. L. Payne" of Company I, 55th Georgia Inf. into one file. Not having *complete* records on either man, they apparently didn't notice the duplications.

third—*the signatures*

The handwriting analyst determined that the signatures were those of two men, each of whom had written his name twice. Since each pair appeared on a set of two vouchers referring to the same payment (for *four* months in one case and for *two* months in the other; $44 and $22 respectively) it's fairly certain we have two signatures for one man and two for the other.

One man's hand was that of a practiced and rather competent penman—clearly an educated person. The other man's execution of his signature was clumsy and hesitant with little consistency in the forming of the letters. Yet the general similarity between the two sets allowed only one plausible conclusion: An unlettered man had written his name by *copying* the signature of another man whose name and initials *sounded* the same as his. In the strict sense, the illiterate man was not really *writing;* he had *copied a design* and, all things considered, reproduced it rather accurately.

The evidence that there were two privates named "H. L. Payne" in Company I of the 55th Georgia is conclusive. The proposition is that one of them—the illiterate man—was the same "Lewis Payne" (Louis Paine) who was hanged in Washington. Before going into this, let's dispose of the question of the identity of the *other* soldier with the same name.

Presuming Paine was on furlough from another regiment in the spring of 1862, his presence in Gwinnett County, Georgia wasn't accidental. He no longer had a home in Florida to return to. The Union lines lay between him and his mother in northern Virginia. He was in Gwinnett County looking for someone he *knew* lived there—presumably a close relative. His original family had lived there before his mother parted from her first husband, John W. Paine, around 1845 and moved to Florida with Jeremiah Smith.

Now, Louis' mother is believed to have been the daughter of Thomas Payne of

Hall County (originally from Virginia) who was listed in the 1850 census (Page 337, #44) as a *shoemaker.* Hall County borders Gwinnett County on the north. The Paynes were numerous in these counties and many were undoubtedly Louis' kin on his mother's side.

The one in which we are interested was "H. L. Payn (Payne)," a *shoemaker* who was living in Gwinnett County with his wife Martha in 1860 (census, Page 675). This was the same "H. L. Payne" who joined the 55th Georgia Infantry on May 7, 1862 and who survived the war and applied for a veteran's pension in 1902. His enlistment was his *first,* prompted by passage of the first Conscription Act in April of that year, making *all* men between 18 and 35 subject to an immediate draft.

In this era when trades were passed down from father to son to grandson, it seems quite plausible that "H. L. Payne," the shoemaker of Gwinnett County, was a grandson of Thomas Payne of Hall County and a nephew of Louis' mother. This would have made him the *first cousin* of Louis Paine. For the sake of this discussion we will refer to him in that relationship. According to his pension application, he was five years older than Louis in 1862.

Both men were shoemakers. The Confederate government's act of 1862 authorizing the detachment of 2,000 shoemakers from their army units to make shoes for the soldiers specified that these should be men experienced in the trade. So young Louis knew how to cobble *before* he entered the army—and this was an occupation which required long training and practice. Since he evidently had a first cousin in Gwinnett County who followed the trade, the logical place for Louis to have learned shoemaking was with this relative during the late 1850's. This also supplies a logical reason for him to have visited Gwinnett County on his furlough in the spring of '62.

The passage of the Conscription Act in April of that year made Louis subject to the draft, but the Bounty and Furlough Act allowed him to choose his new organization and entitled him to a $50 bounty. Thus, both men joined D. A. Lee's Company which was being recruited at Lawrenceville.

Louis seems to have *signed* for his pay *only* while he was with the quartermaster at Knoxville. On all other pay rolls, the paymaster signed for him. He may have written the name "H. L. Payne" less than half a dozen times in his army career.

This point—that he memorized the signature during his five months with the quartermaster in Knoxville in '63, but wrote it less than half a dozen times—becomes a factor in determining whether the illiterate "H. L. Payne" in the 55th Georgia was the same man who signed "L. Paine" to his Oath of Allegiance in Baltimore in March 14, 1865.

single identity of the three Paines

We now have three young men with variations of the name "Hugh Louis Paine" whom we found in different places at different times:

1. *Louis Paine* (or Lewis Payne) who was tried and executed in Washington, who signed his Oath of Allegiance "L. Paine."
2. *Hugh L. Smith* of Bellville, Florida who changed his name to "Louis Paine" prior to the 1860 census.
3. *Private H. L. Payne* (or Paine) of the 55th Georgia Infantry.

In the course of our study we have identified No. 1 as No. 2 by various means. We have also identified No. 2 as No. 3 rather conclusively. Strictly speaking, the conclusion that No. 1 and No. 3 were the same man is well justified by the use of a simple equation: A equals B; B equals C; therefore A equals C.

On the other hand, the comparison of signatures by which Private H. L. Payne can be shown to be the same man who signed his name "L. Paine" in 1865 helps

The Confederate States, Dr.

To H L Payne Pvt.

Co. "D" 55 Ga Vols C. S. Army.

	DOLLARS.	CENTS.
For Monthly Pay, from 1 Jany 1863, to 1 May 1863, being 4 months ... days, at $11 per month,	44	—
For Use and Risk of Horse ... days, at 40 cents per day		
For Bounty		
Deduct, due		
Amount Paid	44	—

I certify that I have endorsed this payment on H L Payne Descriptive Roll.
Lt. J. A. Scates
det'd to Capt Deloige ...

H T Massengale
Captain and A. Q. M.

RECEIVED, Knoxville this 1 June day of June, 1863, from Captain H. T. MASSENGALE, Quartermaster C. S. Army, the sum of Forty Four Dollars $\frac{\quad}{100}$ being the Amount, and in full of the above account.

H. L. Payne

Witness:

SIGNED DUPL'CATES.

FIG. 10.—Confederate Army Pay Receipts Signed "H. L. Payne" (#1)

to increase our understanding of the strange young man whom the War Department hanged. So we proceed with it in spite of the fact that, as evidence, it may be superfluous.

Compare the "H. L. Payne" signature on page 446 with the "L. Paine" on Paine's Oath. In both cases the signature was made by an unlettered man who was otherwise a stranger to the written language. Thus, neither signature was *handwriting* in the literal sense—but the execution of a memorized or copied design. This involved a mental and manual accomplishment which is not readily apparent to us who take literacy for granted and have been writing our names from early childhood. We have long ago forgotten how complicated our own names seemed to us when we first tried to write them as little children. Most of us started by printing the separate letters and worked up to the far more complicated script in a process of learning that took months or years.

When we consider that "H. L. Paine," who could neither read nor write, learned

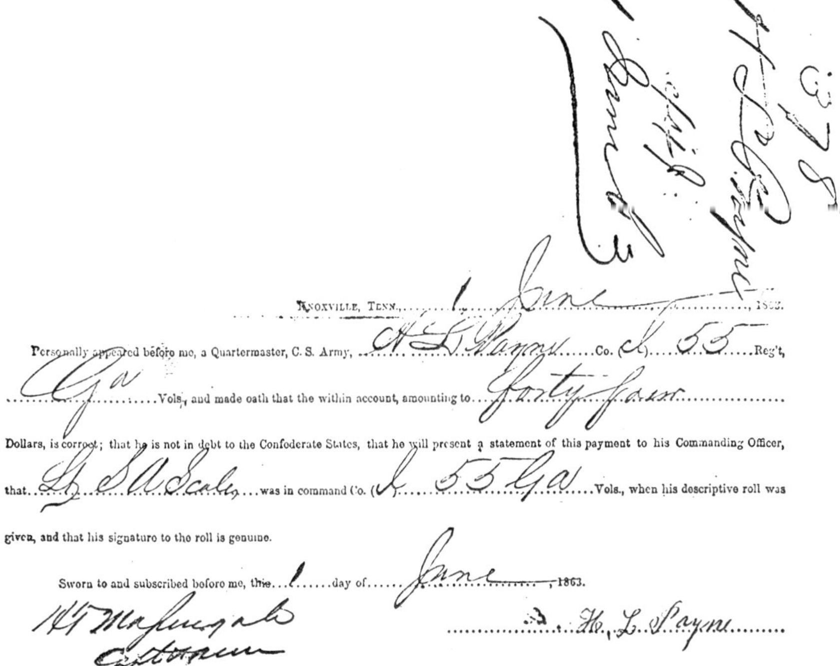
Knoxville, Tenn., 1 June, 1863.

Personally appeared before me, a Quartermaster, C. S. Army, H. L. Payne Co. (I) 55 Reg't, Ga Vols., and made oath that the within account, amounting to Forty four Dollars, is correct; that he is not in debt to the Confederate States, that he will present a statement of this payment to his Commanding Officer, that Lt S U Scales was in command Co. (I) 55 Ga Vols., when his descriptive roll was given, and that his signature to the roll is genuine.

Sworn to and subscribed before me, this 1 day of June, 1863.

Captain

H. L. Payne

Fig. 10.—Confederate Army Pay Receipts Signed "H. L. Payne" (#2)

to imitate his cousin's signature so well that it could readily pass for the other man's, we begin to appreciate his remarkable mental and manual capacities. If, two years later—with little or no practice in the interim—he was still able to write his name *with major variations from the original design,* it would demonstrate a photographic memory almost on the level of genius.

However, signatures of this kind are not ideal for study by the usual criteria of handwriting analysis—though the expert we consulted *did* find some basis for comparison, much to her surprise. An identification depends more heavily upon whether the signature "L. Paine" on the Oath contained any clear indications that the signer had previously learned to inscribe his name "H. L. Payne" (signatures #3 and #4).

Studying the Oath of Allegiance as a whole (see page 152) we note that the clerk had written "Lewis Paine" at the top in an ornate style. This was *not* the familiar spelling of the prisoner's name. As far as we know, he had never written it that way before and had never spelled out "Lewis" before. His signature at the bottom appears rather like an awkward attempt to *copy* the name the way the clerk had written it.

There are at least two peculiarities in the signature "L. Paine" that reveal his recollection of the way he had learned to sign his name in the army.

First there is the initial "L." Studying the letter closely, we find we only *take it to be* an "L" because we *know* the first name written above is "Lewis." The top loop started something like an "I," and swooped downward with confidence—*overconfidence,* in fact. For habit took over and the writer caught himself forming the

The Confederate States, Dr.

To Private H L Payne
Co "I" 55th Ga Vol C. S. Army.

	DOLLARS.	CENTS.
For Monthly Pay, from May 1st 1863, to July 1st 1863, being 2 months x days, at 11 per month,	22	00
For Use and Risk of Horse ..... days, at 40 cents per day		
For Bounty		
Deduct, due		
Amount Paid	22	00

I certify that I have endorsed this payment on H L Paynes Descriptive Roll.

[signature illegible]
Captain and A. Q. M.

RECEIVED Knoxville this 6th day of July, 1863, from Maj McElrath Quartermaster C. S. Army, the sum of ..... Dollars, being the Amount, and in full of the above Account.

Witness: H. L. Payne

[SIGNED DUPLICATES.]

FIG. 10.—Confederate Army Pay Receipts Signed "H. L. Payne" (#3)

first initial he had once learned to make—an *"H."* (Compare with the same stroke in Pvt. H. L. Payne's first initial, #4.) He stopped just in time. The letter he had made could pass for an "L," so he let it stand.

The mistake rattled him a little and it showed in the nervous, smudged lines in the "P" which followed—a compromise between the clerk's "p" and the one "H. L. Payne" made. Then came the "aine" with an unfamiliar "i"—which the clerk made something like an "r" with a dot over it. Uncertain as to whether the clerk had made a greatly deformed "y" or a new letter he hadn't learned, Paine compromised again and made a letter that looked something like an "r" and also something like a "y" with the lower loop greatly abbreviated. Then he finished the "ne" with the clerk's "ne" to refresh his memory. Checking back, he noticed the clerk's dot and put one above the middle of the last name.

Our conclusion from all this is that "L. Paine" was written by an illiterate man who had *memorized* his signature two years earlier as "H. L. Payne."

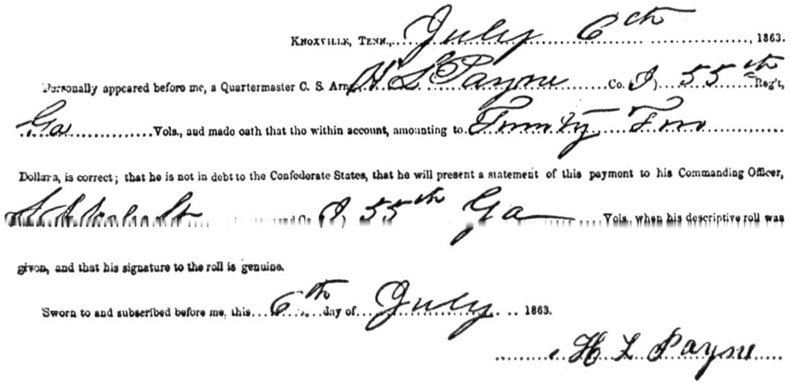

Knoxville, Tenn., July 6th, 1863.

Personally appeared before me, a Quartermaster C. S. Army, H. L. Payne Co. I, 55th Reg't, Ga. Vols., and made oath that the within account, amounting to Twenty Two Dollars, is correct; that he is not in debt to the Confederate States, that he will present a statement of this payment to his Commanding Officer, [illegible] Co. I, 55th Ga. Vols. when his descriptive roll was given, and that his signature to the roll is genuine.

Sworn to and subscribed before me, this 6th day of July 1863.

H. L. Payne

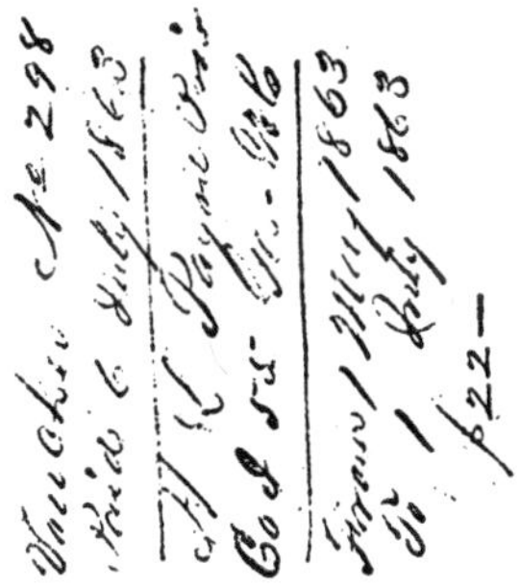

Knoxville No 298
Paid 6 July 1863
H L Payne Pri
Co I 55 Ga Vol
From 1 May 1863
to 1 July 1863
$22—

FIG. 10.—Confederate Army Pay Receipts Signed "H. L. Payne" (#4)

Louis evidently knew how to spell his correct name *orally*. In each of the three instances in which he gave his name to an official to write down, his name was spelled correctly, P-A-I-N-E.

1. The census-taker in Hamilton County in 1860.
2. The officer of D. A. Lee's Company in Lawrenceville, Georgia, who paid him the bounty on May 14, 1862.
3. The provost marshal in Baltimore who made out his Oath of Allegiance on March 14, 1865.

The Oath was signed a month before the assassination. Why, then, did Louis Paine go through this business with his signature? Why didn't he just tell the clerk he thought his name was spelled wrong, or write "H. L. Payne" the way he used to or, better still, just admit he couldn't write?

Because he was in trouble when he took the Oath. He had beaten a colored maid at the Branson house and been arrested. The provost marshal was inclined to give him a break. Rather than being charged and tried for assault and battery, he had a chance to go free by merely signing a paper. To the country boy from Florida—and a former rebel soldier to boot—the Union officer who said to sign the paper meant *sign the paper*. That was the proposition. He couldn't argue about spelling—didn't know the names of the letters. He signed the best he could, waited while the clerk recorded his oath in the register, and was grateful to get out of there with the folded document in his pocket.

In a sense, that signature cost him his life. If the provost marshal had been less lenient (or suspicious of the signature) and turned him over to the civil authorities for trial, he might have spent a couple of months in jail in Baltimore and lived to be an old man.

M— colonel Rath on John Surratt

John Surratt's whereabouts and activities after April 3 (eleven days before the assassination) are screened by a mass of conflicting information—much of which originated with Surratt himself. The revelations of Weichmann, L. C. Baker and the prosecutors at the Surratt Trial in 1867 contributed generously to the confusion—making this conspirator's case a study in itself.

Our view of the situations preceding Lincoln's murder has left the strong impression that John Surratt was a party to that conspiracy in its early stages, but may not have participated in the actual violence of Good Friday, April 14.

His hurried departure for New York immediately upon his return to Washington on April 3 (from Richmond, he said) was prompted, we have assumed, by his belated receipt of the "Watson" letter. But he might have reacted in exactly the same way if he had seen Powell at the Herndon House and learned that L. C. Baker wanted to see him and *why*. In this case, he may never have received and read the "Watson" letter—which would help to explain how it happened to fall into the hands of the War Department prosecutors. *He* knew who "Watson" was, and the nature of the letter is such that he would hardly have left it lying around his home to be found later *if he had received and opened it*.

The assassination was surely the "important business" which caused him to hasten to New York. The Confederacy being in its death throes on April 3, it is very hard to believe Surratt had any genuine spy or courier chores to perform for the rebel government on or after that date.

His arrival in New York on the 4th or 5th seemed to have a connection with Booth's sudden interest in assassination on April 7 (per Chester's testimony) and return to the Capitol on the 8th to prepare for his "performance" at Ford's on the 14th. This theory is supported by his letter to Atzerodt from New York, telling the German to sell the two horses which belonged to Booth but had been stabled by Surratt. The use of either animal to transport an assassin would have been a dead giveaway—as was actually the case with the one-eyed horse Powell used and left where it could be found easily.

There was testimony at the Surratt Trial purporting to show that he had been back in the Capitol on the day of the crime. But most of this has been dismissed as either perjured or mistaken by latterday champions of John Surratt.

On his part, the young man claimed he had left Canada on April 12 to go to Elmira, N. Y., on a Confederate spying mission—and remained in Elmira through the 13th and 14th (SOLD, p. 297). He said that the register of his hotel there for those two days was "mysteriously missing"—implying that the government had purloined the register to conceal proof that he was in Elmira on these days.

But such a conclusion didn't necessarily follow. The object of the prosecutors at the Surratt Trial was to *fail* to convict John Surratt (SOLD, Chapts. XII and XIII).

It may have been that Surratt's name or his alias "John Harrison" was *not* on the hotel register, and its suppression was intended to conceal that he was *not* at the hotel in Elmira on the 12th, 13th and 14th.

Also, his defense counsel in '67 cited the register of the Hotel Webster in Canandaigua, N. Y., to prove that he had checked in there on April 15, the day after the assassination (SOLD, p. 318). The existence of this evidence was not denied, but the Court refused to admit it for the record. It was evidently true—making it seem impossible for Surratt to have left Washington *after* the assassination and yet arrive in west central New York State any time the following day.

Now, Rath's statement that John Surratt was supposed to have killed Grant but lost his nerve and "escaped from the city," "*before* the murder of Lincoln" throws a little different light on the matter. If this were true—that he was in Washington the day of the crime but left on the 6 P.M. train, the one Grant took—the possibility that he could have reached Canandaigua within the next 24 hours would be excellent!

The reason for taking Colonel Rath's information on this matter seriously was the probability that he had obtained it from a man who *knew* all the details of Powell's primary and secondary assignments for the night of April 14—Thomas Eckert.

Although Atzerodt told Colonel Wells he had not seen John Surratt since "about a week before the murder," Surratt was the *only* "conspirator" who was an old friend of his. So, if he knew he had been in town and a party to the plot he might have denied it to help him escape.

The most concrete evidence against Surratt, of course, is the "Watson" letter—in view of our conclusion that L. C. Baker masterminded the assassination from New York City. On the circumstantial side, we have his flight (implying guilt) and continued hiding abroad for a year and a half after Stanton revoked the reward for him in November, '65. The War Department's reluctance to extradite him and extraordinary measures *not* to convict him at his trial suggest a mutual guilt and agreement not to expose one another.

A final, more subtle incrimination is seen in the absence of any determined effort on his part to clear his mother's name, although that was a cause for which there would have been wide popular support. His lecture at Rockville would have been a good forum from which to launch such a crusade—but he seemed to be more interested in showing that he himself was as pure as snow.

N— dr. Gillette's journal

In her book *Red Cross Reveries,*[1] Mrs. Amy Gillette Bassett gave some particulars of Paine's story as told to her grandfather, based upon notations in Dr. Gillette's personal journal. From these it seems Louis told the clergyman a rather different version of how Powell became involved in the "conspiracy" than he had told Doster.

He told Dr. Gillette that the "head of the house" where he stayed in Baltimore was a party to the kidnap plot; that he (as Powell) had been a member of the Confederate secret service and had traveled between Richmond, Washington and Baltimore for months before the tragedy, conferring with prominent men in the latter city. These men kept him in funds and encouraged him with "dreams of future glory."

These assertions do not agree with Doster's account, the findings of our study or the known activities of Lewis Powell as a member of Mosby's Command. Had

[1] Published by Stackpole Books, Harrisburg, Pa., 1961.

Paine forgotten what he had told Doster? Or was this the more respectable version of Lewis Powell's connection with the plot he wanted conveyed to Rev. Powell?

This observation of Dr. Gillette's seems significant: "Of the actual events at the Seward house he seemed to have only a confused memory."

After leaving Seward's "the revulsion came and he saw the crime in the light of reality. . . . Under the awakening to what he had done Payne seemed to reach an indifference as to what might happen to him." He hid in a tree all night and, *the next morning,* made his way back to the Surratt house. *"He was found there."*

He was *found* there! Again the question raised by Colonel Rath's version of the story that Paine was *found* in Mrs. Surratt's cellar! In this case, no mystery of where he had been for three days; no extraordinary coincidence of his arrival during the raid. He had gone to Surratt's on Saturday. He was *found* there on Monday night. In this particular at least, Dr. Gillette's recollection of the story confirmed Colonel Rath's.

In Paine's statement that the "head of the house" where he stayed in *Baltimore* was a party to the kidnap plot, Dr. Gillette may have simply named the wrong city —meaning to say that the head of the Surratt house was in the kidnap plot. But, within only a few hours of his talk with Dr. Gillette, the prisoner had made a sworn statement before witnesses that Mrs. Surratt had nothing to do with either the kidnap or assassination plots. And he repeated the same statement to the clergyman several times. He had surely said *Baltimore* and *meant* Baltimore.

The boardinghouse in Baltimore was Branson's, of course—unless Paine meant Powell had stayed at *another* establishment whose head *was* in on the kidnap scheme. There is one other possibility:

At the Trial we were lead to believe that Mrs. Branson was the head of her house and that she had only one daughter, Margaret. Then Archives documents revealed the existence of her daughter Mary, whose name had been kept out of the proceedings by all concerned, including Louis Paine. There was another member of the Branson family whose name and very existence were also concealed. This was Joseph Branson, husband of the landlady and father of her daughters. According to the 1870 census for Baltimore's 10th Ward, *he* was the head of the house.

Paine's reference to this man (or so it seems) during his last hours may have been a minor revelation. If Joseph Branson was involved in the kidnap plot *and Paine knew it,* we have the possibility that the prisoner had at least a general idea of what his cousin had been up to—that, when arrested and accused, he could have put two and two together and know he had been selected as the stand-in for a real conspirator. We also see that the War Department may have had *another* club to hold over Margaret Branson to persuade her to testify that their boarder "Lewis Payne" was the same man as the Lewis Powell she had met at Gettysburg.

In this writer's opinion, Dr. Gillette qualifies as an *unimpeachable* witness. Thus all his statements are taken as the truth, as he heard it or saw it. One which he made from the pulpit two days after the executions appears to be formidable new evidence against Mrs. Surratt. The clergyman was describing his visits to the cells of the other condemned prisoners: [2]

"His next call was on Atzerodt. He [Atzerodt] at once commenced remarks *which criminated Mrs. Surratt,* but was gently reminded that higher duties now devolved upon him . . ."

The prisoner was persuaded to think, rather, of preparations to meet his God. He confessed that "he had been steeped in sin; the victim of base passions, and *the wiles of artful designing men.*" The Lutheran clergyman who attended Atzerodt through the night said "he professed to have found peace with Heaven."

Dr. Gillette could hardly have been mistaken as to Atzerodt's meaning, since he

---

[2] The Washington *Chronical,* July 10, 1865.

admonished him to raise his thoughts above recriminations. And the German had been present during the final preparations for the murder of Lincoln. He was well able to *know* whether Mrs. Surratt was a party to it.

Colonel Doster, though an honorable witness, was indignant at the conviction of the widow on what appeared to him to be weak, circumstantial evidence. He didn't want to believe her guilty. *His* report was that Atzerodt, like Paine, had maintained Mrs. Surratt was innocent. And when he quoted Herold as saying, "That old lady is as deep in as any of us," he attributed it to the young man's jealousy at the progress the widow's lawyers seemed to be making in discrediting the charges against her (Doster, pp. 276-77).

Tabulation of the votes of the three men who died with Mrs. Surratt might be stated as follows regarding her guilt or innocence:

Paine. Disqualified by bias in her favor; also by lack of information.

Atzerodt. Disqualified by the offsetting testimony of two reliable witnesses.

Herold. A valid, informed vote. Guilty.

O— elder George C. Powell obituary and eulogy

The following obituary[1] is inserted here, having been received by the printer too late to be placed in the report on Deceased Ministers:

Elder G. C. Powell was born in Burke county, Ga., December 13th, 1809, near Botsford meeting-house. He was immersed by Rev. John Blackston into Mount Paran church, Crawford county, Ga., December 28th, 1828. He was married in 1830, and licensed to preach in Talbot by Antioch church, and was ordained in Russell county, Alabama, at Liberty church, in 1847, Elders Reuben Thornton, Willis Jones and Thomas Granberry acting as the presbytery. In 1848 he was called to Beulah church, in Stewart county, Ga., and in 1859 he moved to Florida and settled near Bellville. He preached for Providence church, Bradford county, one year at least, during which a number were added to the church, five of whom became ministers. In January, 1868, he moved to Lake Jessup, in Orange county, where he lived and labored until his death, which occurred at West Opopka, Orange county, at the residence of his son-in-law, H. L. Meeks, November, 1881, at the age of 72, less one month.

Living and dying as he did, far away from the place of his birth, but little can be written of his early life, and his parentage. Like many of the youths of his day, he had not many advantages for getting an education, but was reared, doubtless, morally, and formed no vicious habits.

Elder Powell was physically a fine specimen of manhood. He was above medium height and not bowed till age caused him to stoop some. He was a man of commanding appearance.

Mentally, too, Bro. Powell ranked above the majority of men and though his education was limited, yet by his reading, thought and observation, he became a strong man in the Scriptures. At times he was very impressive, both in the matter and manner of his efforts. The following points were made during the memorial se[r]v-

[1] This valuable record was located by Mr. Rollin S. Armour, Secretary Treasurer of the Baptist Historical Society of Florida, Stetson University, DeLand, Fla. and forwarded by Mr. Howard P. Wright of Jacksonville. Its source is *Florida Baptist Convention Annual*, 1881; pp. 34-35.

ices, conducted at Antioch church, during the union meeting in January, 1882, in memory of Elder Powell:

He was emphatically a man of meekness. Commanding in appearance; above the most of his associates in the ministry, in his mental ability; "moving, (as was said by one brother in the memorial services) ahead of civilization, spending most of his life as a pioneer minister," and under such circumstances as would often cause him to be complimented; yet meekness ever shone conspicuously in his life, in all relations. Geo. C. Powell was as much a stranger to fear as men ever are, yet he was no brawler, or braggart, but quiet, gentle as a woman,—devoid of all spirit of arrogance or vanity.

Beautifully blended with his meekness, was his firmness, and adherence to principles. No "reed shaken with the wind," was he, nor was he "carried about by every wind of doctrine." He was understandingly a Baptist, in the full meaning of the word, and loved the truths couched in the Word, as properly understood, and loving them he was not ashamed of them, nor did shrink from preaching them, not in a combative spirit, but with a spirit of meekness.

He was catholic in spirit, willing, and contending that all should have the right to believe whatever desired, while he claimed the same—and what he believed he swerved not from.

Then too, a consistent Christian life, is the legacy in part left by this deceased minister, to family, to his denomination, to his surviving brethren in the ministry. Long, eventful, and for the most part spent in a state of society rude, formative, with low standard of piety, was his life, yet "his foot never slipped." History can record no dark spot in his life. Even his mistakes were small and fewer than most men. He never compromised his calling or his standing by any improper alliances in politics or business. Truly may it be said of his faith (and consequent life), "by it, he being dead, yet speaketh."

To all the above, we add, as might, and would be inferred from the foregoing, he was a missionary. He was so in fact, in reality, in principle, in practice, in preaching, and giving. He did not, he was not the man, to sail under false colors. He felt the force of his Lord's command, he was fully imbued with the spirit of the word "go," and he went, long and faithfully, against difficulties, with struggles, poverty, opposition, he went.

Servant of God, well done,
Enter thy master's joy;
The battle fought, the victory won,
Rest from thy loved employ.

P— Louis Paine's army records

There are two situations which give foundation for the theory that the records of the Florida unit in which Louis Paine served his first 12-month hitch were destroyed in the War Department.

On May 22 of the Trial, Colonel R. B. Treat was called as a prosecution witness and testified that the archives of the Confederate Government had been surrendered by General Joseph Johnson and had been shipped to Washington in several boxes—being placed in the custody of Acting Assistant Secretary of War *Thomas Eckert*.

Colonel Treat was followed on the witness stand by Eckert himself, who stated that he had received the boxes the day before and they purported to be the records of the Confederate War Department. He said some of them had been opened under his direction (Pitman, p. 52).

It is obvious, then, that the Confederate Army archives were at Eckert's disposal in the War Department from the time of their delivery there on May 21, and no one else had prior access to them.

The second situation is the curious coincidence that the army file of William Wilder Smith—Louis Paine's brother—*also* lacks the records of his first enlistment. Like Paine, his records begin with his *re-enlistment* in 1862. On March 14 of that year he enrolled in the Florida 5th Infantry at Jasper, Hamilton County, and the muster-in roll carries the notation that the $50 bounty was due him (Confederate Army Records, National Archives). Since he had been discharged from his original organization and was ready to re-enlist by March 14, 1862, his first unit must have been one recruited quite early in 1861.

In the same connection, we have already noted that *all* the records on the army service of Benjamin Powell (Lewis Powell's brother and Louis Paine's cousin) are missing—though Paine said he was killed at Murfreesboro, and Paine was in a good position to know.

Now, it would be almost impossible to remove the references to only *one* man from the rosters, pay rolls, muster rolls, etc. of a Confederate company without the removal being evident. The only way of destroying this evidence that there *was* a Florida soldier named Louis Paine (who was hanged under the name of his cousin, Lewis Powell) would have been to destroy the records of the *whole company.*

If this were done, the first year's records of men who had changed to other organizations in 1862 would be missing—and the *entire* war record of men who remained in the company would be lost.

In the cases of William Wilder Smith and Benjamin Powell, we may have an example of each situation. For these two men were kinsmen of Louis Paine and, like him, residents of Hamilton County, Florida when the war began. It is reasonable to suppose they all joined the same unit originally.

Records of Paine's later service in the 55th Georgia may have escaped destruction in the War Department either because they were not taken to Washington immediately after the war ended—or because of the twist of circumstances by which Paine's name was carried on the rolls of the 55th as "H. L. Payne."

Q— H. L. Meeks

The first step in trying to determine if H. L. Meeks was really Rev. Powell's son-in-law was to consult the census schedules for Orange County in 1870 and 1880, and inquire if any documents concerning him were on file at the county court.

Each source furnished information on a man whose name was similar to that of H. L. Meeks. In each case, it was evidently a *different* Meeks; the available information on each of the three indicated that he was *not* married to a daughter of Rev. Powell's. The 1870 census for Orange County contained this listing:

Name	*Age*	*Occupation*	*Where Born*
Henry L. Meeks	23	Farm laborer	Ga.
Sarah C. Meeks	24	Housekeeping	Ala.
Laura V. Meeks	4		Fla.
Thomas E. Meeks	1		Fla.

This Meeks didn't match up with Lewis Powell as to age or birth state. But these points weren't significant, since Powell (if he were Meeks) could be expected to have given false information to the census taker. The important fact was that Rev. Powell had no daughter named "Sarah C." He *did* have a daughter "Angeline" who, curiously, was born in Alabama and was 24 in 1870, if she was still alive, but she had married a man named Joseph Fields in Georgia in 1858. The different first name and initial of this Mr. Meeks' wife is conclusive—unless the researcher is so determined to believe she was "Angeline" that he assumes she had lost her first husband and children and *changed* her first name.

In any case, the question of whether this Henry L. Meeks was the man in whose Apopka home Rev. Powell died is fairly well settled by the fact that he and his family moved out of Orange County between 1870 and 1880 and were not listed in the latter census. The 1880 census for Orange County contained this listing:

Name	*Age*	*Relation-ship*	*Occupa.*	*Born*	*Father Born*	*Mother Born*
Meeks, Henry	51		Farmer	Ga.	Ga.	Ga.
Meeks, Martha	49	wife		Ga.	Ga.	Ga.
Meeks, Emily	14	dau.		Fla.	Ga.	Ga.
Meeks, Martha	12	dau.		Fla.	Ga.	Ga.
Meeks, William	10	son		Fla.	Ga.	Ga.

Now here was a "Meeks" who was living in Orange County only a year before Rev. Powell's death. But that was the only point on which he qualified as a minister's "son-in-law, H. L. Meeks." Again, Rev. Powell had no daughter named "Martha." And this man was using the name of "Henry Meeks" in 1880; if his middle initial were "L." he *could* have been using the name "H. L. Meeks" by the following year. But, by his 50's, the average man has usually settled upon *one way* of giving or signing his name.

The third source of information was the record of a marriage performed in Orange County on December 5, 1872 by Rev. George C. Powell—joining "Mr. Henry L. Meeks and Miss Martha D. Kirkland of Orange County" in matrimony.[1]

This was probably not the marriage of "Henry Meeks" (1880 census) to his wife Martha. All three of their children had been born before 1872, and the birthplaces tended to indicate the couple had married in Georgia and had their family after moving to Florida.

It *could* have been the re-marriage of "Henry L. Meeks" in the 1870 census—if his first wife "Sarah C." died between 1870 and 1872 and he hastened to find another one. *Or,* it could have been the marriage of the "H. L. Meeks" in whose home Rev. Powell died—*if* his first name was "Henry" and *if* he was living in Orange County in 1872. The census taker didn't find him there in 1880. In any case, a marriage to "Martha Kirkland" wouldn't have made him the Rev. Powell's son-in-law.

On the basis of the information available at this time, the writer assumes that neither the two census listings nor the marriage record referred to the "H. L. Meeks" who was living in Apopka in 1881. Yet, late in 1880 or early in 1881 (presumably after the death of his wife Patience, since she wasn't mentioned in his obituary as a survivor) Powell left the farm of his son-in-law Isaiah D. Hart and daughter Minerva and moved in with the "H. L. Meeks"—his son-in-law who was evidently not a son-in-law—and died there. This man's residence in Orange County in 1881—since it was not recorded in the 1880 census—can be explained by 1) his having settled at Apopka *after* the 1880 census and after the death of Patience Powell, or

[1] Certified copy of the marriage license furnished the author by Mr. Herbert Law, Chief Clerk of County Judge's Court, Orange County, Fla.

2) by his having avoided the census taker in 1880 by the simple expedient of being absent from the county during the census.

The logical precaution of looking in the 1890 census to see if both "Henry Meeks" and "H. L. Meeks" were still in Orange County was frustrated by the fire in Washington which destroyed most of the census records for that year. Otherwise, conditions are favorable for finding conclusive, documented answers to the "H. L. Meeks" riddle—since it falls within the period in which there were vast improvements in the making and preserving of public records.

notes to chapters——

key to abbreviations

The following works are those cited most frequently as sources of published information on the Lincoln assassination and the Conspiracy Trial. Those listed are referred to in the Table of References by the *author's name* or *abbreviated book title* shown in the left-hand column below. In addition, the "Lincoln Assassination Suspects" file in the National Archives is shortened to "LAS File."

ANGLE	Angle, Paul M. (ed.). *The Lincoln Reader.* Rutgers University Press, 1947.
BAKER	Baker, General L. C. *History of the United States Secret Service.* Philadelphia, 1867.
BARCLAY	*Trial of the Assassins and Conspirators, etc.* Philadelphia: Barclay & Co., 1865.
BATES	Bates, David Homer. *Lincoln in the Telegraph Office.* New York: The Century Co., 1907.
CONRAD	Conrad, Earl. *The Governor and His Lady.* New York: G. P. Putnam's Sons, 1960.
DEWITT	DeWitt, David Miller. *The Assassination of Abraham Lincoln and Its Expiation.* New York, 1909.
DOSTER	Doster, William E. *Lincoln and Episodes of the Civil War.* New York: G. P. Putnam's Sons, 1915.
SOLD	Eisenschiml, Otto. *In the Shadow of Lincoln's Death.* New York: Wilfred Funk, Inc., 1940.
WWLM	Eisenschiml, Otto. *Why Was Lincoln Murdered?* Boston: Little, Brown Co., 1937.
MOGELEVER	Mogelever, Jacob. *Death To Traitors.* New York: Doubleday & Co. Inc., 1960.
PETERSON	*The Trial of the Assassins and Conspirators, etc.* Philadelphia: T. B. Peterson & Bros., 1865.
PITMAN	Pitman, Benn (ed.). *The Assassination of President Lincoln and the Trial of the Conspirators.* Cincinnati: Moore, Wilstach & Baldwin, 1865.
RUGGLES	Ruggles, Eleanor. *Prince of Players, Edwin Booth.* New York: W. W. Norton & Co., Inc., 1953.
THOMAS & HYMAN	Thomas, Benjamin P., and Hyman, Harold M. *Stanton, The Life and Times of Lincoln's Secretary of War.* New York: Alfred A. Knopf, 1962.
WILSON	Wilson, Francis. *John Wilkes Booth.* Boston: Houghton Mifflin Co., 1929.

notes to chapter one

1. Eisenschiml, WWLM, p. 370.

2. Otto Eisenschiml, *Why Was Lincoln Murdered?* (Boston: Little Brown & Co., 1937)

3. Otto Eisenschiml, *In The Shadow Of Lincoln's Death* (New York: Wilfred Funk, Inc., 1940).

notes to chapter two

1. Peterson, p. 63.
2. WWLM, p. 197.
3. National Archives, LAS file, H. S. Olcott to H. L. Burnett, April 25, 1865.
4. *Ibid.*, Olcott to Burnett, April 25, 1865.
5. *Ibid.*, memo dated April 24, 1865.

notes to chapter three

1. Peterson, p. 75, testimony of Major H. W. Smith.
2. Angle, p. 531, quotes Diary of Gideon Welles.
3. WWLM, pp. 6-8, quotes *Official Records,* Series I, Vol. 46, Part 3, pp. 780-81.
4. WWLM, p. 195, quotes *Official Records,* Series I, Vol. 46, Part 3, p. 783.
5. Peterson, p. 63.
6. *Ibid.*, p. 61.

notes to chapter four

1. Baker, p. 563.
2. *Ibid.*, p. 524.
3. Mogelever, p. 331.
4. Baker, p. 524.
5. *Ibid.*, p. 525.
6. *Ibid.*, Chap. XXXV.
7. *Ibid.*, Chap. XXXVI.
8. Mogelever, p. 337.
9. National Archives, LAS file.
10. Peterson, p. 75; Pitman, p. 158.
11. *Ibid.*, p. 25; *ibid.*, p. 115.
12. Peterson, p. 75.

notes to chapter five

1. National Archives, Army and Air Corps Branch, Lincoln Assassination Suspects file.
2. National Archives, LAS file. Statement transcript dated April 25; routed Col. Wells to Gen. Augur, May 2; routed Gen. Augur to Col. Burnett, May 5.
3. *Ibid.*, undated report, Col. John A. Foster.
4. *Ibid.*, Major W. H. Wiegel to Col. John A. Foster, April 18, re Paine in Baltimore. *Also,* Col. John Woolley to Col. Burnett, May 26; refers to arrest of Branson family in Baltimore on April 28 at Stanton's order.
5. Peterson, pp. 51-52.
6. *Ibid.*, p. 74, testimony of Richard Morgan.

notes to chapter six

1. Doster, pp. 257-68.
2. WWLM, p. 235.
3. Peterson, p. 128. Detective John E. Roberts' testimony implied Paine confessed guilt to him, as Doster stated.

notes to chapter seven

1. Thomas and Hyman, p. 430.

notes to chapter eight

1. Peterson, p. 18.
2. National Archives, LAS file; see facsimile in Appendix.
3. Baker, p. 44.
4. National Archives, LAS file; original longhand draft of Devoe telegram.
5. *Ibid.*, statement of detective expenses headed "Schedule of Vouchers." Approved July 3, 1865, by C. A. Dana.
6. Peterson, p. 77.
7. *Ibid.*, p. 75.
8. *Ibid.*, p. 74.
9. National Archives, LAS file, statement by John S. Brophy dated July 7, 1865.
10. Doster, p. 281.
11. National Archives, LAS file. Anna Surratt statement dated April 28; Honora Fitzpatrick statement, same date.
12. *Ibid.*, Anna Surratt statement.
13. *Ibid.*, Olcott to Burnett, April 28, 1865.
14. *Ibid.*, Honora Fitzpatrick statement, April 28, 1865.
15. *Ibid.*, Mrs. Surratt interrogation by R. B., April 17, 1865.
16. *Ibid.*, Olcott to Burnett, April 28.
17. WWLM, pp. 48-49.
18. *Ibid.*, p. 48.
19. Peterson, p. 25.
20. *The Reporter,* Washington, D. C., July 24, 1867, p. 286. Verbatim proceedings of the Surratt Trial; testimony of Richard C. Morgan, identified as formerly chief clerk to Col. Olcott.
21. National Archives, LAS file. Both the Devoe and Sampson depositions are dated April 18, 1865.
22. DeWitt, David Miller, *Judicial Murder of Mary E. Surratt* (Baltimore: 1895), p. 7.
23. National Archives, LAS file, "Schedule of Vouchers" approved by C. A. Dana, July 3, 1865.
24. Baker, pp. 525-28.
25. Peterson, p. 76.
26. Same reference as Note 20.
27. *Ibid.*, p. 279.
28. *Ibid.*, p. 279.
29. Barclay, p. 100.
30. Peterson, pp. 167-69.
31. Doster, p. 271.
32. SOLD, p. 129, facsimile reproduction of Stanton's order.
33. Pitman, p. 122.
34. *Ibid.*, p. 121.
35. Peterson, p. 75.
36. National Archives, LAS file, Major Field's receipt for Paine, April 18.
37. SOLD, p. 108. Quoting DeWitt's *Assassination, Etc.*, p. 173; another perjurer, James B. Merritt, confessed in 1866 that he had received $6000 from the government for his false testimony regarding Jefferson Davis.
38. Peterson, p. 76; Pitman, p. 159.

39. National Archives, LAS file, Gleason statement dated April 18, 1865.
40. *The Reporter*, Washington, D. C., III (June 17-Sept. 3, 1867), 280.
41. Peterson, p. 146.
42. Peterson, p. 143; Pitman, p. 42. Alleged translation of cipher letter read into the court record June 5, 1865.
43. Peterson, p. 142; Pitman, p. 31.

notes to chapter nine

1. National Archives, LAS file, Major Seward to Col. Burnett, May 3, 1865.
2. Roscoe, Theodore, *The Web of Conspiracy* (New York: Prentice-Hall, Inc., 1959).
3. Angle, p. 530; quoting Gideon Welles' *Diary*.
4. *Ibid.*, p. 530.
5. See this volume, Chapter 3.
6. Peterson, p. 75.
7. Pitman, p. 157.
8. Peterson, p. 82.
9. Pitman, p. 157.
10. Peterson, p. 18.
11. WWLM, p. 151.
12. Baker, p. 482.
13. *Ibid.*, p. 485.
14. WWLM, p. 425.
15. *Ibid.*, p. 431.
16. SOLD, chaps. XI and XII.
17. Doster, p. 268.

notes to chapter ten

1. National Archives, LAS file, John P. Brophy statement, July 7, 1865.
2. Peterson, p. 102, A. S. Howell testimony.
3. National Archives, LAS file, memo May 14, Holt to Stanton.
4. WWLM, p. 473.
5. Peterson, p. 24.
6. Mudd, Nettie, *The Life of Dr. Samuel A. Mudd.*
7. Peterson, pp. 68-69.
8. *Ibid.*, p. 117, following testimony of Captain F. Monroe.
9. National Archives, LAS file. Undated summary of "testimony" by Col. Foster states "Wood" visited Surratt's a second time (in March) and "at *this* time he called himself a Baptist minister." Weichmann statement to Col. W. P. Wood of Old Capitol April 30 is identical with this.
10. Peterson, p. 116.
11. National Archives, LAS file, Anna Surratt interrogation April 28.
12. *Ibid.*, interrogation of Mrs. Surratt dated April 17, 1865.
13. Peterson, p. 89.
14. *Ibid.*, pp. 147-48.
15. National Archives, LAS file, undated statement by Col. Wm. P. Wood re his interview with Miss Fitzpatrick on April 18.
16. *Ibid.*, Col. Foster's report dated April 28.
17. Peterson, p. 81.
18. National Archives, LAS file, Col. John Woolley letter to Col. Burnett dated May 26.

19. *Ibid.*, Mrs. M. A. Branson statement to Col. Woolley, May 1.
20. *Ibid.*, Major W. H. Wiegel in Baltimore to Col. Foster, April 18.
21. Peterson, pp. 124-25; Margaret Branson testimony.
22. *Restoration of Ford's Theatre;* U.S. Dept. of Interior report (Washington, D.C., 1963). List of productions at Ford's during 1865, p. 121.
23. Peterson, pp. 43-44, testimony of G. W. Bunker.
24. *Ibid.*, p. 69.
25. *Ibid.*, p. 195, wire cited by Bingham in summation.
26. Asia Booth Clark, *The Unlocked Book* (New York: G. P. Putnam's Sons, 1938).
27. Peterson, p. 208.

notes to chapter eleven

1. Peterson, p. 131.
2. National Archives, LAS file, undated summary of "testimony respecting Lewis Payne, alias Wood" by Col. John A. Foster.
3. Peterson, p. 206.
4. *Ibid.*, pp. 68-69, testimony of Ethan Horner.
5. *Ibid.*, p. 43, G. W. Bunker.
6. *Ibid.*, p. 66.
7. *Ibid.*, pp. 47-49, re-examined, p, 82.
8. Pitman, pp. 74-75.
9. Peterson, p. 169.
10. *Ibid.*, pp. 68-69, Ethan Horner.
11. *Ibid.*, p. 206, Atzerodt "confession" to the Rev. Butler.
12. National Archives, LAS file, affidavit of Frank Monroe.
13. Peterson, p. 23.

notes to chapter twelve

1. Doster, p. 268.
2. Peterson, p. 125.
3. Doster, pp. 264-66.
4. Peterson, p. 168.

notes to chapter thirteen

1. Peterson, pp. 155-56.
2. *Ibid.*, pp. 167-69.
3. Doster, p. 272.
4. *Florida Baptist Convention Annual*, 1881.
5. National Archives, Army and Air Corps Branch, Confederate Army records.
6. *Soldiers of Florida*, published by the Board of State Institutions, State of Florida, May 14, 1903, pp. 77-79.
7. National Archives, Confederate Army records.
8. *Ibid.*
9. National Archives, Army and Air Corps Branch, Union records of prisoners of war.
10. Barclay, p. 100.
11. Peterson, p. 153.

12. *Ibid.*
13. Pitman, p. 308.
14. Doster, p. 268.

notes to chapter fourteen

1. National Archives, LAS file, Baltimore Provost Marshal Col. John Woolley to Col. H. S. Burnett, May 26, 1865.
2. *Ibid.*
3. Doster, p. 268.
4. Peterson, p. 125.
5. National Archives, same as Note 1.
6. National Archives, LAS file, Col. John Woolley to Secretary of War, dated May 1, 1865 (B-428, JAO).
7. *Ibid.* Though transmitted and received as one of the four documents Woolley forwarded to Stanton, the "Stevens" letter (dated April 27)—addressed to "Lt. Col. Saml. B. Lawrence"—is filed separately as No. 877M, AGO.
8. *Ibid.*, Woolley to Stanton.
9. *Ibid.* Same as Note 7.
10. National Archives, LAS file, Provost Marshal H. B. Smith to Major W. H. Wiegel, April 21, 1865.
11. National Archives, LAS file, Major Wiegel to Col. John A. Foster, April 18.
12. National Archives, LAS file, Samuel S. Bond to Col. Burnett, June 3, 1865.
13. National Archives, Union records of prisoners of war.

notes to chapter fifteen

1. Florida Baptist Convention Annual, 1881, pp. 34-35, Rev. Powell obituary.
2. National Archives, Confederate Army records.
3. *Ibid.*
4. *Ibid.*
5. Barclay, p. 100.
6. National Archives, Union records of prisoners of war.
7. *Ibid.*
8. *Ibid.*
9. *Official Records,* Ser. 1, Vol. XXXIII, p. 1081.
10. Virgil Carrington Jones, *Gray Ghosts and Rebel Raiders,* (New York: Henry Holt & Co., 1956).
11. *Ibid.*, Chapter VII.
12. Brooke Payne, *The Paynes of Virginia,* (Richmond: William Byrd Press, 1937), p. 418.
13. John W. Munson, *Reminiscences of a Mosby Guerrilla,* (New York, 1906).
14. *Ibid.*, p. 231.
15. Virgil Carrington Jones, *Ranger Mosby* (University of North Carolina Press, 1944), pp. 230-31.
16. National Archives, LAS file, JAGO, W-396, 1865.
17. *Ibid.*, Weichmann statement to Col. Wood, April 30, 1865.
18. Bates, Chap. XXVII, "Payne the Assassin."
19. Mogelever, pp. 166-67.
20. Peterson, p. 24.
21. Baker, p. 477.
22. Peterson, p. 63.
23. *Ibid.*, p. 62.

24. National Archives, LAS file.
25. *Ibid.*, Atzerodt "confession" to Col. Wells, April 25.
26. Peterson, p. 59, Fletcher testimony.
27. *Ibid.*, p. 195, Bingham argument.
28. *Ibid.*, pp. 68-69, Ethan J. Harner testimony.
29. SOLD, p. 58.
30. Peterson, p. 43, G. W. Bunker.
31. *Ibid.*, p. 47, Samuel Knapp Chester testimony.
32. WWLM, p. 209.
33. *Ibid.* p. 209.
34. Wilson, p. 71.
35. Peterson, p. 147, J. T. Hollahan.
36. Baker, p. 478.
37. National Archives, LAS file, Atzerodt "confession" to Col. Wells, April 25.
38. Peterson, p. 124, Matthew J. Pope testimony.
39. *Ibid.*, p. 59, John Fletcher.
40. National Archives, LAS file, same as Note 37.
41. Same as Note 37.
42. Peterson, p. 87, John L. Caldwell testimony.
43. *Ibid.*, p. 206.
44. National Archives, LAS file, M. J. Pope statement, April 27.
45. Peterson, p. 124.
46. National Archives, LAS file.
47. *Ibid.*, undated summary of "testimony" by Col. John Foster so states.
48. Peterson, p. 62; Pitman, p. 159. In the former the stenographer reduced the testimony to a brief summary; Pitman has minute details of the animal's exhausted condition.
49. *Ibid.*
50. National Archives, LAS file, Samuel Hopkins to Gen. Augur, April 19.
51. Baker, pp. 556-57.
52. *Surratt Trial*, Vol. III, pp. 156-57.
53. SOLD, p. 366.
54. Doster, pp. 270-71.

notes to chapter sixteen

1. Wilson, pp. 50-54.
2. *Ibid.*, p. 41.
3. Ruggles, pp. 72-73.
4. *Ibid.*, p. 80.
5. *Ibid.*, p. 80, quoting *The Unlocked Book*, by Asia Booth Clarke, p. 379.
6. Wilson, p. 15.
7. Ruggles, p. 123.
8. Wilson, pp. 50-54.
9. Ruggles, p. 119.
10. WWLM, p. 50, quoting Sam Arnold article, *The Lincoln Plot*, Baltimore *American*, 1902.
11. Peterson, p. 116.
12. Ruggles, p. 200; SOLD, p. 158, quoting Doster.
13. Ruggles, p. 177.
14. Wilson, p. 39.
15. Peterson, pp. 17-18.
16. *Ibid.*, p. 45.

17. National Archives, LAS file, Atzerodt "confession" to Col. Wells, April 25.
18. Peterson, p. 62.
19. Wilson, p. 49.
20. Peterson, p. 43; G. W. Bunker.
21. SOLD, p. 13.
22. *Ibid.*, p. 50.
23. Peterson, p. 166.
24. *Ibid.*, p. 46.
25. National Archives, LAS file, Foster memo on Chester.
26. Pitman, p. 5.
27. Peterson, p. 69.
28. Wilson, p. 143.
29. WWLM, p. 50.
30. Angle, p. 526.
31. Wilson, quotes Deery article on pp. 82-84.
32. Jim Bishop, *The Day Lincoln Was Shot,* p. 99.
33. Peterson, p. 36.
34. *Ibid.*, p. 50.
35. WWLM, Chap. XXVI, "The Case Against the Radicals."
36. *Records of the Columbia Society,* Washington, D. C., XXVII, 147-48.
37. Ruggles, p. 179.
38. WWLM, Chap. IX.
39. Peterson, p. 29, John Lloyd testimony.
40. WWLM, p. 297.
41. National Archives, LAS file, statement by Mrs. E. R. Quesenberry, May 16.
42. Wilson, p. 169.
43. *Ibid.*, Chaps. XV and XVI.
44. WWLM, p. 377, National Archives document.
45. Peterson, pp. 29-30, John Lloyd testimony.
46. *Ibid.*, p. 116.
47. *Ibid.*, p. 29.
48. Wilson, p. 168.
49. Peterson, p. 93, B. F. Gwynn testimony.
50. *Ibid.*, p. 29, John Lloyd testimony.
51. Wilson, pp. 209-17, Miss Holloway's account quoted in full by Wilson with permission of the Confederate Museum, Richmond, Va.
52. Peterson, pp. 57-59.
53. SOLD, Chap. III.
54. *Ibid.*, p. 40.
55. *Ibid.*, p. 40.
56. Baker, pp. 499-501.

notes to chapter seventeen

1. Baker, p. 582.
2. WWLM, p. 190, quoting *Recollections of President Lincoln,* by L. E. Chittenden (New York: Harper & Bros., 1891), pp. 189-90.
3. *Ibid.*, p. 190.
4. WWLM, p. 190; quoting *Impeachment Investigation,* 40th Congress, p. 111.
5. Baker, p. 693.
6. *Ibid.*, p. 539.
7. Mogelever, p. 417.
8. Baker, p. 527.
9. Mogelever, p. 366.

10. Baker, p. 526.
11. *Ibid.*, p. 496.
12. *Ibid.*, pp. 495-97.
13. *Ibid.*, pp. 425-28.
14. *Ibid.*, pp. 432-38.
15. Peterson, p. 57.
16. *Ibid.*, p. 59.
17. *Ibid.*, p. 81.
18. Baker, pp. 495-97.
19. Baker, pp. 525-28.
20. *Ibid.*, p. 527.
21. WWLM, p. 121; quoting O'Beirne papers.
22. *Ibid.*, pp. 122-23.
23. Baker, p. 494.
24. WWLM, p. 128, quoting O'Beirne papers.
25. Mogelever, p. 417.
26. Baker, p. 533.
27. WWLM, p. 127, quoting *Recollections of War Times,* by Albert G. Riddle (New York, 1895), pp. 334-35.
28. WWLM, p. 134, quoting Executive Document No. 90, 39th Congress.
29. Baker, p. 527.
30. WWLM, p. 124, quoting *Impeachment Investigation,* p. 487.
31. Peterson, p. 57.
32. Pitman, p. 91.
33. Peterson, p. 58.
34. Baker, p. 496.
35. WWLM, pp. 474-75.
36. Peterson, p. 57.
37. *Ibid.*, p. 113.
38. Baker, p. 535.
39. SOLD, p. 182.
40. Doster, pp. 276-77.
41. Baker, p. 535.
42. Peterson, p. 63.
43. WWLM, Chap. XXIX, "The Case Against Stanton."
44. Conrad, pp. 350-52.
45. *Ibid.*, p. 351.
46. Mogelever, pp. 385-86.
47. *Ibid.*, p. 419, quoting the Washington *Star*, July 6, 1868.
48. Baker, p. 701.
49. WWLM, pp. 144-45.
50. *Ibid.*, pp. 138-52.
51. WWLM, pp. 431-32.
52. James D. Richardson (ed.), *Messages and Papers of the Presidents* (Bureau of National Literature and Art, 1908), pp. 710-56.
53. SOLD, pp. 223-24, WWLM, pp. 409-11.
54. *Civil War Times,* August, 1961.
55. *Ibid.*, p. 17.
56. *Ibid.*, pp. 12-13.

notes to chapter eighteen

1. Thomas and Hyman, p. 420.
2. SOLD, p. 34.

3. Thomas and Hyman, p. 421.
4. WWLM, p. 144.
5. Peterson, p. 72.
6. *The Web of Conspiracy* by Theodore Roscoe.
7. Bates, p. 50.
8. WWLM, pp. 162-64.
9. *Ibid.*, p. 63.
10. *Ibid.*, p. 60.
11. *Ibid.*, p. 56.
12. *Ibid.*, Chap. III.
13. Bates, p. 323.
14. WWLM, pp. 33-34.
15. *Ibid.*, p. 449.
16. Angle, pp. 520-25, quoting Frederick W. Seward, *Reminiscences of a War-Time Statesman and Diplomat* (New York: Putnam, 1916).
17. WWLM, p. 43.
18. *Ibid.*, p. 43.
19. *Ibid.*, p. 42.
20. *The Web Of Conspiracy*, Theodore Roscoe.
21. WWLM, p. 37.
22. Angle, p. 531, quoting Gideon Welles' *Diary*.
23. WWLM, p. 38, quoting Boston *Sunday Post*, April 11, 1915.
24. *Ibid.*, pp. 78-80.
25. Civil War Times, August, 1961, p. 11.

notes to chapter nineteen

1. Death warrant of "Lewis Payne," in document collection at U. S. Military Academy, West Point. Photocopy supplied author by Ann K. Harlow, Chief, Readers Service Division, USMA Library.
2. National Archives, LAS file, transcript of Mrs. Branson's statement dated May 1, 1865.
3. *Ibid;* Major Wm. H. Wiegel, APM, to Col. John A. Foster, April 18, 1865.
4. Peterson, p. 25; Weichmann testimony.
5. *Ibid.*
6. National Archives, LAS file, transcript of Mrs. Surratt interrogation, dated April 17, 1865.
7. *Soldiers of Florida* (Board of State Institutions, 1903), pp. 77-79.
8. Florida Baptist Convention *Annual*, 1881.
9. *Encyclopedia Americana*, p. 222.
10. Elmer T. Clark, *The Small Sects in America* (Nashville: 1937), p. 202. Quoting circular of Rocky Spring Primitive Baptist Church, Holmes County, Miss., April, 1839.
11. Charles Hill Ryland, *The Baptists of Virginia*, (Baptist Board of Missions and Education, Richmond, Va., 1955), p. 245.
12. *Ibid.*, p. 243.
13. Barclay, p. 100.
14. Peterson, p. 157.
15. *American Baptist Register* (American Baptist Publication Society, Philadelphia, 1852).
16. Doster, p. 268.
17. Ryland, *The Baptists of Virginia*, p. 299.
18. Peterson, p. 25.

19. Henry Kyd Douglas, *I Rode With Stonewall* (University of North Carolina Press, Chapel Hill, 1940), pp. 342-45.
20. John A. Gray, *The Fate of the Lincoln Conspirators, McClure's Magazine,* XXXVII (October, 1911), 626-36.
21. SOLD, p. 101.
22. Doster, p. 277.
23. WWLM, p. 294, facsimile No. 15 in documents section.
24. *Ibid.,* p. 129.
25. Barclay, p. 100.
26. Extract from Dr. Gillette's journal. Typed copy supplied the author by his granddaughter, Mrs. Amy Gillette Bassett.
27. Amy Gillette Bassett, *Red Cross Reveries* (Harrisburg, Pa.: Stackpole Books, 1961), p. 92.
28. *Ibid.,* pp. 88-89.
29. Barclay, p. 100.
30. *Ibid.*
31. *Red Cross Reveries,* Bassett, p. 91.

notes to chapter twenty

1. The Rev. Powell's obituary; see Appendix O.
2. Amy Gillette Bassett, Memorandum to Gen. McArthur, dated Feb. 2, 1934, in collection at USMA Library, West Point.
3. National Archives; File AGO 112S, 1869.
4. Osborne H. Oldroyd, *Assassination* etc. (Wash., D. C., 1901), p. 211.

index——

index

A

B

C

D

T

ST. MARY'S COLLEGE OF MARYLAND LIBRARY
ST. MARY'S CITY, MARYLAND

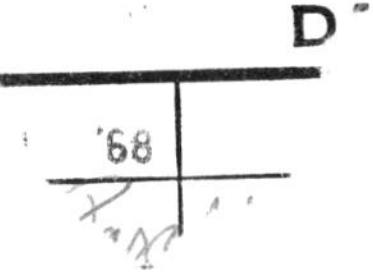